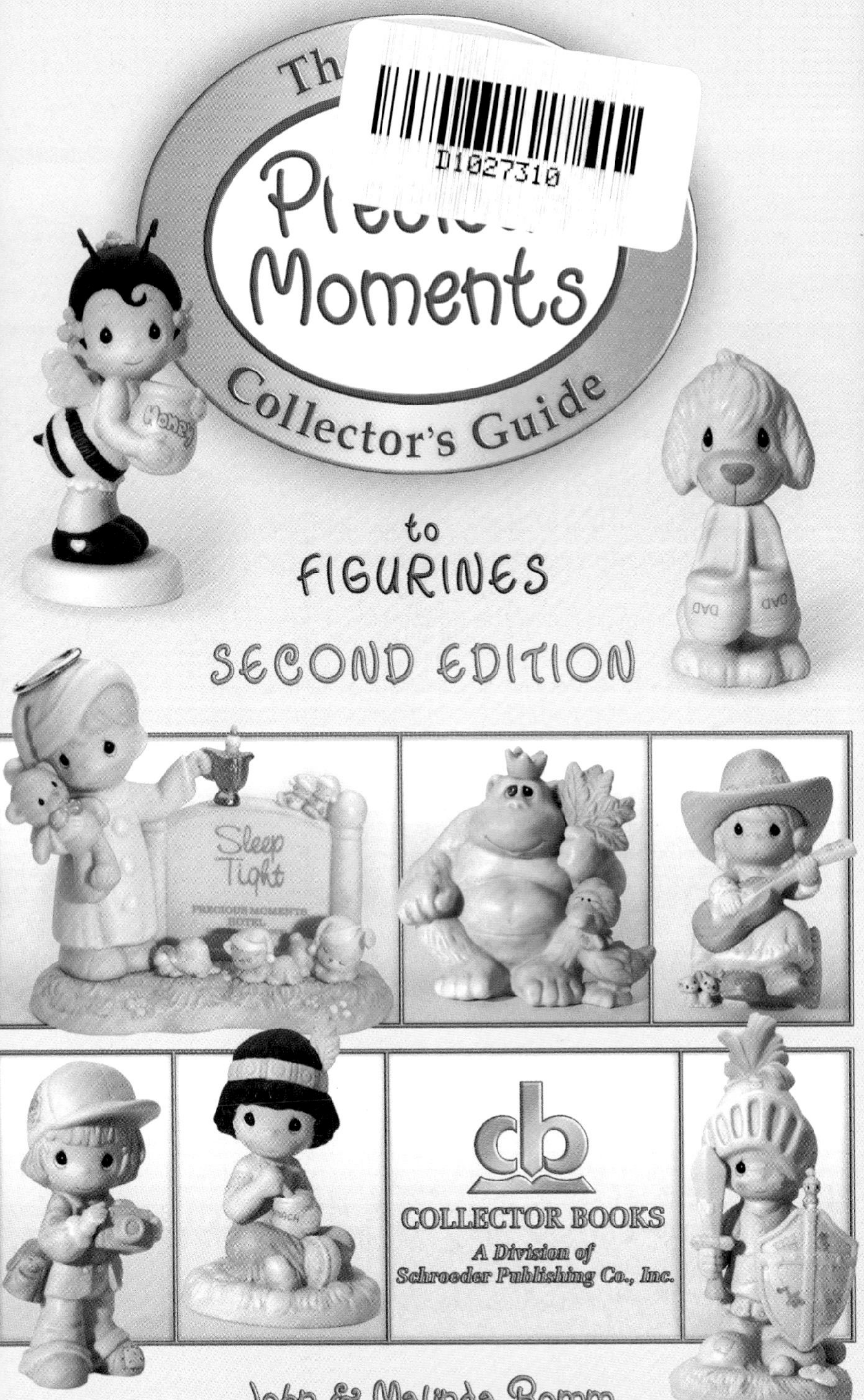

John & Malinda Bomm

Front cover: *You're A Honey,* 795283; *Animal Collection B,* E-9267B; *Sleep Tight,* 542636; *To My Favorite Fan,* 521043; *Hallelujah Hoedown,* 163864; *Focusing In On Those Precious Moments,* C-0018; *Lord, Keep Me In Teepee Top Shape,* PM-912; *He's The Healer Of Broken Hearts,* 100080; *Onward Christian Soldiers,* E-0523.
Back cover: *Dance Of The Lion,* 791121.

Cover design by Beth Summers
Book design by Terri Hunter

COLLECTOR BOOKS
P.O. Box 3009
Paducah, Kentucky 42002-3009

www.collectorbooks.com

The current values in this book should be used only as a guide. They are not intended to set prices, which vary from one section of the country to another. Auction prices as well as dealer prices vary greatly and are affected by condition as well as demand. Neither the authors nor the publisher assume responsibility for any losses that might be incurred as a result of consulting this guide.

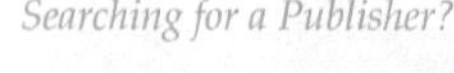

Searching for a Publisher?

We are always looking for people knowledgeable within their fields. If you feel that there is a real need for a book on your collectible subject and have a large comprehensive collection, contact Collector Books.

Proudly printed and bound in the United States of America.

Stand Beside Her And Guide Her, 106671

Contents

Make Everything A Masterpiece, 4001571

A Note From The Authors

Prices listed in this publication are guidelines only. Pricing is determined by location, condition of item, coloring, with or without box, and of course, demand. The authors of this book take no responsibility for variations in pricing. Pricing should be used only as a generalization, not an actual.

Thanks For A Quarter Century Of Loving, Caring And Sharing, 108602

Acknowledgments

Malinda and I wish to thank our mother for all the input, information collecting, and phone calling she had to do to make this book possible. She spent many, many hours of work helping put this book together.

An extra special thank you goes to Janet Cox and Karen Bardwell from Enesco, Inc. Without their help this book would not have been completed. They have backed us up by sending us all the information they could find, beg, steal, or borrow from their vast library. We send a super thank you to both of them.

Thank you to Robert Marchant and Tracey Wardell, members of Sharing The Magic Precious Moments Club in Orlando, Florida, and Brenda Miller for lending us pictures of some of the pieces we could not find.

Thank you to Ginny Gully and Limited of Michigan.

If anyone has any information not found in this book, please contact John and Malinda Bomm at pmguides@hotmail.com.

Dear Friend, My Love For You Will Never Fade Away, 114018

About The Authors

John and Malinda Bomm are residents of Orlando, Florida. John was born in Amityville, New York in 1962. He, his younger brother, and parents stayed in New York until 1972 when his father was transferred to Pennsylvania. They lived in the beautiful Amish country there for three years until John's father was transferred again, this time to New Jersey. John completed his education in New Jersey and at the age of 16 started working for Pathmark Supermarkets as a cart boy and cashier. When John turned 18 he started building a race car, one of his passions through his growing years. He is now a "stay-at-home" dad taking care of his four children.

Malinda was born in 1962 on Naha Air Force Base in Okinawa, Japan. Her father was an Air Force Master Sergeant at the time. Her mother was a native of Okinawa. Malinda and her parents lived in Okinawa for nine years until they moved to Langley Air Force Base in Virginia. Malinda completed her education at Tabb High School in Virginia. She moved to New Jersey in 1987 where she met John Bomm. When John's parents moved to Florida, John and Malinda made the move with them. They were married on Valentine's Day, 1991, and several years later adopted four children: Eric, 14; Gerard, 12; Ramey, 9; and Sirjesim, 8. Malinda is now a health claims examiner for a large city agency.

Through Malinda, John developed a love of Precious Moments collectibles. Malinda and John's collection has expanded from five Precious Moments figurines to approximately 900 pieces, including bisque figurines, dolls, plates, water globes, and much more. Several rooms in their house showcase their collection. They authored *The Official Precious Moments Collector's Guide to Company Dolls,* also published by Collector Books, in 2003.

Adopting A Life Of Love, 108527

The Story Of Precious Moments

Samuel John Butcher was born on January 1, 1939. He was the third of five children who grew up in a very poor family. As a child, he spent hours underneath the dining room table writing stories and illustrating them. Even in kindergarten, his dream of becoming an artist was evident, when he illustrated *Little Black Sambo* and made a box with a movie crank that worked like a movie screen — the whole school admired it. At this young age his talent was recognized by both family and friends.

Sam Butcher

When Sam was in high school in the fall of 1957, he met Katie Cushman, whom he married on December 27, 1959. They had five children: Jon, Philip, Tammy, Debbie, and Timmy. Though life was very busy, Sam continued following his dream of becoming an artist.

Over the years Sam found the Lord and devoted his life to him. His strong spiritual commitment led him to employment at the International Child Evangelism Fellowship in Grand Rapids, Michigan. It was there that he learned how to study the Bible, and his desire to spread God's love to others grew. It was also there that he met Bill Biel, who later became his dear friend and business partner. In 1971 Sam and Bill decided to leave their jobs and go out on their own as commercial artists. With no money, a bit of poster paint, and the talents God gave them, they formed their own company, "Jonathan & David," with Sam as illustrator and Bill as designer.

In 1975 Sam and Bill were invited to attend the Christian Booksellers Convention in Anaheim, California. It was then that they began preparing greeting cards featuring teardrop-eyed children, and Bill came up with the name "Precious Moments." This idea was a huge success at the convention, and their tiny booth was overrun with customers — $10,000 worth of orders were placed. All the men needed was the money to produce the cards and fill the orders. They went to the bank with orders in hand, but were turned down. They decided to try the Christian Businessmen's Association, who told them to put their trust in the Lord. And eventually, Sam met a wealthy man who offered to loan him $25,000 to start up his business.

That first year (1975) Sam's and Bill's first major projects were Christmas cards and Bicentennial cards. To offset their costs and help pay bills, they also painted Christmas scenes on store windows and garages. During the second CBA convention in Atlantic City, Sam and Bill introduced four posters: *Jesus Loves Me, Praise the Lord Anyhow, Prayer Changes Things,* and *God Is Love.* At the same time, their Precious Moments

Prayer Changes Things, E-1375B

Marching Ahead To Another 25 Years of Precious Moments, 108544

greeting cards ministry continued to grow in acceptance to those associated with the growing company of Jonathan & David. Through all the struggles, Sam and Bill kept their senses of humor, and asked the Lord to guide and direct them in sharing the Gospel through the ministry of the Precious Moments greeting cards.

Early in 1978, Sam and Bill were both in the studio when a man by the name of Eugene Freedman called. He was the president and chief executive officer of Enesco Imports Corporation, a company heavily involved in the giftware industry, headquartered in the Chicago suburb of Elk Grove Village. Freedman had seen some of the Precious Moments cards, including *I Will Make You Fishers Of Men.* Freedman wanted to know if Sam and Bill would be interested in making Precious Moments into three-dimensional art through porcelain figurines.

I Will Make You Fishers Of Men, 522139

Sam and Bill had a special relationship. Sam was an artist, not a businessman. The two decided to part ways in March of 1984. Sam sold his interest in Jonathan & David, Inc., the greeting card company, to Bill. They remained friends for many years.

Jesus Loves Me, E-1372G

The Enesco Beginning

Eugene Freedman

By 1978, when Eugene ("Gene") Freedman approached Sam Butcher and Bill Biel about making Precious Moments into porcelain figurines, Enesco Imports Corporation had been involved in the giftware industry for many years. Freedman had served in the U.S. Navy in the South Pacific during World War II, and when he returned from the service, he was not sure just what he wanted to do with his life. He worked in Milwaukee for a while in a dismantling defense production plant.

In the late 1940s, Freedman took a job as a salesman for a Milwaukee firm that manufactured miniatures. He became familiar with many companies that are still customers of Enesco today. In the early 1950s he started his own company which produced injection molded plastics as well as decorative figurines. The company grew to a point where he needed a partner to help run the business.

In 1958, Freedman left this firm and embarked upon another new venture. He and six employees purchased the N. Shure Company, a large wholesale merchandising catalog operation. This later evolved into Enesco Imports Corp., a natural phonetic progression from the initials of the original company, N. S. Co.

On a trip to the Orient, Freedman made a stopover in Los Angeles for a spring gift show. There, a friend brought him some greeting cards and posters that featured illustrations of children with soulful, teardop eyes, the Precious Moments cards. He was so taken by these drawings that he immediately thought of someone who could capture in clay the warmth and expressions of these special little children — Yasuhei Fujioka-San of Nagoya, Japan.

Freedman called Sam Butcher and Bill Biel, and pleaded with them to come to Enesco in Chicago. Coincidentally, both men were in the process of finding someone to make their prints into porcelain figurines. Freedman traveled to Japan and returned with a porcelain figurine of a girl and boy sitting on a tree stump (*Love One Another*). He brought it to Sam and Bill at their office. Sam fell to his knees and cradled the little figurine in his hands, whispering "Look Bill, look." It was a great thrill to see his artwork transformed.

Sam and Bill did not commit themselves that day, but they did take the figurine home with them and told Freedman they would give him their decision at a later date. Freedman was back in the Orient when he received word that Sam and Bill loved the figurine but wanted to work directly with the sculptor. The arrangements were made. Even though Sam and Fujioka-San did not speak the same language, their love of art became a common factor, and they quickly became friends.

Sam's first trip to the Orient to meet the artist that would be transforming his drawings into figurines was an experience that made a deep impact on his life. Sam and Fujioka-San worked on the Precious Moments sculptures for hours and hours, day after day. Though they could not communicate verbally, the two artists had an apparent "heart to heart" connection.

The next step for Freedman, now that the artist and sculptor were together, was to find a factory to produce the figurines. Although the models were being sculpted in Japan,

Precious Moments From The Beginning, 110238

the cost of production there was rising due to the increase in the standard of living. Freedman turned to a long-time friend, Paul Chang, who had worked for Enesco Imports at one time. Chang struck an agreement with Fujioka-San to establish a ceramic factory, Pearl Taiwan, in Miaoli, Taiwan. This became the home of many skilled ceramists and the place where Precious Moments figurines were first manufactured.

There were 21 original Precious Moments figurines painstakingly and endearingly produced at the Pearl Taiwan factory. They were shipped to Chicago, where they were introduced to the giftware trade in the fall of 1978. In addition to *Love One Another* (E-1376), the figurines in the first presentation were: *Love Lifted Me* (E-1375A); *Prayer Changes Things* (E-1375B); *Jesus Loves Me* (E-1372G and E-1372B, both girl and boy figurines); *Jesus Is The Light* (E-1373G); *Smile, God Loves You* (E-1373B); *He Leadeth Me* (E-1377A); *God Loveth A Cheerful Giver* (E-1378); *Love Is Kind* (E-1379A); *God Understands* (E-1379B); *O, How I Love Jesus* (E-1380B); *His Burden Is Light* (E-1380G); *Jesus Is The Answer* (E-1381R); *We Have Seen His Star* (E-2010); *Come Let Us Adore Him* (E-2011); *Praise The Lord Anyhow* (E-1374B); *He Careth For You* (E-1377B); *Make A Joyful Noise* (E-1374G); *Jesus Is Born* (E-2809); and *Unto Us A Child Is Born* (E-2013). The little Precious Moments children, with their messages of hope, love, faith, and trust, were very well received.

Enesco Imports Corporation pays very close attention to detail, especially with their Precious Moments pieces. The company had been a reputable giftware manufacturer until that point, but because of the strong public response and quick popularity of Precious Moments figurines, Enesco soon became known as a producer of collectibles as well. Consumers were instantly drawn to Precious Moments figurines, whose messages of loving, caring, and sharing are cherished by collectors today. Annual releases are always eagerly anticipated by consumers.

Yasuhei Fujioka-San

Errors And Variations

Item #	Name and Valuable Information
12238	*Clown Figurines* (A-B-C-D) On many of these clowns the inscription was written as "CROWN."
12262	*I Get A Bang Out Of You* This figurine has been found with *Lord Keep Me On The Ball* understamp.
12416	*Have A Heavenly Christmas* (Ornament) On some of the 1987 wreaths the words "Heaven Bound" are upside down.
102229	*O Worship The Lord* Many collectors have found this piece missing the "O."
111155	*Faith Takes The Plunge* Some of the figurines that debuted in 1988 and 1989 had smiles and some had frowns.
115231	*You Are My Main Event* The strings on the balloons are sometimes pink instead of white.
128708	*Owl Be Home For Christmas* (Ornament) This 1996 ornament has been found with the date missing.
136204	*It's A Girl* Pieces have been found with one shoe not painted.
136255	*Age 6* On some pieces, the heart with the age number is missing. Most pieces that should have decals are often missing them, but this piece has the entire heart missing.
183873	*Age 10* Some pieces are missing the bowling pins.
192368	*Give Ability A Chance* Has been found without the Easter Seals Lily mark.
260940	*From The Time I Spotted You I Knew We'd Be Friends* The word "Know" has been found on some pieces instead of "Knew." The monkeys on some pieces are very dark brown instead of light brown.
261130	*Have You Any Room For Jesus* The word "Bowling" has been found misspelled on the calendar.
306843	*20 Years And The Vision's Still The Same* On a small number of the commemorative figurines, the Sword and Eyeglasses marks both appear.
306916	*Friendship Hits The Spot* Many pieces have been found with the table missing. Decals were incorrectly spelled "Freindship."

Item #	Name and Valuable Information
520748	*Friendship Hits The Spot* Variation one has a misspelling: *Freindship Hits The Spot*. On variation two, the table between the two girls is missing.
520756	*Jesus Is The Only Way* Dates have been omitted on some and have been placed incorrectly on others.
520772	*Many Moons In Same Canoe, Blessum You* Over the years, the Indians' hair has been darkened.
520802	*My Days Are Blue Without You* Some pieces have a frown or puckered mouth instead of a smile.
522279	*A Reflection Of His Love* Pieces have been found with a white or blue water reflection in the fountain.
522317	*Merry Christmas, Deer* All figurines with the Bow and Arrow mark had no Precious Moments logo.
523011	*There's A Christian Welcome Here* On some of the Chapel Exclusive pieces, the angel's hair hides his right eyebrow.
523704	*May Your Christmas Be A Happy Home* (Ornament) This ornament shows a boy wearing either a yellow or blue shirt. The yellow shirt is considered the variation.
524352	*What The World Needs Now* Pieces have been found with the Bible missing from the table.
524425	*May Only Good Things Come Your Way* Some pieces have the butterfly on top of the net while others have the butterfly on the right side of the net, upside-down.
526053	*Pretty As A Princess* On some pieces one point on the princess's crown is not painted gold.
527106	*He Is Not Here For He Is Risen As He Said* On the sign outside the tomb some exclusives pieces read "Math" instead of "Matt."
528609	*Sending My Love Your Way* Variation one, the kite held by the girl is missing its stripes. Variation two, the kitten is sometimes missing completely.
529540	*Park Bench* Pieces were found glazed over and unpainted.
531634	*Who's Gonna Fill Your Shoes?* Some pieces have been found with no bows on the girl's shoes.

Item #	Name and Valuable Information
531952	*Dropping In For The Holidays* Pieces have been found with the "Egg Nog" and the decal upside-down. The cup of this piece came in either pink or blue.
730068	*The Future Is In Our Hands* On some pieces, the girl is holding a cardinal instead of a bluebird.
B-0102	*A Smile's The Cymbal Of Joy* The word "Cymbal" was misspelled "Symbol" on some Charter Member Figurines.
E-0202	*But Love Goes On Forever* Some of these pieces were reproduced after production was ended. Those pieces were sent to Canada and are identified with the Dove mark.
E-0535	*Love Is Patient — Boy* (Ornament) Some pieces have been found with the "Merry Christmas" upside down.
E-1373B	*Smile, God Loves You* The boy sometimes has a black eye and sometimes a brown eye.
E-1374B	*Praise The Lord Anyhow* On some pieces the puppy has a brown nose and on some it has a black nose.
E-1377B	*He Careth For You* The inscriptions on E-1377A (*He Leadeth Me*) and this piece were sometimes swapped.
E-2013	*Unto Us A Child Is Born* Pieces have been reported with the words placed on the pages incorrectly.
E-2362	*Baby's First Christmas* (Ornament) In variation one, the girl's straight hair appears curly. In variation two, the girl has curly hair, but the decal on the bottom of the piece is missing.
E-2372	*Baby's First Christmas* (Ornament) The inscription did not come with the first pieces that were produced. Right before the piece was suspended, an inscription was included.
E-2395	*Come Let Us Adore Him* (set of 11) The original set included a boy holding a lamb. Later he was replaced by a shepherd wearing a turban.
E-2805	*Wishing You A Season Filled With Joy* The figurine with the dove year mark shows a dog with both eyes painted black instead of one single painted eye.
E-2837	*Groom* Two different molds were used for this piece; on one, the boy's hands are hidden by his sleeves, and on the other, the boy's hands can be seen.

Item #	Name and Valuable Information
E-2854	*God Blessed Our Year Together With So Much Love And Happiness* "God Blessed Our Years" (plural) is the error on some of the decals of these first anniversary pieces.
E-3110B	*Loving Is Sharing — Boy* Pieces have been found with the dog missing or with the boy's lollipop unpainted.
E-3111	*Be Not Weary In Well Doing* Some pieces had the inscription printed as *Be Not Weary And Well Doing.*
E-4724	*Rejoicing With You* Sometimes the "e" in Bible is covered by the girl's hand.
E-5200	*Bear Ye One Another's Burdens* The original figurine shows the boy with a smile yet others have been found with a little circle mouth.
E-5214	*Prayer Changes Things* In some cases, the words "Holy Bible" were put on the back of the book. Some were found with "Holy Bible" on the figurine upside down.
E-5379	*Isn't He Precious* This piece has been seen completely without paint.
E-5624	*They Followed The Star* (set of 3) It has been noted that the camels originally came without blankets.
E-5629	*Let The Heavens Rejoice* The Precious Moments decal is missing on some of the pieces.
E-7156R	*I Believe In Miracles* The variation is the lack of the inscribed "Sam B" on the bottom of the pieces. The boy's head is also smaller on some.
E-9266 & E-9266B	*Our Love Is Heaven-Scent* *I'm Falling For Somebunny* Both pieces were made with the incorrect inscription *Somebunny Cares.*
E-9268	*Nobody's Perfect!* On this figurine, the boy has either a smile or a frown on his face.
PM-831	*Dawn's Early Light* A Dove mark has been found on the bottom of some of these pieces.
PM-961	*Teach Us To Love One Another* Pieces have been found with decals upside down.
PM-971	*You Will Always Be A Treasure To Me* Has been found with a heart mark.

The Original "21"

The original 21 figurines were introduced in 1979.

Jesus Loves Me (boy), E-1372B

Jesus Loves Me (girl), E-1372G

Smile, God Loves You, E-1373B

Jesus Is The Light, E-1373G

Praise The Lord Anyhow, E-1374B

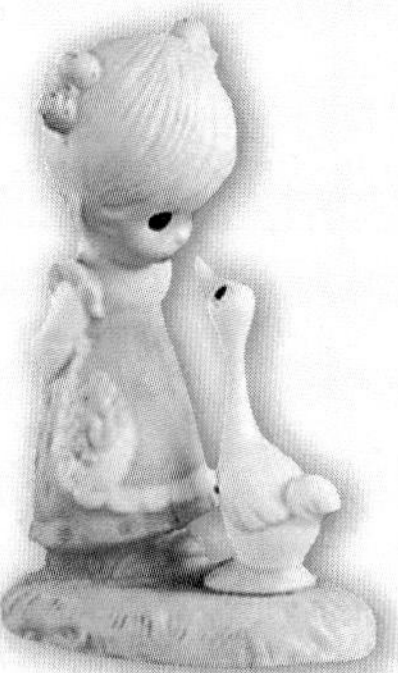

Make A Joyful Noise, E-1374G

Love Lifted Me, E-1375A

Prayer Changes Things, E-1375B

Love One Another, E-1376

He Leadeth Me, E-1377A

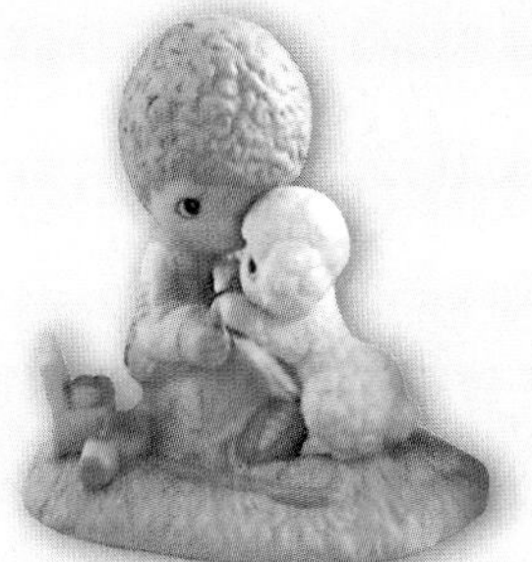
He Careth For You, E-1377B

God Loveth A Cheerful Giver, E-1378

Love Is Kind, E-1379A

God Understands, E-1379B

O, How I Love Jesus, E-1380B

His Burden Is Light, E-1380G

Jesus Is The Answer, E-1381

We Have Seen His Star, E-2010

Come Let Us Adore Him, E-2011

Jesus Is Born, E-2012

Unto Us A Child Is Born, E-2013

Precious Moments Figurines' Stories

Onward Christian Soldiers, E-0523

Sam could hardly wait to paint this idea. This little soldier carried the message to Sam to keep going when things got tough.

His Eye Is On The Sparrow, E-0530

This figurine was first made as a card for a man who Sam had met. It was later made into a figurine. The man's son had committed suicide after returning home from war. The family was sent many cards at the death of their son, but Sam's card really touched them. The painting helped the family know that God had it in his hands from the very beginning.

Praise The Lord Anyhow, E-1374B

Philip, Sam's second son, was the inspiration for this figurine. Sam said you couldn't spend much time with Philip before you threw up your hands lovingly and said, "Praise The Lord Anyhow!"

Love One Another, E-1376

This was the first Precious Moments drawing. Tammy, Sam's daughter, sat by "Uncle Bill" on a stool back-to-back and the love she portrayed for Uncle Bill was the inspiration for the first Precious Moments figurine. The original art was stolen from the Jonathan & David Company.

God Loveth A Cheerful Giver, E-1378

Debbie, Sam's daughter, inspired this piece. Sam will probably never forget Debbie, with her box full of puppies, asking him if any of his friends needed a pet.

Love Is Kind, E-1379A

Sam's son, Timmy, was the subject for this figurine. Timmy is a boy who liked to spend a lot of his time alone with nature when he was small. He also enjoys painting and music.

Make A Joyful Noise, E-1374G

This figurine is one of the original "21" introduced in 1978. Sam and Bill were driving on a country road when they came across a woman with a bumper sticker on her car that read, "Honk If You Love Jesus." Sam honked the car horn; she looked up, forgetting the instruction on her bumper sticker, thinking they were very rude young men. She gave them a dirty look and mouthed some nasty words. He pointed to the sticker, honked again, and drove away. Sam was inspired by this and created the image of a little girl nose-to-nose with a goose. It was originally called *Honk If You Love Jesus*. The title was changed before production.

O, How I Love Jesus, E-1380B

Through Sam's ministry with the Child Evangelism Fellowship, he met a very special member of the Pitt River Indians. This man had a difficult childhood. He learned to overcome his problems and became an excellent teacher. This figurine was dedicated to that man from the mountains of Northern California.

God Sends the Gift Of His Love, E-6613

Sam's grandniece inspired him to create this piece. She looked precious in her frilly Christmas dress her mom made for her. Sam felt the little child was God's special gift to her parents.

I Believe In Miracles, E-7156

Sam's former partner, Bill, was given no hope for his eyesight, but through prayer Bill's sight was restored. This figurine also became the official gift of Child's Wish, an organization for terminally ill children.

His Burden Is Light, E-1380G

This little Indian girl figurine is another result of Sam's experience with the Pitt River Indians. Though life was not easy for them, the Indians kept their traditional ways and never gave their burdens to the Lord. As time went on they left their old traditions and embraced the Lord.

To God Be The Glory, E-2823

Sam will never forget the day he saw Fujioka-San's sculpture of *To God Be The Glory*. He says it captures the story of his life. He feels that the Lord has been good to him and has blessed all his work.

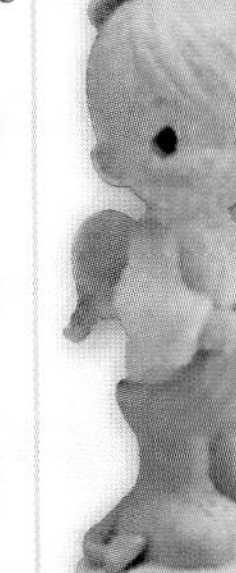

Part of Me Wants To Be Good, 12149

A very special young man, Albern Cuidad, who lived in the Philippines, was the inspiration for this figurine. He was always getting into trouble but he was so loveable you couldn't help but like him. He often said, "Please forgive me, I really meant to be good." The little boy in the figurine *Part of Me Wants To Be Good* is modeled after Albern.

I'm Sending You A White Christmas, E-2829

Sam's mother was born in Michigan, but moved to Florida at an early age. After the death of her father, her mother moved the family back to Michigan. Sam's mother was only five years old and had never seen snow. The first time she saw snow, his mother was found packing snowballs in a box to mail to her relatives in Florida.

Lord, I'm Coming Home, 100110

A collector who was a winner in one of the company's idea contests inspired this figurine. Her brother, who loved to play ball, died at the young age of 19. Sam was moved by the collector's story and her idea for a figurine, so he created this piece.

God Bless The Day We Found You, 100145

Heather was the adopted daughter of the Butchers. She was five years old when she was adopted. They were struggling to make ends meet but knew they wanted her for a daughter. Because of his love for Heather, Sam created *God Bless The Day We Found You,* to celebrate the love that comes with an adopted child.

The Lord Giveth, And The Lord Taketh Away, 100226

After a trip to the Philippines, Sam arrived home and found total chaos. He found his wife Kate standing beside the tipped-over birdcage looking at bird feathers all over the floor. The cat had eaten the canary. Though it was a sad experience, Sam envisioned this figurine, *The Lord Giveth And The Lord Taketh Away.*

No Tears Past The Gate, 101826

No Tears Past The Gate was painted to comfort Sam's assistant in the Philippines, Levi, whose sister was dying. She was 18 when she died. The painting was presented to Levi just a few weeks afterwards. Levi became one of Sam's most devoted workers. He was promoted to manager, then vice-president, and later president of the company.

Only One Life To Offer, 325309

While speaking at a Bible camp, Sam met a young man named Larry who had been in and out of trouble. Sam took him under his wing and listened to him as he explained his feelings of anger. Sam helped turn this young man around. Larry completed Bible school and went into youth ministry. When Larry was less than 40 years old, he called Sam and asked for money for an operation; he had stomach cancer. The surgery was not successful. He died, leaving a wife and two children. This figurine was dedicated to him.

The Good Lord Will Always Uphold Us, 325325

A special friend of Sam's was a missionary in South Africa. Even though she had had rheumatoid arthritis since childhood, she faithfully served the Lord. This figurine was designed to honor Sam's faithful friend, Lory Burg.

Heaven Must Have Sent You, 521388

Nancy Laptad, an employee in Sam's office, was always there when he needed financial advice. Nancy, though she was seen on a daily basis, did not realize how important she was. The figurine was dedicated to Nancy because she was always there when she was needed.

Merry Christmas, Deer, 522317

A five-year-old girl adopted from an orphanage wanted all her Christmas gifts except one sent to her friends at the orphanage. All she wanted to keep was a stuffed reindeer. On the way home from delivering the toys, her reindeer got stuck in the door of a subway train and was lost forever. Several years ago, this lady wrote to Sam and asked him to help her find the Precious Moments ornament of a little reindeer with a teddy bear on his back. Sam sent the ornament from his private collection. The story inspired Sam to create this figurine of a little girl hanging ornaments on the antlers of a reindeer.

Hello, Lord, It's Me Again, PM-811

Jon, Sam's oldest son, inspired this figurine after a romantic setback. Sam envisioned this little guy with a Dear Jon letter. He is on the phone and there is a tear running down his cheek. He's saying, *Hello Lord, It's Me Again*. Jon later found Patti and married her.

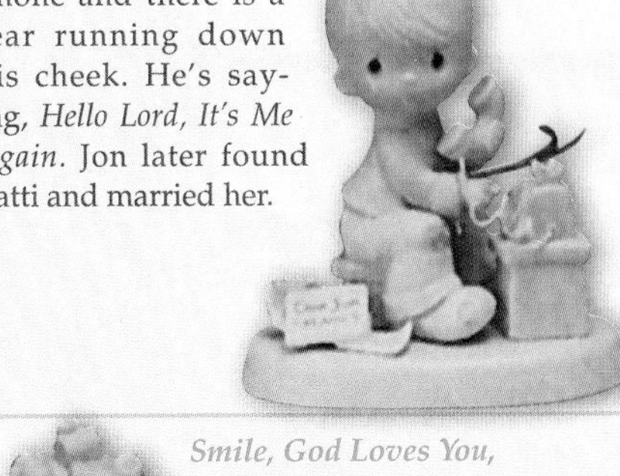

Smile, God Loves You, PM-821

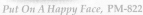

Sam believes that outward appearances don't matter and that "you can't judge a book by its cover."

Count Your Many Blessings, 879274

Sam designed this figurine for a collector named Penny who lived in Canada. She gave Sam Canadian pennies and bugged him for years to make a figurine of her. At the 2000 Collectors' Christmas Weekend she was asked to come on stage. As she was helping Sam she picked up a cloth and found her figurine, *Count Your Many Blessings*.

Put On A Happy Face, PM-822

This figurine was made to inspire collectors to show their happy side. Sam says it's really hard to take off your mask and show a "sunny side." This little clown figurine became an instant success and won the hearts of collectors.

Collecting Friends Along The Way, PM-002

Sam has met many people that have been touched by the Precious Moments collection, and he says it brings him joy to see how much the figurines mean to them. This figurine was designed to honor all the special people in our lives, be they family, friends, or club members. There are 20 animals sculpted on the figurine in commemoration of the twentieth anniversary of the club.

Trust In The Lord To The Finish, PM-842

Sam began the painting for this figurine on his way to the Philippines. His youngest brother, Hank, always loved driving race cars.

Grandma's Prayer, PM-861

This figurine is a loving tribute to Sam's grandmother, who reminded Sam often that she was praying for him.

The Lord Is My Shepherd, PM-851

Sam's daughter, Debbie, was the inspiration for this figurine. She has a warm sensitive spirit and has contributed greatly to the Precious Moments line. She could handle all the very difficult problems in her life. This piece is a symbol of God's promise that, he, as the Good Shepherd, is always there to meet our every need.

I'm Following Jesus, PM-862

After encountering a jobless Filipino friend, Carlito, Sam was inspired to create this figurine. Carlito and his family trusted the Lord to take care of their needs. Eventually, Carlito got his own cab, which has a sign in the window that reads, "I'm Following Jesus."

I Love To Tell The Story, PM-852

Inspired by the old Christian song, this piece was dedicated to Pastor Royal Blue who led Sam to the Lord Jesus. The child is speaking to a lamb, which symbolizes a pastor feeding God's flock with the bread of life, the word of God.

Focusing In On Those Precious Moments, C-0018

Sam attended a collectibles show in Edison, New Jersey, in the spring of 1999. He presented this special version of the 1998 club figurine to Rosemarie who belongs to the Happiness Is Belonging Club and the Precious Moments Collectible Treasures website. Sam states, "She is one of the most giving, kindest people and has a huge giving heart."

How To Clean Your Precious Moments

A Tub Full Of Love, 112313

Here are some tips to help keep your collection clean and safe. The most important thing is to keep your pieces in a safe, smoke-free area, and out of direct sunlight. Enesco recommends hand washing your pieces using warm water, any mild soap, and to wipe them with a damp cloth. Place something soft underneath the area in which you are working just in case the piece gets dropped. When finished, wipe the item off with a soft towel and set it aside to dry completely. If you have intentions of reselling the pieces, try to keep all the original packaging. There is a higher resale value on the secondary market if everything is complete.

What Is Sam Butcher's Signature Worth?

No one can put a value on Sam Butcher's signature on a Precious Moments figurine. Appraisers have set a higher value on a signed piece since he is the artist. The system they seem to use averages out to approximately $30.00 on easily acquired pieces and approximately $50.00 on pieces that are harder to find. With certain special pieces the price could go up to an additional $100.00. Eugene Freedman's signature does not increase the value of a piece, yet Yasuhei Fujioka-San's signature could add $25.00 and Shuhei Fujioka's (his brother) could add $15.00.

SamB

Annual Production Marks

The annual production marks, located on the bottoms of the bases of Precious Moments figurines, reveal the year of the figurine's production and symbolize an inspirational message.

UM No Mark, before 1981

▲ Triangle, Mid-1981
Symbol of the Holy Trinity — God the Father, God the Son, and God the Holy Ghost.

Hourglass, 1982
Represents the time we have on earth to serve the Lord.

Fish, 1983
Earliest symbol used by believers of the early apostolic church.

Cross, 1984
Symbol of Christianity recognized worldwide.

Dove, 1985
Symbol of love and peace.

Olive Branch, 1986
Symbol of peace and understanding.

Cedar Tree, 1987
Symbol of strength, beauty, and preservation.

Flower, 1988
Represents God's love for his children.

Bow & Arrow, 1989
Represents the power of the Bible.

Flame, 1990
For those who have gone through the fire of life and found comfort in believing.

Vessel, 1991
A reminder of God's love which flows through the vessel of life.

G-Clef, 1992
Symbolizes the harmony of God's love.

Butterfly, 1993
Represents the rebirth of man who comes from darkness into the light.

Trumpet, 1994
Represents loving, caring, and sharing; also signified a battle cry and a herald of victory.

Ship, 1995
Ships, which are mentioned many times in the Scriptures, symbolically portray a message of hope.

Heart, 1996
Symbol of love.

Sword, 1997
From Hebrews 4:12, *For the Word of God is quick and powerful, and sharper than any two edged sword.*

Eyeglasses, 1998
Symbolizes Precious Moments' twentieth year and "the vision's still the same."

Star, 1999
From Matthew 2:2, *Where is He who has been born King of the Jews? For we have seen His star in the East and have come to worship Him.*

Egg, 2000
From Sam Butcher: *I have chosen the egg because it symbolizes the new millennium and a new beginning. Just as we know little of what the twenty-first century will bring, no one knows what is taking place inside an egg. Nor will they completely understand until it is hatched and God's wonderful plan is revealed. The egg speaks of birth, of new things to come — things known only to God alone.*

Sandal, 2001
The sandal represents our journey with the Lord.

Cross in Heart, 2002
Keeping faith in his heart, Sam chose a cross surrounded by a heart to symbolize faith. It is representative of the importance of faith now and in the next century.

Crown, 2003
The crown represents glory, dignity, and sovereignty. This is what Sam Butcher feels Precious Moments is all about.

Three-Petal Flower, 2004
In the world of Precious Moments, each petal in this flower symbolizes part of the message "loving, caring, and sharing."

Bread, 2005
Jesus said to them, *I am the bread of life; he who comes to me shall not hunger, and he who believes in me shall never thirst.* John 6:35

House, 2006
From Psalm 122:1-2, *I was glad when they said to me, Let us go to the house of the Lord! Our feet have been standing within your gates, O Jerusalem.*

Special Production Marks

Diamond
Appears on #103004, *We Belong To The Lord.*

Rosebud
Appears on #525049, *Good Friends Are Forever.*

Easter Seals Lily
Appears on annual figurines that benefit Easter Seals.

Flag
Appears on 1991 editions of *Bless Those Who Serve Their Country* figurines.

Flag
Appears on 1992 editions of *Bless Those Who Serve Their Country* figurines.

Four-Star Flag
Appears on 2002 *America Forever* series.

Know The Secondary Market

How do you find out about the production of Precious Moments pieces? Where do you start searching for these items? Precious Moments figurines have been produced since 1978. Finding outdated pieces can be difficult or easy, depending on the piece for which you are searching. The secondary market is the place to find these difficult Suspended, Retired, or Closed pieces.

The secondary market helps when a piece is no longer available at retail stores or at the retirement of the piece. When a piece is Retired, production is stopped on that piece. As the piece is sold out in the stores it becomes almost impossible to purchase. This same piece becomes more valuable on the secondary market and the collector is more willing to pay a higher price, thus increasing the value of the item. The collector today has more opportunity in the market because of the Internet. Most collectors have computers and can go to different websites that deal with the secondary market. The collector can check out these sites to purchase some of those difficult to find pieces. We have listed some of these on page 426.

There are several ways to end the production of a piece. When a piece is Retired, the mold is broken and cannot be produced again. No notice is given to the collector when a piece is Retired. The collector is given only a small amount of time to purchase a piece that will be pulled out of production. Suspended pieces are temporarily taken out of production but can be brought back into production at a later date with a change of some sort to the piece. Dated figurines or pieces with a limited production time are called Closed pieces. They were produced for a limited time, possibly for one year, or in a limited quantity.

In addition to these pieces there are others produced for certain occasions or events. These are called Special Event, Limited Edition, and Club Member Exclusive figurines. Dated Annual means that the piece was issued for one year and includes a date on the figurine; Annuals were issued for one year only, but do not have dates on them. The ongoing, or Open, pieces can be purchased at retail dealers or on Internet sites. Pieces produced before mid-1981 had no symbol on the understamp and are called Unmarked (UM). Precious Moments plates and ornaments were not marked until 1984.

Know the item you are purchasing on the secondary market and examine it for damage. Watch for dings, hairline cracks, paint discoloration, or other damage. Watch for fakes! There are some out there. Know your collection, read price guides, know what you are looking at. Only you can determine what you want in your collection — with or without boxes, damaged pieces bought at a good price, or pieces in mint condition. It's all up to you.

How To Use Your Precious Moments Price Guide

Many collectors confuse the copyright date with the date of issue. You must refer to the annual production symbol, not the date, to determine what year your pieces were manufactured. This price guide shows the suggested retail price for each piece. It lists when it was introduced and shows the changes in production symbols for the piece.

This guide lists items in the index at the back of the book in numerical order. The pieces manufactured from 1982 to the present are numbered on the understamp. If you do not know the number but do know the name of the piece, check the general index in the back of the book. The quickest and most accurate means of identification is the item number that appears on the understamp of most items manufactured from 1982 to the present. This number also appears in ads, brochures, and catalogs.

Remember: Errors are made all the time; unmarked pieces can sometimes be pieces that were just not marked.

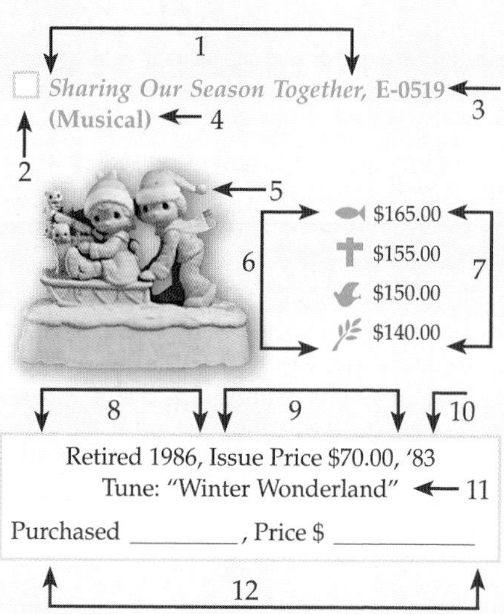

1. **Title** — Spiritual name given to the piece.
2. **Checkbox for inventory** — Box to check to keep track of a personal collection.
3. **Item Number** — The quickest and most accurate means of identification; appears on the understamp of most items.
4. **Object** — Tells whether item is something other than a figurine — ornament, musical, frame, plate, plaque, box, etc. (If nothing is listed in parentheses, it is a figurine).
5. **Picture** — Photo of the item. We did not have photos of all items, but included any information known about the piece .
6. **Production symbols** — Annual Production Symbols; shows all symbols used for a particular figurine.
7. **Secondary market value** — The cost of the item when it is sold on the secondary market, according to production mark.
8. **Production status** — States if the piece has been Suspended or Retired, is a Limited Edition, Annual or Dated Annual, Club Member Exclusive, Special Event, or Open (still available). Date is included if known.
9. **Issue price** — The cost of the item at the time it was first introduced.
10. **Year introduced** — Lists the year the piece was first issued.
11. **Collector information** — Gives important facts about the piece: series, number in set, or name of tune played by musical pieces.
12. **Purchase information** — Gives the collector space to record information on the purchase date and price for each piece.

General Figurines

☐ *Sharing Our Season Together,* E-0501

$190.00
$180.00
$173.00
$168.00

Suspended 1986, Issue Price $50.00, '83

Purchased __________, Price $ ____________

☐ *Jesus Is The Light That Shines,* E-0502

$77.00
$72.00
$68.00
$62.00

Suspended 1986, Issue Price $22.50, '83

Purchased ______ , Price $_______________

☐ *Blessings From My House To Yours,* E-0503

$92.00
$82.00
$77.00
$72.00

Suspended 1986, Issue Price $27.00, '83

Purchased __________, Price $____________

☐ *Christmastime Is For Sharing,* E-0504

$128.00
$118.00
$110.00
$105.00
$102.00
$100.00
$98.00
$93.00

Retired 1990, Issue Price $37.00, '83

Purchased __________, Price $____________

☐ *Christmastime Is For Sharing,* E-0505 (Plate)

UM $87.00

Dated Annual 1983, Issue Price $85.00
Series: *Joy Of Christmas,* Second Issue

Purchased __________, Price $____________

☐ *Surrounded With Joy,* E-0506

$90.00
$88.00
$83.00
$80.00
$78.00
$75.00
$72.00

Retired 1989, Issue Price $21.00, '83

Purchased __________, Price $____________

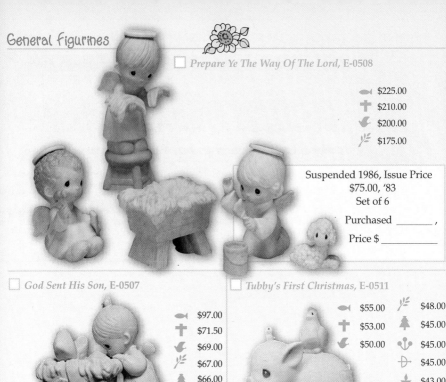

☐ *Prepare Ye The Way Of The Lord, E-0508*

- $225.00
- $210.00
- $200.00
- $175.00

Suspended 1986, Issue Price $75.00, '83
Set of 6

Purchased ______,

Price $ __________

☐ *God Sent His Son, E-0507*

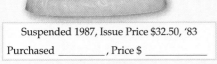

- $97.00
- $71.50
- $69.00
- $67.00
- $66.00

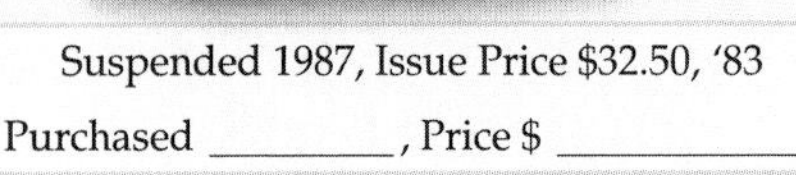

Suspended 1987, Issue Price $32.50, '83

Purchased ________, Price $ ___________

☐ *Bringing God's Blessing To You, E-0509*

- $100.00
- $95.00
- $90.00
- $88.00
- $85.00

Suspended 1987, Issue Price $35.00, '83

Purchased ________, Price $ ___________

☐ *Tubby's First Christmas, E-0511*

- $55.00
- $53.00
- $50.00
- $48.00
- $45.00
- $45.00
- $45.00
- $43.00
- $40.00
- $40.00
- $35.00

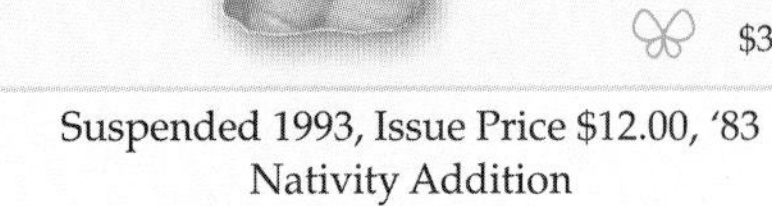

Suspended 1993, Issue Price $12.00, '83
Nativity Addition

Purchased ________, Price $ ___________

☐ *It's A Perfect Boy, E-0512*

- $75.00
- $73.00
- $68.00
- $63.00
- $60.00
- $58.00
- $55.00
- $53.00
- $53.00

Suspended 1990, Issue Price $18.50, '83
Nativity Addition

Purchased ________, Price $ ___________

☐ *Surround Us With Joy*, E-0513 (Ornament)

$75.00

Error: Missing date — add $40.00 to value.

Dated Annual 1983, Issue Price $9.00, '83

Purchased ____________,

Price $________________

☐ *Mother Sew Dear*, E-0514 (Ornament)

$36.00	$20.00
$29.00	$20.00
$29.00	$20.00
$29.00	$20.00
$26.00	$19.00
$25.00	$19.00
$24.00	$19.00
$23.00	$19.00
$22.00	$19.00
$21.00	$19.00

Error: Also exists with a stamped ink cross; add $32.00 to value.

Retired 2002, Issue Price $9.00, '83

Purchased _________, Price $ ____________

☐ *To A Special Dad*, E-0515 (Ornament)

$50.00	$38.00
$48.00	$35.00
$45.00	$30.00

Error: Also exists with a stamped ink cross; add $50.00 to value.

Suspended 1988, Issue Price $9.00, '83

Purchased _________, Price $ ____________

☐ *The Purr-fect Grandma*, E-0516 (Ornament)

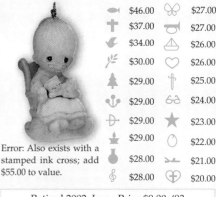

$46.00	$27.00
$37.00	$27.00
$34.00	$26.00
$30.00	$26.00
$29.00	$25.00
$29.00	$24.00
$29.00	$23.00
$29.00	$22.00
$28.00	$21.00
$28.00	$20.00

Error: Also exists with a stamped ink cross; add $55.00 to value.

Retired 2002, Issue Price $9.00, '83

Purchased _________, Price $ ____________

☐ *The Perfect Grandpa*, E-0517 (Ornament)

$48.00	$35.00
$42.00	$32.00
$39.00	$30.00
$37.00	$29.00

Error: Also exists with a stamped ink cross; add $50.00 to value.

Suspended 1990, Issue Price $9.00, '83

Purchased _________, Price $ ____________

☐ *Blessed Are The Pure In Heart*, E-0518 (Ornament)

$45.00

Dated Annual 1983, Issue Price $9.00, '83
"Baby's First Christmas"

Purchased _________, Price $ ____________

☐ *Sharing Our Season Together*, E-0519 (Musical)

$165.00

$155.00

$150.00

$140.00

Retired 1986, Issue Price $70.00, '83
Tune: "Winter Wonderland"

Purchased ______________,

Price $_________________

☐ *Wee Three Kings,* **E-0520 (Musical)**

$140.00
$130.00
$120.00
$110.00

Suspended 1986, Issue Price $60.00, '83
Tune: "We Three Kings"

Purchased ________, Price $ ____________

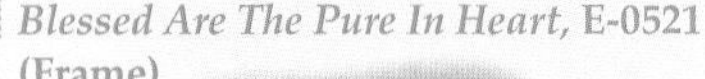

☐ *Blessed Are The Pure In Heart,* **E-0521 (Frame)**

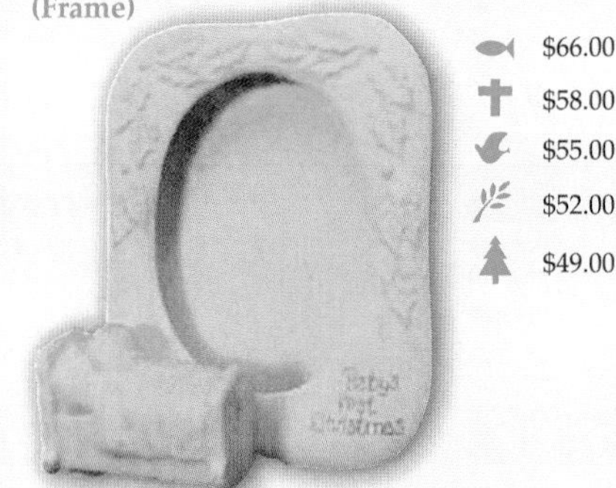

$66.00
$58.00
$55.00
$52.00
$49.00

Suspended 1987, Issue Price $18.00, '83
"Baby's First Christmas"

Purchased ________, Price $ ____________

☐ *Surrounded With Joy,* **E-0522 (Bell)**

$65.00

Error: Has been reported missing date; add $45.00 to value.

Dated Annual 1983, Issue Price $18.00, '83

Purchased ________,

Price $ ____________

☐ *Onward Christian Soldiers,* **E-0523**

UM $260.00
$60.00
$57.00
$56.00
$55.00
$54.00
$53.00
$52.00
$51.00
$50.00
$49.00
$48.00
$47.00
$46.00
$45.00
$44.00
$43.00
$42.00
$42.00
$40.00
$40.00

Though very rare, unmarked pieces could have been produced in any of the years of production. Consider Fish as the first mark. Also exists with a decal fish; add $115.00 to value.

Retired 2002, Issue Price $24.00, '83

Purchased ________, Price $ ____________

☐ *You Can't Run Away From God,* **E-0525**

$175.00
$98.00
$95.00
$93.00
$90.00
$88.00
$86.00
$85.00

Error: Also exists with a decal fish; add $125.00 to value.

Retired 1989, Issue Price $28.50, '83

Purchased ________, Price $ ____________

☐ *He Upholdeth Those Who Fall,* **E-0526**

UM $155.00
$100.00
$95.00
$90.00

Unmarked pieces could have been produced in any of the years of production. Consider Fish as the first mark. Also exists with a removable inked fish; add $120.00 to value.

Suspended 1985, Issue Price $28.50, '83

Purchased ________,

Price $ ____________

His Eye Is On The Sparrow, E-0530

Mark	Price
Fish	$130.00
Cross	$126.00
Dove	$123.00
Olive Branch	$122.00
Cedar Tree	$120.00

Retired 1987, Issue Price $28.50, '83

Purchased ________, Price $ ___________

O Come All Ye Faithful, E-0531 (Ornament)

Mark	Price
Fish	$55.00
Cross	$53.00
Dove	$50.00
Olive Branch	$48.00

Suspended 1986, Issue Price $9.00, '83

Purchased ________, Price $ ___________

Let Heaven And Nature Sing, E-0532 (Ornament)

Mark	Price
Fish	$48.00
Cross	$45.00
Dove	$43.00
Olive Branch	$40.00

Retired 1986, Issue Price $9.00, '83

Purchased ________, Price $ ___________

Suspended 1986, Issue Price $9.00, '83

Purchased ________, Price $ ___________

Tell Me The Story Of Jesus, E-0533 (Ornament)

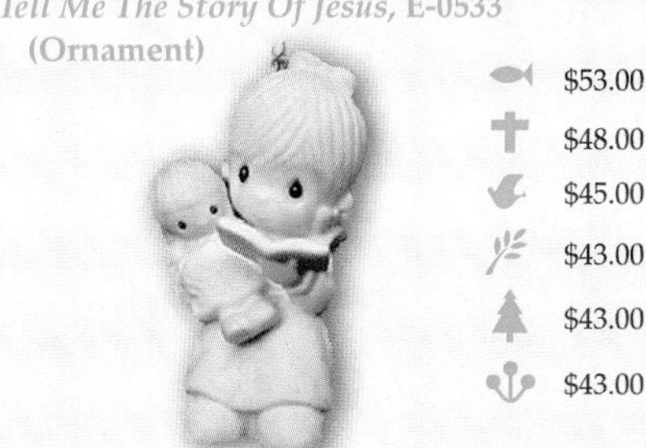

Mark	Price
Fish	$53.00
Cross	$48.00
Dove	$45.00
Olive Branch	$43.00
Cedar Tree	$43.00
Flower	$43.00

Suspended 1988, Issue Price $9.00, '83

Purchased ________, Price $ ___________

To Thee With Love, E-0534 (Ornament)

Mark	Price
Fish	$50.00
Cross	$45.00
Dove	$42.00
Olive Branch	$40.00
Cedar Tree	$39.00
Flower	$35.00
Bow & Arrow	$34.00

Retired 1989, Issue Price $9.00, '83

Purchased ________, Price $ ___________

Love Is Patient, E-0535 (Ornament)

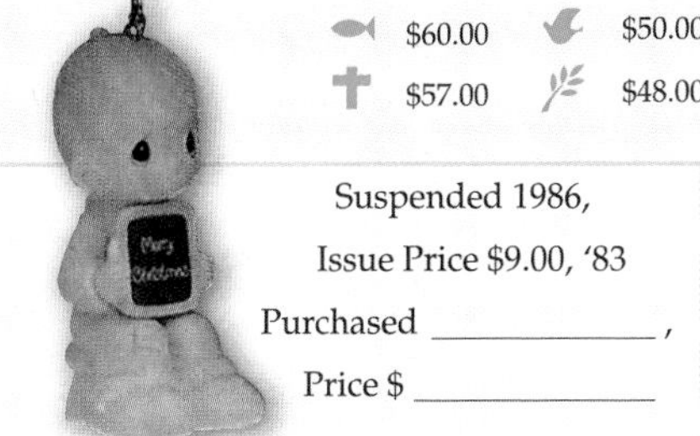

Mark	Price
Fish	$60.00
Cross	$57.00
Dove	$50.00
Olive Branch	$48.00

Suspended 1986,

Issue Price $9.00, '83

Purchased ___________,

Price $ ___________

Love Is Patient, E-0536 (Ornament)

Mark	Price
Fish	$65.00
Cross	$60.00
Dove	$58.00
Olive Branch	$58.00

☐ *Jesus Is The Light That Shines*, E-0537 (Ornament)

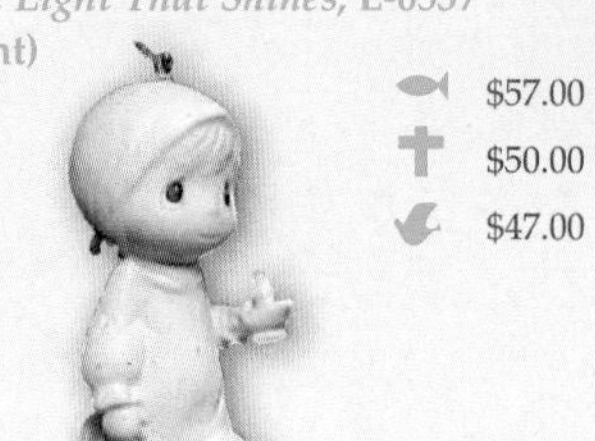

Mark	Price
Fish	$57.00
Cross	$50.00
Dove	$47.00

Suspended 1985, Issue Price $9.00, '83

Purchased ________, Price $ ___________

☐ *Wee Three Kings*, E-0538 (Plate)

Mark	Price
UM	$47.00
Cross	$46.00
Dove	$45.00
Olive Branch	$43.00

Limited Ed. 15,000, Issue Price $40.00, '83
Series: *Christmas Collection* – Third Issue;
Individually Numbered

Purchased ________, Price $ ___________

☐ *Katie Lynne*, E-0539 (Doll)

Mark	Price
UM	$210.00
Fish	$185.00
Cross	$183.00
Dove	$180.00
Olive Branch	$178.00
Cedar Tree	$176.00
Anchor	$175.00

Suspended 1988, Issue Price $150.00, '83

Purchased ________, Price $ ___________

☐ *Jesus Loves Me*, E-1372B

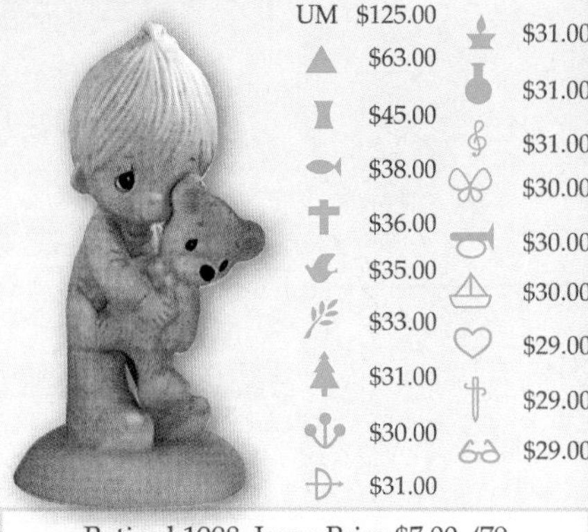

Mark	Price
UM	$125.00
Triangle	$63.00
Hourglass	$45.00
Fish	$38.00
Cross	$36.00
Dove	$35.00
Olive Branch	$33.00
Cedar Tree	$31.00
Anchor	$30.00
Bow & Arrow	$31.00
Flame	$31.00
Vessel	$31.00
G-Clef	$31.00
Butterfly	$30.00
Trumpet	$30.00
Ship	$30.00
Heart	$29.00
Sword	$29.00
Eyeglasses	$29.00

Retired 1998, Issue Price $7.00, '79
One of the Original "21"

Purchased ________, Price $ ___________

☐ *Jesus Loves Me*, E-1372G

Mark	Price
UM	$130.00
Triangle	$80.00
Hourglass	$70.00
Fish	$60.00
Cross	$55.00
Dove	$52.00
Olive Branch	$49.00
Cedar Tree	$47.00
Anchor	$45.00
Bow & Arrow	$42.00
Flame	$40.00
Vessel	$38.00
G-Clef	$38.00
Butterfly	$36.00
Trumpet	$35.00
Ship	$34.00
Heart	$33.00
Sword	$32.00
Eyeglasses	$31.00
Star	$30.00
Egg	$30.00
Plow	$30.00
Cross in Heart	$30.00
Crown	$30.00

Retired 2003, Issue Price $7.00, '79
One of the Original "21"

Purchased ________, Price $ ___________

☐ *Smile, God Loves You*, E-1373B

Mark	Price
UM	$120.00
Triangle	$70.00
Hourglass	$65.00
Fish	$60.00
Cross	$50.00

There is a brown eye variation, which is actually a very pale black eye.

Retired 1984, Issue Price $7.00, '79
One of the Original "21"

Purchased ________, Price $ ___________

☐ *Jesus Is The Light, E-1373G*

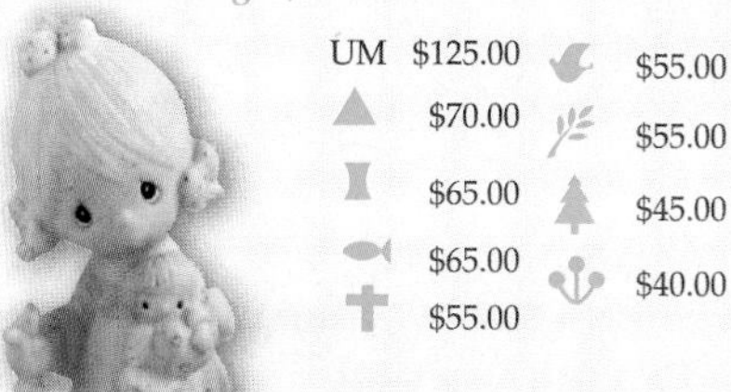

Mark	Price	Mark	Price
UM	$125.00	[Dove]	$55.00
[Triangle]	$70.00	[Olive Branch]	$55.00
[Hourglass]	$65.00	[Cedar Tree]	$45.00
[Fish]	$65.00	[Anchor]	$40.00
[Cross]	$55.00		

Retired 1988, Issue Price $7.00, '79
One of the Original "21"
Purchased ________, Price $ __________

☐ *Love Lifted Me, E-1375A*

Mark	Price	Mark	Price
UM	$155.00	[Fish]	$90.00
[Triangle]	$95.00	[Cross]	$88.00
[Hourglass]	$90.00	[Dove]	$88.00
		[Olive Branch]	$88.00
		[Cedar Tree]	$80.00
		[Anchor]	$75.00
		[Bow & Arrow]	$73.00
		[Flame]	$70.00
		[Vessel]	$70.00
		[G-Clef]	$70.00
		[Butterfly]	$65.00

Retired 1993, Issue Price $11.00, '79
One of the Original "21"
Purchased ________, Price $ __________

☐ *Praise The Lord Anyhow, E-1374B*

There are variations in the color of the dog's nose (brown or black) and variations in the color of the ice cream.

Mark	Price
UM	$125.00
[Triangle]	$110.00
[Hourglass]	$85.00

Retired 1982, Issue Price $8.00, '79
One of the Original "21"
Purchased ________, Price $ __________

☐ *Prayer Changes Things, E-1375B*

Mark	Price
UM	$230.00
[Triangle]	$175.00
[Hourglass]	$173.00
[Fish]	$170.00
[Cross]	$165.00

Suspended 1984, Issue Price $11.00, '79
One of the Original "21"
Purchased ________, Price $ __________

☐ *Make A Joyful Noise, E-1374G*

Figurine has experienced mold shrinkage problems; variations in the position of the goose are common.

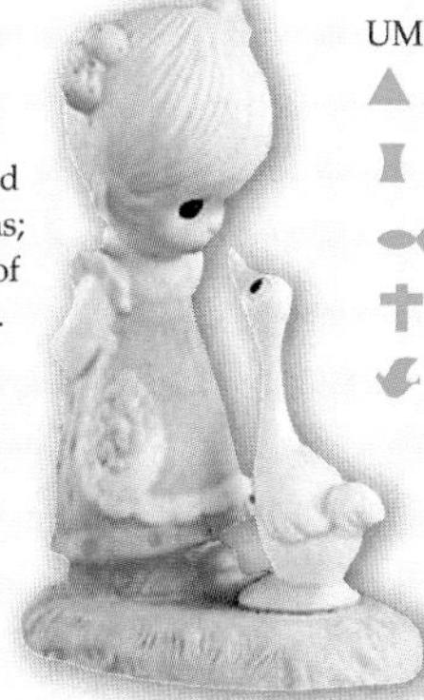

Mark	Price	Mark	Price	Mark	Price	Mark	Price
UM	$115.00	[Olive Branch]	$50.00	[G-Clef]	$35.00	[Eyeglasses]	$35.00
[Triangle]	$70.00	[Cedar Tree]	$45.00	[Butterfly]	$35.00	[Star]	$35.00
[Hourglass]	$70.00	[Anchor]	$45.00	[Trumpet]	$35.00	[Egg]	$35.00
[Fish]	$60.00	[Bow & Arrow]	$42.00	[Ship]	$35.00		
[Cross]	$58.00	[Flame]	$40.00	[Heart]	$35.00		
[Dove]	$55.00	[Vessel]	$35.00	[Sword]	$35.00		

Retired 2000, Issue Price $8.00, '79
One of the Original "21"
Purchased ________, Price $ __________

Love One Another, E-1376

UM $130.00
$72.00
$55.00
$50.00
$48.00
$46.00
$45.00
$45.00
$45.00
$44.00
$42.00
$40.00
$40.00
$40.00
$40.00
$40.00
$40.00
$40.00
$40.00
$40.00
$40.00
$40.00
$40.00
$40.00
$40.00
$40.00

Open, Issue Price $10.00, '79
One of the Original "21"

Purchased ________, Price $ ____________

He Leadeth Me, E-1377A

UM $160.00
$120.00
$100.00
$100.00
$95.00

Classic variation: the incorrect inspirational title, *He Careth For You*, is on the understamp decal of some unmarked pieces. This is one of the most difficult to find of all the classic variations. The few known sales are in the $350.00 range. Reintroduced in 1998 with a color change as E-1377R — November 19 on QVC and November 21 at DSRs and Century Circle Retailers.

Suspended 1984, Reintroduced 1998,
Retired 1998, Issue Price $9.00, '79
One of the Original "21"

Purchased ________, Price $ ____________

He Careth For You, E-1377B

Classic variation: The incorrect inspiration title, *He Leadeth Me* is on the understamp decal of some unmarked pieces. This is a more difficult variation to find than the variation of E-1377A. Known sale at $600.00.

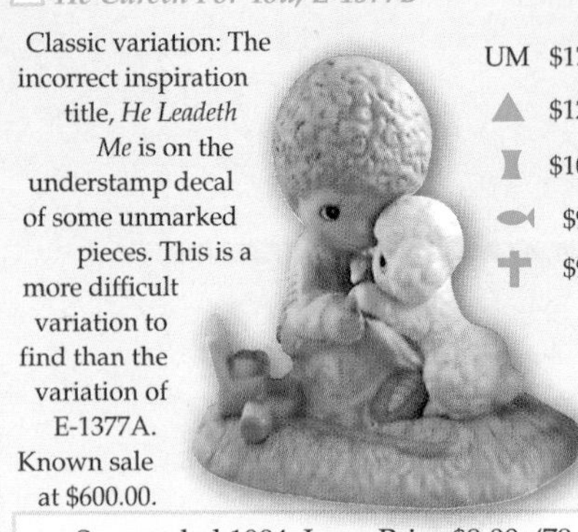

UM $170.00
$125.00
$100.00
$98.00
$95.00

Suspended 1984, Issue Price $9.00, '79
One of the Original "21"

Purchased ________, Price $ ____________

He Leadeth Me, E-1377R

Brought back with a color change for 11/21/98 Turn Back The Clock Event Celebration. Retired after the event.

$40.00

Retired 1998, Issue Price $9.00, '98

Purchased ________, Price $ ____________

God Loveth A Cheerful Giver, E-1378

UM $2,000.00

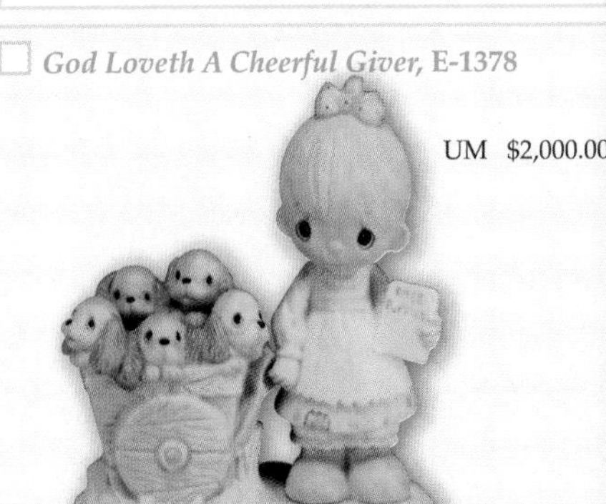

Retired 1981, Issue Price $15.00, '79
One of the Original "21"

Purchased ________, Price $ ____________

Love Is Kind, E-1379A

UM $150.00
▲ $110.00
⧗ $95.00
Fish $90.00
Cross $88.00

Suspended 1984, Reintroduced 1998, Retired 1998, Issue Price $8.00, '79
One of the Original "21"
Purchased ________, Price $ ____________

God Understands, E-1379B

UM $135.00
▲ $105.00
⧗ $98.00
Fish $95.00
Cross $90.00

Suspended 1984, Issue Price $8.00, '79
One of the Original "21"
Purchased ________, Price $ ____________

God Understands, E-1379BR

Flower $35.00

Retired 2001, Issue Price $19.50, '01
Back To School Event
Purchased ________, Price $ ____________

Love Is Kind, E-1379R

Eyeglasses $65.00

Piece retired immediately after event. Color change for reintroduction. Precious Moments Twentieth Anniversary understamp.

Retired 1998, Issue Price $8.00, '98
Turn Back The Clock Event Celebration
Purchased ________, Price $ ____________

O, How I Love Jesus, E-1380B

UM $160.00
▲ $140.00
⧗ $125.00
Fish $120.00
Cross $110.00

Retired 1984, Issue Price $8.00, '79
One of the Original "21"
Purchased ________, Price $ ____________

His Burden Is Light, E-1380G

UM $165.00
▲ $145.00
⧗ $130.00
Fish $125.00
Cross $115.00

Retired 1984, Issue Price $8.00, '79
One of the Original "21"
Purchased ________, Price $ ____________

☐ *Jesus Is The Answer*, E-1381

UM $190.00
▲ $165.00
⌶ $150.00
Fish $140.00
Cross $135.00

E-1381 was re-sculpted and reintroduced in April 1992 as E-1381R. E-1381R was subsequently retired in 1996.

Suspended 1984, Reintroduced 1992, Retired 1996, Issue Price $11.50, '79
One of the Original "21"
Purchased ________, Price $ __________

☐ *Jesus Is The Answer*, E-1381R

G-Clef $80.00
Butterfly $70.00
Trumpet $68.00
Ship $65.00
Heart $63.00

Retired 1996, Issue Price $55.00, '92
St. Jude Children's Research Hospital Exclusive
Purchased ________, Price $ __________

☐ *We Have Seen His Star*, E-2010

UM $155.00
▲ $130.00
⌶ $115.00
Fish $100.00
Cross $95.00

Suspended 1984, Issue Price $8.00, '79
One of the Original "21"
Purchased__________,
Price $ __________

☐ *Come Let Us Adore Him*, E-2011

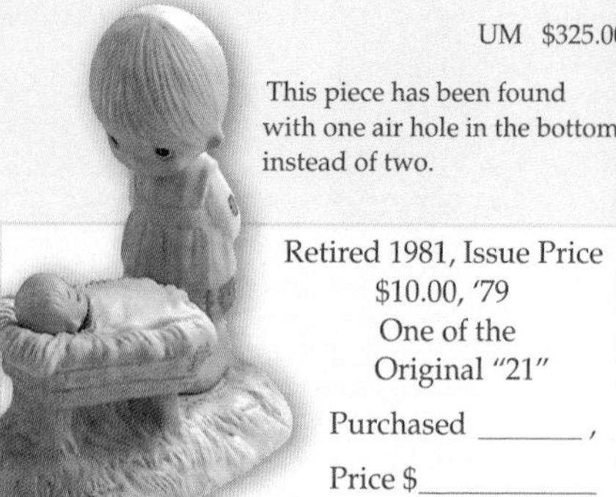

UM $325.00

This piece has been found with one air hole in the bottom instead of two.

Retired 1981, Issue Price $10.00, '79
One of the Original "21"
Purchased ______,
Price $__________

☐ *Jesus Is Born*, E-2012

UM $175.00
▲ $155.00
⌶ $150.00
Fish $140.00
Cross $135.00

Suspended 1984, Issue Price $12.00, '79
One of the Original "21"
Purchased ________, Price $ __________

☐ *Unto Us A Child Is Born*, E-2013

UM $175.00
▲ $155.00
⌶ $150.00
Fish $140.00
Cross $135.00

Suspended 1984, Issue Price $12.00, '79
One of the Original "21"
Purchased ________, Price $ __________

Joy To The World, E-2343 (Ornament)

Mark	Price
UM	$65.00
[Cross]	$60.00
[Dove]	$55.00
[Olive Branch]	$50.00
[Cedar Tree]	$45.00
[Flower]	$40.00

Suspended 1988, Issue Price $9.00, '82

Purchased ________, Price $ __________

Joy To The World, E-2344 (Candle Climbers)

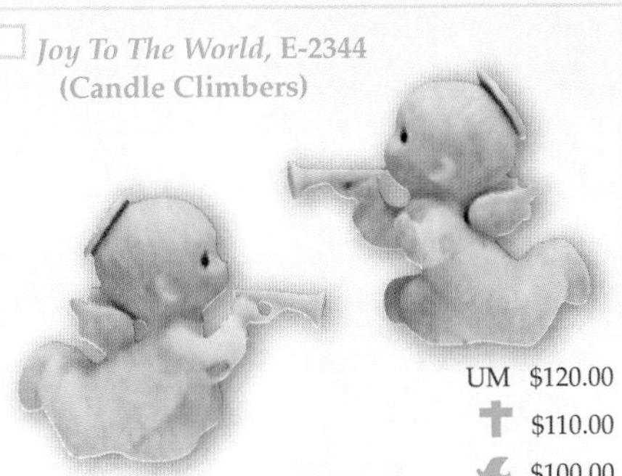

Mark	Price
UM	$120.00
[Cross]	$110.00
[Dove]	$100.00

Suspended 1985, Issue Price $20.00, '82
Set of 2

Purchased ________, Price $ __________

May Your Christmas Be Cozy, E-2345

Mark	Price
[Hourglass]	$85.00
[Fish]	$78.00
[Cross]	$60.00

Suspended 1984, Issue Price $23.00, '82

Purchased ________, Price $ __________

Let Heaven And Nature Sing, E-2346 (Musical)

Mark	Price
UM	$180.00
[Hourglass]	$160.00
[Fish]	$145.00
[Cross]	$140.00
[Dove]	$138.00
[Olive Branch]	$130.00
[Cedar Tree]	$125.00
[Flower]	$120.00
[Bow & Arrow]	$115.00

Unmarked pieces could have been produced in any of the years of production. Consider Hourglass as the first mark.

Suspended 1989, Issue Price $50.00, '82
Tune: "Joy To The World"

Purchased ________, Price $ __________

Let Heaven And Nature Sing, E-2347 (Plate)

Mark	Price
UM	$45.00
[Cross]	$42.00
[Dove]	$42.00
[Olive Branch]	$42.00

Limited Ed. 15,000, Issue Price $40.00, '82
Series: *Christmas Collection* — Second Issue, Individually Numbered

Purchased ________, Price $ __________

May Your Christmas Be Warm, E-2348

Mark	Price
[Hourglass]	$160.00
[Fish]	$150.00
[Cross]	$145.00
[Dove]	$140.00
[Olive Branch]	$135.00
[Cedar Tree]	$130.00
[Flower]	$125.00

Suspended 1988, Issue Price $30.00, '82

Purchased ________, Price $ __________

Tell Me The Story Of Jesus, E-2349

$140.00
$125.00
$115.00
$105.00

This is a favorite of many collectors and is scarce on the secondary market.

Suspended 1985, Issue Price $30.00, '82
Purchased ________, Price $ ___________

Dropping In For Christmas, E-2350

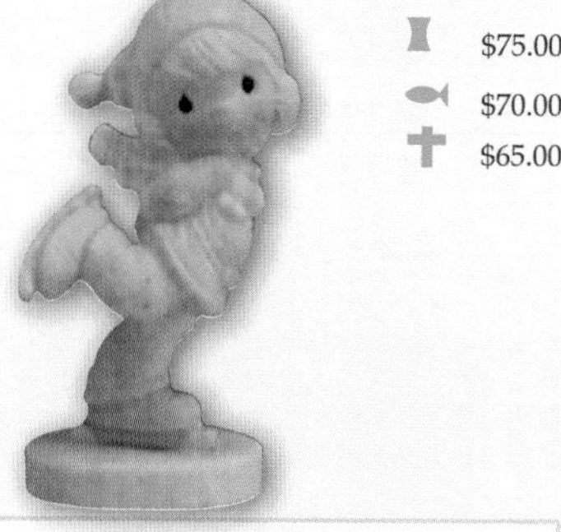

$75.00
$70.00
$65.00

Suspended 1984, Issue Price $18.00, '82
Purchased ________, Price $ ___________

Holy Smokes, E-2351

$150.00
$140.00
$130.00
$120.00
$110.00
$100.00

Retired 1987, Issue Price $27.00, '82
Purchased ________, Price $ ___________

O Come All Ye Faithful, E-2352 (Musical)

UM $200.00
$165.00
$155.00
$150.00

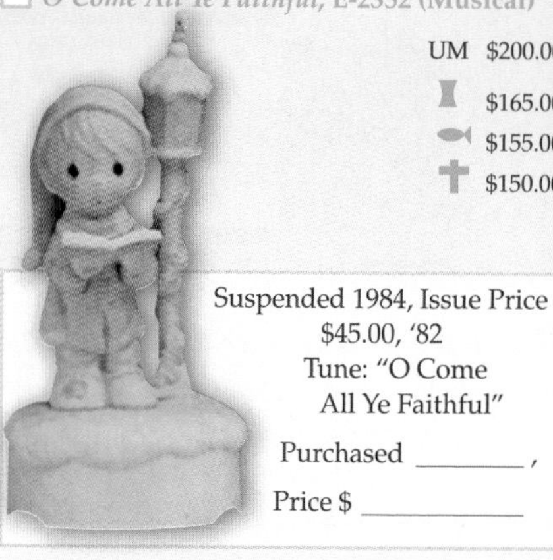

Suspended 1984, Issue Price $45.00, '82
Tune: "O Come All Ye Faithful"
Purchased ________,
Price $ ___________

O Come All Ye Faithful, E-2353

$110.00
$100.00
$95.00
$90.00
$85.00

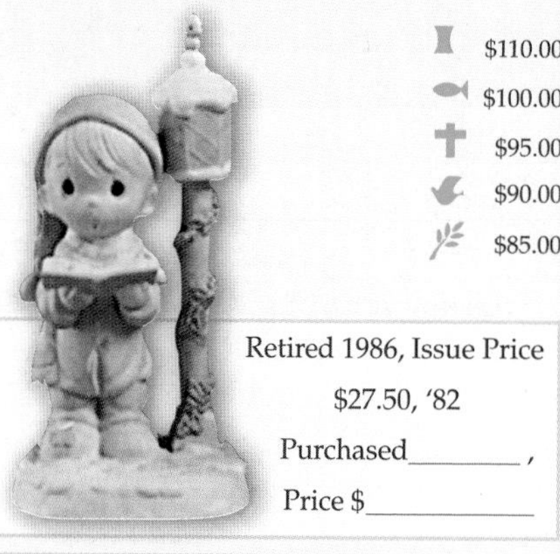

Retired 1986, Issue Price $27.50, '82
Purchased________,
Price $___________

I'll Play My Drum For Him, E-2355 (Musical)

$235.00
$225.00
$215.00

Suspended 1984, Issue Price $45.00, '82
Tune: "Little Drummer Boy"
Purchased ________, Price $ ___________

I'll Play My Drum For Him, E-2356

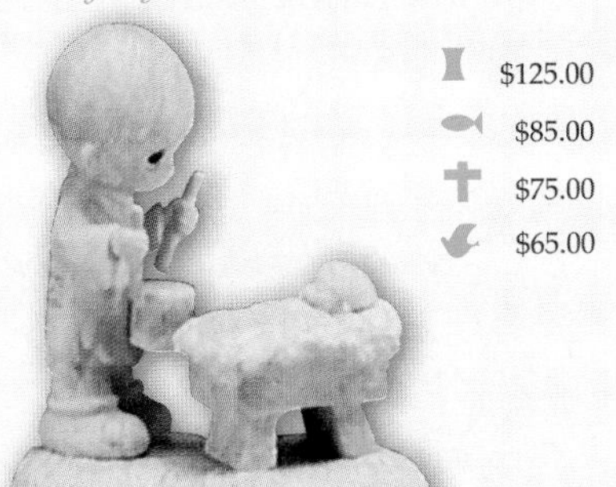

Mark	Price
Hourglass	$125.00
Fish	$85.00
Cross	$75.00
Dove	$65.00

Suspended 1985, Issue Price $30.00, '82

Purchased ________, Price $ __________

I'll Play My Drum For Him, E-2359 (Ornament)

Mark	Price
Hourglass	$86.00

Prototypes were dated. The actual production piece was not.

Dated Annual 1982, Issue Price $9.00, '82

Purchased ________, Price $ __________

I'll Play My Drum For Him, E-2357 (Plate)

UM $65.00

Dated Annual 1982, Issue Price $40.00, '82

Series: *Joy Of Christmas* — First Issue

Purchased ________, Price $ __________

I'll Play My Drum For Him, E-2360

Hourglass	$50.00	G-Clef	$36.00
Fish	$48.00	Butterfly	$34.00
Cross	$46.00	Trumpet	$34.00
Dove	$44.00	Ship	$32.00
Olive Branch	$42.00	Heart	$32.00
Cedar Tree	$42.00	Sword	$30.00
Anchor	$40.00	Eyeglasses	$30.00
Bow & Arrow	$40.00	Star	$28.00
Flame	$38.00	Egg	$28.00
Vessel	$36.00	Bowtie	$28.00

Retired 2001, Issue Price $16.00, '82

Nativity Addition

Purchased ________, Price $ __________

I'll Play My Drum For Him, E-2358 (Bell)

UM $65.00

Dated Annual 1982, Issue Price $17.00, '82

Purchased ________, Price $ __________

Christmas Joy From Head To Toe, E-2361

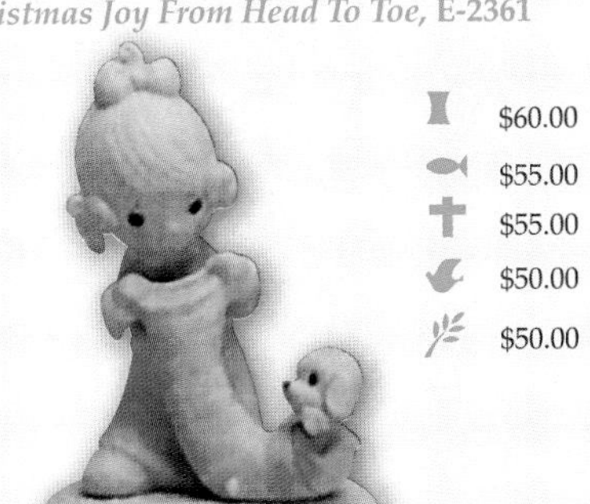

Mark	Price
Hourglass	$60.00
Fish	$55.00
Cross	$55.00
Dove	$50.00
Olive Branch	$50.00

Suspended 1986, Issue Price $25.00, '82

Purchased ________, Price $ __________

☐ *Baby's First Christmas*, E-2362 (Ornament)

UM	$50.00
Cross	$45.00
Dove	$42.00
Olive Branch	$40.00
Cedar Tree	$38.00
Flower	$35.00

Suspended 1988, Issue Price $9.00, '82

Purchased ________, Price $ ___________

☐ *The First Noel*, E-2365

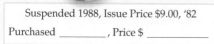

UM	$85.0
Hourglass	$70.0
Fish	$70.0
Cross	$68.0

Suspended 1984, Issue Price $16.00, '82
Nativity Addition

Purchased ________, Price $ ___________

☐ *Camel*, E-2363

Cedar Tree	$35.00
Flower	$35.00
Bow & Arrow	$35.00
Flame	$35.00
Vessel	$35.00
G-Clef	$35.00
Butterfly	$35.00
Trumpet	$35.00
Ship	$35.00
Heart	$35.00
Sword	$35.00
Eyeglasses	$35.00
Star	$35.00
Egg	$35.00
Sandal	$35.00
Cross in Heart	$35.00
Crown	$35.00

Retired 2003, Issue Price $20.00, '82
Nativity Addition

Purchased ________, Price $ ___________

☐ *The First Noel*, E-2366

UM	$87.0
Hourglass	$78.0
Fish	$75.0
Cross	$65.0

Suspended 1984, Issue Price $16.00, '82
Nativity Addition

Purchased ________, Price $ ___________

☐ *Goat*, E-2364

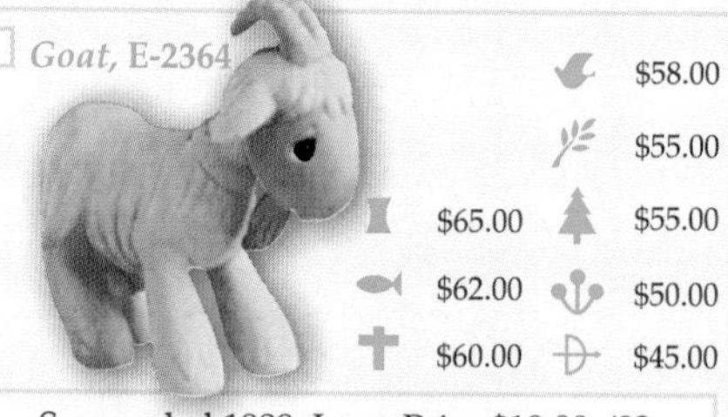

Hourglass	$65.00
Fish	$62.00
Cross	$60.00
Dove	$58.00
Olive Branch	$55.00
Cedar Tree	$55.00
Flower	$50.00
Bow & Arrow	$45.00

Suspended 1989, Issue Price $10.00, '82
Nativity Addition

Purchased ________, Price $ ___________

☐ *The First Noel*, E-2367 (Ornament)

Hourglass	$87.00
Fish	$78.00
Cross	$75.00

Suspended 1984, Issue Price $9.00, '83

Purchased ________, Price $ ___________

☐ *The First Noel*, E-2368 (Ornament)

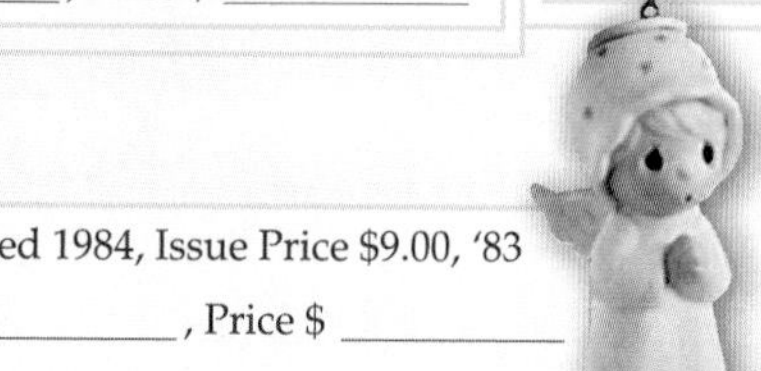

Mark	Price
Hourglass	$87.00
Fish	$78.00
Cross	$75.00

Suspended 1984, Issue Price $9.00, '83

Purchased ________, Price $ ___________

Dropping In For Christmas, E-2369 (Ornament)

UM $75.00
$55.00
$53.00
$50.00
$48.00
$45.00

Retired 1986, Issue Price $9.00, '82

Purchased ________, Price $ __________

Unicorn, E-2371 (Ornament)

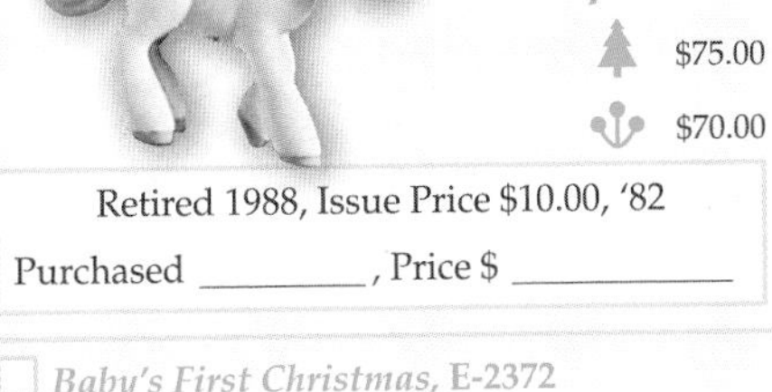

UM $100.00
$95.00
$90.00
$85.00
$80.00
$75.00
$70.00

Retired 1988, Issue Price $10.00, '82

Purchased ________, Price $ __________

Baby's First Christmas, E-2372 (Ornament)

Exists with and without title, *Baby's First Christmas*, in unmarked version. Titled piece is rarer; add $10.00 to value.

UM $45.00
$40.00
$35.00

Suspended 1985, Issue Price $9.00, '82

Purchased ________, Price $ __________

Bundles Of Joy, E-2374

Retired 1993, Issue Price $27.50, '82

Purchased ________, Price $ __________

$135.00	$95.00	$80.00	$65.00
$105.00	$90.00	$75.00	$60.00
$100.00	$85.00	$70.00	$55.00

Dropping Over For Christmas, E-2375

$135.00
$115.00
$105.00
$95.00
$90.00
$85.00
$80.00
$75.00
$70.00
$65.00

Retired 1991, Issue Price $30.00, '82

Purchased ________, Price $ __________

Dropping Over For Christmas, E-2376 (Ornament)

$65.00
$50.00
$45.00
$40.00

Retired 1985, Issue Price $9.00, '82

Purchased ________, Price $ __________

Our First Christmas Together, E-2377

$110.00
$100.00
$90.00
$85.00

Suspended 1985, Issue Price $35.00, '82

Purchased ________, Price $ __________

☐ *Our First Christmas Together*, **E-2378 (Plate)**

UM	$45.00
Cross	$40.00
Dove	$40.00

Suspended 1985, Issue Price $30.00, '82
Purchased ________, Price $ ___________

☐ *Mouse With Cheese*, **E-2381 (Ornament)**

Hourglass	$125.00
Fish	$100.00
Cross	$100.00

Suspended 1984, Issue Price $9.00, '82
Purchased ________, Price $ ___________

☐ *O Holy Night*, **E-2381R**

Crown	$15.00

Open, Issue Price $15.00, '03
Mini Nativity Addition
Purchased ________, Price $ ___________

☐ *Our First Christmas Together*, **E-2385 (Ornament)**

Hourglass	$55.00
Fish	$50.00
Cross	$48.00
Dove	$45.00
Olive Branch	$42.00
Cedar Tree	$38.00
Flower	$35.00
Bow & Arrow	$32.00
Flame	$28.00
Vessel	$25.00

Suspended 1991, Issue Price $10.00, '82
Purchased ________, Price $ ___________

☐ *Camel, Donkey, And Cow*, **E-2386 (Ornaments)**

UM	$100.00
Hourglass	$98.00
Fish	$95.00
Cross	$90.00
Dove	$88.00

Unmarked pieces could have been produced in any of the years of production. Mixed sets of Unmarked/Hourglass marks are common.

Suspended 1984, Issue Price $25.00
Set of 3
Purchased ________, Price $ ___________

☐ *House Set And Palm Tree*, **E-2387**

Hourglass	$135.00
Fish	$100.00
Cross	$95.00
Dove	$92.00
Olive Branch	$87.00
Cedar Tree	$87.00
Flower	$87.00
Bow & Arrow	$85.00
Flame	$85.00
Vessel	$85.00
G-Clef	$85.00
Butterfly	$83.00
Trumpet	$83.00
Ship	$83.00
Heart	$78.00
Sword	$78.00
Eyeglasses	$75.00
Star	$75.00
Egg	$75.00
Sandal	$75.00
Cross in Heart	$75.00
Crown	$75.00
[mark]	$75.00
[mark]	$75.00

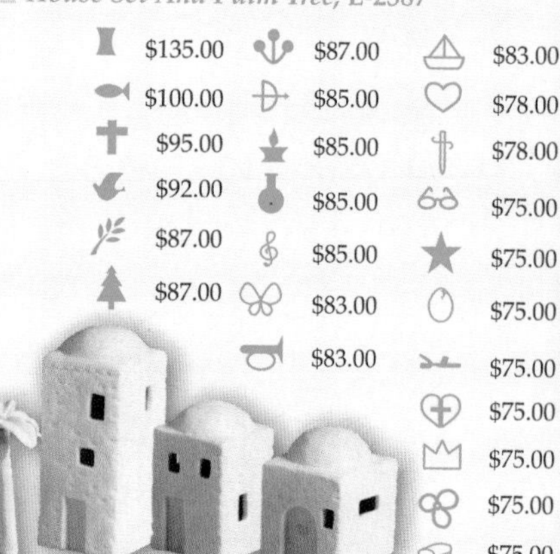

Mini nativity addition. Some Hourglass sets were shipped with the pink house having no mark; add $50.00 to value.

Open, Issue Price $45.00, '82
Set of 4
Mini Nativity Addition
Purchased ________, Price $ ___________

☐ *Come Let Us Adore Him*, E-2395 (Mini Nativity)

$155.00	$140.00	$140.00
$155.00	$140.00	$140.00
$150.00	$140.00	$140.00
$150.00	$140.00	
$145.00	$140.00	
$145.00	$140.00	
$140.00	$140.00	

Classic variation, termed the "Turban Nativity." The shepherd holding a lamb was replaced in some Hourglass sets with a shepherd wearing a turban. "Turban Boy" shepherds were also shipped individually to retailers as replacement pieces, so collectors were sometimes able to add the "Turban Boy" as a twelfth piece to this 11-piece mini nativity set. For the "Turban Nativity" the value is $225.00. The individual "Turban Boy" piece is valued at $95.00. Add $95.00 to the value of the mini nativity if the "Turban Boy" is added as a twelfth piece.

Open, Issue Price $80.00, '82
Set of 11
Purchased ________, Price $ ____________

☐ *Come Let Us Adore Him*, E-2800 (Nativity)

UM $200.00	$170.00	$160.00
$185.00	$165.00	$155.00

This set was resculpted; the new version is #104000.

Discontinued 1985, Issue Price
$60.00, '80
Set of 9
Purchased ______________,
Price $ ________________

☐ *Jesus Is Born*, E-2801

UM $410.00
$380.00
$355.00
$340.00
$320.00

Suspended 1984, Issue Price $37.50, '80
Purchased ________, Price $ ____________

☐ *Christmas Is A Time To Share*, E-2802

UM $120.00
$100.00
$85.00
$80.00
$75.00
$75.00

Piece was Suspended in 1984, yet exists with the 1985 Dove annual production symbol.

Suspended 1984, Issue Price $20.00, '80
Purchased ________, Price $ ____________

☐ *Crown Him Lord Of All*, E-2803

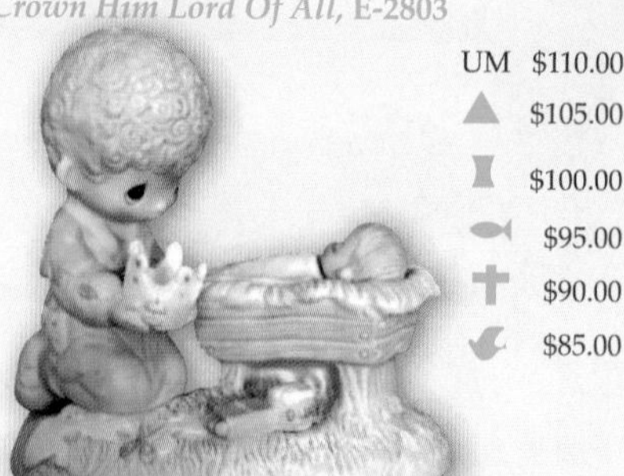

UM	$110.00
▲	$105.00
Hourglass	$100.00
Fish	$95.00
Cross	$90.00
Dove	$85.00

Piece was suspended in 1984, yet exists with the 1985 Dove annual production symbol.

Suspended 1984, Issue Price $20.00, '80

Purchased ________, Price $ ___________

☐ *Peace On Earth*, E-2804

UM	$165.00
▲	$160.00
Hourglass	$155.00
Fish	$150.00
Cross	$145.00

Suspended 1984, Reintroduced 1999, Retired 1999, Issue Price $20.00, '80

Purchased ________, Price $ ___________

☐ *Peace On Earth*, E-2804R

This is a revision of E-2804 of the boy angel on globe with teddy bear, which was Suspended in 1984. This version features a girl angel with a cat. The globe also sits square on the base instead of being tilted.

★	$60.00

Retired 1999, Issue Price $50.00, '99
Catalog Exclusive

Purchased ________, Price $ ___________

☐ *Wishing You A Season Filled With Joy*, E-2805

No mark thru cross, only one dog's eye painted. Dove exists with both one and two eyes painted.

UM	$130.00
▲	$125.00
Hourglass	$120.00
Fish	$117.00
Cross	$113.00
Dove	$110.00

Retired 1985, Issue Price $20.00, '80

Purchased ________, Price $ ___________

☐ *Christmas Is A Time To Share*, E-2806 (Musical)

UM	$195.00
▲	$170.00
Hourglass	$160.00
Fish	$155.00
Cross	$150.00

Retired 1984, Issue Price $35.00, '80
Tune: "Away In A Manger"

Purchased ________, Price $ ___________

☐ *Crown Him Lord Of All*, E-2807 (Musical)

UM	$140.00
▲	$130.00
Hourglass	$125.00
Fish	$118.00
Cross	$110.00

Suspended 1984, Issue Price $35.00, '80
Tune: "O Come All Ye Faithful"

Purchased ________, Price $ ___________

Unto Us A Child Is Born, E-2808 (Musical)

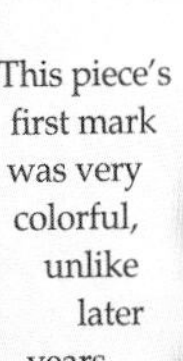
This piece's first mark was very colorful, unlike later years.

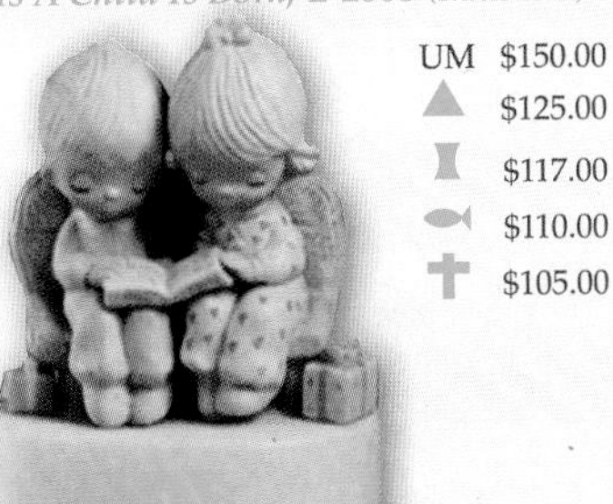

UM	$150.00
Triangle	$125.00
Hourglass	$117.00
Fish	$110.00
Cross	$105.00

Suspended 1984, Issue Price $35.00, '80
Tune: "Jesus Loves Me"

Purchased _________, Price $ ____________

Jesus Is Born, E-2809 (Musical)

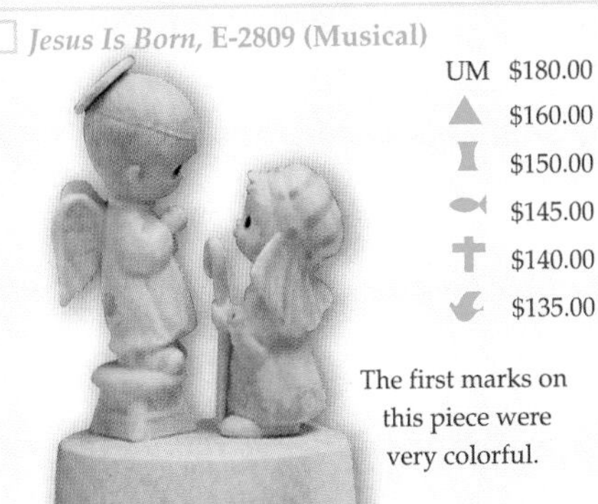

UM	$180.00
Triangle	$160.00
Hourglass	$150.00
Fish	$145.00
Cross	$140.00
Dove	$135.00

The first marks on this piece were very colorful.

Suspended 1985, Issue Price $35.00, '80
Tune: "Hark! The Herald Angels Sing"

Purchased _________, Price $ ____________

Come Let Us Adore Him, E-2810 (Musical)

UM	$165.00
Triangle	$147.00
Hourglass	$138.00
Fish	$135.00
Cross	$132.00
Dove	$129.00
Olive Branch	$125.00
Cedar Tree	$122.00
Flower	$119.00
Bow & Arrow	$117.00
Flame	$113.00
Vessel	$110.00
G-Clef	$110.00
Butterfly	$110.00

Suspended 1993, Issue Price $45.00, '80
Tune: "Joy To The World"

Purchased _________, Price $ ____________

You Have Touched So Many Hearts, E-2821

Fish	$85.00
Cross	$75.00
Dove	$67.00
Olive Branch	$65.00
Cedar Tree	$63.00
Flower	$60.00
Bow & Arrow	$58.00
Flame	$55.00
Vessel	$53.00
G-Clef	$53.00
Butterfly	$50.00
Trumpet	$50.00
Ship	$50.00
Heart	$48.00

Suspended 1996, Issue Price $25.00, '84

Purchased _________, Price $ ____________

This Is Your Day To Shine, E-2822

Fish	$157.00
Cross	$113.00
Dove	$105.00
Olive Branch	$97.00
Cedar Tree	$95.00
Flower	$90.00

Retired 1988, Issue Price $37.50, '84

Purchased _________, Price $ ____________

To God Be The Glory, E-2823

Fish	$132.00
Cross	$98.00
Dove	$92.00
Olive Branch	$88.00
Cedar Tree	$83.00

Suspended 1987, Issue Price $40.00, '84

Purchased _________, Price $ ____________

To God Be The Glory, E-2823R

$55.00

The frame was changed to gold and the flowers were changed to roses.

Retired 2000, Issue Price $45.00, '00

Purchased ________, Price $ ___________

To A Very Special Mom, E-2824

$62.00 $57.00 $52.00 $50.00

$48.00 $47.00 $47.00 $43.00 $42.00 $42.00 $40.00

$40.00 $40.00 $40.00 $40.00 $40.00 $40.00 $40.00 $40.00 $40.00 $40.00 $40.00

This is a popular piece for Mother's Day.

Retired 2003, Issue Price $27.50, '84

Purchased ________, Price $ ___________

To A Very Special Sister, E-2825

$82.00 $66.00 $62.00 $60.00 $60.00 $60.00 $58.00 $55.00

$55.00 $54.00 $54.00 $52.00 $52.00 $52.00 $52.00 $52.00 $52.00 $52.00

Retired 2001, Issue Price $37.50, '84

Purchased ________, Price $ ___________

May Your Birthday Be A Blessing, E-2826

This piece has been found with brown eyes.

$110.00 $95.00 $90.00 $88.00

Suspended 1986, Reintroduced 2000, Retired 2000, Issue Price $37.50, '84

Purchased ________, Price $ ___________

May Your Birthday Be A Blessing, E-2826R

Limited Ed. 25,000, Issue Price $75.00, '00

Individually Numbered

Came with a photo frame

$75.00

Purchased ________, Price $ ___________

I Get A Kick Out Of You, E-2827

$240.00 $220.00 $200.00 $190.00

Suspended 1986, Issue Price $50.00, '84

Purchased ________, Price $ ___________

Precious Memories, E-2828

$140.00 $90.00 $85.00

$85.00 $80.00 $77.00

$77.00 $75.00 $72.00 $72.00 $70.00 $70.00 $68.00 $68.00 $66.00 $66.00 $66.00

Retired 1999, Issue Price $45.00, '84

Purchased ________, Price $ ___________

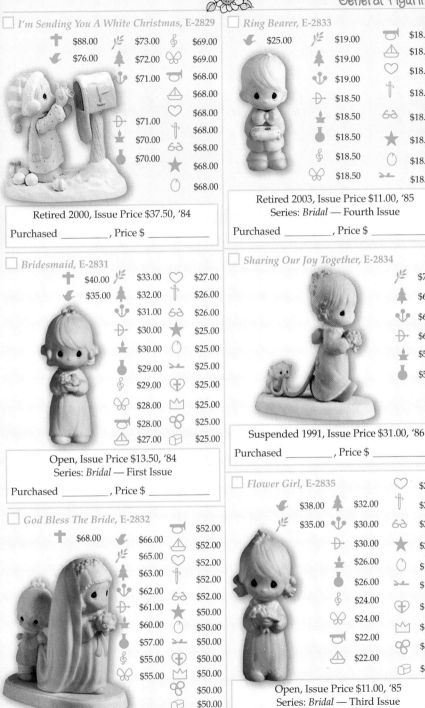

☐ *I'm Sending You A White Christmas, E-2829*

$88.00
$76.00
$73.00
$72.00
$71.00
$71.00
$70.00
$70.00
$69.00
$69.00
$68.00
$68.00
$68.00
$68.00
$68.00
$68.00
$68.00
$68.00

Retired 2000, Issue Price $37.50, '84

Purchased _________, Price $ ____________

☐ *Bridesmaid, E-2831*

$40.00
$35.00
$33.00
$32.00
$31.00
$30.00
$30.00
$29.00
$29.00
$28.00
$28.00
$27.00
$27.00
$26.00
$26.00
$25.00
$25.00
$25.00
$25.00
$25.00
$25.00
$25.00
$25.00
$25.00

Open, Issue Price $13.50, '84
Series: *Bridal* — First Issue

Purchased _________, Price $ ____________

☐ *God Bless The Bride, E-2832*

$68.00
$66.00
$65.00
$63.00
$62.00
$61.00
$60.00
$57.00
$55.00
$55.00
$52.00
$52.00
$52.00
$52.00
$52.00
$50.00
$50.00
$50.00
$50.00
$50.00
$50.00
$50.00
$50.00

Open, Issue Price $35.00 '84

Purchased _________, Price $ ____________

☐ *Ring Bearer, E-2833*

$25.00
$19.00
$19.00
$19.00
$18.50
$18.50
$18.50
$18.50
$18.50
$18.50
$18.50
$18.50
$18.50
$18.50
$18.50
$18.50
$18.50
$18.50
$18.50

Retired 2003, Issue Price $11.00, '85
Series: *Bridal* — Fourth Issue

Purchased _________, Price $ ____________

☐ *Sharing Our Joy Together, E-2834*

$70.00
$64.00
$62.00
$60.00
$58.00
$55.00

Suspended 1991, Issue Price $31.00, '86

Purchased _________, Price $ ____________

☐ *Flower Girl, E-2835*

$38.00
$35.00
$32.00
$30.00
$30.00
$26.00
$26.00
$24.00
$24.00
$22.00
$22.00
$21.00
$21.00
$20.00
$20.00
$19.00
$19.00
$19.00
$19.00
$19.00
$19.00
$19.00

Open, Issue Price $11.00, '85
Series: *Bridal* — Third Issue

Purchased _________, Price $ ____________

Groomsman, E-2836

$40.00
$37.00
$35.00
$34.00
$34.00
$32.00
$32.00
$30.00
$30.00
$28.00
$28.00
$28.00
$27.00
$27.00
$25.00
$25.00
$25.00
$25.00
$25.00
$25.00
$25.00
$25.00
$25.00
$25.00

Open, Issue Price $13.50, '84
Series: *Bridal* — Third Issue
Purchased ________, Price $ ____________

Groom, E-2837

$40.00
$37.00
$35.00
$35.00
$32.00
$32.00
$30.00
$30.00
$30.00
$30.00
$30.00
$30.00
$30.00
$30.00
$30.00
$30.00
$30.00
$30.00
$30.00
$30.00

Termed the "No Hands Groom" during the first year of production (Olive Branch), this piece was first produced with no hands. The mold was changed for the subsequent years (Cedar Tree to present) to show the boy's hands.

Open, Issue Price $15.00, '86
Series: *Bridal* — Sixth Issue
Purchased ________, Price $ ____________

Baby's First Step, E-2840

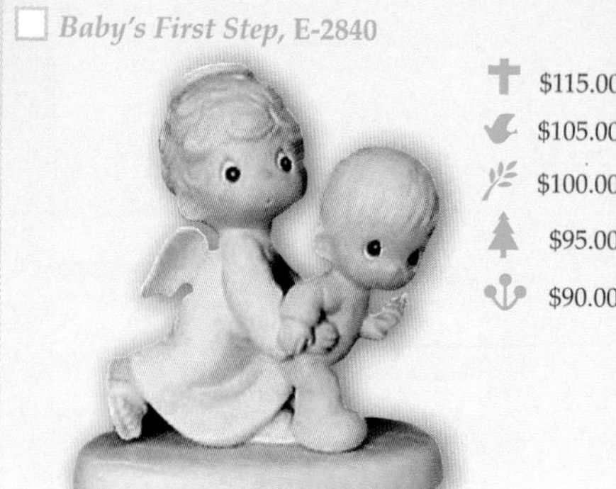

$115.00
$105.00
$100.00
$95.00
$90.00

Suspended 1988, Issue Price $35.00, '84
Series: *Baby's First* — First Issue
Purchased ________, Price $ ____________

Baby's First Picture, E-2841

$200.00
$190.00
$180.00

Retired 1986, Issue Price $45.00, '84
Series: *Baby's First* — Second Issue
Purchased ________, Price $ ____________

This Is the Day Which The Lord Hath Made, E-2838

$235.00

Annual 1987, Issue Price $175.00, '87
Series: *Bridal*
Eighth & Final Issue
Purchased__________,
Price $______________

Junior Bridesmaid, E-2845

$35.00
$32.00
$30.00
$29.00
$28.00
$27.00
$27.00
$25.00
$25.00
$25.00
$25.00
$25.00
$25.00
$25.00
$25.00
$25.00
$25.00
$25.00
$25.00
$25.00

Open, Issue Price $12.50, '86
Series: *Bridal* — Fifth Issue

Purchased ________, Price $ __________

Bride, E-2846

$40.00
$38.00
$36.00
$35.00
$34.00
$33.00
$33.00
$32.00
$32.00
$31.00
$31.00
$30.00
$30.00
$30.00
$30.00
$30.00
$30.00
$30.00
$30.00

Open, Issue Price $18.00, '87
Series: *Bridal* — Seventh Issue

Purchased ________, Price $ __________

Love Is Kind, E-2847 (Plate)

UM $50.00
$47.00

Limited Ed. 15,000, Issue Price $40.00, '84
Series: *Inspired Thoughts* — Fourth Issue
Individually Numbered

Purchased ________, Price $ __________

Loving Thy Neighbor, E-2848 (Plate)

$45.00

This was the first plate with an embossed mark.

Limited Ed. 15,000, Issue Price $40.00, '84
Series: *Mother's Love* — Fourth Issue
Individually Numbered

Purchased ________, Price $ __________

Mother Sew Dear, E-2850 (Doll)

UM $400.00
$400.00
$400.00

Retired 1985, Issue Price $350.00, '84

Purchased ________, Price $ __________

Kristy, E-2851 (Doll)

$225.00
$225.00
$225.00
$200.00
$200.00
$175.00

Suspended 1989, Issue Price $150.00, '84

Purchased ________, Price $ __________

☐ *Baby Figurines, E-2852*

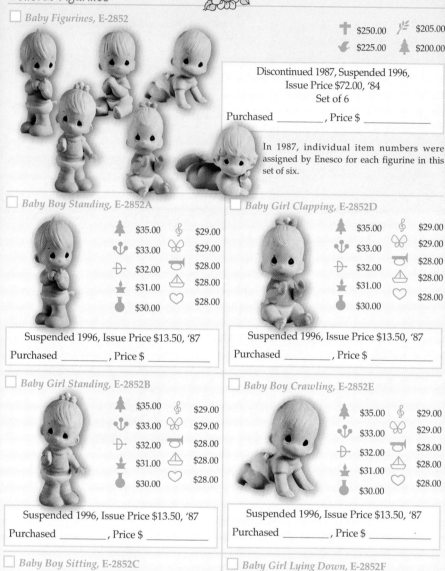

Cross	$250.00	Olive Branch	$205.00
Dove	$225.00	Cedar Tree	$200.00

Discontinued 1987, Suspended 1996,
Issue Price $72.00, '84
Set of 6

Purchased ________, Price $ __________

In 1987, individual item numbers were assigned by Enesco for each figurine in this set of six.

☐ *Baby Boy Standing, E-2852A*

Cedar Tree	$35.00	G-Clef	$29.00
Flower	$33.00	Butterfly	$29.00
Bow & Arrow	$32.00	Trumpet	$28.00
Flame	$31.00	Ship	$28.00
Vessel	$30.00	Heart	$28.00

Suspended 1996, Issue Price $13.50, '87

Purchased ________, Price $ __________

☐ *Baby Girl Clapping, E-2852D*

Cedar Tree	$35.00	G-Clef	$29.00
Flower	$33.00	Butterfly	$29.00
Bow & Arrow	$32.00	Trumpet	$28.00
Flame	$31.00	Ship	$28.00
Vessel	$30.00	Heart	$28.00

Suspended 1996, Issue Price $13.50, '87

Purchased ________, Price $ __________

☐ *Baby Girl Standing, E-2852B*

Cedar Tree	$35.00	G-Clef	$29.00
Flower	$33.00	Butterfly	$29.00
Bow & Arrow	$32.00	Trumpet	$28.00
Flame	$31.00	Ship	$28.00
Vessel	$30.00	Heart	$28.00

Suspended 1996, Issue Price $13.50, '87

Purchased ________, Price $ __________

☐ *Baby Boy Crawling, E-2852E*

Cedar Tree	$35.00	G-Clef	$29.00
Flower	$33.00	Butterfly	$29.00
Bow & Arrow	$32.00	Trumpet	$28.00
Flame	$31.00	Ship	$28.00
Vessel	$30.00	Heart	$28.00

Suspended 1996, Issue Price $13.50, '87

Purchased ________, Price $ __________

☐ *Baby Boy Sitting, E-2852C*

Cedar Tree	$35.00	G-Clef	$29.00
Flower	$33.00	Butterfly	$29.00
Bow & Arrow	$32.00	Trumpet	$28.00
Flame	$31.00	Ship	$28.00
Vessel	$30.00	Heart	$28.00

Suspended 1996, Issue Price $13.50, '87

Purchased ________, Price $ __________

☐ *Baby Girl Lying Down, E-2852F*

Cedar Tree	$35.00	G-Clef	$29.00
Flower	$33.00	Butterfly	$29.00
Bow & Arrow	$32.00	Trumpet	$28.00
Flame	$31.00	Ship	$28.00
Vessel	$30.00	Heart	$28.00

Suspended 1996, Issue Price $13.50, '87

Purchased ________, Price $ __________

☐ *God Blessed Our Years Together With So Much Love & Happiness, E-2853*

$70.00 · $63.00 · $62.00 · $62.00 · $58.00 · $58.00 · $56.00 · $56.00 · $54.00 · $54.00 · $52.00 · $52.00 · $50.00 · $50.00 · $50.00 · $50.00 · $50.00 · $50.00 · $50.00 · $50.00 · $50.00 · $50.00 · $50.00

Open, Issue Price $35.00, '84

Purchased ________, Price $ ____________

☐ *God Blessed Our Years Together With So Much Love & Happiness, E-2856*

$80.00 · $78.00 · $76.00 · $76.00 · $75.00 · $73.00 · $73.00 · $72.00 · $71.00 · $70.00 · $69.00 · $68.00 · $68.00

Suspended 1996, Issue Price $35.00, '84

Purchased ________, Price $ ____________

☐ *God Blessed Our Year Together With So Much Love & Happiness, E-2854*

Error: Add $75.00 to value if title says "Years."

$70.00 · $65.00 · $63.00 · $62.00 · $61.00 · $60.00 · $58.00 · $56.00 · $54.00 · $53.00 · $52.00 · $51.00 · $50.00 · $50.00 · $50.00 · $50.00 · $50.00

Retired 2000, Issue Price $35.00, '84

Purchased ________, Price $ ____________

☐ *God Blessed Our Years Together With So Much Love & Happiness, E-2857*

$67.00 · $63.00 · $60.00 · $58.00 · $58.00 · $57.00 · $56.00 · $56.00 · $55.00 · $55.00 · $54.00 · $54.00 · $53.00 · $53.00 · $52.00 · $52.00 · $50.00 · $50.00

Retired 2001, Issue Price $35.00, '84

Purchased ________, Price $ ____________

☐ *God Blessed Our Years Together With So Much Love & Happiness, E-2855*

$75.00 · $70.00 · $68.00 · $68.00 · $67.00 · $67.00 · $67.00 · $65.00 · $65.00 · $65.00 · $65.00 · $63.00 · $63.00

Suspended 1996,
Issue Price $35.00, '84

Purchased ________, Price $ ____________

God Blessed Our Years Together With So Much Love & Happiness, E-2859

[Cross]	$82.00	[Flame]	$74.00
[Dove]	$77.00	[Vessel]	$73.00
[Olive Branch]	$76.00	[G-Clef]	$73.00
[Cedar Tree]	$75.00	[Butterfly]	$72.00
[Anchor]	$75.00	[Trumpet]	$72.00
[Bow & Arrow]	$74.00	[Ship]	$70.00
		[Heart]	$70.00

Suspended 1996, Issue Price $35.00, '84

Purchased ________, Price $ ___________

God Blessed Our Years Together With So Much Love & Happiness, E-2860

[Cross]	$80.00	[Olive Branch]	$75.00	[Butterfly]	$63.00
[Dove]	$78.00	[Cedar Tree]	$75.00	[Trumpet]	$62.00
		[Anchor]	$70.00	[Ship]	$62.00
		[Bow & Arrow]	$70.00	[Heart]	$60.00
		[Flame]	$68.00	[Sword]	$60.00
		[Vessel]	$65.00	[Eyeglasses]	$55.00
		[G-Clef]	$65.00	[Star]	$55.00
				[Egg]	$52.00
				[symbol]	$52.00

Retired 2001, Issue Price $35.00, '84

Purchased ________, Price $ ___________

Blessed Are The Pure In Heart, E-3104

UM	$60.00	[Hourglass]	$49.00	[Dove]	$45.00
[Triangle]	$50.00	[Fish]	$48.00	[Olive Branch]	$45.00
		[Cross]	$45.00	[Cedar Tree]	$43.00
				[Anchor]	$43.00
				[Bow & Arrow]	$40.00
				[Flame]	$39.00
				[Vessel]	$39.00

Suspended 1991, Issue Price $9.00, '80

Purchased ________, Price $ ___________

He Watches Over Us All, E-3105

UM	$80.00
[Triangle]	$75.00
[Hourglass]	$70.00
[Fish]	$65.00
[Cross]	$55.00

Suspended 1984, Issue Price $11.00, '80

Purchased ________, Price $ ___________

Mother Sew Dear, E-3106

UM	$50.00	[Fish]	$36.00	[G-Clef]	$35.00
[Triangle]	$46.00	[Cross]	$36.00	[Butterfly]	$35.00
[Hourglass]	$38.00	[Dove]	$36.00	[Trumpet]	$35.00
		[Olive Branch]	$36.00	[Ship]	$35.00
		[Cedar Tree]	$35.00	[Heart]	$35.00
		[Anchor]	$35.00	[Sword]	$35.00
		[Bow & Arrow]	$35.00	[Eyeglasses]	$35.00
		[Flame]	$35.00	[Star]	$35.00
		[Vessel]	$35.00	[Egg]	$35.00
				[symbol]	$35.00
				[Heart]	$35.00
				[Crown]	$35.00

Retired 2003, Issue Price $13.00, '80

Purchased ________, Price $ ___________

Blessed Are The Peacemakers, E-3107

UM	$115.00
[Triangle]	$115.00
[Hourglass]	$95.00
[Fish]	$90.00
[Cross]	$80.00
[Dove]	$75.00

Retired 1985, Issue Price $13.00, '80

Purchased ________, Price $ ___________

☐ *Walking By Faith*, E-3117

UM	$135.00	✝	$100.00	🏺	$90.00
▲	$115.00	🕊	$98.00	𝄞	$87.00
⧗	$105.00	🌿	$97.00	🦋	$87.00
🐟	$100.00	🌲	$96.00	🎺	$85.00
		⚓	$95.00	⛵	$85.00
		🏹	$93.00	♡	$85.00
		🔥	$91.00	🗡	$85.00
				👓	$85.00
				★	$85.00
				🥚	$85.00

Retired 2000, Issue Price $35.00, '80

Purchased ________, Price $ ___________

☐ *Eggs Over Easy*, E-3118

UM	$135.00
▲	$105.00
⧗	$85.00
🐟	$75.00

Some collectors have said the eggs are missing from their pieces.

Retired 1983, Issue Price $13.00, '80

Purchased ________, Price $ ___________

☐ *It's What's Inside That Counts*, E-3119

UM	$135.00
▲	$125.00
⧗	$105.00
🐟	$100.00
✝	$95.00

Look for this piece with either the Triangle mark or Unmarked because of the darker colors.

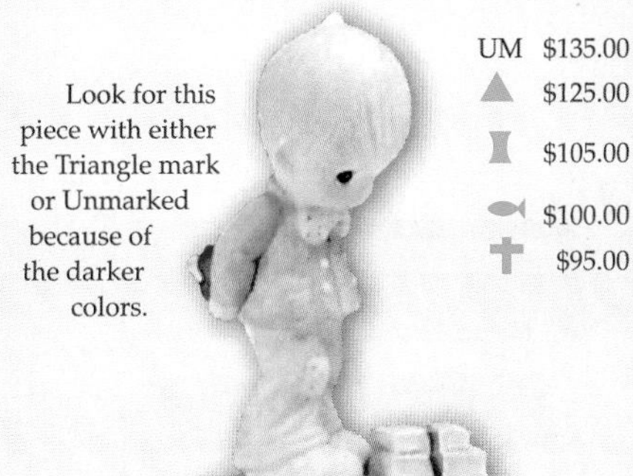

Suspended 1984, Issue Price $13.00, '80

Purchased ________, Price $ ___________

☐ *To Thee With Love*, E-3120

UM	$90.00
▲	$65.00
⧗	$63.00
🐟	$60.00
✝	$58.00
🕊	$55.00
🌿	$53.00
🌲	$50.00

Piece was Suspended in 1986, yet exists with the 1987 Cedar Tree annual production symbol.

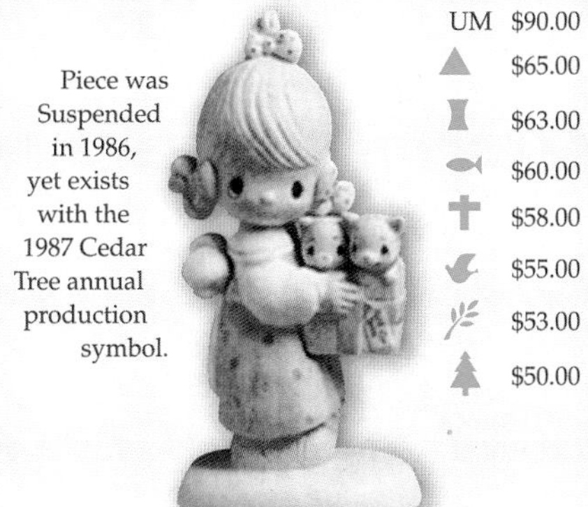

Suspended 1986, Issue Price $13.00, '80

Purchased ________, Price $ ___________

☐ *The Lord Bless You And Keep You*, E-4720

UM	$42.50
▲	$40.00
⧗	$38.00
🐟	$35.00
✝	$34.00
🕊	$33.00
🌿	$32.00
🌲	$31.00

Suspended 1987, Issue Price $14.00, '81

Purchased ________, Price $ ___________

The Lord Bless You And Keep You, E-4721

UM	$75.00	[Fish]	$48.00	[Ship]	$35.00
[Triangle]	$50.00	[Cross]	$47.00	[Heart]	$35.00
[Hourglass]	$49.00	[Dove]	$46.00	[Sword]	$35.00
		[Olive Branch]	$45.00	[Eyeglasses]	$35.00
		[Cedar Tree]	$44.00	[Star]	$35.00
		[Flower]	$43.00	[Egg]	$35.00
		[Bow & Arrow]	$42.00	[Sandal]	$35.00
		[Flame]	$41.00	[Heart]	$35.00
		[Vessel]	$40.00	[Crown]	$35.00
		[G-Clef]	$35.00	[Clover]	$35.00
		[Butterfly]	$35.00	[Box]	$35.00
		[Trumpet]	$35.00		

Open, Issue Price $14.00, '81

Purchased ________, Price $ ___________

The Lord Bless You And Keep You, E-4721B

Limited Ed., Issue Price $40.00, '00
Came with a version of *Don't Sweat the Small Stuff* by Richard Carlson, PhD [Star] $40.00

Purchased ________, Price $ ___________

The Lord Bless You And Keep You, E-4721D

[Egg]	$35.00	[Heart]	$35.00
[Sandal]	$35.00	[Crown]	$35.00

Open, Issue Price $35.00, '00

Purchased __________,

Price $_______________

The Lord Bless You And Keep You, E-4721DB

Limited Ed., Issue Price $40.00, '00
Came with a version of *Don't Sweat the Small Stuff by* Richard Carlson, PhD [Star] $40.00

Purchased ________, Price $ ___________

Love Cannot Break A True Friendship, E-4722

UM	$140.00
[Triangle]	$130.00
[Hourglass]	$120.00
[Fish]	$105.00
[Cross]	$98.00
[Dove]	$95.00

Suspended 1985, Issue Price $22.50, '81

Purchased ________, Price $ ___________

Peace Amid The Storm, E-4723

UM	$100.00
[Triangle]	$90.00
[Hourglass]	$75.00
[Fish]	$70.00
[Cross]	$65.00

Suspended 1984, Issue Price $22.50, '81

Purchased ________, Price $ ___________

Rejoicing With You, E-4724

UM	$83.00	[Cross]	$73.00	[Bow & Arrow]	$60.00
[Triangle]	$80.00	[Dove]	$70.00	[Flame]	$59.00
[Hourglass]	$78.00	[Olive Branch]	$67.00	[Vessel]	$58.00
[Fish]	$75.00	[Cedar Tree]	$65.00	[G-Clef]	$58.00
		[Flower]	$62.00	[Butterfly]	$57.00
				[Trumpet]	$57.00
				[Ship]	$56.00
				[Heart]	$56.00
				[Sword]	$56.00
				[Eyeglasses]	$55.00
				[Star]	$55.00
				[Egg]	$55.00
				[Sandal]	$55.00
				[Heart]	$55.00
				[Crown]	$55.00
				[Clover]	$55.00
				[Box]	$55.00

Classic Variation: "No E" or "Bibl Error." During the first years of production the "e" was missing from the word Bible. Some Hourglass & Fish pieces also have this variation.

Open, Issue Price $25.00, '81

Purchased ________, Price $ ___________

Peace On Earth, E-4725

UM	$115.00
▲	$80.00
⧗	$65.00
🐟	$60.00
✝	$60.00

Unmarked and Triangle pieces are very dark and colorful.

Suspended 1984, Issue Price $25.00, '81

Purchased ________, Price $ ___________

Peace On Earth, E-4726 (Musical)

UM	$150.00
▲	$125.00
⧗	$115.00
🐟	$110.00
✝	$105.00

Suspended 1984, Issue Price $45.00, '81
Tune: "Jesus Loves Me"

Purchased ________, Price $ ___________

Bear Ye One Another's Burdens, E-5200

UM	$110.00
▲	$95.00
⧗	$80.00
🐟	$75.00
✝	$73.00

Suspended 1984, Issue Price $20.00, '81

Purchased ________, Price $ ___________

Love Lifted Me, E-5201

UM	$110.00
▲	$85.00
⧗	$80.00
🐟	$75.00
✝	$70.00

Suspended 1984, Issue Price $25.00, '81

Purchased ________, Price $ ___________

Thank You For Coming To My Ade, E-5202

UM	$150.00
▲	$118.00
⧗	$108.00
🐟	$105.00
✝	$105.00

Suspended 1984, Issue Price $22.50, '81

Purchased ________, Price $ ___________

Let Not The Sun Go Down Upon Your Wrath, E-5203

UM	$170.00
▲	$140.00
⧗	$135.00
🐟	$130.00
✝	$125.00

Suspended 1984, Issue Price $22.50, '81

Purchased ________, Price $ ___________

☐ *The Hand That Rocks The Future*, E-5204 (Musical)

UM $110.00
$100.00
$95.00
$90.00
$90.00
$87.00
$85.00
$83.00
$80.00
$78.00
$75.00
$72.00
$69.00
$67.00
$65.00
$65.00
$65.00
$65.00
$65.00
$65.00
$65.00
$65.00

Retired 2001, Issue Price $30.00, '81
Tune: "Mozart's Lullaby"
Purchased ________, Price $ ___________

☐ *My Guardian Angel*, E-5205 (Musical)

UM $130.00
$115.00
$105.00
$100.00
$95.00
$90.00

Suspended 1985, Issue Price $22.50, '81
Tune: "Brahms' Lullaby"
Purchased ________, Price $ ___________

☐ *My Guardian Angel*, E-5206 (Musical)

UM $135.00
$125.00
$115.00
$105.00
$100.00
$90.00
$85.00
$80.00
$80.00

Suspended 1988, Issue Price $22.50, '81
Tune: "Brahms' Lullaby"
Purchased ________, Price $ ___________

☐ *My Guardian Angel*, E-5207 (Nightlight)

UM $255.00
$185.00

Suspended 1984, Issue Price $30.00, '81
Purchased ________, Price $ ___________

☐ *Jesus Loves Me*, E-5208 (Bell)

UM $50.00
$47.00
$45.00

Suspended 1985, Issue Price $15.00, '81
Purchased ________, Price $ ___________

☐ *Jesus Loves Me*, E-5209 (Bell)

UM $50.00
$47.00
$45.00

Suspended 1985, Issue Price $15.00, '81
Purchased ________, Price $ ___________

Prayer Changes Things, E-5210 (Bell)

UM	$51.00
[Cross]	$47.00

Suspended 1984, Issue Price $15.00, '81

Purchased ________, Price $ __________

God Understands, E-5211 (Bell)

UM	$45.00
[Cross]	$40.00

Retired 1984, Issue Price $15.00, '81

Purchased ________, Price $ __________

To A Special Dad, E-5212

UM	$85.00
[Triangle]	$55.00
[Hourglass]	$50.00
[Fish]	$47.00
[Cross]	$45.00
[Dove]	$45.00
[Olive Branch]	$43.00
[Cedar Tree]	$42.00
[Anchor]	$41.00
[Bow & Arrow]	$40.00
[Flame]	$39.00
[Vessel]	$39.00
[G-Clef]	$38.00
[Butterfly]	$37.00
[Trumpet]	$37.00
[Ship]	$37.00
[Heart]	$37.00
[Sword]	$37.00
[Eyeglasses]	$37.00

Suspended 1998, Issue Price $20.00, '81

Purchased ________, Price $ __________

God Is Love, E-5213

This piece was re-sculpted in 1985 and reintroduced on 11/28/99 as E-5213R.

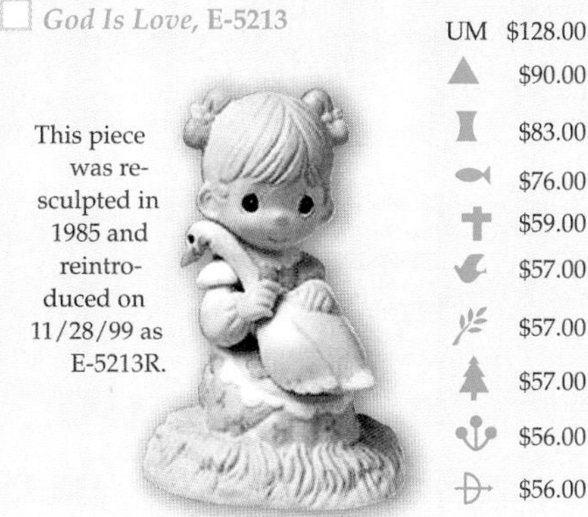

UM	$128.00
[Triangle]	$90.00
[Hourglass]	$83.00
[Fish]	$76.00
[Cross]	$59.00
[Dove]	$57.00
[Olive Branch]	$57.00
[Cedar Tree]	$57.00
[Anchor]	$56.00
[Bow & Arrow]	$56.00

Suspended 1989, Reintroduced 1999, Retired 1999, Issue Price $17.00, '81

Purchased ________, Price $ __________

God Is Love, E-5213R

Retired 1999, Issue Price $17.00, '99

[Star]	$30.00

Purchased ________, Price $ __________

Prayer Changes Things, E-5214

UM	$176.00
[Triangle]	$171.00
[Hourglass]	$155.00
[Fish]	$95.00
[Cross]	$90.00
[Dove]	$85.00

Classic variation: "Backwards Bible." The first production of this figurine had the words "Holy Bible" inscribed on the back cover. Pieces with this error exist in Unmarked and Triangle versions. Reportedly, Unmarked and Triangle pieces also exist where the title is correctly placed, but these may be considered extremely rare. The value for "Backwards Bible" Unmarked is $168.00; "Backwards Bible" with Triangle is $160.00; "Backwards Bible" with Hourglass is $140.00; and correct Hourglass, $140.00. Pieces were Suspended in 1984 yet exist with the 1985 Dove annual production symbol.

Suspended 1984, Issue Price $35.00, '81

Purchased ________, Price $ __________

Love One Another, E-5215 (Plate)

UM $55.00

Limited Ed. 15,000, Issue Price $40.00, '81
Series: *Inspired Thoughts* – First Issue, Individually Numbered

Purchased ________, Price $ ___________

The Lord Bless You and Keep You, E-5216 (Plate)

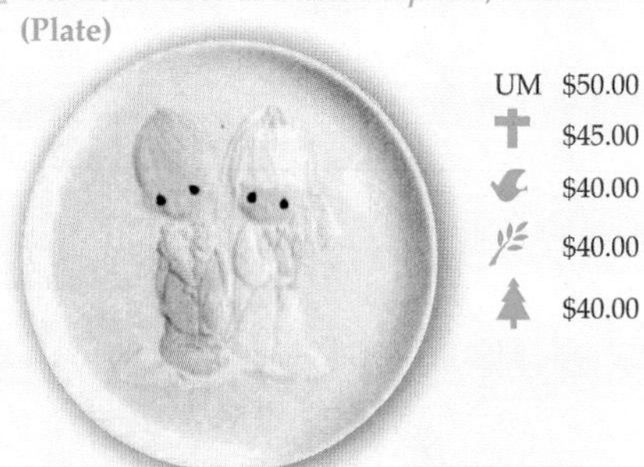

UM	$50.00
[Cross]	$45.00
[Dove]	$40.00
[Olive Branch]	$40.00
[Cedar Tree]	$40.00

Suspended 1987, Issue Price $30.00, '81

Purchased ________, Price $ ___________

Mother Sew Dear, E-5217 (Plate)

UM $50.00

Limited Ed. 15,000, Issue Price $40.00, '81
Series: *Mother's Love* – First Issue, Individually Numbered

Purchased ________, Price $ ___________

May Your Christmas Be Blessed, E-5376

In 1984, "Holy Bible" was written on the back of the book, but was omitted in 1985.

[Cross]	$65.00
[Dove]	$60.00
[Olive Branch]	$55.00

Suspended 1986, Issue Price $37.50, '84

Purchased ________, Price $ ___________

Love Is Kind, E-5377

[Cross]	$80.00
[Dove]	$78.00
[Olive Branch]	$75.00
[Cedar Tree]	$73.00

Retired 1987, Issue Price $27.50, '84

Purchased ________, Price $ ___________

Joy To The World, E-5378

[Cross]	$55.00
[Dove]	$50.00
[Olive Branch]	$47.00
[Cedar Tree]	$46.00
[Anchor]	$45.00
[Bow & Arrow]	$45.00

Suspended 1989, Issue Price $18.00, '84
Nativity Addition

Purchased ________, Price $ ___________

☐ *Isn't He Precious*, E-5379

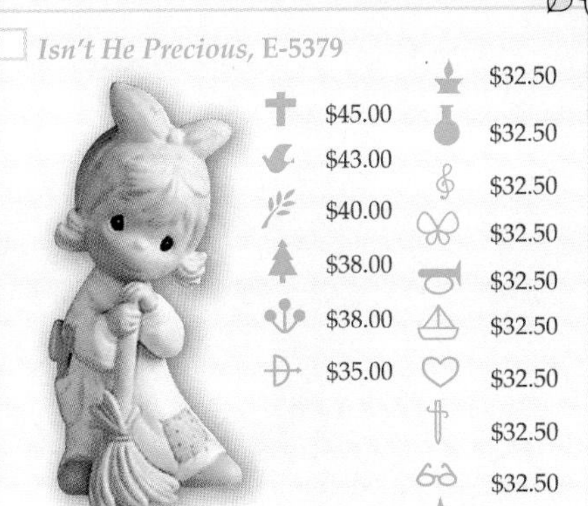

$45.00
$43.00
$40.00
$38.00
$38.00
$35.00
$32.50
$32.50
$32.50
$32.50
$32.50
$32.50
$32.50
$32.50
$32.50
$32.50
$32.50

With the opening of a new production facility in Indonesia, numerous pieces of unpainted figurines were inadvertently shipped to retailers.

Retired 2000, Issue Price $20.00, '84
Nativity Addition
Purchased ________, Price $ ____________

☐ *A Monarch Is Born*, E-5380

$85.00
$80.00
$78.00

Suspended 1986, Issue Price $33.00, '84
Purchased ________, Price $ ____________

☐ *His Name Is Jesus*, E-5381

$120.00
$110.00
$105.00
$100.00

Suspended 1987, Issue Price $45.00, '84
Purchased ________, Price $ ____________

☐ *Wishing You A Merry Christmas*, E-5383

$35.00
$35.00

Dated Annual 1984, Issue Price $17.00, '84
Purchased ________, Price $ ____________

☐ *For God So Loved The World*, E-5382

$140.00
$110.00
$105.00

Suspended 1986, Issue Price $70.00, '84
Deluxe Four-piece Nativity
Purchased __________,
Price $______________

I'll Play My Drum For Him, E-5384

$30.00 $28.00 $27.00 $26.00 $25.00 $24.00 $23.00 $22.00 $21.00 $20.00

$20.00 $20.00 $20.00 $20.00 $20.00 $20.00 $20.00 $20.00 $20.00

Retired 2002, Issue Price $10.00, '84
Mini Nativity Addition

Purchased ________, Price $ ___________

Oh Worship The Lord, E-5385

$68.00 $65.00 $62.00

Suspended 1986, Issue Price $10.00, '84
Mini Nativity Addition

Purchased ________, Price $ ___________

Oh Worship The Lord, E-5386

$74.00 $72.00 $70.00

Suspended 1986, Issue Price $10.00, '84
Mini Nativity Addition

Purchased ________, Price $ ___________

Wishing You A Merry Christmas, E-5387 (Ornament)

$35.00

Dated Annual 1984, Issue Price $10.00, '84

Purchased ________, Price $ ___________

Joy To The World, E-5388 (Ornament)

$50.00 $48.00 $45.00 $43.00

Retired 1987, Issue Price $10.00, '84

Purchased ________, Price $ ___________

Peace On Earth, E-5389 (Ornament)

$37.00 $35.00 $33.00

Suspended 1986, Issue Price $10.00, '84

Purchased ________, Price $ ___________

May God Bless You With A Perfect Holiday Season, E-5390 (Ornament)

$30.00 $28.00 $25.00 $24.00 $23.00 $22.00

Suspended 1989, Issue Price $10.00, '84

Purchased ________, Price $ ___________

☐ *Love Is Kind*, E-5391 (Ornament)

$40.00
$30.00
$28.00
$27.00
$26.00
$25.00

Suspended 1989, Issue Price $10.00, '84
Purchased ________, Price $ __________

☐ *Blessed Are The Pure In Heart*, E-5392 (Ornament)

$35.00

Dated Annual 1984, Issue Price $10.00, '84
"Baby's First Christmas"
Purchased ________, Price $ __________

☐ *Wishing You A Merry Christmas*, E-5393 (Bell)

$45.00

Dated Annual 1984, Issue Price $19.00, '84
Purchased ________, Price $ __________

☐ *Wishing You A Merry Christmas*, E-5394 (Musical)

$130.00
$122.00
$110.00

Suspended 1986, Issue Price $55.00, '84
Tune: "We Wish You A Merry Christmas"
Purchased ________, Price $ __________

☐ *Unto Us A Child Is Born*, E-5395 (Plate)

UM $50.00
$45.00

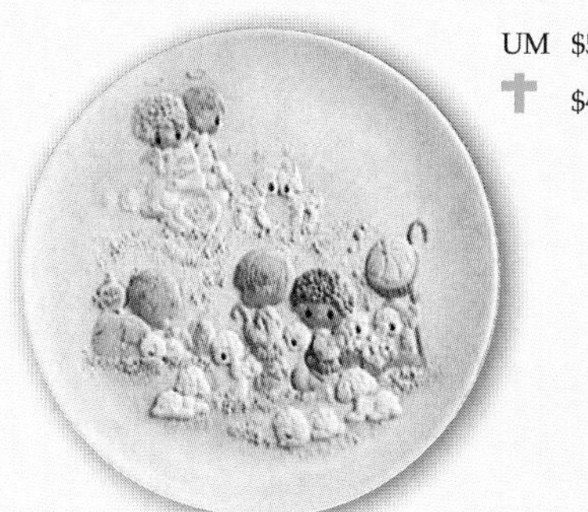

Limited Ed. 15,000, Issue Price $40.00, '84
Series: *Christmas Collection* – Fourth Issue, Individually Numbered
Purchased ________, Price $ __________

☐ *The Wonder Of Christmas*, E-5396 (Plate)

$50.00

Dated Annual 1984, Issue Price $40.00, '84
Series: *Joy Of Christmas* — Third Issue
Purchased ________, Price $ __________

Timmy, E-5397 (Doll)

$165.00
$160.00
$155.00
$155.00
$150.00
$150.00
$150.00
$150.00

Look for the mark on the back of his neck.

Suspended 1991, Issue Price $125.00, '84
Purchased ________, Price $ ___________

Come Let Us Adore Him, E-5619

UM $60.00
$55.00
$50.00
$45.00
$40.00
$35.00

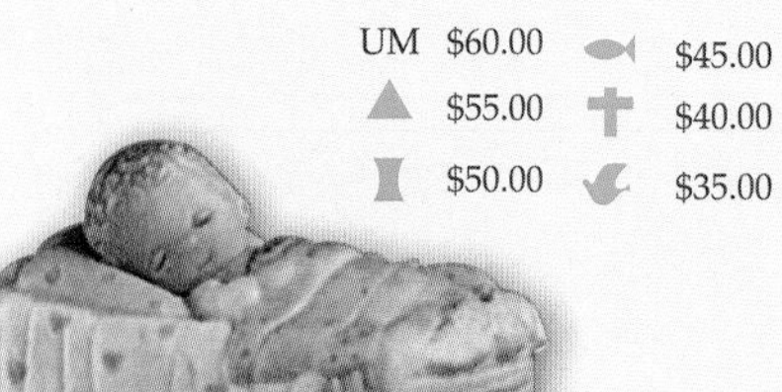

Suspended 1985, Issue Price $10.00, '81
Purchased ________, Price $ ___________

We Have Seen His Star, E-5620 (Bell)

UM $45.00
$40.00
$38.00

Suspended 1985, Issue Price $15.00, '81
Purchased ________, Price $ ___________

Donkey, E-5621

UM $35.00
$35.00
$35.00
$30.00
$30.00
$28.00
$28.00
$26.00
$25.00
$23.00
$23.00
$23.00
$21.00
$21.00
$20.00
$20.00
$20.00
$18.00
$18.00
$18.00
$18.00

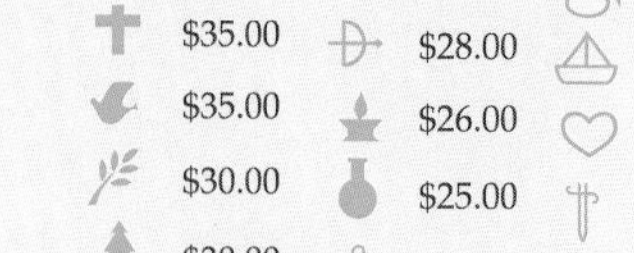

Retired 2003, Issue Price $6.00, '81
Nativity Addition
Purchased ________, Price $ ___________

Let The Heavens Rejoice, E-5622 (Bell)

UM $225.00

Dated Annual 1981, Issue Price $15.00, '81
Purchased ________, Price $ ___________

Jesus Is Born, E-5623 (Bell)

UM $60.00
$47.00

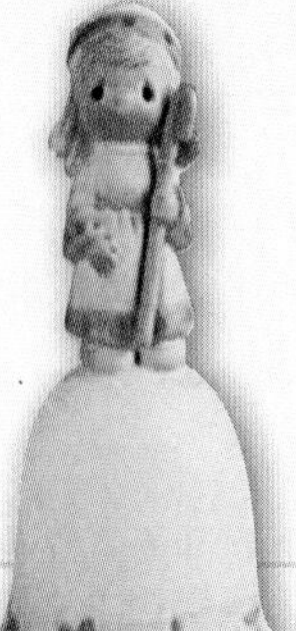

Suspended 1984,
Issue Price $15.00, '81
Purchased ________, Price $ ___________

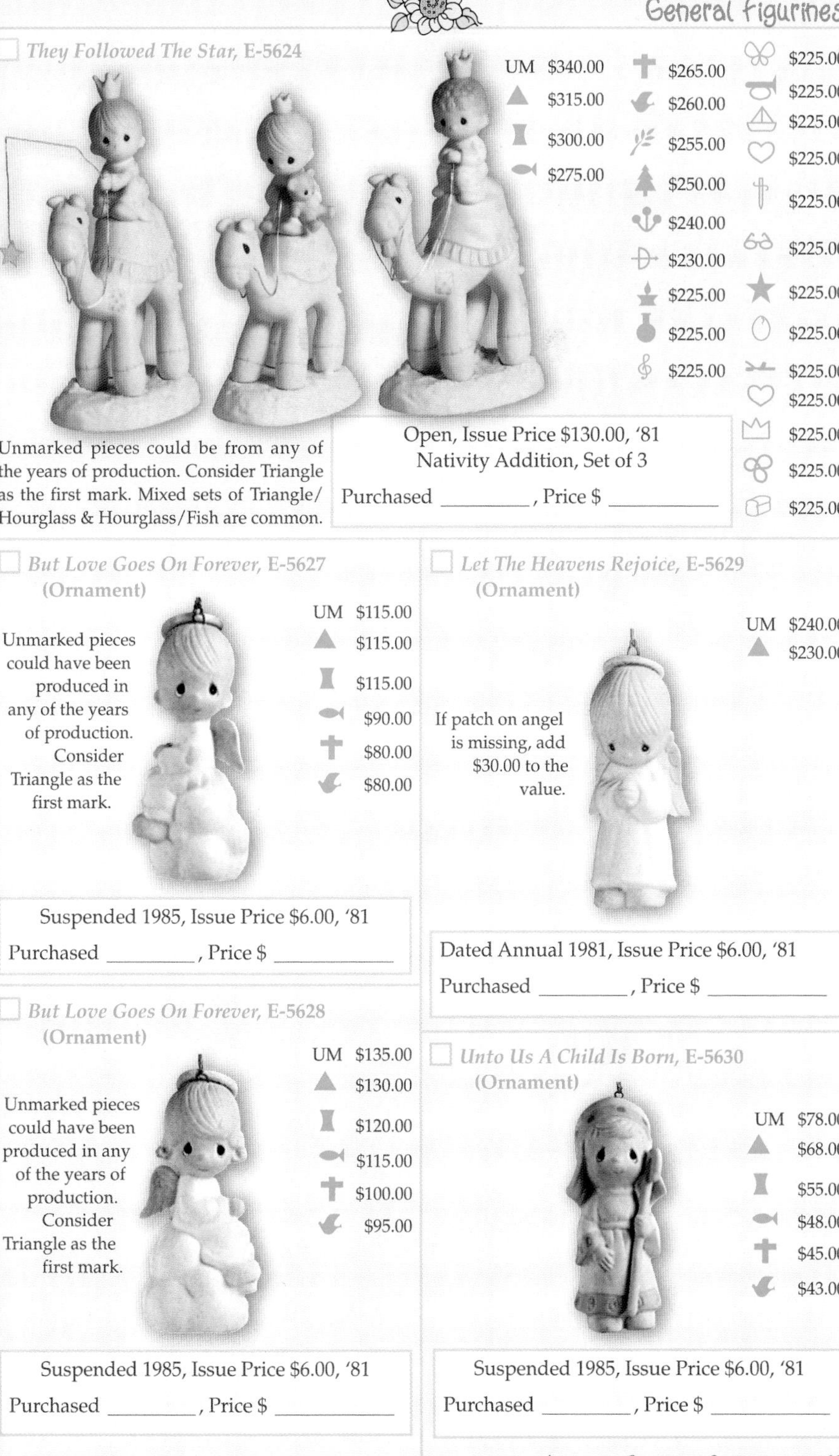

They Followed The Star, E-5624

UM $340.00
$315.00
$300.00
$275.00
$265.00
$260.00
$255.00
$250.00
$240.00
$230.00
$225.00
$225.00
$225.00
$225.00
$225.00
$225.00
$225.00
$225.00
$225.00
$225.00
$225.00
$225.00
$225.00
$225.00
$225.00
$225.00
$225.00

Unmarked pieces could be from any of the years of production. Consider Triangle as the first mark. Mixed sets of Triangle/Hourglass & Hourglass/Fish are common.

Open, Issue Price $130.00, '81
Nativity Addition, Set of 3
Purchased ________, Price $ ___________

But Love Goes On Forever, E-5627 (Ornament)

UM $115.00
$115.00
$115.00
$90.00
$80.00
$80.00

Unmarked pieces could have been produced in any of the years of production. Consider Triangle as the first mark.

Suspended 1985, Issue Price $6.00, '81
Purchased ________, Price $ ___________

But Love Goes On Forever, E-5628 (Ornament)

UM $135.00
$130.00
$120.00
$115.00
$100.00
$95.00

Unmarked pieces could have been produced in any of the years of production. Consider Triangle as the first mark.

Suspended 1985, Issue Price $6.00, '81
Purchased ________, Price $ ___________

Let The Heavens Rejoice, E-5629 (Ornament)

UM $240.00
$230.00

If patch on angel is missing, add $30.00 to the value.

Dated Annual 1981, Issue Price $6.00, '81
Purchased ________, Price $ ___________

Unto Us A Child Is Born, E-5630 (Ornament)

UM $78.00
$68.00
$55.00
$48.00
$45.00
$43.00

Suspended 1985, Issue Price $6.00, '81
Purchased ________, Price $ ___________

Baby's First Christmas, E-5631 (Ornament)

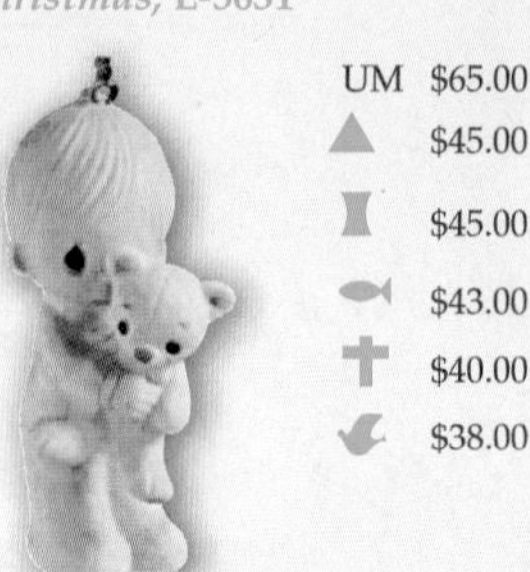

Unmarked pieces could have been produced in any of the years of production. Consider Triangle as the first mark.

UM	$65.00
Triangle	$45.00
Hourglass	$45.00
Fish	$43.00
Cross	$40.00
Dove	$38.00

Suspended 1985, Issue Price $6.00, '81

Purchased ________, Price $ ___________

Baby's First Christmas, E-5632 (Ornament)

Unmarked pieces could have been produced in any of the years of production. Consider Triangle as the first mark.

UM	$74.00
Triangle	$70.00
Hourglass	$59.00
Fish	$45.00
Cross	$36.00
Dove	$35.00

Suspended 1985, Issue Price $6.00, '81

Purchased ________, Price $ ___________

Come Let Us Adore Him, E-5633 (Ornaments)

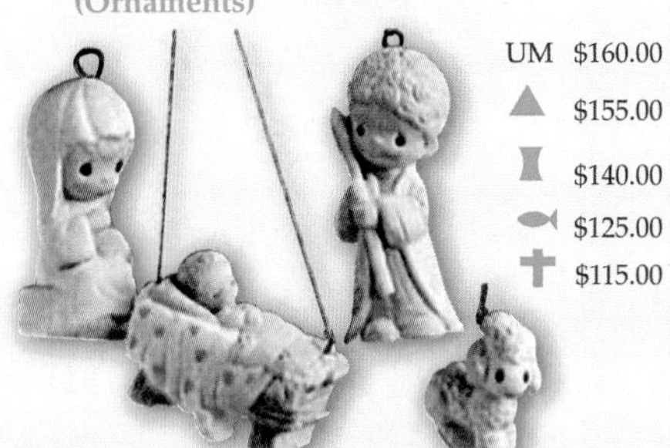

UM	$160.00
Triangle	$155.00
Hourglass	$140.00
Fish	$125.00
Cross	$115.00

Unmarked pieces could have been produced in any of the years of production. Consider Triangle as the first mark. Mixed sets of Triangle/Hourglass & Hourglass are common.

Suspended 1984, Issue Price $22.00, '81
Set of 4 — Mary, Jesus, Joseph, and Lamb

Purchased ________, Price $ ___________

Wee Three Kings, E-5634 (Ornaments)

UM	$165.00
Triangle	$150.00
Hourglass	$140.00
Fish	$130.00
Dove	$120.00

Unmarked pieces could have been produced in any of the years of production. Consider Triangle as the first mark. Mixed sets of Triangle/Hourglass & Hourglass are common.

Suspended 1984, Issue Price $19.00, '81
Set of 3

Purchased ________, Price $ ___________

Wee Three Kings, E-5635

UM	$165.00
Triangle	$130.00
Hourglass	$100.00
Fish	$95.00
Cross	$85.00
Dove	$83.00
Olive Branch	$83.00
Cedar Tree	$80.00
Flower	$79.00
Bow & Arrow	$78.00
Flame	$77.00
Vessel	$76.00
G-Clef	$75.00
Butterfly	$75.00
Trumpet	$75.00
Ship	$75.00
Heart	$75.00
Sword	$75.00
Eyeglasses	$75.00
Star	$75.00
Egg	$75.00
Sandal	$75.00
Heart	$75.00
Crown	$75.00
Clover	$75.00
Box	$75.00

Although scarce, Unmarked pieces could have been produced in any of the years of production. Consider Triangle as the first mark.

Open, Issue Price $40.00, '81
Nativity Addition, Set of 3

Purchased ________, Price $ ___________

☐ *Rejoice O Earth*, E-5636

UM	$83.00
Triangle	$75.00
Hourglass	$73.00
Fish	$72.00
Cross	$70.00
Dove	$68.00
Olive Branch	$65.00
Cedar Tree	$60.00
Flower	$55.00
Bow & Arrow	$53.00
Flame	$50.00
Vessel	$48.00
G-Clef	$45.00
Butterfly	$42.00
Trumpet	$40.00
Ship	$38.00
Heart	$35.00
Sword	$35.00
Eyeglasses	$35.00
Star	$35.00

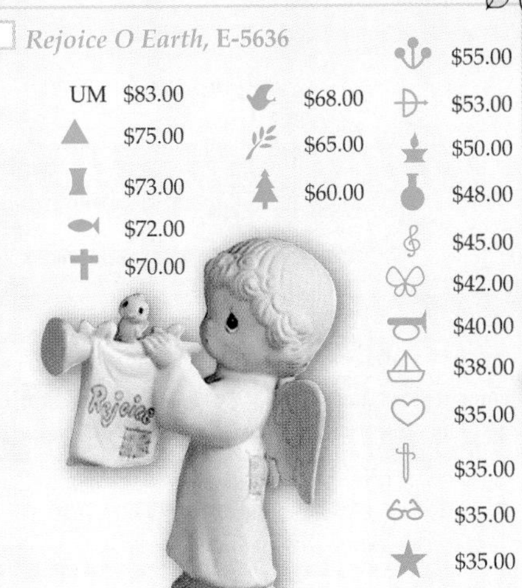

Unmarked pieces could have been produced in any of the years of production. Consider Triangle as the first mark.

Retired 1999, Issue Price $15.00, '81
Nativity Addition
Purchased ________, Price $ __________

☐ *The Heavenly Light*, E-5637

UM	$83.00
Triangle	$75.00
Hourglass	$73.00
Fish	$72.00
Cross	$70.00
Dove	$68.00
Olive Branch	$65.00
Cedar Tree	$60.00
Flower	$55.00
Bow & Arrow	$53.00
Flame	$50.00
Vessel	$48.00
G-Clef	$45.00
Butterfly	$42.00
Trumpet	$40.00
Ship	$38.00
Heart	$35.00
Sword	$35.00
Eyeglasses	$35.00
Star	$35.00
Egg	$35.00
Sandal	$35.00

Unmarked pieces could have been produced in any of the years of production. Consider Triangle as the first mark.

Retired 2001, Issue Price $15.00, '81
Nativity Addition
Purchased ________, Price $ __________

☐ *Cow With Bell*, E-5638

UM	$55.00
Cross	$48.00
Dove	$46.00
Olive Branch	$43.00
Cedar Tree	$40.00
Flower	$40.00
Bow & Arrow	$38.00
Flame	$38.00
Vessel	$35.00
G-Clef	$35.00
Butterfly	$32.50
Trumpet	$32.50
Ship	$32.50
Heart	$32.50
Sword	$32.50
Eyeglasses	$32.50
Star	$32.50
Egg	$32.50
Sandal	$32.50
Heart	$32.50
Crown	$32.50
Clover	$32.50
Cube	$32.50

Open, Issue Price $16.00, '84
Nativity Addition
Purchased ________, Price $ __________

☐ *Isn't He Wonderful*, E-5639

UM	$75.00
Triangle	$70.00
Hourglass	$50.00
Fish	$45.00
Cross	$42.00
Dove	$36.00

Unmarked pieces could have been produced in any of the years of production. Consider Triangle as the first mark.

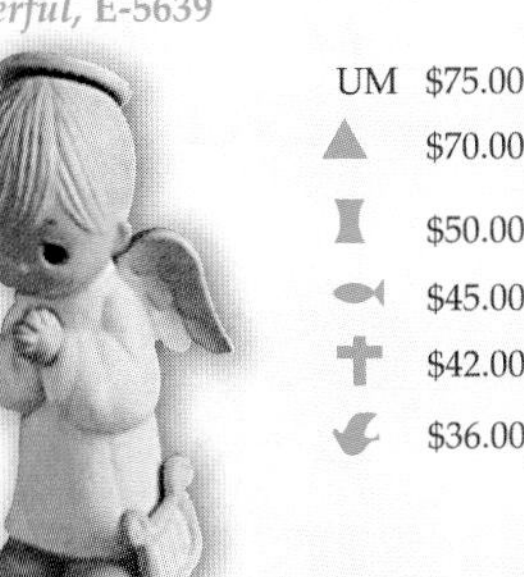

Suspended 1985, Issue Price $12.00, '81
Nativity Addition
Purchased ________, Price $ __________

☐ *Isn't He Wonderful*, E-5640

UM	$75.00
Triangle	$70.00
Hourglass	$50.00
Fish	$45.00
Cross	$42.00
Dove	$36.00

Unmarked pieces could have been produced in any of the years of production. Consider Triangle as the first mark.

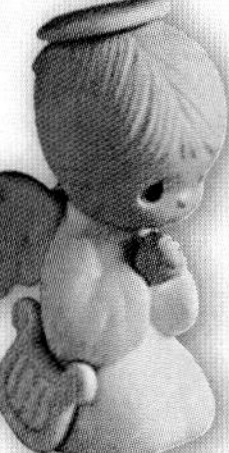

Suspended 1985, Issue Price $12.00, '81
Nativity Addition
Purchased ________, Price $ __________

They Followed The Star, E-5641

Mark	Price
UM	$280.00
▲ (Triangle)	$265.00
(Hourglass)	$215.00
(Fish)	$200.00
(Cross)	$195.00
(Dove)	$190.00

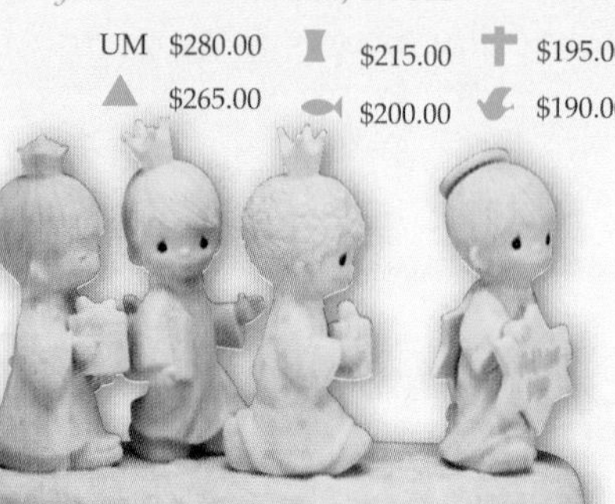

Unmarked pieces could have been produced in any of the years of production. Consider Triangle as the first mark.

Suspended 1985, Issue Price $75.00, '81
Nativity Addition

Purchased ________, Price $ ___________

Silent Knight, E-5642 (Musical)

Mark	Price
UM	$575.00
▲ (Triangle)	$545.00
(Hourglass)	$465.00
(Fish)	$460.00
(Cross)	$430.00
(Dove)	$425.00

Unmarked pieces could have been produced in any of the years of production. Consider Triangle as the first mark. Exists in a double mark, Triangle/Hourglass. This is the only musical that does not have a figurine similar to it.

Suspended 1985, Issue Price $45.00, '81
Tune: "Silent Night"

Purchased ________, Price $ ___________

Nativity Wall, E-5644

Mark	Price
UM	$165.00
▲ (Triangle)	$155.00
(Hourglass)	$153.00
(Fish)	$150.00
(Cross)	$145.00
(Dove)	$140.00
(Olive Branch)	$135.00
(Cedar Tree)	$130.00
(Flower)	$128.00
(Bow & Arrow)	$125.00
(Flame)	$123.00
(Vessel)	$120.00
(G-Clef)	$120.00
(Butterfly)	$120.00
(Trumpet)	$120.00
(Ship)	$120.00
(Heart)	$120.00
(Sword)	$120.00
(Eyeglasses)	$120.00
(Star)	$120.00
(Egg)	$120.00
(Sandal)	$120.00
(Cross in Heart)	$120.00
(Crown)	$120.00
(Three Circles)	$120.00
(Box)	$120.00

Unmarked pieces could have been produced in any of the years of production. Consider Triangle as the first mark.

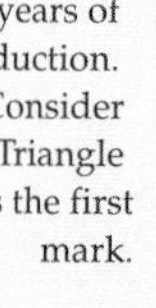

Open, Issue Price $60.00, '81
Nativity Addition, two sections of wall

Purchased_____, Price $ ___________

Rejoice O Earth, E-5645 (Musical)

Mark	Price
▲ (Triangle)	$148.00
(Hourglass)	$105.00
(Fish)	$100.00
(Cross)	$100.00
(Dove)	$95.00
(Olive Branch)	$90.00
(Cedar Tree)	$85.00
(Flower)	$83.00

Retired 1988, Issue Price $35.00, '81
Tune: "Joy To The World"

Purchased ________, Price $ ___________

Come Let Us Adore Him, E-5646 (Plate)

UM $50.00

Limited Ed. 15,000, Issue Price $40.00, '81
Series: *Christmas Collection* — First Issue

Purchased ________, Price $ ___________

But Love Goes On Forever, E-6118 (Candle Climbers)

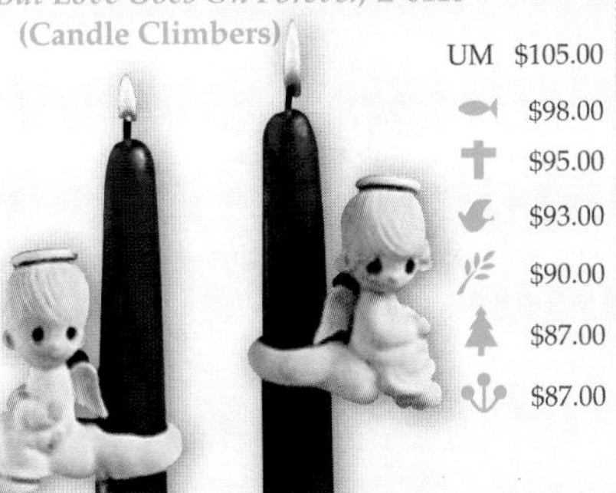

UM $105.00
$98.00
$95.00
$93.00
$90.00
$87.00
$87.00

Suspended 1988, Issue Price $14.00, '81
Set of 2

Purchased _________, Price $ ___________

We Have Seen His Star, E-6120 (Ornament)

UM $75.00
$68.00
$55.00
$50.00
$50.00

Retired 1984, Issue Price $6.00, '81

Purchased _________, Price $ ___________

Mikey, E-6214B (Doll)

UM $225.00
$215.00
$200.00
$200.00

Suspended 1985, Issue Price $150.00, '81

Purchased _________, Price $ ___________

Debbie, E-6214G (Doll)

UM $250.00
$245.00
$242.00
$225.00

Suspended 1985, Issue Price $150.00, '81

Purchased _________, Price $ ___________

God Sends The Gift Of His Love, E-6613

$65.00
$63.00
$59.00
$58.00
$55.00

Suspended 1987, Issue Price $22.50, '84

Purchased _________,

Price $ ___________

Collection Plaque, E-6901 (Plaque)

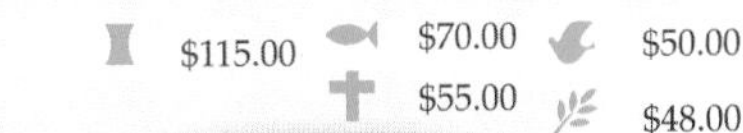

$115.00
$70.00
$55.00
$50.00
$48.00

Found with a double mark, Hourglass/Fish.

Suspended 1986, Issue Price $19.00, '82

Purchased _________, Price $ ___________

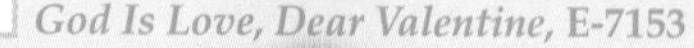

God Is Love, Dear Valentine, E-7153

- $46.00
- $39.00
- $37.00
- $35.00
- $33.00
- $30.00

Suspended 1986, Issue Price $16.00, '82

Purchased ________, Price $ __________

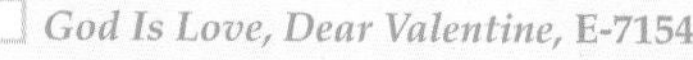

God Is Love, Dear Valentine, E-7154

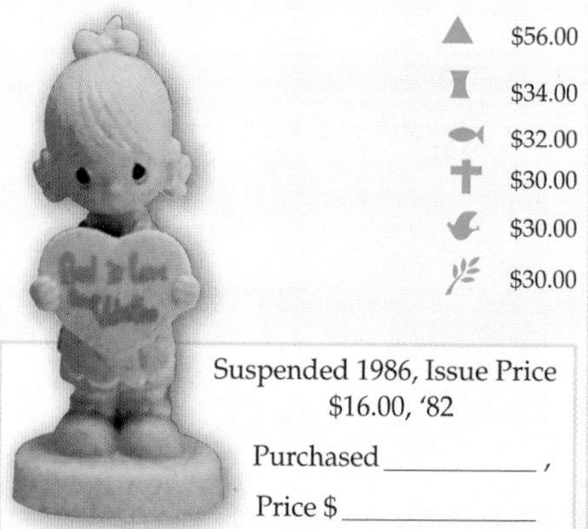

- $56.00
- $34.00
- $32.00
- $30.00
- $30.00
- $30.00

Suspended 1986, Issue Price $16.00, '82

Purchased __________,

Price $ __________

Thanking Him For You, E-7155

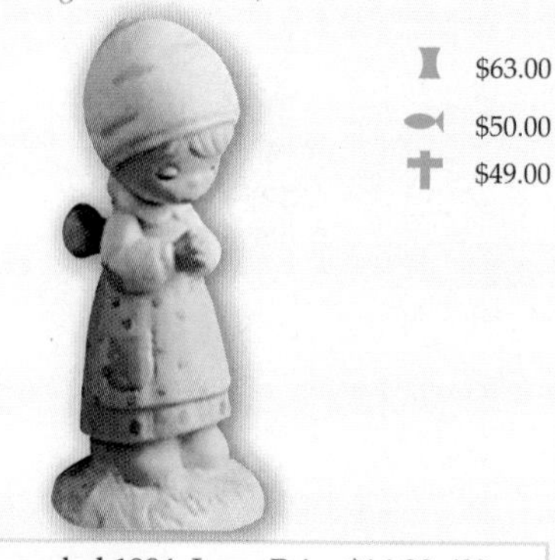

- $63.00
- $50.00
- $49.00

Suspended 1984, Issue Price $16.00, '82

Purchased ________, Price $ __________

I Believe In Miracles, E-7156

- $78.00
- $70.00
- $55.00
- $53.00

Suspended 1985, Reintroduced 1987, Retired 1992, Issue Price $17.00, '82

Purchased ________, Price $ __________

I Believe In Miracles, E-7156R

- $65.00
- $65.00
- $55.00
- $52.00
- $50.00

First introduced in 1982 as E-7156, the original version of this figurine has the boy holding a yellow chick. E-7156 was Suspended in 1985, and in 1987 was resculpted and returned to production as E-7156R. Among the changes made was the addition of the incised "Sam B" on the base of the figurine and a change in the color of the chick, from yellow to blue. The resculpted piece is considerably larger than the original version. During the early part of production in 1987 (Cedar Tree), the molds from the Suspended piece, E-7156, were pulled and used along with the molds for the new Reintroduced piece, E-7156R. Shipments of the figurines crafted from the old Suspended mold but with the new blue painting of the chick were made before the error was discovered. These pieces are the rare version. All rare versions have the Cedar Tree symbol. The values of these rare version pieces are $155.00 each.

Retired 1992, Issue Price $22.50, '87

Purchased ________, Price $ __________

There Is Joy In Serving Jesus, E-7157

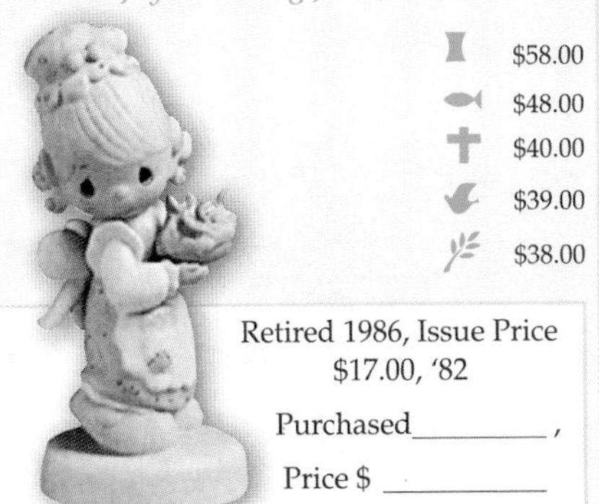

- $58.00
- $48.00
- $40.00
- $39.00
- $38.00

Retired 1986, Issue Price $17.00, '82

Purchased__________, Price $ __________

Love Beareth All Things, E-7158

- $62.00
- $55.00
- $50.00
- $49.00
- $48.00
- $47.00
- $46.00
- $45.00
- $45.00
- $45.00
- $45.00
- $45.00
- $45.00
- $45.00
- $45.00
- $45.00
- $45.00
- $45.00
- $45.00
- $45.00
- $45.00
- $45.00
- $45.00
- $45.00
- $45.00
- $45.00

Open, Issue Price $25.00, '82

Purchased __________, Price $ __________

Lord Give Me Patience, E-7159

- $66.00
- $50.00
- $47.00
- $45.00

There have been reports of no decal on the sign; add $75.00 to the value for these pieces.

The Perfect Grandpa, E-7160

- $85.00
- $75.00
- $73.00
- $68.00
- $65.00

Suspended 1986, Issue Price $25.00, '82

Purchased __________, Price $ __________

His Sheep Am I, E-7161

Unmarked pieces could have been produced in any of the years of production. Consider the Hourglass as the first mark.

- UM $125.00
- $90.00
- $80.00
- $75.00

Suspended 1984, Issue Price $25.00, '82

Purchased __________, Price $ __________

Love Is Sharing, E-7162

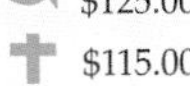

- $145.00
- $125.00
- $115.00

Suspended 1984, Issue Price $25.00, '82

Purchased __________, Price $ __________

Suspended 1985, Issue Price $25.00, '82

Purchased __________, Price $ __________

☐ *God Is Watching Over You*, E-7163

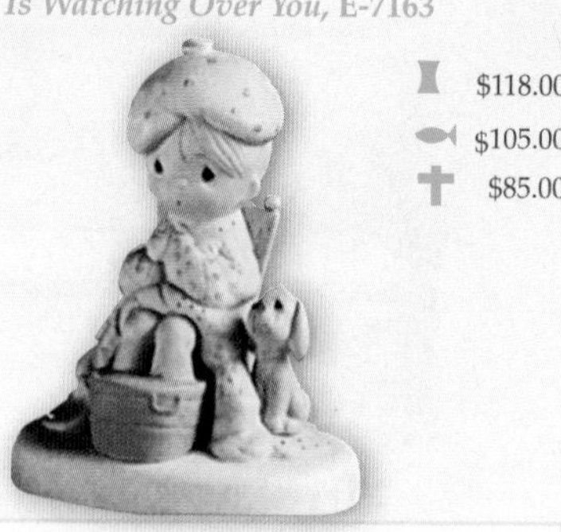

Hourglass	$118.00
Fish	$105.00
Cross	$85.00

Suspended 1984, Issue Price $27.50, '82

Purchased ________, Price $ __________

☐ *Bless This House*, E-7164

Hourglass	$310.00
Fish	$255.00
Cross	$220.00

Suspended 1984, Issue Price $45.00, '82

Purchased ________, Price $ __________

☐ *Let The Whole World Know*, E-7165

UM	$175.00
Hourglass	$155.00
Fish	$135.00
Cross	$110.00
Dove	$100.00
Olive Branch	$95.00
Cedar Tree	$85.00

Unmarked pieces could have been produced in any of the years of production. Consider the Hourglass as the first mark.

Suspended 1987, Issue Price $45.00, '82

Purchased ________, Price $ __________

☐ *The Lord Bless You And Keep You*, E-7166 (Frame)

Hourglass	$65.00
Fish	$55.00
Cross	$55.00
Dove	$50.00
Olive Branch	$49.00
Cedar Tree	$48.00
Anchor	$47.00
Bow & Arrow	$46.00
Flame	$45.00
Vessel	$44.00
G-Clef	$43.00
Butterfly	$42.00

Suspended 1993, Issue Price $22.50, '82

Purchased ________, Price $ __________

☐ *The Lord Bless You And Keep You*, E-7167 (Box)

Hourglass	$68.00
Fish	$65.00
Cross	$55.00
Dove	$50.00

Suspended 1985, Issue Price $22.50, '82

Purchased ________, Price $ __________

☐ *My Guardian Angel*, E-7168 (Frame)

Hourglass	$85.00
Fish	$76.00
Cross	$72.00

Suspended 1984, Issue Price $18.00, '82

Purchased ________, Price $ __________

My Guardian Angel, E-7169 (Frame)

$80.00
$75.00
$70.00

Suspended 1984, Issue Price $18.00, '82
Purchased ________, Price $ __________

Jesus Loves Me, E-7170 (Frame)

$65.00
$63.00
$60.00
$58.00

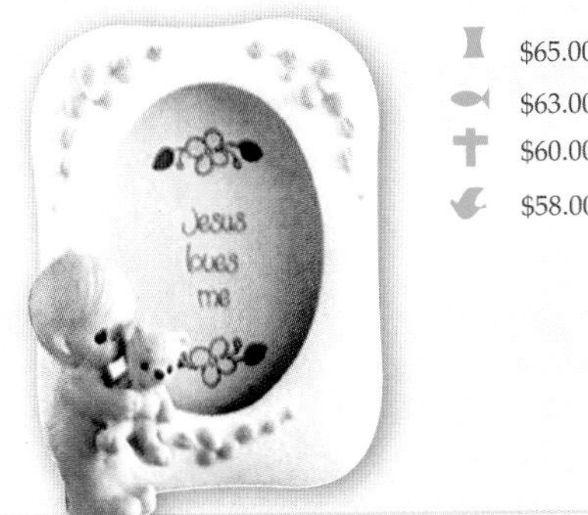

Suspended 1985, Issue Price $17.00, '82
Purchased ________, Price $ __________

Jesus Loves Me, E-7171 (Frame)

$78.00
$75.00
$72.00
$69.00

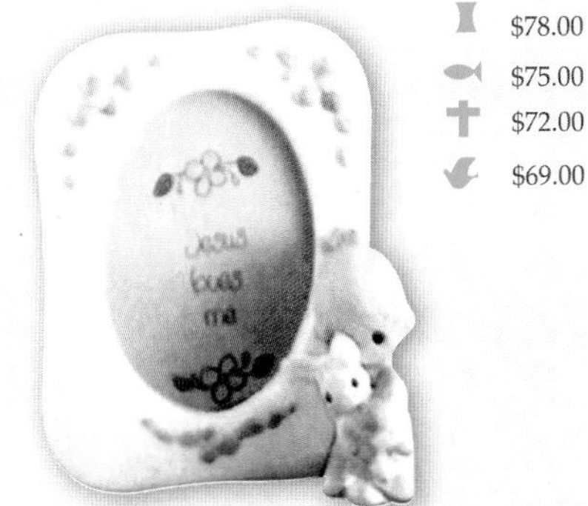

Suspended 1985, Issue Price $17.00, '82
Purchased ________, Price $ __________

Rejoicing With You, E-7172 (Plate)

UM $40.00
$35.00
$35.00

Suspended 1985, Issue Price $30.00, '82
Purchased ________, Price $ __________

The Purr-fect Grandma, E-7173 (Plate)

UM $47.00
$40.00

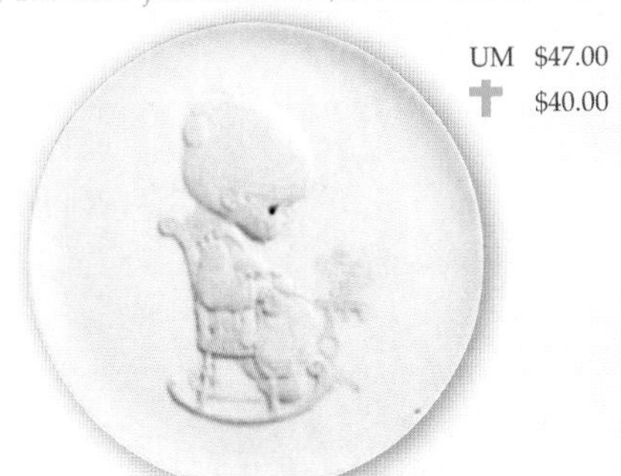

Limited Ed. 15,000, Issue Price $40.00, '82
Series: *Mother's Love* — Second Issue,
Individually Numbered
Purchased ________, Price $ __________

Make A Joyful Noise, E-7174 (Plate)

UM $45.00
$45.00

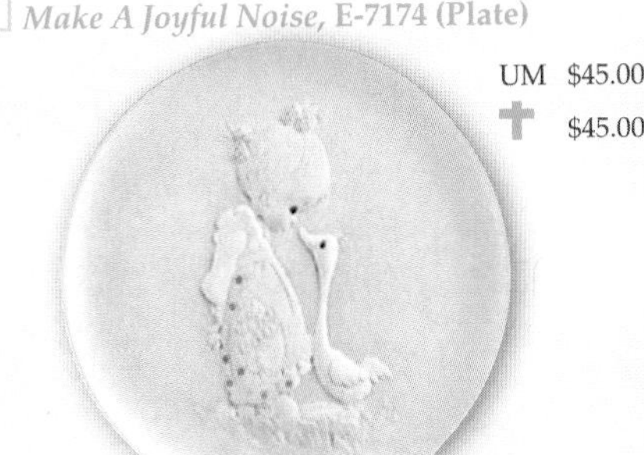

Limited Ed. 15,000, Issue Price $40.00, '82
Series: *Inspired Thoughts* — Second Issue,
Individually Numbered
Purchased ________, Price $ __________

☐ ***The Lord Bless You And Keep You, E-7175***
(Bell)

UM $40.00
$35.00
$30.00

Suspended 1985, Issue Price $17.00, '82

Purchased ________, Price $ ____________

☐ ***The Lord Bless You And Keep You, E-7176***
(Bell)

UM $55.00
$47.00
$43.00

Suspended 1985, Issue Price $17.00, '82

Purchased ________, Price $ ____________

☐ ***The Lord Bless You And Keep You, E-7177***
(Frame)

$55.00
$50.00
$48.00
$47.00
$46.00
$45.00

Suspended 1987, Issue Price $18.00, '82

Purchased ________, Price $ ____________

☐ ***The Lord Bless You And Keep You, E-7178***
(Frame)

$65.00
$62.00
$60.00
$55.00
$53.00
$50.00

Suspended 1987, Issue Price $18.00, '82

Purchased ________, Price $ ____________

☐ ***The Lord Bless You And Keep You, E-7179***
(Bell)

UM $70.00
$65.00
$63.00
$60.00
$58.00
$55.00
$54.00
$53.00
$52.00
$51.00
$50.00

Suspended 1993, Issue Price $22.50, '82

Purchased ________, Price $ ____________

☐ ***The Lord Bless You And Keep You, E-7180***
(Musical)

UM $115.00
$95.00
$90.00
$90.00
$85.00
$85.00
$85.00
$85.00
$85.00
$85.00
$85.00
$85.00
$85.00
$85.00
$85.00
$85.00
$85.00
$85.00
$85.00

Retired 2001, Issue Price $55.00, '82
Tune: "Wedding March"

Purchased ________, Price $ ____________

Mother Sew Dear, E-7181 (Bell)

UM	$70.00
Cross	$55.00
Dove	$54.00
Olive Branch	$53.00
Cedar Tree	$52.00
Flower	$50.00

Suspended 1988, Issue Price $17.00, '82

Purchased ________, Price $ ___________

Mother Sew Dear, E-7182 (Musical)

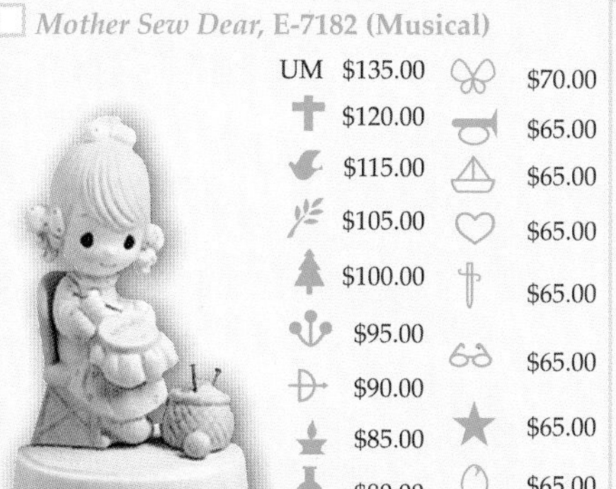

UM	$135.00	Butterfly	$70.00
Cross	$120.00	Trumpet	$65.00
Dove	$115.00	Ship	$65.00
Olive Branch	$105.00	Heart	$65.00
Cedar Tree	$100.00	Sword	$65.00
Flower	$95.00	Eyeglasses	$65.00
Bow & Arrow	$90.00	Star	$65.00
Flame	$85.00	Egg	$65.00
Vessel	$80.00	Bird	$65.00
G-Clef	$75.00		

Retired 2001, Issue Price $35.00, '82
Tune: "You Light Up My Life"

Purchased ________, Price $ ___________

The Purr-fect Grandma, E-7183 (Bell)

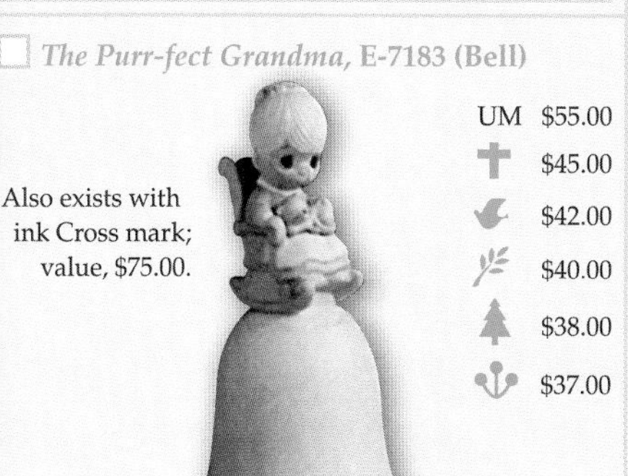

Also exists with ink Cross mark; value, $75.00.

UM	$55.00
Cross	$45.00
Dove	$42.00
Olive Branch	$40.00
Cedar Tree	$38.00
Flower	$37.00

Suspended 1988, Issue Price $17.00, '82

Purchased ________, Price $ ___________

The Purr-fect Grandma, E-7184 (Musical)

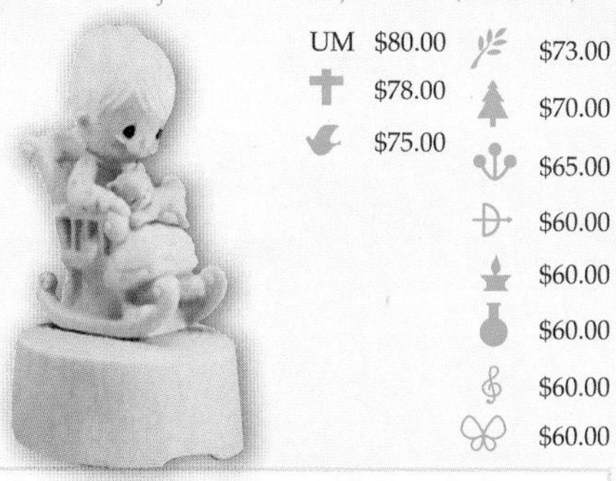

UM	$80.00	Olive Branch	$73.00
Cross	$78.00	Cedar Tree	$70.00
Dove	$75.00	Flower	$65.00
		Bow & Arrow	$60.00
		Flame	$60.00
		Vessel	$60.00
		G-Clef	$60.00
		Butterfly	$60.00

Suspended 1993, Issue Price $35.00, '82
Tune: "Always In My Heart"

Purchased ________, Price $ ___________

Love Is Sharing, E-7185 (Musical)

Hourglass	$175.00
Fish	$165.00
Cross	$155.00
Dove	$150.00
Olive Branch	$145.00

Retired 1985, Issue Price $40.00, '82
Tune: "School Days"

Purchased ________, Price $ ___________

Let The Whole World Know, E-7186 (Musical)

UM	$150.00
Hourglass	$133.00
Fish	$125.00
Cross	$115.00
Dove	$110.00
Olive Branch	$105.00

Suspended 1986, Issue Price $60.00, '82
Tune: "What A Friend We Have In Jesus"

Purchased ________, Price $ ___________

Mother Sew Dear, E-7241 (Frame)

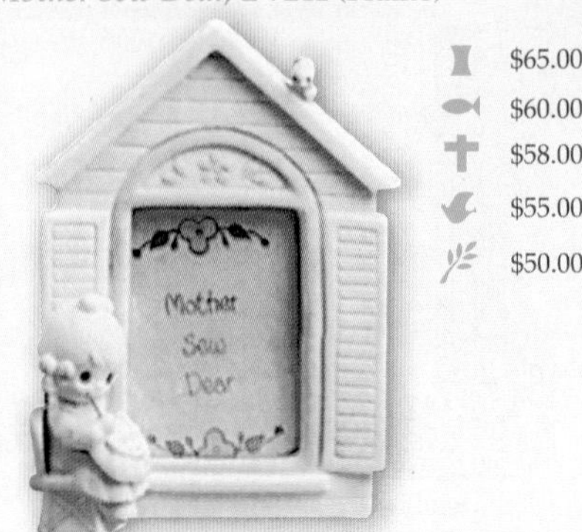

Hourglass	$65.00
Fish	$60.00
Cross	$58.00
Dove	$55.00
Olive Branch	$50.00

Suspended 1986, Issue Price $18.00, '82

Purchased ________, Price $ ___________

Tammy, E-7267G (Doll)

UM $600.00

Individually numbered on foot. Comes with certificate of authenticity.

Limited Ed. 5,000, Issue Price $300.00, '82

Purchased ________, Price $ ___________

The Purr-fect Grandma, E-7242 (Frame)

Hourglass	$55.00
Fish	$50.00
Cross	$48.00
Dove	$46.00
Olive Branch	$45.00
Cedar Tree	$44.00
Flower	$42.00

Suspended 1988, Issue Price $18.00, '82

Purchased ________, Price $ ___________

But Love Goes On Forever, E-7350 (Retailer's Dome)

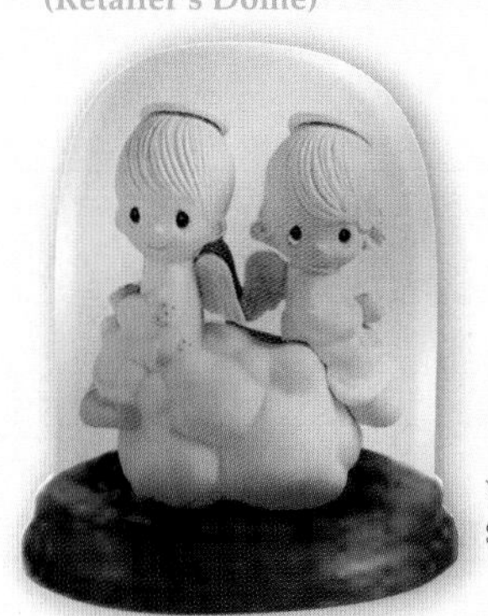

UM $765.00

Cross $750.00

Without dome, $675.00.

Special Gift, '84

Purchased ________, Price $ ___________

Cubby, E-7267B (Doll)

UM $475.00

Individually numbered on foot. Comes with certificate of authenticity.

Limited Ed. 5,000, Issue Price $200.00, '82

Purchased ________, Price $ ___________

Love Is Patient, E-9251

Fish	$93.00
Cross	$63.00
Dove	$60.00

Also exists with Cross decal; value $86.00.

Suspended 1985, Issue Price $35.00, '83

Purchased ________, Price $ ___________

Forgiving Is Forgetting, E-9252

[Fish]	$85.00
[Cross]	$75.00
[Dove]	$70.00
[Olive Branch]	$68.00
[Cedar Tree]	$65.00
[Flower]	$63.00
[Bow & Arrow]	$60.00

Suspended 1989, Issue Price $37.50, '83

Purchased ________, Price $ ___________

The End Is In Sight, E-9253

Unmarked pieces could have been produced in any of the years of production, however it is known many were released in the first year of

UM	$140.00
[Hourglass]	$85.00
[Fish]	$75.00
[Cross]	$70.00
[Dove]	$67.00

Suspended 1985, Issue Price $25.00, '83

Purchased ________, Price $ ___________

Praise The Lord Anyhow, E-9254

UM	$110.00
[Hourglass]	$105.00
[Fish]	$100.00
[Cross]	$95.00
[Dove]	$93.00
[Olive Branch]	$88.00
[Cedar Tree]	$83.00
[Flower]	$78.00
[Bow & Arrow]	$75.00
[Flame]	$73.00
[Vessel]	$70.00
[G-Clef]	$68.00
[Butterfly]	$65.00
[Trumpet]	$60.00

Classic variation: "Inked Fish." During 1983, the Fish mark appeared as part of the understamp decal on many pieces. Pieces were also produced that did not have a Fish mark at all – incised or decal. When this occurred we can only speculate that an attempt was made to correct it by actually drawing the Fish mark on the bottom of the piece. This inked symbol can be washed off, creating an unmarked piece. The value for pieces with the erasable inked Fish mark is $182.00.

Retired 1994, Issue Price $35.00, '82

Purchased ________, Price $ ___________

Bless You Two, E-9255

[Fish]	$50.00
[Cross]	$50.00
[Dove]	$50.00
[Olive Branch]	$50.00
[Cedar Tree]	$45.00
[Flower]	$45.00
[Bow & Arrow]	$45.00
[Flame]	$45.00
[Vessel]	$45.00
[G-Clef]	$45.00
[Butterfly]	$45.00
[Trumpet]	$45.00
[Ship]	$45.00
[Heart]	$45.00
[Sword]	$45.00
[Eyeglasses]	$45.00
[Star]	$45.00
[Egg]	$45.00
[Bow Tie]	$45.00
[Cross in Heart]	$45.00
[Crown]	$45.00
[Clover]	$45.00
[Cube]	$45.00

Open, Issue Price $21.00, '83

Purchased ________, Price $ ___________

The Hand That Rocks The Future, E-9256 (Plate)

UM	$45.00
[Cross]	$45.00

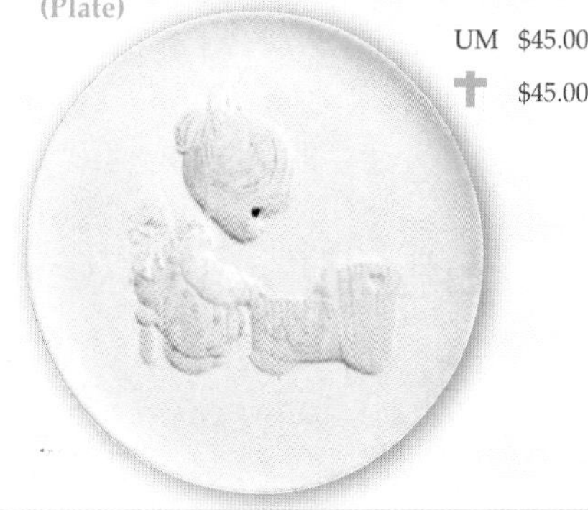

Limited Ed. 15,000, Issue Price $40.00, '83
Series: *Mother's Love* — Third Issue, Individually Numbered

Purchased ________, Price $ ___________

I Believe In Miracles, E-9257 (Plate)

UM $45.00
$45.00

Limited Ed. 15,000, Issue Price $40.00, '83
Series: *Inspired Thoughts* — Third Issue, Individually Numbered

Purchased ________, Price $ ____________

We Are God's Workmanship, E-9258

$60.00
$45.00
$43.00
$40.00
$38.00
$35.00
$35.00
$35.00
$35.00
$35.00
$35.00
$35.00
$35.00
$35.00
$35.00
$35.00
$35.00
$35.00
$35.00
$35.00

Retired 2001, Issue Price $19.00, '83

Purchased ________, Price $ ____________

We're In It Together, E-9259

$95.00
$75.00
$70.00
$70.00
$68.00
$66.00
$63.00
$60.00
$55.00

Suspended 1990, Issue Price $24.00, '83

Purchased ________, Price $ ____________

God's Promises Are Sure, E-9260

Also exists with a stamped Fish. This has been a favorite of angel collectors.

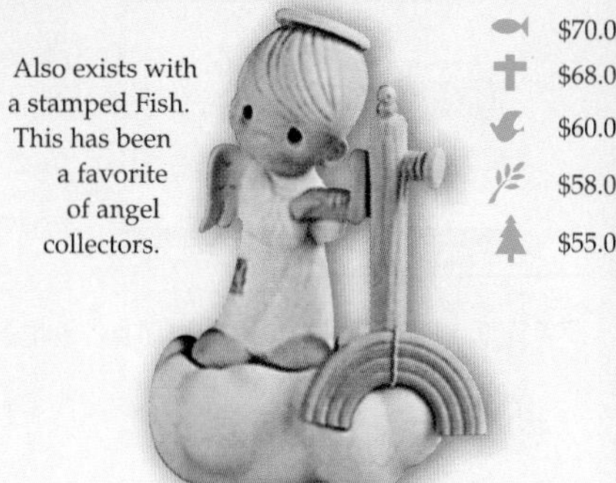

$70.00
$68.00
$60.00
$58.00
$55.00

Suspended 1987, Issue Price $30.00, '83
Series: *Heavenly Halos*

Purchased ________, Price $ ____________

Seek Ye The Lord, E-9261

Most figurines with the Fish annual production symbol do not have the "h" in the word "he" in the inscription on the graduate's scroll

$45.00
$42.00
$40.00
$40.00

Suspended 1986, Issue Price $21.00, '83

Purchased ________, Price $ ____________

Seek Ye The Lord, E-9262

Most figurines with the Fish annual production symbol do not have the "h" in the word "he" in the inscription on the graduate's scroll

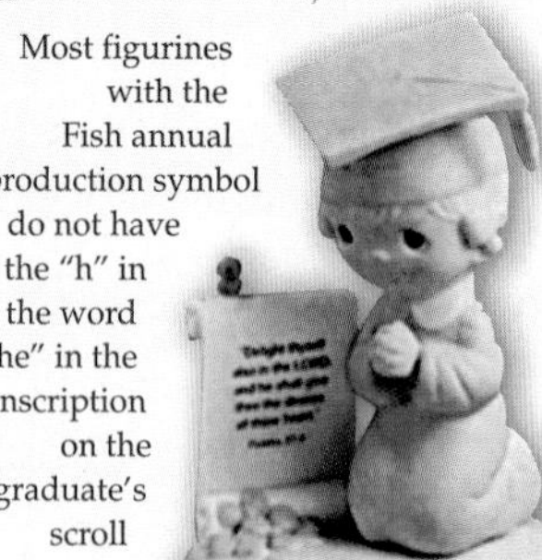

$67.00
$60.00
$57.00
$55.00

Suspended 1986, Issue Price $21.00, '83

Purchased ________, Price $ ____________

How Can Two Walk Together Except They Agree, E-9263

$165.00
$125.00
$120.00
$118.00

Suspended 1985, Issue Price $35.00, '83

Purchased ________, Price $ ___________

Press On, E-9265

$98.00
$85.00
$80.00
$75.00
$72.00
$70.00
$68.00
$68.00
$68.00
$67.00
$67.00
$66.00
$66.00
$66.00
$66.00
$65.00
$65.00
$65.00

Retired 1999, Issue Price $40.00, '83

Purchased ________, Price $ ___________

Our Love Is Heaven-Scent, E-9266 (Box)

UM $55.00
$50.00
$48.00
$44.00
$42.00
$40.00
$38.00

Some understamp decals have the title *Somebunny Cares;* add $50.00 for these pieces.

I'm Falling For Somebunny, E-9266B (Box)

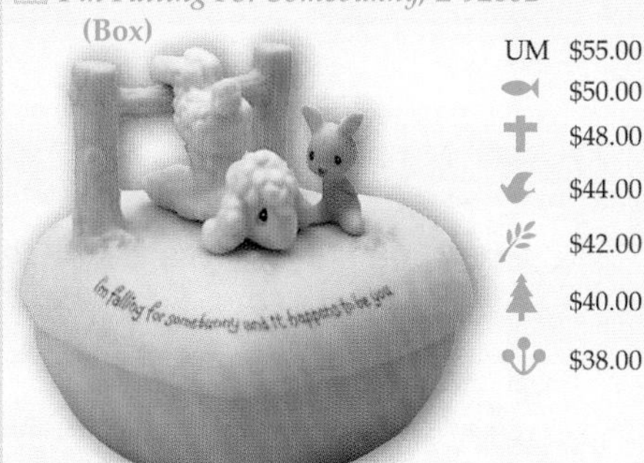

I'm falling for somebunny and it happens to be you

UM $55.00
$50.00
$48.00
$44.00
$42.00
$40.00
$38.00

Some understamp decals have the title *Somebunny Cares;* add $50.00 for these pieces.

Suspended 1988, Issue Price $13.50, '83

Purchased ________, Price $ ___________

Animal Collection, E-9267

UM $155.00
$140.00
$135.00
$130.00
$125.00
$123.00

Note: The Animal Collection was shipped to retailers in sets of six. Consequently they do not have individual boxes. In 1988, individual Enesco item numbers were assigned to each figurine in the set. Some Cedar Tree symbol pieces have an A-F suffix.

Suspended 1991, Issue Price $39.00, '83
Set of 6

Purchased ________, Price $ ___________

Suspended 1988, Issue Price $13.50, '83

Purchased ________, Price $ ___________

☐ *Animal Collection A,* E-9267A

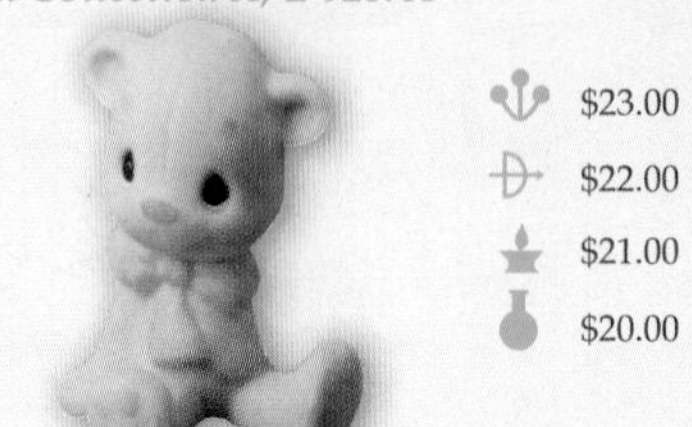

- $23.00
- $22.00
- $21.00
- $20.00

Suspended 1991, Issue Price $8.50, '88

Purchased ________, Price $ ___________

☐ *Animal Collection B,* E-9267B

- $23.00
- $22.00
- $21.00
- $20.00

Suspended 1991, Issue Price $8.50, '88

Purchased ________, Price $ ___________

☐ *Animal Collection C,* E-9267C

- $23.00
- $22.00
- $21.00
- $20.00

Suspended 1991, Issue Price $8.50, '88

Purchased ________, Price $ ___________

☐ *Animal Collection D,* E-9267D

- $23.00
- $22.00
- $21.00
- $20.00

Suspended 1991, Issue Price $8.50, '88

Purchased ________, Price $ ___________

☐ *Animal Collection E,* E-9267E

- $23.00
- $22.00
- $21.00
- $20.00

Suspended 1991, Issue Price $8.50, '88

Purchased ________, Price $ ___________

☐ *Animal Collection F,* E-9267F

- $23.00
- $22.00
- $21.00
- $20.00

Suspended 1991, Issue Price $8.50, '88

Purchased ________, Price $ ___________

☐ *Nobody's Perfect!* E-9268

- $90.00
- $88.00
- $85.00
- $80.00
- $78.00
- $75.00
- $70.00
- $68.00
- $65.00

Classic variation: "Smiling Dunce." The first Hourglass pieces produced are known as "Smiling Dunces" or "Smiley" and appeared with a smile. An "O" shaped mouth is on the normal piece. The value of the "Smiley" is $495.00.

Retired 1990, Issue Price $21.00, '83

Purchased ________, Price $ ___________

Let Love Reign, E-9273

$250.00
$70.00
$68.00
$65.00
$60.00
$60.00

Retired 1987, Issue Price $27.50, '83

Purchased ________, Price $ __________

Taste And See That The Lord Is Good, E-9274

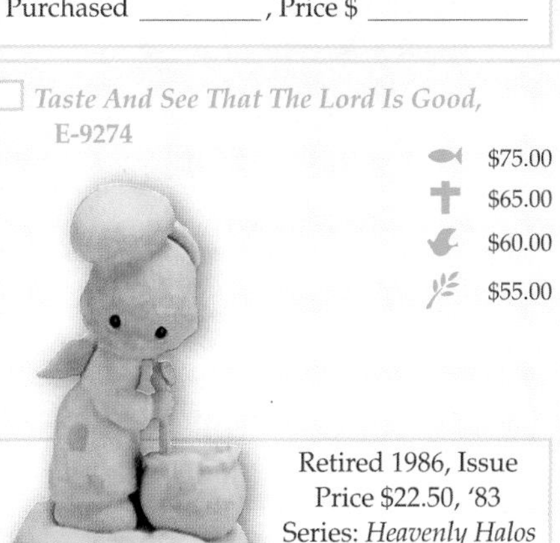

$75.00
$65.00
$60.00
$55.00

Retired 1986, Issue Price $22.50, '83
Series: *Heavenly Halos*

Purchased ________,
Price $__________

Jesus Loves Me, E-9275 (Plate)

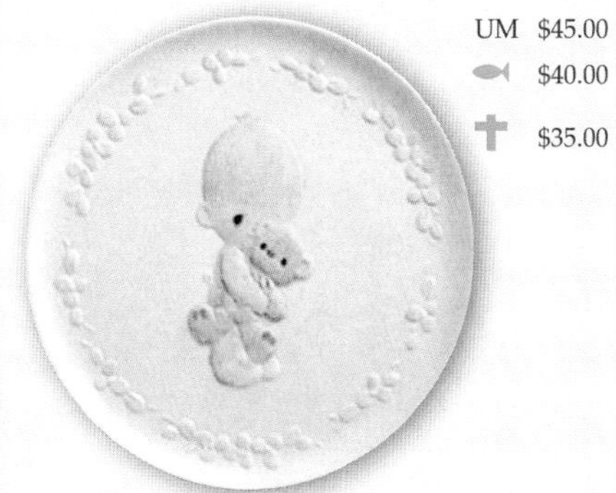

UM $45.00
$40.00
$35.00

Suspended 1984, Issue Price $30.00, '83

Purchased ________, Price $ __________

Jesus Loves Me, E-9276 (Plate)

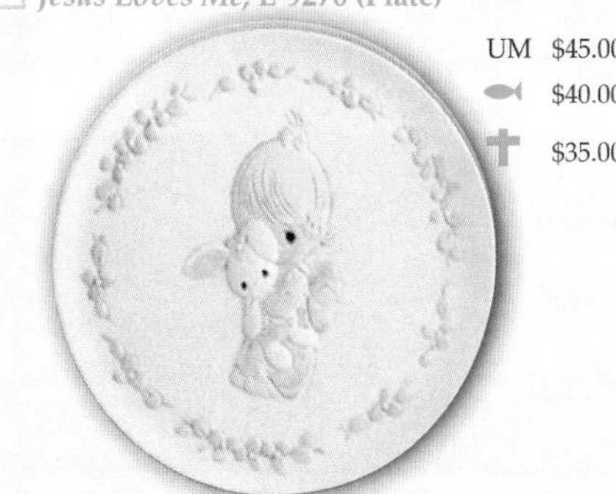

UM $45.00
$40.00
$35.00

Suspended 1984, Issue Price $30.00, '83

Purchased ________, Price $ __________

Jesus Loves Me, E-9278

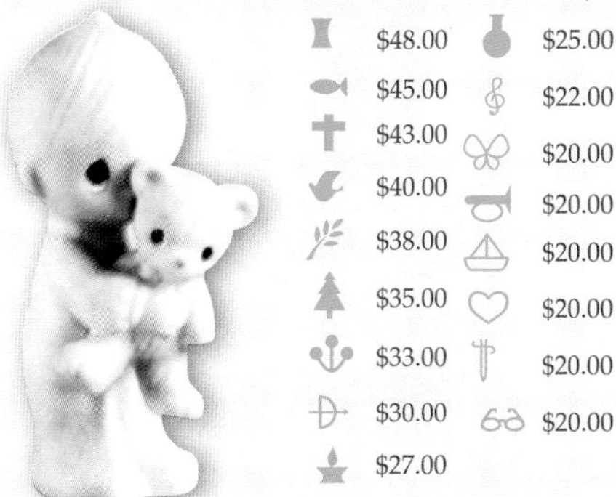

$48.00
$45.00
$43.00
$40.00
$38.00
$35.00
$33.00
$30.00
$27.00
$25.00
$22.00
$20.00
$20.00
$20.00
$20.00
$20.00
$20.00

Retired 1998, Issue Price $9.00, '83

Purchased ________, Price $ __________

Jesus Loves Me, E-9279

$48.00
$45.00
$43.00
$40.00
$38.00
$35.00
$33.00
$30.00
$27.00
$25.00
$22.00
$20.00
$20.00
$20.00
$20.00
$20.00
$20.00
$20.00
$20.00

Retired 2000, Issue Price $9.00, '83

Purchased ________, Price $ __________

Jesus Loves Me, E-9280 (Box)

$55.00
$50.00
$48.00
$45.00

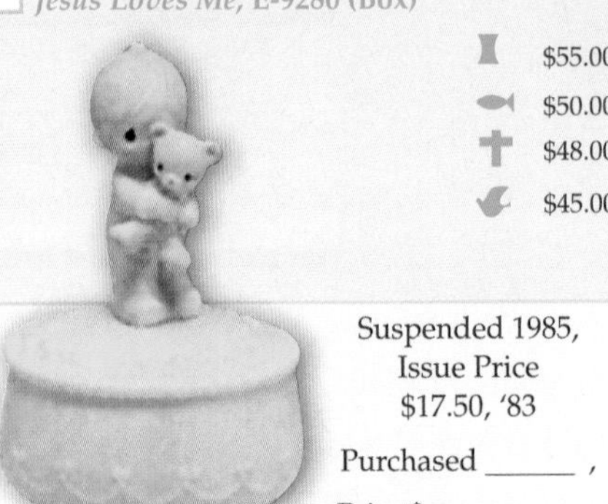

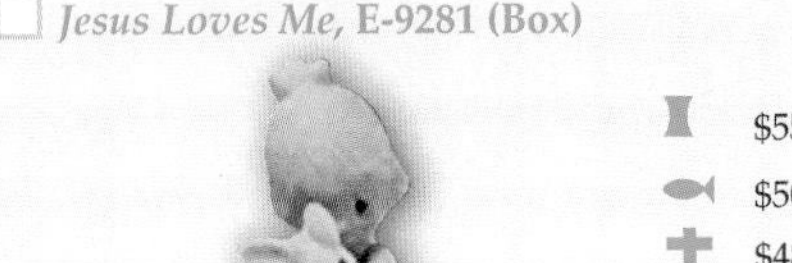

Suspended 1985, Issue Price $17.50, '83

Purchased ______ , Price $___________

Jesus Loves Me, E-9281 (Box)

$55.00
$50.00
$48.00
$45.00

Suspended 1985, Issue Price $17.50, '83

Purchased ________ , Price $ ___________

To Some Bunny Special, E-9282

UM $52.00
$48.00
$45.00
$40.00
$38.00
$36.00

Unmarked pieces could have been produced in any of the years of production. Consider Fish as the first mark. Letter "A" suffix added to item number in 1988.

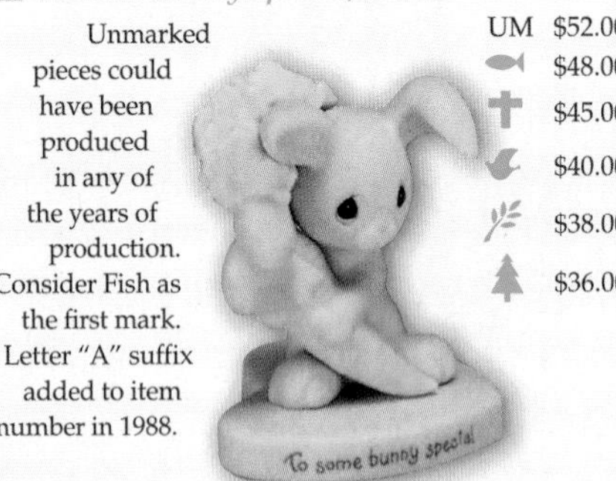

Suspended 1990, Issue Price $8.00, '83

Purchased ________ , Price $ ___________

Suspended 1990, Issue Price $8.00, '83

Purchased ________ , Price $ ___________

To Some Bunny Special, E-9282A

$38.00
$35.00
$33.00

Suspended 1990, Issue Price $10.50, '88

Purchased ______ ,

Price $___________

You're Worth Your Weight In Gold, E-9282

UM $52.00
$48.00
$45.00
$40.00
$38.00
$36.00

Unmarked pieces could have been produced in any of the years of production. Consider Fish as the first mark. Letter "B" suffix added to item number in 1988.

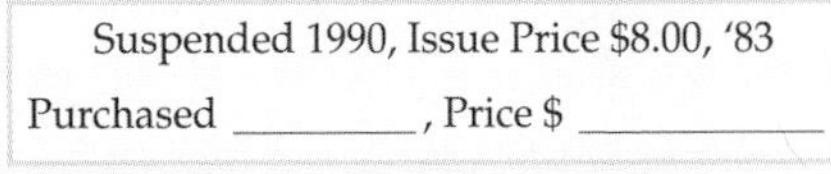

Suspended 1990, Issue Price $8.00, '83

Purchased ________ , Price $ ___________

You're Worth Your Weight In Gold, E-9282B

$38.00
$35.00
$33.00

Suspended 1990, Issue Price $10.50, '88

Purchased ______ ,

Price $ __________

Especially For Ewe, E-9282

Unmarked pieces could have been produced in any of the years of production. Consider Fish as the first mark. Letter "C" suffix added to item number in 1988.

UM $52.00
$48.00
$45.00
$40.00
$38.00
$36.00

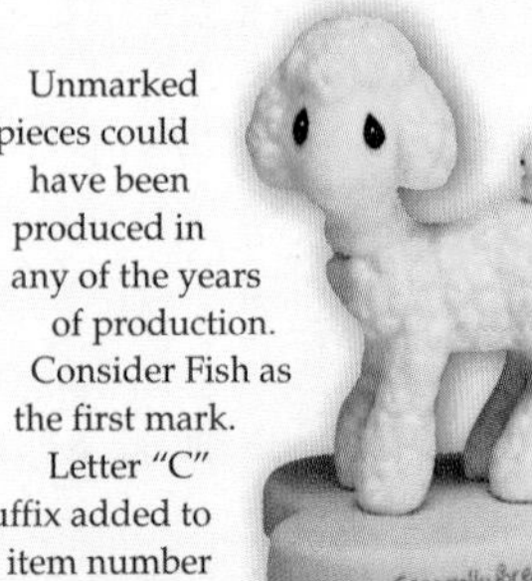

☐ *Especially For Ewe, E-9282C*

$38.00

$35.00

$33.00

Suspended 1990, Issue Price $10.50, '88

Purchased _________, Price $ ___________

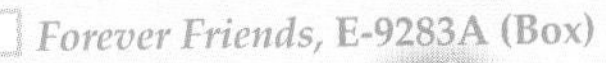

☐ *Forever Friends, E-9283A (Box)*

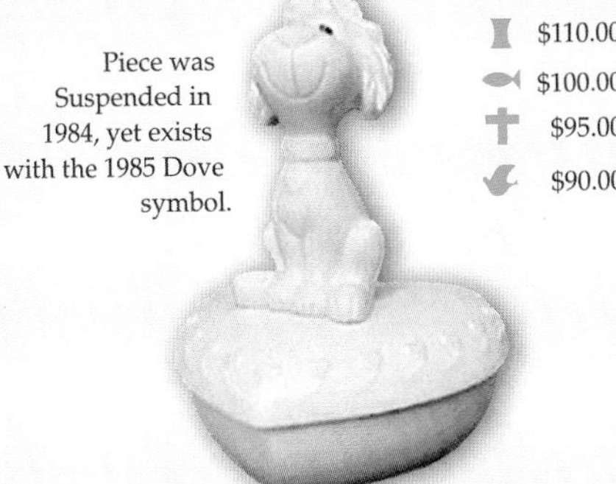

Piece was Suspended in 1984, yet exists with the 1985 Dove symbol.

$110.00

$100.00

$95.00

$90.00

Suspended 1984, Issue Price $15.00, '83

Purchased _________, Price $ ___________

☐ *Forever Friends, E-9283B (Box)*

Also exists with decal of Hourglass. Value is $135.00.

$115.00

$100.00

$90.00

Suspended 1984, Issue Price $15.00, '83

Purchased _________, Price $ ___________

Retired 2003, Issue Price $50.00, '97

Purchased _________, Price $ ___________

☐ *If God Be For Us, Who Can Be Against Us? E-9285*

$95.00

$80.00

$75.00

Suspended 1985, Issue Price $27.50, '83

Purchased _________, Price $ ___________

☐ *Peace On Earth, E-9287*

$195.00

$185.00

$175.00

$160.00

Suspended 1986, Reintroduced 1997, Issue Price $37.50, '83

Purchased _________, Price $ ___________

☐ *And A Child Shall Lead Them, E-9287R*

$65.00

$62.00

$60.00

$60.00

$58.00

$58.00

$55.00

$55.00

Redesigned and brought back from suspension. Original title was *Peace On Earth.*

☐ *Sending You A Rainbow, E-9288*

Fish	$95.00
Cross	$90.00
Dove	$85.00
Olive Branch	$80.00

Suspended 1986, Issue Price $22.50, '83
Series: *Heavenly Halos*

Purchased ________, Price $ ___________

☐ *Trust In The Lord, E-9289*

Fish	$85.00
Cross	$80.00
Dove	$78.00
Olive Branch	$70.00
Tree	$65.00

Suspended 1987, Issue Price $20.00, '83
Series: *Heavenly Halos*

Purchased ________, Price $ ___________

☐ *Collecting Life's Most Precious Moments, 11547 (Medallion)*

Crown	$40.00

Available only at the Donald E. Stephens Convention Center through Krause Publications.

Limited Ed. 3,500, Issue Price $33.00, '03

Purchased ________, Price $ ___________

☐ *Love Covers All, 12009*

Cross	$80.00	Anchor	$70.00
Dove	$78.00	Bow & Arrow	$68.00
Olive Branch	$75.00	Flame	$65.00
Tree	$73.00	Vessel	$62.00

Suspended 1991, Issue Price $27.50, '85

Purchased ________, Price $ ___________

☐ *Loving You, 12017 (Frame)*

Cross	$60.00
Dove	$56.00
Olive Branch	$55.00
Tree	$53.00

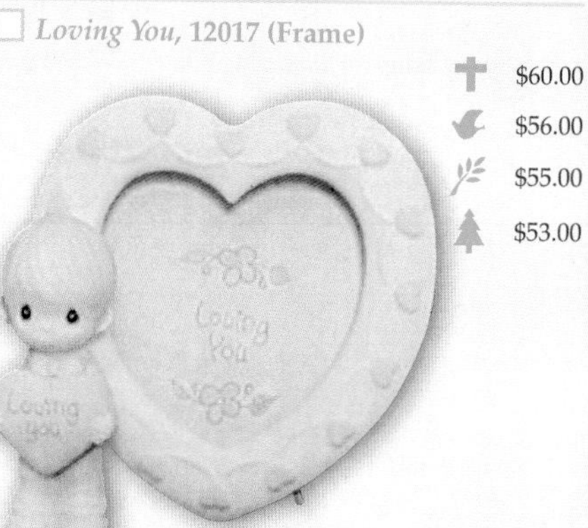

Suspended 1987, Issue Price $19.00, '85

Purchased ________, Price $ ___________

☐ *Loving You, 12025 (Frame)*

Cross	$60.00
Dove	$56.00
Olive Branch	$55.00
Tree	$53.00

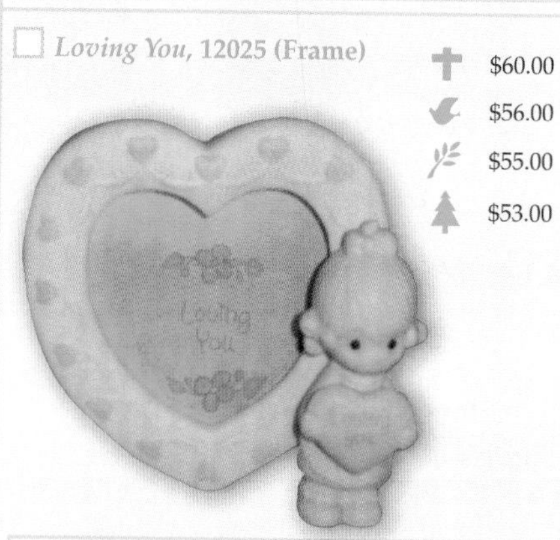

Suspended 1987, Issue Price $19.00, '85

Purchased ________, Price $ ___________

God's Precious Gift, 12033 (Frame)

$110.00
$95.00
$90.00

Suspended 1987, Issue Price $19.00, '85

Purchased ________, Price $ ____________

God's Precious Gift, 12041 (Frame)

$55.00
$50.00
$48.00
$45.00
$43.00
$40.00
$38.00
$35.00

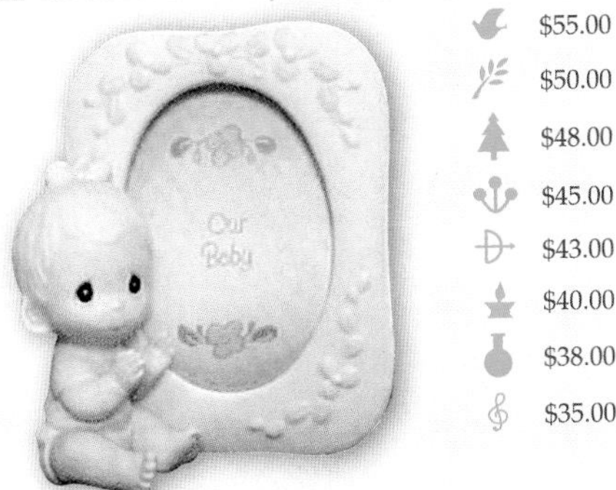

Suspended 1992, Issue Price $19.00, '85

Purchased ________, Price $ ____________

The Voice Of Spring, 12068

$250.00
$250.00

Annual 1985, Issue Price $30.00, '85
Series: *The Four Seasons* — First Issue

Purchased ________, Price $ ____________

Summer's Joy, 12076

$125.00
$115.00

Annual 1985, Issue Price $30.00, '85
Series: *The Four Seasons* — Second Issue

Purchased ________, Price $ ____________

Autumn's Praise, 12084

$85.00
$75.00

Annual 1986, Issue Price $30.00, '86
Series: *The Four Seasons* — Third Issue

Purchased ________, Price $ ____________

Winter's Song, 12092

$145.00
$125.00

Annual 1986, Issue Price $30.00, '86
Series: *The Four Seasons* — Fourth Issue

Purchased ________, Price $ ____________

☐ *The Voice Of Spring*, 12106 (Plate)

✝ $68.00
🕊 $58.00

Annual 1985, Issue Price $40.00, '85
Series: *The Four Seasons* — First Issue
Purchased ________, Price $ ___________

☐ *Summer's Joy*, 12114 (Plate)

✝ $58.00
🕊 $48.00

Annual 1985, Issue Price $40.00, '85
Series: *The Four Seasons* — Second Issue
Purchased ________, Price $ ___________

☐ *Autumn's Praise*, 12122 (Plate)

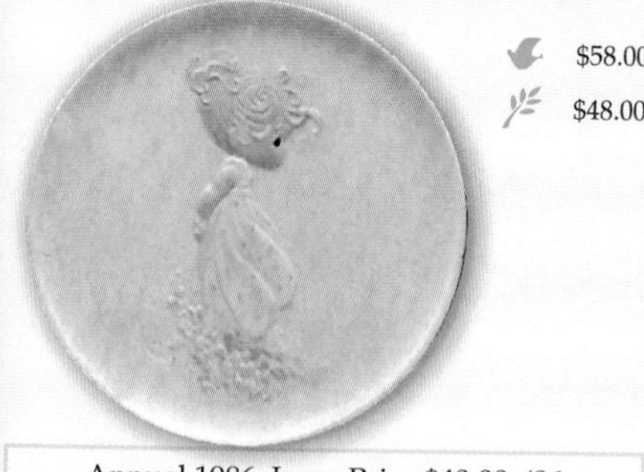

🕊 $58.00
🌿 $48.00

Annual 1986, Issue Price $40.00, '86
Series: *The Four Seasons* — Third Issue
Purchased ________, Price $ ___________

☐ *Winter's Song*, 12130 (Plate)

🕊 $58.00
🌿 $48.00

Annual 1986, Issue Price $40.00, '86
Series: *The Four Seasons* — Fourth Issue
Purchased ________, Price $ ___________

☐ *Part Of Me Wants To Be Good*, 12149

✝ $90.00
🕊 $85.00
🌿 $80.00
🌲 $79.00
⚓ $78.00
🏹 $77.00

Suspended 1989, Issue Price $19.00, '85
Purchased ________, Price $ ___________

☐ *This Is The Day The Lord Has Made*, 12157

Error: The first pieces were produced with the error *This Is The Day Which The Lord Has Made.* The inscription was changed to omit the word "which."

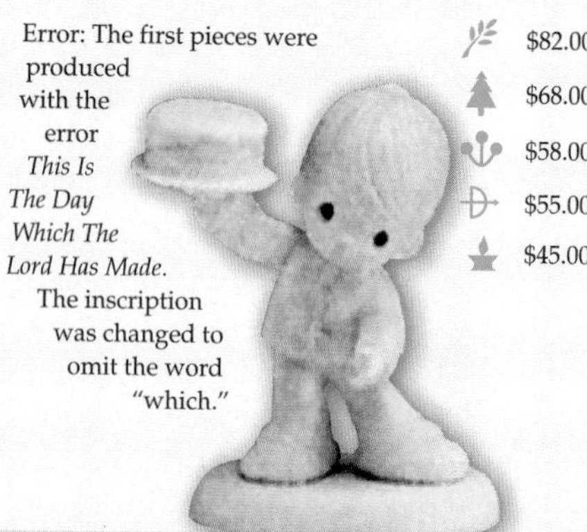

🌿 $82.00
🌲 $68.00
⚓ $58.00
🏹 $55.00
🕯 $45.00

Suspended 1990, Issue Price $20.00, '87
Purchased ________, Price $ ___________

Lord, Keep My Life In Tune, 12165 (Musical)

- $155.00
- $145.00
- $140.00
- $135.00
- $130.00

Suspended 1989, Issue Price $37.50, '85
Tune: "Amazing Grace"
Series: *"Rejoice In The Lord" Band* — Set of 2

Purchased ________, Price $ ____________

Baby's First Haircut, 12211

- $170.00
- $150.00
- $140.00

Suspended 1987, Issue Price $32.50, '85
Series: *Baby's First* — Third Issue

Purchased ________, Price $ ____________

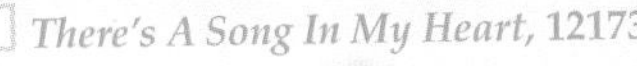

There's A Song In My Heart, 12173

- $58.00
- $55.00
- $50.00
- $49.00
- $48.00
- $46.00

Suspended 1989, Issue Price $11.00, '85
Series: *"Rejoice In The Lord" Band*

Purchased ________, Price $ ____________

Get Into The Habit Of Prayer, 12203

- $45.00
- $40.00
- $35.00

Suspended 1986, Issue Price $19.00, '85

Purchased ________, Price $ ____________

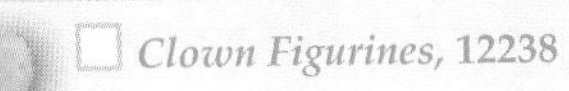

Clown Figurines, 12238

- $160.00
- $152.00
- $140.00

Classic variation: "Clowns" was misspelled "Crowns" on the understamp decal of some sets. Value for the "Crowns" set of four is $225.00.

Discontinued 1987, Issue Price $54.00, '85
Set of 4 miniatures

Purchased ________, Price $ ____________

Clown Figurine, 12238A

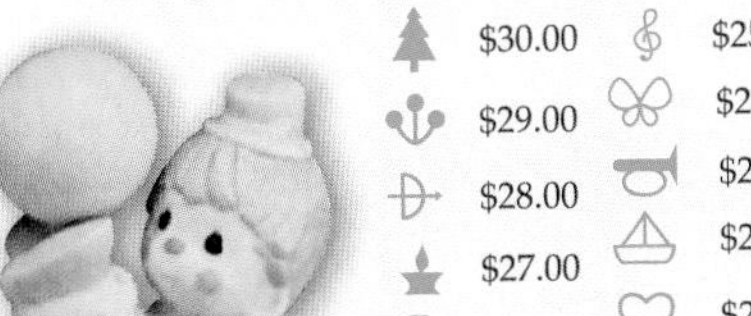

- $30.00
- $29.00
- $28.00
- $27.00
- $26.00
- $25.00
- $24.00
- $23.00
- $22.00
- $21.00

Suspended 1996, Issue Price $16.00, '87

Purchased ________, Price $ ____________

☐ *Clown Figurine, 12238B*

Tree	$30.00	G-Clef	$25.00
Anchor	$29.00	Butterfly	$24.00
Bow & Arrow	$28.00	Trumpet	$23.00
Flame	$27.00	Ship	$22.00
Flask	$26.00	Heart	$21.00

Suspended 1996, Issue Price $16.00, '87

Purchased ________, Price $ ___________

☐ *Clown Figurine, 12238C*

Tree	$30.00	G-Clef	$25.00
Anchor	$29.00	Butterfly	$24.00
Bow & Arrow	$28.00	Trumpet	$23.00
Flame	$27.00	Ship	$22.00
Flask	$26.00	Heart	$21.00

Suspended 1996, Issue Price $16.00, '87

Purchased ________, Price $ ___________

☐ *Clown Figurine, 12238D*

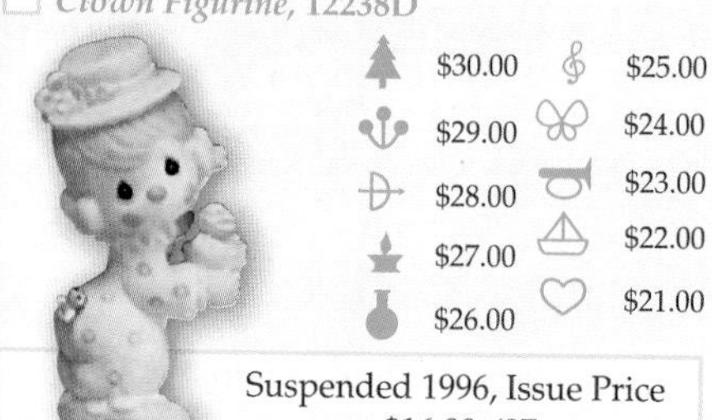

Tree	$30.00	G-Clef	$25.00
Anchor	$29.00	Butterfly	$24.00
Bow & Arrow	$28.00	Trumpet	$23.00
Flame	$27.00	Ship	$22.00
Flask	$26.00	Heart	$21.00

Suspended 1996, Issue Price $16.00, '87

Purchased ________, Price $ ___________

☐ *Precious Moments Last Forever, 12246* (Medallion)

This is the first medallion introduced in the Precious Moments collection. It was a gift to new club members.

Cross	$100.00

Annual 1984, Issue Price $10.00, '84
Sharing Season Gift

Purchased ________, Price $ ___________

☐ *Love Covers All, 12254* (Thimble)

Dove	$20.00	Anchor	$16.00
Olive Branch	$18.00	Bow & Arrow	$15.00
Tree	$17.00	Flame	$14.00

Suspended 1990, Issue Price $5.50, '85

Purchased____________,
Price $ ____________

☐ *I Get A Bang Out Of You, 12262*

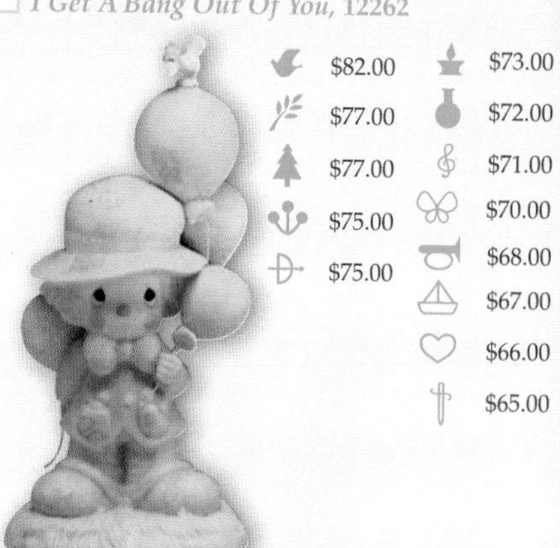

Dove	$82.00	Flame	$73.00
Olive Branch	$77.00	Flask	$72.00
Tree	$77.00	G-Clef	$71.00
Anchor	$75.00	Butterfly	$70.00
Bow & Arrow	$75.00	Trumpet	$68.00
		Ship	$67.00
		Heart	$66.00
		Sword	$65.00

Retired 1997, Issue Price $30.00, '85
Series: *Clown* — First Issue

Purchased ________, Price $ ___________

☐ *Lord Keep Me On The Ball, 12270*

Olive Branch	$70.00	Flask	$55.00
Tree	$65.00	G-Clef	$53.00
Anchor	$62.00	Butterfly	$48.00
Bow & Arrow	$60.00	Trumpet	$45.00
Flame	$58.00	Ship	$45.00
		Heart	$45.00
		Sword	$45.00
		Eyeglasses	$45.00

Suspended 1998, Issue Price $30.00, '86
Series: *Clown* — Fourth Issue

Purchased ________, Price $ ___________

It Is Better To Give Than To Receive, 12297

$150.00
$140.00
$135.00

Suspended 1987, Issue Price $19.00, '85

Purchased _________, Price $ ___________

You Can Fly, 12335

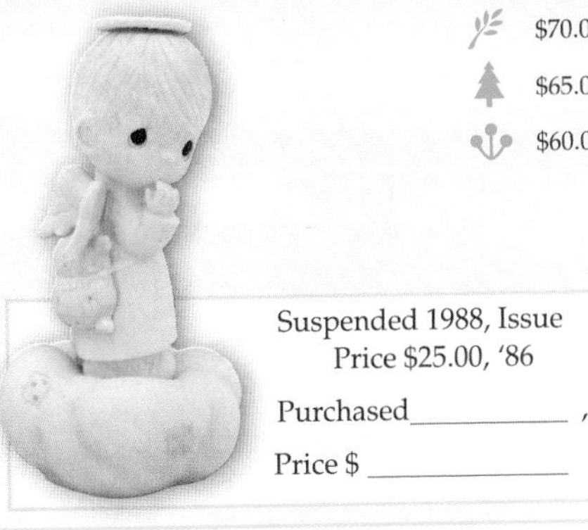

$70.00
$65.00
$60.00

Suspended 1988, Issue Price $25.00, '86

Purchased____________,

Price $ ____________

Love Never Fails, 12300

$60.00
$57.00
$57.00
$57.00
$50.00
$50.00
$50.00
$48.00
$48.00
$48.00
$45.00
$45.00
$45.00
$45.00
$45.00
$45.00

Retired 2000, Issue Price $25.00, '85

Purchased _________, Price $ ___________

Jesus Is Coming Soon, 12343

$60.00
$55.00

Suspended 1986, Issue Price $22.50, '85

Purchased _________, Price $ ___________

God Bless Our Home, 12319

$82.00
$77.00
$77.00
$75.00
$75.00
$73.00
$72.00
$71.00
$70.00
$68.00
$67.00
$66.00
$65.00
$65.00

Retired 1998, Issue Price $40.00, '85

Purchased _________, Price $ ___________

Halo, And Merry Christmas, 12351

$190.00
$165.00
$155.00
$150.00

Suspended 1988, Issue Price $40.00, '85

Purchased _________, Price $ ___________

☐ *Happiness Is The Lord, 12378*

$45.00
$40.00
$37.00
$36.00
$35.00
$34.00

Suspended 1990, Issue Price $15.00, '85
Series: *"Rejoice In The Lord" Band*

Purchased ________, Price $ ___________

☐ *Lord Give Me A Song, 12386*

$45.00
$40.00
$37.00
$36.00
$35.00
$34.00

Suspended 1990, Issue Price $15.00, '85
Series: *"Rejoice In The Lord" Band*

Purchased ________, Price $ ___________

☐ *He Is My Song, 12394*

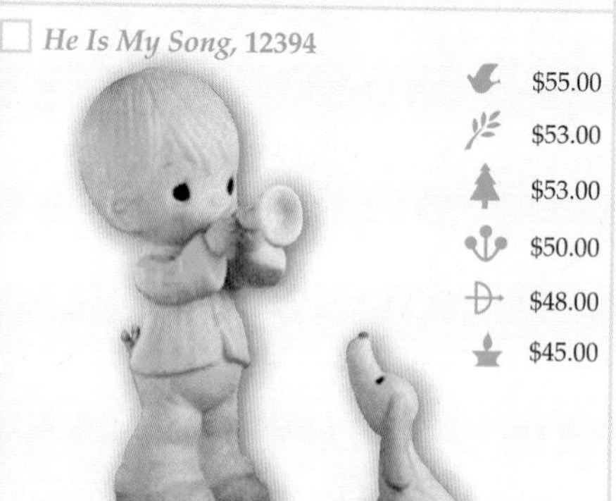

$55.00
$53.00
$53.00
$50.00
$48.00
$45.00

Suspended 1990, Issue Price $17.50, '85
Series: *"Rejoice In The Lord" Band* – Set of 2

Purchased ________, Price $ ___________

☐ *We Saw A Star, 12408* (Musical)

$125.00
$115.00
$105.00

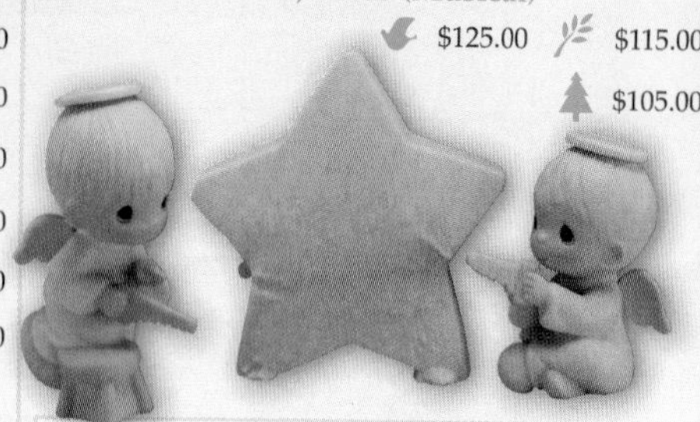

Suspended 1987, Issue Price $50.00, '85
Tune: "Joy To The World" — Set of 3

Purchased ________, Price $ ___________

☐ *Have A Heavenly Christmas, 12416* (Ornament)

$45.00
$40.00
$38.00
$35.00
$33.00
$33.00
$33.00
$30.00
$30.00
$30.00
$28.00
$28.00
$25.00

There are Cedar Tree pieces with two hooks from the Retailer's Wreath, #111465 (see page 142). There are also some ornaments, again from the Retailer's Wreath, that have the inscription "Heaven Bound" upside down.

Suspended 1998, Reintroduced 1998,
Retired 1998, Issue Price $12.00, '85

Purchased ________, Price $ ___________

☐ *Have A Heavenly Journey, 12416R*

$35.00

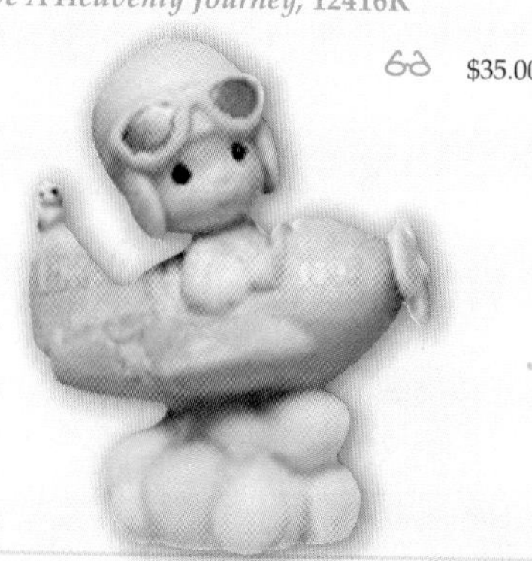

Dated Annual 1998, Issue Price $25.00, '98
Care-A-Van Exclusive

Purchased ________, Price $ ___________

Aaron, 12424 (Doll)

$145.00
$140.00

Suspended 1986, Issue Price $135.00, '85
Purchased ________, Price $ __________

Bethany, 12432 (Doll)

$145.00
$140.00

Suspended 1986, Issue Price $135.00, '85
Purchased ________, Price $ __________

Waddle I Do Without You, 12459

$83.00
$80.00
$77.00
$75.00
$73.00

Retired 1989, Issue Price $30.00, '85
Series: *Clown* — Second Issue
Purchased ________, Price $ __________

The Lord Will Carry You Through, 12467

$68.00
$65.00
$60.00

Retired 1988, Issue Price $30.00, '86
Series: *Clown* — Third Issue
Purchased ________, Price $ __________

P.D., 12475 (Doll)

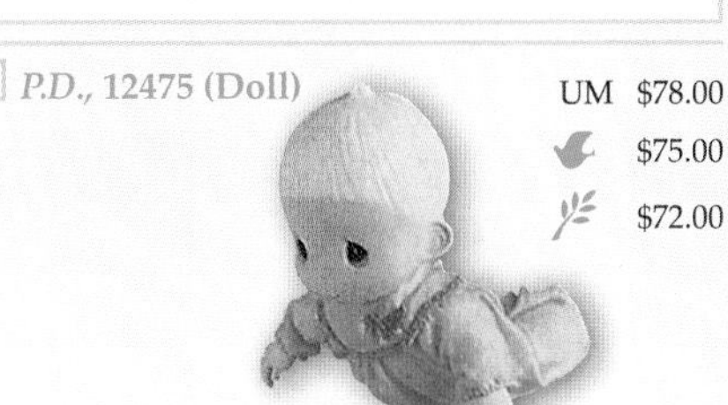

UM $78.00
$75.00
$72.00

Suspended 1986, Issue Price $50.00, '85
Purchased ________, Price $ __________

Trish, 12483 (Doll)

UM $78.00
$75.00
$72.00

Suspended 1986, Issue Price $50.00, '85
Purchased ________, Price $ __________

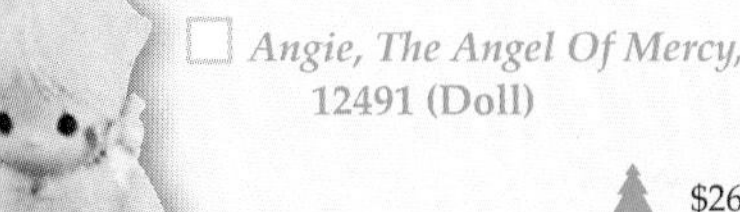

Angie, The Angel Of Mercy, 12491 (Doll)

$260.00

Limited Ed. 12,500, Issue Price $160.00, '87
Individually Numbered
Purchased ________, Price $ __________

☐ *Lord Keep My Life In Tune*, 12580 (Musical)

$250.00
$245.00
$240.00
$235.00
$230.00

Suspended 1990, Issue Price $37.50, '87
Tune: "I'd Like To Teach The World To Sing"
Series: *"Rejoice In The Lord" Band* — Set of 2

Purchased ________, Price $ ___________

☐ *Mother Sew Dear*, 13293 (Thimble)

$25.00
$23.00
$20.00
$19.00
$19.00
$17.00
$17.00
$16.00
$15.00
$13.00
$13.00
$11.00
$10.00
$10.00
$10.00

Retired 1999, Issue Price $5.50, '85

Purchased ________, Price $ ___________

☐ *The Purr-fect Grandma*, 13307 (Thimble)

$25.00
$23.00
$20.00
$19.00
$19.00
$17.00
$17.00
$16.00
$15.00
$13.00
$13.00
$11.00
$10.00
$10.00
$10.00

Retired 1999, Issue Price $5.50, '85

Purchased ________, Price $ ___________

☐ *Tell Me The Story Of Jesus*, 15237 (Plate)

$95.00

Dated Annual 1985, Issue Price $40.00, '85
Series: *Joy Of Christmas* — Fourth Issue

Purchased ________, Price $ ___________

☐ *May Your Christmas Be Delightful*, 15482

$65.00
$62.00
$60.00
$59.00
$58.00
$57.00
$56.00
$55.00
$53.00
$52.00

Suspended 1994, Issue Price $25.00, '85

Purchased ________, Price $ ___________

☐ *Honk If You Love Jesus*, 15490

$40.00
$36.00
$33.00
$31.00
$30.00
$29.00
$28.00
$28.00
$28.00
$26.00
$26.00
$25.00
$25.00
$25.00
$23.00
$23.00
$23.00

Retired 2001, Issue Price $13.00, '85
Nativity Addition — Set of 2

Purchased ________, Price $ ___________

☐ *God Sent You Just In Time*, 15504 (Musical)

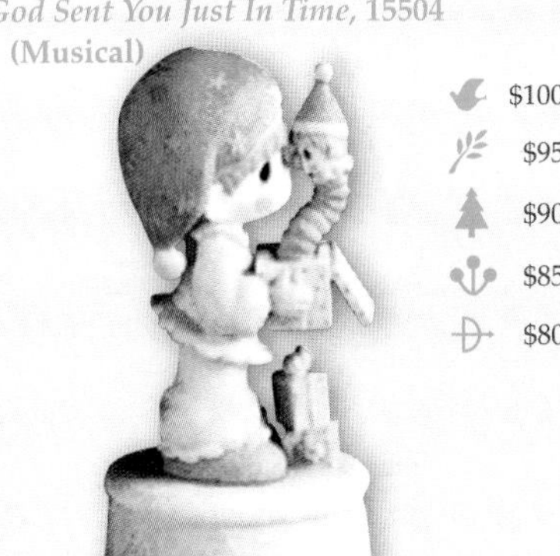

$100.00
$95.00
$90.00
$85.00
$80.00

Retired 1989, Issue Price $45.00, '85
Tune: "We Wish You A Merry Christmas"
Purchased ________, Price $ ____________

☐ *Baby's First Christmas*, 15539

$45.00

Dated Annual 1985, Issue Price $13.00, '85
Purchased ________, Price $ ____________

☐ *Baby's First Christmas*, 15547

$30.00

Dated Annual 1985, Issue Price $13.00, '85
Purchased ________, Price $ ____________

☐ *God Sent His Love*, 15768 (Ornament)

$30.00

Dated Annual 1985, Issue Price $10.00, '85
Purchased ________, Price $ ____________

☐ *May You Have The Sweetest Christmas*, 15776

$60.00
$58.00
$55.00
$53.00
$52.00
$50.00
$48.00
$45.00

Suspended 1992, Issue Price $17.00, '85
Series: *Family Christmas Scene* — First Issue
Purchased ________, Price $ ____________

☐ *The Story Of God's Love*, 15784

$65.00
$60.00
$59.00
$58.00
$57.00
$56.00
$55.00
$54.00

Suspended 1992, Issue Price $22.50, '85
Series: *Family Christmas Scene* — Second Issue
Purchased ________, Price $ ____________

Tell Me A Story, 15792

Unmarked pieces are known to exist.

- $30.00
- $29.00
- $28.00
- $27.00
- $26.00
- $25.00
- $24.00
- $23.00

Suspended 1992, Issue Price $10.00, '85
Series: *Family Christmas Scene* — Third Issue
Purchased ________, Price $ __________

God Gave His Best, 15806

- $60.00
- $48.00
- $45.00
- $43.00
- $40.00
- $38.00
- $35.00
- $33.00

Suspended 1992, Issue Price $13.00, '85
Series: *Family Christmas Scene* — Fourth Issue
Purchased ________, Price $ __________

Silent Night, 15814 (Musical)

- $110.00
- $105.00
- $100.00
- $98.00
- $95.00
- $90.00
- $87.00
- $86.00

Suspended 1992, Issue Price $37.50, '85
Tune: "Silent Night"
Series: *Family Christmas Scene* — Fifth Issue
Purchased ________, Price $ __________

May Your Christmas Be Happy, 15822 (Ornament)

- $48.00
- $45.00
- $43.00
- $42.00
- $40.00

Suspended 1989, Issue Price $10.00, '85
Purchased ________, Price $ __________

Happiness Is The Lord, 15830 (Ornament)

- $35.00
- $33.00
- $32.00
- $31.00
- $30.00

Suspended 1989, Issue Price $10.00, '85
Purchased ________, Price $ __________

May Your Christmas Be Delightful, 15849 (Ornament)

- $40.00
- $36.00
- $35.00
- $34.00
- $33.00
- $32.00
- $31.00
- $30.00
- $28.00

Suspended 1993, Reintroduced 1999,
Issue Price $10.00, '85
Purchased ________, Price $ __________

May Your Christmas Be Delightful, 15849R (Ornament)

★ $30.00

Limited Ed., Issue Price $20.00, '99

Purchased ________, Price $ __________

Honk If You Love Jesus, 15857 (Ornament)

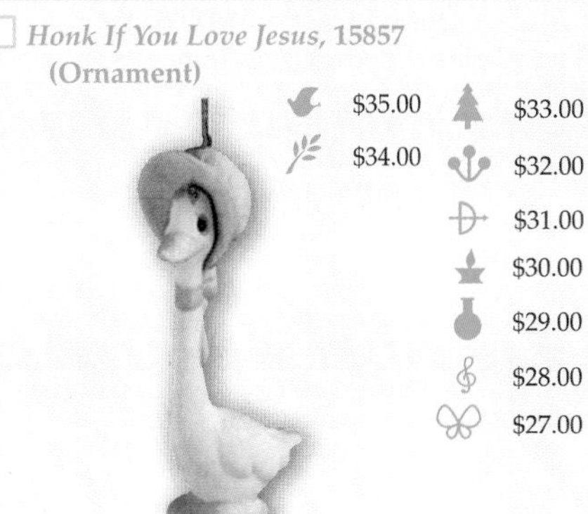

$35.00 $34.00 $33.00 $32.00 $31.00 $30.00 $29.00 $28.00 $27.00

Suspended 1993, Issue Price $10.00, '85

Purchased ________, Price $ __________

God Sent His Love, 15865 (Thimble)

$36.00

Dated Annual 1985, Issue Price $5.50, '85

Purchased ________, Price $ __________

God Sent His Love, 15873 (Bell)

$35.00

Dated Annual 1985, Issue Price $19.00, '85

Purchased ________, Price $ __________

God Sent His Love, 15881

$45.00

Dated Annual 1985, Issue Price $17.00, '85

Purchased ________, Price $ __________

Baby's First Christmas, 15903 (Ornament)

$30.00

Dated Annual 1985, Issue Price $10.00, '85

Purchased ________, Price $ __________

Baby's First Christmas, 15911 (Ornament)

Mark	Price
[Dove]	$30.00

Dated Annual 1985, Issue Price $10.00, '85

Purchased ________, Price $ __________

May Your Birthday Be Warm, 15938

[Dove]	$36.00	[Ship]	$20.00
[Olive Branch]	$30.00	[Heart]	$20.00
[Cedar Tree]	$28.00	[Sword]	$20.00
[Flower]	$27.00	[Eyeglasses]	$20.00
[Bow & Arrow]	$25.00	[Star]	$18.00
[Flame]	$25.00	[Egg]	$18.00
[Vessel]	$23.00	[Sandal]	$18.00
[G-Clef]	$23.00	[Cross in Heart]	$15.00
[Butterfly]	$22.00	[Crown]	$15.00
[Trumpet]	$21.00	[Clover]	$15.00
		[Box]	$15.00

Open, Issue Price $10.00, '86
Series: *Birthday Circus Train* — Infant

Purchased ________, Price $ __________

Happy Birthday Little Lamb, 15946

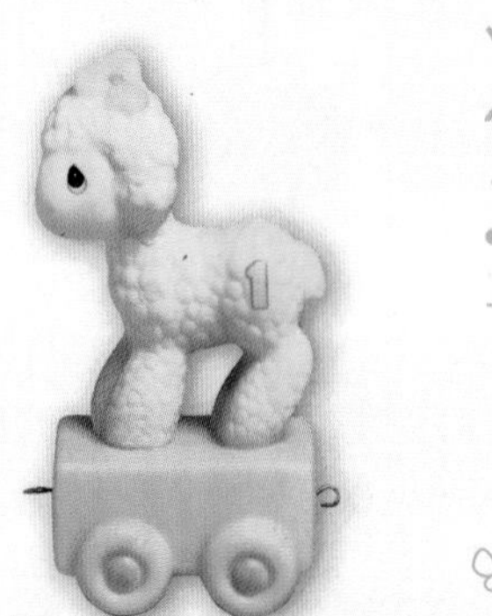

Mark	Price
[Dove]	$36.00
[Olive Branch]	$30.00
[Cedar Tree]	$28.00
[Flower]	$27.00
[Bow & Arrow]	$25.00
[Flame]	$25.00
[Vessel]	$23.00
[G-Clef]	$23.00
[Butterfly]	$22.00

Heaven Bless Your Special Day, 15954

[Dove]	$45.00	[Ship]	$25.00
[Olive Branch]	$40.00	[Heart]	$23.00
[Cedar Tree]	$35.00	[Sword]	$23.00
[Flower]	$30.00	[Eyeglasses]	$20.00
[Bow & Arrow]	$28.00	[Star]	$20.00
[Flame]	$28.00	[Egg]	$20.00
[Vessel]	$26.00	[Sandal]	$17.50
[G-Clef]	$26.00	[Cross in Heart]	$17.50
[Butterfly]	$26.00	[Crown]	$17.50
[Trumpet]	$25.00	[Clover]	$17.50
		[Box]	$17.50

Open, Issue Price $11.00, '86
Series: *Birthday Circus Train* — Age 3

Purchased ________, Price $ __________

God Bless You On Your Birthday, 15962

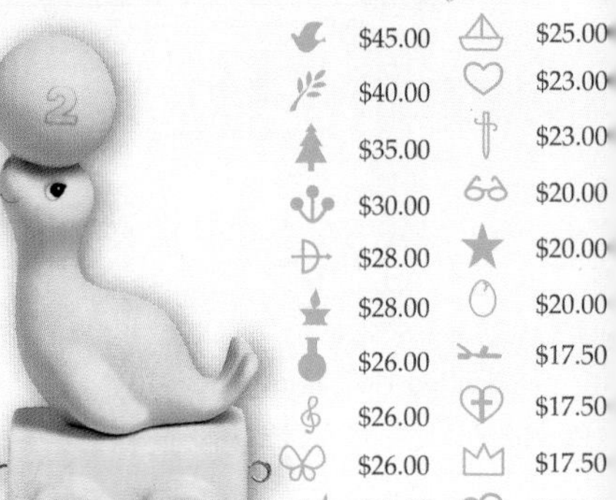

[Dove]	$45.00	[Ship]	$25.00
[Olive Branch]	$40.00	[Heart]	$23.00
[Cedar Tree]	$35.00	[Sword]	$23.00
[Flower]	$30.00	[Eyeglasses]	$20.00
[Bow & Arrow]	$28.00	[Star]	$20.00
[Flame]	$28.00	[Egg]	$20.00
[Vessel]	$26.00	[Sandal]	$17.50
[G-Clef]	$26.00	[Cross in Heart]	$17.50
[Butterfly]	$26.00	[Crown]	$17.50
[Trumpet]	$25.00	[Clover]	$17.50
		[Box]	$17.50

Open, Issue Price $11.00, '86
Series: *Birthday Circus Train* — Age 2

Purchased ________, Price $ __________

[Trumpet]	$21.00	[Eyeglasses]	$20.00	[Cross in Heart]	$15.00
[Ship]	$20.00	[Star]	$18.00	[Crown]	$15.00
[Heart]	$20.00	[Egg]	$18.00	[Clover]	$15.00
[Sword]	$20.00	[Sandal]	$18.00	[Box]	$15.00

Open, Issue Price $10.00, '86
Series: *Birthday Circus Train* — Age 1

Purchased ________, Price $ __________

May Your Birthday Be Gigantic, 15970

$45.00 · $40.00

$38.00 · $35.00 · $35.00 · $33.00 · $33.00 · $30.00 · $28.00 · $28.00 · $28.00

$25.00 · $25.00 · $25.00 · $25.00 · $23.00 · $23.00 · $20.00 · $20.00 · $20.00 · $20.00

Open, Issue Price $12.50, '86
Series: *Birthday Circus Train* — Age 4
Purchased _________, Price $ ___________

Bless The Days Of Our Youth, 16004

$50.00 · $48.00

$45.00 · $43.00 · $40.00 · $38.00 · $35.00 · $33.00 · $30.00 · $28.00 · $28.00

$25.00 · $25.00 · $25.00 · $22.50 · $22.50 · $22.50 · $22.50 · $22.50 · $22.50 · $22.50

Open, Issue Price $15.00, '86
Series: *Birthday Circus Train*
Purchased _________, Price $ ___________

This Day Is Something To Roar About, 15989

$45.00

$40.00 · $38.00 · $35.00 · $33.00 · $33.00 · $30.00 · $30.00 · $30.00 · $28.00 · $28.00

$25.00 · $25.00 · $25.00 · $22.50 · $22.50 · $22.50 · $22.50 · $22.50 · $22.50 · $22.50

Open, Issue Price $13.50, '86
Series: *Birthday Circus Train* — Age 5
Purchased _________, Price $ ___________

Baby's First Trip, 16012

$325.00 · $300.00 · $285.00 · $275.00

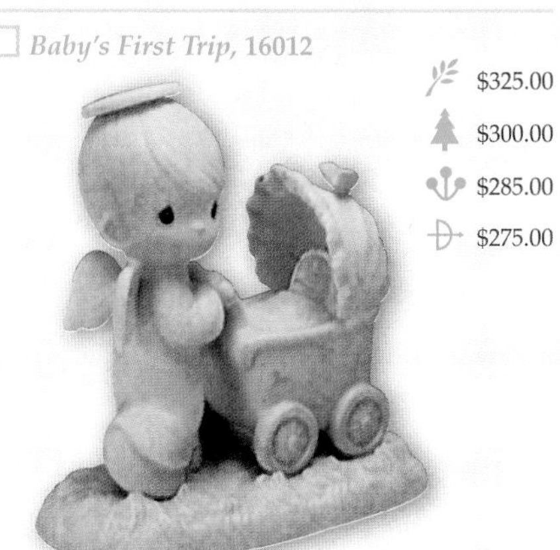

Suspended 1989, Issue Price $32.50, '86
Series: *Baby's First* — Fourth Issue
Purchased _________, Price $ ___________

Keep Looking Up, 15997

$45.00 · $40.00 · $38.00 · $35.00 · $33.00 · $33.00 · $30.00 · $30.00

$30.00 · $28.00 · $28.00 · $25.00

$25.00 · $25.00 · $22.50

$22.50 · $22.50 · $22.50

$22.50 · $22.50 · $22.50

Open, Issue Price $13.50, '86
Series: *Birthday Circus Train* — Age 6
Purchased _________, Price $ ___________

☐ *God Bless You With Rainbows*, 16020 (Nightlight)

$125.00
$120.00
$115.00
$110.00
$105.00

Suspended 1989, Issue Price $45.00, '86

Purchased ________, Price $ ____________

☐ *To My Favorite Paw*, 100021

$85.00
$60.00
$55.00
$50.00

Suspended 1988, Issue Price $22.50, '86

Purchased ________, Price $ ____________

☐ *To My Deer Friend*, 100048

$110.00
$85.00
$83.00
$80.00
$75.00
$73.00
$70.00
$68.00
$65.00
$65.00
$63.00
$60.00
$58.00
$55.00
$55.00
$55.00
$50.00
$50.00

Retired 2003, Issue Price $33.00, '87

Purchased ________, Price $ ____________

☐ *Sending My Love*, 100056

$65.00
$60.00
$55.00
$50.00
$49.00
$48.00
$47.00

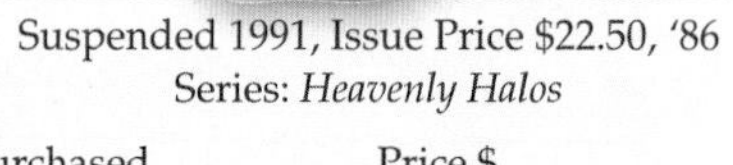

Suspended 1991, Issue Price $22.50, '86
Series: *Heavenly Halos*

Purchased ________, Price $ ____________

☐ *O Worship The Lord*, 100064

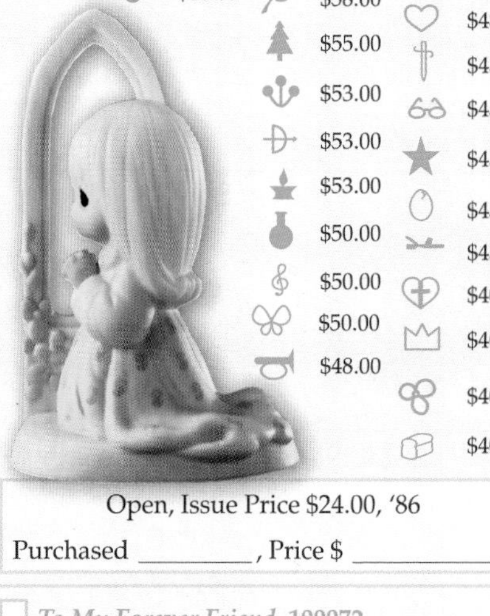

$60.00
$58.00
$55.00
$53.00
$53.00
$53.00
$50.00
$50.00
$50.00
$48.00
$48.00
$48.00
$45.00
$45.00
$45.00
$45.00
$45.00
$40.00
$40.00
$40.00
$40.00

Open, Issue Price $24.00, '86

Purchased ________, Price $ ____________

☐ *To My Forever Friend*, 100072

$125.00
$98.00
$87.00
$83.00
$80.00
$75.00
$73.00
$70.00
$70.00
$70.00
$68.00
$68.00
$65.00
$65.00
$60.00
$60.00
$60.00
$55.00
$55.00
$55.00
$55.00

Open, Issue Price $33.00, '86

Purchased ________, Price $ ____________

He's The Healer Of Broken Hearts, 100080

$100.00 · $90.00 · $88.00 · $85.00 · $83.00 · $80.00 · $78.00 · $75.00 · $70.00 · $70.00 · $65.00 · $65.00 · $60.00 · $60.00

Retired 1999, Issue Price $33.00, '87

Purchased ________, Price $ ___________

Make Me A Blessing, 100102

$108.00 · $95.00 · $90.00 · $85.00 · $80.00

Retired 1990, Issue Price $35.00, '87

Purchased ________, Price $ ___________

Lord, I'm Coming Home, 100110

$95.00 · $90.00 · $87.00 · $85.00 · $83.00 · $80.00 · $75.00 · $70.00 · $65.00 · $60.00 · $55.00 · $55.00 · $53.00 · $50.00 · $48.00 · $45.00 · $45.00 · $40.00 · $35.00

Retired 2003, Issue Price $22.50, '86

Purchased ________, Price $ ___________

Lord Keep Me On My Toes, 100129

$75.00 · $65.00 · $58.00 · $55.00

Retired 1988, Issue Price $22.50, '86

Purchased ________, Price $ ___________

The Joy Of The Lord Is My Strength, 100137

$120.00 · $110.00 · $95.00 · $85.00 · $80.00 · $75.00 · $73.00 · $70.00 · $70.00 · $70.00 · $68.00 · $68.00 · $65.00 · $65.00 · $65.00 · $55.00 · $55.00 · $55.00 · $55.00 · $55.00 · $55.00 · $55.00

Open, Issue Price $35.00, '86

Purchased ________, Price $ ___________

God Bless The Day We Found You, 100145

$100.00 · $90.00 · $85.00 · $80.00 · $75.00

Suspended 1990, Reintroduced 1995,
Issue Price $40.00, '86

Purchased ________, Price $ ___________

☐ *God Bless The Day We Found You, 100145R*

- $85.00
- $80.00
- $75.00
- $73.00
- $70.00
- $68.00
- $65.00
- $65.00
- $65.00

Redesigned and brought back from Suspension with the original title.

Retired 2002, Issue Price $60.00, '95

Purchased ________, Price $ ___________

☐ *God Bless The Day We Found You, 100153*

- $100.00
- $90.00
- $85.00
- $80.00
- $75.00

Suspended 1990, Reintroduced 1995, Issue Price $40.00, '86

Purchased ________, Price $ ___________

☐ *God Bless The Day We Found You, 100153R*

- $80.00
- $78.00
- $75.00
- $73.00
- $70.00
- $65.00
- $65.00
- $65.00
- $65.00

Redesigned and brought back from Suspension with the original title.

☐ *Serving The Lord, 100161*

- $65.00
- $60.00
- $57.00
- $56.00
- $55.00
- $50.00

Suspended 1990, Issue Price $19.00, '86

Purchased ________, Price $ ___________

☐ *I'm A Possibility, 100188*

- $90.00
- $78.00
- $75.00
- $73.00
- $65.00
- $60.00
- $55.00
- $50.00

Retired 1993, Issue Price $22.00, '86

Purchased ________, Price $ ___________

☐ *The Spirit Is Willing, But The Flesh Is Weak, 100196*

- $70.00
- $68.00
- $67.00
- $63.00
- $59.00

Retired 1991, Issue Price $19.00, '87

Purchased ________, Price $ ___________

Retired 2002, Issue Price $60.00, '95

Purchased ________, Price $ ___________

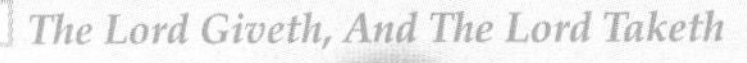

☐ *The Lord Giveth, And The Lord Taketh Away, 100226*

$115.00
$105.00
$100.00
$95.00
$93.00
$90.00
$88.00
$85.00
$80.00

Retired 1995, Issue Price $33.50, '87

Purchased ________, Price $ ____________

☐ *Friends Never Drift Apart, 100250*

$85.00 $73.00 $65.00
$70.00 $73.00 $65.00
$75.00 $68.00 $65.00
$65.00
$65.00
$65.00
$65.00
$65.00
$65.00
$65.00

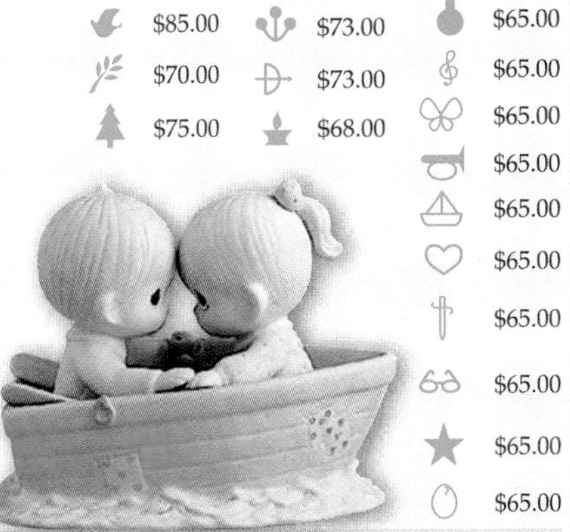

Retired 2000, Issue Price $35.00, '86

Purchased ________, Price $ ____________

☐ *Help, Lord, I'm In A Spot, 100269*

$75.00
$74.00
$73.00
$70.00

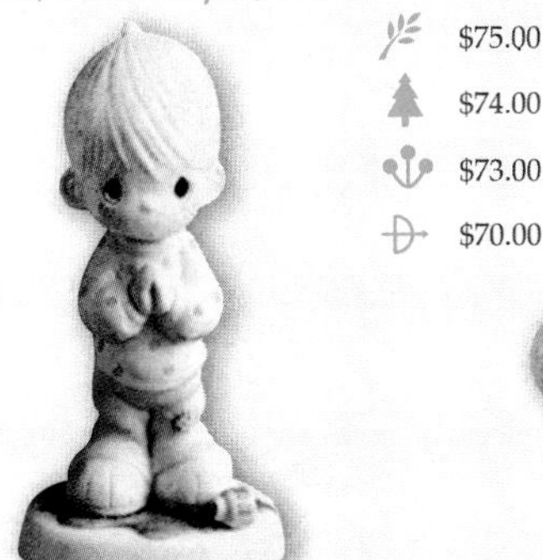

Retired 1989, Issue Price $18.50, '86

Purchased ________, Price $ ____________

☐ *He Cleansed My Soul, 100277*

$60.00 $55.00 $45.00 $40.00
$50.00 $44.00 $40.00
$40.00 $40.00
$40.00 $40.00
$40.00 $40.00
$40.00 $40.00
$40.00
$40.00
$40.00
$40.00
$40.00
$40.00

Has been found with the Bible inscription missing.

Open, Issue Price $24.00, '86

Purchased ________, Price $ ____________

☐ *Heaven Bless You, 100285 (Musical)*

$125.00
$95.00
$92.00
$90.00
$88.00
$87.00
$85.00
$82.00
$80.00

Suspended 1993, Issue Price $45.00, '86
Tune: "Brahms' Lullaby"

Purchased ________, Price $ ____________

☐ *Serving The Lord, 100293*

$65.00 $55.00
$60.00 $53.00
$50.00
$45.00

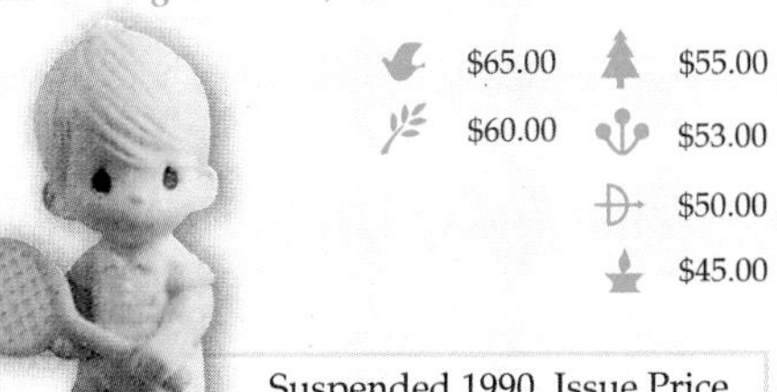

Suspended 1990, Issue Price $19.00, '86

Purchased ____________,

Price $ ____________

Bong Bong, 100455 (Doll)

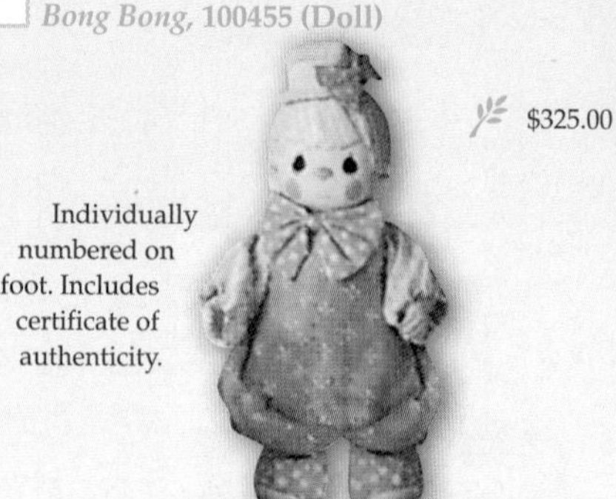

$325.00

Individually numbered on foot. Includes certificate of authenticity.

Limited Ed. 12,000, Issue Price $150.00, '86

Purchased ________, Price $ ___________

Candy, 100463 (Doll)

$325.00

Individually numbered on foot. Includes certificate of authenticity.

Limited Ed. 12,000, Issue Price $150.00, '86

Purchased ________, Price $ ___________

God Bless Our Family, 100498

$80.00 $75.00 $68.00 $70.00 $65.00 $65.00 $65.00 $60.00 $60.00 $60.00 $55.00 $55.00 $55.00

Retired 1999, Issue Price $35.00, '87

Purchased ________, Price $ ___________

God Bless Our Family, 100501

$75.00 $70.00 $65.00 $73.00 $68.00 $65.00 $60.00 $60.00 $58.00 $58.00 $55.00 $55.00 $55.00

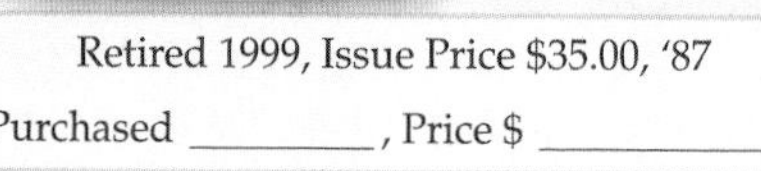

Retired 1999, Issue Price $35.00, '87

Purchased ________, Price $ ___________

Scent From Above, 100528

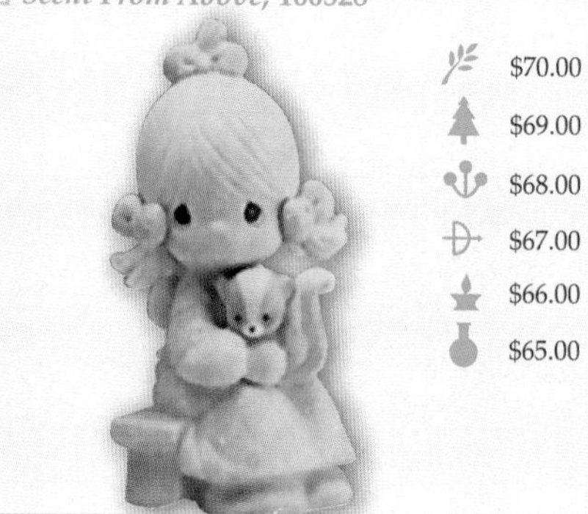

$70.00 $69.00 $68.00 $67.00 $66.00 $65.00

Retired 1991, Issue Price $19.00, '87

Purchased ________, Price $ ___________

I Picked A Special Mom, 100536

$85.00 $75.00

Annual 1987, Issue Price $37.50, '87

Purchased ________, Price $ ___________

Brotherly Love, 100544

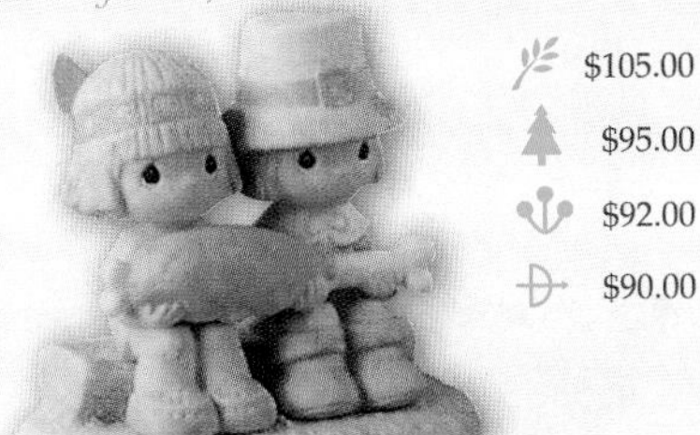

$105.00
$95.00
$92.00
$90.00

Suspended 1989, Issue Price $37.00, '86

Purchased ________, Price $ ____________

God Is Love, Dear Valentine, 100625 (Thimble)

$20.00
$18.00
$17.00
$16.00
$15.00

Suspended 1989, Issue Price $5.50, '86

Purchased ________, Price $ ____________

The Lord Bless You And Keep You, 100633 (Thimble)

$20.00
$20.00
$19.00
$18.00
$17.00
$16.00
$15.00

Suspended 1991, Issue Price $5.50, '86

Purchased ________, Price $ ____________

Four Seasons, 100641 (Thimbles)

$150.00
$95.00

Annual 1986, Issue Price $20.00, '86
Set of 4

Purchased ________, Price $ ____________

Clowns, 100668 (Thimbles)

$63.00
$55.00
$45.00

Suspended 1988, Issue Price $11.00, '86
Set of 2

Purchased ________, Price $ ____________

Cherishing Each Special Moment, 101233

$60.00
$55.00
$50.00

Open, Issue Price $50.00, '02
Series: *Motherhood* — Third and Final Issue

Purchased ________, Price $ ____________

A Penny A Kiss, A Penny A Hug, 101234

$55.00

Limited Ed., Issue Price $35.00, '01
Authorized Retailer Event, 3/2/01

Purchased ________,
Price $ ____________

101234C Limited Ed., '02
Canadian Event Exclusive $60.00

Purchased ________, Price $ ____________

☐ *So You Finally Met Your Match, Congratulations,* 101493

$25.00
$23.00
$20.00
$20.00
$20.00

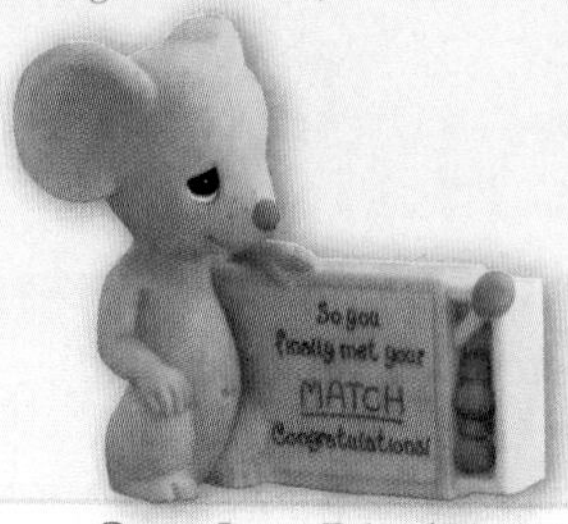

Open, Issue Price $20.00, '02
Series: *Animal Affections*
Purchased ________, Price $ ____________

☐ *You Are A Real Cool Mommy!* 101495

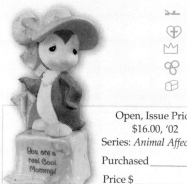

$25.00
$23.00
$20.00
$20.00
$20.00

Open, Issue Price
$16.00, '02
Series: *Animal Affections*
Purchased __________ ,
Price $ ____________

☐ *Rats, I Missed Your Birthday,* 101496

$25.00
$20.00
$20.00
$20.00
$20.00

Open, Issue Price $20.00, '02
Series: *Animal Affections*
Purchased ________, Price $ ____________

☐ *It's What's Inside That Counts,* 101497

$38.00
$35.00
$35.00
$35.00
$35.00

Open, Issue Price
$35.00, '02
Purchased____________,
Price $____________

☐ *You're An All Star Graduate,* 101498

$27.00
$25.00
$25.00
$25.00
$25.00

Open, Issue Price
$25.00, '02
Purchased __________ ,
Price $ ____________

☐ *You're An All Star Graduate,* 101499

$27.00
$25.00
$25.00
$25.00
$25.00

Open, Issue Price
$25.00, '02
Purchased____________,
Price $ ____________

☐ *The Sweetest Baby Boy,* 101500

$19.00
$17.50
$17.50
$17.50
$17.50

Open, Issue Price $17.50, '02
Purchased ________, Price $ ____________

The Sweetest Baby Girl, 101501

$19.00
$17.50
$17.50
$17.50
$17.50

Open, Issue Price $17.50, '02

Purchased ________, Price $ __________

I'm A Big Sister, 101502

$22.00
$20.00
$20.00
$20.00
$20.00

Open, Issue Price $20.00, '02

Purchased __________,

Price $ ____________

I'm A Big Brother, 101503

$22.00
$20.00
$20.00
$20.00
$20.00

Open, Issue Price $20.00, '02

Purchased _________ ,

Price $ _________

Precious Grandma, 101504

$27.00
$25.00
$25.00
$25.00
$25.00

Open, Issue Price $25.00, '02

Purchased ________, Price $ _________

Precious Grandpa, 101505

$27.00
$25.00
$25.00
$25.00
$25.00

Open, Issue Price $25.00, '02

Purchased ________, Price $ __________

My Love Spills Over For You Mom, 101513

$40.00
$38.00

Comes with "Pampered Mom Coupon Book," designed to be personalized

Retired 2002, Issue Price $35.00, '02

Purchased _________,

Price $ _________

Loads Of Love For My Mommy, 101514

$40.00
$38.00

Comes with "Pampered Mom Coupon Book," designed to be personalized

Retired 2002, Issue Price $35.00, '02

Purchased ________,

Price $ _________

☐ *January — Snowdrop, "Pure And Gentle,"* 101515

$45.00
$43.00
$40.00
$40.00
$40.00

Open, Issue Price $40.00, '02
Series: *Calendar Girls*
Purchased ________, Price $ ___________

☐ *February — Carnation, "Bold And Brave,"* 101517

$45.00
$43.00
$40.00
$40.00
$40.00

Open, Issue Price $40.00, '02
Series: *Calendar Girls*
Purchased ________, Price $ ___________

☐ *March — Violet, "Modest,"* 101518

$45.00
$43.00
$40.00
$40.00
$40.00

Open, Issue Price $40.00, '02
Series: *Calendar Girls*
Purchased ________, Price $ ___________

☐ *April — Lily, "Virtuous,"* 101519

$45.00
$43.00
$40.00
$40.00
$40.00

Open, Issue Price $40.00, '02
Series: *Calendar Girls*
Purchased ________, Price $ ___________

☐ *May — Hawthorn, "Bright And Hopeful,"* 101520

$45.00
$43.00
$40.00
$40.00
$40.00

Open, Issue Price $40.00, '02
Series: *Calendar Girls*
Purchased ________, Price $ ___________

☐ *June — Rose, "Beautiful,"* 101521

$45.00
$43.00
$40.00
$40.00
$40.00

Open, Issue Price $40.00, '02
Series: *Calendar Girls*
Purchased ________, Price $ ___________

July — Daisy, "Wide-Eyed And Innocent," 101522

- $45.00
- $43.00
- $40.00
- $40.00
- $40.00

Open, Issue Price $40.00, '02
Series: *Calendar Girls*

Purchased ________, Price $ __________

August — Poppy, "Peaceful," 101523

- $45.00
- $43.00
- $40.00
- $40.00
- $40.00

Open, Issue Price $40.00, '02
Series: *Calendar Girls*

Purchased ________, Price $ __________

September — Morning Glory, "Easily Contented," 101525

- $45.00
- $43.00
- $40.00
- $40.00
- $40.00

Open, Issue Price $40.00, '02
Series: *Calendar Girls*

Purchased ________, Price $ __________

October — Cosmos, "Ambitious," 101526

- $45.00
- $43.00
- $40.00
- $40.00
- $40.00

Open, Issue Price $40.00, '02
Series: *Calendar Girls*

Purchased ________, Price $ __________

November — Chrysanthemum, "Sassy And Cheerful," 101527

- $45.00
- $43.00
- $40.00
- $40.00
- $40.00

Open, Issue Price $40.00, '02
Series: *Calendar Girls*

Purchased ________, Price $ __________

December — Holly, "Full Of Foresight," 101528

- $45.00
- $43.00
- $40.00
- $40.00
- $40.00

Open, Issue Price $40.00, '02
Series: *Calendar Girls*

Purchased ________, Price $ __________

Friends Are Never Far Behind, 101543

$110.00

Limited Ed. 5,000, Issue Price $45.00, '02
Series: *Smiles Forever* — Fifth Issue

Purchased ________, Price $ ___________

Love Is On Its Way, 101544

$145.00
$130.00

Limited Ed. 5,000, Issue Price $30.00, '02
Series: *Smiles Forever* — First Issue

Purchased ________, Price $ ___________

Lord, Help Me Clean Up My Act, 101545

$100.00

Limited Ed. 5,000, Issue Price $30.00, '02
Series: *Smiles Forever* — Second Issue

Purchased ________, Price $ ___________

Our Love Is Heaven Scent, 101546

$100.00

Limited Ed. 5,000, Issue Price $30.00, '02
Series: *Smiles Forever* — Fourth Issue

Purchased ________, Price $ ___________

Life Never Smelled So Sweet, 101547

$100.00

Limited Ed. 5,000, Issue Price $30.00, '02
Series: *Smiles Forever* — Third Issue

Purchased ________, Price $ ___________

Planting The Seeds Of Love, 101548

$150.00

Limited Ed. 7,500, Issue Price $99.50, '02
CCR Exclusive

Purchased ________, Price $ ___________

Precious Moments In Paradise, 101549

$55.00

Limited Ed., Issue Price $45.00, '02
CCR Exclusive
Purchased ________, Price $ __________

A Beary Warm Aloha! 101550 (Ornament)

$22.00

Limited Ed., Issue Price $15.00, '02
CCR Exclusive
Purchased ________, Price $ __________

Where The Deer And The Antelope Play, 101552

$37.00
$35.00
$35.00

Retired 2004, Issue Price $28.00, '02
Purchased ________, Price $ __________

Nurses Are Blessed With Patients, 101554

$20.00
$20.00

Open, Issue Price
$20.00, '02
Series: *Little Moments*
Purchased __________ ,
Price $__________

Dew Remember Me, 101555

$48.00

Limited Ed. 5,000, Issue Price $40.00, '02
Syndicated Catalog Exclusive
Purchased ________, Price $ __________

Our First Christmas Together, 101702 (Musical)

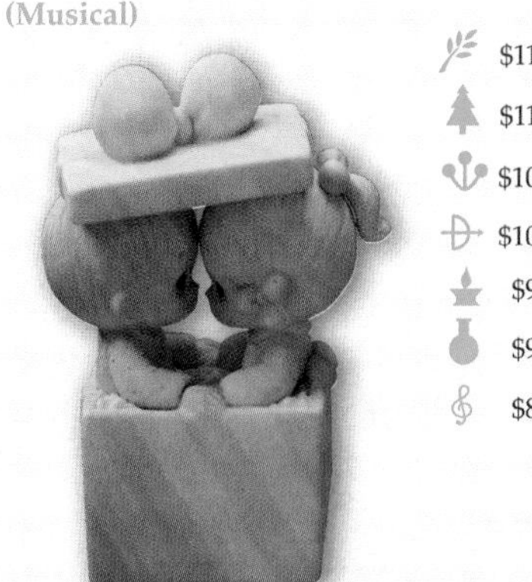

$115.00
$110.00
$105.00
$100.00
$95.00
$90.00
$85.00

Retired 1992, Issue Price $50.00, '86
Tune: "We Wish You A Merry Christmas"
Purchased ________, Price $ __________

No Tears Past The Gate, 101826

$105.00 $85.00 $75.00

$74.00 $73.00 $72.00 $71.00

$70.00 $70.00 $70.00 $70.00 $70.00 $70.00 $70.00 $70.00 $70.00 $70.00 $70.00 $70.00

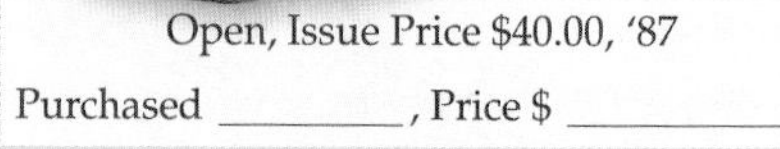

Open, Issue Price $40.00, '87

Purchased ________, Price $ ___________

I'm Sending You A White Christmas, 101834 (Plate)

$60.00

Dated Annual 1986, Issue Price $45.00, '86

Series: *Christmas Love* — First Issue

Purchased ________, Price $ ___________

Smile Along The Way, 101842

$175.00 $140.00 $138.00

$135.00 $130.00 $125.00

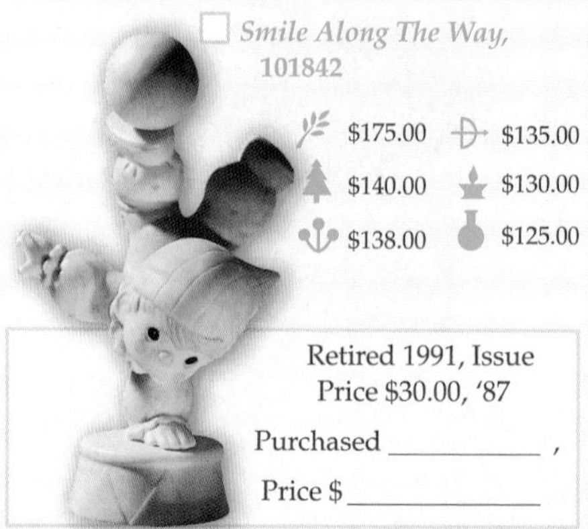

Retired 1991, Issue Price $30.00, '87

Purchased __________ ,

Price $ __________

Lord, Help Us Keep Our Act Together, 101850

$125.00 $115.00 $105.00

$100.00 $95.00 $90.00

Retired 1992, Issue Price $35.00, '87

Purchased __________ ,

Price $ __________

O Worship The Lord, 102229

$55.00 $52.00

$50.00 $48.00 $45.00 $45.00 $45.00 $45.00 $45.00

$45.00 $45.00 $40.00 $40.00 $40.00 $40.00 $40.00 $40.00 $40.00 $40.00

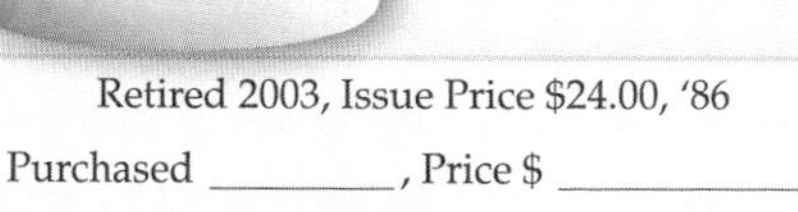

Retired 2003, Issue Price $24.00, '86

Purchased ________, Price $ ___________

Connie, 102253 (Doll)

$285.00

Limited Ed. 7,500, Issue Price $160.00, '86

Individually Numbered

Purchased ________, Price $ ___________

☐ *Shepherd Of Love, 102261*

$35.00
$33.00
$30.00
$28.00
$28.00
$25.00
$25.00
$25.00
$20.00
$20.00
$20.00
$20.00
$20.00
$20.00
$18.50
$18.50
$18.50
$18.50
$18.50
$18.50

Open, Issue Price $10.00, '86
Mini Nativity Addition
Purchased ________, Price $ ___________

☐ *Shepherd Of Love, 102288 (Ornament)*

$40.00
$38.00
$36.00
$34.00
$33.00
$32.00
$31.00
$30.00

Suspended 1993, Issue Price $10.00, '86
Purchased ________, Price $ ___________

☐ *Mini Animals, 102296*

$40.00
$38.00
$36.00
$35.00
$34.00
$33.00
$32.00

Suspended 1992, Issue Price $13.50, '86
Mini Nativity Addition
Set of 3 – Sheep, Bunny, and Turtle
Purchased ________, Price $ ___________

☐ *Wishing You A Cozy Christmas, 102318 (Bell)*

$30.00

Dated Annual 1986, Issue Price $20.00, '86
Purchased ________, Price $ ___________

☐ *Wishing You A Cozy Christmas, 102326 (Ornament)*

$30.00

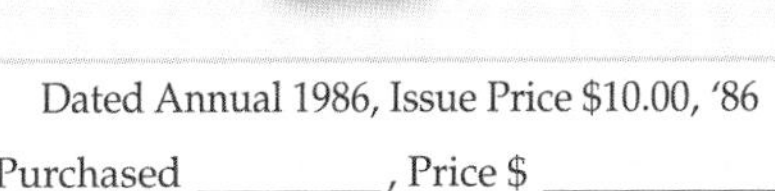

Dated Annual 1986, Issue Price $10.00, '86
Purchased ________, Price $ ___________

☐ *Wishing You A Cozy Christmas, 102334 (Thimble)*

$20.00

Dated Annual 1986, Issue Price $5.50, '86
Purchased ________, Price $ ___________

Wishing You A Cozy Christmas, 102342

$35.00

Dated Annual 1986, Issue Price $18.00, '86

Purchased ________, Price $ ____________

Our First Christmas Together, 102350 (Ornament)

$28.00

Dated Annual 1986, Issue Price $10.00, '86

Purchased ________, Price $ ____________

Wedding Arch, 102369

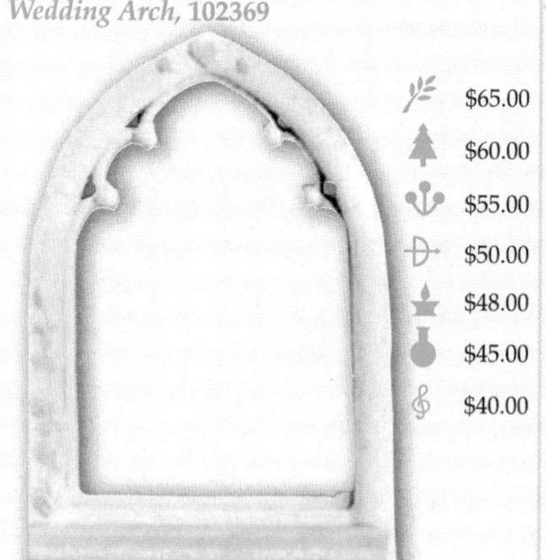

$65.00
$60.00
$55.00
$50.00
$48.00
$45.00
$40.00

Suspended 1992, Issue Price $22.50, '86

Purchased ________, Price $ ____________

Trust And Obey, 102377 (Ornament)

$32.00 $22.00
$30.00 $22.00
$30.00 $21.00
$28.00 $21.00
$25.00 $20.00
$25.00 $20.00
$23.00 $20.00
$23.00 $20.00

Retired 2001, Issue Price $10.00, '86

Purchased ________, Price $ ____________

Love Rescued Me, 102385 (Ornament)

$32.00 $22.00
$30.00 $22.00
$30.00 $21.00
$28.00 $21.00
$25.00 $20.00
$25.00 $20.00
$23.00 $20.00
$23.00 $20.00

Retired 2001, Issue Price $10.00, '86

Purchased ________, Price $ ____________

Love Rescued Me, 102393

$65.00 $45.00
$60.00 $45.00
$58.00 $42.00
$55.00 $40.00
$54.00 $40.00
$50.00 $40.00
$48.00 $40.00

Retired 1999, Issue Price $22.50, '86

Purchased ________, Price $ ____________

Angel Of Mercy, 102407 (Ornament)

$55.00
$50.00
$48.00
$45.00
$43.00
$40.00
$40.00
$40.00
$38.00
$38.00
$35.00
$35.00
$35.00
$33.00
$33.00
$33.00
$33.00
$33.00
$32.50
$32.50

Open, Issue Price $10.00, '86

Purchased ________, Price $ __________

It's A Perfect Boy, 102415 (Ornament)

$30.00
$28.00
$25.00
$23.00

Suspended 1989, Issue Price $10.00, '86

Purchased ________, Price $ __________

Lord, Keep Me On My Toes, 102423 (Ornament)

$45.00
$43.00
$41.00
$40.00
$40.00

Retired 1990, Issue Price $10.00, '86

Purchased ________, Price $ __________

Serve With A Smile, 102431 (Ornament)

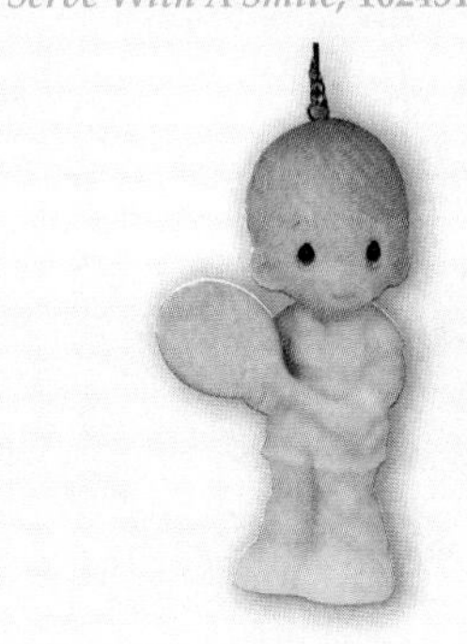

$30.00
$25.00
$23.00

Suspended 1988, Issue Price $10.00, '86

Purchased ________, Price $ __________

Serve With A Smile, 102458 (Ornament)

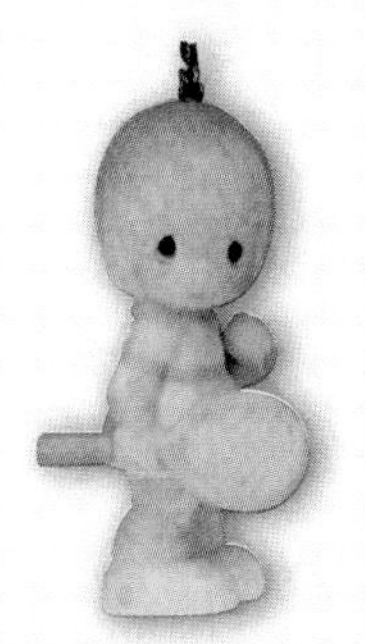

$35.00
$33.00
$30.00

Suspended 1988, Issue Price $10.00, '86

Purchased ________, Price $ __________

Reindeer, 102466 (Ornament)

First ornament in the Birthday Collection. Left off the retailer order form, they were in the stores and gone before the collectors knew about them.

$160.00

Dated Annual 1986, Issue Price $11.00, '86
Series: *Birthday Collection*

Purchased ________, Price $ __________

Rocking Horse, 102474 (Ornament)

$40.00
$38.00
$36.00
$35.00
$33.00
$30.00

Suspended 1991, Issue Price $10.00, '86

Purchased ________, Price $ ___________

Angel Of Mercy, 102482

$55.00
$50.00
$48.00
$45.00
$43.00
$43.00
$40.00
$40.00
$38.00
$38.00
$38.00
$35.00
$35.00
$35.00
$35.00
$32.50
$32.50
$32.50
$32.50
$32.50

Open, Issue Price $20.00, '86

Purchased ________, Price $ ___________

Sharing Our Christmas Together, 102490

$70.00 $68.00 $65.00

Suspended 1988, Issue Price $37.00, '86

Purchased ________, Price $ ___________

Baby's First Christmas, 102504 (Ornament)

$30.00

Dated Annual 1986, Issue Price $10.00, '86

Purchased ________, Price $ ___________

Baby's First Christmas, 102512 (Ornament)

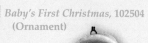

$28.00

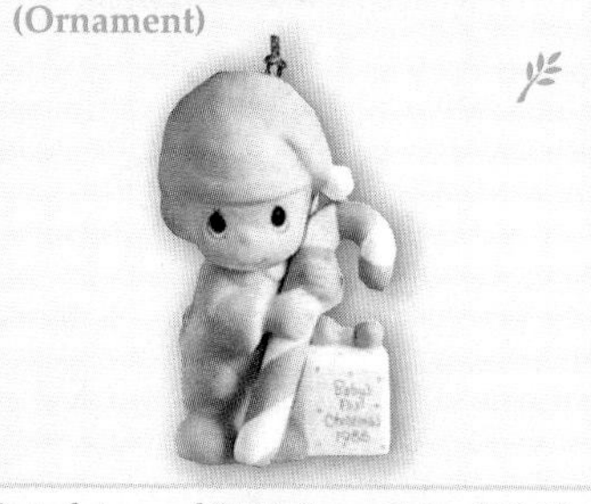

Dated Annual 1986, Issue Price $10.00, '86

Purchased ________, Price $ ___________

Let's Keep In Touch, 102520 (Musical)

$130.00
$127.00
$120.00
$115.00
$110.00
$108.00
$105.00
$100.00
$98.00
$95.00
$95.00
$95.00
$95.00
$95.00

Retired 1999, Issue Price $65.00, '86

Tune: "Be A Clown"

Purchased ________, Price $ ___________

☐ *We Are All Precious In His Sight*, 102903

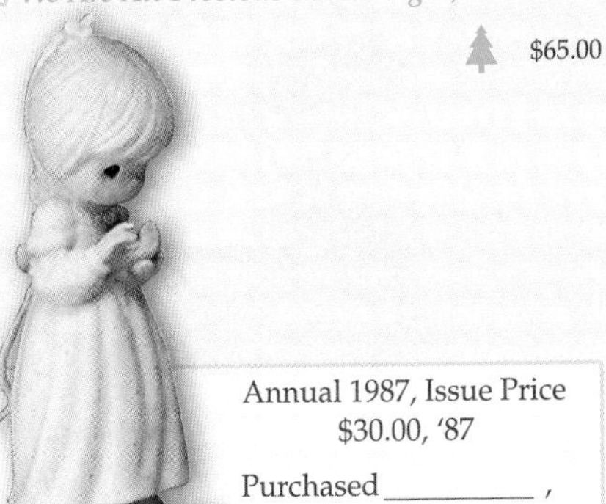

$65.00

Annual 1987, Issue Price $30.00, '87

Purchased __________ ,

Price $ __________

☐ *God Bless America*, 102938R

$45.00

$40.00

$40.00

$40.00

$40.00

This piece features a second mark, the 4 Star Flag. A portion of the proceeds went to benefit the victims of September 11th and the Precious Moments September 11th Relief Fund.

Retired 2004, Issue Price $40.00, '02
Series: *America Forever*

Purchased __________, Price $ __________

☐ *Mom, You're A Sweetheart*, 102913

$30.00

Limited Ed., Issue Price $19.99, '02
Avon Exclusive

Purchased __________, Price $ __________

☐ *My Peace I Give Unto Thee*, 102954 (Plate)

$55.00

Dated Annual 1987, Issue Price $45.00, '87
Series: *Christmas Love* — Second Issue

Purchased __________, Price $ __________

☐ *God Bless America*, 102938

$75.00

Annual 1986, Reintroduced 2001,
Issue Price $30.00, '86
Series: *America Forever*

Purchased __________, Price $ __________

☐ *It's The Birthday Of A King*, 102962

$40.00

$38.00

$35.00

$33.00

Suspended 1989, Issue Price $19.00, '86
Nativity Addition

Purchased __________, Price $ __________

I Would Be Sunk Without You, 102970

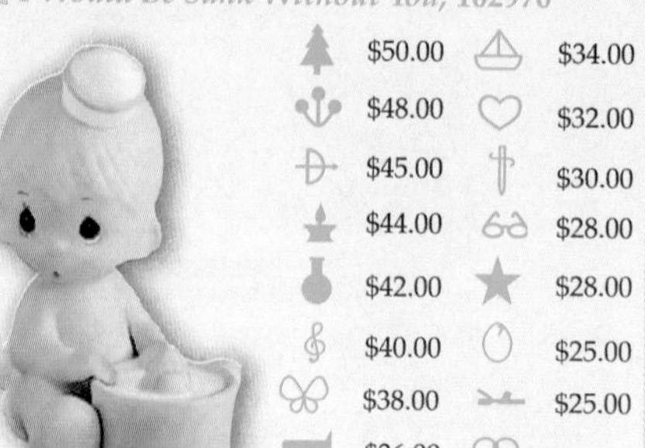

	$50.00		$34.00
	$48.00		$32.00
	$45.00		$30.00
	$44.00		$28.00
	$42.00		$28.00
	$40.00		$25.00
	$38.00		$25.00
	$36.00		$25.00

Retired 2002, Issue Price $15.00, '87

Purchased ________, Price $ ___________

We Belong To The Lord, 103004

$225.00

Without Bible $200.00

The Damien-Dutton Society for Leprosy Aid operates two gift shops and all of the profits go back to this charity. This figurine was a special edition produced for and sold by the Damien-Dutton Society. Comes with a leatherbound Bible.

Special Piece, Issue Price $50.00, '86

Damien-Dutton Piece

Purchased ________, Price $ ___________

Living Each Day With Love, 103175

$65.00

$60.00

Limited Ed. 7,500, Issue Price $49.95, '02

Series: *Rose Petal*

GoCollect.com/Century Circle Exclusive

Purchased ________, Price $ ___________

You Are The Rose In My Bouquet, 103176

$65.00

$60.00

Limited Ed. 7,500, Issue Price $40.00, '02

Series: *Rose Petal* — First Issue

GoCollect.com/CCR Exclusive

Purchased ________, Price $ ___________

A Smile Is Cherished In The Heart, 103177

$65.00

$60.00

Open, Issue Price $40.00, '02

Series: *Rose Petal*

GoCollect.com/CCR Exclusive

Purchased ________, Price $ ___________

Hang Onto Your Happiness, 103178

$30.00

$25.00

Open, Issue Price $16.00, '03

Japanese Exclusive

Purchased ________, Price $ ___________

We Are The Sheep Of His Pasture, 103180

$30.00

$25.00

Open, Issue Price $16.00, '03
Japanese Exclusive

Purchased ______ ,

Price $ ________

Life's Blessings Are Bountiful, 103184

$30.00

$25.00

Open, Issue Price $16.00, '03
Japanese Exclusive

Purchased ________ ,

Price $ ________

The Dawn Of A New Beginning, 103181

$30.00

$25.00

Open, Issue Price $16.00, '03
Japanese Exclusive

Purchased ______ ,

Price $ ________

Ringing In A Year Of Good Health, 103185

$30.00

$25.00

Open, Issue Price $16.00, '03
Japanese Exclusive

Purchased ________ , Price $ ________

Good Fortune Is Just Around The Corner, 103182

$30.00

$25.00

Open, Issue Price $16.00, '03
Japanese Exclusive

Purchased ________ ,

Price $ ________

Strength Comes From Within, 103186

$30.00

$25.00

Open, Issue Price $16.00, '03
Japanese Exclusive

Purchased ________ ,

Price $ ________

Life Is No Boar With You, 103183

$30.00

$25.00

Open, Issue Price $16.00, '03
Japanese Exclusive

Purchased ______ , Price $ ________

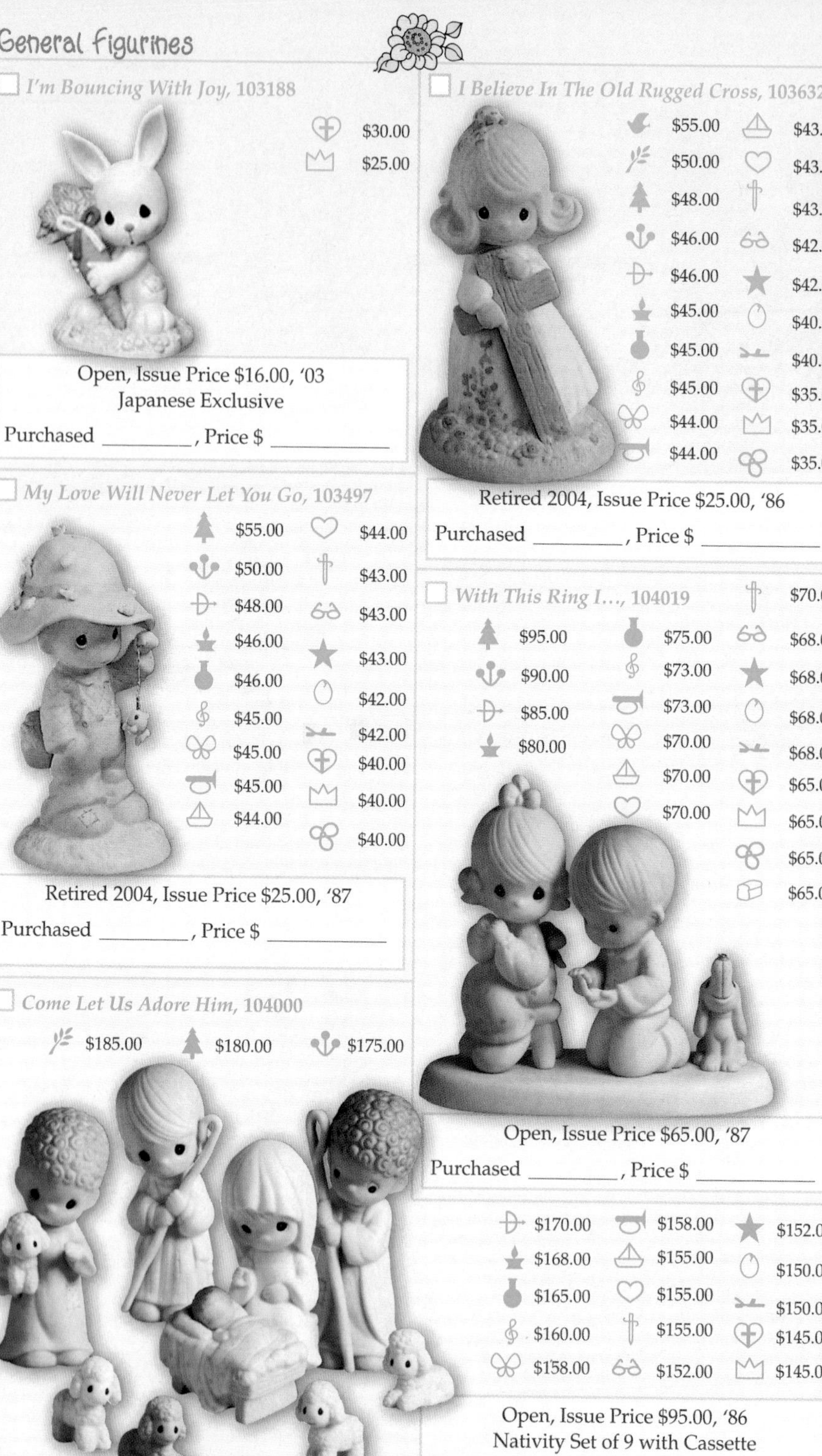

☐ *I'm Bouncing With Joy, 103188*

$30.00
$25.00

Open, Issue Price $16.00, '03
Japanese Exclusive
Purchased ________, Price $ ___________

☐ *I Believe In The Old Rugged Cross, 103632*

$55.00 $43.00
$50.00 $43.00
$48.00 $43.00
$46.00 $42.00
$46.00 $42.00
$45.00 $40.00
$45.00 $40.00
$45.00 $35.00
$44.00 $35.00
$44.00 $35.00

Retired 2004, Issue Price $25.00, '86
Purchased ________, Price $ ___________

☐ *My Love Will Never Let You Go, 103497*

$55.00 $44.00
$50.00 $43.00
$48.00 $43.00
$46.00 $43.00
$46.00 $42.00
$45.00 $42.00
$45.00 $40.00
$45.00 $40.00
$44.00 $40.00

Retired 2004, Issue Price $25.00, '87
Purchased ________, Price $ ___________

☐ *With This Ring I..., 104019*

$95.00 $75.00 $70.00
$90.00 $73.00 $68.00
$85.00 $73.00 $68.00
$80.00 $70.00 $68.00
$70.00 $68.00
$70.00 $65.00
$65.00
$65.00
$65.00

Open, Issue Price $65.00, '87
Purchased ________, Price $ ___________

☐ *Come Let Us Adore Him, 104000*

$185.00 $180.00 $175.00

$170.00 $158.00 $152.00
$168.00 $155.00 $150.00
$165.00 $155.00 $150.00
$160.00 $155.00 $145.00
$158.00 $152.00 $145.00

Open, Issue Price $95.00, '86
Nativity Set of 9 with Cassette
Purchased ________, Price $ ___________

☐ *Love Is The Glue That Mends, 104027*

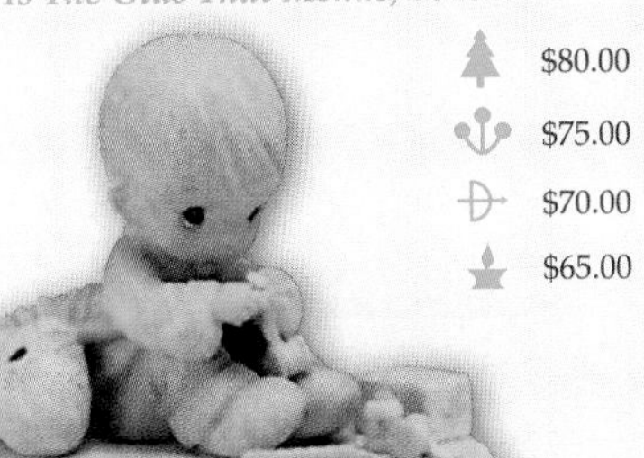

$80.00
$75.00
$70.00
$65.00

Suspended 1990, Issue Price $33.50, '87
Purchased ________, Price $ __________

☐ *Cheers To The Leader, 104035*

$73.00
$70.00
$65.00
$63.00
$60.00
$55.00
$50.00
$48.00
$45.00
$43.00
$40.00

Retired 1997, Issue Price $22.50, '87
Purchased ________, Price $ __________

☐ *May Your Holidays Sparkle With Joy, 104202*

$40.00

Open, Issue Price $35.00, '02
Purchased ________, Price $ __________

☐ *May Your Holidays Sparkle With Joy, 104203 (Ornament)*

$25.00

Dated Annual 2002, Issue Price $20.00, '02
Purchased__________ ,
Price $ __________

☐ *Baby's First Christmas, 104204 (Ornament)*

$25.00

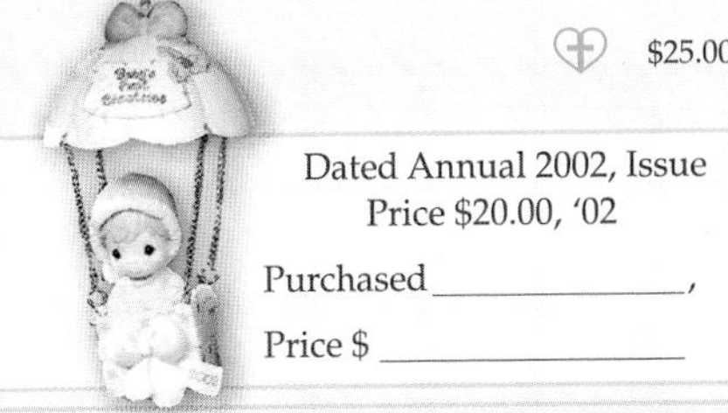

Dated Annual 2002, Issue Price $20.00, '02
Purchased__________,
Price $ __________

☐ *Baby's First Christmas, 104206 (Ornament)*

$25.00

Dated Annual 2002, Issue Price $20.00, '02
Purchased__________,
Price $ __________

☐ *Our First Christmas Together, 104207 (Ornament)*

$30.00

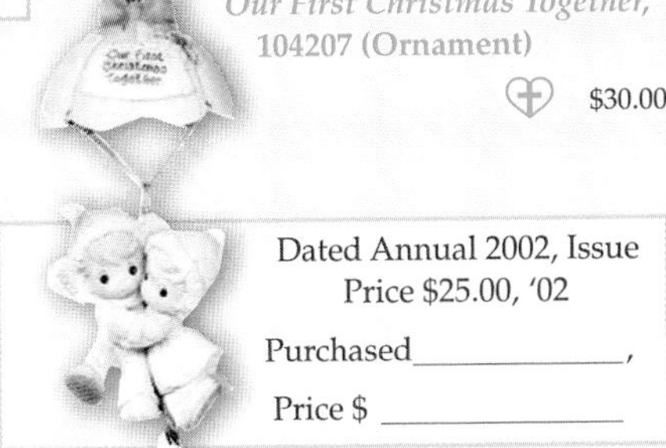

Dated Annual 2002, Issue Price $25.00, '02
Purchased__________,
Price $ __________

☐ *Home Sweet Home, 104208 (Ornament)*

$35.00

Dated Annual 2002, Issue Price $30.00, '02
Purchased __________ ,
Price $ __________

☐ *There's Sno-One Like You,* 104209 (Ornament)

$33.00

Dated Annual 2002, Issue Price $19.00, '02
Series: *Birthday Collection*
Purchased __________ ,
Price $ ____________

☐ *Jesus Is Born,* 104210

$45.00
$43.00
$40.00
$40.00

Open, Issue Price $40.00, '03
Nativity Addition
Purchased ________ ,
Price $__________

☐ *Hark, The Harold Angel Sings,* 104211

$25.00 $20.00
$23.00 $20.00

Open, Issue Price $20.00, '02
Mini Nativity Addition
Purchased________ ,
Price $ __________

☐ *You Are My Christmas Special,* 104215

$115.00

Annual 2002, Issue Price $100.00, '02
Purchased ________, Price $ __________

☐ *...And To All A Good Night,* 104217

$60.00
$58.00

Retired 2003, Issue Price $55.00, '02
Series: *Christmas Remembered* — Third Issue
Purchased ________, Price $ __________

☐ *Merry Christ-Miss,* 104218

$38.00
$35.00
$35.00
$35.00

Open, Issue Price $35.00, '02
Purchased __________ ,
Price $ __________

☐ *Friends Share A Special Bond,* 104219

$48.00
$45.00
$45.00
$45.00

Open, Issue Price $45.00, '02
Purchased ________, Price $ __________

You're O.K. Buy Me, 104267

Heart	$43.00
Crown	$40.00
Clover	$37.50
Cube	$37.50

Open, Issue Price $37.50, '02

Purchased ________, Price $ ___________

Your Love Is Just So Comforting, 104268

Heart	$38.00
Crown	$35.00
Clover	$35.00
Cube	$35.00

Open, Issue Price $35.00, '02

Purchased ________, Price $ ___________

I'm So Lucky To Have You As A Daughter, 104269

Heart	$37.00
Crown	$35.00
Clover	$35.00
Cube	$35.00

Open, Issue Price $35.00, '02

Purchased ________, Price $ ___________

I Get A Cluck Out Of You, 104270

Heart	$45.00
Crown	$43.00
Clover	$40.00

Retired 2004, Issue Price $40.00, '02
Series: *Country Lane Collection*

Purchased ________, Price $ ___________

Owl Always Be There For You, 104271

Heart	$28.00
Crown	$27.00
Clover	$25.00
Cube	$25.00

Open, Issue Price $25.00, '02

Purchased ________, Price $ ___________

You Cane Count On Me, 104273

Heart	$44.00

Limited Ed. 9,000, Issue Price $35.00, '02
GCC Fall Exclusive

Purchased ________, Price $ ___________

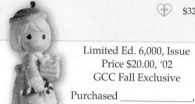

☐ *You Cane Count On Me, 104274 (Ornament)*

$32.00

Limited Ed. 6,000, Issue Price $20.00, '02
GCC Fall Exclusive

Purchased ________,

Price $________

☐ *Life's Ups 'N Downs Are Smoother With You, 104275*

$33.00
$30.00
$30.00

Comes with tart burner, tea light candle, and bayberry scented tart.

Limited Ed., Issue Price $30.00, '03
Gift To Go

Purchased ________, Price $ ________

☐ *Twogether We Can Move Mountains, 104276*

$80.00
$80.00

Annual 2002, Issue Price $80.00, '02
Boys & Girls Club Commemorative

Purchased ________, Price $ ________

☐ *A Journey Of Hope, 104277*

$45.00
$45.00

Open, Issue Price $45.00, '04

Purchased ________,

Price $ ________

☐ *His Love Is Reflected In You, 104279*

$85.00
$85.00

Limited Ed., Issue Price $85.00, '03

Purchased ________, Price $ ________

☐ *Carry A Song In Your Heart, 104281*

$45.00

Limited Ed. 8,500, Issue Price $35.00, '02
CCR & DSR Exclusive

Purchased ________,

Price $ ________

Hugs Can Tame The Wildest Heart, 104282

$55.00

Limited Ed. 8,500, Issue Price $35.00, '02
CCR & DSR Exclusive

Purchased ________, Price $ ___________

A Mother's Love Is From Above, 104311

$40.00
$40.00
$40.00

Open, Issue Price $40.00, '03
Series: *Motherhood*

Purchased ________, Price $ ___________

Happy Days Are Here Again, 104396

$65.00
$60.00
$58.00
$56.00

Suspended 1990, Issue Price $25.00, '87

Purchased________ ,

Price $___________

Friends To The End, 104418

UM $48.00
$32.00
$29.00
$27.00
$25.00
$22.00
$19.00

Suspended 1993, Issue Price $15.00, '88

Purchased ________, Price $ ___________

Bear The Good News Of Christmas, 104515 (Ornament)

$35.00

Dated Annual 1987, Issue Price $11.00, '87
Series: *Birthday Collection*

Purchased ________, Price $ ___________

Come Let Us Adore Him, 104523

$600.00

Dealers Only Promotional Pieces,
Issue Price $400.00, '88
Nativity With Backdrop & Video — Set of 9

Purchased ________, Price $ ___________

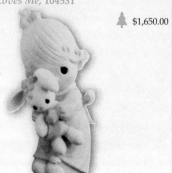

☐ *Jesus Loves Me, 104531*

$1,650.00

Limited Ed. 1,000, Issue Price $500.00, '88
Easter Seals, Lily Understamp,
Individually Numbered

Purchased ________, Price $ ___________

☐ *Lots Of Good Things Are Coming Your Way, 104778*

$50.00

Limited Ed., Issue Price $45.00, '03
Kirlin's Exclusive

Purchased ________, Price $ ___________

☐ *Lots Of Good Things Are Coming Your Way, 104780 (Ornament)*

$30.00

Limited Ed., Issue
Price $20.00, '03
Kirlin's Exclusive

Purchased ________ ,

Price $ ___________

☐ *There's Sno-One Quite Like You, 104781*

$25.00

$25.00

Limited Ed., Issue Price $25.00, '02
Gift To Go
Series: *Little Moments*

Purchased ________, Price $ ___________

☐ *The True Spirit Of Christmas Guides The Way, 104784*

$125.00

Limited Ed. 5,000, Issue Price $125.00, '02
DSR Exclusive

Purchased ________, Price $ ___________

☐ *No One's Sweeter Than Mom, 104785 (Ornament)*

$22.00

$20.00

$18.50

$18.50

Open, Issue Price
$18.50, '02
Series: *Family Ornament*, Mom

Purchased ___________ ,

Price $ ___________

Papas Make The Season Bright, 104786 (Ornament)

Heart	$22.00
Crown	$20.00
Clover	$18.50
Box	$18.50

Open, Issue Price $18.50, '02
Series: *Family Ornament*, Dad

Purchased ________ ,

Price $ ____________

Making The Holidays Special, 104788 (Ornament)

Heart	$22.00	Clover	$18.50
Crown	$20.00	Box	$18.50

Open, Issue Price $18.50, '02
Series: *Family Ornament*, Grandma

Purchased __________ ,

Price $ _____________

Delivering Lots Of Love, 104789 (Ornament)

Heart	$22.00	Clover	$18.50
Crown	$20.00	Box	$18.50

Open, Issue Price $18.50, '02
Series: *Family Ornament*, Grandpa

Purchased __________ ,

Price $ _____________

Bringing Bouquets Of Love, 104790 (Ornament)

Heart	$22.00	Clover	$18.50
Crown	$20.00	Box	$18.50

Open, Issue Price $20.00, '02
Series: *Family Ornament*, Daughter

Purchased ____________ ,

Price $ _______________

Packed With Love, 104791 (Ornament)

Heart	$22.00	Clover	$18.50
Crown	$20.00	Box	$18.50

Open, Issue Price $18.50, '02
Series: *Family Ornament*, Son

Purchased _____________ ,

Price $ ________________

Overflowing With Holiday Joy, 104792 (Ornament)

Heart	$22.00	Clover	$18.50
Crown	$20.00	Box	$18.50

Open, Issue Price $18.50, '02
Series: *Family Ornament*, Toddler Daughter

Purchased ___________ ,

Price $ ______________

Holiday Surprises Come In All Sizes, 104793 (Ornament)

Heart	$22.00	Clover	$18.50
Crown	$20.00	Box	$18.50

Open, Issue Price $18.50, '02
Series: *Family Ornament*, Toddler Son

Purchased ___________ ,

Price $ _____________

Hooked On the Holidays, 104794 (Ornament)

Heart	$22.00	Clover	$18.50
Crown	$20.00	Box	$18.50

Open, Issue Price $18.50, '02
Series: *Family Ornament*, Dog

Purchased ____________ ,

Price $ _______________

Hanging Out For The Holidays, 104796 (Ornament)

$22.00	$18.50
$20.00	$18.50

Open, Issue Price $18.50, '02
Series: *Family Ornament*, Cat
Purchased ________ ,
Price $ ________

I Trust In The Lord For My Strength, 104798

$27.00
$25.00
$25.00
$25.00

Open, Issue Price $25.00, '02
Purchased ________ , Price $ ________

I'd Jump Through Hoops For You, 104799

$27.00
$25.00
$25.00
$25.00

Open, Issue Price $25.00, '02
Purchased ________ , Price $ ________

You're A Perfect 10, 104800

$27.00
$25.00
$25.00
$25.00

Open, Issue Price $25.00, '02
Purchased ________ , Price $ ________

You're A Perfect Match, 104801

$27.00
$25.00
$25.00
$25.00

Open, Issue Price $25.00, '02
Purchased ________ , Price $ ________

Your Spirit Is An Inspiration, 104802

$27.00
$25.00
$25.00
$25.00

Open, Issue Price $25.00, '02
Purchased ________ , Price $ ________

Serving Up Fun, 104803

$27.00
$25.00
$25.00
$25.00

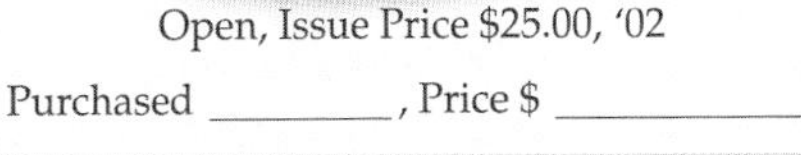

Open, Issue Price $25.00, '02

Purchased ________, Price $ ___________

A Tub Full Of Love, 104817

$55.00
$52.00
$50.00
$48.00
$45.00
$43.00
$41.00
$40.00
$38.00
$35.00
$35.00
$35.00

Suspended 1998, Issue Price $22.50, '87

Purchased ________, Price $ ___________

Sitting Pretty, 104825

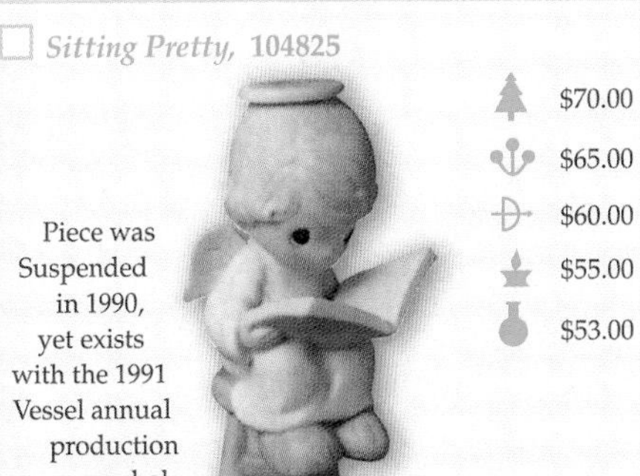

$70.00
$65.00
$60.00
$55.00
$53.00

Piece was Suspended in 1990, yet exists with the 1991 Vessel annual production symbol.

Suspended 1990, Issue Price $22.50, '87

Purchased ________, Price $ ___________

Mom, You're A Sweetheart, 104850

$30.00

Limited Ed., Issue Price $19.99, '02
Avon Exclusive

Purchased ________, Price $ ___________

Have I Got News For You, 105635

$65.00
$60.00
$55.00
$53.00
$50.00

Suspended 1991, Issue Price $22.50, '87
Nativity Addition

Purchased ________, Price $ ___________

Something's Missing When You're Not Around, 105643

$72.00
$66.00
$63.00
$60.00

Suspended 1991, Issue Price $32.50, '88

Purchased ________, Price $ ___________

To Tell The Tooth You're Special, 105813

$225.00
$200.00
$190.00
$185.00

Suspended 1990, Issue Price $38.50, '87

Purchased ________, Price $ ___________

Hallelujah Country, 105821

$95.00
$90.00
$80.00
$75.00
$70.00
$65.00
$60.00
$58.00
$55.00
$53.00
$52.00
$52.00
$50.00
$50.00

Retired 2000, Issue Price $35.00, '88

Purchased ________, Price $ ___________

Showers Of Blessings, 105945

$45.00
$35.00
$34.00
$33.00
$32.00
$31.00
$30.00

Retired 1993, Issue Price $16.00, '87
Series: *Birthday Collection*

Purchased ________, Price $ ___________

Brighten Someone's Day, 105953

$33.00
$32.00
$31.00
$30.00
$28.00
$27.00
$25.00

Suspended 1993, Issue Price $12.50, '88
Series: *Birthday Collection*

Purchased ________, Price $ ___________

The Heart Of The Home Is Love, 106109

$60.00

Limited Ed. 1,300, Issue Price $35.00, '02
Chapel Exclusive
2002 Licensee Event Exclusive

Purchased ________, Price $ ___________

We're Pulling For You, 106151

$85.00
$75.00
$70.00
$68.00
$65.00

Suspended 1991, Issue Price $40.00, '87

Purchased ________, Price $ ___________

☐ *God Bless You Graduate, 106194*

$60.00 · $55.00 · $50.00 · $48.00 · $45.00 · $45.00 · $43.00 · $40.00 · $40.00 · $40.00

$40.00 · $40.00 · $40.00 · $38.00 · $38.00 · $38.00 · $38.00 · $35.00 · $35.00 · $35.00

Open, Issue Price $20.00, '86

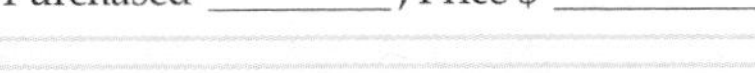

Purchased ________, Price $ __________

☐ *Congratulations, Princess, 106208*

$75.00 · $70.00 · $62.00 · $58.00 · $55.00 · $53.00 · $50.00 · $50.00 · $48.00

$45.00 · $45.00 · $43.00 · $43.00 · $40.00 · $40.00 · $40.00 · $40.00

Retired 2002, Issue Price $20.00, '86

Purchased ________, Price $ __________

☐ *Lord, Help Me Make The Grade, 106216*

$65.00 · $60.00 · $55.00 · $50.00

Suspended 1990, Issue Price $25.00, '87

Purchased ________, Price $ __________

☐ *God Shed His Grace On Thee, 106632*

$75.00 · $65.00

Limited Ed., Issue Price $60.00, '02

Purchased ________ ,

Price $ __________

☐ *Stand Beside Her And Guide Her, 106671*

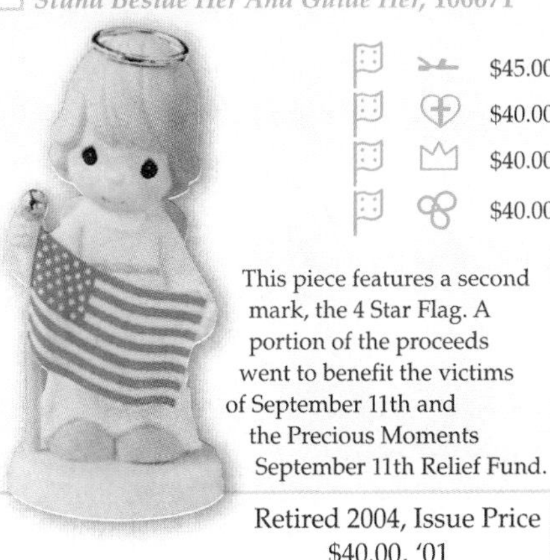

$45.00 · $40.00 · $40.00 · $40.00

This piece features a second mark, the 4 Star Flag. A portion of the proceeds went to benefit the victims of September 11th and the Precious Moments September 11th Relief Fund.

Retired 2004, Issue Price $40.00, '01

Series: *America Forever*

Purchased ________, Price $ __________

☐ *Land Of The Free, Home Of The Brave, 106672*

UM $55.00

Limited Ed. 1,100, Issue Price $35.00, '03

2003 Licensee Show And Collectors' Event Piece

Purchased ________ ,

Price $ __________

☐ *Heaven Bless Your Togetherness, 106755*

$125.00 $100.00 $90.00
$105.00 $95.00 $90.00
$90.00 $90.00
$90.00
$90.00
$90.00
$90.00
$90.00

Retired 1999, Issue Price $65.00, '88

Purchased ________, Price $ ___________

☐ *Precious Memories, 106763*

$58.00
$75.00 $68.00 $58.00
$73.00 $65.00 $55.00
$70.00 $63.00 $55.00
$61.00 $50.00
$50.00
$50.00
$50.00
$50.00
$50.00
$50.00
$50.00

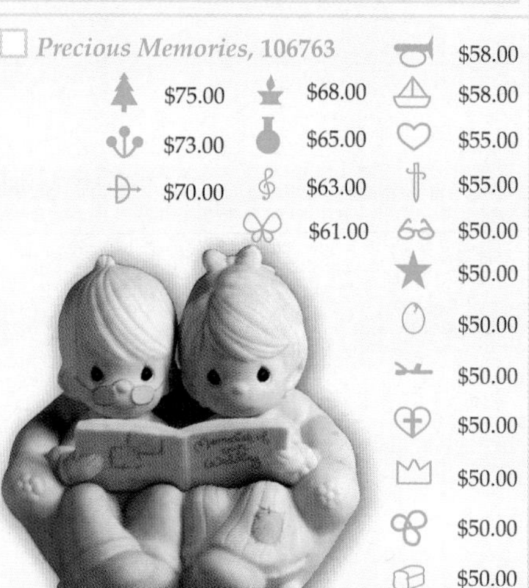

Open, Issue Price $37.50, '88

Purchased ________, Price $ ___________

☐ *Puppy Love Is From Above, 106798*

$85.00
$80.00
$78.00

$74.00 $65.00 $63.00
$70.00 $60.00 $60.00

Retired 1995, Issue Price $45.00, '88

Purchased ________, Price $ ___________

☐ *Happy Birthday Poppy, 106836*

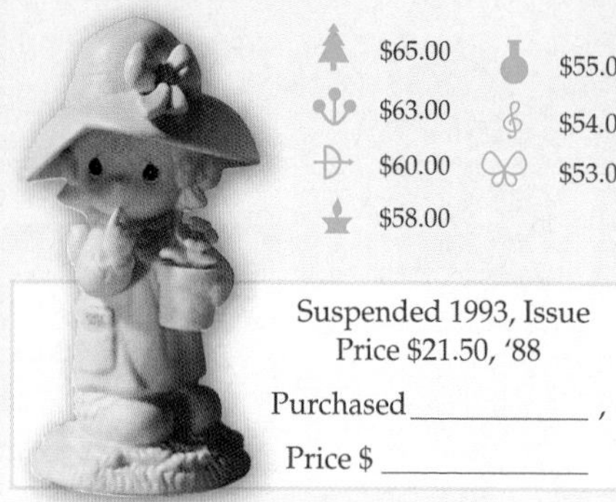

$65.00 $55.00
$63.00 $54.00
$60.00 $53.00
$58.00

Suspended 1993, Issue Price $21.50, '88

Purchased ___________,

Price $ ___________

☐ *Sew In Love, 106844*

$84.00 $80.00 $75.00
$68.00
$65.00
$64.00
$62.00
$60.00
$60.00
$60.00
$60.00

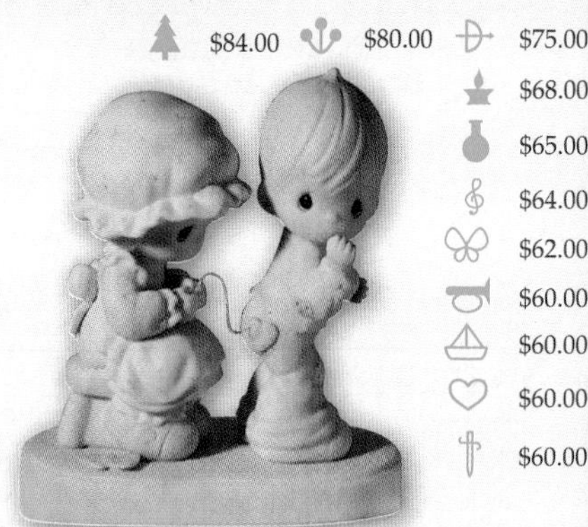

Retired 1997, Issue Price $45.00, '88

Purchased ________, Price $ ___________

☐ *He Walks With Me, 107999*

$125.00
$50.00

Annual 1987, Issue Price $25.00, '87
Easter Seals Commemorative, Lily Understamp

Purchased ___________,

Price $___________

☐ *They Followed The Star, 108243*

$140.00
$130.00
$125.00
$120.00
$120.00
$120.00
$120.00
$120.00
$120.00
$120.00
$120.00
$120.00
$120.00
$120.00
$120.00
$120.00
$120.00

Suspended, Issue Price $75.00, '87
Mini Nativity Addition, Set of 3
Purchased ________, Price $ __________

☐ *Your Love Fills My Heart, 108522*

$50.00
$50.00

Limited Ed., Issue Price
$50.00, '03
Purchased ____________ ,
Price $ _____________

☐ *Family's Fur-ever, 108526*

$35.00
$35.00
$35.00
$35.00

Open, Issue Price $35.00, '03
Purchased __________ ,
Price $ _____________

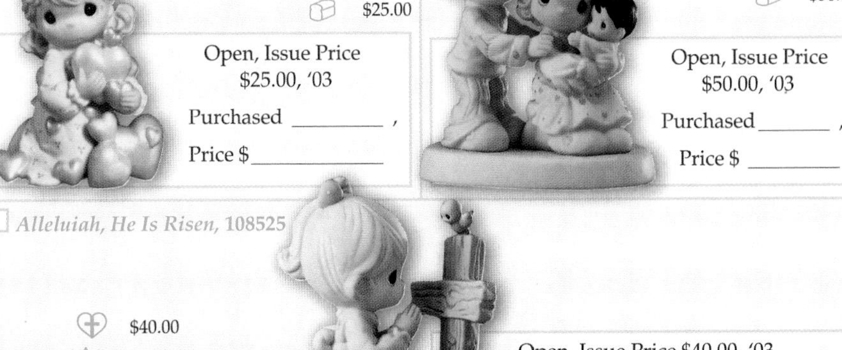

☐ *Overflowing With Love, 108523*

$25.00
$25.00
$25.00
$25.00

Open, Issue Price
$25.00, '03
Purchased ________ ,
Price $___________

☐ *Adopting A Life Of Love, 108527*

$50.00
$50.00
$50.00
$50.00

Open, Issue Price
$50.00, '03
Purchased______ ,
Price $ ________

☐ *Alleluiah, He Is Risen, 108525*

$40.00
$40.00
$40.00
$40.00

Open, Issue Price $40.00, '03
Purchased______, Price $__________

My Most Precious Mom-ents Are With You (Mom), 108528

$40.00
$40.00
$40.00
$40.00

Open, Issue Price $40.00, '03

Purchased ______ ,

Price $________

Collecting Life's Most Precious Moments, 108531

$50.00
$50.00
$50.00
$50.00

Limited Ed., Issue Price $50.00, '03
25th Anniversary Commemorative

Purchased ________, Price $ __________

Collecting Life's Most Precious Moments, 108532 (Ornament)

$25.00 $25.00
$25.00 $25.00

Open, Issue Price $25.00, '03
25th Anniversary Commemorative

Purchased ______ ,

Price $________

Just For Your Knowledge, I'll Miss You At College, 108533

$40.00 $40.00
$40.00 $40.00

Open, Issue Price $40.00, '03

Purchased __________ ,

Price $__________

Wishing You A Birthday Fit For A Princess, 108534

$25.0
$25.0
$25.0
$25.0

Open, Issue Price $25.00, '03

Purchased __________ ,

Price $ __________

I-rish You Lots Of Luck, 108535

$30.0
$30.0
$30.0
$30.0

Open, Issue Price $30.00, '03

Purchased __________ ,

Price $ __________

Grounds For A Great Friendship, 108536

$50.0
$50.0
$50.0
$50.0

Open, Issue Price $50.00, '03

Purchased ________, Price $ __________

Friends Always Deserve Special Treatment, 108538

$50.00
$50.00
$50.00
$50.00

Open, Issue Price $50.00, '03

Purchased ________, Price $ ___________

I'm So Glad I Spotted You As A Friend, 108539

$25.00
$25.00
$25.00
$25.00

Open, Issue Price $25.00, '03

Purchased ___________,

Price $ _____________

May Your Faith Grow With Daily Care, 108540

$40.00 $40.00
$40.00 $40.00

Open, Issue Price $40.00, '03

Purchased_______ ,

Price $ ________

Forever In Our Hearts, 108541

$35.00
$35.00
$35.00
$35.00

Open, Issue Price $35.00, '03

Purchased ___________,

Price $_____________

Simple Pleasures Are Life's True Treasures, 108542

$75.00
$75.00

Limited Ed., Issue Price $75.00, '02

Purchased ________, Price $ ___________

Marching Ahead To Another 25 Years Of Precious Moments, 108544

$325.00

Limited Ed. 5,000,
Issue Price $325.00, '03
Precious Moments
25th Anniversary
CCR Exclusive

Purchased ________, Price $ ___________

You Bring Me Out Of My Shell, 108546

Crown	$45.00
Clover	$45.00
Box	$45.00

Open, Issue Price $45.00, '03
Series: *Sea Of Friendship*
Purchased ________, Price $ __________

Water I Do Without You? 108547

Heart	$45.00
Crown	$45.00
Clover	$45.00
Box	$45.00

Open, Issue Price $45.00, '03
Series: *Sea Of Friendship*
Purchased ________, Price $ __________

I'm Filled With Love For You, 108548

Crown	$45.00
Clover	$45.00
Box	$45.00

Open, Issue Price $45.00, '03
Series: *Sea Of Friendship*
Purchased ________, Price $ __________

I'd Be Lost Without You, 108592

Heart	$75.0

Limited Ed. 7,500, Issue Price $45.00, '03
Series: *Endangered Species* — Third Issue
Purchased ________, Price $ __________

Have You Herd How Much I Love You? 108593

Crown	$75.0

Limited Ed. 7,500, Issue Price $45.00, '03
Series: *Endangered Species* — Sixth Issue
Purchased ________, Price $ __________

Stay With Me A Whale, 108595

Heart	$75.00

Limited Ed. 7,500, Issue Price $45.00, '03
Series: *Endangered Species* — First Issue
Purchased ________, Price $ __________

Everything's Better When Shared Together, 108597

$75.00

Limited Ed. 7,500, Issue Price $45.00, '03
Series: *Endangered Species* — Second Issue

Purchased ________, Price $ ___________

Head And Shoulders Above The Rest, 108598

$75.00

Limited Ed. 7,500, Issue Price $45.00, '03
Series: *Endangered Species* — Fourth Issue

Purchased ________, Price $ ___________

Together Fur-Ever, 108600

$75.00

Limited Ed. 7,500, Issue Price $45.00, '03
Series: *Endangered Species* — Fifth Issue

Purchased ________, Price $ ___________

Thanks For A Quarter Century Of Loving, Caring And Sharing, 108602

$100.00
$100.00

Limited Ed., Issue Price $100.00, '02
Precious Moments 25th Anniversary
CCR Exclusive

Purchased ________, Price $ ___________

Love Is The True Reward, 108603

$37.50
$35.00

Limited Ed., Issue Price $37.50, '03
GCC Exclusive

Purchased ________, Price $ ___________

I Love You Knight And Day, 108604

$28.00
$25.00

Comes with votive holder.

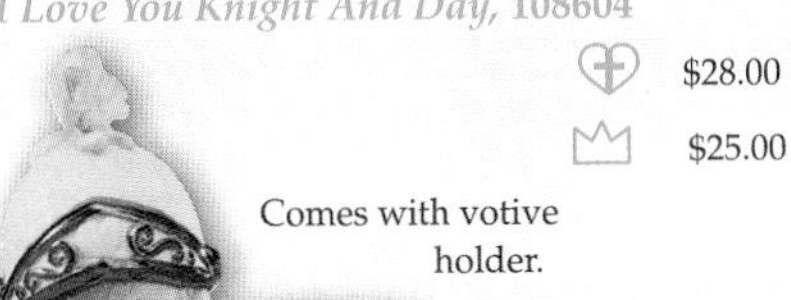

Retired 2003, Issue Price $25.00, '03

Purchased ________, Price $ ___________

☐ *Mom Hits A Home Run Every Day, 108606*

$100.00

Precious Moments Day at Wrigley Field, May 12, 2002.

Limited Ed. 10,000, '02

Purchased________ ,

Price $__________

☐ *The Greatest Gift Is A Friend, 109231*

$65.00 $63.00 $60.00 $58.00 $55.00 $53.00 $50.00 $48.00 $45.00 $45.00 $45.00 $45.00 $45.00

Retired 1999, Issue Price $30.00, '87

Purchased ________ , Price $ __________

☐ *Baby's First Christmas, 109401 (Ornament)*

$42.00

Dated Annual 1987, Issue Price $12.00, '87

Purchased__________ ,

Price $__________

☐ *Baby's First Christmas, 109428 (Ornament)*

$42.00

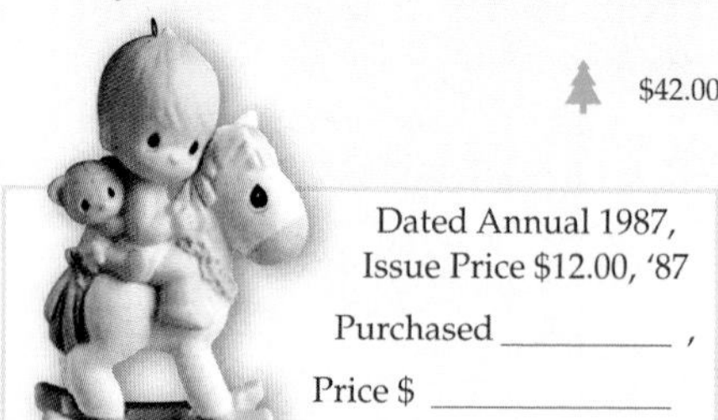

Dated Annual 1987, Issue Price $12.00, '87

Purchased __________ ,

Price $ __________

☐ *Isn't Eight Just Great, 109460*

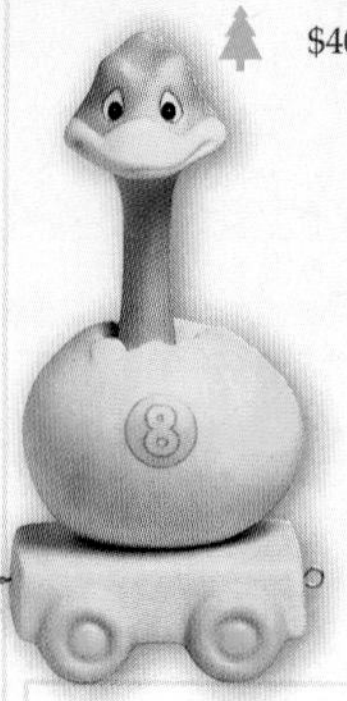

$40.00 $38.00 $35.00 $33.00 $30.00 $28.00 $28.00 $28.00 $25.00 $25.00 $25.0 $23.0 $23.0 $23.0 $23.0 $22.5 $22.5 $22.5 $22.5

Open, Issue Price $18.50, '88
Series: *Birthday Circus Train* — Age 8

Purchased ________ , Price $ __________

☐ *Wishing You Grr-eatness, 109479*

$40.00 $38.00 $35.00 $33.00 $30.00 $28.00 $28.00 $28.00 $25.00 $25.00 $25.0 $23.0 $23.0 $23.0 $23.0 $22.5 $22.5 $22.5 $22.5

Open, Issue Price $18.50, '88
Series: *Birthday Circus Train* — Age 7

Purchased ________ , Price $ __________

☐ *Believe The Impossible, 109487*

$95.0 $75.0 $70.0 $69.0 $68.0

Suspended 1991, Issue Price $35.00, '88

Purchased ________ , Price $ __________

Believe The Impossible, 109487R

$55.00

$50.00

Limited Ed., Issue Price $45.00, '00
Care-A-Van Exclusive

Purchased ________, Price $ __________

Happiness Divine, 109584

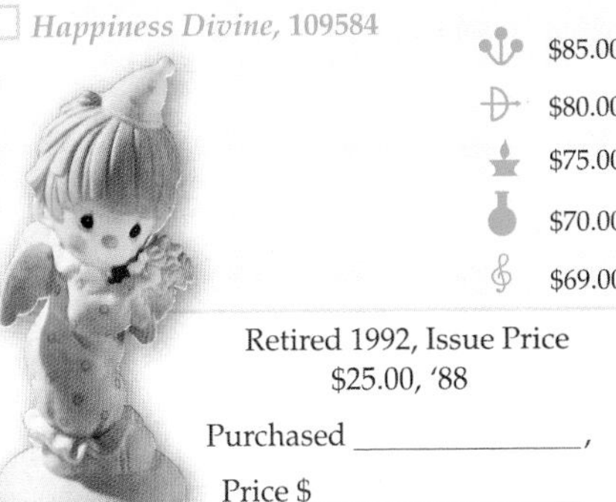

$85.00

$80.00

$75.00

$70.00

$69.00

Retired 1992, Issue Price $25.00, '88

Purchased ______________,

Price $ ______________

Peace On Earth, 109746 (Musical)

$150.00

$150.00

$145.00

$143.00

$140.00

$138.00

Suspended 1993, Issue Price $100.00, '88
Tune: "Hark! The Herald Angels Sing"

Purchased ________, Price $ __________

Wishing You A Yummy Christmas, 109754

$75.00 $70.00

$73.00 $65.00

$60.00

$58.00

$58.00

$55.00

Suspended 1994, Issue Price $35.00, '87

Purchased ________, Price $ __________

Love Is The Best Gift Of All, 109770 (Ornament)

$45.00

Dated Annual 1987, Issue Price $11.00, '87

Purchased ________, Price $ __________

We Gather Together To Ask The Lord's Blessing, 109762

$325.00 $305.00 $294.00

$310.00 $300.00 $293.00

$305.00 $295.00 $292.00

$291.00

Retired 1995, Issue Price $130.00, '87
Family Thanksgiving Set, Set of 6 plus cassette

Purchased ________, Price $ __________

There were reports of sets having two fathers or mothers instead of one of each. This does not increase the value.

☐ *Meowie Christmas, 109800*

$60.00
$58.00
$55.00
$53.00
$50.00
$48.00
$48.00
$45.00
$45.00
$43.00
$42.00
$40.00
$40.00

Retired 2000, Issue Price $30.00, '88
Purchased ________, Price $ ________

☐ *Oh What Fun It Is To Ride, 109819*

$150.00
$140.00
$135.00
$132.00
$130.00
$125.00
$123.00
$120.00
$118.00
$115.00
$115.00
$115.00

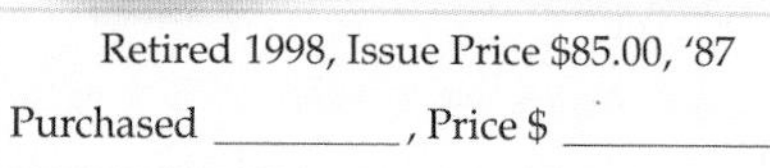

Retired 1998, Issue Price $85.00, '87
Purchased ________, Price $ ________

☐ *Love Is The Best Gift Of All, 109835 (Bell)*

$30.00

Dated Annual 1987, Issue Price $22.50, '87
Purchased ________, Price $ ________

☐ *Love Is The Best Gift Of All, 109843 (Thimble)*

$35.00

Dated Annual 1987, Issue Price $6.00, '87
Purchased ________,
Price $________

☐ *Wishing You A Happy Easter, 109886*

$55.00
$53.00
$50.00
$48.00
$48.00
$45.00
$45.00
$45.00
$43.00
$43.00
$40.00
$40.00
$40.00

Retired 1999, Issue Price $23.00, '88
Purchased ________, Price $ ________

☐ *Wishing You A Basket Full Of Blessings, 109924*

$55.00
$53.00
$50.00
$48.00
$48.00
$45.00
$45.00
$45.00
$43.00
$43.00
$40.00
$40.00
$40.00

Retired 1999, Issue Price $23.00, '88
Purchased ________, Price $ ________

Sending You My Love, 109967

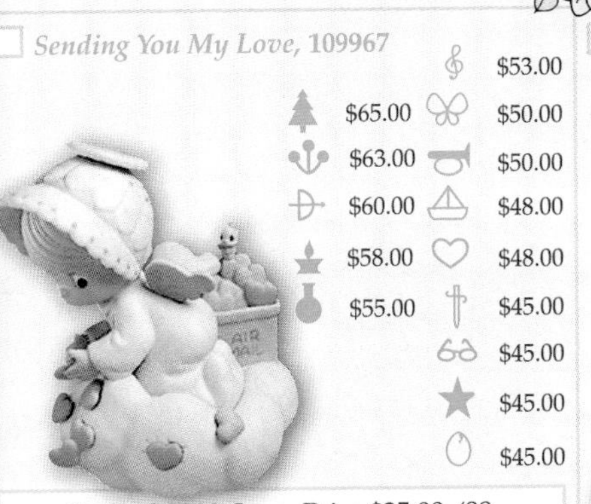

$65.00
$63.00
$60.00
$58.00
$55.00
$53.00
$50.00
$50.00
$48.00
$48.00
$45.00
$45.00
$45.00
$45.00

Retired 2000, Issue Price $35.00, '88
Series: *Heavenly Halos*

Purchased ________, Price $ ___________

Mommy I Love You, 109975

$48.00
$45.00
$43.00
$40.00
$40.00
$40.00
$38.00
$38.00
$35.00
$35.00
$35.00
$33.00
$33.00
$33.00
$30.00
$30.00
$30.00

Retired 2003, Issue Price $30.00, '87

Purchased ________, Price $ ___________

January, 109983

$85.00
$80.00
$78.00
$75.00
$73.00
$70.00
$68.00
$68.00
$65.00
$65.00
$58.00
$55.00
$55.00
$50.00
$50.00
$50.00

Retired 2002, Issue Price $37.50, '88
Series: *Calendar Girls*

Purchased ________, Price $ ___________

February, 109991

$75.00
$70.00
$68.00
$65.00
$63.00
$60.00
$58.00
$55.00
$53.00
$50.00
$48.00
$45.00
$43.00
$43.00
$40.00
$40.00

Retired 2002, Issue Price $27.50, '88
Series: *Calendar Girls*

Purchased ________, Price $ ___________

March, 110019

$75.00
$70.00
$68.00
$65.00
$63.00
$60.00
$58.00
$55.00
$53.00
$50.00
$48.00
$45.00
$43.00
$43.00
$40.00
$40.00

Retired 2002, Issue Price $37.50, '88
Series: *Calendar Girls*

Purchased ________, Price $ ___________

April, 110027

$125.00
$115.00
$110.00
$105.00
$100.00
$95.00
$85.00
$80.00
$75.00
$70.00
$65.00
$60.00
$55.00
$50.00
$45.00
$45.00

Retired 2002, Issue Price $30.00, '88
Series: *Calendar Girls*

Purchased ________, Price $ ___________

May, 110035

$125.00
$115.00
$110.00
$105.00
$100.00
$95.00
$85.00
$80.00
$75.00
$70.00
$65.00
$60.00
$55.00
$50.00
$45.00
$45.00

Retired 2002, Issue Price $25.00, '88
Series: *Calendar Girls*
Purchased ________, Price $ __________

June, 110043

$130.00
$120.00
$115.00
$110.00
$105.00
$100.00
$95.00
$90.00
$85.00
$80.00
$75.00
$70.00
$65.00
$60.00
$55.00
$55.00

Retired 2002, Issue Price $40.00, '88
Series: *Calendar Girls*
Purchased ________, Price $ __________

July, 110051

$85.00
$80.00
$77.00
$75.00
$73.00
$70.00
$65.00
$63.00
$60.00
$60.00
$58.00
$58.00
$55.00
$55.00
$53.00
$53.00

Retired 2002, Issue Price $35.00, '88
Series: *Calendar Girls*
Purchased ________, Price $ __________

August, 110078

$85.00
$80.00
$76.00
$73.00
$70.00
$68.00
$65.00
$63.00
$60.00
$60.00
$58.00
$58.00
$55.00
$55.00
$55.00
$55.00

Retired 2002, Issue Price $40.00, '88
Series: *Calendar Girls*
Purchased ________, Price $ __________

September, 110086

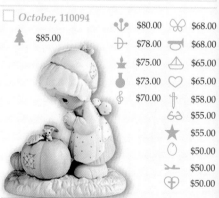

$85.00
$80.00
$75.00
$70.00
$68.00
$65.00
$63.00
$60.00
$58.00
$58.00
$53.00
$51.00
$50.00
$48.00
$48.00
$45.00

Retired 2002, Issue Price $27.50, '88
Series: *Calendar Girls*
Purchased ________, Price $ __________

October, 110094

$85.00
$80.00
$78.00
$75.00
$73.00
$70.00
$68.00
$68.00
$65.00
$65.00
$58.00
$55.00
$55.00
$50.00
$50.00
$50.00

Retired 2002, Issue Price $35.00, '88
Series: *Calendar Girls*
Purchased ________, Price $ __________

November, 110108

$105.00
$95.00
$90.00
$85.00
$80.00
$75.00
$70.00
$65.00
$60.00
$55.00
$50.00
$45.00
$45.00
$40.00
$40.00

Retired 2002, Issue Price $32.50, '88
Series: *Calendar Girls*

Purchased ________, Price $ __________

December, 110116

$90.00
$85.00
$80.00
$75.00
$73.00
$70.00
$68.00
$65.00
$60.00
$55.00
$53.00
$50.00
$48.00
$45.00
$43.00

Retired 2002, Issue Price $27.50, '88
Series: *Calendar Girls*

Purchased ________, Price $ __________

Precious Moments From The Beginning, 110238

$175.00
$175.00

Limited Ed., Issue Price $175.00, '03
25th Anniversary Celebration CCR Exclusive

Purchased ________, Price $ __________

God Loveth A Cheerful Giver, 110239 (Ornament)

$25.00
$25.00
$25.00
$25.00

Open, Issue Price $25.00, '03
25th Anniversary Celebration
CCR Exclusive

Purchased ________, Price $ __________

I Just Go Bats Over You, 110260

$20.00
$20.00
$20.00
$20.00

Open, Issue Price $20.00, '03
Series: *Animal Affections*

Purchased ________, Price $ __________

It's Down Hill All The Way, Congratulations, 110261

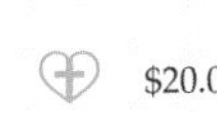
$20.00
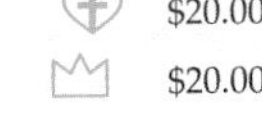
$20.00

Open, Issue Price $20.00, '03
Series: *Animal Affections*

Purchased ________, Price $ __________

Are You Lonesome Tonight? 110262

$20.00 $20.00
$20.00 $20.00

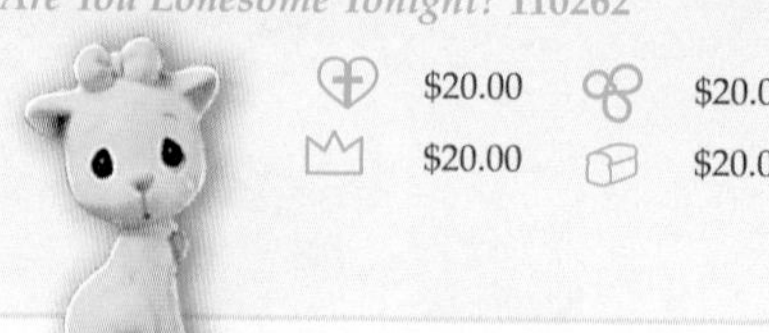

Open, Issue Price $20.00, '03
Series: *Animal Affections*
Purchased ________ ,
Price $ ________

Remember To Reach For The Stars, 110263

$20.00 $20.00
$20.00 $20.00

Open, Issue Price $20.00, '03
Series: *Animal Affections*
Purchased________ ,
Price $ ________

I Love You A Bushel And A Peck, 110265

$20.00
$20.00
$20.00
$20.00

Open, Issue Price $20.00, '03
Series: *Animal Affections*
Purchased ________, Price $ ________

A Chip Off The Old Block, 110266

$20.00
$20.00
$20.00
$20.00

Open, Issue Price $20.00, '03
Series: *Animal Affections*
Purchased ________, Price $ ________

A Mother's Love Is Beyond Measure, 110267

$27.50
$27.50

Retired 2003, Issue Price
$27.50, '03
Purchased ________ ,
Price $ ________

My Heart Belongs To You, 110268

$125.00
$125.00

First "mature" or "elongated" figurine to feature both boy and girl.

Limited Ed., Issue Price $125.00, '03
Purchased ________, Price $ ________

Friendship Is Always A Sweet Surprise, 110269

$35.00
$35.00

Limited Ed., Issue Price $35.00, '02
Carlton Cards Exclusive
Purchased ________, Price $ ________

☐ *Reisen In Deutschland, 110270 (Medallion)*

UM $300.00

This piece was given to members who went to Germany in 2002.

Limited Ed. 106, Gift, '02
Germany Tour Exclusive – May 2002

Purchased ________, Price $ ____________

☐ *Love Is The Best Gift Of All, 110930*

$35.00

Dated Annual 1987, Issue Price $22.50, '87

Purchased __________,

Price $____________

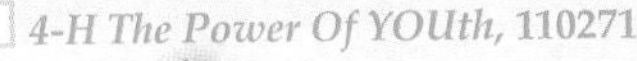

☐ *4-H The Power Of YOUth, 110271*

UM $35.00
$30.00

Limited Ed., Issue Price $30.00, '02
Chapel Exclusive,
4-H Commemorative

Purchased____________,

Price $____________

☐ *I'm A Possibility, 111120 (Ornament)*

$40.00 $35.00
$38.00 $33.00

Suspended 1990, Issue Price $11.00, '87

Purchased __________,

Price $ ____________

☐ *Love Is A Heavenly Song, 110367*

$125.00
$125.00
$125.00
$125.00

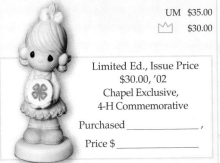

Open, Issue Price $125.00, '03
Easter Seals Exclusive
Series: *Heaven's Grace*
Second Issue

Purchased______,

Price $ __________

☐ *Faith Takes The Plunge, 111155*

$75.00 $45.00
$55.00 $45.00
$50.00 $45.00
$48.00 $45.00
$43.00
$43.00
$40.00
$40.00

At some point during the 1988 production, the expression on the face was changed from a smile to a "determined frown." The smiling piece is often referred to as the "Smiling Plunger." Value for Cedar Tree Smiling is $50.00. Flower Smiling is valued at $48.00.

Suspended 1998, Issue Price $27.50, '88

Purchased ________, Price $ ____________

☐ *Wish You Were Hare, 110447*

$40.00
$40.00
$40.00

Open, Issue Price $40.00, '03

Purchased ________, Price $ ____________

'Tis The Season, 111163

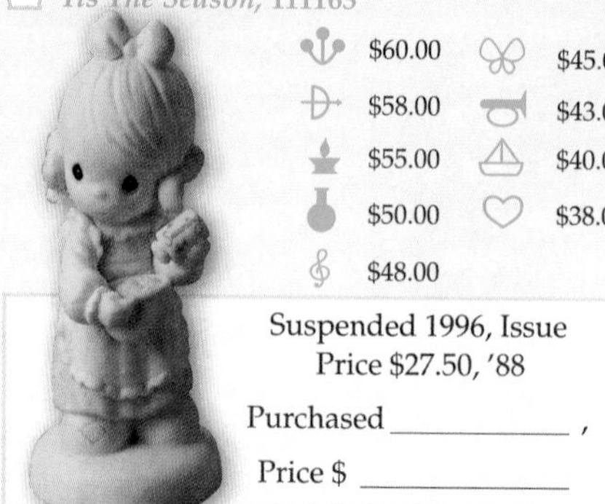

$60.00 $45.00
$58.00 $43.00
$55.00 $40.00
$50.00 $38.00
$48.00

Suspended 1996, Issue Price $27.50, '88

Purchased ________ ,

Price $ ________

O Come, Let Us Adore Him, 111333

$240.00 $230.00
$235.00 $225.00
$220.00

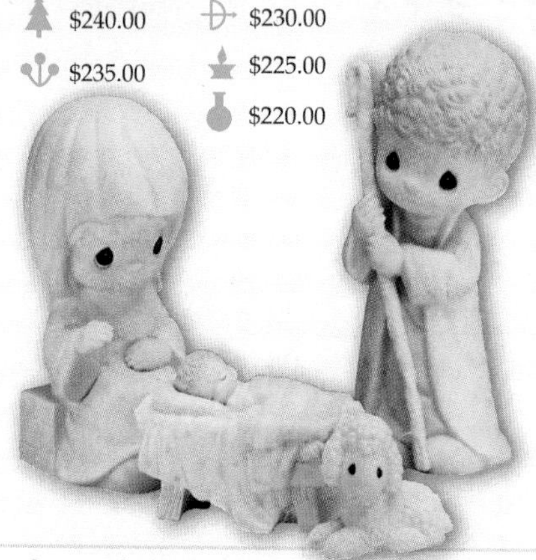

Suspended 1991, Issue Price $200.00, '87
Large (9") Nativity, Set of 4

Purchased ________ , Price $ ________

Ma-Holo-Day Wishes For You, 111413

$50.00

2002 Collector's Weekend, December 6 – 8.

Limited Ed. 1,200, Issue Price $35.00, '02
Chapel Exclusive

Purchased ________ , Price $ ________

Retailer's Wreath, 111465

$200.00

On some wreaths, the *Have a Heavenly Christmas* ornament has the inscription "Heaven Bound" upside down. The value for the wreath with this error is $200.00.

Promotional Item, Issue Price $150.00, '87
Purchased ________ , Price $ ________

You're Worth Waiting On, 111749

UM $35.00
$35.00
$35.00

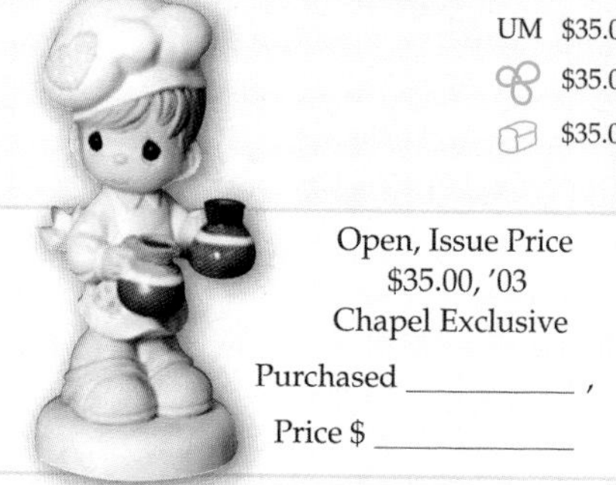

Open, Issue Price $35.00, '03
Chapel Exclusive

Purchased ________ ,

Price $ ________

Everybody's Grandmother, 111752

UM $50.00
$50.00
$50.00

Open, Issue Price $50.00, '03
Chapel Exclusive

Purchased ________ , Price $ ________

☐ *Heather (If You Could Only See Heaven),* 111753

UM $40.00
$40.00
$40.00

Open, Issue Price
$40.00, '03
Chapel Exclusive
Purchased ______ ,
Price $__________

☐ *Fairytales Can Come True,* 111754

UM $100.00
$100.00
$100.00

Open, Issue Price $100.00, '03
Chapel Exclusive
Purchased ________, Price $ __________

☐ *Every Precious Moment Needs A Smile,* 111757

UM $35.00
$35.00
$35.00

Open, Issue Price $35.00, '03
Chapel Exclusive
Purchased ________, Price $ __________

☐ *Holding Him Close To My Heart,* 111760

UM $30.00
$30.00
$30.00

Open, Issue Price
$30.00, '03
Chapel Exclusive
Purchased__________ ,
Price $ __________

☐ *Holding Him Close To My Heart,* 111762 (Ornament)

UM $20.00
$20.00
$20.00

Open, Issue Price
$20.00, '03
Chapel Exclusive
Purchased__________,
Price $ __________

☐ *Welcome And God Bless You,* 111765 (Plaque)

UM $45.00

Open, Issue Price $45.00, '03
Chapel Exclusive
Purchased ________, Price $ __________

☐ *Mommy's Little Angel* (Brunette), 111869

$25.00
$25.00
$25.00
$25.00

Open, Issue Price
$25.00, '03
Purchased __________ ,
Price $__________

☐ *Mommy's Little Angel* (Blonde), 111870

$25.00
$25.00
$25.00
$25.00

Open, Issue Price $25.00, '03
Purchased_____________ ,
Price $ _____________

☐ *A Time To Wish You A Merry Christmas*, 111895

$50.00
$50.00

Open, Issue Price $50.00, '04
Purchased _________, Price $ ____________

☐ *Your Love Means The World To Me*, 111896

$50.00
$50.00

Open, Issue Price $50.00, '04
Purchased ________ ,
Price $ ___________

☐ *With A Little Help From Above*, 111897

$50.00
$50.00

Open, Issue Price $50.00, '04
Purchased _________ ,
Price $ ___________

☐ *Simple Pleasures Make Holiday Treasures*, 111898

$125.00 $125.00
$125.00

Open, Issue Price $125.00, '03
Set of 5
Purchased _________, Price $ ___________

☐ *The Lord Bless You And Keep You*, 111904

$125.00
$100.00
$75.00
$75.00

Open, Issue Price $70.00, '03
Japanese Exclusive, Set of 5
Purchased _________, Price $ ___________

Mommy, I Love You, 112143

$75.00
$65.00
$60.00
$55.00
$53.00
$50.00
$48.00
$40.00
$38.00
$35.00

$45.00
$45.00
$43.00
$43.00
$40.00

Retired 2001, Issue Price $22.50, '88

Purchased ________, Price $ ___________

A Tub Full Of Love, 112313

$55.00
$53.00
$50.00

$48.00
$45.00
$45.00
$40.00

$40.00
$40.00
$40.00
$38.00
$38.00
$38.00
$35.00
$35.00
$35.00
$35.00
$35.00
$35.00

Open, Issue Price $22.50, '87

Purchased ________, Price $ ___________

Retailer's Wreath Bell, 112348 (Ornament)

$70.00

Promotional Item, '87

Purchased___________,

Price $ ___________

You Have Touched So Many Hearts, 112356 (Ornament)

$35.00
$30.00
$28.00

$25.00
$25.00
$25.00
$23.00
$23.00
$20.00
$20.00

Retired 1997, Issue Price $11.00, '87

Purchased ________, Price $ ___________

Waddle I Do Without You, 112364 (Ornament)

$40.00
$38.00
$35.00
$30.00
$28.00
$25.00

$25.00
$25.00
$23.00
$23.00
$23.00
$20.00
$20.00

Retired 1999, Issue Price $11.00, '87

Purchased ________, Price $ ___________

I'm Sending You A White Christmas, 112372 (Ornament)

$33.00
$30.00
$25.00

$23.00
$20.00
$19.00

Suspended 1992, Issue Price $11.00, '87

Purchased ___________,

Price $ ___________

He Cleansed My Soul, 112380 (Ornament)

$45.00
$43.00

$40.00
$38.00
$35.00
$33.00
$30.00

$28.00
$28.00
$25.00
$25.00
$20.00
$20.00

Retired 1999, Issue Price $12.00, '87

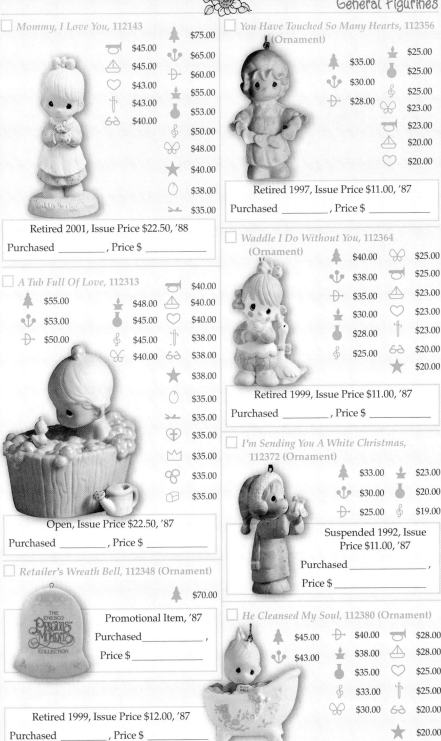

Purchased ________, Price $ ___________

Our First Christmas Together, 112399 (Ornament)

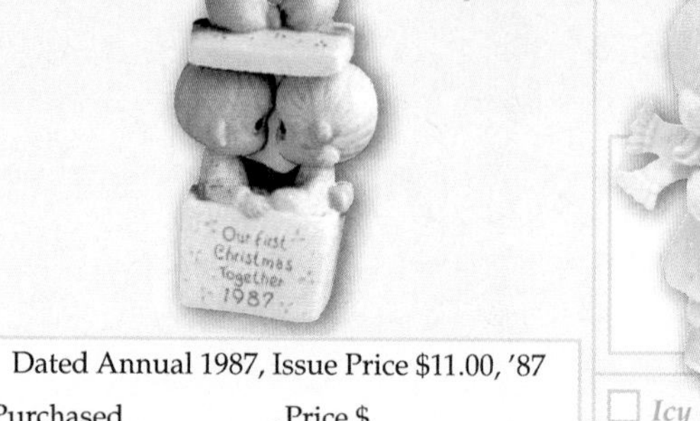

$30.00

Dated Annual 1987, Issue Price $11.00, '87

Purchased ________, Price $ ___________

I'm Sending You A White Christmas, 112402 (Musical)

$140.00
$138.00
$135.00
$130.00
$125.00
$120.00
$115.00

Retired 1993, Issue Price $55.00, '87
Tune: "White Christmas"

Purchased ________, Price $ ___________

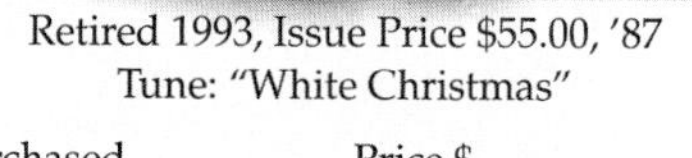

You Have Touched So Many Hearts, 112577 (Musical)

$100.00
$95.00
$93.00
$90.00
$85.00
$83.00
$80.00
$78.00
$75.00
$70.00

Suspended 1996, Issue Price $50.00, '88
Tune: "Everybody Loves Somebody"

Purchased ________, Price $ ___________

Icy Good Times Ahead, 112839

$40.00

Dated Annual 2003, Issue Price $35.00, '03

Purchased ________,

Price $ ___________

Icy Good Times Ahead, 112840 (Ornament)

$25.00

Dated Annual 2003, Issue Price $20.00, '03

Purchased ___________,

Price $ ___________

Our First Christmas Together, 112841 (Ornament)

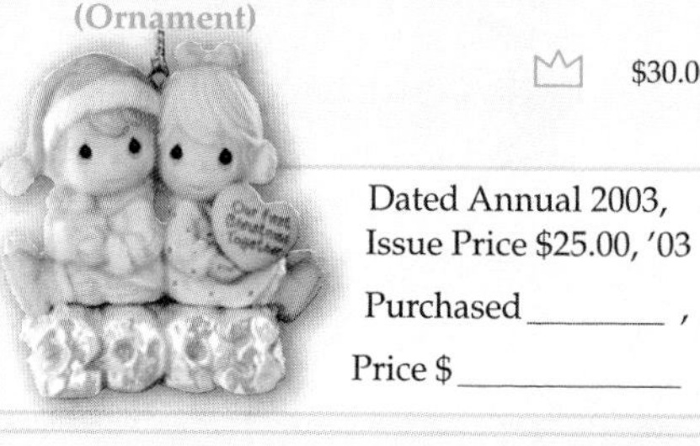

$30.00

Dated Annual 2003, Issue Price $25.00, '03

Purchased ________,

Price $ ___________

Baby's First Christmas, 112842 (Ornament)

$25.00

Dated Annual 2003, Issue Price $20.00, '03

Purchased ________,

Price $ ___________

Baby's First Christmas, 112843 (Ornament)

$25.00

Dated Annual 2003, Issue Price $20.00, '03

Purchased___________,

Price $ ___________

A Nurse's Care Is The Best Medicine, 112845

$30.00
$30.00
$30.00

Open, Issue Price
$30.00, '03

Purchased ________,

Price $ ________

Everyday Hero, 112857

$30.00
$30.00
$30.00

Open, Issue Price
$30.00, '03

Purchased ________,

Price $ ________

Take A Note, You're Great! 112858

$30.00
$30.00
$30.00

Open, Issue Price
$30.00, '03

Purchased ________,

Price $ ________

Coach, You're A Real Sport, 112859

$30.00
$30.00
$30.00

Open, Issue Price
$30.00, '03

Purchased ________,

Price $ ________

Teacher, You're A Precious Work Of Art, 112861

$30.00
$30.00
$30.00

Open, Issue Price
$30.00, '03

Purchased ________,

Price $ ________

It's Only Gauze I Care, 112862

$30.00
$30.00
$30.00

Open, Issue Price
$30.00, '03

Purchased ________,

Price $ ________

Bearing Gifts Of Great Joy, 112863

$35.00
$35.00
$35.00

Open, Issue Price
$35.00, '03
Nativity Addition

Purchased ________,

Price $ ________

I Can't Give You Anything But Love, 112864

$30.00
$30.00
$30.00

Open, Issue Price
$30.00, '03

Purchased ________,

Price $ ________

☐ *To A Niece With A Bubbly Personality, 112870*

Crown	$30.00
Clover	$30.00
Box	$30.00

Open, Issue Price $25.00, '03

Purchased ________ ,

Price $ ____________

☐ *Squashed With Love, 112874*

Crown	$45.00
Clover	$45.00
Box	$45.00

Open, Issue Price $45.00, '03

Purchased ________ , Price $ __________

☐ *I-cy Potential In You, 112875 (Ornament)*

Crown	$30.00
Clover	$30.00
Box	$30.00

Dated Annual 2003, Issue Price $30.00, '03

Purchased ________ ,

Price $ ____________

☐ *May The Holidays Keep You Bright Eyed And Bushy Tailed, 112876 (Ornament)*

Crown	$20.00

Dated Annual 2003, Issue Price $20.00, '03

Series: *Birthday Collection*

Purchased ________ ,

Price $ ____________

☐ *God Rest Ye Merry Gentlemen, 112878*

Crown	$55.00
Clover	$55.00

Retired 2004, Issue Price $55.00, '03

Series: *Christmas Remembered*

Purchased ________ , Price $ __________

☐ *May Your Heart Be Filled With Christmas Joy, 112880*

Crown	$50.00
Clover	$50.00
Box	$50.00

Open, Issue Price $50.00, '03

Series: *Christmas Remembered* – 4th Edition

Purchased ________ , Price $ __________

☐ *Warmest Wishes For The Holidays, 112881*

Crown	$50.00
Clover	$50.00
Box	$50.00

Open, Issue Price $50.00, '03

Purchased ________ , Price $ __________

You're A Gem Of A Friend, 112882

$37.50
$37.50
$37.50

Open, Issue Price $37.50, '03

Purchased ________ ,

Price $ ____________

Joy Is The Music Of Angels, 112966

$125.00
$125.00
$125.00
$125.00

Open, Issue Price $125.00, '03

Easter Seals – Series: *Heaven's Grace* – 3rd Edition

Purchased ________, Price $ ____________

Hope Is A Gentle Melody, 112967

$125.00
$125.00

Open, Issue Price $125.00, '04

Easter Seals – Series: *Heaven's Grace* – 4th Edition

Purchased ________, Price $ ____________

Happines Is A Song From Heaven, 112969

$125.00
$125.00

Open, Issue Price $125.00, '04

Easter Seals – Series: *Heaven's Grace* – 5th Edition

Purchased ________, Price $ ____________

Mom, I Always Have A Ball With You, 112995

$80.00

Figurine given at "Precious Moments Day," May 5, 2003, at Wrigley Field, Chicago, Illinois.

Limited Ed. 10,000, Gift, '03

Purchased ________, Price $ ____________

A Mother's Love Is Beyond Measure, 113037

$30.00
$30.00

Retired 2003, Issue Price $30.00, '03

Purchased ________, Price $ ____________

A Mother's Story Is One Of Love, 113369C

$40.00

$40.00

Limited Ed., Issue Price $40.00, '03 Carlton Cards Exclusive

Purchased ________, Price $ ___________

Hold On To Your Faith, 113946

$35.00

$35.00

$35.00

Open, Issue Price $35.00, '03

Purchased ________, Price $ ___________

I Love You Forever And Always, 113944

$65.00

$65.00

$65.00

Limited Ed., Issue Price $65.00, '03

Purchased ________, Price $ ___________

Hold On To Your Faith, 113947

$35.00

$35.00

$35.00

Open, Issue Price $35.00, '03

Purchased ________, Price $ ___________

You Have A Certain Glow About You, 113945

$32.50

$32.50

$32.50

Limited Ed., Issue Price $32.50, '03

Purchased ________, Price $ ___________

This Little Light Of Mine, I'm Gonna Let It Shine, 113949

$35.00

$35.00

$35.00

Limited Ed., Issue Price $35.00, '03

Purchased ________, Price $ ___________

☐ *To My Forever Friend*, 113956 (Ornament)

$35.00 $25.00
$30.00 $24.00
$29.00 $23.00
$28.00 $22.00
$27.00 $21.00
$26.00 $20.00

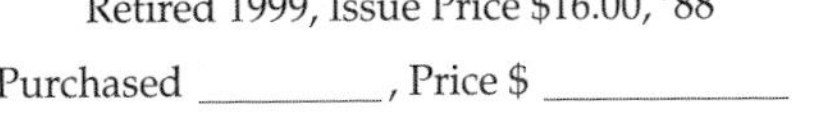

Retired 1999, Issue Price $16.00, '88
Purchased ________, Price $ __________

☐ *A Child Is A Gift Of God*, 113962

$45.00
$45.00
$45.00

Open, Issue Price $45.00, '03
Purchased ________, Price $ __________

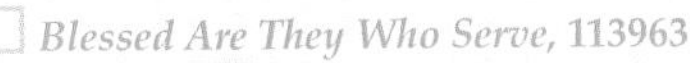

☐ *Blessed Are They Who Serve*, 113963

$30.00
$30.00
$30.00

Open, Issue Price $30.00, '03
Purchased ________,
Price $__________

☐ *Smile Along The Way*, 113964 (Ornament)

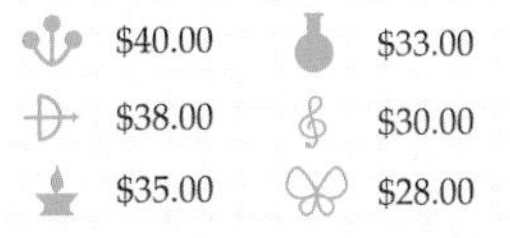

$40.00 $33.00
$38.00 $30.00
$35.00 $28.00

Suspended 1993, Issue Price $15.00, '88
Purchased ________, Price $ __________

☐ *You Shall Receive A Crown Of Glory*, 113965

$35.00
$35.00
$35.00

Limited Ed., Issue Price $35.00, '03
Purchased ________, Price $ __________

☐ *His Blessings Are Without Measure*, 113966

$40.00
$40.00
$40.00

Open, Issue Price $40.00, '03
Purchased ________,
Price $ __________

☐ *God Sent You Just In Time*, 113972 (Ornament)

$40.00
$38.00
$35.00
$33.00

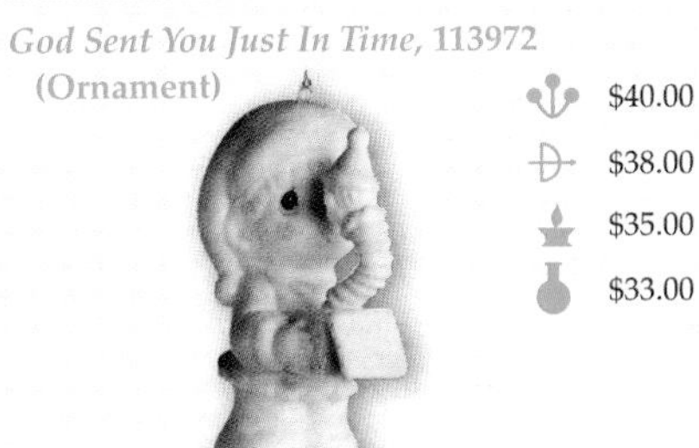

Suspended 1991, Issue Price $13.50, '88
Purchased ________, Price $ __________

Rejoice O Earth, 113980 (Ornament)

$40.00
$38.00
$35.00
$33.00

Retired 1991, Issue Price $13.50, '88
Purchased ________, Price $ ____________

Glad We See Eye To Eye, 113991

$27.50
$27.50
$27.50

Open, Issue Price $27.50, '03
Purchased ________, Price $ ____________

Cheers To The Leader, 113999 (Ornament)

$35.00
$34.00
$32.00
$30.00

Suspended 1991, Issue Price $13.50, '88
Purchased____________,
Price $_______________

My Love Will Never Let You Go, 114006

$35.00
$34.00
$32.00
$30.00

Suspended 1991, Issue Price $13.50, '88
Purchased ____________ ,
Price $_______________

If The Shoe Fits, Buy It! 114010

$40.00
$40.00
$40.00

Open, Issue Price $40.00, '03
Purchased ________, Price $ ____________

I'm Sorry, 114011

$30.00
$30.00
$30.00

Open, Issue Price $30.00, '03
Purchased ________, Price $ ____________

No Rest For The Weary, 114012

$35.00
$35.00
$35.00

Open, Issue Price $35.00, '03
Purchased ________, Price $ ____________

☐ *You Are The Sunshine Of My Life*, 114013

$35.00
$35.00
$35.00

Open, Issue Price $35.00, '03
Purchased ________, Price $ ____________

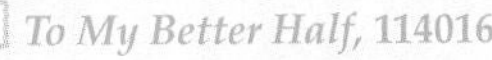

☐ *To My Better Half*, 114016

$35.00
$35.00
$35.00

Open, Issue Price $35.00, '03
Purchased ________, Price $ ____________

☐ *This Too Shall Pass*, 114014

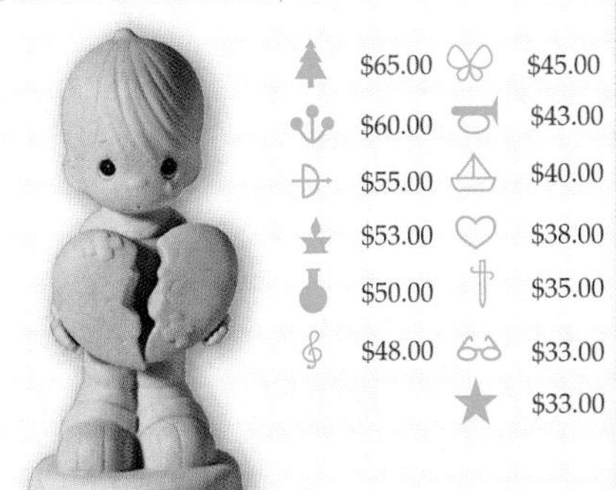

$65.00
$60.00
$55.00
$53.00
$50.00
$48.00
$45.00
$43.00
$40.00
$38.00
$35.00
$33.00
$33.00

Retired 1999, Issue Price $23.00, '88
Purchased ________, Price $ ____________

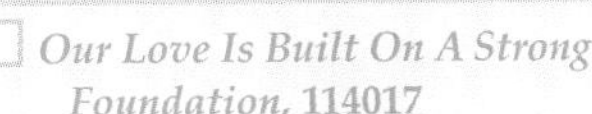

☐ *Our Love Is Built On A Strong Foundation*, 114017

$35.00
$35.00
$35.00

Open, Issue Price $35.00, '03
Purchased ________, Price $ ____________

☐ *You're Due For A Lifetime Of Happiness*, 114015

$37.50
$37.50
$37.50

Open, Issue Price $37.50, '03
Purchased ________, Price $ ____________

☐ *Dear Friend, My Love For You Will Never Fade Away*, 114018

$60.00
$60.00
$60.00

Open, Issue Price $60.00, '03
Purchased ________, Price $ ____________

☐ *Friends Of A Feather Shop Together, 114019*

$55.00
$55.00
$55.00

Open, Issue Price $55.00, '03
Purchased ________, Price $ ____________

☐ *Let's Always Preserve Our Friendship, 114020*

$37.50
$37.50
$37.50

Open, Issue Price $37.50, '03
Purchased ________, Price $ ____________

☐ *Happy Birthday To Our Love, 114021*

$50.00
$50.00
$50.00

Open, Issue Price $50.00, '03
Purchased ________, Price $ ____________

☐ *The Good Lord Has Blessed Us Tenfold, 114022*

$245.00
$230.00

Annual 1988, Issue Price $90.00, '88
Tenth Anniversary Commemorative
Purchased ________, Price $ ____________

☐ *Nothing Is Stronger Than Our Love, 114023*

$30.00
$30.00
$30.00

Open, Issue Price $30.00, '03
Purchased ________, Price $ ____________

☐ *You Arrr A Treasure To Me, 114026*

$50.00
$50.00
$50.00

Open, Issue Price $50.00, '03
Purchased ________, Price $ ____________

☐ *Hope Blooms In A Garden Of Glory,* 114027

Crown	$45.00
Clover	$45.00
Box	$45.00

Open, Issue Price $45.00, '03
Series: *Spring Is In Bloom*

Purchased ________, Price $ ___________

☐ *Kindness Of Spirit Knows No Bounds,* 114028

Crown	$45.00
Clover	$45.00
Box	$45.00

Open, Issue Price $45.00, '03
Series: *Spring Is In Bloom*

Purchased ________, Price $ ___________

☐ *Humble Prayers Make Hearts Bloom,* 114029

Crown	$45.00
Clover	$45.00
Box	$45.00

Open, Issue Price $45.00, '03
Series: *Spring Is In Bloom*

Purchased ________, Price $ ___________

☐ *Dreams Bloom With A Seed Of Faith,* 114031

Crown	$45.00
Clover	$45.00
Box	$45.00

Open, Issue Price $45.00, '03
Series: *Spring Is In Bloom*

Purchased ________, Price $ ___________

☐ *I Love You More Every Day,* 114032

Crown	$35.00
Clover	$35.00
Box	$35.00

Open, Issue Price $35.00, '03

Purchased ________, Price $ ___________

☐ *Friends Make Life More Fun,* 114918

Crown	$80.00

Limited Ed., Issue Price $80.00, '03
Boys & Girls Club Commemorative

Purchased ________, Price $ ___________

☐ *I Will Never Leaf You, 114958*

$40.00

Open, Issue Price
$40.00, '05

Purchased ____ ,

Price $ _______

☐ *You Are My Main Event, 115231*

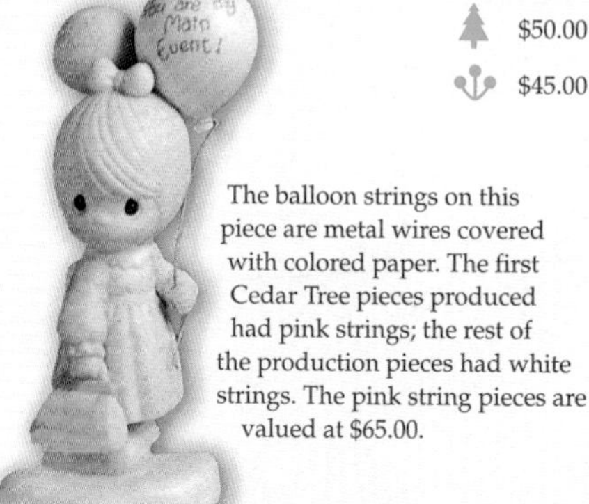

$50.00

$45.00

The balloon strings on this piece are metal wires covered with colored paper. The first Cedar Tree pieces produced had pink strings; the rest of the production pieces had white strings. The pink string pieces are valued at $65.00.

Annual 1988, Issue Price $30.00, '88
Special Event

Purchased ________, Price $ ___________

☐ *Your Love Reigns Forever In My Heart, 115248*

$45.00

$45.00

$45.00

Open, Issue Price $45.00, '03
Chapel Exclusive

Purchased ________, Price $ ___________

☐ *Some Bunny's Sleeping, 115274*

$30.00 $25.00

$28.00 $24.00

$27.00 $23.00

$26.00 $22.00

$21.00

Suspended 1996, Issue Price $15.00, '88
Nativity Addition

Purchased ________, Price $ ___________

☐ *Baby's First Christmas, 115282 (Ornament)*

$30.00

Dated Annual 1988, Issue Price $15.00, '88

Purchased ________, Price $ ___________

☐ *Our First Christmas Together, 115290*

$85.00

$75.00

$70.00

$65.00

Suspended 1991, Issue Price $50.00, '88

Purchased ________, Price $ ___________

☐ *Time To Wish You A Merry Christmas, 115304 (Bell)*

$38.00

Dated Annual 1988, Issue Price $25.00, '88

Purchased ____________ ,

Price $ ______________

☐ *Time To Wish You A Merry Christmas, 115312 (Thimble)*

$35.00

Dated Annual 1988, Issue Price $7.00, '88

Purchased ______________ ,

Price $ ________________

☐ *Time To Wish You A Merry Christmas, 115320 (Ornament)*

$48.00

Dated Annual 1988, Issue Price $13.00, '88

Purchased ____________ ,

Price $______________

☐ *Time To Wish You A Merry Christmas, 115339*

$50.00

Dated Annual 1988, Issue Price $24.00, '88

Purchased ________ ,

Price $ ____________

☐ *Blessed Are They That Overcome, 115479*

Easter Seals Lily missing on all decals.

$35.00

$30.00

☐ *You Are Such A Heavenly Host, 115625*

$37.50

Limited Ed. 5,000, Issue Price $37.50, '03
2003 Fall Catalog Exclusive

Purchased__________ ,

Price $ ____________

☐ *Let's Sea Where This Friendship Takes Us, 115654*

$45.00

$45.00

Open, Issue Price $45.00, '04
Series: *Sea Of Friendship*, Fourth Series

Purchased_________ ,

Price $ ___________

☐ *La Quinceañera, 115871*

$45.00

$45.00

$45.00

Annual 1988, Issue Price $27.50, '88

Purchased ________ , Price $ ___________

Open, Issue Price $45.00, '03

Purchased ________ , Price $ ___________

☐ *Love From The First Impression* — Boy, 115898

$30.00

$30.00

Includes a coupon book that can be personalized.

Open, Issue Price $30.00, '04

Purchased ________, Price $ __________

☐ *Love From The First Impression* — Girl, 115899

$30.00

$30.00

Includes a coupon book that can be personalized.

Open, Issue Price $30.00, '04

Purchased ________, Price $ __________

☐ *Mommy & Me* — Boy, 115900

$25.00

$25.00

$25.00

Open, Issue Price $25.00, '04

Purchased ________, Price $ __________

☐ *Mommy & Me* — Girl, 115901

$25.00

$25.00

$25.00

Open, Issue Price $25.00, '04

Purchased ____________,

Price $ ____________

☐ *Grandma & Me* — Boy, 115902

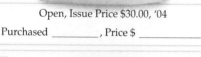

$25.00

$25.00

$25.00

Open, Issue Price $25.00, '04

Purchased ____________,

Price $ ____________

☐ *Grandma & Me* — Girl, 115903

$25.00

$25.00

$25.00

Open, Issue Price $25.00, '04

Purchased ____________,

Price $ ____________

☐ *Godmother & Me* — Boy, 115904

$25.00

$25.00

$25.00

Open, Issue Price $25.00, '04

Purchased __________,

Price $ ____________

☐ *Godmother & Me — Girl, 115905*

$25.00
$25.00

Open, Issue Price $25.00, '04
Purchased ________, Price $ __________

☐ *Like Father, Like Son, 115906*

$55.00
$55.00

Open, Issue Price $55.00, '04
Purchased ________, Price $ __________

☐ *How Do You Spell Mom, 115907*

$37.50 $37.50

Retired 2004, Issue Price $37.50, '04
Purchased ________, Price $ __________

☐ *Our Love Was Meant To Be, 115909*

$50.00
$50.00

Open, Issue Price $50.00, '04
Purchased ________, Price $ __________

☐ *A Whole Year Filled With Special Moments — First Anniversary, 115910*

$50.00
$50.00

Open, Issue Price $50.00, '04
Purchased ________, Price $ __________

☐ *Our Love Still Sparkles In Your Eyes — 25th Anniversary, 115911*

$50.00
$50.00

Open, Issue Price $50.00, '04
Purchased ________, Price $ __________

We Share A Love Forever Young — 50th Anniversary, 115912

$50.00

$50.00

Open, Issue Price $50.00, '04

Purchased ________, Price $ ___________

You Are The Apple Of My Eye, 115915

$37.50

$37.50

Limited Ed. 7,500, Issue Price $37.50, '04
Series: *Fruitful Delights*

Purchased ________, Price $ ___________

Orange You The Sweetest Thing, 115913

$37.50

$37.50

Limited Ed. 7,500, Issue Price $37.50, '04
Series: *Fruitful Delights*

Purchased ________, Price $ ___________

You're A-peeling To Me, 115914

$37.50

$37.50

Limited Ed. 7,500, Issue Price $37.50, '04
Series: *Fruitful Delights*

Purchased ________, Price $ ___________

You're Pear-fectly Sweet, 115917

$37.50

$37.50

Limited Ed. 7,500, Issue Price $37.50, '04
Series: *Fruitful Delights*

Purchased ________, Price $ ___________

You're Just Peachy, 115918

$37.50

$37.50

Limited Ed. 7,500, Issue Price $37.50, '04
Series: *Fruitful Delights*

Purchased ________, Price $ ___________

Girls Rule, 115919

$35.00

$35.00

Open, Issue Price $35.00, '04

Purchased ________, Price $ __________

Sixteen... Sweet! 115920

$37.50

$37.50

Open, Issue Price $37.50, '04

Purchased________ ,

Price $__________

A Bright And Shining Moment, 115921

$35.00

Limited Ed., Issue Price $35.00, '04

CCR & DSR Event Piece

Purchased ________ ,

Price $ __________

May Love Blossom Around You, 115922

$150.00

$150.00

Limited Ed. 7,500, Issue Price $150.00, '04

Purchased ________, Price $ __________

A Special Moment Just For You, 115923

$45.00

Limited Ed., Issue Price $45.00, '04

CCR Exclusive

Purchased ________, Price $ __________

May Love Blossom Around You, 115925 (Ornament)

$20.00

Limited Ed., Issue Price $35.00, '04

CCR Exclusive

Purchased ________, Price $ __________

☐ *Happiness Is Being A Mom, 115926*

$50.00
$50.00

Limited Ed., Issue Price $50.00, '04
Carlton Cards and American Greetings
Early Release

Purchased ________, Price $ ___________

☐ *Express Who You Are And You'll Be A Star, 116611*

$35.00
$35.00

Open, Issue Price $35.00, '04
2004 Authorized Dealer Exclusive

Purchased ________, Price $ ___________

☐ *Friends Let You Be You, 116612*

$50.00
$50.00

Limited Ed., Issue Price $30.00, '04
2004 *PM Rocks* Tour Exclusive

Purchased__________,

Price $ ___________

☐ *Christmas Around The World, 116710*

$35.00

Limited Ed. 1,100, Issue Price $35.00, '03
2003 Christmas Event

Purchased ________, Price $ ___________

☐ *Praise Him With The Sound Of The Trumpet, 116712*

$37.50
$37.50

Open, Issue Price $37.50, '04
Chapel Exclusive

Purchased ________, Price $ ___________

☐ *It's Your Birthday, Live It Large, 116945*

$25.00
$25.00
$25.00

Open, Issue Price $25.00, '03
Series: *Birthday Train* — Age 14

Purchased ________, Price $ ___________

☐ *It's Your Birthday, Go Bananas,* 116946

$25.00

$25.00

$25.00

Open, Issue Price
$25.00, '03
Series: *Birthday Train* — Age 15

Purchased ________, Price $ ___________

☐ *16 And Feline Fine,* 116948

$25.00

$25.00

$25.00

Open, Issue Price $25.00, '03
Series: *Birthday Train* — Age 16

Purchased ________, Price $ ___________

☐ *A Banner Of Hope, A Symbol Of Pride,* 117581

$40.00

Open, Issue Price $40.00, '05

Purchased ________, Price $ ___________

☐ *S'Mitten With The Christmas Spirit,* 117784 (Ornament)

UM $24.00

Dated Annual 2004,
Issue Price
$24.00, '04

Purchased ________ ,

Price $ ___________

☐ *S'Mitten With The Christmas Spirit,* 117785

$35.00

Dated Annual 2004, Issue Price $35.00, '04

Purchased ________, Price $ ___________

☐ *Our First Christmas Together,* 117786 (Ornament)

$25.00

Dated Annual 2004,
Issue Price $25.00, '04

Purchased ________ ,

Price $___________

☐ *Baby's First Christmas — Boy,* 117787 (Ornament)

$20.00

Dated Annual 2004, Issue
Price $20.00, '04

Purchased ________ ,

Price $___________

Baby's First Christmas — Girl, 117788 (Ornament)

$20.00

Dated Annual 2004, Issue Price $20.00, '04

Purchased ____________ ,

Price $ ______________

Thoughts Of You Are So Heartwarming, 117789 (Ornament)

$30.00

Dated Annual 2004, Issue Price $30.00, '04

Purchased _________ ,

Price $ ____________

Beaver-y Good This Year, 117790 (Ornament)

$20.00

$20.00

Open, Issue Price $20.00, '04

Purchased _________ ,

Price $ ____________

Wise Men Still Seek Him, 117791

$20.00

$20.00

Open, Issue Price $20.00, '04
Mini Nativity Addition

Purchased ________, Price $ ___________

Tidings Of Comforter & Joy, 117792

$50.00

$50.00

Open, Issue Price $50.00, '04

Purchased ________, Price $ ___________

Bringing You The Gift Of Peace, 117793

$45.00

$45.00

Limited Ed. 10,000, Issue Price $45.00, '04
Series: *Heavenly Angels*

Purchased ______ ,

Price $__________

Simple Joys Put A Song In Your Heart, 117794

$45.00

$45.00

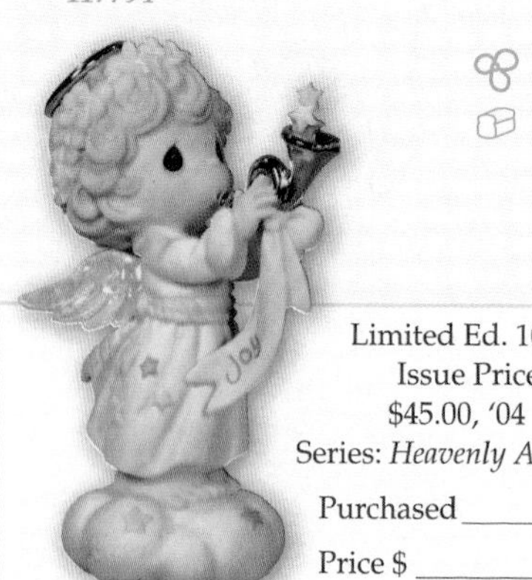

Limited Ed. 10,000, Issue Price $45.00, '04
Series: *Heavenly Angels*

Purchased ________ ,

Price $ ___________

All Wrapped Up With Love, 117795

$45.00
$45.00

Limited Ed. 10,000, Issue Price $45.00, '04
Series: *Heavenly Angels*
Purchased_______ ,
Price $___________

A Little Help Goes A Long Way, 117796

$45.00
$45.00

Open, Issue Price $45.00, '04
Purchased ________, Price $ ___________

I'm Gonna Stick With You, 117797

$40.00
$40.00

Open, Issue Price $40.00, '04
Purchased ________, Price $ ___________

T'was The Night Before Christmas, 117798

$125.00
$125.00

Limited Ed., Issue Price $125.00, '04
Set of 4
Purchased ________, Price $ ___________

Dance To Your Own Beat, 117799

$30.00
$30.00

Open, Issue Price $30.00, '04
Purchased______ ,
Price $ __________

Remember, We're In It Together, 117800

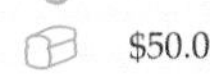

$50.00
$50.00

Open, Issue Price $50.00, '04
Purchased ________, Price $ ___________

A Grandma's Love Is One Size Fits All, 117801

$35.00
$35.00

Open, Issue Price
$35.00, '04
Purchased ________ ,
Price $__________

Beautiful And Blushing, My Baby's Now A Bride, 117802

$50.00
$50.00

Open, Issue Price $50.00, '04
Purchased ________ , Price $ __________

There's Snow Place Like Home, 118129

$40.00
$40.00

Limited Ed., Issue Price $40.00, '04
Purchased ________ , Price $ __________

Crown Him King Of Kings, 118262

$32.50
$32.50

Open, Issue Price
$32.50, '04
Nativity Addition
Purchased ________ ,
Price $__________

Crown Him King Of Kings, 118263

$32.50
$32.50

Open, Issue Price $32.50, '04
Nativity Addition
Purchased ________ , Price $ __________

Crown Him King Of Kings, 118264

$32.50
$32.50

Open, Issue Price $32.50, '04
Nativity Addition
Purchased ________ , Price $ __________

Note To Self: Take Time For Me, 118266

$37.50
$37.50

Open, Issue Price
$37.50, '04
Purchased ________ ,
Price $ __________

☐ *Happy Hula Days, 118267 (Ornament)*

$20.00

$20.00

Open, Issue Price $20.00, '04

Purchased ___________,

Price $___________

☐ *You Make My Heart Soar, 118316*

$35.00

$35.00

Open, Issue Price $35.00, '04

Purchased _________, Price $ ___________

☐ *I'm There For You Rain Or Shine, 118361*

$32.50

$32.50

Open, Issue Price $32.50, '04

Purchased___________,

Price $___________

☐ *A Mother's Arms Are Always Open, 118444*

$50.00

$50.00

$50.00

Open, Issue Price $50.00, '04

Purchased _________, Price $ ___________

☐ *Bringing You My Heart, 118728*

$50.00

$50.00

Open, Issue Price $50.00, '04

Purchased _________, Price $ ___________

☐ *Loving, 118872*

☐ *Caring, 118873*

☐ *Sharing, 118874*

Set of three pieces that fit together to form heart-shaped base. Values given are for each piece.

$50.00 $50.00

Limited Ed. 3,500, Issue Price $40.00, '03
eBay Exclusive

Purchased _________, Price $ ___________

Our Friendship's In The Bag, 119094

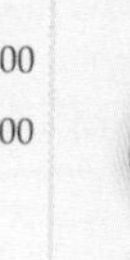

$30.00
$30.00

Open, Issue Price
$30.00, '04
Purchased _________ ,
Price $ ___________

You've Made An Impression On Me, 119434

$37.50
$37.50

Open, Issue Price
$37.50, '04
Purchased _________ ,
Price $ ___________

May Your Dreams Be Warm & Fuzzy, 119374

$35.00
$35.00

Comes with 11-ounce cocoa mug.

Open, Issue Price $35.00, '04
Set of 2
Purchased _________ , Price $ ___________

Sisters In Purple, 119435

$40.00
$40.00

Open, Issue Price $40.00, '04
Purchased _________ , Price $ ___________

Birthday Train Frame, 119424

Holds 2" x 3" Photo of your precious little one
As your child grows this frame can be moved next to the Birthday Train figurine that represents their age.
Great for School Pictures

$20.00
$20.00

Open, Issue Price $20.00, '04
Series: *Birthday Train*
Purchased _________ , Price $ ___________

Take My Hand, 119460

$40.00

Includes "Pop Tab" keeper box.

Limited Ed., Issue Price
$40.00, '05
Ronald McDonald House Charities
Purchased _________ , Price $ ___________

Heavenly Angels, 119559

Set of three: *Bringing You The Gift Of Peace*, 117793; *Simple Joys Put A Song In Your Heart*, 117794; and *All Wrapped Up With Love*, 117795. See pages 164 – 165.

$175.00
$175.00

Limited Ed. 10,000, Issue Price $175.00, '04
Purchased ________, Price $ __________

You Are Always Here, 119642

$45.00
$45.00

Open, Issue Price $45.00, '04
Chapel Exclusive
Purchased ________, Price $ __________

Uphold His Name, 119643

$30.00
$30.00

Open, Issue Price
$30.00, '04
Chapel Exclusive
Purchased __________,
Price $ __________

Messenger Of Love, 119837

$20.00
$20.00

Open, Issue Price
$20.00, '04
Purchased __________,
Price $ __________

Messenger Of Love, 119838

$20.00
$20.00

Open, Issue Price
$20.00, '04
Purchased __________,
Price $ __________

Uphold His Name, 119839 (Ornament)

$20.00
$20.00

Open, Issue Price
$20.00, '04
Purchased __________,
Price $ __________

Baby (Boy Standing), 119916

$17.50
$17.50

Open, Issue Price
$17.50, '04
Purchased __________,
Price $ __________

Baby (Boy Kneeling), 119917

$17.50
$17.50

Open, Issue Price
$17.50, '04
Purchased __________,
Price $ __________

Baby (Girl Sitting), 119918

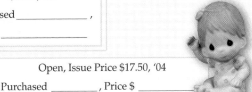

$17.50
$17.50

Open, Issue Price $17.50, '04
Purchased ________, Price $ __________

Baby (Girl Standing), 119919

$17.50

$17.50

Open, Issue Price
$17.50, '04

Purchased _________,

Price $___________

Baby (Boy Crawling), 119920

$17.50

$17.50

Open, Issue Price
$17.50, '04

Purchased ________, Price $ __________

Baby (Girl Crawling), 119921

$17.50

$17.50

Open, Issue Price
$17.50, '04

Purchased ________, Price $ __________

You Have The Sweetest Smile, 120007

$32.50

$32.50

Open, Issue Price $32.50, '04

Purchased ________, Price $ __________

Mom, Thanks For Always Supporting Our Team, 120008

$50.00

$50.00

Special gift for Precious Moments Day, May 9, 2004, at Wrigley Field.

Limited Ed., Issue Price $50.00, '04
Boys and Girls Club of America

Purchased ________, Price $ __________

My Last One For You, 120104

$37.50

$37.50

Special Issue, Issue Price $37.50, '04

Purchased ________, Price $ __________

Purse-suit Of Happiness, 120105

$37.50

$37.50

Open, Issue Price $37.50, '04

Purchased ________, Price $ __________

☐ *Love Is The Color Of Rainbows, 120106*

$50.00
$50.00

One Year of Production, Issue Price $50.00, '04
Purchased ________, Price $ __________

☐ *There's More To Life Than Nine To Five, 120107*

$40.00
$40.00

Open, Issue Price $40.00, '04
Purchased ________, Price $ __________

☐ *Tossing A Little Luck Your Way, 120108*

$35.00
$35.00

Open, Issue Price $35.00, '04
Purchased ______,
Price $ ________

☐ *Just A Little Paws For A Warm Welcome, 120109*

$25.00
$25.00

Open, Issue Price $25.00, '04
Purchased ________, Price $ __________

☐ *Blessed With A Miracle, 120110*

$55.00
$55.00

Open, Issue Price $55.00, '04
Purchased ________, Price $ __________

☐ *"Stressed" Is "Desserts" Spelled Backwards, 120112*

$35.00
$35.00

Open, Issue Price $35.00, '04
Purchased ________, Price $ __________

Wishing You The Sweetest Birthday, 120113

$35.00

$35.00

Open, Issue Price $35.00, '04

Purchased ________ ,

Price $ ____________

Safely Home, 120114

$40.00

$40.00

Open, Issue Price $40.00, '04

Purchased ________ , Price $ ____________

On A Wing And A Prayer, 120115

$40.00

$40.00

Open, Issue Price $40.00, '04

Purchased ________ , Price $ ____________

Open Your Eyes To All His Blessings, 120116

$40.00

$40.00

Open, Issue Price $40.00, '04

Purchased ________ , Price $ ____________

I'd Go Anywhere With You, 120117

$35.00

$35.00

Open, Issue Price $35.00, '04

Purchased ________ , Price $ ____________

I Am Me! 120118

$32.50

$32.50

Open, Issue Price $32.50, '04

Purchased ________ , Price $ ____________

Our Friendship Has Always Been Write On, 120119

$25.00

$25.00

Comes with a diary.

Open, Issue Price $25.00, '04

Purchased ________, Price $ ___________

Love Grows Where You Plant It, 120120

$32.50

$32.50

Open, Issue Price $32.50, '04

Purchased ________, Price $ ___________

You Bet Your Boots I Love You, 120121

$30.00

$30.00

Gift set includes porcelain boot vase.

Retired, Issue Price $30.00, '04

Purchased ________, Price $ ___________

I've Got A Crush On You, 120122

$30.00

$30.00

Open, Issue Price $30.00, '04

Purchased ________, Price $ ___________

Sharing Fun And Games Together, 120123

$80.00

$80.00

Annual 2004, Issue Price $80.00, '04
Boys and Girls Club of America Commemorative

Purchased ________, Price $ ___________

Always On The Ball, 120124

$35.00

$35.00

Open, Issue Price $35.00, '04

Purchased__________ ,

Price $__________

☐ *Love Blooms Eternal*, 127019

$45.00
$40.00

Dated Annual 1995, Issue Price $35.00, '95
Series: *Dated Cross* — First Issue

Purchased ________, Price $ ___________

☐ *Congratulations, You Earned Your Stripes*, 127809

$30.00
$28.00
$25.00
$20.00
$20.00
$18.00
$18.00
$18.00

Retired 2002, Issue Price $15.00, '95
Series: *Two By Two*

Purchased ________, Price $ ___________

☐ *He Shall Lead The Children Into The 21st Century*, 127930

Available exclusively at the Enesco "A Toast To 2000" Millennium Event held at 4,500 retail locations across the country on 10/29/99. Two artists' proofs (127930A) were sold through silent auction at each location to benefit breast cancer awareness. These were unmarked and are valued at $200.00.

$175.00

Limited Ed. 1999, Issue Price $160.00, '99
Set of 5

Purchased ________, Price $ ___________

☐ *An Event Showered With Love*, 128295A, 128295B, 128295C, 128295D (Ornament)

$110.00

Dated Annual 1994, Issue Price $30.00, '94
Regional Event — Wisconsin, New York, Texas, and California
Approximately 1,000 each distributed

Purchased ________, Price $ ___________

☐ *Dreams Really Do Come True*, 128309

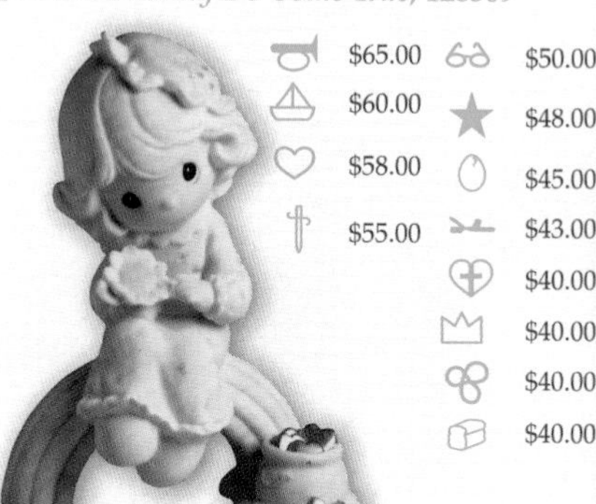

$65.00
$60.00
$58.00
$55.00
$50.00
$48.00
$45.00
$43.00
$40.00
$40.00
$40.00
$40.00

Open, Issue Price $37.50, '95

Purchased ________, Price $ ___________

Another Year And More Grey Hares, 128686

[Trumpet] $35.00 · [Ship] $33.00 · [Heart] $30.00 · [Sword] $28.00 · [Eyeglasses] $25.00 · [Star] $25.00 · [Egg] $23.00 · [Bow] $23.00 · [Cross in Heart] $20.00 · [Crown] $20.00

Retired 2003, Issue Price $17.50, '95
Series: *Birthday Collection*

Purchased ________, Price $ ___________

Happy Hula Days, 128694

[Ship] $35.00 · [Heart] $34.00 · [Sword] $33.00 · [Eyeglasses] $32.50 · [Star] $32.50 · [Egg] $32.50 · [Bow] $32.50 · [Cross in Heart] $32.50 · [Crown] $32.50 · [Clover] $32.50 · [Cube] $32.50

Open, Issue Price
$30.00, '95

Purchased ______,

Price $___________

Owl Be Home For Christmas, 128708 (Ornament)

[Heart] $22.00

Dated Annual 1996, Issue Price $18.50, '96
Series: *Birthday Collection*

Purchased ___________,

Price $ ______________

Take Time To Smell The Flowers, 128899 (Ornament)

UM $10.00

Annual 1995, Issue Price
$7.50, '95
Easter Seals
Commemorative

Purchased ________, Price $ ___________

Love Vows To Always Bloom, 129097

[Ship] $72.00 · [Heart] $70.00 · [Sword] $70.00 · [Eyeglasses] $70.00 · [Star] $70.00 · [Egg] $70.00 · [Bow] $70.00 · [Cross in Heart] $70.00 · [Crown] $70.00 · [Clover] $70.00 · [Cube] $70.00

Open, Issue Price $70.00, '96
Series: *To Have And To Hold*

Purchased ________, Price $ ___________

I Give You My Love Forever True, 129100

[Trumpet] $78.00 · [Ship] $70.00 · [Heart] $70.00 · [Sword] $70.00 · [Eyeglasses] $70.00 · [Star] $70.00 · [Egg] $70.00 · [Bow] $70.00 · [Cross in Heart] $70.00 · [Crown] $70.00 · [Clover] $70.00 · [Cube] $70.00

Open, Issue Price $70.00, '95

Purchased ________, Price $ ___________

He Graces The Earth With Abundance, 129119

- ★ $55.00
- $53.00
- $50.00
- $50.00
- $50.00
- $50.00

Retired 2004, Issue Price $50.00, '99
Series: *New Four Seasons — Fall*
Purchased ________, Price $ __________

Beside The Still Waters, 129127

- ★ $60.00
- $58.00
- $55.00
- $53.00
- $50.00
- $50.00

Retired 2004, Issue Price $50.00, '00
Series: *New Four Seasons — Summer*
Purchased ________, Price $ __________

He Covers The Earth With His Glory, 129135

- $55.00
- $53.00
- $50.00
- $50.00
- $50.00

Retired 2004, Issue Price $50.00, '00
Series: *New Four Seasons — Winter*
Purchased ________, Price $ __________

The Beauty Of God Blooms Forever, 129143

- $55.00
- $53.00
- $50.00
- $50.00
- $50.00

Retired 2004, Issue Price $50.00, '00
Series: *New Four Seasons — Spring*
Purchased ________, Price $ __________

He Hath Made Everything Beautiful In His Time, 129151 (Plate)

- $50.00

Dated Annual 1995, Issue Price $50.00, '95
Series: *Mother's Day* — Second Issue
Purchased ________, Price $ __________

Grandpa's Island, 129259

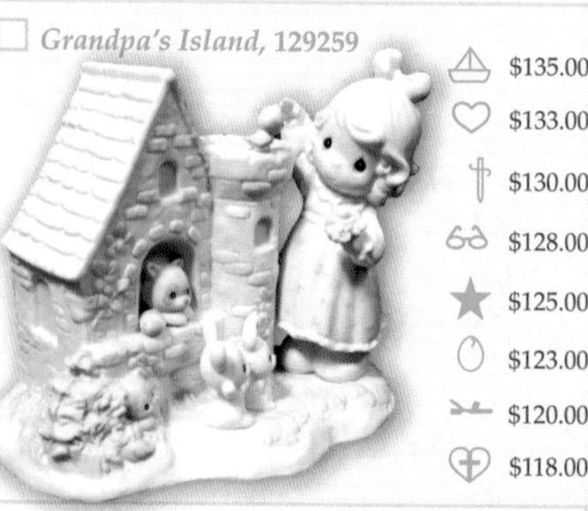

- $135.00
- $133.00
- $130.00
- $128.00
- ★ $125.00
- $123.00
- $120.00
- $118.00

Suspended 2002, Issue Price $100.00, '95
Chapel Exclusive
Purchased ________, Price $ __________

☐ *Lighting The Way To A Happy Holiday,* 129267

$45.00
$33.00
$40.00
$38.00

Retired 1998, Issue Price $30.00, '95
Chapel Exclusive

Purchased ________, Price $ ___________

☐ *Lighting The Way To A Happy Holiday,* 129275 (Ornament)

$30.00
$28.00
$25.00
$25.00
$20.00

Suspended 1999, Issue Price $20.00, '95
Chapel Exclusive

Purchased ________, Price $ ___________

☐ *Love Letters In The Sand,* 129488

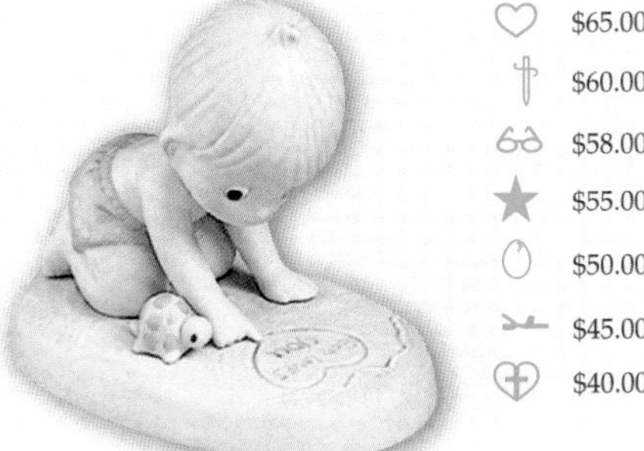

$65.00
$60.00
$58.00
$55.00
$50.00
$45.00
$40.00

Retired 2002, Issue Price $35.00, '97

Purchased ________, Price $ ___________

☐ *Gone But Never Forgotten,* 135976

UM $55.00
$53.00
$50.00
$50.00
$50.00
$50.00

Open, Issue Price $50.00, '00
Chapel Exclusive

Purchased ________, Price $ ___________

☐ *He Is My Salvation,* 135984

$48.00
$45.00

A portion of the proceeds from the sales of this figurine was donated to the Salvation Army.

Retired 2004, Issue Price $45.00, '00

Purchased ________, Price $ ___________

☐ *Heaven Must Have Sent You,* 135992

UM $65.00
$60.00
$55.00
$50.00
$48.00
$45.00
$45.00

Suspended 2002, Issue Price $45.00, '96
Chapel Exclusive

Purchased ________, Price $ ___________

Going To The Chapel, 136018

Mark	Price
UM	$25.00
	$25.00
	$25.00
	$25.00

Open, Issue Price $25.00, '02
Chapel Exclusive
Purchased ________, Price $ __________

Age 1, 136190

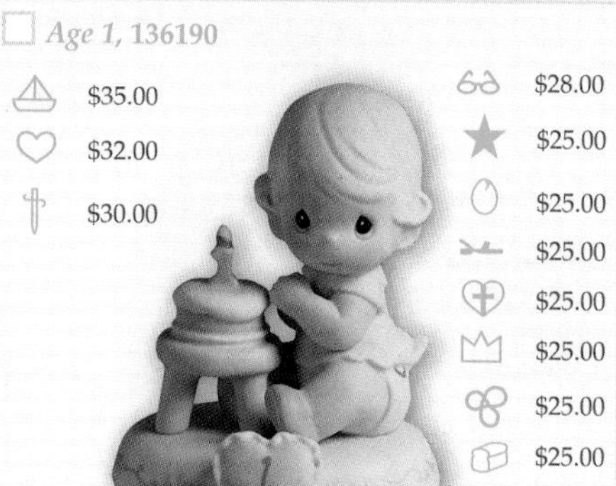

Price
$35.00
$32.00
$30.00
$28.00
$25.00
$25.00
$25.00
$25.00
$25.00
$25.00
$25.00

Open, Issue Price $25.00, '95
Series: *Growing In Grace* (Blonde)
Purchased ________, Price $ __________

Age 1, 136190B

$25.00
$25.00
$25.00
$25.00

Open, Issue Price $25.00, '02
Series: *Growing In Grace* (Brunette)
Purchased ________, Price $ __________

It's A Girl, 136204

$35.00
$32.00
$30.00
$28.00
$25.00
$25.00
$25.00
$25.00
$25.00
$25.00
$25.00

Open, Issue Price $22.50, '95
Series: *Growing In Grace* (Blonde)
Purchased ________, Price $ __________

It's A Girl, 136204B

$25.00
$25.00
$25.00
$25.00

Open, Issue Price $22.50, '02
Series: *Growing In Grace* (Brunette)
Purchased ________, Price $ __________

Age 2, 136212

$35.00
$32.00
$30.00
$28.00
$25.00
$25.00
$25.00
$25.00
$25.00
$25.00
$25.00

Open, Issue Price $25.00, '95
Series: *Growing In Grace* (Blonde)
Purchased ________, Price $ __________

☐ *Age 2, 136212B*

Mark	Price
[heart with cross]	$25.00
[crown]	$25.00
[flower]	$25.00
[box]	$25.00

Open, Issue Price $25.00, '02
Series: *Growing In Grace* (Brunette)
Purchased ________, Price $ __________

☐ *Age 3, 136220*

Mark	Price
[sailboat]	$35.00
[heart]	$32.00
[sword]	$30.00
[eyeglasses]	$28.00
[star]	$25.00
[egg]	$25.00
[arrow]	$25.00
[heart with cross]	$25.00
[crown]	$25.00
[flower]	$25.00
[box]	$25.00

Open, Issue Price $25.00, '95
Series: *Growing In Grace* (Blonde)
Purchased ________, Price $ __________

☐ *Age 3, 136220B*

Mark	Price
[heart with cross]	$25.00
[crown]	$25.00
[flower]	$25.00
[box]	$25.00

Open, Issue Price $25.00, '02
Series: *Growing In Grace* (Brunette)
Purchased ________, Price $ __________

☐ *Age 4, 136239*

Mark	Price
[sailboat]	$35.00
[heart]	$32.00
[sword]	$30.00
[eyeglasses]	$30.00
[star]	$30.00
[egg]	$30.00
[arrow]	$30.00
[heart with cross]	$30.00
[crown]	$30.00
[flower]	$30.00
[box]	$30.00

Open, Issue Price $27.50, '95
Series: *Growing In Grace* (Blonde)
Purchased ________, Price $ __________

☐ *Age 4, 136239B*

Mark	Price
[heart with cross]	$30.00
[crown]	$30.00
[flower]	$30.00
[box]	$30.00

Open, Issue Price $27.50, '95
Series: *Growing In Grace* (Brunette)
Purchased ________, Price $ __________

☐ *Age 5, 136247*

Mark	Price
[sailboat]	$35.00
[heart]	$32.00
[sword]	$30.00
[eyeglasses]	$30.00
[star]	$30.00
[egg]	$30.00
[arrow]	$30.00
[heart with cross]	$30.00
[crown]	$30.00
[flower]	$30.00
[box]	$30.00

Open, Issue Price $27.50, '95
Series: *Growing In Grace* (Blonde)
Purchased ________, Price $ __________

☐ *Age 5, 136247B*

- $30.00
- $30.00
- $30.00
- $30.00

Open, Issue Price $27.50, '95
Series: *Growing In Grace* (Brunette)
Purchased ________, Price $ ____________

☐ *Age 16, 136263*

- $55.00
- $50.00
- $48.00
- $45.00
- $45.00
- $45.00
- $45.00
- $45.00
- $45.00
- $45.00
- $45.00

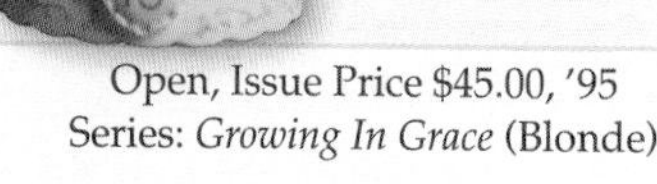

Open, Issue Price $45.00, '95
Series: *Growing In Grace* (Blonde)
Purchased ________, Price $ ____________

☐ *Age 6, 136255*

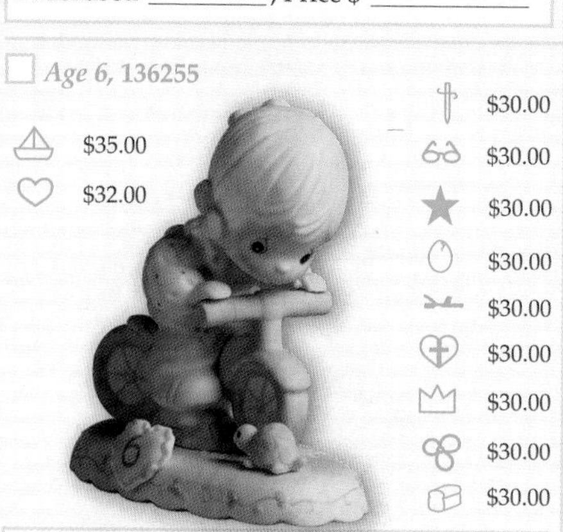

- $35.00
- $32.00
- $30.00
- $30.00
- $30.00
- $30.00
- $30.00
- $30.00
- $30.00
- $30.00
- $30.00

Open, Issue Price $30.00, '95
Series: *Growing In Grace* (Blonde)
Purchased ________, Price $ ____________

☐ *Age 6, 136255B*

- $30.00
- $30.00
- $30.00
- $30.00

Open, Issue Price $30.00, '95
Series: *Growing In Grace* (Brunette)
Purchased ________, Price $ ____________

☐ *Age 16, 136263B*

- $45.00
- $45.00
- $45.00
- $45.00

Open, Issue Price $45.00, '95
Series: *Growing In Grace* (Brunette)
Purchased ________, Price $ ____________

☐ *You Will Always Be Our Hero, 136271*

- $50.00
- $40.00

Annual 1995, Issue Price $40.00, '95
Celebrating 50th Anniversary of WWII
Purchased ________, Price $ ____________

Love Makes The World Go 'Round, 139475

$400.00

Limited Ed. 15,000, Issue Price $200.00, '95
Century Circle Exclusive
Individually Numbered
Purchased _________, Price $ ____________

Where Would I Be Without You, 139491

UM $20.00

Open, Issue Price
$20.00, '97
Series: *Little Moments*
Purchased _____________,
Price $_______________

All Things Grow With Love, 139505

UM $20.00

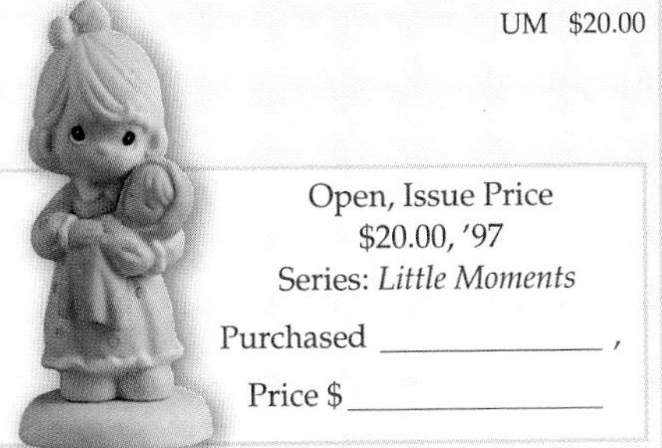

Open, Issue Price
$20.00, '97
Series: *Little Moments*
Purchased _____________,
Price $_______________

You're The Berry Best, 139513

UM $20.00

Open, Issue Price 20.00, '97
Series: *Little Moments*
Purchased _____________,
Price $_______________

You Make The World A Sweeter Place, 139521

UM $20.00

Open, Issue Price
$20.00, '97
Series: *Little Moments*
Purchased _____________,
Price $_______________

You're Forever In My Heart, 139548

UM $20.00

Open, Issue Price $20.00, '97
Series: *Little Moments*
Purchased _________, Price $ ____________

Birthday Wishes With Hugs And Kisses, 139556

UM $20.00

Open, Issue Price
$20.00, '97
Series: *Little Moments*
Purchased _____________,
Price $_______________

You Make My Spirit Soar, 139564

UM $20.00

Open, Issue Price $20.00, '97
Series: *Little Moments*
Purchased _____________,
Price $_______________

He Covers The Earth With His Beauty, 142654

$42.00

Dated Annual 1995, Issue Price $30.00, '95

Purchased ________, Price $ ____________

He Covers The Earth With His Beauty, 142662 (Ornament)

$30.00

Dated Annual 1995, Issue Price $17.00, '95

Purchased ________, Price $ ____________

He Covers The Earth With His Beauty, 142670 (Plate)

$60.00

Dated Annual 1995, Issue Price $50.00, '95
Series: *The Beauty Of Christmas*
Second Issue

Purchased ________, Price $ ____________

He Covers The Earth With His Beauty, 142689 (Ornament)

$40.00

Dated Annual 1995, Issue Price $30.00, '95

Purchased ________, Price $ ____________

Our First Christmas Together, 142700 (Ornament)

$25.00

Dated Annual 1995, Issue Price $18.50, '95

Purchased ________, Price $ ____________

Baby's First Christmas, 142719 (Ornament)

$25.00

Dated Annual 1995, Issue Price $17.50, '95

Purchased ________, Price $ ____________

Baby's First Christmas, 142727 (Ornament)

$25.00

Dated Annual 1995, Issue Price $17.50, '95

Purchased ________, Price $ ____________

Come Let Us Adore Him, 142735

$55.00 $50.00 $50.00 $50.00
$53.00 $50.00 $50.00 $50.00
$50.00 $50.00 $50.00

Open, Issue Price $50.00, '95
Three-piece Nativity Starter Set with Booklet

Purchased _________, Price $ ___________

Come Let Us Adore Him, 142743

$40.00 $38.00 $35.00
$35.00
$35.00
$35.00
$35.00
$35.00
$35.00
$35.00
$35.00

Open, Issue Price $35.00, '95
Mini Figurines, 2¾" tall, Set of 3

Purchased _________, Price $ ___________

I'll Give Him My Heart, 150088

$70.00
$68.00
$65.00
$60.00

Retired 1998, Issue Price $40.00, '95

Purchased _________, Price $ ___________

Making A Trail To Bethlehem, 142751

$35.00 $32.50
$32.50 $32.50

Retired 1998, Issue Price $30.00, '95
Nativity Addition

Purchased _________, Price $ ___________

Soot Yourself To A Merry Christmas, 150096

$55.00
$50.00
$48.00
$45.00
$40.00

Retired 1999, Issue Price $35.00, '95

Purchased _________, Price $ ___________

Sailabration Cruise, 150061

This piece was given to those who went on a Precious Moments cruise in 1995.

$475.00

Limited Ed., 1995, Gift, '95

Purchased _________, Price $ ___________

Making Spirits Bright, 150118

$55.00
$48.00
$45.00
$40.00

Retired 1998, Issue Price $37.50, '95
Purchased ________ ,
Price $ ________

Joy From Head To Mistletoe, 150126 (Ornament)

$25.00 | $19.00
$22.00 | $19.00
$20.00 | $19.00
$20.00 | $19.00
$20.00 | $18.50
$18.50

Open, Issue Price $17.00, '95
Purchased ________ , Price $ ________

Merry Chrismoose, 150134 (Ornament)

$30.00

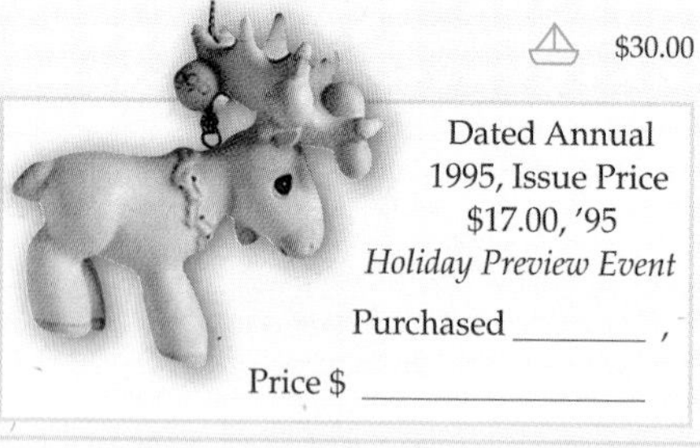

Dated Annual 1995, Issue Price $17.00, '95
Holiday Preview Event
Purchased ________ ,
Price $ ________

You're "A" Number One In My Book, Teacher, 150142 (Ornament)

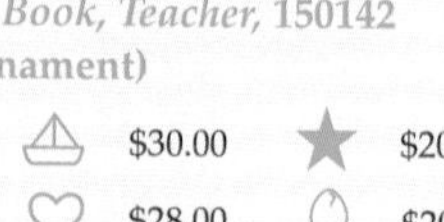

$30.00 | $20.00
$28.00 | $20.00
$25.00 | $20.00
$23.00 | $20.00

Train Station, 150150 (Nightlight)

$125.00 $115.00 $105.00

Retired 1997, Issue Price $100.00, '95
Series: *Sugar Town*
Purchased ________ , Price $ ________

Sam, 150169

$35.00

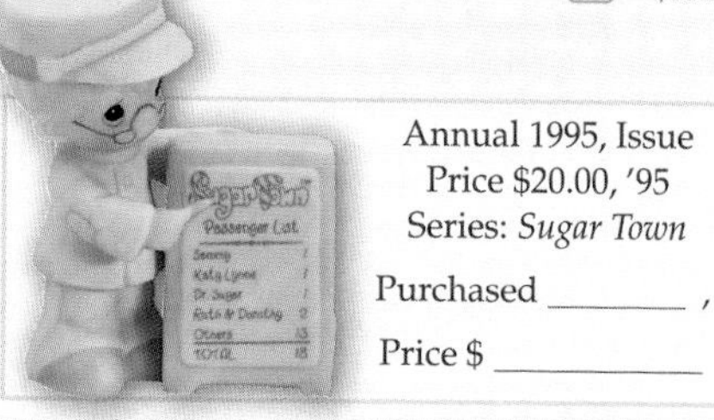

Annual 1995, Issue Price $20.00, '95
Series: *Sugar Town*
Purchased ________ ,
Price $ ________

Railroad Crossing Sign, 150177

$18.00
$15.00
$13.00

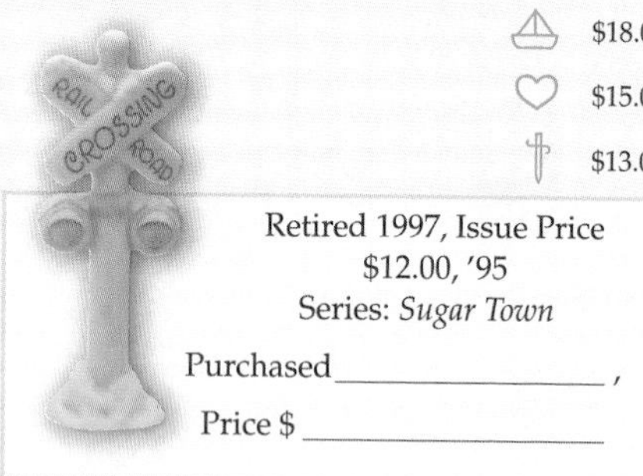

Retired 1997, Issue Price $12.00, '95
Series: *Sugar Town*
Purchased ________ ,
Price $ ________

Retired 2002, Issue Price $17.00, '95
Purchased ________ , Price $ ________

☐ *Train Station Set, 150193*

△ $275.00 ♡ $250.00 † $240.00

Retired 1997, Issue Price $190.00, '95
Series: *Sugar Town*, Set of 6 (Train Station, Railroad Crossing Sign, Luggage Cart, Sam, Tammy & Debbie, and Donny)

Purchased ______________,

Price $ ________________

☐ *Luggage Cart, 150185*

△ $25.00

♡ $20.00

† $18.00

Retired 1997, Issue Price $13.00, '95
Series: *Sugar Town*

Purchased________ ,

Price $ ____________

☐ *Bus Stop Sign, 150207*

♡ $12.00

△ $13.00 † $11.00

Retired 1997, Issue Price $8.50, '95
Series: *Sugar Town*

Purchased ________________ ,

Price $ ________________

☐ *Fire Hydrant, 150215*

♡ $10.00

△ $12.00 † $8.00

Retired 1997, Issue Price $5.00, '95
Series: *Sugar Town*

Purchased ________, Price $ ___________

☐ *Bird Bath, 150223*

△ $13.00

♡ $10.00

† $10.00

☐ *God Bless Our Home, 150231 (Ornament)*

△ $55.00

Issued in *Sugar Town* boxes.

Out Of Production, Issue Price $19.95, '95
Series: *Sugar Town*

Purchased ________, Price $ ___________

☐ *Even The Heavens Shall Praise Him, 150312*

👓 $135.00

Limited Ed. 15,000, Issue Price $125.00, '98
Century Circle Exclusive

Purchased ________, Price $ ___________

Retired 1997, Issue Price $8.50, '95
Series: *Sugar Town*

Purchase _________, Price $ ___________

Joy To The World, 150320 (Ornament)

$25.00
$30.00 $25.00
$28.00 $25.00

Retired 1999, Issue Price $20.00, '95

Purchased ________,

Price $ ________

Sugar Town Enhancement Set, 152269

$68.00
$65.00
$63.00

Retired 1997, Issue Price $45.00, '95
Series: *Sugar Town*, Set of 5
(Fire Hydrant, Bench, Bus Stop Sign, Bird Bath, and Street Sign)

Purchased ________, Price $ ________

He Loves Me, 152277

$550.00

Limited Ed. 2,000, Issue Price $500.00, '96
Easter Seals,
Lily Understamp
Individually Numbered

Purchased______,

Price $ ________

You Can Always Count On Me, 152579 (Ornament)

$10.00

Annual 1996, Issue Price $6.50, '96
Easter Seals Commemorative

Purchased ________,

Price $________

Joy To The World, 153338 (Ornament)

$30.00 $25.00
$28.00 $25.00

Retired 1999, Issue Price $20.00, '96

Purchased ________,

Price $ ________

An Event Filled With Sunshine And Smiles, 160334A – H (Ornament)

$75.00

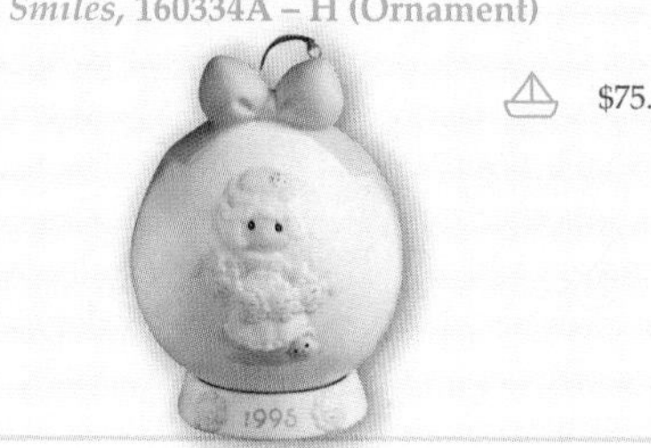

Dated Annual 1995, Issue Price $35.00, '95
Regional Event — Illinois, California, New Jersey, Missouri, Maryland, Florida, Ohio, and Canada (add $25 to value for Canada)

Purchased ________, Price $ ________

Sugar Town Express, 152595 (Musical)

Retired 1997, Issue Price $75.00, '95
Series: *Sugar Town*, Set of 3 plus track
Tunes: "Jingle Bells," "We Wish You A Merry Christmas," and "Santa Claus Is Coming To Town"

Purchased ________, Price $ ________

UM $95.00

☐ *You Are Always There For Me, 163597*

Mark	Price
♡	$65.00
†	$63.00
👓	$60.00
★	$58.00
⬯	$55.00
bow	$55.00

Retired 2001, Issue Price $50.00, '97

Purchased ________, Price $ ___________

☐ *You Are Always There For Me, 163600*

Mark	Price
△	$60.00
♡	$55.00
†	$55.00
👓	$55.00
★	$55.00
⬯	$55.00
bow	$55.00
♡✝	$50.00
♔	$50.00
☘	$50.00
cube	$50.00

Open, Issue Price $50.00, '96

Purchased ________, Price $ ___________

☐ *You Are Always There For Me, 163619*

Mark	Price
♡	$60.00
†	$55.00
👓	$55.00
★	$55.00
⬯	$55.00
bow	$55.00
♡✝	$50.00
♔	$50.00
☘	$50.00
cube	$50.00

Open, Issue Price $50.00, '97

Purchased ________, Price $ ___________

☐ *You Are Always There For Me, 163627*

Mark	Price
△	$60.00
♡	$50.00
†	$50.00
👓	$50.00
★	$50.00
⬯	$50.00
bow	$50.00
♡✝	$50.00
♔	$50.00

Retired 2003, Issue Price $50.00, '96

Purchased ________, Price $ ___________

☐ *You Are Always There For Me, 163635*

Mark	Price
♡	$55.00
†	$53.00
👓	$50.00
★	$50.00
⬯	$50.00
bow	$50.00
♡✝	$50.00
♔	$50.00
☘	$50.00
cube	$50.00

Open, Issue Price $50.00, '96

Purchased ________, Price $ ___________

☐ *Baby Girl Personalized, 163651G*

Mark	Price
△	$32.50

Open, Issue Price $32.50, '95

Purchased ________, Price $ ___________

Baby Boy Personalized, **163651B**

$32.50

Open, Issue Price $32.50, '95

Purchased ________, Price $ ____________

Birthday Personalized, **163686**

$42.50

$42.50

Open, Issue Price $42.50, '95

Purchased ________, Price $ ____________

I'd Goat Anywhere With You, **163694**

$25.00 $20.00

$22.00 $18.00

$15.00

$15.00

$15.00

$15.00

Retired 2002, Issue Price $10.00, '96
Series: *Two By Two*

Purchased ________, Price $ ____________

Jennifer, **163708**

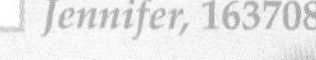

$35.00

$30.00

Suspended 1996, Issue Price $20.00, '96
Series: *Sammy's Circus*

Purchased ________, Price $ ____________

Of All The Mothers I Have Known, There's None As Precious As My Own, **163716 (Plate)**

$40.00

Dated Annual 1996, Issue Price $37.50, '96
Series: *Mother's Day* — Third Issue

Purchased ________, Price $ ____________

Blessed Are They With A Caring Heart, **163724**

$60.00

Limited Ed., Issue Price $55.00, '99
Century Circle Exclusive

Purchased ________, Price $ ____________

Standing In The Presence Of The Lord, 163732

△ $50.00
♡ $40.00

Dated Annual 1996, Issue Price $37.50, '96
Series: *Dated Cross* — Second Issue

Purchased ________, Price $ ___________

Age 7, 163740

△ $45.00
♡ $43.00
† $40.00
$38.00
★ $35.00
⬯ $35.00
$35.00
$35.00
$35.00
$32.50
$32.50

Open, Issue Price $32.50, '96
Series: *Growing In Grace* (Blonde)

Purchased ________, Price $ ___________

Age 7, 163740B

$35.00
$33.00
$32.50
$32.50

Open, Issue Price $32.50, '02
Series: *Growing In Grace* (Brunette)

Purchased ________, Price $ ___________

Age 8, 163759

△ $45.00
♡ $43.00
† $40.00
$38.00
★ $35.00
⬯ $35.00
$35.00
$35.00
$35.00
$32.50
$32.50

Open, Issue Price $32.50, '96
Series: *Growing In Grace* (Blonde)

Purchased ________, Price $ ___________

Age 8, 163759B

$35.00
$33.00
$32.50
$32.50

Open, Issue Price $32.50, '02
Series: *Growing In Grace* (Brunette)

Purchased ________, Price $ ___________

Take It To The Lord In Prayer, 163767

△ $50.00
♡ $48.00
† $45.00
$43.00
★ $40.00
⬯ $35.00
$35.00

Retired 2001, Issue Price $30.00, '96

Purchased ________, Price $ ___________

☐ *The Sun Is Always Shining Somewhere,* 163775

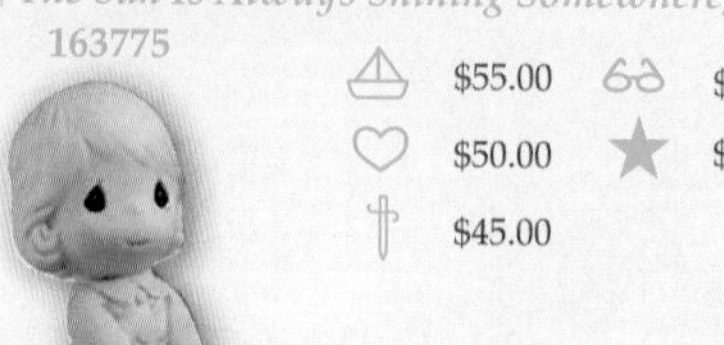

Mark	Price	Mark	Price
[sailboat]	$55.00	[eyeglasses]	$40.00
[heart]	$50.00	[star]	$40.00
[sword]	$45.00		

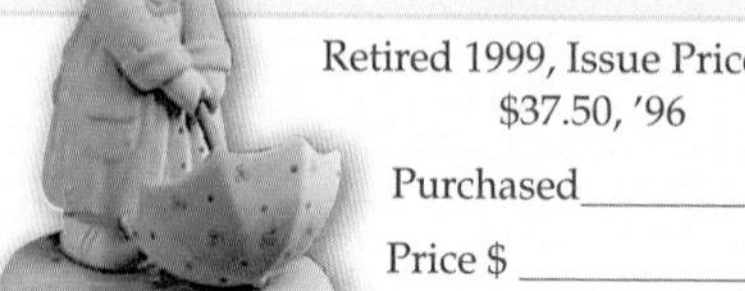

Retired 1999, Issue Price $37.50, '96

Purchased________ ,

Price $ ____________

☐ *A Year Of Blessings,* 163783

Mark	Price	Mark	Price
[sailboat]	$75.00	[sword]	$70.00
[heart]	$70.00	[eyeglasses]	$70.00
		[star]	$70.00
		[egg]	$70.00
		[trumpet]	$70.00
		[heart with cross]	$70.00
		[crown]	$70.00
		[flower]	$70.00
		[cube]	$70.00

Open, Issue Price $70.00, '96
Series: *To Have And To Hold*

Purchased ________, Price $ ___________

☐ *Each Hour Is Precious With You,* 163791

Mark	Price	Mark	Price
[sailboat]	$75.00	[sword]	$70.00
[heart]	$70.00	[eyeglasses]	$70.00
		[star]	$70.00
		[egg]	$70.00
		[trumpet]	$70.00
		[heart with cross]	$70.00
		[crown]	$70.00
		[flower]	$70.00
		[cube]	$70.00

Open, Issue Price $70.00, '96
Series: *To Have And To Hold*

Purchased ________, Price $ ___________

☐ *Ten Years Heart To Heart,* 163805

Mark	Price	Mark	Price
[sailboat]	$75.00	[star]	$70.00
[heart]	$70.00	[egg]	$70.00
[sword]	$70.00	[trumpet]	$70.00
[eyeglasses]	$70.00	[heart with cross]	$70.00
		[crown]	$70.00
		[flower]	$70.00
		[cube]	$70.00

Open, Issue Price $70.00, '96
Series: *To Have And To Hold*

Purchased ________, Price $ ___________

☐ *A Silver Celebration To Share,* 163813

Mark	Price	Mark	Price
[sailboat]	$75.00	[sword]	$70.00
[heart]	$70.00	[eyeglasses]	$70.00
		[star]	$70.00
		[egg]	$70.00
		[trumpet]	$70.00
		[heart with cross]	$70.00
		[crown]	$70.00
		[flower]	$70.00
		[cube]	$70.00

Open, Issue Price $70.00, '96
Series: *To Have And To Hold*

Purchased ________, Price $ ___________

☐ *Sharing The Gift Of 40 Precious Years,* 163821

Mark	Price	Mark	Price
[sailboat]	$75.00	[sword]	$70.00
[heart]	$70.00	[eyeglasses]	$70.00
		[star]	$70.00
		[egg]	$70.00
		[trumpet]	$70.00
		[heart with cross]	$70.00
		[crown]	$70.00
		[flower]	$70.00
		[cube]	$70.00

Open, Issue Price $70.00, '96
Series: *To Have And To Hold*

Purchased ________, Price $ ___________

Precious Moments To Remember, 163848

$75.00 $70.00
$70.00 $70.00
$70.00
$70.00
$70.00
$70.00
$70.00
$70.00
$70.00

Open, Issue Price $70.00, '96
Series: *To Have And To Hold*
Purchased ________, Price $ __________

Sowing Seeds Of Kindness, 163856

$40.00 $37.50
$39.00 $37.50
$38.00 $37.50
$37.50
$37.50
$37.50
$37.50

Retired 2004, Issue Price $37.50, '96
Series: *Growing In God's Garden Of Love*
First Issue
Purchased ________, Price $ __________

Hallelujah Hoedown, 163864

$75.00
$50.00

Annual 1996, Issue Price $32.50, '96
Spring Celebration
Purchased ________, Price $ __________

His Presence Is Felt In The Chapel, 163872

UM $45.00
$40.00
$35.00

Retired 1998, Issue Price $25.00, '96
Chapel Exclusive
Purchased ________, Price $ __________

His Presence Is Felt In The Chapel, 163880
(Ornament)

UM $28.00
$25.00

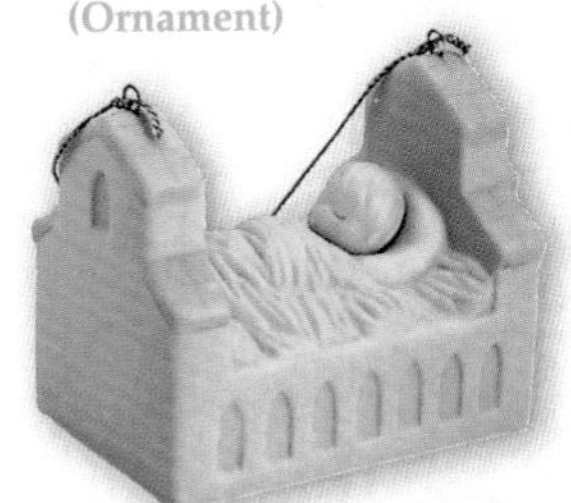

Suspended 1997, Issue Price $17.50, '96
Chapel Exclusive
Purchased ________, Price $ __________

It May Be Greener, But It's Just As Hard To Cut, 163899

$55.00
$50.00
$48.00
$45.00
$43.00
$40.00
$40.00

Retired 2001, Issue Price $37.50, '96
Purchased ________, Price $ __________

☐ *God's Love Is Reflected In You, 175277*

♡ $225.00

Limited Ed. 15,000, Issue Price $150.00, '96
Century Circle Exclusive
Individually Numbered

Purchased ________, Price $ ___________

☐ *Some Plant, Some Water, But God Giveth The Increase, 176958*

♡ $45.00
† $44.00
$43.00
★ $42.00
$40.00
$40.00
$40.00
$40.00
$40.00

Retired 2004, Issue Price $37.50, '96
Series: *Growing In God's Garden of Love*
Second Issue

Purchased ________, Price $ ___________

☐ *A Perfect Display Of 15 Happy Years, 177083 (Medallion)*

$400.00

This Medallion was given to the attendees of the 1995 Local Club Chapter Convention. This is the fifth in the collection.

Convention Gift, '95

Purchased ________, Price $ ___________

☐ *Peace On Earth, 177091 (Ornament)*

UM $35.00

Limited Ed. 15,000, Issue Price $25.00, '95
Century Circle Exclusive

Purchased ________, Price $ ___________

☐ *Peace On Earth… Anyway, 183342*

♡ $45.00

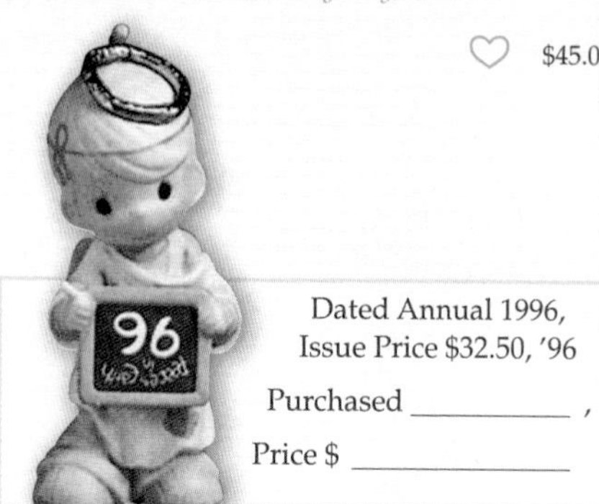

Dated Annual 1996,
Issue Price $32.50, '96

Purchased __________ ,

Price $ ___________

☐ *Peace On Earth… Anyway, 183350 (Ornament)*

♡ $40.00

Dated Annual 1996,
Issue Price $30.00, '96

Purchased________ ,

Price $ ___________

☐ *Peace On Earth… Anyway, 183369 (Ornament)*

♡ $22.00

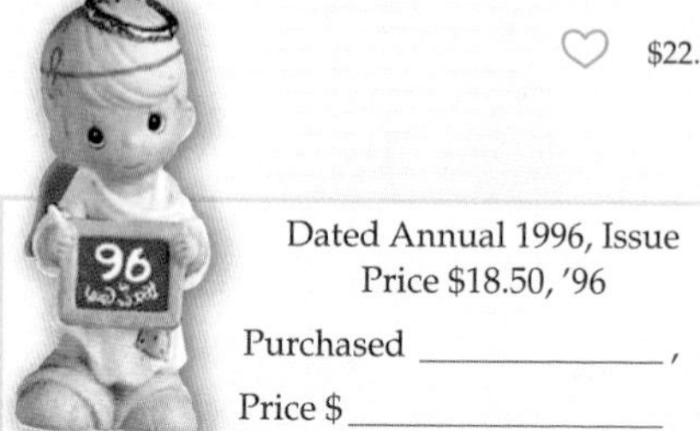

Dated Annual 1996, Issue Price $18.50, '96

Purchased ___________ ,

Price $ ___________

☐ *Peace On Earth… Anyway*, 183377 (Plate)

♡ $55.00

Dated Annual 1996, Issue Price $50.00, '96
Series: *Beauty Of Christmas* — Third Issue

Purchased ________, Price $ __________

☐ *Angels On Earth*, 183776

Mark	Price
♡	$55.00
†	$50.00
👓	$48.00
★	$48.00
◯	$45.00
⋈	$45.00

Retired 2001, Issue Price $40.00, '96

Purchased ________, Price $ __________

☐ *Snowbunny Loves You Like I Do*, 183792

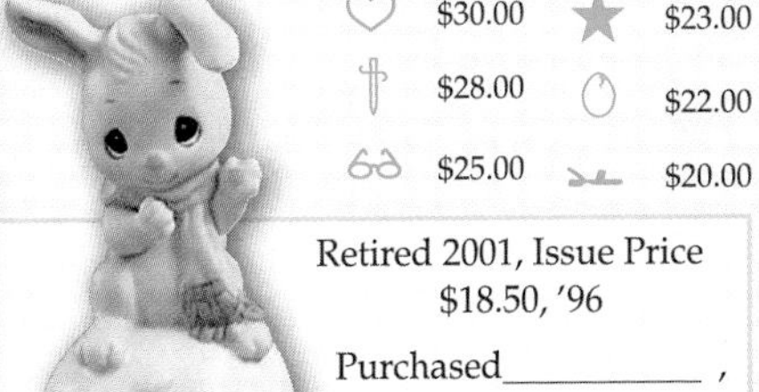

Mark	Price	Mark	Price
♡	$30.00	★	$23.00
†	$28.00	◯	$22.00
👓	$25.00	⋈	$20.00

Retired 2001, Issue Price $18.50, '96

Purchased__________ ,

Price $__________

☐ *The Most Precious Gift Of All*, 183814

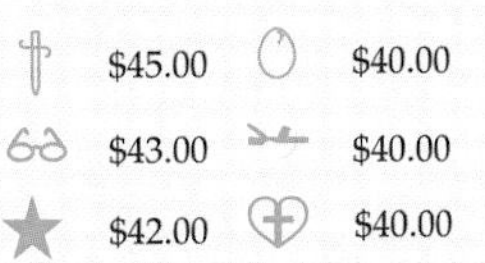

Mark	Price	Mark	Price
†	$45.00	◯	$40.00
👓	$43.00	⋈	$40.00
★	$42.00	♡✝	$40.00

☐ *The Most Precious Gift Of All*, 183814S

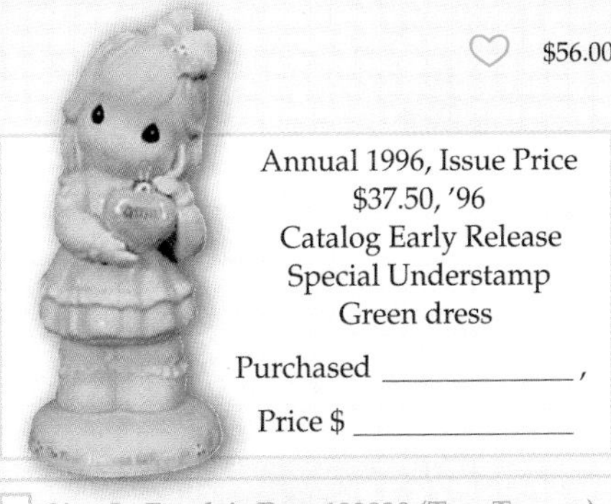

♡ $56.00

Annual 1996, Issue Price $37.50, '96
Catalog Early Release
Special Understamp
Green dress

Purchased __________ ,

Price $ __________

☐ *Sing In Excelsis Deo*, 183830 (Tree Topper)

Mark	Price
♡	$135.00
†	$130.00
👓	$125.00
★	$125.00

Retired 1999, Issue Price $125.00, '96

Purchased ________, Price $ __________

☐ *You're Just Too Sweet To Be Scary*, 183849

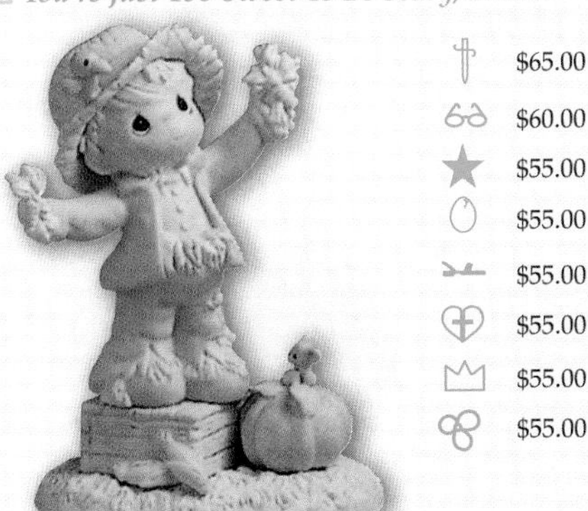

Mark	Price
†	$65.00
👓	$60.00
★	$55.00
◯	$55.00
⋈	$55.00
♡✝	$55.00
♔	$55.00
✿	$55.00

Retired 2004, Issue Price $55.00, '97

Purchased ________, Price $ __________

Retired 2001, Issue Price $37.50, '97
Pink dress

Purchased ________, Price $ __________

☐ *Color Your World With Thanksgiving,* 183857

♡ $75.00
† $73.00
👓 $70.00

Retired 1998, Issue Price $50.00, '96
Purchased ________, Price $ __________

☐ *Age 10,* 183873

♡ $45.00
† $43.00
👓 $40.00
★ $40.00
🔥 $40.00
🏹 $40.00
♡✚ $40.00
♔ $40.00
☘ $40.00
◫ $40.00

Open, Issue Price $35.00, '96
Series: *Growing In Grace* (Blonde)
Purchased ________, Price $ __________

☐ *Age 9,* 183865

♡ $35.00
† $33.00
👓 $30.00
★ $30.00
🔥 $30.00
🏹 $30.00
♡✚ $30.00
♔ $30.00
☘ $30.00
◫ $30.00

Open, Issue Price $30.00, '96
Series: *Growing In Grace* (Blonde)
Purchased ________, Price $ __________

☐ *Age 10,* 183873B

♡✚ $40.00
♔ $40.00
☘ $40.00
◫ $40.00

Open, Issue Price $35.00, '02
Series: *Growing In Grace* (Brunette)
Purchased ________, Price $ __________

☐ *Age 9,* 183865B

♡✚ $30.00
♔ $30.00
☘ $30.00
◫ $30.00

Open, Issue Price $30.00, '02
Series: *Growing In Grace* (Brunette)
Purchased ________, Price $ __________

☐ *God's Precious Gift,* 183881 (Ornament)

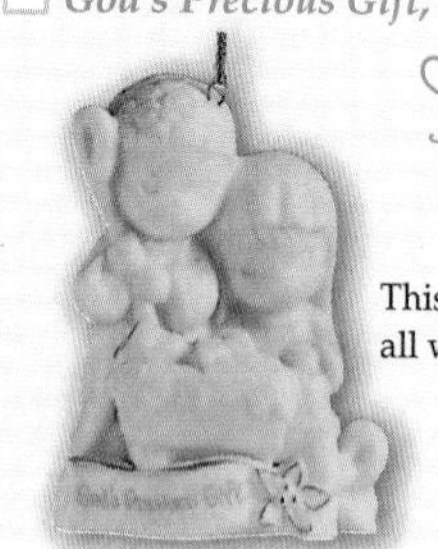

This piece is all white.

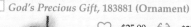

♡ $25.00
† $23.00
👓 $22.00
★ $21.00
🔥 $20.00
🏹 $20.00
♡✚ $20.00
♔ $20.00
☘ $20.00

Suspended 2004, Issue Price $20.00, '96
Purchased ________, Price $ __________

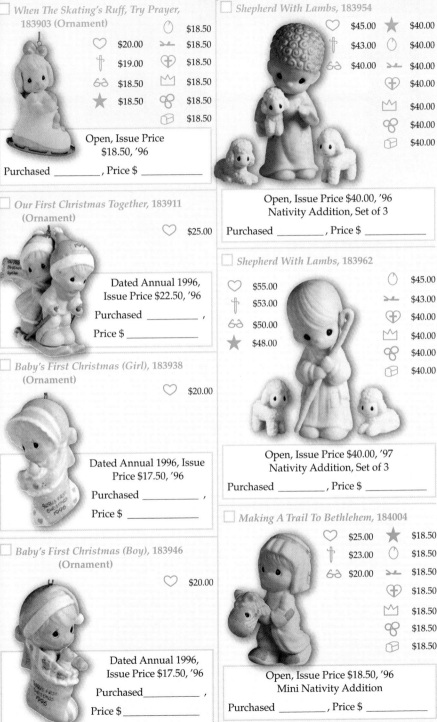

When The Skating's Ruff, Try Prayer, 183903 (Ornament)

$20.00, $19.00, $18.50, $18.50, $18.50, $18.50, $18.50, $18.50, $18.50, $18.50, $18.50

Open, Issue Price $18.50, '96

Purchased ________, Price $ __________

Our First Christmas Together, 183911 (Ornament)

$25.00

Dated Annual 1996, Issue Price $22.50, '96

Purchased ________,

Price $ __________

Baby's First Christmas (Girl), 183938 (Ornament)

$20.00

Dated Annual 1996, Issue Price $17.50, '96

Purchased ________,

Price $ __________

Baby's First Christmas (Boy), 183946 (Ornament)

$20.00

Dated Annual 1996, Issue Price $17.50, '96

Purchased________,

Price $__________

Shepherd With Lambs, 183954

$45.00, $43.00, $40.00, $40.00, $40.00, $40.00, $40.00, $40.00, $40.00, $40.00

Open, Issue Price $40.00, '96
Nativity Addition, Set of 3

Purchased ________, Price $ __________

Shepherd With Lambs, 183962

$55.00, $53.00, $50.00, $48.00, $45.00, $43.00, $40.00, $40.00, $40.00, $40.00

Open, Issue Price $40.00, '97
Nativity Addition, Set of 3

Purchased ________, Price $ __________

Making A Trail To Bethlehem, 184004

$25.00, $23.00, $20.00, $18.50, $18.50, $18.50, $18.50, $18.50, $18.50, $18.50

Open, Issue Price $18.50, '96
Mini Nativity Addition

Purchased ________, Price $ __________

☐ *All Sing His Praises*, 184012

$36.00
$34.00
$32.50
$32.50
$32.50
$32.50
$32.50
$32.50
$32.50
$32.50

Open, Issue Price $32.50, '96
Nativity Addition
Purchased ________, Price $ __________

☐ *Sugar Town Skating Sign*, 184020

$25.00

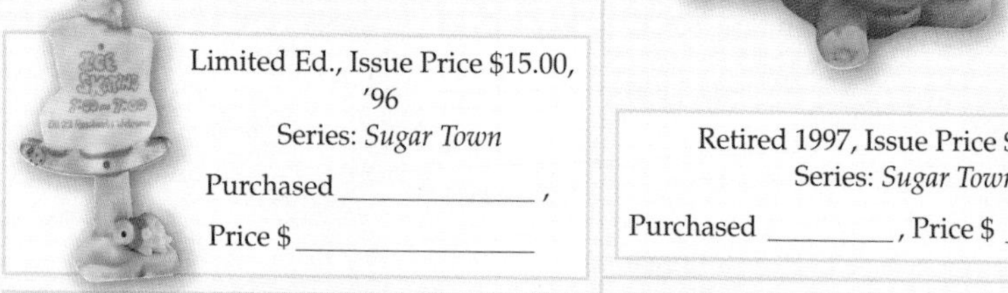

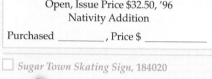

Limited Ed., Issue Price $15.00, '96
Series: *Sugar Town*
Purchased ____________,
Price $ ______________

☐ *Sugar Town Tree*, 184039 (Lighted)

$80.00
$70.00

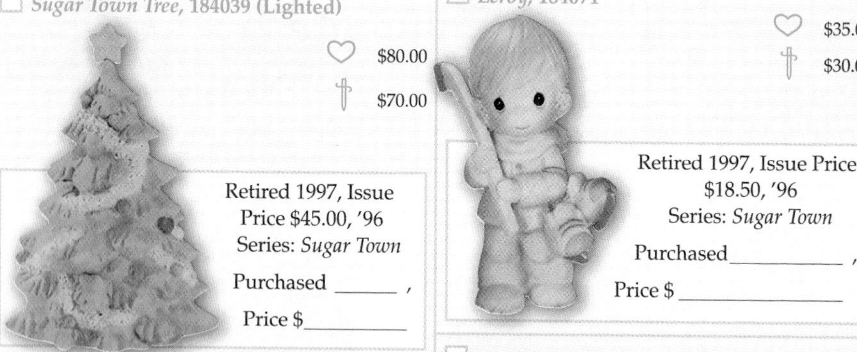

Retired 1997, Issue Price $45.00, '96
Series: *Sugar Town*
Purchased _____,
Price $__________

☐ *Sugar Town Skating Pond*, 184047

$60.00
$55.00

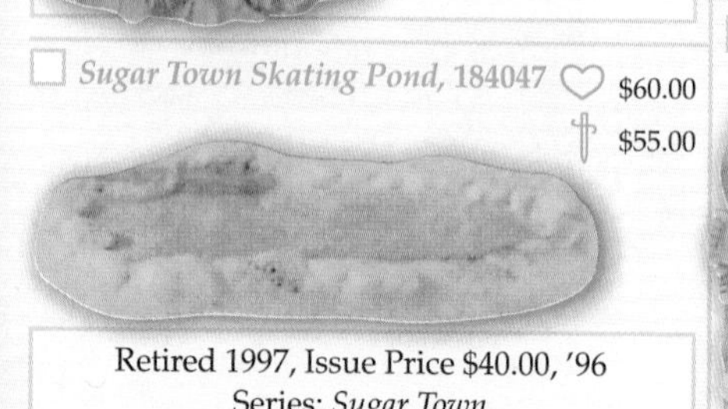

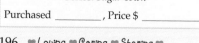

Retired 1997, Issue Price $40.00, '96
Series: *Sugar Town*
Purchased ________, Price $ __________

☐ *Mazie*, 184055

$35.00
$32.00

Retired 1997, Issue Price $18.50, '96
Series: *Sugar Town*
Purchased ___________,
Price $______________

☐ *Cocoa*, 184063

$15.00
$12.00

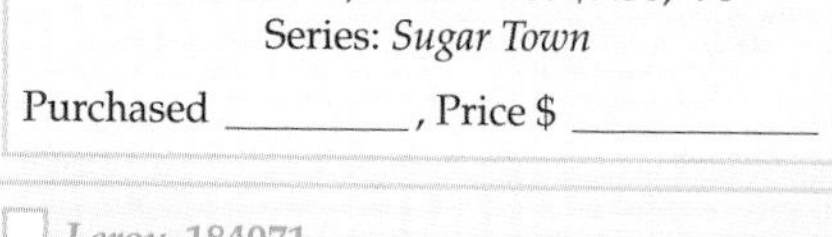

Retired 1997, Issue Price $7.50, '96
Series: *Sugar Town*
Purchased ________, Price $ __________

☐ *Leroy*, 184071

$35.00
$30.00

Retired 1997, Issue Price $18.50, '96
Series: *Sugar Town*
Purchased__________,
Price $ _____________

☐ *Hank And Sharon*, 184098

$35.00
$33.00

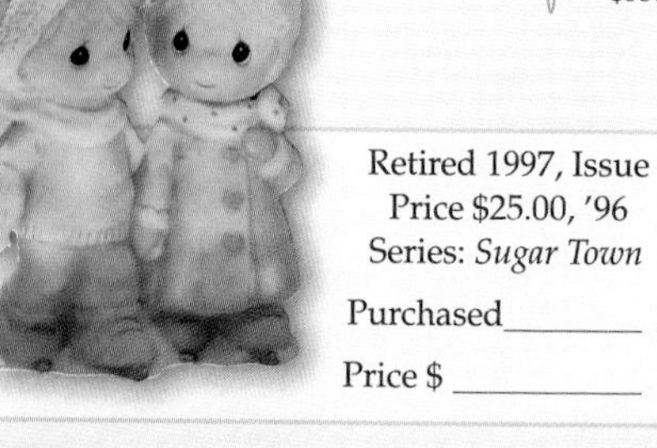

Retired 1997, Issue Price $25.00, '96
Series: *Sugar Town*
Purchased_______,
Price $ _________

Sugar Town Skating Pond Set, 184128

♡ $275.00

† $265.00

Retired 1997, Issue Price $184.50, '97
Set of 7
(Warming Hut, Mazie, Hank And Sharon, Leroy, Cocoa, Sugar Town Skating Sign, and Sugar Town Skating Pond)

Purchased ________, Price $ ___________

Train Station, 184101 (Ornament)

♡ $25.00

Limited Ed., Issue Price $18.50, '96
Series: *Sugar Town*

Purchased _______ ,

Price $ __________

Hot Cocoa Stand, 184144

♡ $22.00

† $20.00

Retired 1997, Issue Price $15.00, '96
Series: *Sugar Town*

Purchased ____________,

Price $ ______________

Flagpole, 184136

♡ $22.00

† $20.00

Retired 1997, Issue Price $15.00, '96
Series: *Sugar Town*

Purchased ___________ ,

Price $______________

Bonfire, 184152

♡ $20.00

† $17.00

Retired 1997, Issue Price $10.00, '96
Series: *Sugar Town*

Purchased ________, Price $ ___________

Sugar Town Enhancement Set, 184160

♡ $60.00

† $60.00

Retired 1997, Issue Price $40.00, '96
Series: *Sugar Town*, Set of 3 (Hot Cocoa Stand, Flagpole, and Bonfire)

Purchased ________, Price $ ___________

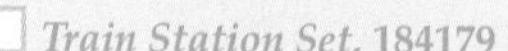

☐ *Train Station Set,* 184179

$230.00 $225.00

$215.00

Retired 1997, Issue Price $170.00, '96
Series: *Sugar Town,* Set of 6 (Train Station, Donny, Luggage Cart, Tammy and Debbie, Railroad Crossing Sign, and Sam)

Purchased ________, Price $ ___________

☐ *Doctor's Office Set,* 184187

$250.00 $245.00

$240.00

Retired 1997, Issue Price $170.00, '96
Series: *Sugar Town,* Set of 6 (Doctor's Office, Sugar and Her Doghouse, Jan, Dr. Sam Sugar, Leon and Evelyn Mae, and Free Christmas Puppies)

Purchased ________, Price $ ___________

☐ *Sam's House Set, 184195*

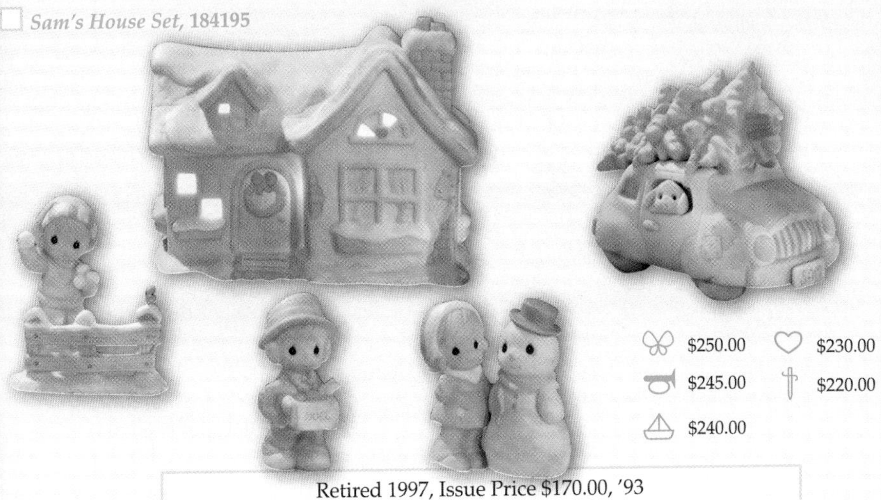

$250.00 $230.00
$245.00 $220.00
$240.00

Retired 1997, Issue Price $170.00, '93
Series: *Sugar Town*, Set of 6
(Sam's House, Fence, Sam's Car, Sammy, Katy Lynne, and Dusty)
Purchased ________, Price $ ________

☐ *May The Sun Always Shine On You,* 184217

$55.00

Limited Ed., Issue Price $37.50, '96
Century Circle Event Exclusive
Purchased ________, Price $ ________

☐ *Winter Wishes Warm The Heart,* 184241 (Ornament)

UM $35.00

Limited Ed., Issue Price
$20.00, '00
Avon Exclusive
Purchased ________,
Price $________

☐ *A Bouquet From God's Garden Of Love,* 184268

$48.00
$45.00
$43.00
$40.00
$40.00
$40.00

Retired 2001, Issue Price $37.50, '97
Series: *Growing In God's Garden Of Love*
Third Issue
Purchased ________, Price $ ________

☐ *Love Makes The World Go 'Round,* 184209 (Ornament)

$45.00

Limited Ed. 19 96, Issue
Price $22.50, '96
Century Circle Exclusive
Purchased ________,
Price $________

Warm Hands, Warm Heart, Warm Wishes, 191353

$90.00

Limited Ed. 1,200, Issue Price $45.00, '01
Chapel Exclusive, 2001 Christmas Event

Purchased ________, Price $ ____________

Warming Hut, 192341 (Nightlight)

♡ $73.00

† $70.00

Retired 1997, Issue Price $60.00, '96
Series: *Sugar Town*

Purchased ________, Price $ ____________

Give Ability A Chance, 192368

♡ $38.00

† $35.00

None of these pieces have the Easter Seals Lily on them.

Annual 1997, Issue Price $30.00, '97
Easter Seals Commemorative

Purchased ________, Price $ ____________

Love Is Universal, 192376

♡ $525.00

† $510.00

Limited Ed. 2,000, Issue Price $500.00, '97
Easter Seals — Lily Understamp
Individually Numbered

Purchased ________, Price $ ____________

Give Ability A Chance, 192384 (Ornament)

UM $9.00

Dated Annual 1997, Issue Price $6.00, '96
Easter Seals Commemorative

Purchased ________,

Price $ ____________

Passenger Car, 192406

UM $35.00

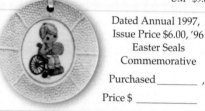

Dated Annual 1996, Issue Price $27.50, '96
Series: *Sugar Town*

Purchased ________, Price $ ____________

You Are A Lifesaver To Me, 204854

♡ $48.00 $40.00

† $45.00 ★ $38.00

$35.00

Retired 2000, Issue Price $35.00, '97

Purchased ____________,

Price $ ________________

☐ *The Lord Is Our Chief Inspiration, 204862*

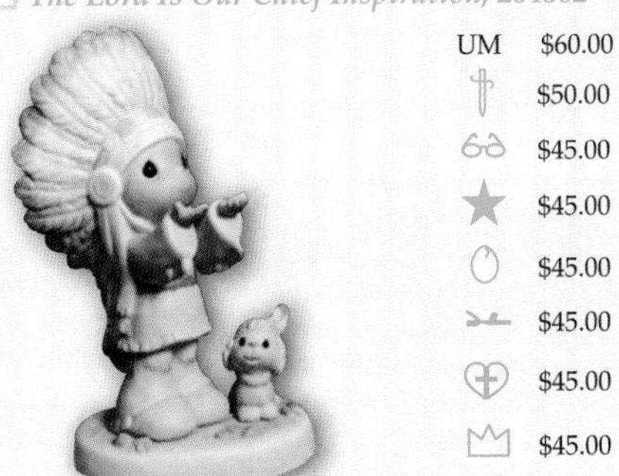

UM $60.00
† $50.00
👓 $45.00
★ $45.00
⬯ $45.00
⋈ $45.00
♡✚ $45.00
♔ $45.00

Retired 2003, Issue Price $45.00, '96
Chapel Exclusive

Purchased ________, Price $ ___________

☐ *The Lord Is Our Chief Inspiration, 204870*

UM $300.00
† $275.00

Limited Ed., Issue Price $250.00, '96
Chapel Exclusive, One Year of Production

Purchased ________, Price $ ___________

☐ *Coleenia, 204889*

UM $45.00
† $40.00
👓 $38.00
★ $35.00
⬯ $35.00
⋈ $35.00
♡✚ $35.00

Retired 2002, Issue Price $32.50, '96
Chapel Exclusive

Purchased ________, Price $ ___________

☐ *A Mother's Love Is From Above, 210408*

♔ $40.00

Limited Ed., Issue Price $40.00, '03
Carlton Cards Exclusive

Purchased ________, Price $ ___________

☐ *The Most Precious Gift Of Them All, 212520 (Ornament)*

♡ $35.00

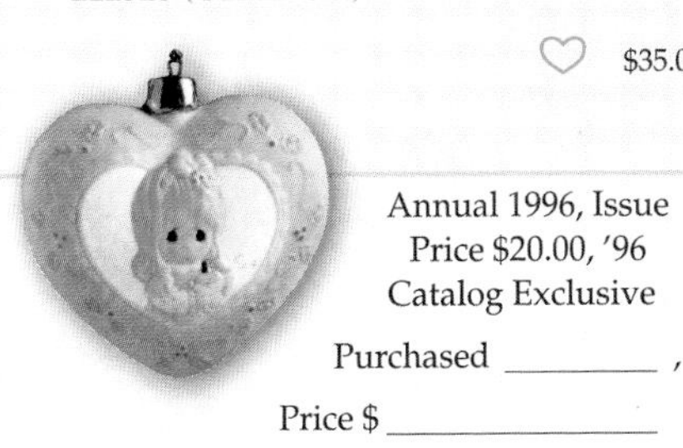

Annual 1996, Issue
Price $20.00, '96
Catalog Exclusive

Purchased ________,

Price $ ___________

☐ *This World Is Not My Home (I'm Just A Passin' Thru), 212547*

UM $110.00
👓 $100.00
★ $95.00

Gospel cassette tape was included with this figurine.

Retired 1999, Issue Price $85.00, '97
Chapel Exclusive
Honors Albert E. Brumley

Purchased ________, Price $ ___________

Your Precious Spirit Comes Shining Through, 212563, 212563A and 212563B

$135.00

Dated Annual 1996, Issue Price $35.00, '96
Regional Event — Knoxville, Indianapolis, and Minneapolis

Purchased ________, Price $ ____________

Wee Three Kings, 213624

$65.00 $62.00 $60.00 $58.00 $56.00 $56.00 $55.00 $55.00 $55.00 $55.00

Open, Issue Price $55.00, '96
Mini Nativity Addition, Set of 3

Purchased ________, Price $ ____________

Sugar Town Accessories, 212725

$25.00

Retired 1997, Issue Price $20.00, '97
Series: *Sugar Town*, Set of 8 (3 Trees, 2 Bushes, Fence, Wreath, and Garland)

Purchased ________, Price $ ____________

Friendship Is Always A Sweet Surprise, 217273

$35.00 $35.00

Limited Ed., Issue Price $35.00, '04
Carlton Cards Exclusive

Purchased ________, Price $ ____________

Shepherd And Sheep, 213616

$30.00 $28.00 $25.00 $25.00 $25.00 $25.00 $25.00 $25.00 $25.00

Open, Issue Price $22.50, '97
Mini Nativity Addition, Set of 2

Purchased ________, Price $ ____________

A Mother's Story Is One Of Love, 220226

$40.00 $40.00

Open, Issue Price $40.00, '02
Carlton Cards Exclusive

Purchased ________, Price $ ____________

Always In His Care, 225290 (Ornament)

UM $12.00

Ornament is shaped like the Easter Seals Lily.

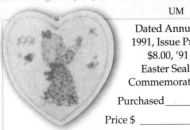

Dated Annual 1990, Issue Price $8.00, '90
Easter Seals Commemorative

Purchased ________________,
Price $________________

Happiness Is Being A Mom, 226228

$50.00

Limited Ed., Issue Price $50.00, '04

Purchased ________,
Price $________

The Enesco Precious Moments Collection, 230448 (Plaque)

UM $15.00

Open, Issue Price $15.00, '88

Purchased ________, Price $ ________

Sharing A Gift Of Love, 233196 (Ornament)

UM $12.00

Dated Annual 1991, Issue Price $8.00, '91
Easter Seals Commemorative

Purchased ______,
Price $ ________

A Universal Love, 238899 (Ornament)

UM $12.00

Annual 1992, Issue Price $8.00, '92
Easter Seals Commemorative

Purchased ________, Price $ ________

Special Times With Mom Create Memories Of A Lifetime, 239260

$50.00

Limited Ed., Issue Price $50.00, '05
Carlton Cards Exclusive

Purchased ________, Price $ ________

It Is No Secret What God Can Do, 244570 (Ornament)

UM $10.00

Dated Annual 1994, Issue Price $6.50, '94
Easter Seals Commemorative

Purchased ________, Price $ ________

☐ *You're My Number One Friend, 250112* (Ornament)

UM $12.00

Dated Annual 1993, Issue Price $8.00, '93
Easter Seals Commemorative

Purchased ________, Price $ ___________

☐ *Lead Me To Calvary, 260916*

$40.00

Dated Annual 1997, Issue Price $37.50, '97
Series: *Dated Cross* — Third Issue

Purchased ________, Price $ ___________

☐ *Age 11, 260924*

$45.00
$43.00
$40.00
$40.00
$40.00
$40.00
$40.00
$40.00
$40.00
$40.00

Open, Issue Price $37.50, '97
Series: *Growing In Grace* (Blonde)

Purchased ________, Price $ ___________

☐ *Age 11, 260924B*

$40.00
$40.00
$40.00
$40.00

Open, Issue Price $37.50, '02
Series: *Growing In Grace* (Brunette)

Purchased ________, Price $ ___________

☐ *Age 12, 260932*

$45.00
$43.00
$40.00
$40.00
$40.00
$40.00
$40.00
$40.00
$40.00
$40.00

Open, Issue Price $37.50, '97
Series: *Growing In Grace* (Blonde)

Purchased ________, Price $ ___________

☐ *Age 12, 260932B*

$40.00
$40.00
$40.00
$40.00

Open, Issue Price $37.50, '02
Series: *Growing In Grace* (Brunette)

Purchased ________, Price $ ___________

From The Time I Spotted You I Knew (Know) We'd Be Friends, 260940

The "Know" error occurred on all Heart marks and the first production run of the Sword marks.

Mark	Price
Heart	$45.00
Sword	$40.00
Eyeglasses	$35.00
Star	$30.00
Egg	$25.00

Retired 2000, Issue Price $20.00, '97
Series: *Birthday Collection*

Purchased ________, Price $ __________

Friends From The Very Beginning, 261068

Mark	Price
Heart	$60.00
Sword	$55.00
Eyeglasses	$55.00
Star	$55.00
Egg	$55.00

Retired 2000, Issue Price $50.00, '97

Purchased ________, Price $ __________

You Have Touched So Many Hearts (Blonde), 261084

Mark	Price
Heart	$55.00
Sword	$53.00
Eyeglasses	$50.00
Star	$48.00
Egg	$45.00
Bow & Arrow	$44.00
Flower	$43.00
Crown	$40.00
Clover	$40.00
Cube	$40.00

Open, Issue Price $37.50, '97

Purchased ________, Price $ __________

You Have Touched So Many Hearts (Brunette), 261084B

Mark	Price
Bow & Arrow	$50.00
Flower	$45.00
Crown	$40.00
Clover	$40.00

Suspended 2004, Issue Price $40.00, '01

Purchased __________ ,

Price $ __________

Hogs And Kisses, 261106

Mark	Price
Eyeglasses	$60.00
Star	$57.00
Egg	$55.00
Bow & Arrow	$53.00
Flower	$50.00
Crown	$50.00
Clover	$50.00
Cube	$50.00

Open, Issue Price $50.00, '99
Series: *Country Lane Collection*

Purchased ________, Price $ __________

Hogs And Kisses, 261106S

UM $155.00

Limited Ed. 1,500, Gift, '98
Chapel Understamp, Swap 'N Sell Weekend
Series: *Country Lane Collection*

Purchased ________, Price $ __________

Lettuce Pray, 261122

Mark	Price
Heart	$25.00
Sword	$23.00
Eyeglasses	$22.00
Star	$21.00

Retired 1999, Issue Price $17.50, '97

Purchased ________, Price $ __________

Have You Any Room For Jesus, 261130

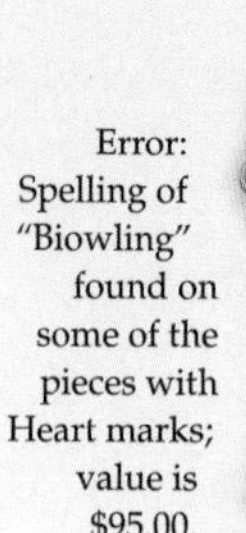

Error: Spelling of "Biowling" found on some of the pieces with Heart marks; value is $95.00.

$50.00
$47.00
$45.00
$43.00
$40.00
$38.00

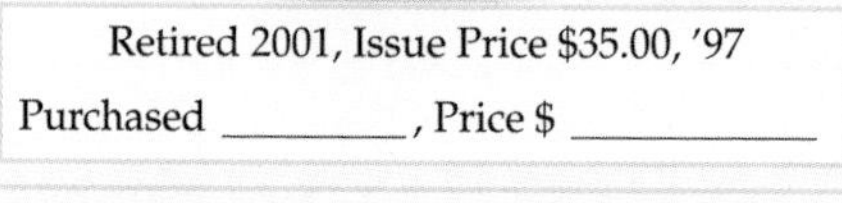

Retired 2001, Issue Price $35.00, '97
Purchased ________, Price $ __________

Say I Do, 261149

$65.00
$60.00
$60.00
$60.00
$60.00
$60.00
$60.00
$60.00
$60.00
$60.00

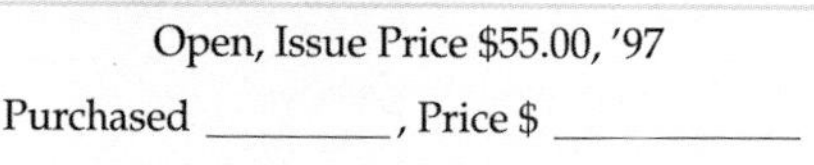

Open, Issue Price $55.00, '97
Purchased ________, Price $ __________

We All Have Our Bad Hair Days, 261157

$40.00
$35.00
$35.00
$35.00
$35.00
$35.00
$35.00

Retired 2002, Issue Price $35.00, '97
Purchased ________, Price $ __________

Bless Your Little Tutu, 261173

UM $20.00

Open, Issue Price $20.00, '97
Series: *Sports — Little Moments*
Purchased ____________,
Price $ ____________

January, 261203

UM $20.00

Open, Issue Price $20.00, '96
Series: *Birthstone — Little Moments*
Purchased ____________,
Price $ ____________

May, 261211

UM $20.00

Open, Issue Price $20.00, '96
Series: *Birthstone — Little Moments*
Purchased ____________,
Price $____________

September, 261238

UM $20.00

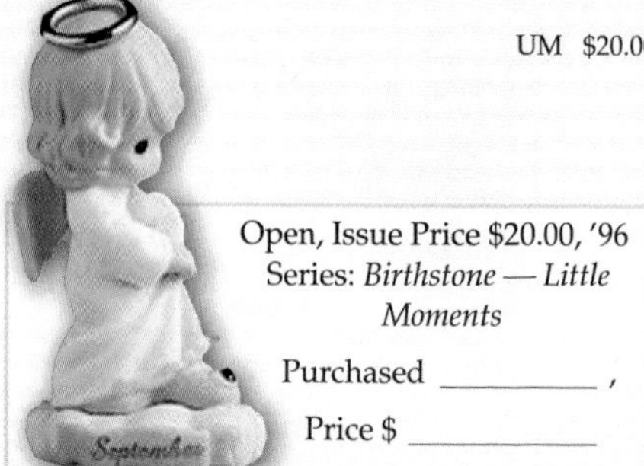

Open, Issue Price $20.00, '96
Series: *Birthstone — Little Moments*
Purchased ____________,
Price $ ____________

☐ *February*, 261246

UM $20.00

Open, Issue Price
$20.00, '96
Series: *Birthstone — Little Moments*

Purchased ____________,

Price $ ____________

☐ *June*, 261254

UM $20.00

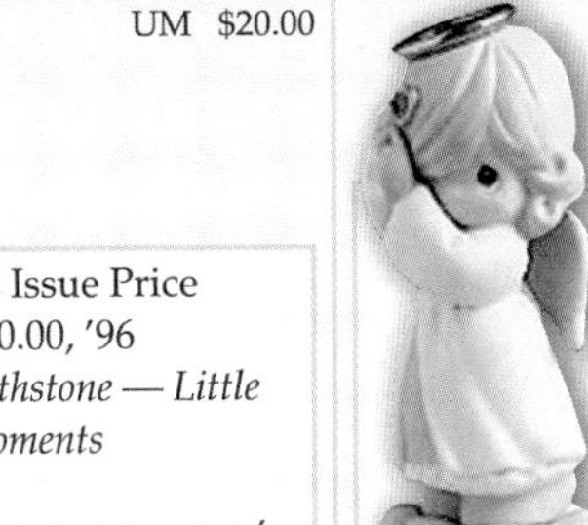

Open, Issue Price
$20.00, '96
Series: *Birthstone — Little Moments*

Purchased ____________,

Price $ ____________

☐ *October*, 261262

UM $20.00

Open, Issue Price
$20.00, '96
Series: *Birthstone — Little Moments*

Purchased ____________,

Price $ ____________

☐ *March*, 261270

UM $20.00

Open, Issue Price
$20.00, '96
Series: *Birthstone — Little Moments*

Purchased ____________,

Price $ ____________

☐ *July*, 261289

UM $20.00

Open, Issue Price
$20.00, '96
Series: *Birthstone — Little Moments*

Purchased ____________,

Price $ ____________

☐ *November*, 261297

UM $20.00

Open, Issue Price
$20.00, '96
Series: *Birthstone — Little Moments*

Purchased ____________,

Price $ ____________

☐ *April*, 261300

UM $20.00

Open, Issue Price
$20.00, '96
Series: *Birthstone — Little Moments*

Purchased ____________,

Price $ ____________

☐ *August*, 261319

UM $20.00

Open, Issue Price
$20.00, '96
Series: *Birthstone — Little Moments*

Purchased ____________,

Price $ ____________

☐ *December, 261327*

UM $20.00

Open, Issue Price $20.00, '96
Series: *Birthstone — Little Moments*
Purchased__________ ,
Price $ __________

☐ *We're So Hoppy You're Here, 261351*

Sword $45.00

Annual 1997, Issue Price $32.50, '97
Spring Celebration Event (April 26, 1997)
Purchased ________, Price $ __________

☐ *Happiness To The Core, 261378*

Mark	Value
Heart	$45.00
Sword	$40.00

Annual 1997, Issue Price $37.50, '97
Catalog Exclusive
Purchased ________, Price $ __________

☐ *Blessed Are Thou Amongst Women, 261556*

This piece has been found double marked with both Eyeglasses and Star.

Mark	Value
Eyeglasses	$215.00
Star	$200.00

Annual 1999, Issue Price $175.00, '99
1998 Fall Show Exclusive
Purchased_____ ,
Price $ ________

☐ *The Lord Is The Hope Of Our Future, 261564*

This piece was paired with a copy of the book *Chicken Soup for the Soul* as a limited edition graduation promotion (261564B) in 2000. Issue price was $45.00; value (Egg mark) is $45.00.

Mark	Value
Heart	$45.00
Sword	$43.00
Eyeglasses	$40.00
Star	$40.00
Egg	$40.00
Bow & Arrow	$40.00
Cross in Heart	$40.00
Crown	$40.00
Flower	$40.00
Box	$40.00

Open, Issue Price $40.00, '97
Purchased ________, Price $ __________

☐ *The Lord Is The Hope Of Our Future, 261564L*

This piece was paired with a copy of the book *Chicken Soup for the Soul* as a limited edition graduation promotion (261564G) in 2000. Issue price was $45.00; value (Egg mark) is $45.00.

Mark	Value
Egg	$40.00
Bow & Arrow	$40.00
Cross in Heart	$40.00
Crown	$40.00
Flower	$40.00
Box	$40.00

Open, Issue Price $40.00, '00
Purchased ________, Price $ __________

☐ *We Have The Sweetest Times Together,* 261580

$125.00
$120.00

Limited Ed. 10,000, Issue Price $100.00, '01

Purchased ________, Price $ __________

☐ *In God's Beautiful Garden Of Love,* 261599 (Ornament)

$65.00

Limited Ed., Issue Price $50.00, '97
Century Circle Exclusive

Purchased ________,

Price $ __________

☐ *Crown Him Lord Of All,* 261602

UM $45.00
$35.00
$35.00
$35.00
$35.00
$35.00
$35.00
$35.00
$35.00

Open, Issue Price $45.00, '97
Chapel Exclusive

Purchased ________, Price $ __________

Dated Annual 1997, Issue Price $30.00, '97
Regional Event — San Jose, Cleveland, Houston, and Philadelphia

Purchased ________, Price $ __________

☐ *Crown Him Lord Of All,* 261610 (Ornament)

UM $35.00
$30.00
$28.00
$25.00
$25.00
$25.00
$25.00
$25.00
$25.00
$25.00

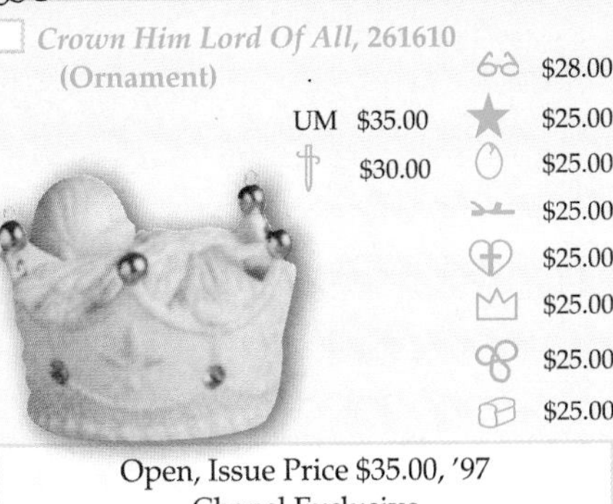

Open, Issue Price $35.00, '97
Chapel Exclusive

Purchased ________, Price $ __________

☐ *In God's Beautiful Garden Of Love,* 261629

$175.00

Limited Ed. 15,000,
Issue Price $150.00, '97
Century Circle Exclusive

Purchased _____,

Price $ __________

☐ *Sweet Sixteen,* 266841 (Medallion)

$350.00

Given to attendees of the 1996 Local Club Chapter Convention. Sixth medallion in the collection.

Convention Gift, '96

Purchased ________, Price $ __________

☐ *A Festival Of Precious Moments,* 270741, 270741A, 270741B, and 270741G

$80.00

☐ *Seeds Of Love From The Chapel, 271586*

Mark	Price
UM	$42.00
∞	$40.00
★	$35.00

Retired 1999, Issue Price $30.00, '97
Chapel Exclusive
Purchased ________, Price $ ___________

☐ *Make A Joyful Noise, 272450*

Mark	Price
♡	$35.00
†	$33.00
∞	$30.00
★	$30.00
○	$30.00
⋈	$30.00
♡✝	$30.00
♔	$30.00
✿	$30.00

Retired 2004, Issue Price $30.00, '97
Series: *Baby Classics*
Purchased ________, Price $ ___________

☐ *Good Friends Are Forever, 272422*

Mark	Price
♡	$36.00
†	$33.00
∞	$31.00
★	$30.00
○	$30.00
⋈	$30.00
♡✝	$30.00
♔	$30.00
✿	$30.00

Retired 2004, Issue Price $30.00, '97
Series: *Baby Classics*
Purchased ________, Price $ ___________

☐ *I Believe In Miracles, 272469*

Mark	Price
♡	$30.00
†	$28.00
∞	$28.00
★	$27.00
○	$26.00
⋈	$26.00
♡✝	$26.00

Retired 2002, Issue Price $25.00, '97
Series: *Baby Classics*
Purchased ________, Price $ ___________

☐ *We Are God's Workmanship, 272434*

Mark	Price
♡	$30.00
†	$28.00
∞	$25.00
★	$25.00
○	$25.00
⋈	$25.00
♡✝	$25.00
♔	$25.00
✿	$25.00

Retired 2004, Issue Price $25.00, '97
Series: *Baby Classics*
Purchased ________, Price $ ___________

☐ *God Loveth A Cheerful Giver, 272477*

Mark	Price
♡	$35.00
†	$30.00
∞	$28.00

Retired 1998, Issue Price $25.00, '97
Series: *Baby Classics*
Purchased ________, Price $ ___________

You Have Touched So Many Hearts, 272485

$30.00 $28.00 $28.00 $27.00 $26.00 $25.00 $25.00 $25.00 $25.00

Retired 2004, Issue Price $25.00, '97
Series: *Baby Classics*
Purchased ________ Price $ ___________

Love Is Sharing, 272493

$33.00 $30.00 $28.00 $28.00 $27.00 $27.00 $27.00

Retired 2002, Issue Price $25.00, '97
Series: *Baby Classics*
Purchased ________, Price $ ___________

Love One Another, 272507

$35.00 $33.00 $32.00 $32.00 $30.00 $30.00 $30.00 $30.00 $30.00

Retired 2004, Issue Price $30.00, '97
Series: *Baby Classics*
Purchased ________, Price $ ___________

Happy Birthday Jesus, 272523

$40.00 $38.00 $36.00 $35.00 $35.00 $35.00 $35.00 $35.00 $35.00

Open, Issue Price $35.00, '97
Purchased ________, Price $ ___________

Sharing The Light Of Love, 272531

$45.00 $43.00 $40.00 $38.00 $35.00 $35.00 $35.00 $35.00 $35.00

Open, Issue Price $35.00, '97
Purchased ________, Price $ ___________

I Think You're Just Divine, 272558

$45.00 $43.00 $40.00 $40.00 $40.00

First production pieces have the logo missing from the understamp. Also known as *Holy Cow.*

Retired 2001, Issue Price $40.00, '97
Purchased ________, Price $ ___________

Joy To The World, 272566 (Ornament)

Cross	$30.00
Glasses	$28.00
Star	$25.00

Retired 1999, Issue Price $20.00, '97

Purchased ________, Price $ ____________

Palm Trees, Hay Bale And Baby Food, 272582

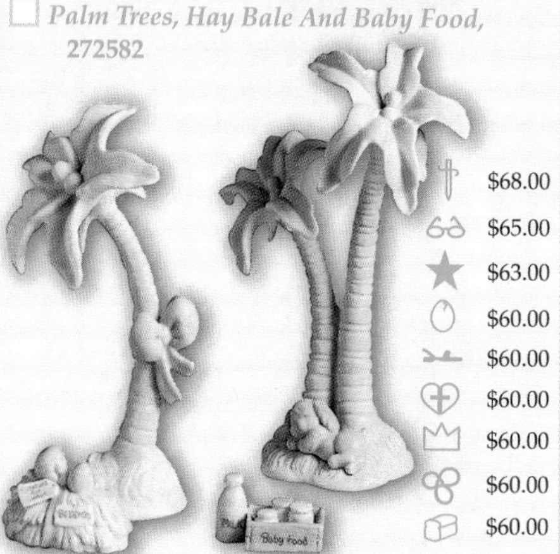

Cross	$68.00
Glasses	$65.00
Star	$63.00
Egg	$60.00
Sword	$60.00
Heart	$60.00
Crown	$60.00
Clover	$60.00
Cube	$60.00

Open, Issue Price $60.00, '97
Nativity Addition, Set of 4

Purchased ________, Price $ ____________

I'm Dreaming Of A White Christmas, 272590

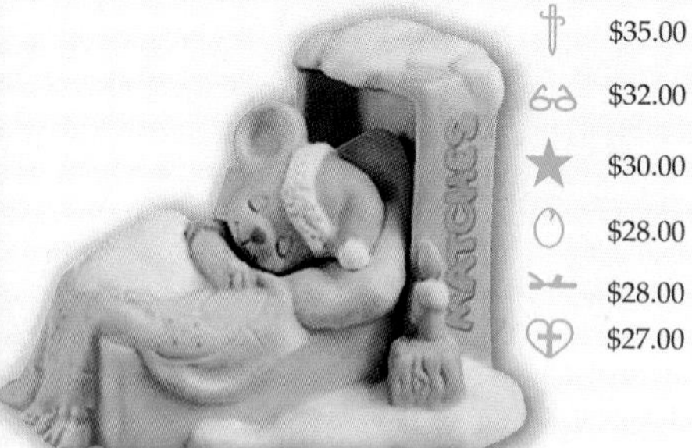

Cross	$35.00
Glasses	$32.00
Star	$30.00
Egg	$28.00
Sword	$28.00
Heart	$27.00

Retired 2002, Issue Price $25.00, '97

Purchased ________, Price $ ____________

You Will Always Be A Winner To Me (Boy), 272612

UM $20.00

Open, Issue Price $20.00, '97
Series: *Sports — Little Moments*

Purchased ________, Price $ ____________

It's Ruff To Always Be Cheery, 272639

UM $20.00

Open, Issue Price $20.00, '97
Series: *Sports — Little Moments*

Purchased ________, Price $ ____________

Age 13, 272647

Cross	$45.00
Glasses	$43.00
Star	$40.00
Egg	$40.00
Sword	$40.00
Heart	$40.00
Crown	$40.00
Clover	$40.00
Cube	$40.00

Open, Issue Price $40.00, '97
Series: *Growing In Grace* (Blonde)

Purchased ________, Price $ ____________

☐ *Age 13, 272647B*

$40.00
$40.00
$40.00
$40.00

Open, Issue Price $40.00, '02
Series: *Growing In Grace* (Brunette)
Purchased ________, Price $ ____________

☐ *Age 14, 272655*

$40.00
$38.00
$37.00
$35.00
$35.00
$35.00
$35.00
$35.00
$35.00

Open, Issue Price $35.00, '97
Series: *Growing In Grace* (Blonde)
Purchased ________, Price $ ____________

☐ *Age 14, 272655B*

$35.00
$35.00
$35.00
$35.00

Open, Issue Price $35.00, '02
Series: *Growing In Grace* (Brunette)
Purchased ________, Price $ ____________

☐ *Age 15, 272663*

$45.00
$40.00
$40.00
$40.00
$40.00
$40.00
$40.00

Open, Issue Price $40.00, '97
Series: *Growing In Grace* (Blonde)
Purchased ________, Price $ ____________

☐ *Age 15, 272663B*

$40.00
$40.00
$40.00
$40.00

Open, Issue Price $40.00, '02
Series: *Growing In Grace* (Brunette)
Purchased ________, Price $ ____________

☐ *Cane You Join Us For A Merry Christmas, 272671*

$40.00

Dated Annual 1997, Issue Price $30.00, '97
Purchased ________, Price $ ____________

☐ *Cane You Join Us For A Merry Christmas,* 272698 (Ornament)

† $30.00

Dated Annual 1997, Issue Price $18.50, '97

Purchased ____________ , Price $ ____________

☐ *Cane You Join Us For A Merry Christmas,* 272701 (Plate)

† $55.00

Dated Annual 1997, Issue Price $50.00, '97
Series: *Beauty Of Christmas* — Fourth Issue

Purchased ________, Price $ ____________

☐ *Cane You Join Us For A Merry Christmas,* 272728 (Ornament)

† $35.00

Dated Annual 1997, Issue Price $30.00, '97

Purchased ________ , Price $____________

☐ *Our First Christmas Together,* 272736 (Ornament)

† $28.00

Dated Annual 1997, Issue Price $20.00, '97

Purchased ________ , Price $ ____________

☐ *Baby's First Christmas (Girl),* 272744 (Ornament)

† $25.00

Dated Annual 1997, Issue Price $18.50, '97

Purchased ____________ , Price $ ____________

☐ *Baby's First Christmas (Boy),* 272752 (Ornament)

† $25.00

Dated Annual 1997, Issue Price $18.50, '97

Purchased____________ , Price $ ____________

☐ *Slow Down For The Holidays,* 272760 (Ornament)

† $25.00

Dated Annual 1997, Issue Price $18.50, '97
Series: *Birthday Collection*

Purchased ________ , Price $____________

☐ *And You Shall See A Star,* 272787

† $45.00
Eyeglasses $40.00
Star $38.00
Egg $35.00
Sailboat $35.00

Retired 2001, Issue Price $32.50, '97
Nativity Addition

Purchased ________, Price $ ____________

☐ *Schoolhouse, 272795 (Nightlight)*

† $115.00

American Flag version. Also came with Canadian flag (same item number).

Retired 1997, Issue Price $80.00, '97
Series: *Sugar Town*
Purchased ________, Price $ __________

☐ *Chuck, 272809*

† $40.00

Dated Annual 1997, Issue Price $22.50, '97
Series: *Sugar Town*
Purchased ________, Price $ __________

☐ *Aunt Cleo, 272817*

† $25.00

Retired 1997, Issue Price $18.50, '97
Series: *Sugar Town*
Purchased ________,
Price $ __________

☐ *Schoolhouse Collector's Set, 272876*

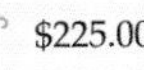

† $225.00

Dated Annual 1997, Issue Price $183.50, '97
Series: *Sugar Town*, Set of 6 (Schoolhouse, Chuck, Aunt Cleo, Aunt Bulah and Uncle Sam, Merry-Go-Round, and Heather)
Purchased ________, Price $ __________

Schoolhouse came in American flag and Canadian flag versions.

☐ *Aunt Bulah And Uncle Sam, 272825*

† $33.00

Retired 1997, Issue Price $22.50, '97
Series: *Sugar Town*
Purchased ________,
Price $ __________

☐ *Heather, 272833*

† $30.00

Retired 1997, Issue Price $20.00, '97
Series: *Sugar Town*
Purchased ________, Price $ __________

☐ *Merry-Go-Round, 272841*

† $30.00

Retired 1997, Issue Price $20.00, '97
Series: *Sugar Town*
Purchased ________, Price $ __________

Puppies On Sled, 272892 (Ornament)

$25.00 $23.00
$24.00 $22.00
$22.00
$20.00

Retired 2002, Issue Price $18.50, '97

Purchased ________, Price $ __________

Bike Rack, 272906

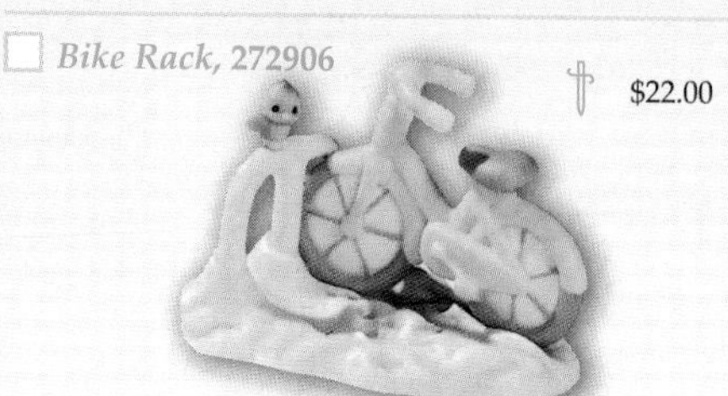

$22.00

Retired 1997, Issue Price $15.00, '97
Series: *Sugar Town*

Purchased ________, Price $ __________

Garbage Can, 272914

$25.00

Retired 1997, Issue Price $20.00, '97
Series: *Sugar Town*

Purchased ________, Price $ __________

Somebody Cares, 272922 (Ornament)

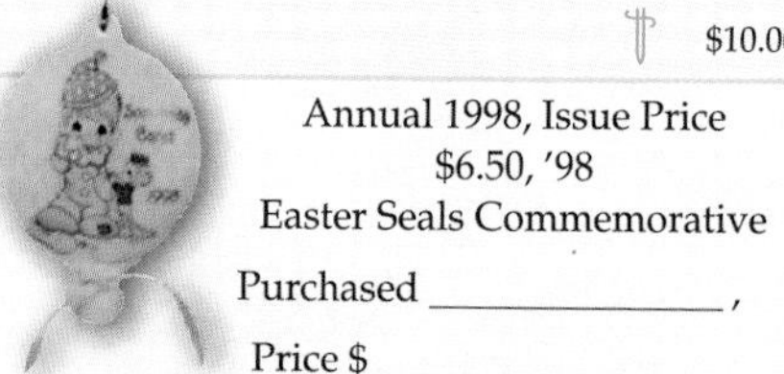

$10.00

Annual 1998, Issue Price
$6.50, '98
Easter Seals Commemorative

Purchased __________,

Price $__________

Pack Your Trunk For The Holidays, 272949 (Ornament)

$25.00

Dated Annual 1997,
Issue Price $20.00, '97
Holiday Preview
Event

Purchased ________,

Price $ __________

My Love Will Keep You Warm, 272957

$45.00 $37.50
$42.00 $37.50
$40.00 $37.50
$38.00 $37.50

Open, Issue Price
$37.50, '98

Purchased ________,

Price $ __________

My Love Will Keep You Warm, 272957S

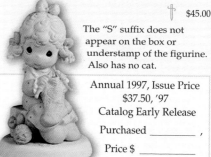

$45.00

The "S" suffix does not appear on the box or understamp of the figurine. Also has no cat.

Annual 1997, Issue Price
$37.50, '97
Catalog Early Release

Purchased ________,

Price $ __________

Sugar Town Skating Pond Collector's Set, 272930

$245.00

Retired 1997, Issue Price $169.50, '97
Series: *Sugar Town*, Set of 6
(Warming Hut, Hank And Sharon, Cocoa,
Mazie, Leroy, and Sugar Town Skating Pond)

Purchased ________, Price $ __________

☐ *My Love Will Keep You Warm, 272965 (Ornament)*

† $38.00

Annual 1997, Issue Price $20.00, '97
Syndicated Catalog Exclusive

Purchased________,
Price $ ________

☐ *Love Grows Here, 272981*

† $575.00

Limited Ed. 2,000, Issue Price $500.00, '98
Easter Seals Commemorative Lily Understamp
Individually Numbered

Purchased________,
Price $ ________

☐ *Cargo Car, 273007*

† $35.00

Dated Annual 1997, Issue Price $27.50, '97
Series: *Sugar Town*

Purchased ________, Price $ ________

☐ *Sugar Town Enhancement Set, 273015*

† $50.00

Retired 1997, Issue Price $43.50, '97
Series: *Sugar Town*, Set of 3 (Bike Rack, Bunnies Caroling, and Garbage Can)

Purchased ________, Price $ ________

☐ *Donkey, Camel, And Cow, 279323*

Mark	Price
†	$35.00
[eyeglasses]	$32.00
★	$31.00
[egg]	$30.00
[sandal]	$30.00
[cross in heart]	$30.00
[crown]	$30.00
[flower]	$30.00
[box]	$30.00

Open, Issue Price $30.00, '97
Mini Nativity Addition, Set of 3

Purchased ________, Price $ ________

☐ *Inn, 283428 (Nightlight)*

Mark	Price
†	$135.00
[eyeglasses]	$130.00
★	$125.00
[egg]	$120.00
[sandal]	$115.00
[cross in heart]	$110.00
[crown]	$105.00
[flower]	$100.00
[box]	$100.00

Open, Issue Price $100.00, '97
Nativity Addition

Purchased ________, Price $ ________

☐ *Nativity Wall, 283436*

Mark	Price
†	$48.00
[eyeglasses]	$45.00
★	$45.00
[egg]	$40.00
[sandal]	$40.00
[cross in heart]	$40.00
[crown]	$40.00
[flower]	$40.00
[box]	$40.00

Open, Issue Price $40.00, '97
Mini Nativity Addition

Purchased ________, Price $ ________

For An Angel You're So Down To Earth, 283444

$22.00 $17.50
$20.00 $17.50
$19.00 $17.50
$18.00 $17.50
$17.50

Open, Issue Price $17.50, '97
Mini Nativity Addition
Purchased ________, Price $ __________

You Will Always Be A Winner To Me (Girl), 283460

UM $20.00

Open, Issue Price $20.00, '97
Series: *Sports — Little Moments*
Purchased __________,
Price $ __________

Cats With Kitten, 291293

$19.00
$22.00 $18.50
$20.00 $18.50
$18.50
$18.50
$18.50
$18.50

Open, Issue Price $18.50, '97
Mini Nativity Addition
Purchased ________, Price $ __________

Nativity Well, 292753

$45.00 $37.00
$40.00 $35.00
$35.00

Retired 2001, Issue Price $30.00, '97
Nativity Addition
Purchased ________,
Price $ __________

Under His Wings I Am Safely Abiding, 306835

$48.00
$45.00

Dated Annual 1998, Issue Price $40.00, '98
Series: *Dated Cross* — Fourth Issue
Purchased ________, Price $ __________

20 Years And The Vision's Still The Same, 306843

$60.00
$55.00

Dated Annual 1998, Issue Price $55.00, '98
Commemorates Twentieth Anniversary Of Precious Moments
Purchased ________, Price $ __________

Friendship Hits The Spot, 306916

$35.00
$32.00
$30.00
$30.00
$30.00
$27.00
$27.00
$27.00

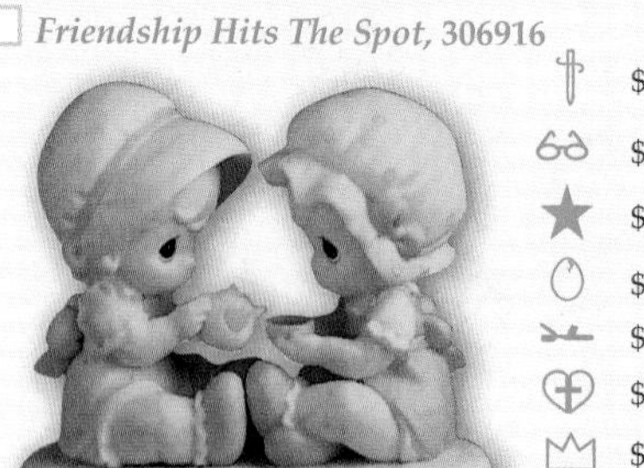

Retired 2004, Issue Price $30.00, '98
Series: *Baby Classics*
Purchased ________, Price $ __________

Loving You Dear Valentine, 306932

Mark	Value
Cross	$30.00
Eyeglasses	$28.00
Star	$25.00
Egg	$25.00
Bow & Arrow	$25.00
Heart	$25.00

Retired 2002, Issue Price $25.00, '98
Series: *Baby Classics*

Purchased ________, Price $ __________

He Cleansed My Soul, 306940

Mark	Value
Cross	$30.00
Eyeglasses	$28.00
Star	$25.00
Egg	$25.00
Bow & Arrow	$25.00
Heart	$25.00
Crown	$25.00
Clover	$25.00

Retired 2004, Issue Price $25.00, '98
Series: *Baby Classics*

Purchased ________, Price $ __________

For The Sweetest Tu-lips In Town, 306959

Mark	Value
Cross	$40.00
Eyeglasses	$38.00
Star	$35.00
Egg	$35.00
Bow & Arrow	$35.00
Heart	$35.00
Crown	$35.00
Clover	$35.00
Loaf	$35.00

Open, Issue Price $35.00, '98

Purchased ________, Price $ __________

For The Sweetest Tu-lips In Town, 306959B

Mark	Value
Heart	$35.00
Crown	$35.00
Clover	$35.00

Suspended 2004, Issue Price $35.00, '02

Purchased ________, Price $ __________

You Are Always On My Mind, 306967

Mark	Value
Cross	$50.00
Eyeglasses	$48.00
Star	$45.00
Egg	$43.00

Retired 2000, Issue Price $37.50, '98

Purchased ________, Price $ __________

Missum You, 306991

Mark	Value
Cross	$55.00
Eyeglasses	$50.00
Star	$48.00
Egg	$46.00
Bow & Arrow	$46.00

Retired 2001, Issue Price $45.00, '98

Purchased ________, Price $ __________

☐ *Charity Begins In The Heart, 307009*

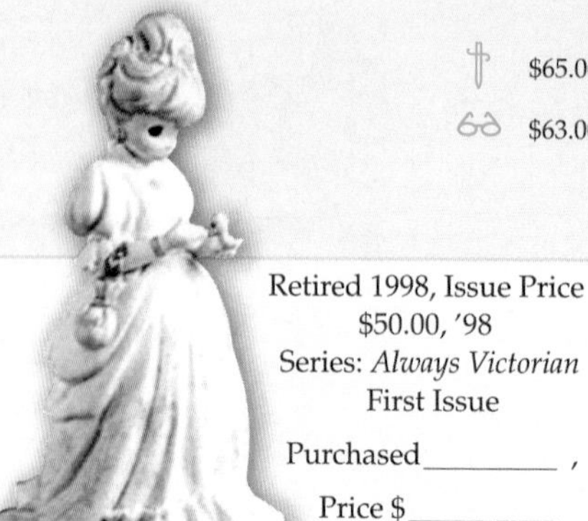

$65.00
$63.00

Retired 1998, Issue Price $50.00, '98
Series: *Always Victorian* First Issue
Purchased________ ,
Price $__________

☐ *You're Just as Sweet As Pie, 307017*

$55.00
$53.00
$50.00
$48.00

Retired 2001, Issue Price $45.00, '98
Series: *Country Lane Collection*
Purchased ________, Price $ ___________

☐ *Oh Taste And See That The Lord Is Good, 307025*

$65.00
$62.00
$60.00
$58.00

Retired 2001, Issue Price $55.00, '98
Series: *Country Lane Collection*
Purchased ________, Price $ ___________

☐ *Fork Over Those Blessings To Others, 307033*

$55.00
$53.00
$50.00
$45.00
$45.00
$45.00
$45.00

Retired 2004, Issue Price $45.00, '98
Series: *Country Lane Collection*
Purchased ________, Price $ ___________

☐ *Nobody Likes To Be Dumped, 307041*

$80.00
$73.00

Retired 1999, Issue Price $65.00, '98
Series: *Country Lane Collection*
Purchased ________, Price $ ___________

☐ *I'll Never Tire Of You, 307068*

$60.00
$55.00

Retired 1999, Issue Price $50.00, '98
Series: *Country Lane Collection*
Purchased ________, Price $ ___________

Peas Pass The Carrots, 307076

6ð	$45.00
★	$43.00
◯	$40.00

Retired 2000, Issue Price $35.00, '98
Series: *Country Lane Collection*

Purchased ________, Price $ ________

Bringing In The Sheaves, 307084 (Musical)

UM	$385.00
†	$365.00
6ð	$285.00

Limited Ed. 12,000, Issue Price $90.00, '98
Series: *Country Lane Collection*
Tune: "Bringing In The Sheaves"

Purchased ________, Price $ ________

Holiday Wishes, Sweety Pie, 312444

UM $28.00

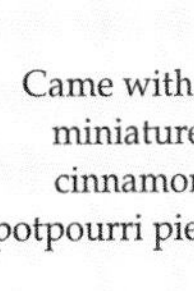

Came with miniature cinnamon potpourri pie.

Limited Ed., Issue Price $20.00, '97
Series: *Little Moments*, Set of 2

Purchased ________, Price $ ________

You're Just Perfect In My Book, 320560

UM $25.00

Open, Issue Price $25.00, '98
Series: *Professionals — Little Moments*

Purchased ________,

Price $ ________

Loving Is Caring, 320579

UM $20.00

Open, Issue Price $20.00, '98
Series: *Professionals — Little Moments*

Purchased ________,

Price $ ________

Loving Is Caring, 320595

UM $20.00

Open, Issue Price $20.00, '98
Series: *Professionals — Little Moments*

Purchased ________,

Price $ ________

You Set My Heart Ablaze, 320625

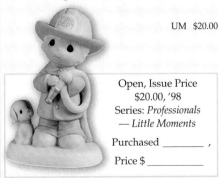

UM $20.00

Open, Issue Price $20.00, '98
Series: *Professionals — Little Moments*

Purchased ________,

Price $ ________

Just The Facts… You're Terrific, 320668

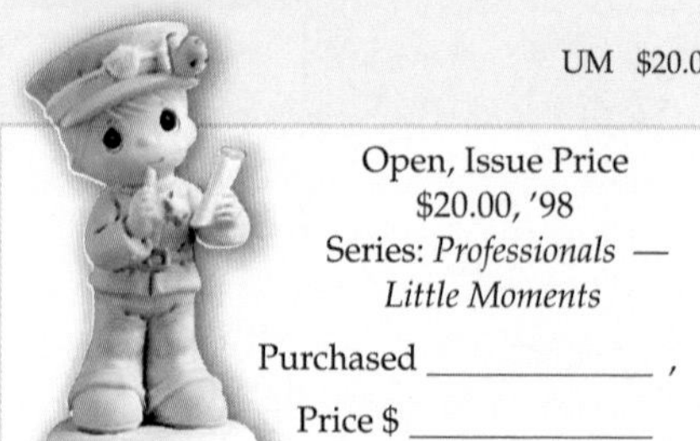

UM $20.00

Open, Issue Price $20.00, '98
Series: *Professionals — Little Moments*

Purchased ____________ ,
Price $ ____________

You Have Such A Special Way Of Caring Each And Every Day, 320706

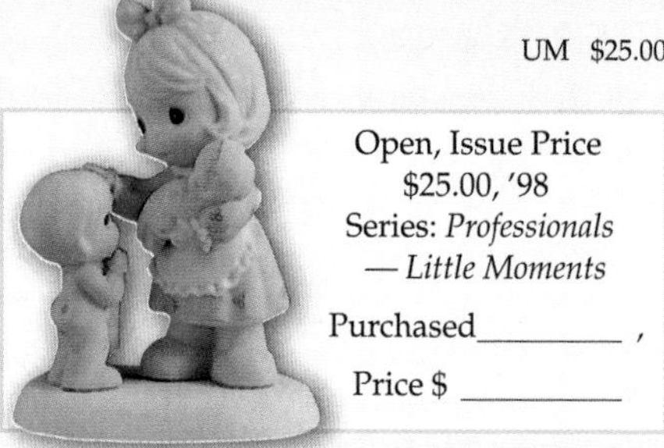

UM $25.00

Open, Issue Price $25.00, '98
Series: *Professionals — Little Moments*

Purchased________ ,
Price $ ________

What Would I Do Without You, 320714

UM $25.00

Open, Issue Price $25.00, '98
Series: *Professionals — Little Moments*

Purchased_______ ,
Price $ ________

Wait Patiently On The Lord, 325279

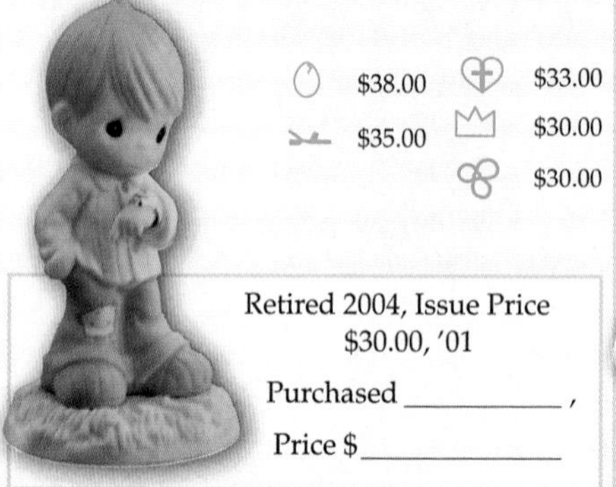

Mark	Price	Mark	Price
[Egg]	$38.00	[Heart]	$33.00
[Bow & Arrow]	$35.00	[Crown]	$30.00
		[Clover]	$30.00

Retired 2004, Issue Price $30.00, '01

Purchased __________ ,
Price $__________

Only One Life To Offer, 325309

Mark	Price
[Cross]	$45.00
[Glasses]	$43.00
[Star]	$40.00
[Egg]	$38.00
[Bow & Arrow]	$38.00

Retired 2001, Issue Price $35.00, '98

Purchased ________, Price $ __________

The Good Lord Will Always Uphold Us, 325325

Mark	Price
[Cross]	$65.00
[Glasses]	$60.00
[Star]	$58.00
[Egg]	$55.00
[Bow & Arrow]	$53.00

Retired 2001, Issue Price $50.00, '98

Purchased ________, Price $ __________

By Grace We Have Communion With God, 325333C

[Egg] $90.00

Piece is a bible holder and comes with a New Testament Bible.

Annual 2000, Issue Price $75.00, '00
Show Special

Purchased ________, Price $ __________

There Are Two Sides To Every Story, 325368

(cross)	$25.00
(glasses)	$22.00
(star)	$20.00
(egg)	$18.00
(bow)	$18.00

Retired 2001, Issue Price $15.00, '98

Purchased ________, Price $ ____________

Life Can Be A Jungle, 325457

(glasses)	$45.00

Annual 1998, Issue Price $37.50, '98
10/31/98 Jungle Jamboree DSR Event Piece

Purchased ________, Price $ ____________

Mom You Always Make Our House A Home, 325465

(cross)	$45.00
(glasses)	$40.00

Limited Ed., Issue Price $37.50, '98
Catalog Exclusive

Purchased ________, Price $ ____________

Mom, You're My Special-Tea, 325473

Early release to retailers attending 1998 Fall Enesco Show. Included a mini *Chicken Soup for the Soul* book.

(glasses)	$30.00
(star)	$27.00

Retired 1999, Issue Price $25.00, '99
Mother's Day 1999

Purchased ________, Price $ ____________

Home Is Where The Heart Is, 325481

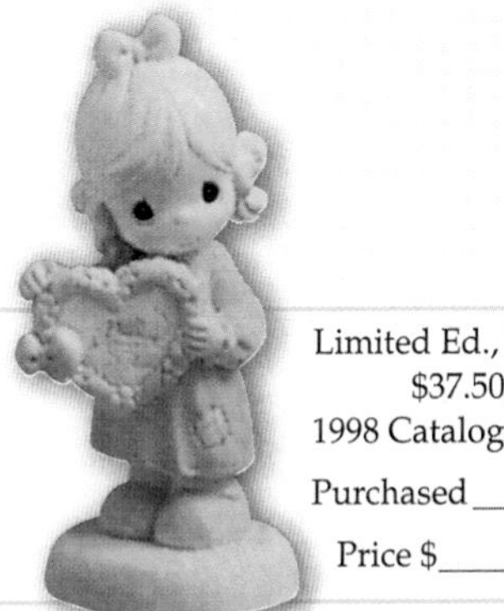

(cross)	$50.00
(glasses)	$45.00

Limited Ed., Issue Price $37.50, '98
1998 Catalog Exclusive

Purchased __________,

Price $__________

Marvelous Grace, 325503

(glasses)	$58.00

Limited Ed., Issue Price $50.00, '98
Century Circle Exclusive

Purchased ________, Price $ ____________

☐ *Our Future Is Looking Much Brighter,* 325511

$450.00

Given to those on the 1998 Precious Moments Cruise.

Dated Annual 1998, Gift, '98
Cruise Piece

Purchased ________, Price $ ___________

☐ *Well, Blow Me Down It's Yer Birthday,* 325538

$60.00
$55.00
$53.00
$52.00
$50.00

Retired 2001, Issue Price $50.00, '98

Purchased ________, Price $ ___________

☐ *Garnet — Color Of Boldness (January),* 335533 (Hinged Box)

$30.00 $25.00
$28.00 $25.00
$25.00 $25.00
$25.00 $25.00

Open, Issue Price
$25.00, '98
Series: *Birthstone Collection*

Purchased ________, Price $ ___________

Open, Issue Price
$25.00, '98
Series: *Birthstone Collection*

Purchased ________, Price $ ___________

☐ *Amethyst — Color Of Faith (February),* 335541 (Hinged Box)

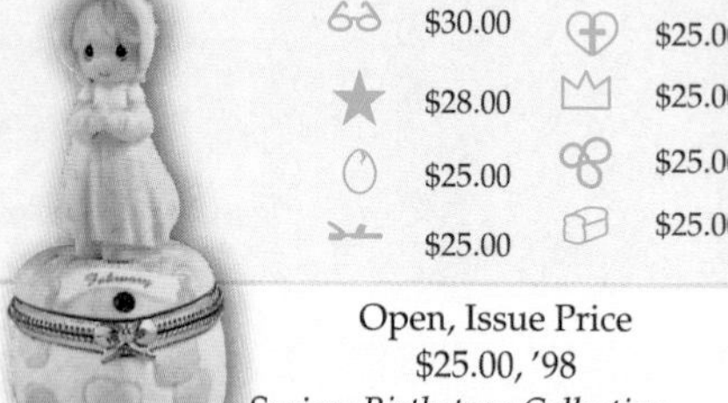

$30.00 $25.00
$28.00 $25.00
$25.00 $25.00
$25.00 $25.00

Open, Issue Price
$25.00, '98
Series: *Birthstone Collection*

Purchased ________, Price $ ___________

☐ *Aquamarine — Color Of Kindness (March),* 335568 (Hinged Box)

$30.00 $25.00
$28.00 $25.00
$25.00 $25.00
$25.00 $25.00

Open, Issue Price
$25.00, '98
Series: *Birthstone Collection*

Purchased ________, Price $ ___________

☐ *Diamond — Color Of Purity (April),* 335576 (Hinged Box)

$30.00 $25.00
$28.00 $25.00
$25.00 $25.00
$25.00 $25.00

Open, Issue Price
$25.00, '98
Series: *Birthstone Collection*

Purchased ________, Price $ ___________

☐ *Emerald — Color Of Patience (May),* 335584 (Hinged Box)

$30.00 $25.00
$28.00 $25.00
$25.00 $25.00
$25.00 $25.00

☐ *Pearl — Color Of Love (June)*, 335592 (Hinged Box)

$30.00 $25.00
$28.00 $25.00
$25.00 $25.00
$25.00 $25.00

Open, Issue Price
$25.00, '98
Series: *Birthstone Collection*
Purchased ____________ ,
Price $ ______________

☐ *Opal — Color Of Happiness (October)*, 335657 (Hinged Box)

$30.00 $25.00
$28.00 $25.00
$25.00 $25.00
$25.00 $25.00

Open, Issue Price
$25.00, '98
Series: *Birthstone Collection*
Purchased ______________ ,
Price $ ________________

☐ *Ruby — Color Of Joy (July)*, 335606 (Hinged Box)

$30.00 $25.00
$28.00 $25.00
$25.00 $25.00
$25.00 $25.00

Open, Issue Price
$25.00, '98
Series: *Birthstone Collection*
Purchased ____________ ,
Price $ _______________

☐ *Topaz — Color Of Truth (November)*, 335665 (Hinged Box)

$30.00 $25.00
$28.00 $25.00
$25.00 $25.00
$25.00 $25.00

Open, Issue Price
$25.00, '98
Series: *Birthstone Collection*
Purchased _____________ ,
Price $ ________________

☐ *Peridot — Color Of Pride (August)*, 335614 (Hinged Box)

$30.00 $25.00
$28.00 $25.00
$25.00 $25.00
$25.00 $25.00

Open, Issue Price
$25.00, '98
Series: *Birthstone Collection*
Purchased _____________ ,
Price $ ________________

☐ *Turquoise — Color Of Loyalty (December)*, 335673 (Hinged Box)

$30.00 $25.00
$28.00 $25.00
$25.00 $25.00
$25.00 $25.00

Open, Issue Price
$25.00, '98
Series: *Birthstone Collection*
Purchased _____________ ,
Price $ ________________

☐ *Sapphire — Color Of Confidence (September)*, 335622 (Hinged Box)

$30.00 $25.00
$28.00 $25.00
$25.00 $25.00
$25.00 $25.00

Open, Issue Price
$25.00, '98
Series: *Birthstone Collection*
Purchased _______ , Price $ ________

☐ *I'm Gonna Let It Shine,* 349852

UM $60.00
$55.00
$53.00
$50.00
$50.00
$50.00
$50.00

Open, Issue Price $50.00, '99
Chapel Exclusive
Purchased ________, Price $ __________

☐ *A Prayer Warrior's Faith Can Move Mountains,* 354406

UM $50.00
$48.00
$45.00
$45.00
$45.00

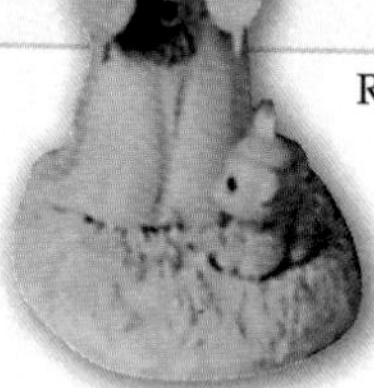

Retired 2002, Issue Price $45.00, '98
Chapel Exclusive
Purchased________,
Price $ __________

☐ *A Prayer Warrior's Faith Can Move Mountains,* 354414

UM $260.00

Limited Ed., Issue Price $250.00, '98
Chapel Exclusive, One Year Production
Purchased ________, Price $ __________

☐ *Catch Ya Later,* 358959

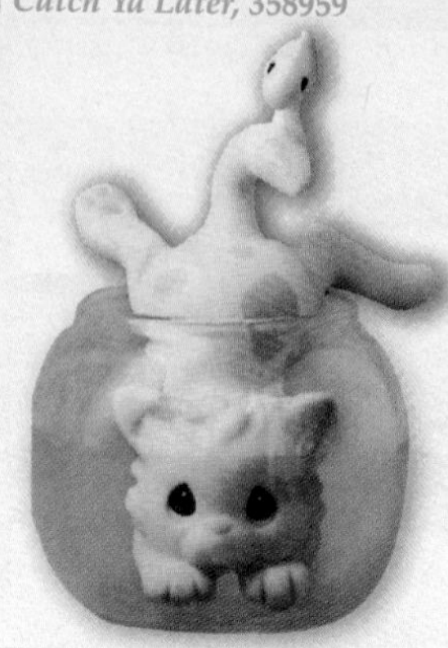

$25.00
$25.00
$25.00
$25.00

Open, Issue Price $25.00, '03
Purchased ________, Price $ __________

☐ *Thank You For The Time We Share,* 384836

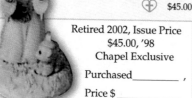

UM $35.00

Limited Ed., Issue Price $22.00, '97
Avon Exclusive
Series: *Little Moments*
Purchased __________,
Price $ __________

☐ *Fountain Of Angels,* 384844

UM $55.00
$53.00
$50.00
$48.00
$45.00
$45.00
$45.00

Retired, Issue Price $45.00, '98
Chapel Exclusive
Purchased ________, Price $ __________

Many Years Of Blessing You, 384887

† $75.00

👓 $70.00

Sent to 61 retailers from 2/15/98 to 4/1/98. Remainders available to retailers who attended Oct. '98 Enesco Show.

Limited Ed., Issue Price $60.00, '98
Commemorates Kirlin Hallmark Fiftieth Anniversary

Purchased ________, Price $ __________

Autumn's Praise, 408751 (Musical)

$225.00

$225.00

Two Year Collectible, Issue Price $200.00, '90
Series: *The Four Seasons*
Tune: "Autumn Leaves"

Purchased ________, Price $ __________

The Voice Of Spring, 408735 (Musical)

$225.00

$225.00

Two Year Collectible, Issue Price $200.00, '90
Series: *The Four Seasons*, Tune: "April Love"

Purchased ________, Price $ __________

Winter's Song, 408778 (Musical)

$225.00

$225.00

Two Year Collectible, Issue Price $200.00, '90
Series: *The Four Seasons*
Tune: "Through The Eyes Of Love"

Purchased ________, Price $ __________

Summer's Joy, 408743 (Musical)

$225.00

$225.00

Two Year Collectible, Issue Price $200.00, '90
Series: *The Four Seasons*
Tune: "You Are My Sunshine"

Purchased ________, Price $ __________

The Voice Of Spring, 408786 (Doll)

$175.00

$175.00

Two Year Collectible, Issue Price $150.00, '90
Series: *The Four Seasons*

Purchased ________, Price $ __________

☐ *Summer's Joy*, 408794 (Doll)

$175.00

$175.00

Two Year Collectible, Issue Price $150.00, '90
Series: *The Four Seasons*
Purchased ________, Price $ ___________

☐ *Autumn's Praise*, 408808 (Doll)

$175.00

$175.00

Two Year Collectible, Issue Price $150.00, '90
Series: *The Four Seasons*
Purchased ________, Price $ ___________

☐ *Winter's Song*, 408816 (Doll)

$175.00

$175.00

Two Year Collectible, Issue Price $150.00, '90
Series: *The Four Seasons*
Purchased ________, Price $ ___________

☐ *May You Have An Old Fashioned Christmas*, 417777 (Musical)

$225.00

$225.00

$225.00

Two Year Collectible, Issue Price $200.00, '91
Tune: "Have Yourself A Merry Christmas"
Purchased ________, Price $ ___________

☐ *May You Have An Old Fashioned Christmas*, 417785 (Doll)

$175.00

$175.00

$175.00

Two Year Collectible, Issue Price $150.00, '91
Purchased ________, Price $ ___________

☐ *You Have Touched So Many Hearts*, 422282 (Musical)

$200.00

$200.00

$200.00

Two Year Collectible, Issue Price $175.00, '91
Tune: "Everybody Loves Somebody"
Purchased ________, Price $ ___________

You Have Touched So Many Hearts, 427527 (Doll)

Mark	Price
Flame	$115.00
Vessel	$115.00
G-Clef	$115.00

Two Year Collectible, Issue Price $90.00, '91

Purchased ________, Price $ ___________

The Eyes Of The Lord Are Upon You (Boy), 429570 (Musical)

Mark	Price
Flame	$75.00
Vessel	$73.00
G-Clef	$70.00
Butterfly	$68.00
Trumpet	$65.00

Suspended 1994, Issue Price $65.00, '91
Tune: "Brahms' Lullaby"

Purchased ________, Price $ ___________

The Eyes Of The Lord Are Upon You (Girl), 429589 (Musical)

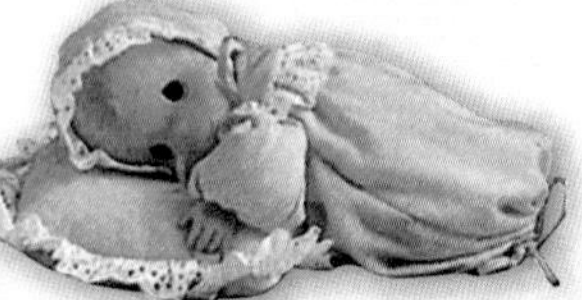

Mark	Price
Flame	$75.00
Vessel	$73.00
G-Clef	$70.00
Butterfly	$68.00
Trumpet	$65.00

Suspended, 1994, Issue Price $65.00, '91
Tune: "Brahms' Lullaby"

Purchased ________, Price $ ___________

20 Years And The Vision's Still The Same, 451312 (Ornament)

Mark	Price
Eyeglasses	$25.00

Limited Ed., Issue Price $22.50, '98
Commemorates Twentieth Anniversary of Precious Moments

Purchased ________, Price $ ___________

Feed My Lambs, 453722

Mark	Price
UM	$75.00
Star	$70.00
Egg	$69.00
Sword	$69.00
Heart	$68.00
Crown	$68.00
Clover	$67.50
Cube	$67.50

Open, Issue Price $67.50, '98
Chapel Exclusive
Shepherd Of The Hills Exclusive

Purchased ________, Price $ ___________

I'm Sending You A Merry Christmas, 455601

Mark	Price
Eyeglasses	$35.00

Dated Annual 1998, Issue Price $30.00, '98

Purchased ________, Price $ ___________

I'm Sending You A Merry Christmas, 455628 (Ornament)

Mark	Price
Eyeglasses	$30.00

Dated Annual 1998, Issue Price $18.50, '98

Purchased ___________,

Price $___________

Our First Christmas Together, 455636 (Ornament)

$28.00

Dated Annual 1998, Issue Price $25.00, '98

Purchased ________, Price $ ___________

Baby's First Christmas (Girl), 455644 (Ornament)

$22.00

Dated Annual 1998, Issue Price $18.50, '98

Purchased ____________,

Price $ ______________

Baby's First Christmas (Boy), 455652 (Ornament)

$22.00

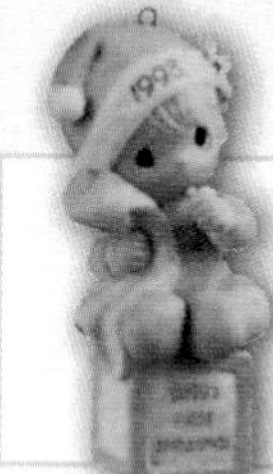

Dated Annual 1998, Issue Price $18.50, '98

Purchased ____________,

Price $ ______________

I'll Be Dog-ged It's That Season Again, 455660 (Ornament)

$22.00

Dated Annual 1998, Issue Price $18.50, '98 Series: *Birthday Collection*

Purchased ________, Price $ ___________

Mornin' Pumpkin, 455687

$55.0

$50.0

Retired 1999, Issue Price $45.00, '98

Purchased ________, Price $ ___________

Praise God From Whom All Blessings Flow, 455695

$50.0

$48.0

$45.0

$43.0

Retired 2001, Issue Price $40.00, '98

Purchased ________, Price $ ___________

Praise The Lord And Dosie-Do, 455733

$55.00

$53.00

$50.00

$50.00

$50.00

$50.00

$50.00

Retired 2004, Issue Price $50.00, '98

Purchased ________, Price $ ___________

☐ *Peas On Earth, 455768*

$50.00
$45.00
$40.00
$38.00

Retired 2001, Issue Price $32.50, '98

Purchased ________, Price $ ___________

☐ *I'm Just Nutty About The Holidays, 455776 (Ornament)*

$25.00
$23.00
$22.00
$20.00
$20.00

Retired 2002, Issue Price $17.50, '98

Purchased ________, Price $ ___________

☐ *Alaska Once More, How's Yer Christmas? 455784*

$40.00
$38.00
$35.00
$35.00
$35.00
$35.00
$35.00
$35.00

Open, Issue Price $35.00, '98

Purchased ________, Price $ ___________

☐ *You Can Always Fudge A Little During The Season, 455792*

$40.00
$38.00
$35.00
$35.00
$35.00
$35.00
$35.00
$35.00

Open, Issue Price $35.00, '98

Purchased ______,

Price $ ________

☐ *Things Are Poppin' At Our House This Christmas, 455806*

$50.00
$48.00
$45.00
$45.00
$45.00
$45.00

Open, Issue Price $45.00, '00

Purchased ________, Price $ ___________

☐ *Wishing You A Yummy Christmas, 455814*

$45.00
$40.00
$38.00
$35.00

Retired 2001, Issue Price $30.00, '98

Purchased ________, Price $ ___________

I Saw Mommy Kissing Santa Claus, 455822

$75.00
$73.00
$70.00
$68.00
$65.00
$65.00
$65.00
$65.00

Open, Issue Price $65.00, '98
Purchased ________, Price $ ___________

Warmest Wishes For The Holidays, 455830

$65.00
$60.00
$58.00
$55.00

Retired 2001, Issue Price $50.00, '99
Purchased ________, Price $ ___________

Time For A Holy Holiday, 455849

$45.00
$40.00
$38.00
$35.00

Retired 2001, Issue Price $35.00, '98
Purchased ________, Price $ ___________

Wishing You A Moo-ie Christmas, 455865

$70.00
$68.00
$65.00
$63.00
$62.00
$61.00
$60.00

Retired 2004, Issue Price $60.00, '99
Series: *Country Lane Collection*
Purchased ________, Price $ ___________

Have A Cozy Country Christmas, 455873

$55.00
$53.00
$50.00
$50.00
$50.00
$50.00
$50.00
$50.00

Open, Issue Price $50.00, '98
Purchased ________, Price $ ___________

Friends Are Forever, Sew Bee It, 455903

$72.00
$70.00
$68.00
$68.00
$66.00

Retired 2002, Issue Price $60.00, '98
Purchased ________, Price $ ___________

☐ *I Now Pronounce You Man And Wife*, 455938

$35.00
$33.00
$31.00
$30.00
$30.00
$30.00
$30.00
$30.00

Open, Issue Price $30.00, '98

Purchased ________, Price $ ___________

☐ *The Light Of The World Is Jesus*, 455954

$35.00
$33.00
$31.00
$30.00
$30.00
$30.00
$30.00
$30.00

Open, Issue Price $30.00, '98
Nativity Addition

Purchased ________, Price $ ___________

☐ *Hang On To That Holiday Feeling*, 455962

$30.00
$28.00
$25.00
$23.00

Retired 2001, Issue Price $17.50, '98
Mini Nativity Addition

Purchased ________, Price $ ___________

☐ *Flight Into Egypt*, 455970

Offered to retailers who attended the 1998 Spring Fling Show.

$90.00

Annual 1998, Issue Price $75.00, '98
Complements Large Nativity, Set of 2

Purchased ________, Price $ ___________

☐ *My True Love Gave To Me*, 455989 (Ornament)

$25.00
$23.00
$22.00
$20.00
$20.00
$20.00
$20.00
$20.00

Open, Issue Price $20.00, '98
Series: *12 Days Of Christmas — Day 1*

Purchased ________, Price $ ___________

☐ *We're Two Of A Kind*, 455997 (Ornament)

$25.00
$23.00
$22.00
$20.00
$20.00
$20.00
$20.00
$20.00

Open, Issue Price $20.00, '98
Series: *12 Days Of Christmas — Day 2*

Purchased ________, Price $ ___________

☐ *Saying "Oui" To Our Love,* 456004 (Ornament)

$25.00 $22.00
$23.00 $20.00
$20.00
$20.00
$20.00
$20.00

Open, Issue Price $20.00, '98
Series: *12 Days Of Christmas — Day 3*
Purchased ________, Price $ __________

☐ *Ringing In The Season,* 456012 (Ornament)

$25.00 $22.00
$23.00 $20.00
$20.00
$20.00
$20.00
$20.00

Open, Issue Price $20.00, '98
Series: *12 Days Of Christmas — Day 4*
Purchased ________, Price $ __________

☐ *The Golden Rings Of Friendship,* 456020 (Ornament)

$25.00 $22.00
$23.00 $20.00
$20.00
$20.00
$20.00
$20.00

Open, Issue Price $20.00, '98
Series: *12 Days Of Christmas — Day 5*
Purchased ________, Price $ __________

☐ *Hatching The Perfect Holiday,* 456039 (Ornament)

$25.0
$23.0
$22.0
$20.0
$20.0
$20.0
$20.0
$20.0

Open, Issue Price $20.00, '98
Series: *12 Days Of Christmas — Day 6*
Purchased ________, Price $ __________

☐ *Swimming Into Your Heart,* 456047 (Ornament)

$25.0
$23.0
$22.0
$20.0
$20.0
$20.0
$20.0
$20.00

Open, Issue Price $20.00, '98
Series: *12 Days Of Christmas — Day 7*
Purchased ________, Price $ __________

☐ *Eight Mice A Milking,* 456055 (Ornament)

$25.00
$23.00
$22.00
$20.00
$20.00
$20.00
$20.00
$20.00

Open, Issue Price $20.00, '98
Series: *12 Days Of Christmas — Day 8*
Purchased ________, Price $ __________

Nine Ladies Dancing With Joy, 456063 (Ornament)

$25.00 $22.00
$23.00 $20.00
$20.00
$20.00
$20.00
$20.00

Open, Issue Price $20.00, '98
Series: *12 Days Of Christmas — Day 9*

Purchased ________, Price $ ___________

Leaping Into The Holidays, 456071 (Ornament)

$25.00 $22.00
$23.00 $20.00
$20.00
$20.00
$20.00
$20.00

Open, Issue Price $20.00, '98
Series: *12 Days Of Christmas — Day 10*

Purchased ________, Price $ ___________

Piping In Perfect Harmony, 456098 (Ornament)

$25.00 $22.00
$23.00 $20.00
$20.00
$20.00
$20.00
$20.00

Open, Issue Price $20.00, '98
Series: *12 Days Of Christmas — Day 11*

Purchased ________, Price $ ___________

Twelve Drummers Drumming Up Fun, 456101 (Ornament)

$25.00 $22.00
$23.00 $20.00
$20.00
$20.00
$20.00
$20.00

Open, Issue Price $20.00, '98
Series: *12 Days Of Christmas — Day 12*

Purchased ________, Price $ ___________

God Loveth A Cheerful Giver, 456225

$2,500.00

Limited Ed. 20, Gift, '98
Loving, Caring & Sharing Contest
Twentieth Anniversary Piece

Purchased ________, Price $ ___________

Sugar Town Post Office Collector's Set, 456217

$275.00

Limited Ed., Issue Price $250.00, '98
Series: *Sugar Town*, Lighted, Set of 7
(Post Office, girl with lights, girl with goose, girl mailing snowball, boy with ice cream, postman in car, girl pushing sleigh of puppies)

Purchased ________, Price $ ___________

☐ *How Can Two Work Together Except They Agree*, 456268 (Ornament)

† $30.00
6ᘐ $28.00

Limited Ed., Issue Price $25.00, '98
Care-A-Van Exclusive
Purchased ________, Price $ ___________

☐ *You Have Mastered The Art Of Caring*, 456276

6ᘐ $50.00

Limited Ed., Issue Price $40.00, '98
Fall Syndicated Catalog
Purchased ________, Price $ ___________

☐ *Heaven Bless You Easter Seal*, 456314

6ᘐ $39.00
★ $37.00

Annual 1999, Issue Price $35.00, '99
Easter Seals Commemorative,
Lily Understamp
Purchased ________, Price $ ___________

☐ *Sharing Our Time Is So Precious*, 456349

★ $120.00

Limited Ed. 15,000, Issue Price $110.00, '99
Century Circle Exclusive
Individually Numbered
Purchased ________, Price $ ___________

☐ *You Are A Dutch-ess To Me (Holland)*, 456373

UM $20.00

Open, Issue Price $20.00, '98
Series: *International — Little Moments*
Purchased ________, Price $ ___________

☐ *Life Is A Fiesta (Spain)*, 456381

UM $20.00

Open, Issue Price $20.00, '98
Series: *International — Little Moments*
Purchased ________, Price $ ___________

☐ *Don't Rome Too Far From Home (Italy), 456403*

UM $20.00

Open, Issue Price $20.00, '98
Series: *International — Little Moments*

Purchased ________ ,
Price $ ________

☐ *You Can't Beat The Red, White And Blue (United States), 456411*

UM $20.00

Open, Issue Price $20.00, '98
Series: *International — Little Moments*

Purchased ________ ,
Price $ ________

☐ *Love's Russian Into My Heart (Russia), 456446*

UM $20.00

Open, Issue Price $20.00, '98
Series: *International — Little Moments*

Purchased ________ ,
Price $ ________

☐ *Hola, Amigo! (Mexico), 456454*

UM $20.00

Open, Issue Price $20.00, '98
Series: *International — Little Moments*

Purchased ________ ,
Price $ ________

☐ *Afri-can Be There For You, I Will Be (Kenya), 456462*

UM $20.00

Open, Issue Price $20.00, '98
Series: *International — Little Moments*

Purchased ________ ,
Price $ ________

☐ *I'd Travel The Highlands To Be With You (Scotland), 456470*

UM $20.00

Open, Issue Price $20.00, '98
Series: *International — Little Moments*

Purchased ________ ,
Price $ ________

☐ *Sure Would Love To Squeeze You (Germany), 456896*

UM $20.00

Open, Issue Price $20.00, '98
Series: *International — Little Moments*

Purchased ________ ,
Price $ ________

☐ *You Are My Amour (France), 456918*

UM $20.00

Open, Issue Price $20.00, '98
Series: *International — Little Moments*

Purchased ________ ,
Price $ ________

☐ *Our Friendship Is Always In Bloom (Japan)*, 456926

UM $20.00

Open, Issue Price $20.00, '98
Series: *International — Little Moments*
Purchased ________,
Price $ ________

☐ *My Love Will Stand Guard Over You (England)*, 456934

UM $20.00

Open, Issue Price $20.00, '98
Series: *International — Little Moments*
Purchased ________,
Price $ ________

☐ *I'm Sending You A Merry Christmas*, 469327 (Plate)

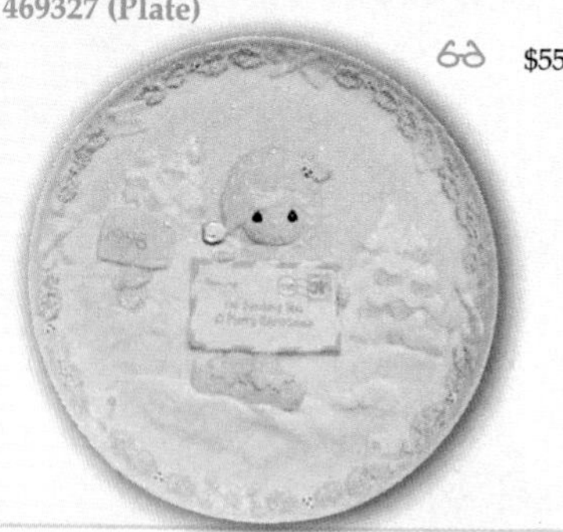

$55.00

Dated Annual 1998, Issue Price $50.00, '98
Series: *Wonder Of Christmas*
Purchased ________, Price $ ________

☐ *May Your Christmas Be Warm*, 470279 (Ornament)

$25.00
$22.00
$20.00
$18.00
$15.00

☐ *We Are All Precious In His Sight*, 475068

$550.00
$525.00

Limited Ed. 2,500, Issue Price $500.00, '99
Easter Seals, Lily Understamp
Individually Numbered
Purchased ________, Price $ ________

☐ *Heaven Bless You Easter Seal*, 475076 (Ornament)

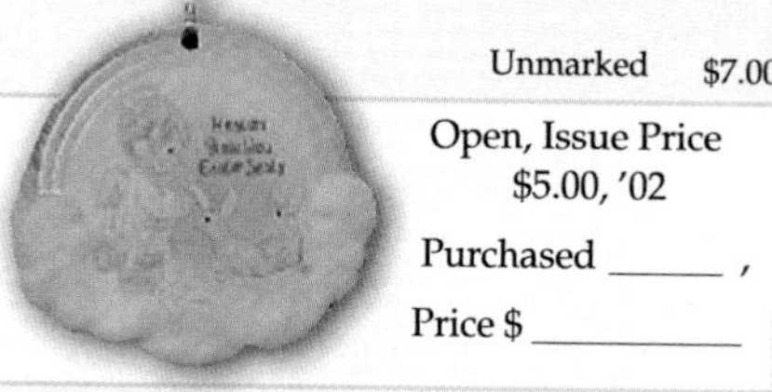

Unmarked $7.00

Open, Issue Price $5.00, '02
Purchased ________,
Price $ ________

☐ *Even The Heavens Shall Praise Him*, 475084 (Ornament)

$40.00

Annual 1998, Issue Price $30.00, '98
Century Circle Exclusive
Purchased ________,
Price $ ________

$15.00 $15.00 $15.00

Open, Issue Price $15.00, '98
Series: *Birthday Circus Train*
Purchased ________, Price $ ________

☐ *Toy Maker, 475092*

UM $60.00

Memorial to Pat Carson's father.

Retired 2001, Issue Price $40.00, '98
Chapel Exclusive
Purchased ________, Price $ ___________

☐ *Toy Maker, 475106 (Ornament)*

UM $40.00

Memorial to Pat Carson's father.

Retired 2001, Issue Price $20.00, '98
Chapel Exclusive
Purchased ___________,
Price $ _____________

☐ *On Our Way To A Special Day, 481602*

$25.00
$22.00
$20.00
$17.50
$17.50
$17.50
$17.50
$17.50

Open, Issue Price $17.50, '99
Japan and CCR Exclusive
Purchased ________, Price $ ___________

☐ *On Our Way To A Special Day, 481610*

$25.00
$22.00
$20.00
$17.50
$17.50
$17.50
$17.50
$17.50

Open, Issue Price $17.50, '99
Japan and CCR Exclusive
Purchased ________, Price $ ___________

☐ *Shiny New And Ready For School, 481629*

$35.00
$30.00
$28.00
$25.00
$20.00
$20.00
$20.00
$20.00

Open, Issue Price $20.00, '99
Japan and CCR Exclusive
Purchased ________, Price $ ___________

☐ *Shiny New And Ready For School, 481637*

$35.00
$30.00
$28.00
$25.00
$20.00
$20.00
$20.00
$20.00

Open, Issue Price $20.00, '99
Japan and CCR Exclusive
Purchased ________, Price $ ___________

Growing In Wisdom, 481645

$40.00 · $35.00 · $30.00 · $25.00 · $22.50 · $22.50 · $22.50 · $22.50

Open, Issue Price $22.50, '99
Japan and CCR Exclusive
Purchased ____________ ,
Price $ ______________

Growing In Wisdom, 481653

$40.00 · $35.00 · $30.00 · $25.00 · $22.50 · $22.50 · $22.50 · $22.50

Open, Issue Price $22.50, '99
Japan and CCR Exclusive
Purchased __________ ,
Price $______________

Love Is The Key, 482242

$45.00 · $40.00

Limited Ed., Issue Price
$30.00, '98
Avon Exclusive
Purchased____________ ,
Price $ ____________

My Universe Is You, 487902

$60.00 · $50.00

Retired 1999, Issue Price $45.00, '99
Purchased ________, Price $ ___________

All Girls Are Beautiful, 481661

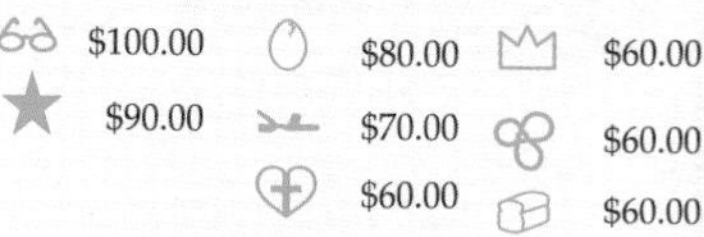

$100.00 · $90.00 · $80.00 · $70.00 · $60.00 · $60.00 · $60.00 · $60.00

Open, Issue Price $60.00, '99
Japan and CCR Exclusive
Set of 5 (Emperor, Empress, and
3 Flower Arrangements)
Purchased _____, Price $ ___________

Make Me Strong, 481688

$100.00 · $90.00 · $80.00 · $70.00 · $60.00 · $60.00 · $60.00 · $60.00

Open, Issue Price $60.00, '99
Japan and CCR Exclusive
Set of 4
(Samurai, Helmet, Bow, and Arrows)
Purchased _______, Price $ ___________

☐ *Believe It Or Knot I Luv You, 487910*

- $45.00
- $40.00
- $35.00
- $35.00
- $35.00
- $35.00
- $35.00
- $35.00

Open, Issue Price $35.00, '99

Purchased _________, Price $ ____________

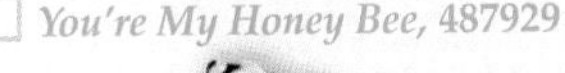

☐ *You're My Honey Bee, 487929*

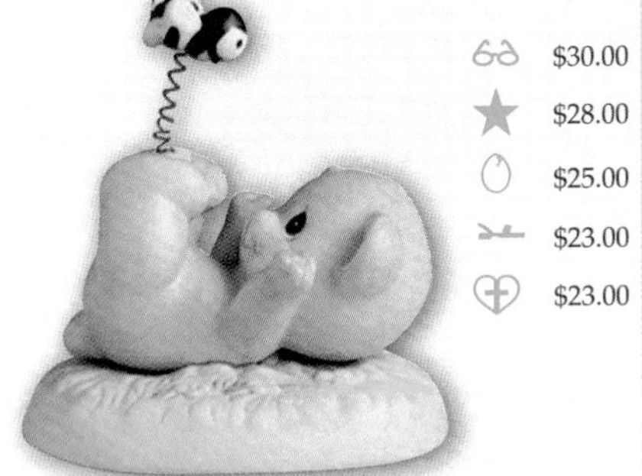

- $30.00
- $28.00
- $25.00
- $23.00
- $23.00

Retired 2001, Issue Price $20.00, '99

Purchased _________, Price $ ____________

☐ *Jesus Is My Lighthouse, 487945 (Lighted)*

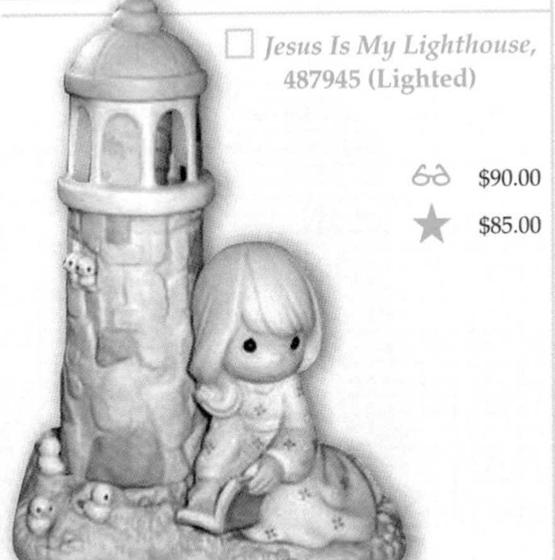

- $90.00
- $85.00

Limited Ed., Issue Price $75.00, '99

Purchased _________, Price $ ____________

☐ *You Can Always Count On Me, 487953*

- $45.00
- $42.00
- $40.00
- $38.00
- $38.00

Retired 2002, Issue Price $35.00, '99

Purchased _________, Price $ ____________

☐ *What Better To Give Than Yourself, 487988*

- $40.00
- $38.00
- $35.00
- $33.00
- $32.00

Retired 2002, Issue Price $30.00, '99

Purchased _________, Price $ ____________

☐ *Take Your Time It's Your Birthday, 488003*

- $30.00
- $28.00
- $26.00
- $25.00
- $25.00
- $25.00
- $25.00
- $25.00

Open, Issue Price $25.00, '99
Series: *Birthday Circus Train* — Age 11

Purchased _________, Price $ ____________

☐ *Give A Grin And Let The Fun Begin,* 488011

$25.00
$25.00
$25.00
$25.00
$25.00
$25.00

Open, Issue Price $25.00, '00
Series: *Birthday Circus Train* — Age 12
Purchased ________, Price $ __________

☐ *You Mean The Moose To Me,* 488038

$25.00
$25.00
$25.00
$25.00
$25.00
$25.00

Open, Issue Price $25.00, '00
Series: *Birthday Circus Train* — Age 13
Purchased ________, Price $ __________

☐ *Mom, You've Given Me So Much,* 488046

$35.00
$35.00
$35.00
$35.00
$35.00
$35.00
$35.00
$35.00

Open, Issue Price $35.00, '99
Purchased ________, Price $ __________

☐ *You Just Can't Replace A Good Friendship,* 488054

$35.00
$35.00
$35.00
$35.00
$35.00
$35.00
$35.00
$35.00

Open, Issue Price $35.00, '99
Purchased ________, Price $ __________

☐ *He'll Carry Me Through,* 488089

$55.00
$50.00
$48.00
$45.00
$45.00

Retired 2004, Issue Price $45.00, '00
Purchased ________, Price $ __________

☐ *Confirmed In The Lord,* 488178

$40.00
$35.00
$30.00
$30.00
$30.00
$30.00
$30.00
$30.00

Open, Issue Price $30.00, '99
Purchased ________, Price $ __________

☐ *You'll Always Be Daddy's Little Girl,* 488224

$55.00
$50.00
$50.00
$50.00
$50.00
$50.00

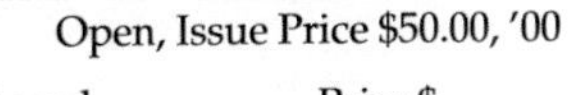

Open, Issue Price $50.00, '00
Purchased ________, Price $ ___________

☐ *Dedicated To God,* 488232

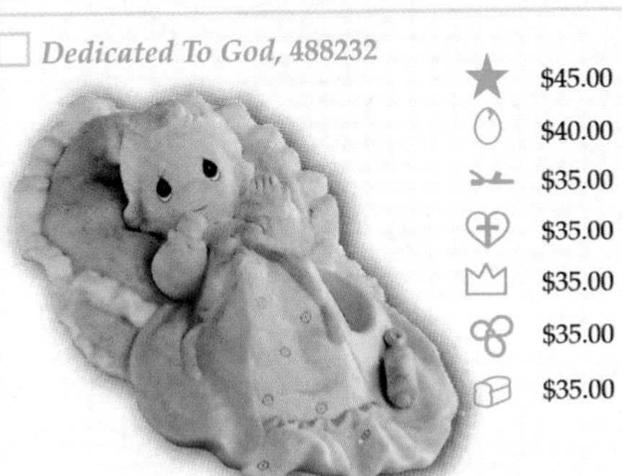

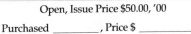

$45.00
$40.00
$35.00
$35.00
$35.00
$35.00
$35.00

Open, Issue Price $35.00, '99
Purchased ________, Price $ ___________

☐ *A Very Special Bond,* 488240

$80.00
$78.00
$75.00
$70.00
$70.00
$70.00
$70.00
$70.00

Open, Issue Price $70.00, '99
Purchased ________, Price $ ___________

☐ *Hope Is Revealed Through God's Word,* 488259

$78.00

Annual, Issue Price $70.00, '98
Series: *Always Victorian*, Second Issue
Purchased ________, Price $ ___________

☐ *Jonah And The Whale,* 488283

UM $25.00

Open, Issue Price $25.00, '99
Series: *Bible Stories — Little Moments*
Purchased ________, Price $ ___________

☐ *Daniel And The Lion's Den,* 488291

UM $25.00

Open, Issue Price $25.00, '99
Series: *Bible Stories — Little Moments*
Purchased ________, Price $ ___________

☐ *Joseph's Special Coat*, 488305

UM $25.00

Open, Issue Price $25.00, '99
Series: *Bible Stories — Little Moments*
Purchased ________, Price $ __________

☐ *You Can't Take It With You*, 488321

$30.00
$28.00
$25.00
$25.00
$25.00
$25.00
$25.00

Retired 2004, Issue Price $25.00, '99
Purchased ________, Price $ __________

☐ *Holiday Surprises Come In All Sizes*, 488348

$30.00
$30.00

Open, Issue Price $30.00, '04
Purchased ________,
Price $ __________

☐ *Always Listen To Your Heart*, 488356

$30.00
$28.00
$25.00
$25.00
$25.00
$25.00
$25.00
$25.00

Suspended 2005, Issue Price $25.00, '99
Purchased ________, Price $ __________

☐ *Purr-fect Friends*, 488364

$40.00

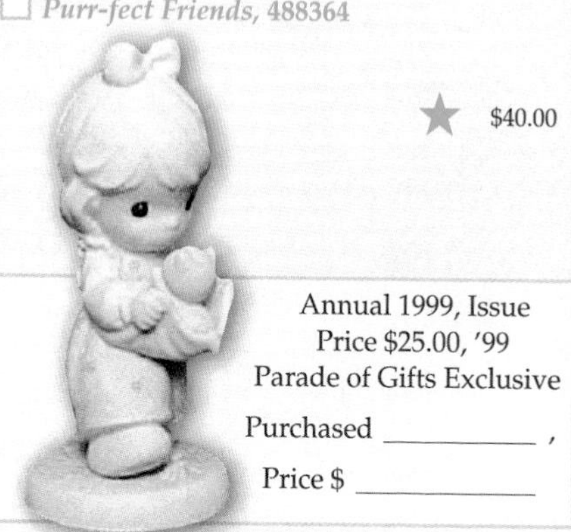

Annual 1999, Issue Price $25.00, '99
Parade of Gifts Exclusive
Purchased ________,
Price $ __________

☐ *You Count*, 488372

$35.00
$30.00
$28.00
$25.00
$25.00
$25.00
$25.00

Retired 2004, Issue Price $25.00, '99
Purchased ________, Price $ __________

☐ *Jesus Loves Me*, 488380 (Hinged Box)

UM $25.00

Open, Issue Price $25.00, '98
Series: Original "21" *Covered Boxes*

Purchased ________, Price $ ________

☐ *Jesus Loves Me*, 488399 (Hinged Box)

UM $25.00

Open, Issue Price $25.00, '98
Series: Original "21" *Covered Boxes*

Purchased ________, Price $ ________

☐ *Make A Joyful Noise*, 488402 (Hinged Box)

UM $25.00

Open, Issue Price $25.00, '98
Series: Original "21" *Covered Boxes*

Purchased ________, Price $ ________

☐ *Love One Another*, 488410 (Hinged Box)

UM $25.00

Open, Issue Price $25.00, '98
Series: Original "21" *Covered Boxes*

Purchased ________, Price $ ________

☐ *His Burden Is Light*, 488429 (Hinged Box)

UM $25.00

Open, Issue Price $25.00, '98
Series: Original "21" *Covered Boxes*

Purchased ________, Price $ ________

☐ *Jesus Is The Light*, 488437 (Hinged Box)

UM $25.00

Open, Issue Price $25.00, '98
Series: Original "21" *Covered Boxes*

Purchased ________, Price $ ________

☐ *Give Your Whole Heart*, 490245

★ $33.00
$30.00

Annual 2000, Issue Price $30.00, '00
Easter Seals Commemorative

Purchased ________, Price $ ________

☐ *God Knows Our Ups And Downs*, 490318

★ $35.00
$30.00
$30.00
$30.00
$30.00
$30.00

Retired 2004, Issue Price $30.00, '99

Purchased ________, Price $ ________

☐ *You Oughta Be In Pictures, 490327*

★ $45.00

Annual 1999, Issue Price $32.50, '99
DSR Event Figurine 5/22/99

Purchased ________,

Price $ ________

☐ *Soap Bubbles, Soap Bubbles, All Is Soap Bubbles, 490342*

UM $40.00

Limited Ed., Issue Price $20.00, '99
Series: *Little Moments — Avon Exclusive*

Purchased ________, Price $ ________

☐ *World's Greatest Student (Boy), 491586*

UM $20.00

Open, Issue Price $20.00, '99
Series: *Trophies — Little Moments*

Purchased ________,

Price $ ________

☐ *World's Sweetest Girl, 491594*

UM $20.00

Open, Issue Price $20.00, '99
Series: *Trophies — Little Moments*

Purchased ________,

Price $ ________

☐ *World's Best Helper (Girl), 491608*

UM $20.00

Open, Issue Price $20.00, '99
Series: *Trophies — Little Moments*

Purchased ________,

Price $ ________

☐ *World's Greatest Student (Girl), 491616*

UM $20.00

Open, Issue Price $20.00, '99
Series: *Trophies — Little Moments*

Purchased ________,

Price $ ________

☐ *You're No. 1 (Girl), 491624*

UM $20.00

Open, Issue Price $20.00, '99
Series: *Trophies — Little Moments*

Purchased ________,

Price $ ________

☐ *You're No. 1 (Boy), 491640*

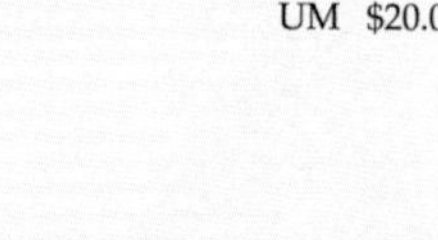

UM $20.00

Open, Issue Price $20.00, '99
Series: *Trophies — Little Moments*

Purchased ________,

Price $ ________

☐ *You Always Stand Behind Me*, **492140**

- $53.00
- $50.00
- $50.00
- $50.00
- $50.00
- $50.00
- $50.00
- $50.00

Open, Issue Price $50.00, '99

Purchased ________, Price $ __________

☐ *Goose Girl*, **495301 (Medallion)**

UM $400.00

Given to those who have been on the annual tour of the Orient factory.

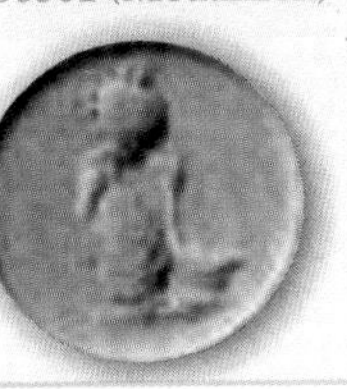

Limited Ed., Gift, '90
1990 Orient Tour Medallion

Purchased ________, Price $ __________

☐ *Have Faith In God*, **505153**

- $65.00
- $60.00
- $55.00

Retired 2002, Issue Price $50.00, '00
Series: *Always Victorian* — Third Issue

Purchased ________,

Price $__________

☐ *Our First Christmas Together*, **520233 (Ornament)**

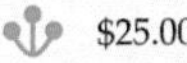

$25.00

Dated Annual 1988, Issue Price $13.00, '88

Purchased ________, Price $ __________

☐ *Baby's First Christmas*, **520241 (Ornament)**

$25.00

Dated Annual 1988, Issue Price $15.00, '88

Purchased ________, Price $ __________

☐ *Rejoice O Earth*, **520268**

- $35.00
- $30.00
- $28.00
- $25.00
- $24.00
- $23.00
- $20.00
- $20.00
- $18.50
- $18.50
- $18.50
- $18.50
- $18.50
- $18.50
- $18.50
- $18.50
- $18.50
- $18.50

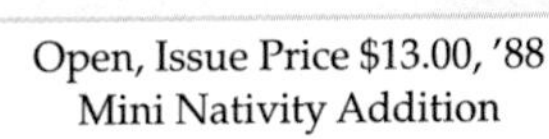

Open, Issue Price $13.00, '88
Mini Nativity Addition

Purchased ________, Price $ __________

☐ *You Are My Gift Come True*, **520276 (Ornament)**

$25.00

Dated Annual 1988, Issue Price $12.50, '88
Tenth Anniversary Commemorative

Purchased ____________,

Price $______________

Merry Christmas, Deer, **520284 (Plate)**

$60.00

Dated Annual 1988, Issue Price $50.00, '88
Series: *Christmas Love* — Third Issue
Purchased ________, Price $ ________

Hang On For The Holly Days, **520292 (Ornament)**

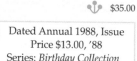

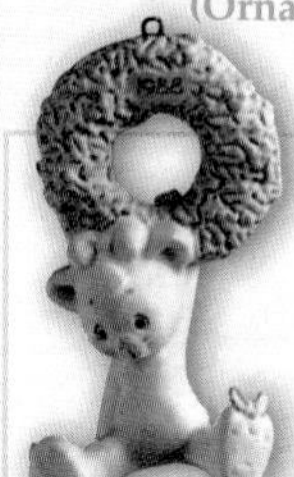

$35.00

Dated Annual 1988, Issue Price $13.00, '88
Series: *Birthday Collection*
Purchased ________,
Price $ ________

Make A Joyful Noise, **520322**

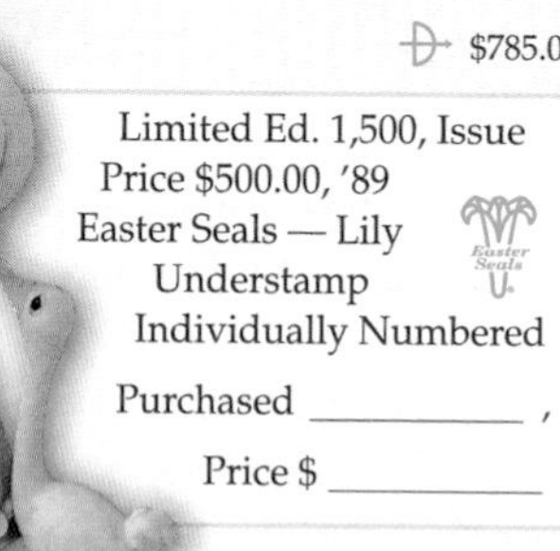

$785.00

Limited Ed. 1,500, Issue Price $500.00, '89
Easter Seals — Lily Understamp
Individually Numbered
Purchased ________,
Price $ ________

Jesus The Savior Is Born, **520357**

	$70.00		$60.00
	$68.00		$55.00
	$65.00		$50.00

Suspended 1993, Issue Price $25.00, '88
Nativity Addition
Purchased ________, Price $ ________

Hippo Holly Days, **520403 (Ornament)**

$25.00

Dated Annual 1995, Issue Price $17.00, '95
Series: *Birthday Collection*
Purchased ________,
Price $ ________

I'm Nuts About You, **520411 (Ornament)**

$25.00

Dated Annual 1992, Issue Price $16.00, '92
Series: *Birthday Collection*
Purchased ________, Price $ ________

Sno-Bunny Falls For You Like I Do, **520438 (Ornament)**

$32.00

Dated Annual 1991, Issue Price $15.00, '91
Series: *Birthday Collection*
Purchased ________,
Price $ ________

Sno-Ball Without You, **520446 (Ornament)**

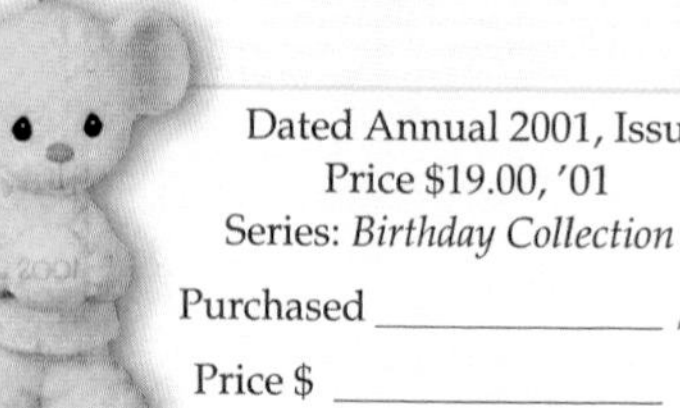

$20.00

Dated Annual 2001, Issue Price $19.00, '01
Series: *Birthday Collection*
Purchased ________,
Price $ ________

Happy Holidaze, 520454 (Ornament)

$25.00 $20.00

$23.00 $20.00

$20.00

Retired 2002, Issue Price $17.50, '98

Purchased__________ ,

Price $ ______________

Christmas Is Ruff Without You, 520462 (Ornament)

$35.00

Dated Annual 1989, Issue Price $13.00, '89

Series: *Birthday Collection*

Purchased ___________ ,

Price $_____________

Take A Bow Cuz You're My Christmas Star, 520470 (Ornament)

$25.00

Annual 1994, Issue Price $16.00, '94

Holiday Preview Event

Purchased ___________ ,

Price $ _______________

Slow Down And Enjoy The Holidays, 520489 (Ornament)

$30.00

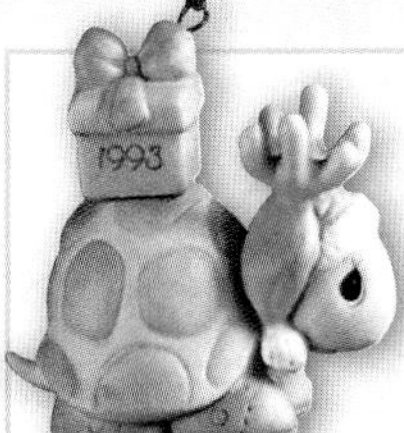

Dated Annual 1993, Issue Price $16.00, '93

Series: *Birthday Collection*

Purchased_______ ,

Price $ __________

Wishing You A Purr-fect Holiday, 520497 (Ornament)

$35.00

Dated Annual 1990, Issue Price $15.00, '90

Series: *Birthday Collection*

Purchased ______, Price $ __________

The Lord Turned My Life Around, 520535

$65.00

$60.00

$58.00

$55.00

$50.00

Suspended 1996, Issue Price $35.00, '92

Purchased _______________,

Price $ _____________

In The Spotlight Of His Grace, 520543

$70.00

$68.00

$65.00

$63.00

$60.00

$58.00

Suspended 1996, Issue Price $35.00, '91

Purchased ____________ ,

Price $ ______________

Lord, Turn My Life Around, 520551

$70.00

$68.00

$65.00

$63.00

$60.00

$58.00

$55.00

$50.00

Suspended 1996, Issue Price $35.00, '90

Purchased ________, Price $ ___________

☐ *You Deserve An Ovation, 520578*

$50.00 $38.00
$48.00 $38.00
$45.00 $37.50
$43.00 $37.50
$40.00 $37.50
$37.50
$37.50
$37.50
$37.50

Open, Issue Price $35.00, '92
Purchased ________, Price $ ___________

☐ *I'm So Glad You Fluttered Into My Life, 520640*

$325.00
$315.00
$310.00
$300.00

Retired 1991, Issue Price $40.00, '89
Purchased ________, Price $ ___________

☐ *My Heart Is Exposed With Love, 520624*

$85.00 $80.00 $75.00
$83.00 $78.00 $70.00
$70.00
$68.00
$68.00
$65.00
$65.00
$63.00

Retired 1999, Issue Price $45.00, '89
Purchased ________, Price $ ___________

☐ *Wishing You A Happy Bear Hug, 520659*

$50.00
$45.00
$40.00

Suspended 1996, Issue Price $27.50, '95
Series: *Birthday Collection*
Purchased ________, Price $ ___________

☐ *A Friend Is Someone Who Cares, 520632*

$95.00
$90.00
$87.00
$85.00
$80.00
$77.00
$75.00
$73.00

Retired 1995, Issue Price $30.00, '89
Purchased ________, Price $ ___________

☐ *Egg-specially For You, 520667*

$85.00 $78.00
$83.00 $75.00
$80.00 $73.00
$70.00
$68.00
$68.00
$65.00
$65.00
$63.00

Retired 1999, Issue Price $45.00, '89
Purchased ________, Price $ ___________

Your Love Is So Uplifting, 520675

$105.00
$100.00
$98.00
$95.00
$93.00
$90.00
$88.00
$85.00
$83.00
$80.00
$78.00

Retired 1998, Issue Price $60.00, '89

Purchased ________, Price $ ____________

Sending You Showers Of Blessings, 520683

$100.00
$95.00
$90.00
$85.00
$80.00

Retired 1992, Issue Price $32.50, '89

Purchased ________, Price $ ____________

Lord, Keep My Life In Balance, 520691 (Musical)

$95.00
$90.00
$85.00

Suspended 1993, Issue Price $60.00, '91
Tune: "Music Box Dancer"

Purchased ________, Price $ ____________

Baby's First Pet, 520705

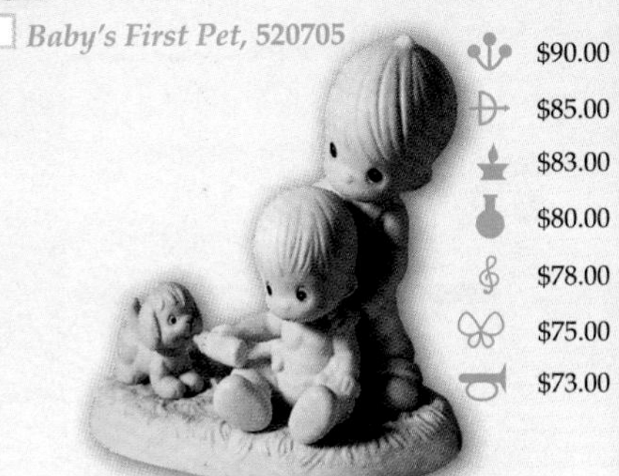

$90.00
$85.00
$83.00
$80.00
$78.00
$75.00
$73.00

Suspended 1994, Issue Price $45.00, '89
Series: *Baby's First* — Fifth Issue

Purchased ________, Price $ ____________

Just A Line To Wish You A Happy Day, 520721

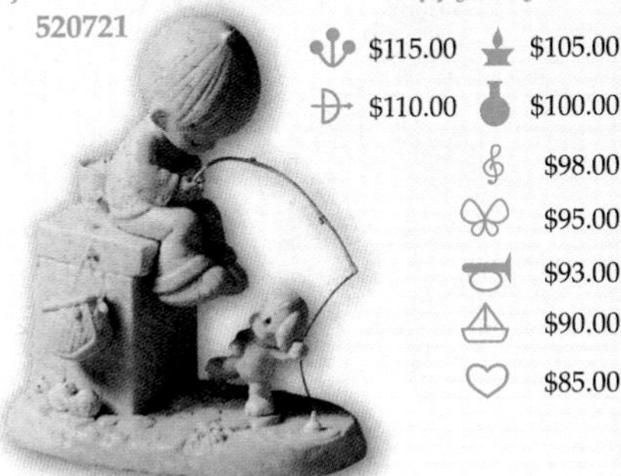

$115.00
$110.00
$105.00
$100.00
$98.00
$95.00
$93.00
$90.00
$85.00

Suspended 1996, Issue Price $65.00, '89

Purchased ________, Price $ ____________

Friendship Hits The Spot, 520748

Errors: Misspelled "Friendship" on boxes and figurines in Trumpet and Ship marks. Several have been found with tables missing.

$98.00
$95.00
$90.00
$85.00
$83.00
$80.00
$78.00
$75.00
$75.00
$75.00
$73.00
$73.00
$73.00

Retired 2000, Issue Price $55.00, '89

Purchased ________, Price $ ____________

☐ *Jesus Is The Only Way, 520756*

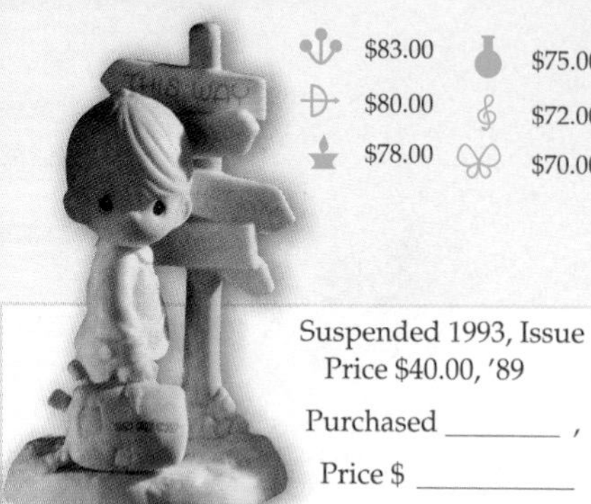

$83.00
$80.00
$78.00
$75.00
$72.00
$70.00

Suspended 1993, Issue Price $40.00, '89
Purchased ________ ,
Price $ ________

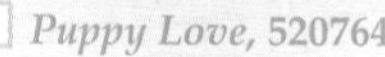

☐ *Puppy Love, 520764*

$35.00
$32.00
$30.00
$27.00
$27.00
$25.00
$25.00
$20.00
$20.00
$20.00
$20.00
$20.00

Retired 2/14/99, Issue Price $12.50, '89
Purchased ________ , Price $ ________

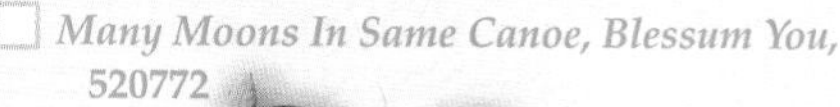

☐ *Many Moons In Same Canoe, Blessum You,* 520772

$350.00
$340.00
$320.00

Retired 1990, Issue Price $50.00, '89
Purchased ________ , Price $ ________

☐ *Wishing You Roads Of Happiness, 520780*

$90.00
$80.00
$78.00
$75.00
$75.00
$75.00
$75.00
$75.00
$75.00
$75.00
$75.00
$75.00
$75.00
$75.00
$75.00
$75.00
$75.00
$75.00
$75.00

Open, Issue Price $60.00, '89
Purchased ________ , Price $ ________

☐ *Someday My Love, 520799*

$83.00
$75.00
$70.00
$68.00
$65.00

Retired 1992, Issue Price $40.00, '89
Purchased ________ , Price $ ________

☐ *My Days Are Blue Without You, 520802*

$110.00
$100.00
$95.00
$90.00

Exists with three variations of the mouth — smiling, frowning, and open. Value for smiling with Flower mark, $125.00; smiling with Bow & Arrow mark, $115.00.

Suspended 1991, Issue Price $65.00, '89
Purchased ________ , Price $ ________

☐ *We Need A Good Friend Through The Ruff Times, 520810*

$60.00
$59.00
$58.00
$57.00

Suspended 1991, Issue Price $35.00, '89
Purchased ________, Price $ ___________

☐ *You Are My Number One, 520829*

$50.00 $36.00
$45.00 $36.00
$42.00 $36.00
$40.00 $36.00
$38.00 $36.00
$36.00

Suspended 1998, Issue Price $25.00, '89
Purchased ________, Price $ ___________

☐ *The Lord Is Your Light To Happiness, 520837*

$65.00 $65.00
$75.00 $65.00 $65.00
$72.00 $65.00 $65.00
$68.00 $65.00 $65.00
$65.00
$65.00
$65.00
$65.00
$65.00
$65.00
$65.00

Open, Issue Price $50.00, '89
Purchased ________, Price $ ___________

☐ *Wishing You A Perfect Choice, 520845*

$83.00 $75.00 $70.00
$80.00 $73.00 $70.00
$78.00 $70.00 $70.00
$70.00 $70.00
$70.00
$70.00
$70.00
$70.00
$70.00
$70.00
$70.00

Open, Issue Price $55.00, '89
Purchased ________, Price $ ___________

☐ *I Belong To The Lord, 520853*

$55.00
$50.00
$40.00
$35.00

Suspended 1991, Issue Price $25.00, '89
Purchased __________,
Price $___________

☐ *Sharing Begins In The Heart, 520861*

$80.00
$50.00

Annual 1989, Issue Price $25.00, '89
1989 Special Event
Purchased ________, Price $ ___________

Blessed Be The Tie That Binds, 520918

$60.00
$55.00
$50.00
$50.00
$50.00
$50.00
$50.00

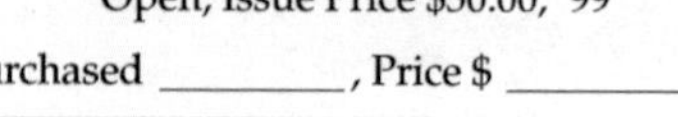

Open, Issue Price $50.00, '99

Purchased ________, Price $ __________

Heaven Bless You, 520934

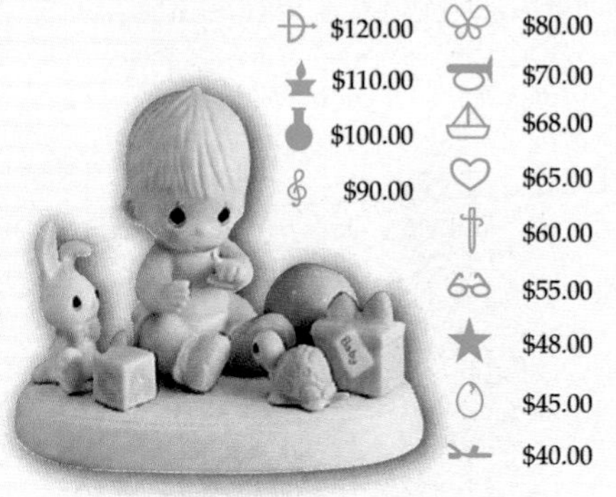

$120.00
$110.00
$100.00
$90.00
$80.00
$70.00
$68.00
$65.00
$60.00
$55.00
$48.00
$45.00
$40.00

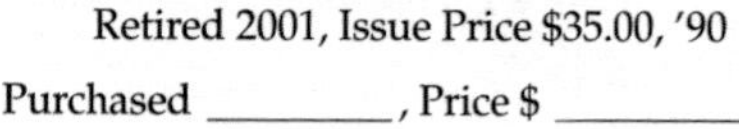

Retired 2001, Issue Price $35.00, '90

Purchased ________, Price $ __________

There Is No Greater Treasure Than To Have A Friend Like You, 521000

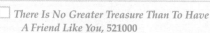

$45.00
$40.00
$38.00
$35.00
$33.00
$33.00
$33.00

Retired 1998, Issue Price $30.00, '93

Purchased ________, Price $ __________

To My Favorite Fan, 521043

$50.00
$48.00
$40.00
$36.00
$30.00

Suspended 1993, Issue Price $16.00, '90
Series: *Birthday Collection*

Purchased ________, Price $ __________

Merry Christmas, Little Lamb, 521078 (Ornament)

$23.00
$20.00
$18.00
$18.00
$18.00
$18.00

Suspended 2003, Issue Price $15.00, '98
Series: *Birthday Circus Train* — Age 1

Purchased ________, Price $ __________

Heaven Bless Your Special Christmas, 521086 (Ornament)

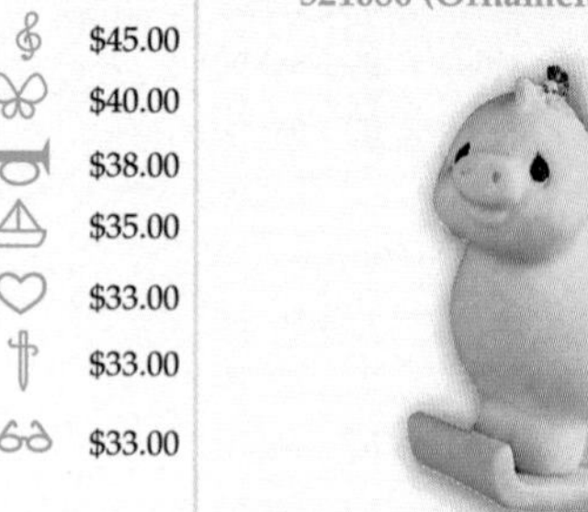

$23.00
$20.00
$18.00
$18.00
$18.00
$18.00

Suspended 2003, Issue Price $15.00, '98
Series: *Birthday Circus Train* — Age 3

Purchased ________, Price $ __________

☐ *God Bless You This Christmas*, 521094 (Ornament)

Mark	Price	Mark	Price
👓	$23.00	⋈	$18.00
★	$20.00	♡	$18.00
◯	$18.00	♛	$18.00

Suspended 2003, Issue Price $15.00, '98
Series: *Birthday Circus Train* — Age 2

Purchased ________, Price $ __________

☐ *May Your Christmas Be Gigantic*, 521108 (Ornament)

Mark	Price	Mark	Price
👓	$23.00	⋈	$18.00
★	$20.00	♡	$18.00
◯	$18.00	♛	$18.00

Suspended 2003, Issue Price $15.00, '98
Series: *Birthday Circus Train* — Age 4

Purchased ________, Price $ __________

☐ *Christmas Is Something To Roar About*, 521116 (Ornament)

Mark	Price	Mark	Price
👓	$23.00	⋈	$18.00
★	$20.00	♡	$18.00
◯	$18.00	♛	$18.00

Suspended 2003, Issue Price $15.00, '98
Series: *Birthday Circus Train* — Age 5

Purchased ________, Price $ __________

☐ *Christmas Keeps Looking Up*, 521124 (Ornament)

Mark	Price	Mark	Price
👓	$23.00	⋈	$18.00
★	$20.00	♡	$18.00
◯	$18.00	♛	$18.00

Suspended 2003, Issue Price $15.00, '98
Series: *Birthday Circus Train* — Age 6

Purchased __________,

Price $ __________

☐ *Hello World*, 521175

Mark	Price	Mark	Price
		🦋	$18.00
⚓	$30.00	📯	$18.00
⊕	$28.00	⛵	$18.00
🔥	$25.00	♡	$18.00
⚱	$23.00	✝	$18.00
𝄞	$20.00	👓	$18.00
		★	$18.00

Retired 1999, Issue Price $13.50, '89
Series: *Birthday Collection*

Purchased ________, Price $ __________

☐ *That's What Friends Are For*, 521183

Mark	Price	Mark	Price
🔥	$73.00	🦋	$60.00
⚱	$70.00	📯	$57.00
𝄞	$65.00	⛵	$55.00
		♡	$55.00
		✝	$55.00
		👓	$55.00
		★	$53.00
		◯	$53.00

Retired 2000, Issue Price $45.00, '90

Purchased ________, Price $ __________

☐ *Lord, Spare Me*, 521191

Mark	Price
♡	$55.00
✝	$50.00
👓	$47.00
★	$45.00
◯	$43.00
⋈	$42.00

Retired 2001, Issue Price $37.50, '97

Purchased ________, Price $ __________

☐ *Hope You're Up And On The Trail Again,* 521205

$65.00
$60.00
$58.00
$55.00
$53.00

Suspended 1993, Issue Price $35.00, '90

Purchased ________, Price $ ___________

☐ *The Fruit Of The Spirit Is Love,* 521213

$55.00
$48.00
$45.00
$43.00
$40.00
$38.00
$35.00

Retired 1999, Issue Price $30.00, '93

Purchased ________, Price $ ___________

☐ *Enter His Court With Thanksgiving,* 521221

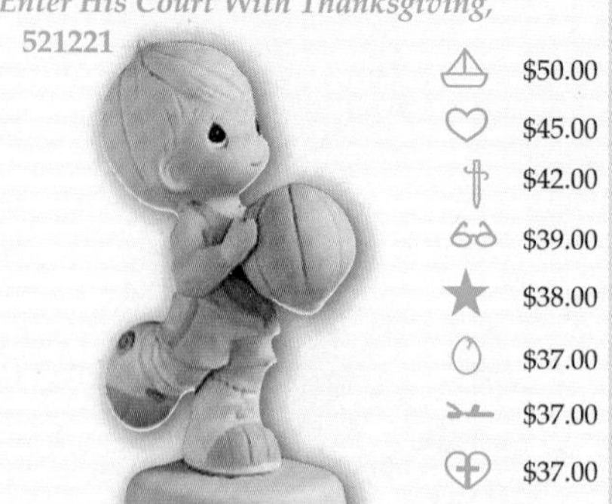

$50.00
$45.00
$42.00
$39.00
$38.00
$37.00
$37.00
$37.00

Retired 2002, Issue Price $35.00, '96

Purchased ________, Price $ ___________

☐ *Take Heed When You Stand,* 521272

Limited Ship mark figurines offered to retailers at Fall 1998 Enesco show.

$82.00
$80.00
$78.00
$75.00
$68.00

Suspended 1994, Issue Price $55.00, '91

Purchased ________, Price $ ___________

☐ *Happy Trip,* 521280

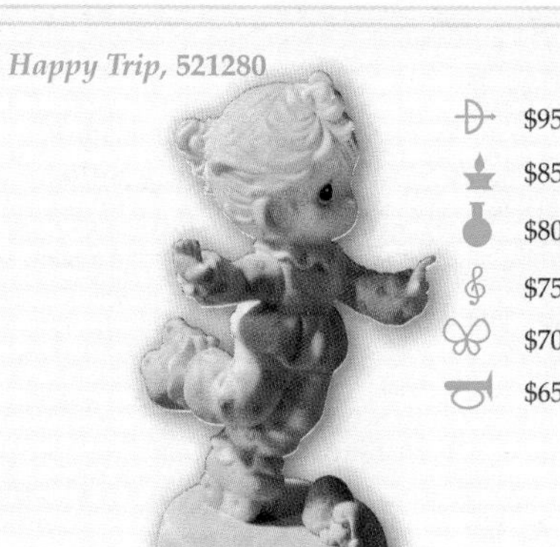

$95.00
$85.00
$80.00
$75.00
$70.00
$65.00

Suspended 1994, Issue Price $35.00, '90

Purchased ________, Price $ ___________

☐ *Hug One Another,* 521299

$80.00
$75.00
$70.00
$70.00
$65.00
$65.00

Retired 1995, Issue Price $45.00, '91

Purchased ________, Price $ ___________

☐ *May All Your Christmases Be White,* 521302 (Ornament)

$40.00 $33.00
$35.00 $30.00
$34.00 $30.00

Suspended 1994,
Issue Price $13.50, '89

Purchased ____________ ,

Price $ ________________

☐ *May All Your Christmases Be White,* 521302R (Ornament)

$30.00

Limited Ed., Issue Price $20.00, '99
Limited To One Year Production

Purchased ________, Price $ ___________

☐ *Yield Not To Temptation,* 521310

$60.00
$55.00
$50.00
$48.00
$45.00

Suspended 1993, Issue Price $27.50, '90

Purchased ____________ ,

Price $ ____________

☐ *Have I Toad You Lately That I Love You?* 521329

$55.00
$50.00

Annual 1996, Issue Price $30.00, '96
Spring Catalog DSR Promo

Purchased ________, Price $ ___________

☐ *Life's Journey Has Its Ups & Downs,* 521345

$35.00
$35.00
$35.00

Retired 2004, Issue Price $35.00, '03

Purchased ________, Price $ ___________

☐ *Heaven Must Have Sent You,* 521388

$80.00
$75.00
$72.00
$70.00
$68.00

Retired 2000, Issue Price $60.00, '98
Series: *Birthday Collection*

Purchased ________, Price $ ___________

☐ *Faith Is A Victory,* 521396

$170.00
$150.00
$143.00
$123.00
$120.00

Retired 1993, Issue Price $25.00, '90

Purchased ________, Price $ ___________

☐ *I'll Never Stop Loving You, 521418*

$75.00
$73.00
$70.00
$68.00
$65.00
$63.00
$60.00
$58.00

Retired 1996, Issue Price $37.50, '90
Purchased ________, Price $ ___________

☐ *To A Very Special Mom And Dad, 521434*

$55.00
$53.00
$50.00

Suspended 1993, Issue Price $35.00, '91
Purchased ________, Price $ ___________

☐ *Lord, Help Me Stick To My Job, 521450*

$75.00
$73.00
$70.00
$68.00
$65.00
$63.00
$60.00
$57.00
$57.00

Retired 1997, Issue Price $30.00, '90
Purchased ________, Price $ ___________

☐ *I'll Weight For You, 521469*

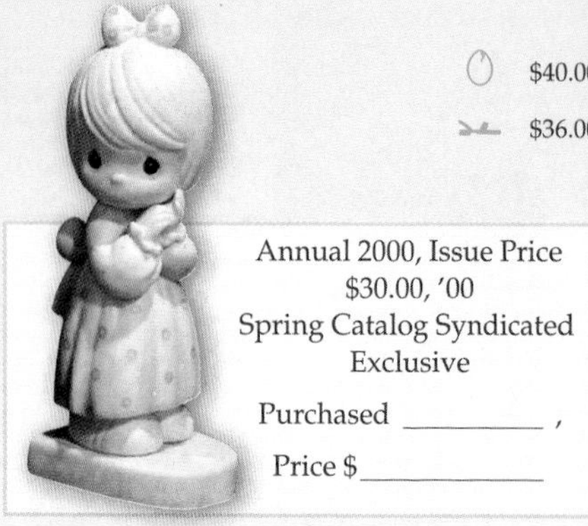

$40.00
$36.00

Annual 2000, Issue Price $30.00, '00
Spring Catalog Syndicated Exclusive
Purchased ________,
Price $___________

☐ *Tell It To Jesus, 521477*

$60.00
$58.00
$55.00
$53.00
$50.00
$45.00
$40.00
$40.00
$40.00
$40.00
$40.00
$40.00
$40.00
$40.00
$40.00

Retired 2003, Issue Price $35.00, '89
Purchased ________, Price $ ___________

☐ *There's A Light At The End Of The Tunnel, 521485*

$85.00
$83.00
$80.00
$78.00
$75.00
$70.00

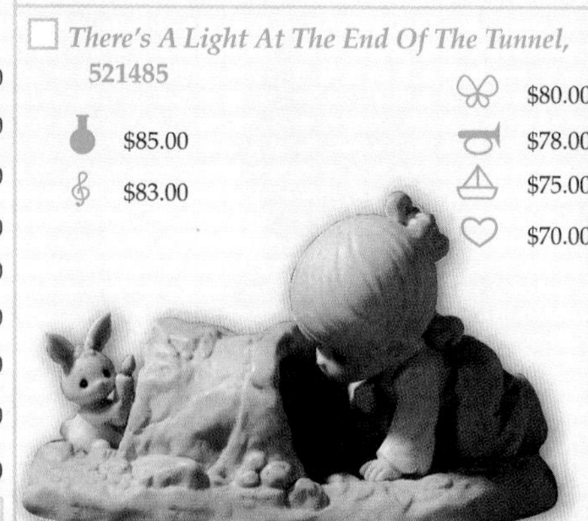

Suspended 1996, Issue Price $55.00, '91
Purchased ________, Price $ ___________

☐ *A Special Delivery, 521493*

$40.00 · $37.00 · $35.00 · $33.00 · $32.50 · $32.50

$32.50 · $32.50 · $32.50 · $32.50 · $32.50 · $32.50 · $32.50 · $32.50 · $32.50

Open, Issue Price $30.00, '91

Purchased ________, Price $ __________

☐ *The Light Of The World Is Jesus, 521507* **(Musical)**

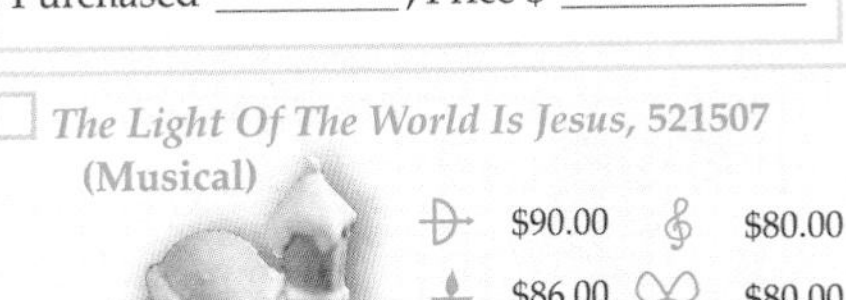

$90.00 · $86.00 · $84.00

$80.00 · $80.00 · $78.00 · $78.00 · $75.00 · $75.00 · $75.00 · $75.00

Retired 1999, Issue Price $60.00, '89
Tune: "White Christmas"

Purchased ________, Price $ __________

☐ *Water-Melancholy Day Without You, 521515*

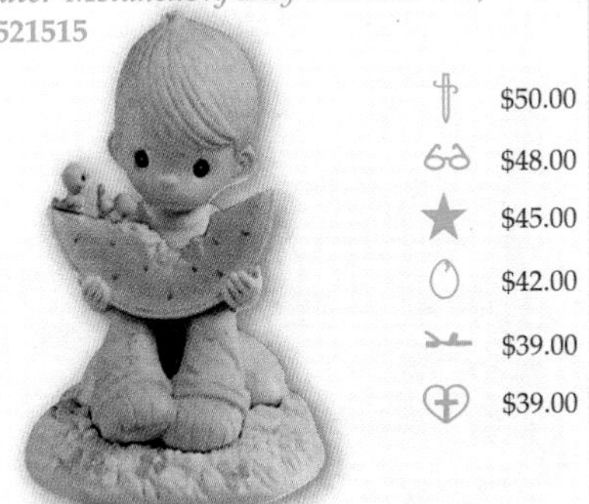

$50.00 · $48.00 · $45.00 · $42.00 · $39.00 · $39.00

Retired 2002, Issue Price $35.00, '98

Purchased ________, Price $ __________

☐ *Our First Christmas Together, 521558* **(Ornament)**

$35.00

Dated Annual 1989, Issue Price $17.50, '89

Purchased ________, Price $ __________

☐ *Glide Through The Holidays, 521566* **(Ornament)**

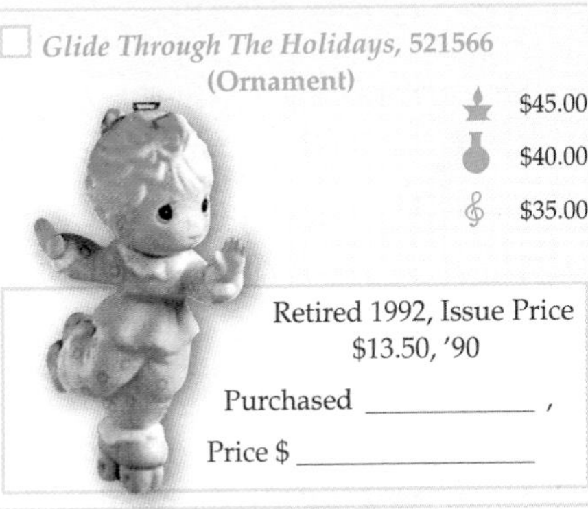

$45.00 · $40.00 · $35.00

Retired 1992, Issue Price $13.50, '90

Purchased __________ ,

Price $ __________

☐ *Dashing Through The Snow, 521574* **(Ornament)**

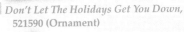

$35.00 · $33.00

$31.00 · $29.00 · $27.00

Suspended 1994, Issue Price $15.00, '90

Purchased ________ ,

Price $ __________

☐ *Don't Let The Holidays Get You Down, 521590* **(Ornament)**

$50.00 · $45.00

$40.00 · $38.00 · $35.00

Retired 1994, Issue Price $15.00, '90

Purchased _______ ,

Price $________

Hope You're Over The Hump, 521671

$38.00
$35.00
$33.00
$30.00

Suspended 1996, Issue Price $17.50, '93
Series: *Birthday Collection*

Purchased ________, Price $ ___________

Thumb-Body Loves You, 521698

$90.00
$85.00
$80.00
$77.00
$75.00
$73.00
$70.00

Suspended 1996, Issue Price $55.00, '91

Purchased ________, Price $ ___________

Shoot For The Stars And You'll Never Strike Out, 521701

$75.00
$73.00
$70.00
$65.00
$60.00
$60.00
$60.00
$60.00
$60.00
$60.00

Open, Issue Price $60.00, '96
Boys & Girls Club Of America Commemorative

Purchased ________, Price $ ___________

My Love Blooms For You, 521728

$65.00
$63.00
$60.00
$58.00
$55.00
$53.00
$50.00
$50.00
$50.00
$50.00
$50.00

Open, Issue Price $50.00, '96

Purchased ________, Price $ ___________

Sweep All Your Worries Away, 521779

$115.00
$100.00
$95.00
$90.00
$85.00
$80.00
$75.00
$70.00

This figurine has been found with the dog missing; values increase by $75.00.

Retired 1996, Issue Price $40.00, '90

Purchased ________, Price $ ___________

Good Friends Are Forever, 521817

$80.00
$75.00
$70.00
$65.00
$60.00
$55.00
$55.00
$55.00
$55.00
$55.00
$55.00
$55.00
$55.00
$55.00
$55.00

Retired 2003, Issue Price $50.00, '90

Purchased ________, Price $ ___________

☐ *May Your Birthday Be Mammoth,* 521825

$30.00

$28.00
$25.00
$25.00
$25.00

$25.00
$25.00
$25.00
$25.00
$25.00
$25.00
$25.00
$25.00
$25.00

Open, Issue Price $25.00, '92
Series: *Birthday Circus Train* — Age 10

Purchased ________, Price $ __________

☐ *Being Nine Is Just Divine,* 521833

$30.00
$28.00

$25.00
$25.00
$25.00
$25.00

$25.00
$25.00
$25.00
$25.00
$25.00
$25.00
$25.00
$25.00

Open, Issue Price $25.00, '92
Series: *Birthday Circus Train* — Age 9

Purchased ________, Price $ __________

☐ *Love Is From Above,* 521841

$75.00
$70.00
$65.00
$65.00
$60.00
$60.00
$60.00
$60.00

Suspended 1996, Issue Price $45.00, '90

Purchased ________, Price $ __________

☐ *The Greatest Of These Is Love,* 521868

$45.00
$38.00
$35.00

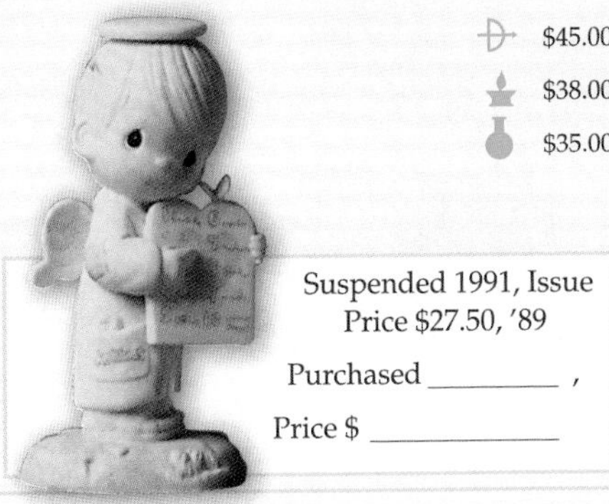

Suspended 1991, Issue Price $27.50, '89

Purchased ________,

Price $ __________

☐ *Pizza On Earth,* 521884

$65.00
$60.00
$58.00
$55.00
$55.00
$55.00

Retired 2001, Issue Price $55.00, '97

Purchased ________, Price $ __________

☐ *Easter's On Its Way,* 521892

$88.00
$85.00

$83.00
$80.00

$80.00
$75.00
$75.00
$73.00
$70.00
$70.00
$70.00

Retired 1999, Issue Price $60.00, '90

Purchased ________, Price $ __________

Hoppy Easter, Friend, 521906

$55.00 $48.00
$53.00 $45.00
$50.00 $43.00
$40.00
$40.00
$40.00
$40.00

Retired 1999, Issue Price $40.00, '91
Purchased ________, Price $ __________

Perfect Harmony, 521914

$70.00
$65.00
$60.00
$55.00
$55.00
$55.00

Retired 1999, Issue Price $55.00, '94
Purchased ________, Price $ __________

Safe In The Arms Of Jesus, 521922

$50.00 $40.00 $35.00
$48.00 $35.00 $35.00
$45.00 $35.00 $35.00
$43.00 $35.00 $35.00
$35.00
$35.00

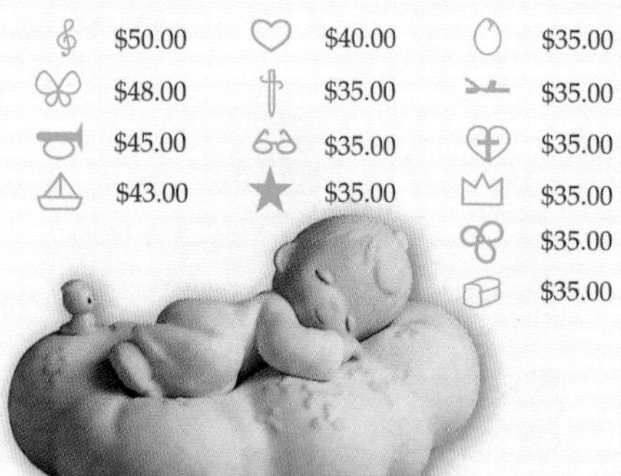

Open, Issue Price $30.00, '93
Child Evangelism Fellowship Piece
Purchased ________, Price $ __________

Wishing You A Cozy Season, 521949

$68.00
$65.00
$63.00
$60.00
$58.00

Suspended 1993, Issue Price $42.50, '89
Purchased ________, Price $ __________

High Hopes, 521957

$50.00
$48.00
$45.00
$43.00
$40.00

Suspended 1993, Issue Price $30.00, '90
Purchased ________, Price $ __________

To A Special Mum, 521965

$53.00 $45.00
$50.00 $45.00
$48.00 $40.00
$40.00
$40.00
$40.00
$40.00

Retired 1999, Issue Price $30.00 '91
Purchased ________, Price $ __________

Caught Up In Sweet Thoughts Of You, 521973

$35.00
$30.00
$30.00
$30.00
$30.00
$30.00
$30.00
$30.00

Open, Issue Price $30.00, '99

Purchased _________, Price $ ____________

Marching To The Beat Of Freedom's Drum, 521981

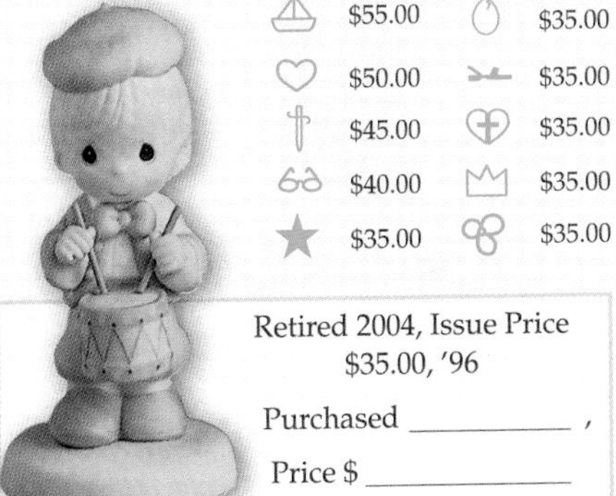

$55.00
$50.00
$45.00
$40.00
$35.00
$35.00
$35.00
$35.00
$35.00
$35.00

Retired 2004, Issue Price $35.00, '96

Purchased ___________,

Price $ ____________

To The Apple Of God's Eye, 522015

$45.00
$43.00
$40.00
$38.00
$37.00
$37.00
$36.00

Retired 1999, Issue Price $32.50, '93

Purchased _________, Price $ ____________

May Your Life Be Blessed With Touchdowns, 522023

$70.00
$68.00
$50.00
$65.00
$63.00
$60.00
$58.00
$50.00
$50.00
$50.00

Retired 1998, Issue Price $45.00, '89

Purchased _________, Price $ ____________

Thank You, Lord, For Everything, 522031

$95.00
$93.00
$90.00
$87.00
$85.00

Suspended 1993, Issue Price $60.00, '89

Purchased _________, Price $ ____________

Now I Lay Me Down To Sleep, 522058

$55.00
$50.00
$48.00
$45.00

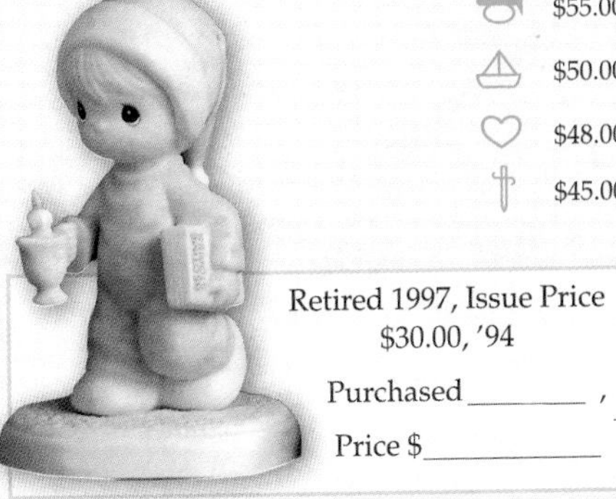

Retired 1997, Issue Price $30.00, '94

Purchased ________,

Price $___________

May Your World Be Trimmed With Joy, 522082

$90.00
$85.00
$80.00
$75.00
$73.00
$70.00

Suspended 1996, Issue Price $55.00, '91

Purchased ________, Price $ ___________

Don't Let The Holidays Get You Down, 522112

$110.00
$105.00
$100.00
$95.00
$90.00

Retired 1993, Issue Price $42.50, '89

Purchased ________, Price $ ___________

There Shall Be Showers Of Blessings, 522090

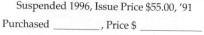

$85.00	$78.00
$82.00	$78.00
$80.00	$75.00
	$75.00
	$75.00
	$75.00
	$75.00
	$75.00

Retired 1999, Issue Price $60.00, '90

Purchased ________, Price $ ___________

Wishing You A Very Successful Season, 522120

$95.00	$93.00	$90.00
		$88.00
		$85.00
		$83.00
		$80.00
		$78.00
		$75.00
		$73.00
		$73.00

Retired 1999, Issue Price $60.00, '89

Purchased ________, Price $ ___________

It's No Yolk When I Say I Love You, 522104

$100.00
$95.00
$90.00
$85.00

Suspended 1994, Issue Price $60.00, '92

Purchased ________, Price $ ___________

I Will Make You Fishers Of Men, 522139

$60.00
$55.00

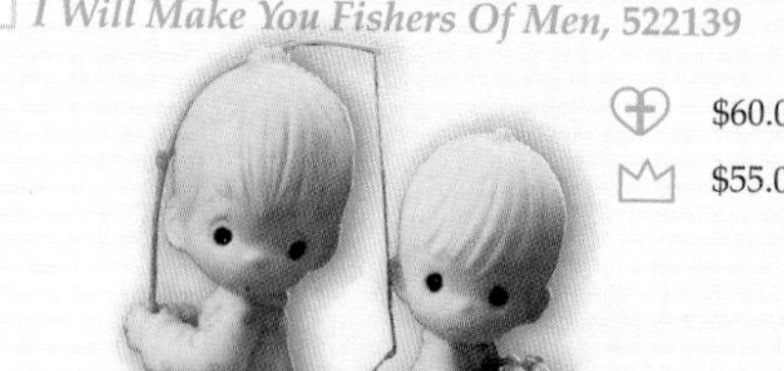

Limited Ed., Issue Price $50.00, '02
Precious Moments 25th Anniversary

Purchased ________, Price $ ___________

☐ *Bon Voyage! 522201*

$135.00
$130.00
$125.00
$120.00
$115.00
$110.00
$105.00
$100.00

Suspended 1996, Issue Price $75.00, '89

Purchased ________, Price $ ___________

☐ *Do Not Open 'Til Christmas, 522244*
(Musical)

$135.00
$130.00
$110.00

Suspended 1994, Issue Price $75.00, '92
Tune: "Toyland"

Purchased ________, Price $ ___________

☐ *He Is The Star Of The Morning, 522252*

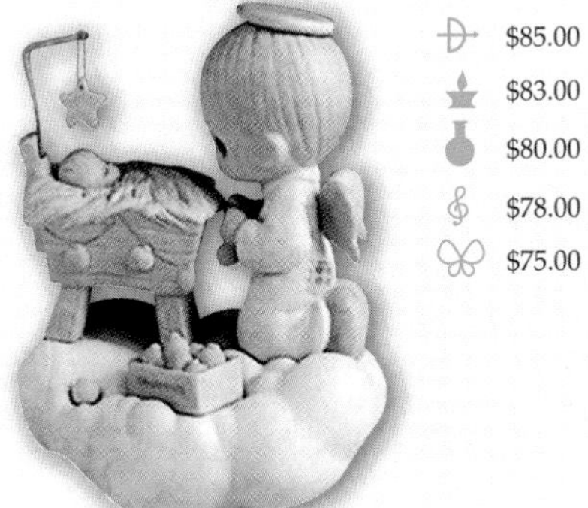

$85.00
$83.00
$80.00
$78.00
$75.00

Suspended 1993, Issue Price $55.00, '89

Purchased ________, Price $ ___________

☐ *To Be With You Is Uplifting, 522260*

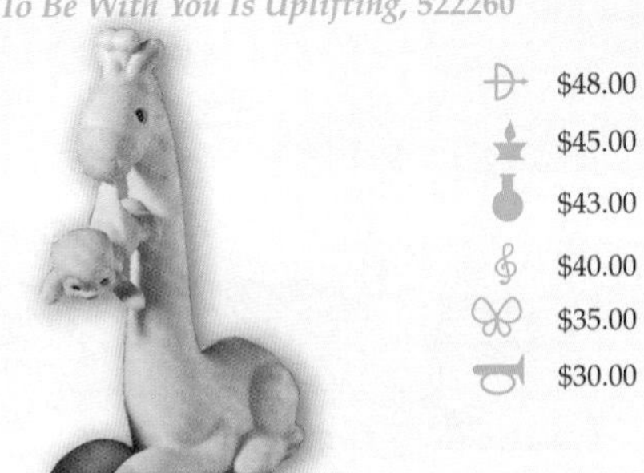

$48.00
$45.00
$43.00
$40.00
$35.00
$30.00

Retired 1994, Issue Price $20.00, '89
Series: *Birthday Collection*

Purchased ________, Price $ ___________

☐ *A Reflection Of His Love, 522279*

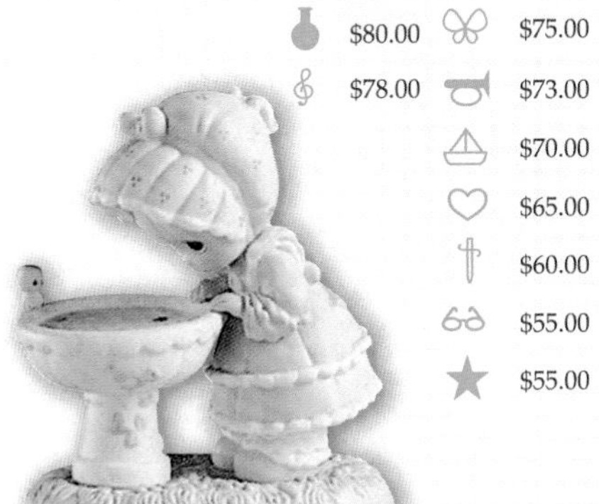

$80.00
$78.00
$75.00
$73.00
$70.00
$65.00
$60.00
$55.00
$55.00

Retired 1999, Issue Price $50.00, '91

Purchased ________, Price $ ___________

☐ *Thinking Of You Is What I Really Like To Do, 522287*

$50.00
$48.00
$45.00
$43.00
$40.00
$38.00
$36.00
$35.00

Suspended 1996, Issue Price $30.00, '90

Purchased ________, Price $ ___________

☐ *Merry Christmas, Deer, 522317*

$105.00 $100.00 $98.00 $95.00 $93.00 $90.00 $87.00 $85.00 $83.00

Retired 1997, Issue Price $50.00, '89

Purchased ________, Price $ ___________

☐ *Somebody Cares, 522325*

$55.00 $48.00

Annual 1998, Issue Price $40.00, '98
Easter Seals Commemorative
Lily Understamp

Purchased ________, Price $ ___________

☐ *Sweeter As The Years Go By, 522333*

$70.00 $68.00 $65.00

Retired 1998, Issue Price $60.00, '96

Purchased ________, Price $ ___________

☐ *His Love Will Shine On You, 522376*

$55.00 $53.00

Annual 1989, Issue Price $30.00, '89
Easter Seals Commemorative,
Lily Understamp

Purchased ________, Price $ ___________

☐ *Oh Holy Night, 522546*

$50.00

Dated Annual 1989, Issue Price $25.00, '89

Purchased ________, Price $ ___________

☐ *Oh Holy Night, 522554 (Thimble)*

$25.00

Dated Annual 1989, Issue Price $7.50, '89

Purchased ________, Price $ ___________

Oh Holy Night, 522821 (Bell)

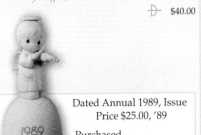

$40.00

Dated Annual 1989, Issue Price $25.00, '89

Purchased __________ ,

Price $ __________

Oh Holy Night, 522848 (Ornament)

$35.00

Dated Annual 1989, Issue Price $13.50, '89

Purchased __________ ,

Price $ __________

Have A Beary Merry Christmas, 522856

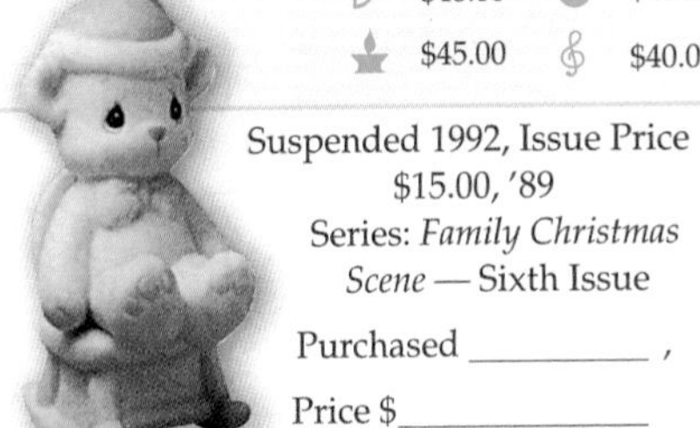

$48.00 $43.00

$45.00 $40.00

Suspended 1992, Issue Price $15.00, '89

Series: *Family Christmas Scene* — Sixth Issue

Purchased __________ ,

Price $ __________

Just A Line To Say You're Special, 522864

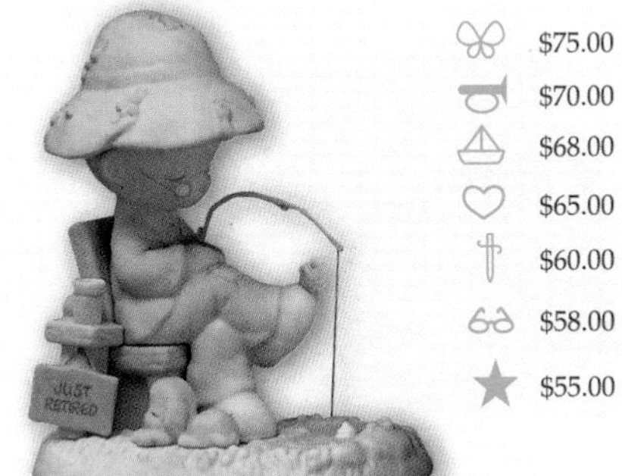

$75.00

$70.00

$68.00

$65.00

$60.00

$58.00

$55.00

Retired 1999, Issue Price $45.00, '95

Purchased __________ , Price $ __________

On My Way To A Perfect Day, 522872

$55.00

$53.00

$50.00

$48.00

$46.00

$46.00

$46.00

Retired 2002, Issue Price $45.00, '97

Purchased __________ , Price $ __________

Make A Joyful Noise, 522910 (Ornament)

$35.00 $28.00

$30.00 $28.00

$25.00

$25.00

$25.00

$25.00

Suspended 1996, Issue Price $15.00, '89

Purchased __________ , Price $ __________

Love One Another, 522929 (Ornament)

$35.00 $30.00 $28.00

$32.00 $30.00 $28.00

$28.00

$25.00

$25.00

$24.00

$24.00

$22.00

$22.00

Retired 2001, Issue Price $17.50, '89

Purchased __________ , Price $ __________

☐ *Friends Never Drift Apart, 522937* (Ornament)

$40.00
$38.00
$36.00
$34.00
$32.00
$30.00

Retired 1995, Issue Price $17.50, '90

Purchased ________, Price $ __________

☐ *Our First Christmas Together, 522945* (Ornament)

$25.00

Dated Annual 1991, Issue Price $17.50, '91

Purchased ________, Price $ __________

☐ *I Believe In The Old Rugged Cross, 522953* (Ornament)

$45.00
$40.00
$37.00
$35.00
$33.00
$33.00

Suspended 1994, Issue Price $15.00, '89

Purchased __________,

Price $ __________

☐ *Isn't He Precious, 522988*

$40.00
$38.00
$36.00
$34.00
$32.00

Suspended 1993, Issue Price $15.00, '89

Mini Nativity Addition

Purchased__________,

Price $ __________

☐ *Some Bunnies Sleeping, 522996*

$30.00
$28.00
$26.00
$24.00

Suspended 1993, Issue Price $12.00, '90

Mini Nativity Addition

Purchased ________, Price $ __________

☐ *May Your Christmas Be A Happy Home, 523003* (Plate)

$65.00

Dated Annual 1989, Issue Price $50.00, '89

Series: *Christmas Love* — Fourth Issue

Purchased ________, Price $ __________

☐ *There's A Christian Welcome Here, 523011*

UM $110.00
$95.00
$90.00
$85.00
$80.00
$75.00

Suspended 1995, Issue Price $45.00, '89

Chapel Exclusive

Purchased ________, Price $ __________

☐ *He Is My Inspiration, 523038*

UM $85.00
$80.00
$75.00
$70.00
$65.00
$60.00
$60.00

Open, Issue Price $60.00, '90
Chapel Exclusive
Purchased ________, Price $ __________

☐ *Peace On Earth, 523062 (Ornament)*

$65.00

Dated Annual 1989, Issue Price $25.00, '89
Series: *Masterpiece Ornament* — First Issue
Purchased ________, Price $ __________

☐ *Jesus Is The Sweetest Name I Know, 523097*

$55.00
$50.00
$48.00
$45.00
$43.00

Suspended 1993, Issue Price $22.50, '89
Nativity Addition
Purchased ________, Price $ __________

☐ *Joy On Arrival, 523178*

$80.00
$78.00
$75.00
$73.00
$70.00
$68.00
$65.00
$60.00
$60.00
$58.00
$58.00
$55.00
$55.00
$55.00
$55.00

Open, Issue Price $50.00, '91
Purchased ________, Price $ __________

☐ *Yes Dear, You're Always Right, 523186*

$70.00

Limited Ed. 5,000, Issue Price $60.00, '99
CCR Exclusive
Individually Numbered
Purchased ________, Price $ __________

☐ *Yes Dear, You're Always Right, 523186E*

Exclusive for "The Limited Edition" store in Merrick, New York. Understamp reads "Premiere Edition of 500," and plate in girl's hand has "The Limited Edition" on it.

$75.00

☐ *Baby's First Christmas, 523194 (Ornament)*

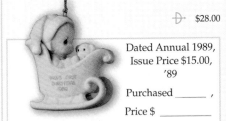

$28.00

Dated Annual 1989, Issue Price $15.00, '89
Purchased ______,
Price $ __________

Baby's First Christmas, 523208 (Ornament)

$28.00

Dated Annual 1989, Issue Price $15.00, '89

Purchased ________ ,

Price $ __________

Happy Trails Is Trusting Jesus, 523224 (Ornament)

$35.00 $30.00

$34.00 $28.00

Suspended 1994, Issue Price $15.00, '91

Purchased ________ ,

Price $ __________

You Have Touched So Many Hearts, 523283

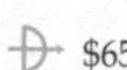 $650.00 $585.00

Limited Ed. 2,000, Issue Price $500.00, '90

Easter Seals, Lily Understamp

Individually Numbered

Purchased ________ ,

Price $ __________

Blessed Are The Merciful, For They Shall Obtain Mercy, 523291 (Wall Hanging)

 $70.00

Limited Ed., Issue Price $55.00, '94

Series: *Beatitudes* — Fifth Issue, One Year Production

Chapel Exclusive, Chapel Window Collection, Individually Numbered

Purchased ________, Price $ __________

He Leads Me Beside The Still Waters, 523305 (Wall Hanging)

UM $70.00

$70.00

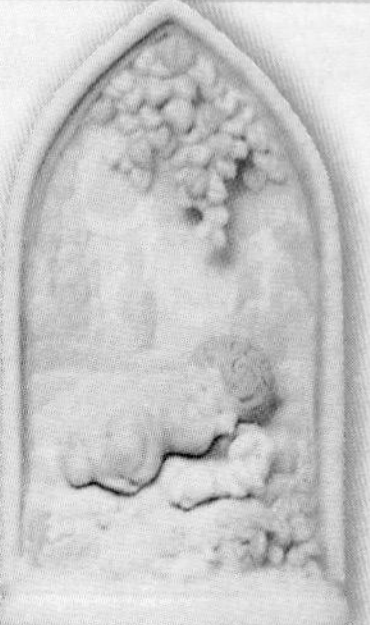

Limited Ed. 7,500, Issue Price $55.00, '97

Series: *23rd Psalm Collection* — Second Issue

Chapel Exclusive, Individually Numbered

Purchased ________, Price $ __________

Blessed Are The Meek, For They Shall Inherit The Earth, 523313 (Wall Hanging)

$70.00

Limited Ed., Issue Price $55.00, '93

Series: *Beatitudes* — Third Issue, One Year Production

Chapel Exclusive, Chapel Window Collection, Individually Numbered

Purchased ________, Price $ __________

Blessed Are They That Hunger And Thirst For Righteousness, 523321 (Wall Hanging)

$70.00

Limited Ed., Issue Price $55.00, '93

Series: *Beatitudes* — Fourth Issue, One Year Production

Chapel Exclusive, Chapel Window Collection, Individually Numbered

Purchased ________, Price $ __________

Blessed Are The Peacemakers, For They Shall Be Called Sons Of God, 523348 (Wall Hanging)

 $70.00

 $70.00

Limited Ed., Issue Price $55.00, 95
Series: *Beatitudes* — Seventh & Final Issue
One Year Production
Chapel Exclusive, Chapel Window Collection, Individually Numbered

Purchased ________, Price $ ___________

I Will Fear No Evil, 523356 (Wall Hanging)

UM $70.00

$70.00

Limited Ed. 7,500, Issue Price $55.00, '98
Series: *23rd Psalm Collection* — Fourth Issue
Chapel Exclusive, Individually Numbered

Purchased ________, Price $ ___________

He Restores My Soul, 523364 (Wall Hanging)

UM $70.00

$70.00

Limited Ed. 7,500, Issue Price $55.00, '98
Series: *23rd Psalm Collection* — Third Issue
Chapel Exclusive, Individually Numbered

Purchased ________, Price $ ___________

You Prepare A Table Before Me, 523372 (Wall Hanging)

UM $70.00

$70.00

Limited Ed. 7,500, Issue Price $55.00, '98
Series: *23rd Psalm Collection* — Fifth Issue
Chapel Exclusive, Individually Numbered

Purchased ________, Price $ ___________

Blessed Are They That Mourn, For They Shall Be Comforted, 523380 (Wall Hanging)

$75.00

Limited Ed., Issue Price $55.00, '92
Series: *Beatitudes* — Second Issue,
One Year Production
Chapel Exclusive, Chapel Window Collection, Individually Numbered

Purchased ________, Price $ ___________

Blessed Are The Pure In Heart, For They Shall See God, 523399 (Wall Hanging)

$70.00

Limited Ed., Issue Price $55.00, '94
Series: *Beatitudes* — Sixth Issue,
One Year Production
Chapel Exclusive, Chapel Window Collection, Individually Numbered

Purchased ________, Price $ ___________

The Lord Is My Shepherd, I Shall Not Want, 523402 (Wall Hanging)

UM $70.00

$70.00

Limited Ed. 7,500, Issue Price $55.00, '97
Series: *23rd Psalm Collection* — First Issue
Chapel Exclusive, Individually Numbered

Purchased ________, Price $ ___________

And I Will Dwell In The House Of The Lord Forever, 523410 (Wall Hanging)

UM $70.00

$70.00

Limited Ed. 7,500, Issue Price $55.00, '98
Series: *23rd Psalm Collection* — Seventh Issue
Chapel Exclusive, Individually Numbered

Purchased ________, Price $ ___________

You Anoint My Head With Oil, 523429 (Wall Hanging)

UM $70.00

$70.00

Limited Ed. 7,500, Issue Price $55.00, '98
Series: *23rd Psalm Collection* — Sixth Issue
Chapel Exclusive, Individually Numbered

Purchased ________, Price $ ___________

Blessed Are The Poor In Spirit, For Theirs Is The Kingdom Of Heaven, 523437 (Wall Hanging)

$85.00

Limited Ed., Issue Price $55.00, '92
Series: *Beatitudes* — First Issue,
One Year Production
Chapel Exclusive, Chapel Window
Collection, Individually Numbered

Purchased ________, Price $ ___________

The Good Lord Always Delivers, 523453

$45.00 $33.00
$43.00 $31.00
$40.00 $31.00
$38.00 $30.00
$35.00 $30.00
$35.00 $30.00
$34.00 $30.00
$33.00 $30.00
$30.00

Open, Issue Price $27.50, '90
(Blonde)

Purchased ________, Price $ ___________

The Good Lord Always Delivers, 523453B

$45.00 $33.00
$43.00 $31.00
$40.00 $31.00
$38.00 $30.00
$35.00 $30.00
$35.00 $30.00
$34.00 $30.00
$33.00 $30.00
$30.00

Open, Issue Price $27.50, '90
(Brunette)

Purchased ________, Price $ ___________

This Day Has Been Made In Heaven, 523496

$53.00 | $40.00
$50.00 | $38.00
$48.00 | $38.00
$45.00 | $35.00
$45.00 | $35.00
$43.00 | $35.00
$43.00 | $35.00
$40.00 | $35.00
$35.00

Open, Issue Price $30.00, '90

Purchased ________, Price $ ___________

God Is Love, Dear Valentine, 523518

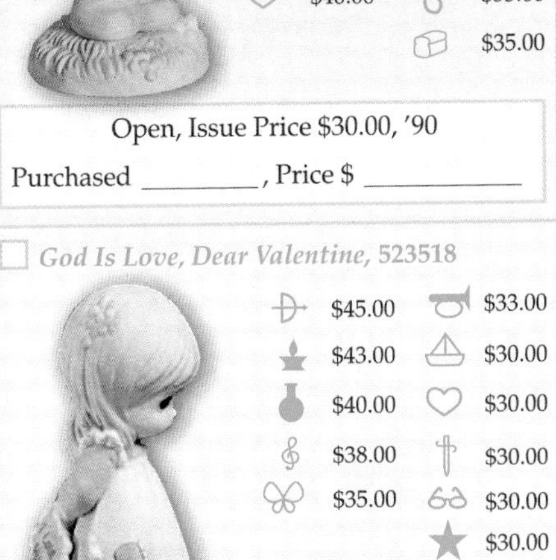

$45.00 | $33.00
$43.00 | $30.00
$40.00 | $30.00
$38.00 | $30.00
$35.00 | $30.00
$30.00

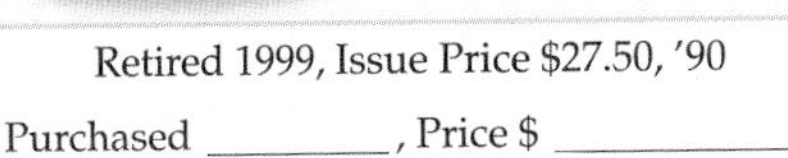

Retired 1999, Issue Price $27.50, '90

Purchased ________, Price $ ___________

I'm A Precious Moments Fan, 523526

$50.00
$45.00

Annual 1990, Issue Price $30.00, '90
Special Event

Purchased ________, Price $ ___________

I Will Cherish The Old Rugged Cross, 523534 (Egg)

$35.00
$33.00

Dated Annual 1991, Issue Price $27.50, '91
Set of 2, Series: *Eggs* – First Issue

Purchased ________, Price $ ___________

You Are The Type I Love, 523542

$55.00 | $50.00
$53.00 | $50.00
$53.00 | $48.00
$50.00 | $48.00
$48.00
$47.00
$47.00
$47.00

Retired 2002, Issue Price $40.00, '92

Purchased ________, Price $ ___________

He Is Our Shelter From The Storm, 523550

$80.00
$78.00
$75.00
$75.00
$75.00
$75.00
$75.00
$75.00

Retired 2004, Issue Price $75.00, '98
Boys & Girls Club of America
Commemorative

Purchased ________, Price $ ___________

I Will Always Love You, 523569

$60.00

$55.00

Limited Ed., Issue Price $45.00, '01
2001 Spring Catalog Exclusive

Purchased ________, Price $ ___________

The Lord Will Provide, 523593

$55.00

$45.00

Annual 1993, Issue Price $40.00, '93

Purchased ________, Price $ ___________

Good News Is So Uplifting, 523615

$90.00

$87.00

$85.00

$83.00

$80.00

$77.00

$77.00

$75.00

$75.00

Retired 1999, Issue Price $60.00, '91

Purchased ________, Price $ ___________

I'm So Glad That God Has Blessed Me With A Friend Like You, 523623

$85.00

$75.00

$70.00

$65.00

Retired 1995, Issue Price $50.00, '93

Purchased ________, Price $ ___________

I Will Always Be Thinking Of You, 523631

$65.00

$55.00

$53.00

$50.00

Retired 1996, Issue Price $45.00, '94

Purchased ________, Price $ ___________

This Day Has Been Made In Heaven, 523682 (Musical)

$90.00

$85.00

$80.00

$75.00

$75.00

$73.00

$73.00

$70.00

$70.00

$65.00

$65.00

$65.00

$65.00

Retired 2003, Issue Price $60.00, '92
Tune: "Amazing Grace"

Purchased ________, Price $ ___________

☐ *May Your Christmas Be A Happy Home,* 523704 (Ornament)

- $35.00

Dated Annual 1990, Issue Price $27.50, '90
Series: *Masterpiece Ornament* — Second Issue
Purchased ________, Price $ ________

☐ *Time Heals,* 523739

- $55.00
- $53.00
- $50.00
- $50.00
- $48.00
- $48.00
- $45.00
- $45.00
- $45.00
- $43.00
- $43.00
- $43.00

Retired 2001, Issue Price $37.50, '90
Purchased ________, Price $ ________

☐ *Blessings From Above,* 523747

- $115.00
- $95.00
- $90.00
- $85.00
- $80.00

Retired 1994, Issue Price $45.00, '90
Purchased ________, Price $ ________

☐ *Just Poppin' In To Say Halo!* 523755

- $70.00
- $68.00
- $65.00
- $63.00
- $60.00
- $55.00

Retired 1999, Issue Price $45.00, '94
Purchased ________, Price $ ________

☐ *I Can't Spell Success Without You,* 523763

- $100.00
- $70.00
- $67.00
- $65.00
- $63.00

Suspended 1994, Issue Price $40.00, '91
Purchased ________, Price $ ________

☐ *Baby's First Christmas,* 523771 (Ornament)

- $25.00

Dated Annual 1990, Issue Price $15.00, '90
Purchased ________,
Price $ ________

☐ *Baby's First Christmas,* 523798 (Ornament)

- $25.00

Dated Annual 1990, Issue Price $15.00, '90
Purchased ________,
Price $ ________

☐ *Wishing You A Yummy Christmas*, 523801 (Plate)

$60.00

Dated Annual 1990, Issue Price $50.00, '90
Series: *Christmas Blessings* — First Issue
Purchased ________, Price $ __________

☐ *Once Upon A Holy Night*, 523828 (Bell)

$40.00

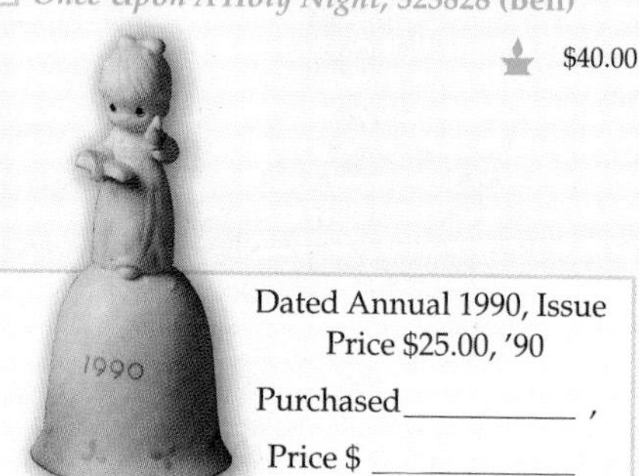

Dated Annual 1990, Issue Price $25.00, '90
Purchased __________ ,
Price $ __________

☐ *Once Upon A Holy Night*, 523836

$45.00

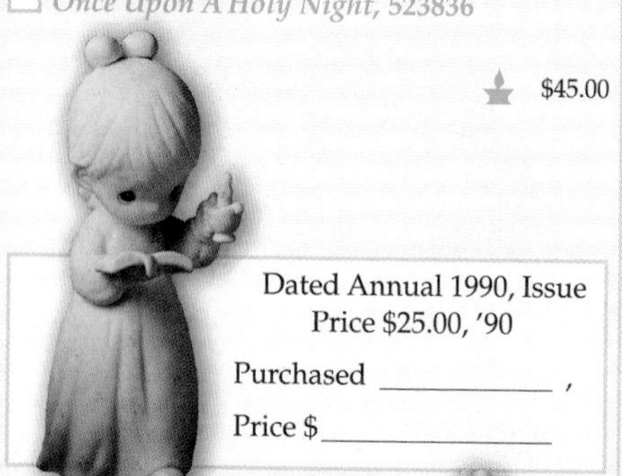

Dated Annual 1990, Issue Price $25.00, '90
Purchased __________ ,
Price $__________

☐ *Once Upon A Holy Night*, 523844 (Thimble)

$25.00

☐ *Once Upon A Holy Night*, 523852 (Ornament)

$30.00

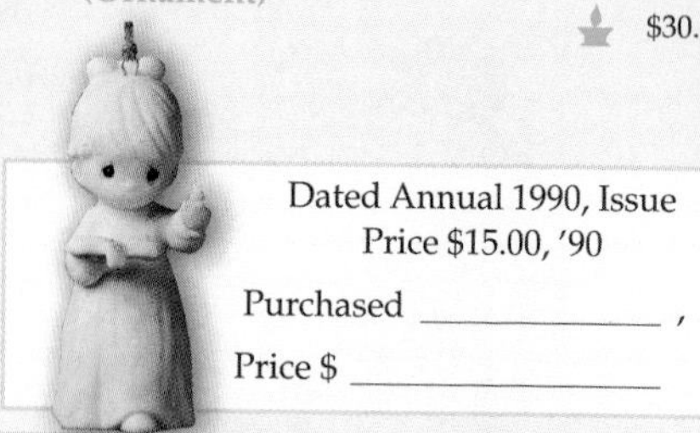

Dated Annual 1990, Issue Price $15.00, '90
Purchased __________ ,
Price $ __________

☐ *Blessings From Me To Thee*, 523860 (Plate)

$55.00

Dated Annual 1991, Issue Price $50.00, '91
Series: *Christmas Blessings* — Second Issue
Purchased ________, Price $ __________

☐ *We Are God's Workmanship*, 523879

$625.00

Limited Ed. 2,000, Issue Price $500.00, '91
Easter Seals, Lily Understamp
Individually Numbered
Purchased ________, Price $ __________

Dated Annual 1990, Issue Price $8.00, '90
Purchased ________, Price $ __________

Love Never Leaves A Mother's Arms, 523941

$50.00
$47.00
$45.00
$45.00
$43.00
$43.00
$40.00
$40.00
$40.00
$40.00
$40.00

Open, Issue Price $40.00, '96

Purchased ________, Price $ ____________

You're The Best Friend On The Block, 524018

$55.00
$53.00
$50.00
$50.00
$50.00

Suspended 2005, Issue Price $50.00, '02

Purchased ________, Price $ ____________

Life's Filled With Little Surprises, 524034

UM $30.00

Limited Ed., Issue Price $22.50, '00
Series: *Little Moments*
Hallmark Gold Crown Exclusive

Purchased ________, Price $ ____________

Baby's First Birthday, 524069

$35.00
$33.00
$30.00
$28.00
$25.00
$25.00
$25.00
$25.00
$25.00
$25.00
$25.00
$25.00
$25.00
$25.00

Open, Issue Price $25.00, '93
Series: *Baby's First* — Eighth & Final Issue

Purchased ________, Price $ ____________

Baby's First Meal, 524077

$55.00
$53.00
$50.00
$48.00
$48.00
$45.00
$45.00
$43.00
$43.00

Retired 1999, Issue Price $35.00, '91
Series: *Baby's First* — Sixth Issue

Purchased ________, Price $ ____________

My Warmest Thoughts Are You, 524085

$120.00
$110.00
$100.00
$95.00
$90.00
$85.00

Retired 1996, Issue Price $55.00, '92

Purchased ________, Price $ ____________

☐ *Missing You, 524107*

$50.00 $40.00
$45.00 $37.50
$37.50

Open, Issue Price $40.00, '01
Purchased ________ ,
Price $ ________

☐ *Sharing Our Christmas Together, 524115*

$125.00
$125.00

Open, Issue Price $125.00, '04
Purchased ________ , Price $ ________

☐ *Good Friends Are For Always, 524123*

$50.00 $43.00
$48.00 $43.00
$45.00 $40.00
$45.00 $40.00
$40.00

Retired 1999, Issue Price $27.50, '91
Purchased ________ ,
Price $ ________

☐ *Good Friends Are For Always, 524131 (Ornament)*

$35.00 $30.00 $25.00
$33.00 $28.00 $25.00

Retired 1997, Issue Price $15.00, '92
Purchased ________ , Price $ ________

☐ *Lord, Teach Us To Pray, 524158*

$45.00

Annual 1994, Issue Price $35.00, '94
National Day Of Prayer
Purchased ________ , Price $ ________

☐ *May Your Christmas Be Merry, 524166*

$40.00

Dated Annual 1991, Issue Price $27.50, '91
Purchased ________ , Price $ ________

☐ *May Your Christmas Be Merry, 524174 (Ornament)*

$38.00

Dated Annual 1991, Issue Price $25.00, '91
Purchased ________ ,
Price $ ________

May Your Christmas Be Merry, 524182 (Bell)

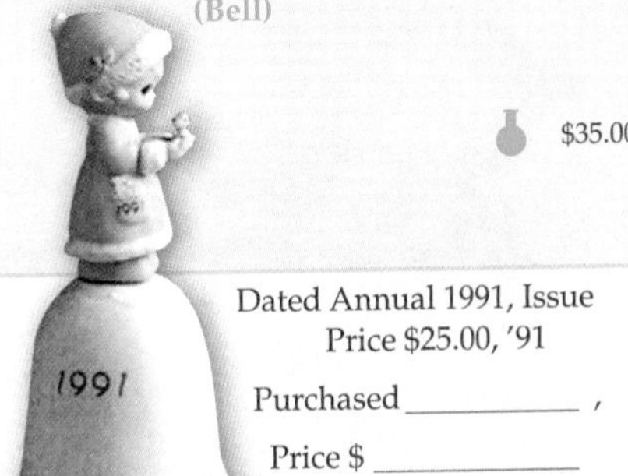

$35.00

Dated Annual 1991, Issue Price $25.00, '91

Purchased __________ ,

Price $ __________

May Your Christmas Be Merry, 524190 (Thimble)

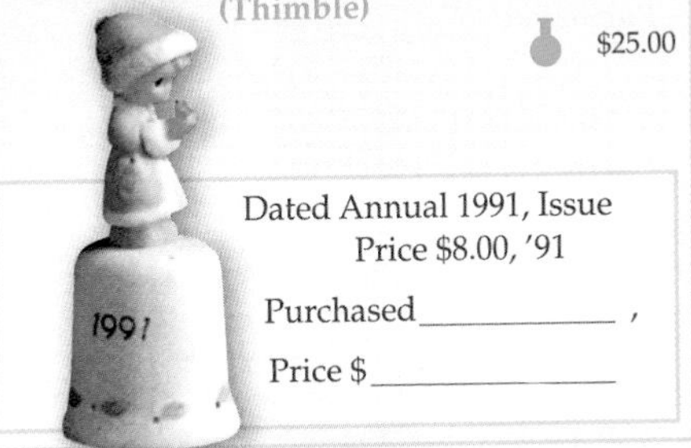

$25.00

Dated Annual 1991, Issue Price $8.00, '91

Purchased __________ ,

Price $ __________

Love Is Color Blind, 524204

$65.00
$65.00
$60.00
$60.00
$60.00
$60.00
$60.00

Retired 2004, Issue Price $60.00, '99
Boys & Girls Club of America Commemorative

Purchased __________ , Price $ __________

Walk In The Sonshine, 524212

$45.00 $38.00
$40.00 $38.00
$39.00 $37.00
$37.00

Retired 2001, Issue Price $35.00, '95

Purchased __________ ,

Price $ __________

He Loves Me, 524263

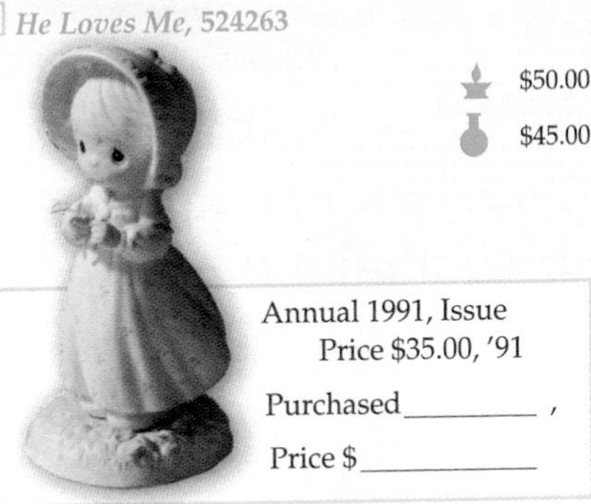

$50.00
$45.00

Annual 1991, Issue Price $35.00, '91

Purchased __________ ,

Price $ __________

Friendship Grows When You Plant A Seed, 524271

$115.00
$95.00
$85.00
$83.00

Retired 1994, Issue Price $40.00, '92

Purchased __________ , Price $ __________

May Your Every Wish Come True, 524298

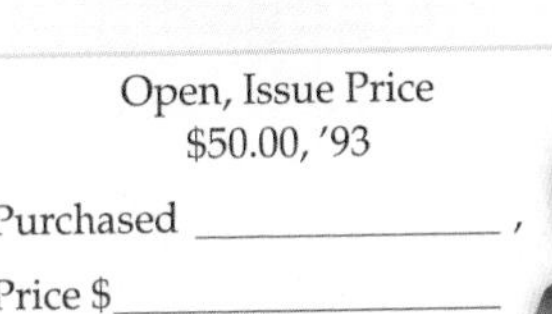

$70.00 $53.00
$68.00 $50.00
$65.00 $50.00
$63.00 $50.00
$60.00 $50.00
$58.00 $50.00
$55.00 $50.00

Open, Issue Price $50.00, '93

Purchased __________ ,

Price $ __________

May Your Birthday Be A Blessing, 524301

$50.00
$48.00
$45.00
$45.00
$43.00
$40.00
$40.00
$38.00
$36.00
$35.00
$35.00
$35.00
$35.00
$35.00
$35.00
$35.00

Open, Issue Price $30.00, '91
(Blonde)

Purchased ________, Price $ ___________

What The World Needs Now, 524352

$87.00
$85.00
$80.00
$78.00
$75.00
$73.00
$70.00

Retired 1997, Issue Price $50.00, '92

Purchased ________, Price $ ___________

May Your Birthday Be A Blessing, 524301B

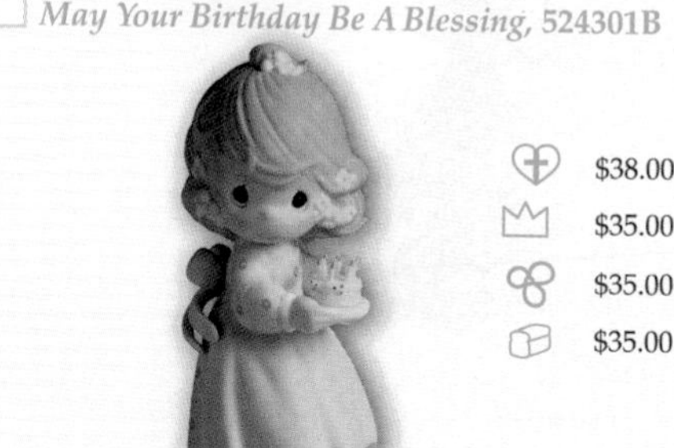

$38.00
$35.00
$35.00
$35.00

Open, Issue Price $35.00, '02
(Brunette)

Purchased ________, Price $ ___________

Something Precious From Above, 524360

$65.00
$63.00
$60.00
$58.00
$55.00
$55.00
$55.00
$55.00
$55.00
$55.00

Open, Issue Price $50.00, '97

Purchased ________, Price $ ___________

Our Friendship Is Soda-licious, 524336

$90.00
$87.00
$85.00
$83.00
$80.00
$78.00
$75.00
$75.00

Retired 1999, Issue Price $65.00, '93

Purchased ________, Price $ ___________

So Glad I Picked You As A Friend, 524379

$50.00
$48.00

Annual 1994, Issue Price $40.00, '94
DSR Spring Catalog Exclusive

Purchased ________, Price $ ___________

Take Time To Smell The Flowers, 524387

$48.00
$40.00

Annual 1995, Issue Price $30.00, '95
Easter Seals Commemorative
Lily Understamp

Purchased ________, Price $ ___________

You Are Such A Purr-fect Friend, 524395

$50.00
$45.00
$43.00
$40.00
$38.00
$36.00
$35.00
$35.00
$35.00
$35.00
$35.00
$35.00
$35.00
$35.00

Open, Issue Price $35.00, '93

Purchased ________, Price $ ___________

Be Fruitful And Multiply, 524409

$60.00
$58.00
$55.00
$50.00
$50.00
$50.00
$50.00

Open, Issue Price $50.00, '99

Purchased ________, Price $ ___________

May Only Good Things Come Your Way, 524425

$50.00
$48.00
$45.00
$43.00
$40.00
$40.00
$40.00
$40.00
$40.00

Retired 1998, Issue Price $30.00, '91

Purchased ________, Price $ ___________

Sealed With A Kiss, 524441

$90.00
$85.00
$80.00
$75.00
$70.00

Retired 1996, Issue Price $50.00, '93

Purchased ________, Price $ ___________

A Special Chime For Jesus, 524468

$55.00
$52.00
$50.00
$48.00
$46.00

Retired 1997, Issue Price $32.50, '93

Purchased ________, Price $ ___________

God Cared Enough To Send His Best, 524476

- $85.00
- $80.00
- $75.00

Retired 1996, Issue Price $50.00, '94

Purchased ________, Price $ ___________

Not A Creature Was Stirring, 524484

- $45.00
- $43.00
- $40.00
- $38.00
- $35.00

Suspended 1994, Issue Price $17.00, '90
Series: *Birthday Collection*, Set of 2

Purchased ________, Price $ ___________

Can't Be Without You, 524492

- $35.00
- $33.00
- $30.00
- $28.00
- $25.00
- $25.00
- $20.00
- $20.00
- $20.00

Retired 1999, Issue Price $16.00, '91
Series: *Birthday Collection*

Purchased ________, Price $ ___________

Oinky Birthday, 524506

- $33.00
- $30.00
- $28.00
- $25.00
- $23.00
- $20.00
- $20.00

Retired 1999, Issue Price $13.50, '94
Series: *Birthday Collection*

Purchased ________, Price $ ___________

Always In His Care, 524522

- $55.00
- $48.00

Limited Ed., Issue Price $30.00, '90
Easter Seals Commemorative
Lily Understamp

Easter Seals

Purchased ________, Price $ ___________

Happy Birthday Dear Jesus, 524875

- $40.00
- $38.00
- $35.00
- $30.00

Suspended 1993, Issue Price $13.50, '90
Nativity Addition

Purchased ________, Price $ ___________

☐ *Christmas Fireplace, 524883*

Mark	Value
Flame	$70.00
Flask	$65.00
G-Clef	$60.00

Suspended 1992, Issue Price $37.50, '90
Series: *Family Christmas Scene*

Purchased ________, Price $ ___________

☐ *It's So Uplifting To Have A Friend Like You, 524905*

Mark	Value
G-Clef	$60.00
Butterfly	$58.00
Trumpet	$55.00
Ship	$53.00
Heart	$50.00
Sword	$48.00
Eyeglasses	$47.00
Star	$47.00

Retired 1999, Issue Price $40.00, '92

Purchased ________, Price $ ___________

☐ *We're Going To Miss You, 524913*

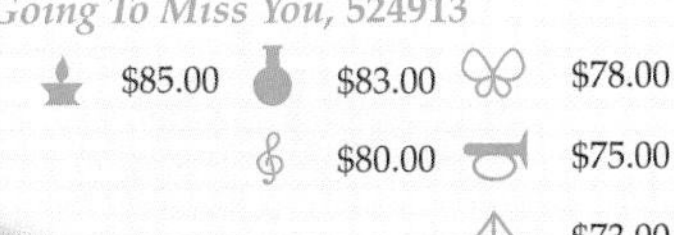

Mark	Value
Flame	$85.00
Flask	$83.00
G-Clef	$80.00
Butterfly	$78.00
Trumpet	$75.00
Ship	$73.00
Heart	$70.00
Sword	$68.00
Eyeglasses	$65.00
Star	$65.00
Egg	$63.00
Bow & Arrow	$63.00

Retired 2001, Issue Price $50.00, '90

Purchased ________, Price $ ___________

☐ *Angels We Have Heard On High, 524921*

There have been many reports of the African-American angel's hand not being painted.

Mark	Value
Flask	$95.00
G-Clef	$90.00
Butterfly	$88.00
Trumpet	$85.00
Ship	$83.00
Heart	$80.00

Retired 1996, Issue Price $60.00, '91

Purchased ________, Price $ ___________

☐ *Good Friends Are Forever, 525049*

Only collectors who attended the 1990 "Good Friends are Forever" Special Event with a friend had the opportunity to be included in a drawing for this special Rosebud decal understamp figurine. Last known sale of this piece was $625.00.

Mark	Value
Rosebud	$600.00

Annual 1990
Special Event

Purchased ________, Price $ ___________

☐ *Bundles Of Joy, 525057 (Ornament)*

Mark	Value
Flame	$30.00

Annual 1990, Issue Price $15.00, '90

Purchased ___________ ,

Price $_______________

Tubby's First Christmas, 525278

$15.00 $10.00
$12.00 $10.00
$10.00 $10.00
$10.00
$10.00

Retired 1999, Issue Price $10.00, '92
Mini Nativity Addition
Purchased _________, Price $ ___________

It's A Perfect Boy, 525286

$25.00 $18.50
$18.50 $18.50
$18.50 $18.50
$18.50
$18.50
$18.50

Retired 1999, Issue Price $16.50, '91
Mini Nativity Addition
Purchased _________, Price $ ___________

May Your Future Be Blessed, 525316

$55.00 $50.00 $48.00
$53.00 $45.00
$44.00
$42.00
$40.00
$40.00
$40.00
$40.00
$40.00
$40.00
$40.00

Open, Issue Price $35.00, '93
Purchased _________, Price $ ___________

Our First Christmas Together, 525324
(Ornament)

$28.00

Dated Annual 1990, Issue Price $17.50, '90
Purchased _________, Price $ ___________

Lord, Keep Me On My Toes, 525332
(Ornament)

$30.00 $25.00
$28.00 $25.00
$23.00
$23.00
$20.00
$20.00
$20.00
$20.00

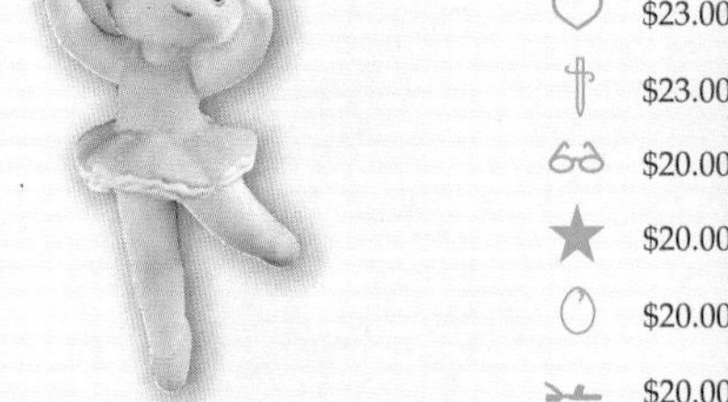

Retired 2001, Issue Price $15.00, '92
Purchased _________, Price $ ___________

Ring Those Christmas Bells, 525898

$165.00
$155.00
$150.00
$140.00
$135.00

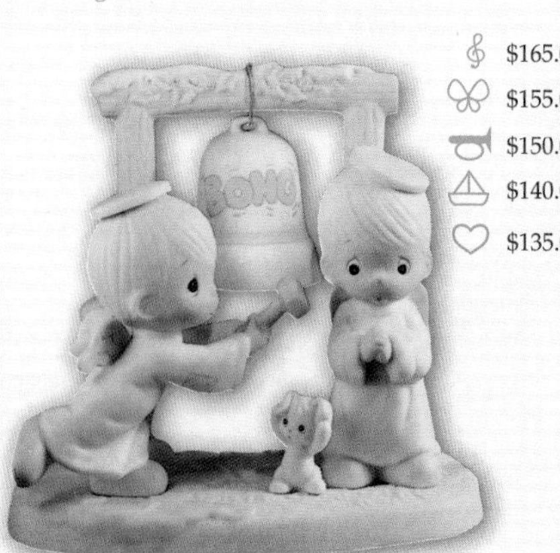

Retired 1996, Issue Price $95.00, '92
Purchased _________, Price $ ___________

We All Need A Friend Through The Ruff Times, 525901

$50.00
$48.00
$45.00
$45.00
$45.00

Open, Issue Price $45.00, '01

Purchased ________, Price $ __________

Let's Put The Pieces Together, 525928

$70.00 $65.00 $63.00
$60.00
$60.00
$60.00
$60.00
$60.00
$60.00

Open, Issue Price $60.00, '98

Purchased ________, Price $ __________

Lord, I'm In It Again, 525944

$60.00
$58.00
$55.00
$50.00
$50.00
$50.00
$50.00

Open, Issue Price $50.00, '99

Purchased ________, Price $ __________

All About Heaven, 525952

$28.00
$25.00
$23.00
$20.00
$20.00

Open, Issue Price $20.00, '01
Mini Nativity Addition

Purchased ________, Price $ __________

We Are God's Workmanship, 525960 (Egg)

$35.00
$30.00

Dated Annual 1992, Issue Price $27.50, '92
Set of 2, Series: *Eggs* – 2nd Issue

Purchased ________, Price $ __________

Going Home, 525979

$80.00 $75.00 $70.00
$78.00 $73.00 $68.00
$65.00
$63.00
$60.00
$60.00
$60.00
$60.00
$60.00
$60.00

Has been found with "Heaven Bound" missing from license plate.

Retired 2004, Issue Price $60.00, '92
Philip Butcher Memorial Figurine

Purchased ________, Price $ __________

You Are Such A Purr-fect Friend, 526010

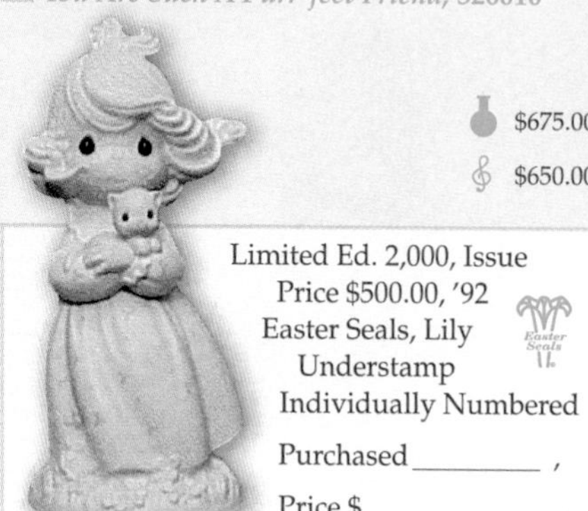

$675.00
$650.00

Limited Ed. 2,000, Issue Price $500.00, '92
Easter Seals, Lily Understamp
Individually Numbered

Purchased ________ ,
Price $ ____________

A Prince Of A Guy, 526037

$48.00 $40.00
$45.00 $38.00
$43.00 $35.00

Retired 2000, Issue Price $35.00, '95

Purchased __________ ,
Price $______________

A Prince Of A Guy, 526037S $35.00

Limited Ed., Issue Price $35.00, '95
1995 Fall Catalog Exclusive

Purchased ________, Price $ ____________

Pretty As A Princess, 526053

$45.00 $35.00
$43.00 $35.00
$40.00 $35.00
$38.00 $35.00
$35.00 $35.00
$35.00

Open, Issue Price $35.00, '95
Catalog Early Release

Purchased ________ ,
Price $ ____________

The Pearl Of Great Price, 526061

$70.0

Annual 1997, Issue Price $50.00, '97
Century Circle Event Exclusive

Purchased ________, Price $ ____________

I'm Completely Suspended With Love, 526096

$30.0

Annual 2001, Issue Price $23.00, '01

Purchased ____________ ,
Price $ ____________

I'm Completely Suspended With Love, 526096S

$35.00 $30.0

Comes with crystal heart-shaped box.

Annual 2001, Issue Price $28.50, '01

Purchased ________, Price $ ____________

I Would Be Lost Without You, 526142

$45.00 $35.0
$43.00 $35.0
$40.00 $33.0
$38.00 $33.0
$33.0

Retired 1999, Issue Price $27.50, '92

Purchased________ ,
Price $____________

Friends To The Very End, 526150

- $75.00
- $73.00
- $70.00
- $68.00
- $65.00

Retired 1997, Issue Price $40.00, '94

Purchased ________, Price $ ___________

Sharing Sweet Moments Together, 526487

- $55.00
- $50.00
- $48.00
- $47.00
- $47.00
- $46.00
- $46.00

Retired 1999, Issue Price $45.00, '94

Purchased ________, Price $ ___________

You Are My Happiness, 526185

- $70.00
- $68.00

Limited Ed., Issue Price $37.50, '92

Purchased ________, Price $ ___________

Bless Those Who Serve Their Country — Navy, 526568

- UM $150.00
- $135.00
- $135.00

Suspended 1992, Issue Price $32.50, '91

Purchased ________, Price $ ___________

You Suit Me To A Tee, 526193

- $55.00
- $50.00
- $48.00
- $45.00
- $43.00
- $40.00

Retired 1999, Issue Price $35.00, '94

Purchased ________, Price $ ___________

Bless Those Who Serve Their Country — Army, 526576

- $50.00
- $48.00

Suspended 1992, Issue Price $32.50, '91

Purchased ________, Price $ ___________

Bless Those Who Serve Their Country — Air Force, 526584

$50.00

$48.00

Suspended 1992, Issue Price $32.50, '91

Purchased ________, Price $ __________

You Can Always Count On Me, 526827

$40.00

$35.00

Annual 1996, Issue Price $30.00, '96
Easter Seals Commemorative
Lily Understamp

Purchased ________, Price $ __________

The Lord Is With You, 526835

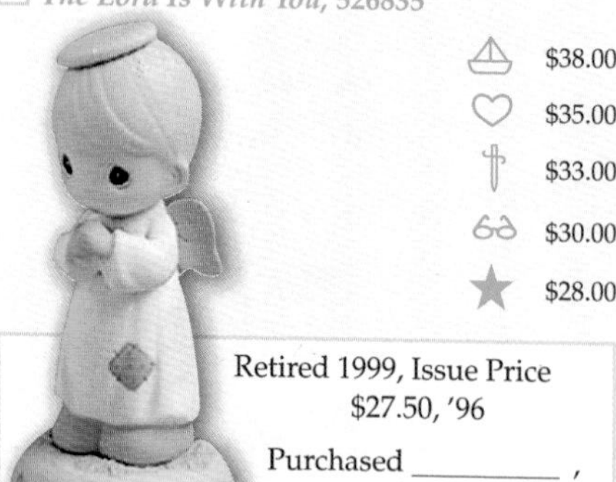

$38.00

$35.00

$33.00

$30.00

$28.00

Retired 1999, Issue Price $27.50, '96

Purchased ________,

Price $ __________

He's Got The Whole World In His Hands, 526886

$625.00

$600.00

Limited Ed. 2,000, Issue Price $500.00, '95
Easter Seals, Lily Understamp
Individually Numbered

Purchased ________, Price $ __________

Wishing You Were Here, 526916 (Musical)

$150.00

$145.00

$140.00

$135.00

$130.00

$125.00

$120.00

Retired 1998, Issue Price $100.00, '93
Tune: "When You Wish Upon A Star"

Purchased ________, Price $ __________

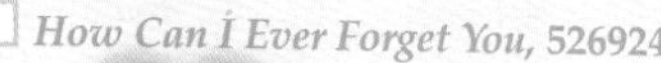

How Can I Ever Forget You, 526924

$35.00	$23.00
$33.00	$23.00
$30.00	$20.00
$28.00	$20.00
$25.00	$20.00
$25.00	$20.00

Retired 2001, Issue Price $15.00, '91
Series: *Birthday Collection*

Purchased ________, Price $ __________

May Your Christmas Be Merry, 526940 (Ornament)

$40.00

Dated Annual 1991, Issue Price $30.00, '91
Series: *Masterpiece Ornament* — Third Issue
Set of 2

Purchased ________, Price $ __________

We Have Come From Afar, 526959

$30.00
$25.00
$20.00
$20.00

Suspended 1994, Issue Price $17.50, '91
Nativity Addition

Purchased ________, Price $ __________

Baby's First Christmas, 527084 (Ornament)

$28.00

Dated Annual 1991, Issue Price $15.00, '91

Purchased __________,

Price $__________

Baby's First Christmas, 527092 (Ornament)

$28.00

Dated Annual 1991, Issue Price $15.00, '91

Purchased __________,

Price $__________

He Is Not Here For He Is Risen As He Said, 527106

UM $115.00
$100.00
$85.00
$80.00
$75.00
$73.00
$70.00
$68.00
$65.00
$63.00
$60.00
$60.00
$60.00

Open, Issue Price $60.00, '93
Chapel Exclusive

Purchased ________, Price $ __________

Sharing A Gift Of Love, 527114

$65.00
$60.00

Annual 1991, Issue Price $30.00, '91
Easter Seals Commemorative
Lily Understamp

Purchased __________,

Price $ __________

You Can Always Bring A Friend, 527122

$60.00
$55.00

Annual 1991, Issue Price $27.50, '91
Special Event

Purchased__________,

Price $ __________

☐ *The Good Lord Always Delivers, 527165* (Ornament)

$35.00
$30.00
$28.00

Suspended 1993, Issue Price $15.00, '91

Purchased ________, Price $ ________

☐ *A Universal Love, 527173*

$95.00
$93.00

Annual 1992, Issue Price $32.50, '92
Easter Seals Commemorative Lily Understamp

Purchased ________, Price $ ________

☐ *Share In The Warmth Of Christmas, 527211* (Ornament)

$33.00
$30.00
$28.00
$25.00
$25.00
$23.00
$23.00
$20.00
$20.00

Retired 2001, Issue Price $15.00, '93

Purchased ________, Price $ ________

☐ *Baby's First Word, 527238*

$45.00
$43.00
$40.00
$38.00
$35.00
$33.00
$30.00
$28.00

Retired 1999, Issue Price $25.00, '92
Series: *Baby's First* — Seventh Issue

Purchased ________, Price $ ________

☐ *Let's Be Friends, 527270*

$40.00
$35.00
$33.00
$30.00
$28.00
$27.00

Retired 1996, Issue Price $15.00, '92
Series: *Birthday Collection*

Purchased ________, Price $ ________

☐ *Bless Those Who Serve Their Country — Girl Soldier, 527289*

$55.00
$48.00

Suspended 1992, Issue Price $32.50, '91

Purchased ________, Price $ ________

☐ *Bless Those Who Serve Their Country — African-American Soldier, 527297*

$55.00
$50.00

Suspended 1992, Issue Price $32.50, '91

Purchased ________, Price $ ________

An Event Worth Wading For, 527319

(mark)	$55.00
(mark)	$50.00

Annual 1992, Issue Price $32.50, '92
Special Event

Purchased ________, Price $ ___________

Onward Christmas Soldiers, 527327
(Ornament)

(mark)	$35.00	(mark)	$30.00
(mark)	$33.00	(mark)	$28.00
		(mark)	$25.00
		(mark)	$23.00
		(mark)	$20.00
		(mark)	$20.00

Retired 2001, Issue Price $16.00, '94

Purchased ________, Price $ ___________

Bless-um You, 527335

(mark)	$50.00
(mark)	$48.00
(mark)	$45.00
(mark)	$43.00
(mark)	$40.00
(mark)	$38.00
(mark)	$38.00

Retired 1998, Issue Price $35.00, '93

Purchased ________, Price $ ___________

Happy Birdie, 527343

(mark)	$33.00
(mark)	$30.00
(mark)	$28.00
(mark)	$25.00
(mark)	$23.00

Suspended 1996, Issue Price $16.00, '92
Series: *Birthday Collection*

Purchased ________, Price $ ___________

You Are My Favorite Star, 527378

(mark)	$115.00
(mark)	$105.00
(mark)	$95.00
(mark)	$90.00
(mark)	$85.00
(mark)	$80.00

Retired 1997, Issue Price $60.00, '92

Purchased ________, Price $ ___________

Baby's First Christmas (Girl), 527475
(Ornament)

(mark)	$30.00

Dated Annual 1992, Issue Price $15.00, '92

Purchased ________, Price $ ___________

☐ *Baby's First Christmas (Boy), 527483 (Ornament)*

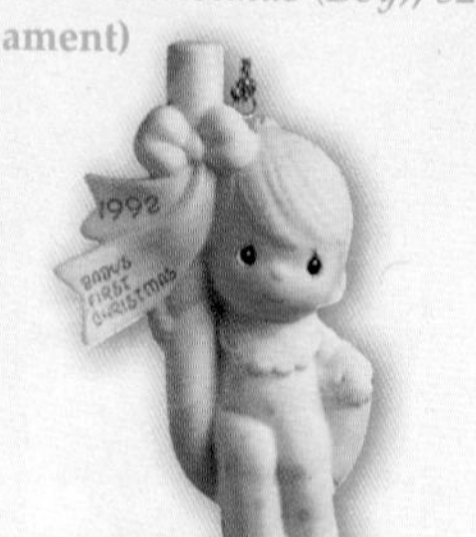

$30.00

Dated Annual 1992, Issue Price $15.00, '92
Purchased ________, Price $ ___________

☐ *Bless Those Who Serve Their Country — Marine, 527521*

$65.00
$60.00

Suspended 1992, Issue Price $32.50, '91
Purchased ________, Price $ ___________

☐ *Bring The Little Ones To Jesus, 527556*

$125.00
$115.00
$105.00
$100.00
$95.00
$90.00
$90.00
$90.00
$90.00
$90.00
$90.00
$90.00
$90.00

Retired 2003, Issue Price $90.00, '92
Child Evangelism Fellowship
Purchased ________, Price $ ___________

☐ *God Bless The USA, 527564*

$45.00
$40.00

Annual 1992, Issue Price $32.50, '92
Purchased ________, Price $ ___________

☐ *Tied Up For The Holidays, 527580*

$65.00
$60.00
$58.00
$55.00

Suspended 1996, Issue Price $40.00, '93
Purchased ________, Price $ ___________

☐ *Bringing You A Merry Christmas, 527599*

$95.00
$90.00
$85.00

Retired 1995, Issue Price $45.00, '93
Purchased ________, Price $ ___________

Wishing You A Ho, Ho, Ho, 527629

$60.00
$58.00
$55.00
$53.00
$50.00
$50.00
$50.00
$50.00
$50.00
$50.00

Retired 2001, Issue Price $40.00, '92

Purchased ________, Price $ __________

Waiting For A Merry Christmas, 527637

$80.00

Retired 2000, Issue Price $65.00, '00

Purchased ________, Price $ __________

You Have Touched So Many Hearts, 527661

$45.00
$43.00
$40.00
$38.00
$37.50
$37.50

Suspended 1996, Issue Price $35.00, '91
DSR Exclusive

Purchased ________, Price $ __________

But The Greatest Of These Is Love, 527688

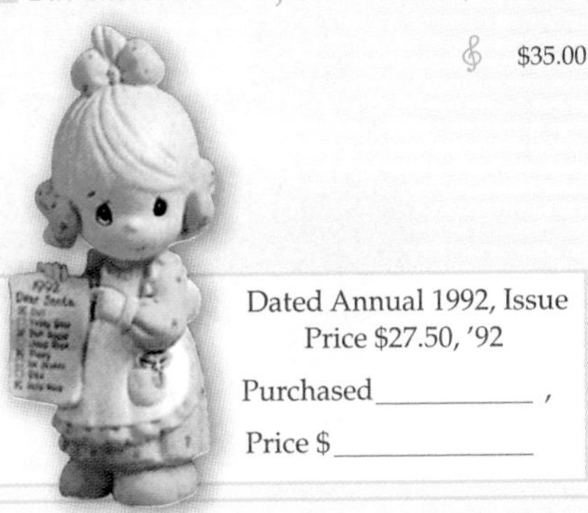

$35.00

Dated Annual 1992, Issue Price $27.50, '92

Purchased __________ ,

Price $ __________

But The Greatest Of These Is Love, 527696 (Ornament)

$35.00

Dated Annual 1992, Issue Price $15.00, '92

Purchased __________ ,

Price $ __________

But The Greatest Of These Is Love, 527718 (Thimble)

$25.00

Dated Annual 1992, Issue Price $8.00, '92

Purchased __________ ,

Price $ __________

But The Greatest Of These Is Love, 527726 (Bell)

$35.00

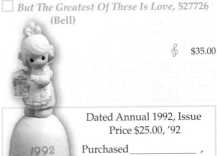

Dated Annual 1992, Issue Price $25.00, '92

Purchased __________ ,

Price $ __________

☐ *But The Greatest Of These Is Love, 527734* (Ornament)

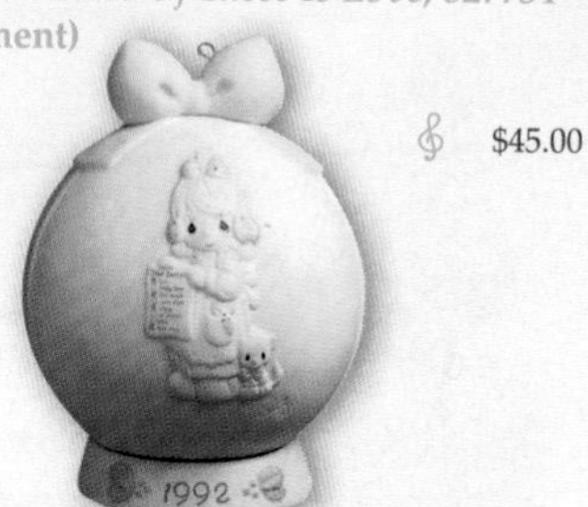

Mark	Price
𝄞	$45.00

Dated Annual 1992, Issue Price $30.00, '92
Series: *Masterpiece Ornament* — Fourth Issue
Set of 2

Purchased ________, Price $ __________

☐ *But The Greatest Of These Is Love, 527742* (Plate)

Mark	Price
𝄞	$60.00

Dated Annual 1992, Issue Price $50.00, '92
Series: *Christmas Blessings* — Third Issue

Purchased ________, Price $ __________

☐ *Wishing You A Comfy Christmas, 527750*

Mark	Price
𝄞	$45.00
🦋	$43.00
📯	$40.00
⛵	$40.00
♡	$38.00
†	$38.00
👓	$35.00
★	$35.00

Retired 1999, Issue Price $27.50, '92
Nativity Addition

Purchased ________, Price $ __________

☐ *I Only Have Arms For You, 527769*

Mark	Price
𝄞	$30.00
🦋	$28.00
📯	$25.00
⛵	$23.00
♡	$20.00
†	$20.00
👓	$20.00

Retired 1998, Issue Price $15.00, '93
Series: *Birthday Collection*

Purchased ________, Price $ __________

☐ *This Land Is Our Land, 527777*

Mark	Price
𝄞	$45.00

Annual 1992, Issue Price $35.00, '92

Purchased ________, Price $ __________

☐ *There's A Christian Welcome Here, 528021* (Ornament)

Mark	Price
UM	$35.00
🦋	$33.00
📯	$30.00
⛵	$28.00
♡	$25.00
†	$25.00

Suspended 1997, Issue Price $22.50, '92
Chapel Exclusive

Purchased ________, Price $ __________

Free Christmas Puppies, 528064

$35.00
$32.00
$30.00
$28.00

Retired 1997, Issue Price $12.50, '94
Series: *Sugar Town*

Purchased ________, Price $ ___________

Nativity Cart, 528072

$35.00
$33.00
$30.00
$28.00
$25.00
$25.00
$23.00
$23.00

Retired 2001, Issue Price $18.50, '94
Nativity Addition

Purchased ________, Price $ ___________

Follow Your Heart, 528080

There have been reports of the decal being on backwards.

$60.00
$50.00

Annual 1995, Issue Price $30.00, '95
Spring Celebration Event

Purchased ________, Price $ ___________

Markie, 528099

$35.00
$33.00
$28.00
$25.00

Suspended 1996, Issue Price $18.50, '94
Series: *Sammy's Circus*

Purchased ______________ ,

Price $ ______________

He Came As The Gift Of God's Love, 528129

$40.00
$38.00
$35.00
$33.00
$30.00
$30.00
$30.00

Open, Issue Price $30.00, '99
Nativity, Set of 4

Purchased ________, Price $ ___________

Have I Got News For You, 528137

$30.00
$28.00
$25.00
$23.00
$23.00
$20.00

Retired 1999, Issue Price $16.00, '94
Mini Nativity Addition

Purchased ________, Price $ ___________

☐ *Circus Tent,* 528196 (Nightlight)

$115.00
$105.00
$98.00
$95.00

Suspended 1996, Issue Price $90.00, '94
Series: *Sammy's Circus*
Purchased ________, Price $ __________

☐ *Sending You A White Christmas,* 528218 (Ornament)

$30.00
$28.00
$25.00
$23.00
$20.00
$20.00
$20.00
$20.00

Retired 2001, Issue Price $16.00, '94
Purchased ____________,
Price $______________

☐ *Bringing You A Merry Christmas,* 528226 (Ornament)

$30.00
$28.00
$25.00
$23.00
$20.00

Suspended 1998, Issue Price $16.00, '94
Purchased __________,
Price $ __________

☐ *I'm Sending My Love Your Way,* 528609

$65.00
$60.00

Annual 1995, Issue Price $40.00, '95
Spring Catalog DSR Promo
Purchased________,
Price $_________

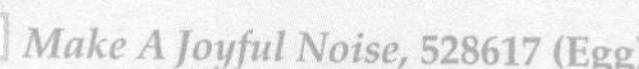

☐ *Make A Joyful Noise,* 528617 (Egg)

$40.00
$35.00

Dated Annual 1993, Issue Price $27.50, '93
Set of 2
Purchased ________, Price $ __________

☐ *To A Very Special Sister,* 528633

$95.00
$85.00
$80.00
$75.00
$73.00
$70.00
$70.00
$68.00
$68.00

Retired 2002, Issue Price $60.00, '94
Purchased ________, Price $ __________

☐ *Sammy,* 528668

$40.00
$35.00
$33.00
$30.00
$25.00

Retired 1997, Issue Price $17.00, '93
Series: *Sugar Town*
Purchased ________, Price $ __________

Alive With The Spirit Of The Season, 528676 (Ornament)

$20.00

$20.00

Open, Issue Price $20.00, '04
Series: *The Legend Of The Christmas Tree*

Purchased __________ ,
Price $ __________

Evergreen Tree, 528684

$40.00

$38.00

$35.00

Retired 1994, Issue Price $15.00, '92
Series: *Sugar Town*

Purchased __________ ,
Price $ __________

It's So Uplifting To Have A Friend Like You, 528846 (Ornament)

$23.00

$30.00 | $20.00

$28.00 | $20.00

$25.00 | $20.00

Retired 1999, Issue Price $16.00, '93

Purchased __________ ,
Price $ __________

America, You're Beautiful, 528862

$65.00

$60.00

Annual 1993, Issue Price $35.00, '93
National Day of Prayer

Purchased __________ ,
Price $ __________

Our First Christmas Together, 528870 (Ornament)

$30.00

Dated Annual 1992, Issue Price $17.50, '92

Purchased __________ , Price $ __________

Friends Never Drift Apart, 529079 (Medallion)

$750.00

Dated Annual 1993, Gift, '93
Fifteenth Anniversary Cruise Piece

Purchased __________ , Price $ __________

America, You're Beautiful, 528862R

A portion of the proceeds from the sales of this figurine benefited the September 11th Relief Fund.

$50.00  $45.00

Retired 2004, Issue Price $35.00, '01
Series: *America Forever*

Purchased __________ ,
Price $ __________

15 Years, Tweet Music Together, 529087 (Medallion)

$75.00

Dated Annual 1993, Gift, '93
Fifteenth Anniversary Convention
Orlando Celebration

Purchased ________, Price $ ____________

A Reflection Of His Love, 529095 (Egg)

$35.00
$30.00

Dated Annual 1994, Issue Price $27.50, '94
Series: *Eggs* — Fourth & Final Issue

Purchased ________, Price $ ____________

Jordan, 529168

$35.00
$30.00
$28.00

Suspended 1996, Issue Price $20.00, '95
Series: *Sammy's Circus*, Set of 2

Purchased ________, Price $ ____________

Dusty, 529176

$35.00
$30.00
$28.00
$25.00

Suspended 1996, Issue Price $22.50, '94
Series: *Sammy's Circus*

Purchased ________, Price $ ____________

Katie, 529184

$35.00
$30.00
$28.00
$25.00

Suspended 1996, Issue Price $17.00, '94
Series: *Sammy's Circus*, Set of 2

Purchased ________, Price $ ____________

Tippy, 529192

$25.00
$23.00
$20.00
$20.00

Suspended 1996, Issue Price $12.00, '94
Series: *Sammy's Circus*

Purchased ________, Price $ ____________

Our First Christmas Together, 529206 (Ornament)

(trumpet) $25.00

Dated Annual 1994, Issue Price $18.50, '94

Purchased ________ ,

Price $ ________

Collin, 529214

(butterfly) $35.00 (sailboat) $28.00
(trumpet) $30.00 (heart) $25.00

Suspended 1996, Issue Price $20.00, '94

Series: *Sammy's Circus*

Purchased _____ ,

Price $ __________

Sammy, 529222

(butterfly) $50.00
(trumpet) $45.00

Dated Annual 1994, Issue Price $20.00, '94

Series: *Sammy's Circus*

Purchased_______ ,

Price $ ___________

My True Love Gave To Me, 529273

(heart) $55.00
(sword) $53.00
(eyeglasses) $50.00
(star) $48.00
(egg) $45.00
(sandal) $43.00
(heart with cross) $43.00

Retired 2002, Issue Price $40.00, '96

Purchased _________, Price $ ___________

Dusty, 529435

(butterfly) $35.00
(trumpet) $30.00
(sailboat) $25.00
(heart) $23.00
(sword) $20.00

Retired 1997, Issue Price $17.00, '93

Series: *Sugar Town*

Purchased _________, Price $ ___________

Doctor's Office Set, 529281

(butterfly) $325.00 (heart) $290.00
(trumpet) $300.00 (sword) $280.00

Retired 1997, Issue Price $150.00, '94

Series: *Sugar Town*, Set of 7 (Doctor's Office, Dr. Sam Sugar, Jan, Stork with Baby Sam, Free Christmas Puppies, Leon and Evelyn Mae, and Sugar And Her Doghouse)

Purchased _________, Price $ _______________

☐ *Sam's Car, 529443*

$45.00
$40.00
$35.00
$30.00
$25.00

Retired 1997, Issue Price $22.50, '93
Series: *Sugar Town*
Purchased ________, Price $ __________

☐ *The Best Gifts Are Loving, Caring and Sharing, 529451 (Ornament)*

$20.00
$20.00

Open, Issue Price $20.00, '04
Series: *The Legend Of Gifts*
Purchased ________,
Price $ __________

☐ *Aunt Ruth & Aunt Dorothy, 529486*

$45.00
$43.00
$40.00

Retired 1994, Issue Price $20.00, '92
Series: *Sugar Town*
Purchased ______,
Price $ __________

☐ *Philip, 529494*

$45.00
$43.00
$40.00

Retired 1994, Issue Price $17.00, '92
Series: *Sugar Town*
Purchased ___________,
Price $ ___________

☐ *Nativity, 529508*

$60.00
$55.00
$50.00

Retired 1994, Issue Price $20.00, '92
Series: *Sugar Town*
Purchased ________, Price $ __________

☐ *Grandfather, 529516*

$40.00
$38.00
$35.00

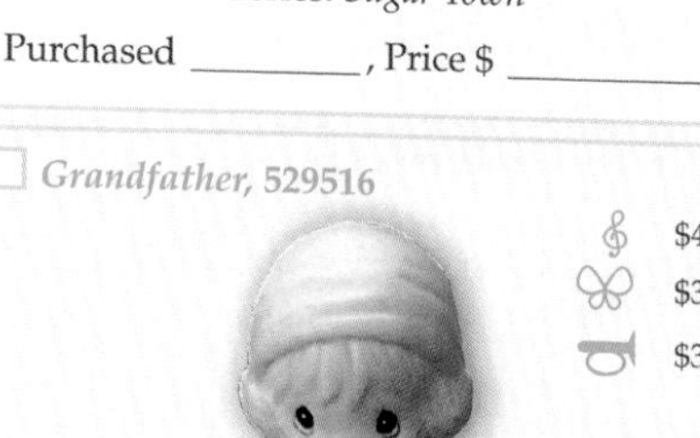

Retired 1994, Issue Price $15.00, '92
Series: *Sugar Town*
Purchased ________, Price $ __________

☐ *Katy Lynne, 529524*

$40.00
$38.00
$35.00
$33.00
$30.00

Retired 1997, Issue Price $20.00, '93
Series: *Sugar Town*
Purchased ________, Price $ __________

Welcome Are Those With Happy Hearts, 529532 (Ornament)

$20.00 $20.00

Open, Issue Price $20.00, '04
Series: *The Legend Of The Wreath*

Purchased ________ ,
Price $____________

Park Bench, 529540

$25.00
$20.00
$18.00

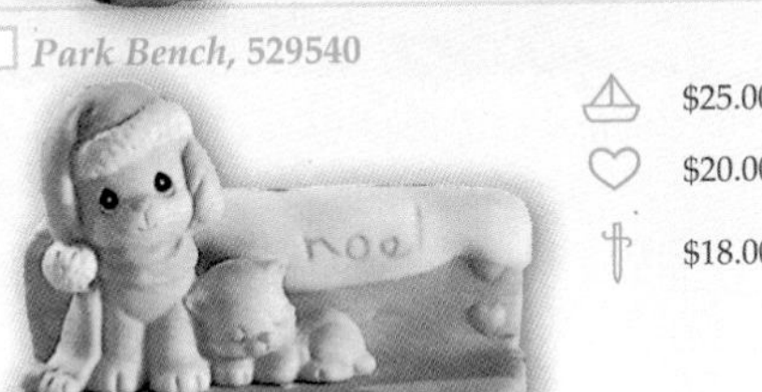

Retired 1997, Issue Price $13.00, '95
Series: *Sugar Town*

Purchased ________, Price $ ____________

Lamp Post, 529559

$21.00
$20.00
$19.00
$18.00

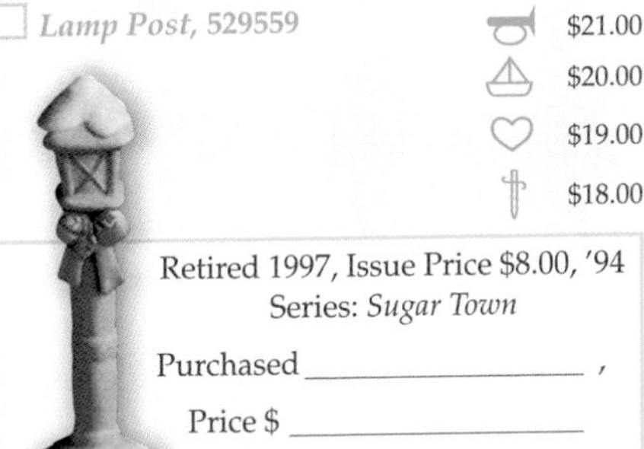

Retired 1997, Issue Price $8.00, '94
Series: *Sugar Town*

Purchased ______________ ,
Price $ ________________

Sam Butcher, 529567

$175.00

Sign reads: "Established 1992. Population 5 and Growing."

Dated Annual 1992, Issue Price $22.50, '92
Series: *Sugar Town*

Purchased ________, Price $ ____________

Sam's House, 529605 (Nightlight)

$115.00 $110.00 $90.00
$110.00 $95.00

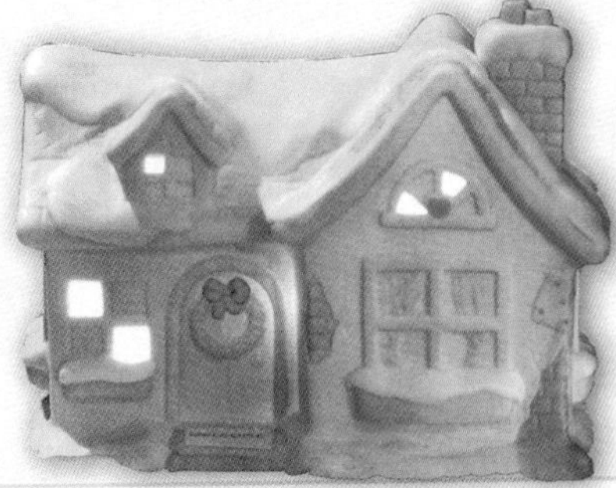

Retired 1997, Issue Price $80.00, '93
Series: *Sugar Town*

Purchased ________, Price $ ____________

Chapel, 529621 (Nightlight)

$160.00
$150.00
$140.00

Retired 1994, Issue Price $85.00, '92
Series: *Sugar Town*

Purchased ________, Price $ ____________

The Magic Starts With You, 529648 (Ornament)

$26.00

Annual 1992, Issue Price $16.00, '92
Open House Event

Purchased __________ ,
Price $ ______________

☐ *Gather Your Dreams, 529680*

$700.00
$680.00

Limited Ed. 2,000, Issue Price $550.00, '93
Easter Seals, Lily Understamp
Individually Numbered

Purchased ________, Price $ ___________

☐ *Stork With Baby Sam, 529788*

$50.00

Annual 1994, Issue Price $22.50, '94
Series: *Sugar Town*

Purchased ________, Price $ ___________

☐ *Fence, 529796*

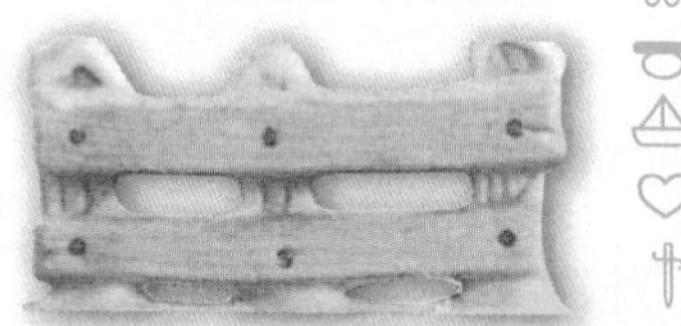

$20.00
$19.00
$18.00
$17.00
$16.00

Retired 1997, Issue Price $10.00, '93
Series: *Sugar Town*

Purchased ________, Price $ ___________

☐ *Leon And Evelyn Mae, 529818*

$30.00
$28.00
$26.00
$24.00

Retired 1997, Issue Price $20.00, '94
Series: *Sugar Town*

Purchased ________, Price $ ___________

☐ *Jan, 529826*

$40.00
$32.00
$28.00
$25.00

Retired 1997, Issue Price $17.00, '94
Series: *Sugar Town*

Purchased ___________ ,

Price $______________

☐ *Sam Butcher With Sugar Town Population Sign, 529842*

$75.00

Annual 1993, Issue Price $22.50, '93
Series: *Sugar Town*

Purchased ________, Price $ ___________

Dr. Sam Sugar, 529850

- $33.00
- $25.00
- $23.00
- $20.00

Retired 1997, Issue Price $17.00, '94
Series: *Sugar Town*

Purchased ________, Price $ __________

Doctor's Office , 529869 (Nightlight)

- $115.00
- $105.00
- $98.00
- $95.00

Retired 1997, Issue Price $80.00, '94
Series: *Sugar Town*

Purchased ________, Price $ __________

Happiness Is At Our Fingertips, 529931

- $75.00
- $70.00

Annual 1993, Issue Price $35.00, '93
Catalog Exclusive

Purchased ________, Price $ __________

Ring Out The Good News, 529966

- $65.00
- $50.00
- $45.00
- $40.00
- $35.00
- $33.00

Retired 1997, Issue Price $27.50, '93
Nativity Addition

Purchased ________, Price $ __________

An Event For All Seasons, 529974 (Ornament)

- $30.00
- $25.00

Annual 1993, Issue Price $15.00, '93
Open House Event

Purchased __________,
Price $ __________

Memories Are Made Of This, 529982

- $50.00
- $45.00

Annual 1994, Issue Price $30.00, '94
Special Event

Purchased ________, Price $ __________

☐ *Wishes For The World, 530018*

★ $45.00

Annual 1999, Issue Price $35.00, '99
Millennium Event Exclusive

Purchased ________, Price $ ________

☐ *You're My Number One Friend, 530026*

𝄞 $45.00
Butterfly $43.00
Trumpet $40.00

Annual 1993, Issue Price $30.00, '93
Easter Seals Commemorative Lily Understamp

Purchased ________,
Price $ ________

☐ *Noah's Ark, 530042 (Nightlight)*

Butterfly	$155.00	Heart	$140.00	★	$133.00
Trumpet	$150.00	Cross	$138.00	Egg	$130.00
Ship	$145.00	Eyeglasses	$135.00	Bow	$130.00
				Heart cross	$130.00

☐ *Sheep, 530077*

Butterfly	$20.00
Trumpet	$18.00
Ship	$16.00
Heart	$15.00
Cross	$14.00
Eyeglasses	$13.00
★	$12.00
Egg	$12.00
Bow	$12.00
Heart cross	$12.00

Retired 2002, Issue Price $10.00, '93
Series: *Two By Two*

Purchased ________, Price $ ________

☐ *Pigs, 530085*

Butterfly	$25.00
Trumpet	$22.00
Ship	$20.00
Heart	$18.00
Cross	$16.00
Eyeglasses	$15.00
★	$15.00
Egg	$15.00
Bow	$15.00
Heart cross	$15.00

Retired 2002, Issue Price $12.00, '93
Series: *Two By Two*

Purchased ________, Price $ ________

☐ *Giraffes, 530115*

Butterfly	$26.00
Trumpet	$25.00
Ship	$23.00
Heart	$22.00
Cross	$20.00
Eyeglasses	$18.00
★	$18.00
Egg	$18.00
Bow	$18.00
Heart cross	$18.00

Retired 2002, Issue Price $16.00, '93
Series: *Two By Two*

Purchased ________, Price $ ________

Retired 2002, Issue Price $125.00, '93
Series: *Two By Two*, Set of 3

Purchased ________,
Price $ ________

☐ *Bunnies, 530123*

$25.00 $20.00
$22.00 $18.00
$16.00
$15.00
$15.00
$15.00
$15.00
$15.00

Retired 2002, Issue Price $9.00, '93
Series: *Two By Two*
Purchased ________, Price $ __________

☐ *Elephants, 530131*

$30.00 $23.00
$28.00 $22.00
$25.00 $20.00
$20.00
$20.00
$20.00
$20.00

Retired 2002, Issue Price $18.00, '93
Series: *Two By Two*
Purchased ________, Price $ __________

☐ *An Event For All Seasons, 530158*

$50.00
$45.00

Annual 1993, Issue Price $30.00, '93
Special Event
Purchased ________, Price $ __________

☐ *Wishing You The Sweetest Christmas, 530166*

$45.00

Dated Annual 1993, Issue Price $25.00, '93
Purchased __________,
Price $ __________

☐ *Wishing You The Sweetest Christmas, 530174 (Bell)*

$35.00

Dated Annual 1993, Issue Price $25.00, '93
Purchased __________,
Price $__________

☐ *Wishing You The Sweetest Christmas, 530182 (Thimble)*

$20.00

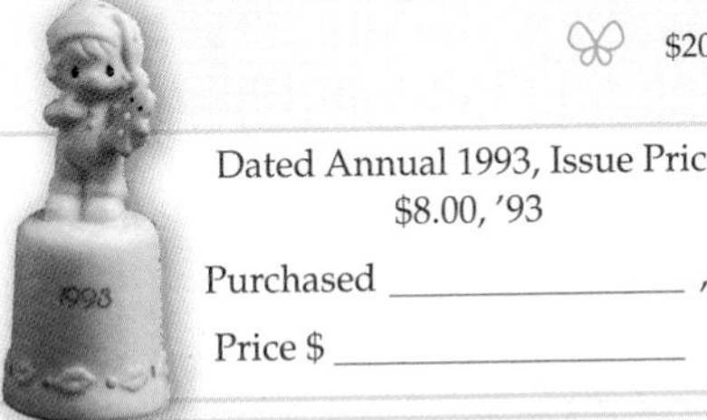

Dated Annual 1993, Issue Price $8.00, '93
Purchased __________,
Price $ __________

☐ *Wishing You The Sweetest Christmas, 530190 (Ornament)*

$35.00

Dated Annual 1993, Issue Price $30.00, '93
Series: *Masterpiece Ornament* — Fifth Issue
Purchased ________,
Price $ __________

☐ *Wishing You The Sweetest Christmas,* 530204 (Plate)

$60.00

Dated Annual 1993, Issue Price $50.00, '93
Series: *Christmas Blessings* — Fourth & Final Issue

Purchased ________, Price $ ___________

☐ *Wishing You The Sweetest Christmas,* 530212 (Ornament)

$40.00

Dated Annual 1993, Issue Price $15.00, '93

Purchased ___________,

Price $___________

☐ *Baby's First Christmas,* 530255 (Ornament)

$30.00

Dated Annual 1994, Issue Price $16.00, '94

Purchased ________,

Price $___________

☐ *Baby's First Christmas,* 530263 (Ornament)

$30.00

Dated Annual 1994, Issue Price $16.00, '94

Purchased___________,

Price $ ___________

☐ *You're As Pretty As A Christmas Tree,* 530387 (Ornament)

$35.00

Dated Annual 1994, Issue Price $30.00, '94
Series: *Masterpiece Ornament* — Sixth Issue
Set of 2

Purchased ________, Price $ ___________

☐ *You're As Pretty As A Christmas Tree,* 530395 (Ornament)

$30.00

Dated Annual 1994, Issue Price $16.00, '94

Purchased ________, Price $ ___________

☐ *You're As Pretty As A Christmas Tree,* 530409 (Plate)

$60.00

Dated Annual 1994, Issue Price $50.00, '94
Series: *Beauty Of Christmas* — First Issue

Purchased ________, Price $ ___________

☐ *You're As Pretty As A Christmas Tree,* 530425

$35.00

Dated Annual 1994, Issue Price $27.50, '94

Purchased ________ ,

Price $ ____________

☐ *Doctor's Office,* 530441 (Ornament)

$25.00

Annual 1995, Issue Price $17.50, '95
Series: *Sugar Town*

Purchased ________ , Price $ ____________

☐ *Sam's House,* 530468 (Ornament)

$25.00

Annual 1994, Issue Price $17.50, '94
Series: *Sugar Town*

Purchased ________ , Price $ ____________

☐ *Chapel,* 530484 (Ornament)

$25.00

Annual 1993, Issue Price $17.50, '93
Series: *Sugar Town*

Purchased______ ,

Price $ __________

☐ *Happy Birthday Jesus,* 530492

$35.00
$33.00
$30.00
$28.00
$25.00
$25.00
$23.00

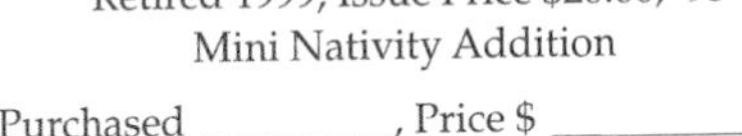

Retired 1999, Issue Price $20.00, '93
Mini Nativity Addition

Purchased ________ , Price $ ____________

☐ *Our First Christmas Together,* 530506 (Ornament)

$30.00

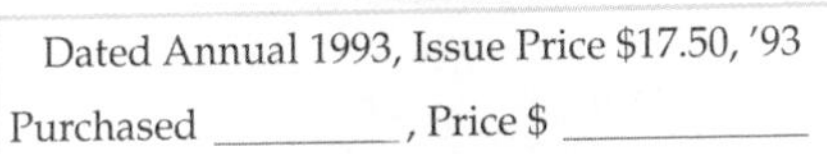

Dated Annual 1993, Issue Price $17.50, '93

Purchased ________ , Price $ ____________

☐ *Serenity Prayer Girl,* 530697

$50.00	$43.00	$38.00
$48.00	$40.00	$38.00
$45.00	$40.00	$37.50
		$37.50
		$37.50
		$37.50

God grant me
The serenity
to accept the things
I cannot change.
The courage to change
the things I can and
The wisdom to know the
difference

Retired 2004, Issue Price $35.00, '94

Purchased ________ , Price $ ____________

☐ *Serenity Prayer Boy, 530700*

$50.00 $48.00 $45.00 $43.00 $40.00 $40.00 $38.00 $38.00 $38.00 $38.00 $38.00

God grant me
The serenity
to accept the things
I cannot change
The courage to change
the things I can and
The wisdom to know t
difference

Retired 2003, Issue Price $35.00, '94

Purchased ________, Price $ ___________

☐ *15 Happy Years Together, What A Tweet!* 530786

$150.00
$135.00

Came with base, display plate, and medallion. Value for G-clef with dome, $225.00. Butterfly with dome, $200.00.

Annual 1993, Issue Price $100.00, '93
Fifteenth Anniversary Commemorative

Purchased ________, Price $ ___________

☐ *15 Years, Tweet Music Together, 530840* (Ornament) $32.00 $25.00

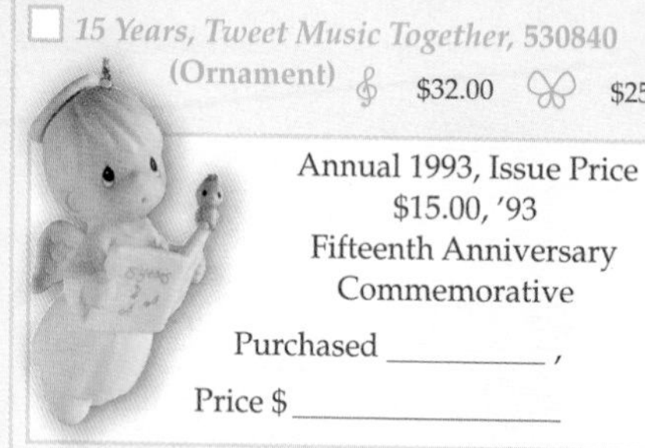

Annual 1993, Issue Price $15.00, '93
Fifteenth Anniversary Commemorative

Purchased ________,

Price $ ___________

☐ *Baby's First Christmas, 530859* (Ornament)

$25.00

Dated Annual 1993, Issue Price $15.00, '93

Purchased ________,

Price $ ___________

☐ *Baby's First Christmas, 530867* (Ornament)

$25.00

Dated Annual 1993, Issue Price $15.00, '93

Purchased _______,

Price $ ___________

☐ *Two By Two Collector's Set, 530948*

$265.00 $260.00 $250.00 $245.00 $235.00 $225.00 $220.00 $215.00 $210.00 $200.00

WELCOME

Retired 2002, Issue Price $190.00, '93
Series: *Two By Two*, Set of 8
(Ark, Bunnies, Pigs, Noah, Noah's Wife, Elephants, Giraffes, and Sheep)

Purchased ________, Price $ ___________

☐ *We Have Come From Afar*, 530913

$25.00 $23.00 $20.00 $20.00 $18.00 $18.00 $15.00

Retired 2001, Issue Price $12.00, '95
Mini Nativity Addition

Purchased ________, Price $ ___________

☐ *I Only Have Ice For You*, 530956

$80.00 $78.00 $75.00 $70.00 $65.00

Retired 1999, Issue Price $55.00, '95

Purchased ________, Price $ ___________

☐ *Sometimes You're Next To Impossible*, 530964

$60.00 $58.00 $55.00 $54.00 $52.00 $50.00 $50.00 $50.00 $50.00 $50.00

Open, Issue Price $50.00, '97

Purchased ________, Price $ ___________

☐ *You Are Always In My Heart*, 530972 (Ornament)

$25.00

Dated Annual 1994, Issue Price $16.00, '94
Series: *Birthday Collection*

Purchased ________, Price $ ___________

☐ *I Still Do*, 530999

$55.00 $50.00 $45.00 $40.00 $35.00 $30.00 $30.00 $30.00 $30.00 $30.00 $30.00 $30.00 $30.00

Open, Issue Price $30.00, '94

Purchased ________, Price $ ___________

☐ *I Still Do*, 531006

$55.00 $50.00 $45.00 $40.00 $35.00 $30.00 $30.00 $30.00 $30.00 $30.00 $30.00 $30.00 $30.00

Open, Issue Price $30.00, '94

Purchased______,

Price $ ________

☐ *My World's Upside Down Without You*, 531014

$20.00 $18.00 $15.00 $15.00 $15.00 $15.00 $15.00 $15.00 $15.00

Open, Issue Price $15.00, '98

Purchased ________, Price $ ___________

Potty Time, 531022

$35.00
$33.00
$30.00
$30.00
$28.00
$28.00
$28.00

Retired 2001, Issue Price $25.00, '97
Purchased ________, Price $ ____________

You Are My Once In A Lifetime, 531030

$60.00
$58.00
$55.00
$53.00
$50.00

Retired 2000, Issue Price $45.00, '98
Purchased ________, Price $ ____________

I Haven't Seen Much Of You Lately, 531057

$28.00
$25.00
$23.00
$22.00
$21.00
$20.00
$18.00
$15.00

Retired 2002, Issue Price $13.50, '96
Series: *Birthday Collection*
Purchased ________, Price $ ____________

What The World Needs Is Love, 531065

$63.00
$60.00
$58.00
$55.00
$53.00
$50.00
$50.00

Retired 1999, Issue Price $45.00, '95
Purchased ________, Price $ ____________

Money's Not The Only Green Thing Worth Saving, 531073

$60.00
$57.00
$55.00

Retired 1996, Issue Price $50.00, '94
Purchased ________, Price $ ____________

It Is No Secret What God Can Do, 531111

$45.00
$43.00
$40.00

Annual 1994, Issue Price $30.00, '94
Easter Seals Commemorative
Lily Understamp
Purchased ________, Price $ ____________

What A Difference You've Made In My Life, 531138

$63.00
$60.00
$58.00
$58.00
$55.00

$55.00
$50.00
$50.00

Retired 2001, Issue Price $50.00, '96

Purchased ________, Price $ ___________

Vaya Con Dios (To Go With God), 531146

$38.00
$35.00
$35.00
$35.00
$35.00
$35.00
$35.00
$35.00
$35.00
$35.00

Retired 2003, Issue Price $32.50, '95

Purchased ________, Price $ ___________

Bless Your Soul, 531162

$43.00
$40.00
$38.00
$35.00
$33.00
$31.00
$30.00
$30.00

Retired 2001, Issue Price $25.00, '95

Purchased ________, Price $ ___________

Wishing You A Bear-ie Merry Christmas, 531200 (Ornament)

$25.00

Dated Annual 1996, Issue Price $17.50, '96
Holiday Preview Event

Purchased ________, Price $ ___________

You Are The Rose Of His Creation, 531243

$650.00
$600.00

Limited Ed. 2,000, Issue Price $500.00, '94
Easter Seals Commemorative
Lily Understamp
Individually Numbered

Purchased ________, Price $ ___________

Bring The Little Ones To Jesus, 531359 (Plate)

$60.00
$55.00

Dated Annual 1994, Issue Price $50.00, '94
Child Evangelism Fellowship

Purchased ________, Price $ ___________

☐ *Llamas, 531375*

$25.00 $22.00
$23.00 $20.00
$18.00
$18.00
$18.00
$18.00
$18.00

Retired 2002, Issue Price $15.00, '94
Series: *Two By Two*
Purchased ________, Price $ __________

☐ *Happy Birthday To Ewe, 531561*

$45.00 $35.00
$43.00 $35.00
$40.00 $35.00
$35.00

Open, Issue Price
$35.00, '99
Purchased __________,
Price $ __________

☐ *You Make Such A Lovely Pair, 531588*

$40.00

Annual 1998, Issue Price
$30.00, '98
GCC Fall Exclusive
Purchased ________,
Price $ __________

☐ *Our Friendship Goes A Long Way, 531626*

$75.00
$70.00

Retired 2002, Issue Price $60.00, '02
Series: *Friendship*
Purchased ________, Price $ __________

☐ *Who's Gonna Fill Your Shoes? 531634*

$48.00 $40.00
$45.00 $40.00
$45.00 $40.00
$43.00 $40.00
$40.00 $40.00

Open, Issue Price
$37.50, '97
Purchased ________,
Price $ __________

☐ *Who's Gonna Fill Your Shoes? 531634S*

$60.00 $55.00

Annual 1996, Issue Price $37.50, '96
1996 Syndicated Catalog Exclusive
Purchased ________, Price $ __________

☐ *Surrounded With Joy, 531677*

$35.00
UM $45.00 $43.00 $35.00
$40.00 $35.00
$38.00 $30.00

Suspended 2001, Issue
Price $30.00, '93
Chapel Exclusive
Purchased __________,
Price $ __________

☐ *Surrounded With Joy, 531685 (Ornament)*

UM $25.00 $17.50
$23.00 $17.50
$20.00 $17.50
$18.00 $17.50
$17.50

Suspended 2002, Issue Price $17.50, '93
Chapel Exclusive
Purchased ________, Price $ __________

You Deserve A Halo – Thank You, 531693

$70.00
$68.00
$65.00
$63.00

Retired 1998, Issue Price $55.00, '96

Purchased ________, Price $ ___________

The Lord Is Counting On You, 531707

$50.00
$48.00
$45.00
$43.00
$43.00
$40.00
$40.00
$38.00
$38.00

Retired 2002, Issue Price $32.50, '94

Purchased ________, Price $ ___________

Thinking Of You Is What I Really Like To Do, 531766 (Plate)

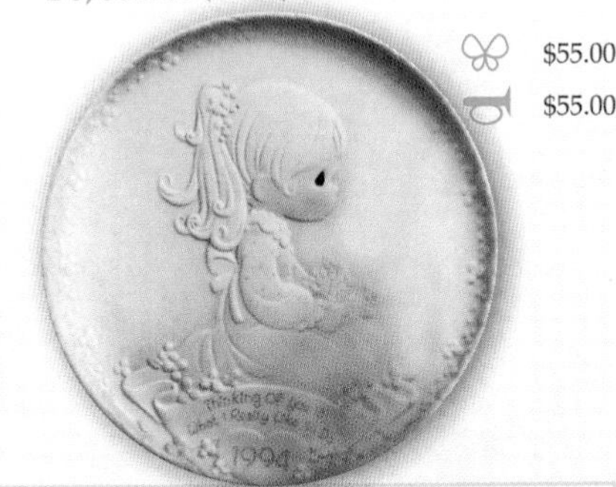

$55.00
$55.00

Dated Annual 1994, Issue Price $50.00, '94
Series: *Mother's Day* — First Issue

Purchased ________, Price $ ___________

Chapel Set, 531773

$325.00
$325.00

Retired 1994, Issue Price $189.00, '93
Series: *Sugar Town*, Set of 7
(Chapel, Sam Butcher, Evergreen Tree, Aunt Ruth & Aunt Dorothy, Philip, Grandfather, and Nativity)

Purchased ________, Price $ ___________

Sam's House Set, 531774

$325.00

Retired 1997, Issue Price $189.00, '93
Series: *Sugar Town*, Set of 7
(Sam's House, Sam's Car, Dusty, Katy Lynne, Sammy, Fence, and Sam Butcher with Sign)

Purchased ________, Price $ ___________

Bunnies Caroling, 531804

$18.00

Retired 1997, Issue Price $10.00, '97
Series: *Sugar Town*

Purchased ________ ,

Price $______________

Tammy And Debbie, 531812

$35.00
$33.00
$30.00

Retired 1997, Issue Price $22.50, '95
Series: *Sugar Town*

Purchased _________ , Price $ _____________

Boughs Of Holly To Make You Jolly, 531820 (Ornament)

$20.00
$20.00

Open, Issue Price $20.00, '04
Series: *The Legend Of Holly*

Purchased ______________ ,

Price $ _________________

Mailbox, 531847

$17.00
$15.00
$13.00
$10.00

Retired 1997, Issue Price $5.00, '94
Series: *Sugar Town*

Purchased _________ , Price $ _____________

May Joy Bloom Within You, 531863 (Ornament)

$20.00
$20.00

Open, Issue Price $20.00, '04
Series: *The Legend Of The Poinsettia*

Purchased _____________ ,

Price $ _______________

Donny, 531871

$30.00
$28.00
$25.00

Retired 1997, Issue Price $22.50, '95
Series: *Sugar Town*

Purchased _________ , Price $ _____________

Death Can't Keep Him In The Ground, 531928

UM $40.00
$30.00

$30.00
$30.00
$30.00
$30.00
$30.00
$30.00
$30.00
$30.00
$30.00

Suspended 2002, Issue Price $30.00, '94
Chapel Exclusive

Purchased _________ , Price $ _____________

Sharing Our Christmas Together, 531944

$40.00
$38.00
$35.00
$35.00
$35.00
$35.00
$35.00

Retired 2003, Issue Price $35.00, '97

Purchased _________ , Price $ _____________

☐ *Dropping In For The Holidays, 531952*

$55.00
$53.00
$50.00
$48.00
$45.00

Pink cup has been found with Ship and Heart marks. Blue cup has been found with Trumpet and Ship marks. The decal has been found upside down.

Retired 1998, Issue Price $40.00, '94
Purchased ________, Price $ __________

☐ *Lord Speak To Me, 531987*

$55.00
$53.00
$50.00
$50.00
$48.00
$48.00
$47.00

Retired 2004, Issue Price $45.00, '99
Purchased ________, Price $ __________

☐ *Hallelujah For The Cross, 532002*

$45.00
$40.00
$38.00
$37.00
$37.00
$37.00

Retired 1999, Issue Price $35.00, '95
Purchased ________, Price $ __________

☐ *Sending You Oceans Of Love, 532010*

$55.00
$53.00
$50.00

Retired 1996, Issue Price $35.00, '95
Purchased ________, Price $ __________

☐ *I Can't Bear To Let You Go, 532037*

$70.00
$68.00
$65.00
$63.00
$60.00
$58.00

Retired 1999, Issue Price $50.00, '95
Purchased ________, Price $ __________

☐ *Who's Gonna Fill Your Shoes? 532061*

$55.00
$53.00
$50.00
$48.00
$45.00
$45.00

There are pennies in the loafers.

Retired 2002, Issue Price $37.50, '98
Catalog Early Release
Purchased ________, Price $ __________

Who's Gonna Fill Your Shoes? 532061S

Special Understamp, "1997 Catalog." This piece has no pennies in loafers.

$60.00
$55.00

Annual 1997, Issue Price $37.50, '97
Catalog Early Release

Purchased __________ ,

Price $__________

A King Is Born, 532088 (Ornament)

UM $35.00 $32.00

Retired 1995, Issue Price $17.50, '94
Chapel Exclusive

Purchased __________ ,

Price $ __________

Lord Help Me To Stay On Course, 532096

$35.00
$35.00
$35.00
$35.00
$35.00
$35.00
$35.00
$35.00
$35.00
$35.00

Retired 2002, Issue Price $35.00, '95

Purchased __________, Price $ __________

The Lord Bless You And Keep You (African-American), 532118

$60.00
$55.00
$50.00
$50.00
$50.00
$50.00
$50.00
$50.00
$50.00
$50.00
$50.00
$50.00
$50.00

Open, Issue Price $40.00, '94

Purchased __________, Price $ __________

The Lord Bless You And Keep You (African-American), 532126

$45.00
$40.00
$35.00
$35.00
$35.00
$35.00
$35.00
$35.00
$35.00
$35.00
$35.00
$35.00
$35.00
$35.00

Open, Issue Price $30.00, '94

Purchased __________,

Price $ __________

The Lord Bless You And Keep You (African-American), 532134

$45.00
$40.00
$35.00
$35.00
$35.00
$35.00
$35.00
$35.00
$35.00
$35.00
$35.00
$35.00
$35.00
$35.00

Open, Issue Price $30.00, '94

Purchased __________,

Price $__________

Street Sign, 532185

$20.00
$18.00
$15.00

Retired 1997, Issue Price $10.00, '95
Series: *Sugar Town*

Purchased __________ ,

Price $ __________

Remember The Sweetest Of The Season, 532193 (Ornament)

$20.00 $20.00

Open, Issue Price $20.00, '04
Series: *The Legend Of The Candy Cane*

Purchased__________,
Price $ __________

Merry Giftness, 532223 (Ornament)

$25.00

Annual 1999, Issue Price $20.00, '99
DSR Exclusive

Purchased ________,
Price $__________

Town Square Clock, 532908

$115.00 $105.00 $100.00 $90.00

Retired 1997, Issue Price $80.00, '94
Series: *Sugar Town*

Purchased ________, Price $ __________

Luke 2:10 – 11, 532916

$50.00 $48.00 $45.00 $43.00 $40.00

Retired 1999, Issue Price $35.00, '94

Purchased ________, Price $ __________

It's Almost Time For Santa, 532932

$85.00

Annual 2001, Issue Price $75.00, '01

Purchased ________, Price $ __________

Curved Sidewalk, 533149

$22.00 $20.00 $18.00 $13.00

Retired 1997, Issue Price $10.00, '94
Series: *Sugar Town*

Purchased ________, Price $ __________

Straight Sidewalk, 533157

$23.00 $21.00 $18.00 $18.00

Retired 1997, Issue Price $10.00, '94
Series: *Sugar Town*

Purchased ________, Price $ __________

Sugar And Her Doghouse, 533165

$30.00 $25.00 $27.00 $23.00

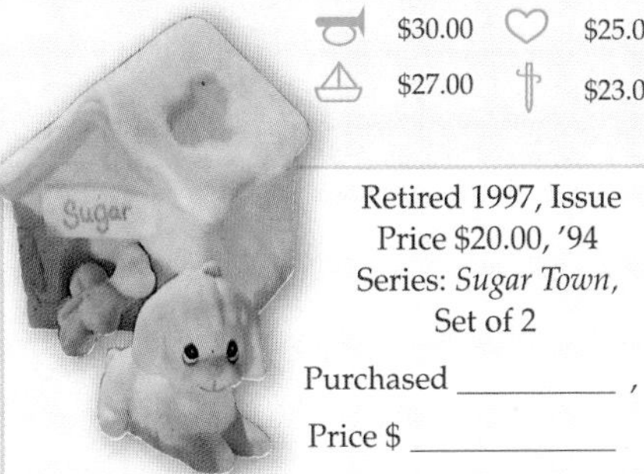

Retired 1997, Issue Price $20.00, '94
Series: *Sugar Town*, Set of 2

Purchased ________,
Price $ __________

☐ *Single Tree, 533173*

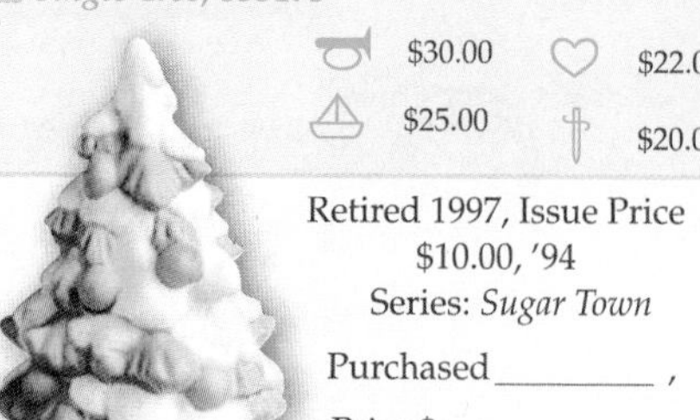

$30.00 $22.00
$25.00 $20.00

Retired 1997, Issue Price $10.00, '94
Series: *Sugar Town*

Purchased ________ ,

Price $ ____________

☐ *Double Tree, 533181*

$35.00
$33.00
$30.00
$28.00

Retired 1997, Issue Price $10.00, '94
Series: *Sugar Town*

Purchased ________ , Price $ ____________

☐ *Cobblestone Bridge, 533203*

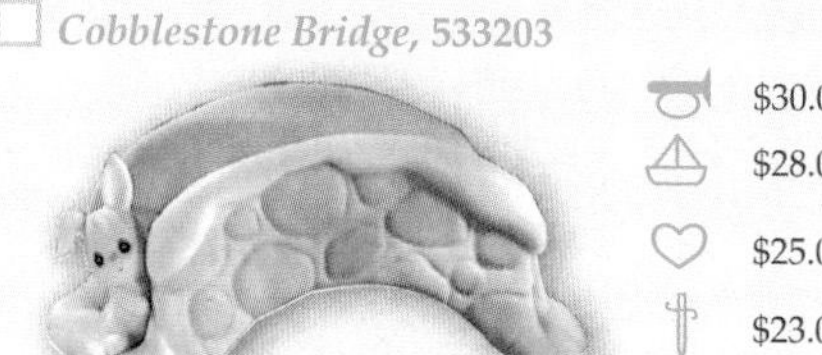

$30.00
$28.00
$25.00
$23.00

Retired 1997, Issue Price $17.00, '94
Series: *Sugar Town*

Purchased ________ , Price $ ____________

☐ *Shear Happiness And Hare Cuts, 539910*

$50.00
$48.00
$45.00
$40.00
$40.00
$40.00
$40.00

Retired 2004, Issue Price $40.00, '99
Series: *Country Lane Collection*

Purchased ________ , Price $ ____________

☐ *Lord, Police Protect Us, 539953*

$55.00
$53.00
$50.00
$48.00
$45.00
$45.00
$45.00
$45.00

Open, Issue Price $45.00, '99

Purchased ________ , Price $ ____________

☐ *His Love Will Uphold The World, 539309*

Early release to retailers attending the Fall 1998 show.

$185.00
$179.00

Annual 1999, Issue Price $150.00, '99
Precious Moments Millennium Piece

Purchased ________ ,

Price $ ____________

☐ *Sharing Our Winter Wonderland, 539988*

★ $85.00

Annual 1999, Issue Price $75.00, '99

Purchased ________, Price $ ___________

☐ *Happy 10th Anniversary, 540013*

UM $55.00

★ $60.00

Annual 1999, Issue Price $45.00, '99
Chapel Exclusive
Tenth Anniversary Commemorative

Purchased ________, Price $ ___________

☐ *Sleep Tight, 542636*

UM $60.00

$58.00

$55.00

$53.00

$50.00

Suspended 2003, Issue Price $45.00, '99
Best Western Hotel Exclusive

Purchased ________, Price $ ___________

☐ *Let's Keep Our Eyes On The Goal, 549975*

$50.00

★ $45.00

Retired 1999, Issue Price $37.50, '98
Canadian Exclusive

Purchased ________, Price $ ___________

☐ *I Pray The Lord My Soul To Keep, 553867*

UM $28.00

Comes with picture frame.

Dated Annual 2001, Issue Price $22.50, '01
National Children's Day Event Exclusive
Series: *Little Moments*

Purchased ________, Price $ ___________

☐ *I Pray The Lord My Soul To Keep, 553875*

UM $28.00

Comes with picture frame.

Dated Annual 2001, Issue Price $22.50, '01
National Children's Day Event Exclusive
Series: *Little Moments*

Purchased ________, Price $ ___________

Slide Into The Next Millennium With Joy, 587761

$45.00
$43.00

Dated Annual 1999, Issue Price $35.00, '99

Purchased _________, Price $ ____________

Slide Into The Next Millennium With Joy, 587788 (Ornament)

$30.00
$28.00

Dated Annual 1999, Issue Price $25.00, '99

Purchased _________, Price $ ____________

Our First Christmas Together, 587796 (Ornament)

$30.00 $28.00

Dated Annual 1999, Issue Price $25.00, '99

Purchased _______ ,

Price $ __________

May Your Wishes For Peace Take Wing, 587818 (Ornament)

$30.00
$28.00

Dated Annual 1999, Issue Price $20.00, '99

Purchased_________ ,

Price $ ___________

Baby's First Christmas (Girl), 587826 (Ornament)

$25.00 $23.0

Dated Annual 1999, Issue Price $18.50, '99

Purchased _____________ ,

Price $ _______________

Baby's First Christmas (Boy), 587834 (Ornament)

$25.00 $23.0

Dated Annual 1999, Issue Price $18.50, '99

Purchased _____________ ,

Price $ _______________

Eat Ham, 587842

$35.0
$30.0
$28.0
$25.0
$25.0
$25.0
$25.0
$25.0

Open, Issue Price $25.00, '99
Series: *Country Lane Collection*

Purchased _________, Price $ ____________

You Brighten My Field Of Dreams, 587850

$65.00 $60.0
$63.00 $60.0
$60.0

Retired 2002, Issue Price $55.00, '99
Series: *Country Lane Collection*

Purchased _________ ,

Price $ ___________

☐ *Witch Way Do You Spell Love? 587869*

$45.00
$40.00
$38.00
$35.00
$30.00

Retired 2002, Issue Price $25.00, '99

Purchased ________, Price $ ___________

☐ *Snow Man Like My Man, 587877*

$65.00
$63.00
$60.00
$58.00
$55.00
$55.00
$55.00
$55.00

Suspended 2005, Issue Price $55.00, '99

Purchased ________, Price $ ___________

☐ *May Your Season Be Jelly And Bright, 587885*

$45.00
$45.00
$43.00
$40.00
$38.00
$38.00
$37.50
$37.50

Open, Issue Price $37.50, '99

Purchased ________, Price $ ___________

☐ *God Loves A Happy Camper, 587893*

$45.00
$42.00
$40.00
$37.50
$37.50
$37.50
$37.50

Open, Issue Price $37.50, '99

Purchased ________, Price $ ___________

☐ *My Life Is A Vacuum Without You, 587907*

$45.00
$42.00
$40.00
$37.50
$37.50
$37.50
$37.50

Suspended 2004, Issue Price $37.50, '99

Purchased ________, Price $ ___________

☐ *RV Haven' Fun Or What, 587915*

$65.00
$60.00
$55.00
$53.00
$50.00

Retired 2002, Issue Price $45.00, '99

Purchased ________, Price $ ___________

☐ *Thank You Sew Much*, 587923

Mark	Price	Mark	Price
[glasses]	$32.00	[heart]	$25.00
★	$30.00	[crown]	$25.00
[egg]	$28.00	[clover]	$25.00
[bow]	$25.00	[box]	$25.00

Open, Issue Price $25.00, '99

Purchased ________ ,

Price $ ____________

☐ *May Your Christmas Be Delightful*, 587931 (Ornament)

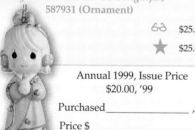

Mark	Price
[glasses]	$25.00
★	$25.00

Annual 1999, Issue Price $20.00, '99

Purchased ____________ ,

Price $ ____________

☐ *Pretty As A Princess*, 587958 (Ornament)

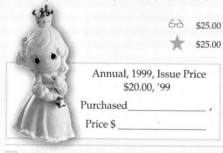

Mark	Price
[glasses]	$25.00
★	$25.00

Annual, 1999, Issue Price $20.00, '99

Purchased ____________ ,

Price $ ____________

☐ *Happy 10th Anniversary*, 588040 (Ornament)

UM $40.00  $35.00

Limited Ed., Issue Price $22.50, '99
Tenth Anniversary Commemorative
One Year Production

Purchased ________ ,

Price $ ____________

☐ *Our Love Will Flow Eternal*, 588059

Mark	Price
UM	$120.00
[egg]	$115.00
[bow]	$105.00
[heart]	$100.00
[crown]	$90.00
[clover]	$90.00
[box]	$90.00

Open, Issue Price $90.00, '99

Purchased ________ , Price $ ____________

☐ *Our Love Will Flow Eternal*, 588059C

UM $120.00 [egg] $115.00 [bow] $105.00

Open, Issue Price $90.00, '99
Chapel Exclusive, Chapel Early Release

Purchased ________ , Price $ ____________

☐ *He Is The Bright Morning Star*, 588067

Mark	Price
UM	$40.00
[egg]	$38.00
[bow]	$35.00
[heart]	$30.00
[crown]	$30.00

Retired 2003, Issue Price $30.00, '99
Chapel Exclusive

Purchased ________ , Price $ ____________

☐ *He Is The Bright Morning Star*, 588075 (Ornament)

Mark	Price	Mark	Price
UM	$28.00	[heart]	$20.00
[egg]	$25.00	[crown]	$20.00
[bow]	$23.00	[clover]	$20.00
		[box]	$20.00

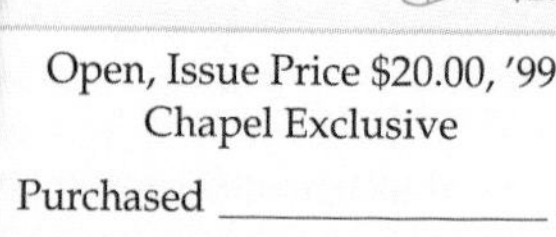

Open, Issue Price $20.00, '99
Chapel Exclusive

Purchased ____________ ,

Price $ ____________

Mom, You're A Royal Gem, 588083

$40.00
$35.00

Annual 1999, Issue Price $30.00, '99
Avon Exclusive
Purchased ________, Price $ ___________

Dear Jon, I Will Never Leave You, 588091

$60.00
$58.00
$55.00
$53.00
$50.00
$50.00
$50.00
$50.00

Retired 2005, Issue Price $50.00, '99
Series: *Country Lane Collection*
Purchased ________, Price $ ___________

I'm Proud To Be An American (Army), 588105

$40.00
$38.00
$35.00
$32.50
$32.50
$32.50
$32.50

Open, Issue Price $32.50, '00
Purchased ________, Price $ ___________

I'm Proud To Be An American (Marine), 588113

$40.00
$38.00
$35.00
$32.50
$32.50
$32.50
$32.50

Open, Issue Price $32.50, '00
Purchased ________, Price $ ___________

I'm Proud To Be An American (Navy), 588121

$40.00
$38.00
$35.00
$32.50
$32.50
$32.50
$32.50

Open, Issue Price $32.50, '00
Purchased ________, Price $ ___________

I'm Proud To Be An American (Coast Guard), 588148

$40.00
$38.00
$35.00
$32.50
$32.50
$32.50
$32.50

Open, Issue Price $32.50, '00
Purchased ________, Price $ ___________

☐ *I'm Proud To Be An American (Air Force), 588156*

Mark	Price	Mark	Price
[Star]	$40.00	[Heart with Cross]	$32.50
[Egg]	$38.00	[Crown]	$32.50
[Bow & Arrow]	$35.00	[Flower]	$32.50
		[Sugar Cube]	$32.50

Open, Issue Price $32.50, '00

Purchased ________,

Price $ __________

☐ *Behold The Lamb Of God, 588164*

Mark	Price
[Star]	$55.00
[Egg]	$53.00
[Bow & Arrow]	$50.00
[Heart with Cross]	$48.00
[Crown]	$48.00
[Flower]	$45.00
[Sugar Cube]	$45.00

Retired 2005, Issue Price $45.00, '99
Nativity Addition

Purchased ________, Price $ __________

☐ *Sammy's Circus Set, 604070*

Mark	Price
[Butterfly]	$350.00
[Trumpet]	$350.00

Retired 1994, Issue Price $200.00, '94
Series: *Sammy's Circus*, Set of 7
(Circus Tent, Markie, Dusty, Sammy, Tippy, Jennifer, & Collin)

Purchased ________, Price $ __________

☐ *Bisque Ornament Holder, 603171*

Mark	Price	Mark	Price
[Trumpet]	$45.00	[Heart]	$40.00
[Ship]	$43.00	[Sword]	$38.00
		[Eyeglasses]	$38.00
		[Star]	$35.00
		[Egg]	$35.00
		[Bow & Arrow]	$33.00
		[Heart with Cross]	$30.00
		[Crown]	$30.00
		[Flower]	$30.00
		[Sugar Cube]	$30.00

Open, Issue Price $30.00, '94

Purchased ________, Price $ __________

☐ *On A Hill Overlooking A Quiet Blue Stream, 603503*

Mark	Price	Mark	Price
		[Ship]	$57.00
UM	$65.00	[Heart]	$55.00
		[Sword]	$53.00
		[Eyeglasses]	$50.00

Unmarked version has 3 verses of poem; Heart version has 4 verses.

Retired 1998, Issue Price $45.00, '94
Chapel Exclusive

Purchased ________, Price $ __________

☐ *Nothing Can Dampen The Spirit Of Caring,* 603864

$55.00 $48.00
$50.00 $45.00
$45.00
$43.00
$43.00
$40.00
$40.00
$40.00

Retired 2002, Issue Price $35.00, '94
Series: *Good Samaritan* — First Issue

Purchased ________, Price $ ___________

☐ *May Your Christmas Be Delightful,* 604135

$45.00
$40.00
$40.00
$40.00
$40.00
$40.00
$40.00

Retired 2002, Issue Price $40.00, '97

Purchased ________, Price $ ___________

☐ *A King Is Born,* 604151

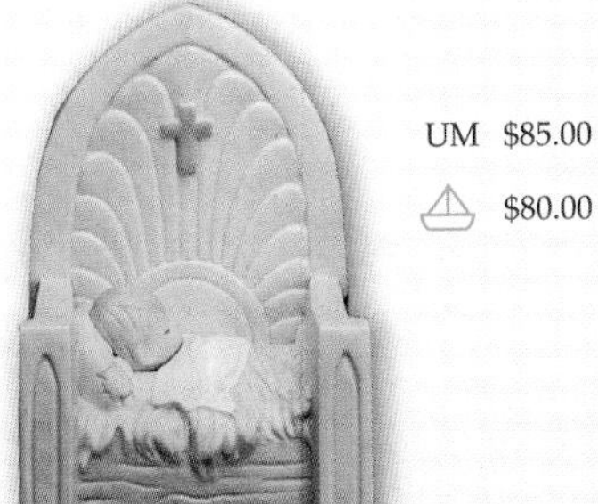

UM $85.00
$80.00

Retired 1995, Issue Price $25.00, '94
Chapel Exclusive

Purchased ________, Price $ ___________

☐ *A Poppy For You,* 604208

$45.00
$40.00
$38.00
$37.00
$37.00

Suspended 1998, Issue Price $35.00, '94

Purchased ________, Price $ ___________

☐ *You're As Pretty As A Christmas Tree,* 604216 (Bell)

$35.00

Dated Annual 1994, Issue Price $27.50, '94

Purchased ________, Price $ ___________

☐ *Rejoice, O Earth,* 617334 (Musical Tree Topper)

$175.00

Annual 1990, Issue Price $125.00, '90
Tune: "Hark! The Herald Angels Sing!"

Purchased ________, Price $ ___________

I Pray The Lord My Soul To Keep, 632430

UM $20.00

Open, Issue Price $20.00, '02
Series: *Little Moments*

Purchased ________, Price $ ________

I Pray The Lord My Soul To Keep, 632431

UM $20.00

Open, Issue Price $20.00, '02
Series: *Little Moments*

Purchased________,

Price $________

Jesus Loves Me, 634735

★ $575.00

$550.00

Limited Ed. 1,500, Issue Price $500.00, '99
Easter Seals
Lily Understamp
Individually Numbered

Purchased ________, Price $ ________

Give Your Whole Heart, 634751 (Ornament)

UM $12.00

Annual 1999, Issue Price $6.50, '99
Easter Seals Commemorative

Purchased ________, Price $ ________

Wishing You An Old Fashioned Christmas, 634778

★ $195.00

Annual 1999, Issue Price $175.00, '99
Set of 6 (Lighted Christmas Tree, Mom With Garland, Dad Hanging Ornaments, Son With Box Of Decorations, Daughter Holding Ornaments, and Baby Crawling)
Series: *Family Christmas*

Purchased ________, Price $ ________

Friendship's A Slice Of Life, 634964

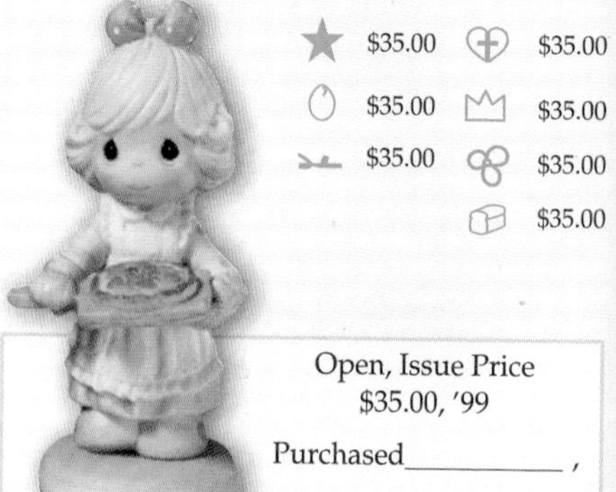

★ $35.00 $35.00

$35.00 $35.00

$35.00 $35.00

$35.00

Open, Issue Price $35.00, '99

Purchased________,

Price $________

Reach For The Stars, 634972

$50.00

Annual 1999, Issue Price $35.00, '99
Signing Tour 1999

Purchased ________, Price $ ___________

Take Time To Smell The Roses, 634980C

$45.00
$45.00

A portion of the proceeds from the sales of this figurine are donated to the United Way.

Open, Issue Price $35.00, '99
Carlton Cards Exclusive

Purchased ________, Price $ ___________

Scootin' Your Way To A Perfect Day, 634999

$35.00

Dated Annual 1999, Issue Price $25.00, '99
Care-A-Van Exclusive

Purchased ________, Price $ ___________

Hail Mary, Full Of Grace — Madonna II, 635006

$80.00
$80.00
$80.00

Open, Issue Price
$80.00, '03

Purchased ________,

Price $ ___________

I Couldn't Make It Without You, 635030

$70.00
$67.00
$65.00
$65.00
$60.00
$60.00
$60.00
$60.00

Limited Ed. 15,000, Issue Price $60.00, '99
Boys & Girls Club of America
Commemorative

Purchased ________, Price $ ___________

Scoopin' Up Some Love, 635049

$35.00

Also found with rainbow sherbet cone, very rare. $350.00.

Limited Ed., Issue Price $35.00, '00
Easter Seals Commemorative
DSR and Century Circle Exclusive

Purchased ________, Price $ ___________

Life's Beary Precious With You, 642673

Mark	Price	Mark	Price
Egg	$30.00	Heart	$25.00
Bow & Arrow	$29.00	Crown	$25.00
		Clover	$25.00
		Sugar Cube	$25.00

Open, Issue Price $25.00, '01

Purchased ____________ ,

Price $____________

You Color Our World With Loving, Caring And Sharing, 644463

★ $45.00

Open, Issue Price $24.00, '99

Tenth Anniversary Chapel Event Exclusive

Purchased ____________ ,

Price $____________

You Color Our World With Loving, Caring And Sharing, 644463C

Mark	Price	Mark	Price	Mark	Price
UM	$40.00	Bow & Arrow	$35.00	Crown	$30.00
Egg	$38.00	Heart	$33.00	Clover	$30.00
				Sugar Cube	$30.00

Open, Issue Price $30.00, '99

Chapel Exclusive

Purchased ________, Price $ ____________

Highway To Happiness, 649457

UM $20.00

Open, Issue Price $20.00, '99

Series: *Highway To Happiness — Little Moments*

Purchased ________ ,

Price $____________

I'll Never Stop Loving You, 649465

UM $20.00

Open, Issue Price $20.00, '99

Series: *Highway To Happiness — Little Moments*

Purchased ________, Price $ ____________

There's No Wrong Way With You, 649473

UM $20.00

Open, Issue Price $20.00, '99

Series: *Highway To Happiness — Little Moments*

Purchased ________, Price $ ____________

God's Children At Play, 649481

UM $20.00

Open, Issue Price $20.00, '99

Series: *Highway To Happiness — Little Moments*

Purchased ________, Price $ ____________

Cross Walk, 649511

UM $20.00

Open, Issue Price $20.00, '99
Series: *Highway To Happiness — Little Moments*

Purchased ________, Price $ __________

Let Him Enter Your Heart, 649554

UM $20.00

Open, Issue Price $20.00, '01
Series: *Highway To Happiness — Little Moments*

Purchased ________, Price $ __________

Go 4 It, 649538

UM $20.00

Open, Issue Price $20.00, '99
Series: *Highway To Happiness — Little Moments*

Purchased ________, Price $ __________

Give'em A Brake For Jesus, 649562

UM $20.00

Open, Issue Price $20.00, '01
Series: *Highway To Happiness — Little Moments*

Purchased ________, Price $ __________

Yield To Him, 649546

UM $20.00

Open, Issue Price $20.00, '01
Series: *Highway To Happiness — Little Moments*

Purchased ________, Price $ __________

Hay Good Lookin', 649732

★ $50.00
Egg $48.00
Sword $45.00
Heart $45.00
Crown $45.00
Clover $45.00

Retired 2004, Issue Price $45.00, '99
Series: *Country Lane Collection*

Purchased ________, Price $ __________

Peace In The Valley, 649929

★ $150.00
Egg $145.00

Limited Ed. 12,500, Issue Price $125.00, '99
1999 Enesco Fall Show Exclusive
Purchased ________, Price $ ____________

Ice See In You A Champion, 649937

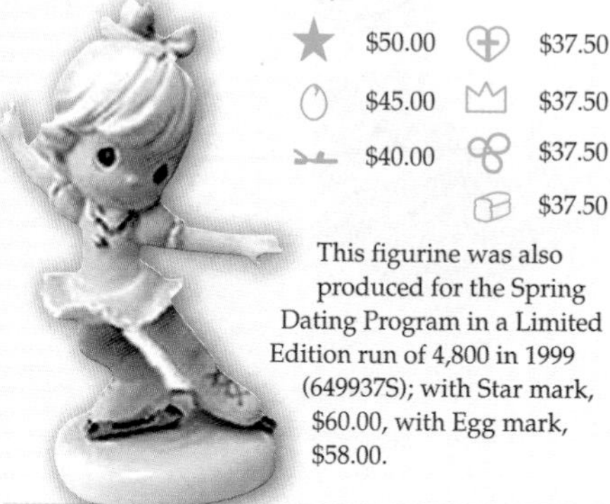

★	$50.00	Heart	$37.50
Egg	$45.00	Crown	$37.50
Bow	$40.00	Clover	$37.50
		Cake	$37.50

This figurine was also produced for the Spring Dating Program in a Limited Edition run of 4,800 in 1999 (649937S); with Star mark, $60.00, with Egg mark, $58.00.

Open, Issue Price $37.50, '00
Canadian Exclusive
Purchased ________, Price $ ____________

Baby Moses, 649953

UM $25.00

Annual 1999, Issue Price $25.00, '00
Series: *Bible Stories — Little Moments*
Purchased ________, Price $ ____________

Ruth & Naomi, 649961

UM $25.00

Open, Issue Price $25.00, '00
Series: *Bible Stories — Little Moments*
Purchased ________, Price $ ____________

The Good Samaritan, 649988

UM $25.00

Open, Issue Price $25.00, '00
Series: *Bible Stories — Little Moments*
Purchased ________, Price $ ____________

The Great Pearl, 649996

UM $25.00

Open, Issue Price $25.00, '00
Series: *Bible Stories — Little Moments*
Purchased ________, Price $ ____________

The Sower And The Seed, 650005

UM $25.00

Open, Issue Price $20.00, '00
Series: *Bible Stories — Little Moments*

Purchased ________, Price $ ____________

Peace On Earth, 679259 (Ornament)

★ $40.00

Limited Ed., Issue Price $25.00, '99
GCC Exclusive

Purchased ________, Price $ ____________

Giving My Heart Freely, 650013

$45.00
$43.00
$40.00
$40.00
$40.00
$40.00

Open, Issue Price $40.00, '01

Purchased ________, Price $ ____________

I Will Love You All Ways, 679704

This is a "Gift-to-Go" figurine with a Tender Tail ornament and matching valentine.

★ $30.00
$28.00

Retired 2000, Issue Price $25.00, '99

Purchased ________, Price $ ____________

David & Goliath, 650064

UM $20.00

Open, Issue Price $20.00, '01
Series: *Bible Stories — Little Moments*

Purchased ________, Price $ ____________

Good Advice Has No Price, 679828

★ $35.00
$33.00
$30.00
$30.00
$30.00
$30.00
$30.00

Open, Issue Price $30.00, '99

Purchased ________, Price $ ____________

☐ *We Knead You Grandma, 679844*

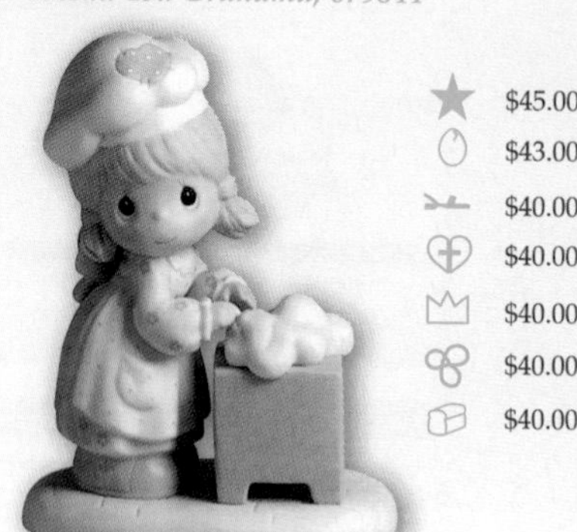

$45.00
$43.00
$40.00
$40.00
$40.00
$40.00
$40.00

Open, Issue Price $40.00, '99
Purchased ________, Price $ ___________

☐ *Bless You, 679879*

$30.00
$28.00
$25.00
$25.00
$25.00
$25.00
$25.00

Open, Issue Price $25.00, '99
Purchased ________, Price $ ___________

☐ *This Day Has Been Made In Heaven, 679852*

$35.00
$33.00
$30.00
$30.00
$30.00
$30.00
$30.00

Open, Issue Price $30.00, '99
Purchased ________, Price $ ___________

☐ *A Tail Of Love, 679976*

$30.00
$28.00
$25.00
$25.00
$23.00
$23.00
$20.00

Open, Issue Price $20.00, '99
Series: *Two By Two*
Purchased ________, Price $ ___________

☐ *Lovingcaringsharing.com, 679860*

$45.00
$43.00
$40.00
$35.00
$35.00
$35.00
$35.00

Open, Issue Price $35.00, '99
Purchased ________, Price $ ___________

☐ *Wishing You A Blow Out Birthday, 680184*

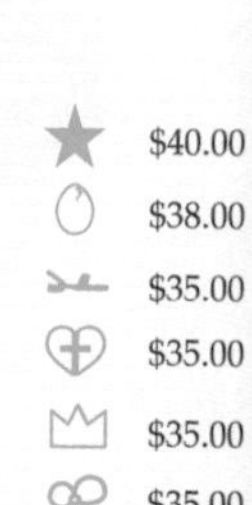

$40.00
$38.00
$35.00
$35.00
$35.00
$35.00
$35.00

Open, Issue Price $35.00, '99
Purchased ________, Price $ ___________

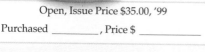

Share In The Celebration, 680761 (Medallion)

UM $225.00

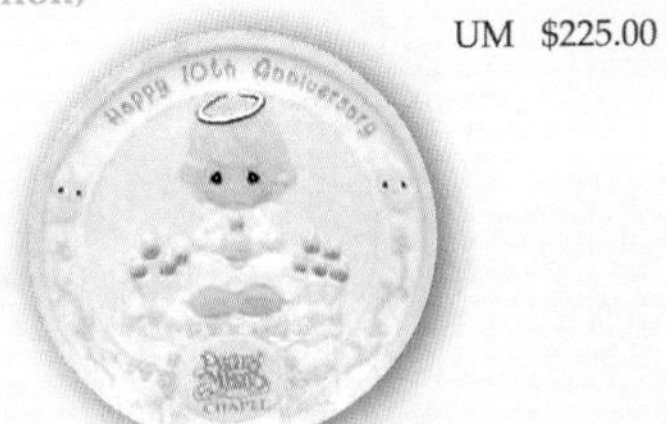

Limited Ed. 1,500, Gift, '99
Chapel Exclusive
Chapel Tenth Anniversary
1999 Licensee Show

Purchased ________, Price $ ___________

Life Is Worth Fighting For (Blonde), 680982

$30.00
$30.00
$30.00
$30.00

Retired 2003, Issue Price $30.00, '00
Breast Cancer Awareness, Benefits NABCO

Purchased ________, Price $ ___________

Life Is Worth Fighting For (Brunette), 680982B

$30.00
$30.00
$30.00
$30.00
$30.00
$30.00

Open, Issue Price $30.00, '00
Breast Cancer Awareness, Benefits NABCO

Purchased ________, Price $ ___________

God Gives Us Memories So That We Might Have Roses In December, 680990

$50.00
$47.00
$45.00
$45.00
$45.00

Retired 2004, Issue Price $45.00, '00
Benefits Compassionate Friends

Purchased ________, Price $ ___________

Precious Moments Will Last Forever, 681008

$45.00
$40.00

Annual 1999, Issue Price $35.00, '99

Purchased ________, Price $ ___________

His Name Is Jesus, 681032

UM $70.00

Limited Ed. 1,500, Issue Price $40.00, '99
1999 Collector's Christmas Weekend

Purchased ________, Price $ ___________

☐ *Let Freedom Ring, 681059*

Figurine was also issued as a limited edition show exclusive for Enesco summer shows (681059E); Star mark, $65.00; Egg mark, $65.00.

★ $55.00
$53.00
$50.00
$48.00
$45.00
$45.00

Retired 2004, Issue Price $45.00, '99
Purchased ________, Price $ ___________

☐ *You Complete My Heart, 681067*

★ $50.00
$48.00
$45.00
$43.00
$42.00

Suspended 2003, Issue Price $37.50, '99
Purchased ________, Price $ ___________

☐ *A Love Like No Other, 681075*

★ $50.00
$48.00
$45.00
$45.00
$45.00
$45.00
$45.00

Open, Issue Price $45.00, '99
Series: *Motherhood — First Issue*
Purchased ________,
Price $ ___________

☐ *You Have The Sweetest Heart, 689548*

★ $30.00
$28.00
$26.00
$25.00
$25.00
$25.00
$25.00

Open, Issue Price $25.00, '99
Purchased ________, Price $ ___________

☐ *The Child That's Born On The Sabbath Day…, 692077*

UM $20.00

Open, Issue Price $20.00, '00
Series: *Thought of the Day — Little Moments*
Purchased ________, Price $ ___________

☐ *Monday's Child Is Fair Of Face, 692085*

UM $20.00

Open, Issue Price $20.00, '00
Series: *Thought of the Day — Little Moments*
Purchased ________, Price $ ___________

Tuesday's Child Is Full Of Grace, 692093

UM $20.00

Open, Issue Price $20.00, '00
Series: *Thought of the Day — Little Moments*
Purchased ________, Price $ __________

Friday's Child Is Loving And Giving, 692123

UM $20.00

Open, Issue Price $20.00, '00
Series: *Thought of the Day — Little Moments*
Purchased ________, Price $ __________

Wednesday's Child Is Full Of Woe, 692107

UM $20.00

Open, Issue Price $20.00, '00
Series: *Thought of the Day — Little Moments*
Purchased ________, Price $ __________

Saturday's Child Works Hard For A Living, 692131

UM $20.00

Open, Issue Price $20.00, '00
Series: *Thought of the Day — Little Moments*
Purchased ________, Price $ __________

Thursday's Child Has Far To Go, 692115

UM $20.00

Open, Issue Price $20.00, '00
Series: *Thought of the Day — Little Moments*
Purchased ________, Price $ __________

Alleluia, He Is Risen, 692409

Mark	Price	Mark	Price
★	$40.00	(cross in heart)	$32.00
(egg)	$38.00	(crown)	$30.00
(plane)	$35.00	(flower)	$30.00
		(box)	$30.00

Open, Issue Price $30.00, '99
Purchased__________,
Price $__________

☐ *I'm Proud To Be An American (Army),* 729876

$40.00
$38.00
$35.00
$33.00
$32.50
$32.50
$32.50

Open, Issue Price $32.50, '99
Purchased ________, Price $ ___________

☐ *I'm Proud To Be An American (Marine),* 729884

$40.00
$38.00
$35.00
$33.00
$32.50
$32.50
$32.50

Open, Issue Price $32.50, '99
Purchased ________, Price $ ___________

☐ *I'm Proud To Be An American (Navy),* 729892

$40.00
$38.00
$35.00
$33.00
$32.50
$32.50
$32.50

Open, Issue Price $32.50, '99
Purchased ________, Price $ ___________

☐ *I'm Proud To Be An American (Coast Guard),* 729906

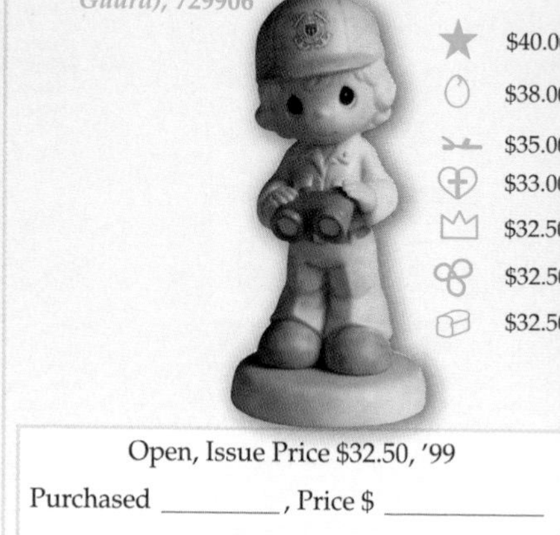

$40.00
$38.00
$35.00
$33.00
$32.50
$32.50
$32.50

Open, Issue Price $32.50, '99
Purchased ________, Price $ ___________

☐ *I'm Proud To Be An American (Air Force),* 729914

$40.00
$38.00
$35.00
$33.00
$32.50
$32.50
$32.50

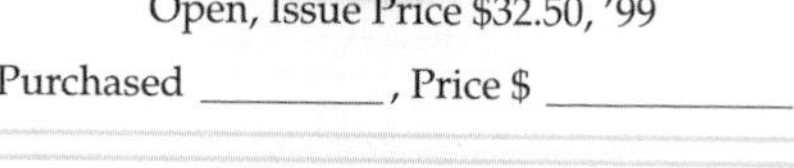

Open, Issue Price $32.50, '99
Purchased ________, Price $ ___________

☐ *I'm Proud To Be An American (Army),* 729922

$40.00
$38.00
$35.00
$33.00
$32.50
$32.50
$32.50

Open, Issue Price $32.50, '99
Purchased ________, Price $ ___________

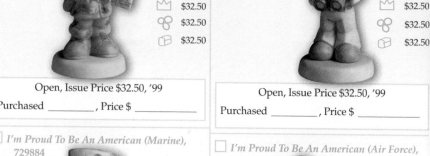

☐ *I'm Proud To Be An American (Marine),* 729930

- $40.00
- $38.00
- $35.00
- $33.00
- $32.50
- $32.50
- $32.50

Open, Issue Price $32.50, '99

Purchased ________, Price $ ___________

☐ *I'm Proud To Be An American (Air Force),* 729965

- $40.00
- $38.00
- $35.00
- $33.00
- $32.50
- $32.50
- $32.50

Open, Issue Price $32.50, '99

Purchased ________, Price $ ___________

☐ *I'm Proud To Be An American (Navy),* 729949

- $40.00
- $38.00
- $35.00
- $33.00
- $32.50
- $32.50
- $32.50

Open, Issue Price $32.50, '99

Purchased ________, Price $ ___________

☐ *I'm Proud To Be An American (Army),* 729973

- $40.00
- $38.00
- $35.00
- $33.00
- $32.50
- $32.50
- $32.50

Open, Issue Price $32.50, '99

Purchased ________, Price $ ___________

☐ *I'm Proud To Be An American (Coast Guard),* 729957

- $40.00
- $38.00
- $35.00
- $33.00
- $32.50
- $32.50
- $32.50

Open, Issue Price $32.50, '99

Purchased ________, Price $ ___________

☐ *I'm Proud To Be An American (Marine),* 730009

- $40.00
- $38.00
- $35.00
- $33.00
- $32.50
- $32.50
- $32.50

Open, Issue Price $32.50, '99

Purchased ________, Price $ ___________

☐ *I'm Proud To Be An American (Navy), 730017*

$40.00
$38.00
$35.00
$33.00
$32.50
$32.50
$32.50

Open, Issue Price $32.50, '99
Purchased ________, Price $ ___________

☐ *Gratitude With Attitude, 730041*

$40.00
$38.00
$35.00
$32.50
$32.50
$32.50

Open, Issue Price $35.00, '01
Purchased ________, Price $ ___________

☐ *I'm Proud To Be An American (Coast Guard), 730025*

$40.00
$38.00
$35.00
$33.00
$32.50
$32.50
$32.50

Open, Issue Price $32.50, '99
Purchased ________, Price $ ___________

☐ *I'm Proud To Be An American (Air Force), 730033*

$40.00
$38.00
$35.00
$33.00
$32.50
$32.50
$32.50

Open, Issue Price $32.50, '99
Purchased ________, Price $ ___________

☐ *The Future Is In Our Hands, 730068*

Randomly produced with a red cardinal rather than a bluebird.

$45.00

Dated Annual 2000, Issue Price $30.00, '00
Purchased ________, Price $ ___________

☐ *The Future Is In Our Hands, 730076 (Ornament)*

Randomly produced with a red cardinal rather than a bluebird.

$30.00

Dated Annual 2000, Issue Price $19.00, '00
Purchased ________, Price $ ___________

☐ *Our First Christmas Together, 730084* (Ornament)

$30.00

Dated Annual 2000, Issue Price $25.00, '00

Purchased ________, Price $ ___________

☐ *Baby's First Christmas (Girl), 730092* (Ornament)

$25.00

Dated Annual 2000, Issue Price $19.00, '00

Purchased __________,

Price $ ____________

☐ *Baby's First Christmas (Boy), 730106* (Ornament)

$25.00

Dated Annual 2000, Issue Price $19.00, '00

Purchased ____________,

Price $____________

☐ *There's Sno-Boredom With You, 730122*

$50.00
$48.00
$45.00
$45.00
$45.00
$45.00

Open, Issue Price $45.00, '00

Purchased ________, Price $ ___________

☐ *Raisin' Cane On The Holidays, 730130*

$45.00
$43.00
$40.00
$38.00

Suspended 2003, Issue Price $35.00, '00

Purchased ________, Price $ ___________

☐ *We're A Family That Sticks Together, 730114*

$65.00

Limited Ed., Issue Price $40.00, '00 Set of 3

Purchased ______________,

Price $______________

☐ *Everything Is Beautiful In Its Own Way, 730149*

Triangle/Egg	$30.00
Bow & Arrow	$28.00
Heart	$25.00
Crown	$25.00
Clover	$25.00
Box	$25.00

Open, Issue Price $25.00, '00

Purchased ________, Price $ __________

☐ *Home-Made Of Love, 730211*

Egg	$52.00
Bow & Arrow	$50.00
Heart	$48.00
Crown	$45.00
Clover	$45.00
Box	$45.00

Open, Issue Price $45.00, '00

Purchased ________, Price $ __________

☐ *I'll Never Let You Down, 730165*

Egg	$58.00	Crown	$50.00
Bow & Arrow	$55.00	Clover	$50.00
Heart	$53.00	Box	$50.00

Open, Issue Price $45.00, '01

Purchased __________,

Price $ __________

☐ *I'm A Reflection Of Your Love, 730238*

UM $30.00

Limited Ed., Issue Price $14.99, '00
Avon Exclusive

Purchased _________,

Price $ __________

☐ *The Peace That Passes Understanding, 730173*

Egg	$150.00	Bow & Arrow	$140.00

☐ *You Have The Beary Best Heart, 730254*

Egg	$45.00	Bow & Arrow	$40.00

Limited Ed., Issue Price $35.00, '01
Authorized Retailer Event 3/10/01
Easter Seals – Lily Understamp

Purchased _________,

Price $__________

Limited Ed. 10,000, Issue Price $100.00, '00
CCR & DSR Exclusive
Set of 7
(Two pilgrims, two Indians, animals, table, and pine tree base which also holds candles)

Purchased _____, Price $ __________

☐ *The Fun Is Being Together, 730262*

$230.00 $220.00

Limited Ed. 10,000, Issue Price $200.00, '00
CCR Exclusive, Individually Numbered

Purchased ________, Price $ ___________

☐ *A Collection Of Precious Moments, 731129*

$35.00
$33.00
$30.00
$28.00
$26.00
$25.00
$25.00

Open, Issue Price $25.00, '00

Purchased ________, Price $ ___________

☐ *Squeaky Clean, 731048*

$55.00
$50.00

Annual 2000, Issue Price $45.00, '00
CCR Event Exclusive

Purchased ________, Price $ ___________

☐ *Sharing Sweet Moments Together, 731579*

$28.00
$25.00

Limited Ed., Issue Price $20.00, '00
Series: *Little Moments*
2000 Sweetest Day Promo

Purchased ________, Price $ ___________

☐ *Take Thyme For Yourself, 731064*

$45.00
$43.00
$40.00
$38.00
$35.00

Suspended 2004, Issue Price $35.00, '01

Purchased ________, Price $ ___________

☐ *Grandma, I'll Never Outgrow You! 731587*

$35.00 $25.00
$30.00 $25.00
$28.00 $25.00

Open, Issue Price
$25.00, '00
Grandparents' Day
Promo

Purchased ________,

Price $ ___________

☐ *Grandma, I'll Never Outgrow You!* 731595

Mark	Price	Mark	Price
Egg	$35.00	Crown	$25.00
Bow & Arrow	$30.00	Flower	$25.00
Heart	$28.00	Box	$25.00

Open, Issue Price $25.00, '00
Grandparents' Day Promo
Purchased ________,
Price $ ________

☐ *Everybody Has A Part,* 731625

Mark	Price	Mark	Price	Mark	Price
Star	$80.00	Bow & Arrow	$70.00	Heart	$65.00
Egg	$75.00			Crown	$55.00

Out of Production, Issue Price $50.00, '00
Japanese Exclusive, Set of 3
Purchased ________, Price $ ________

☐ *Good Fortune,* 731633

Mark	Price	Mark	Price
Star	$30.00	Bow & Arrow	$17.50
Egg	$25.00	Heart	$17.50
		Crown	$17.50

Out of Production, Issue
Price $17.50, '00
Series: *Junishi* —
Japanese Exclusive
Purchased ________,
Price $ ________

☐ *There Shall Be Fountains Of Blessings,* 731668

Mark	Price
UM	$85.00
Egg	$80.00
Heart	$75.00
Crown	$75.00
Flower	$75.00
Box	$75.00

Open, Issue Price $75.00, '00
Chapel Exclusive
Purchased ________, Price $ ________

☐ *Our Loss Is Heaven's Gain,* 731676

Mark	Price	Mark	Price
UM	$45.00	Crown	$35.00
Bow & Arrow	$43.00	Flower	$30.00
Heart	$40.00	Box	$30.00

Open, Issue Price
$30.00, '00
Chapel Exclusive
Purchased ________,
Price $ ________

☐ *Fall Festival,* 732494

Mark	Price	Mark	Price	Mark	Price
Egg	$160.00	Heart	$155.00	Flower	$150.00
Bow & Arrow	$158.00	Crown	$150.00	Box	$150.00

Barn is a nightlight.

Open, Issue Price
$150.00, '00
Set of 7
Purchased ________,
Price $ ________

You Should Be As Proud As A Peacock — Congratulations, 733008

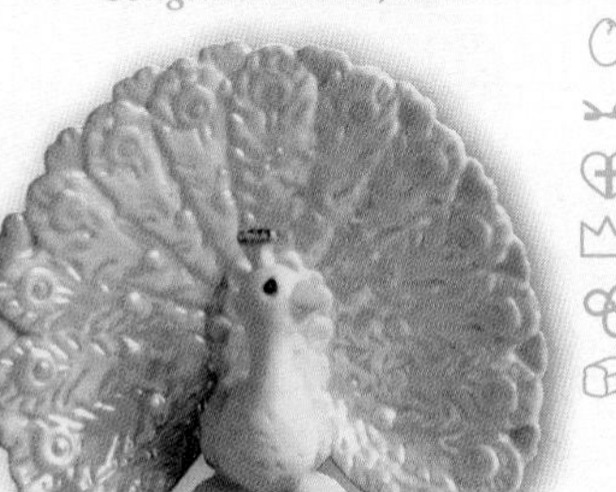

Mark	Price
Egg	$30.00
Bow & Arrow	$30.00
Heart	$27.50
Crown	$27.50
Clover	$27.50
Box	$27.50

Open, Issue Price $27.50, '00

Purchased ________, Price $ ___________

One Good Turn Deserves Another, 737569 (Ornament)

Mark	Price
Egg	$28.00
Bow & Arrow	$25.00
Heart	$23.00
Crown	$20.00
Clover	$20.00
Box	$20.00

Open, Issue Price $20.00, '00
Series: *Precious Scape*

Purchased ________, Price $ ___________

You Have A Special Place In My Heart, 737534

Mark	Price
Egg	$75.00

Limited Ed., Issue Price $55.00, '00
Series: *Christmas Remembered*

Purchased ________, Price $ ___________

Behold The Lord, 737607

Mark	Price
Egg	$30.00
Bow & Arrow	$28.00
Heart	$25.00
Crown	$25.00
Clover	$25.00
Box	$25.00

Open, Issue Price $25.00, '00
Nativity Addition, Set of 3

Purchased ________, Price $ ___________

Sure Could Use Less Hustle And Bustle, 737550

Mark	Price
Egg	$43.00
Bow & Arrow	$40.00
Heart	$37.50
Crown	$37.50
Clover	$37.50
Box	$37.50

Open, Issue Price $37.50, '00
Series: *Christmas Remembered*

Purchased ________, Price $ ___________

Auntie, You Make Beauty Blossom, 737623

Mark	Price
Egg	$30.00
Bow & Arrow	$28.00
Heart	$25.00
Crown	$20.00
Clover	$20.00
Box	$20.00

Open, Issue Price $40.00, '00

Purchased ________, Price $ ___________

☐ *You're A Real Barbe-cutie, 742872*

$38.00
$35.00
$35.00
$35.00
$35.00

Open, Issue Price $35.00, '01
Series: *Special Wishes*
Purchased ________, Price $ ____________

☐ *To The Sweetest Girl In The Cast, 742880*

$40.00
$38.00
$35.00
$35.00
$35.00
$35.00

Open, Issue Price $35.00, '01
Purchased __________,
Price $ ____________

☐ *You Add Sparkle To My Life, 745413*

$35.00

Limited Ed., Issue Price $25.00, '01
Series: *Heavenly Daze* – First Issue
Care-A-Van Exclusive
Purchased ________, Price $ ____________

☐ *A Collection Of Precious Moments, 745510*

$40.00
$35.00

Comes with a copy of the book *Chicken Soup for the Soul.*

Retired 2000, Issue Price $27.00, '99
Set of 2
Purchased ________, Price $ ____________

☐ *Let Earth Receive Her King, 748382*

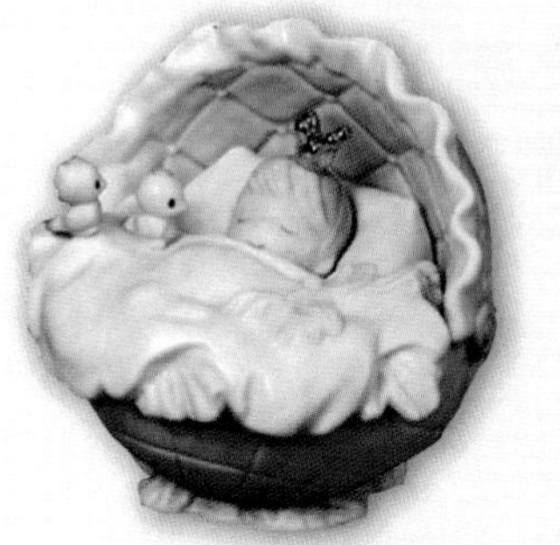

UM $40.00
$39.00
$38.00
$35.00
$33.00
$32.50

Open, Issue Price $32.50, '00
Chapel Exclusive
Purchased ________, Price $ ____________

☐ *Let Earth Receive Her King, 748390* (Ornament)

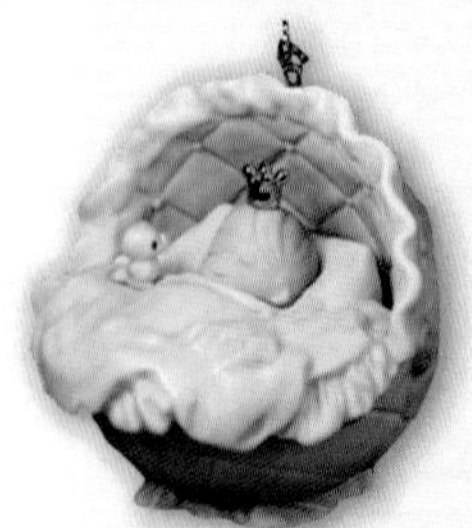

UM $27.50
$27.00
$26.00
$25.00
$25.00
$25.00

Open, Issue Price $25.00, '00
Chapel Exclusive
Purchased ________, Price $ ____________

☐ *Whale Have Oceans Of Fun, 748412*

◯ $250.00

Limited Ed., Gift, '00
2000 Cruise Exclusive

Purchased ________, Price $ __________

☐ *Christmas Street Precious Scape, 750123*

UM $25.00

For displaying pieces.

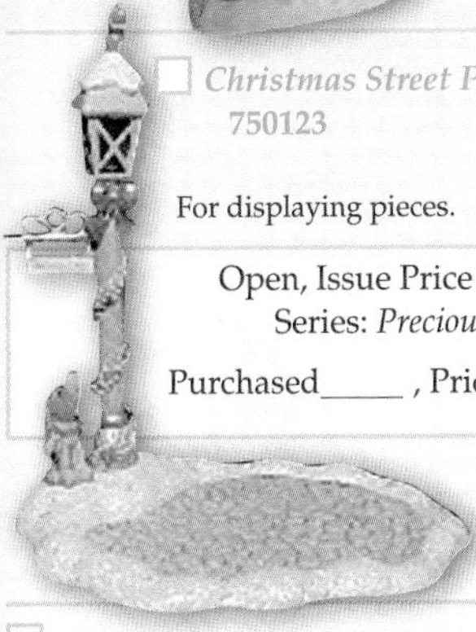

Open, Issue Price $25.00, '00
Series: *Precious Scape*

Purchased_____ , Price $ ________

☐ *You Are Always In My Heart, 768987*

◯ $45.00
$40.00

Limited Ed., Issue Price $40.00, '01

Purchased ________, Price $ __________

☐ *Eat Turkey, 763225*

◯ $35.00 $28.00
$33.00 $35.00
$30.00 $35.00

Open, Issue Price $25.00, '00
Series: *Country Lane Collection*

Purchased ______ ,

Price $ __________

☐ *May Your Days Be Rosy, 781770C*

◯ $45.00

Limited Ed., Issue Price $30.00, '00
Carlton Cards Exclusive

Purchased__________ ,

Price $__________

☐ *You Are Always In My Heart, 768952*

◯ $45.00
$40.00

Limited Ed., Issue Price $40.00, '01

Purchased ________, Price $ __________

☐ *Mr. Fujioka, 781851*

◯ $50.00

Annual 2001, Issue Price $25.00, '01

Purchased __________ ,

Price $ __________

☐ *Your Love Keeps Me Toasty Warm, 788031*

$45.00

Limited Ed., Issue Price $39.95, '00
Winter Syndicated Exclusive
Purchased ________, Price $ __________

☐ *Christmas Trees Precious Scape, 788171*

UM $30.00

Open, Issue Price $30.00, '00
Set of 3
Series: *Precious Scape*
Purchased ________, Price $ __________

☐ *Rhythm And Flute, 791091*

$100.00 $80.00 $60.00
$90.00 $70.00 $60.00

Open, Issue Price $80.00, '00
Series: *Girl's Festival* — Set of 5
CCR Exclusive, Japanese Exclusive
Purchased ________, Price $ __________

☐ *Courteous Service, 791113*

$100.00 $80.00 $60.00
$90.00 $70.00 $60.00

Open, Issue Price $60.00, '00
Series: *Girl's Festival* — Set of 3
CCR Exclusive, Japanese Exclusive
Purchased ________, Price $ __________

☐ *Dance Of The Lion, 791121*

$100.00 $70.00
$90.00 $60.00
$80.00 $60.00

Open, Issue Price $60.00, '00
CCR Exclusive, Japanese Exclusive
Purchased________,
Price $__________

☐ *Different Beats Can Still Come Together*, 791148

$60.00 $55.00
$55.00 $55.00
$55.00

Open, Issue Price $55.00, '01
CCR Exclusive, Japanese Exclusive

Purchased ________, Price $ ____________

☐ *You Are The Queen Of My Heart*, 795151

$60.00

Limited Ed., Issue Price $50.00, '01

Purchased _______ ,

Price $ __________

☐ *You Will Always Be Mine*, 795186

$55.00 $45.00
$50.00 $45.00
$45.00
$45.00

Open, Issue Price $45.00, '01
Set of 2

Purchased ________, Price $ ____________

☐ *You Can't Hide From God*, 795194

$28.00
$25.00
$23.00
$20.00
$20.00
$20.00

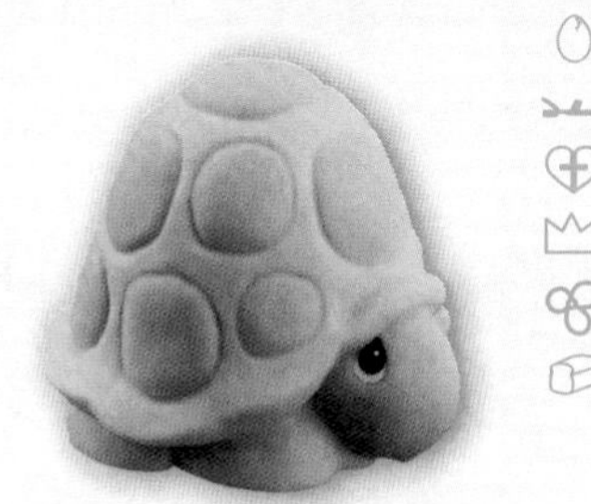

Open, Issue Price $18.50, '01

Purchased ________, Price $ ____________

☐ *The Lord Can Dew Anything*, 795208

$45.00
$40.00
$38.00
$35.00
$35.00

Retired 2004, Issue Price $35.00, '01

Purchased ________, Price $ ____________

☐ *Cherish Every Step*, 795224

$60.00
$55.00
$50.00
$50.00
$50.00
$50.00

Open, Issue Price $50.00, '01
Series: *Motherhood* — Second Issue

Purchased______ ,

Price $__________

☐ *You're A Dandy Mom And I'm Not Lion,* 795232V

$40.00
$35.00

Comes with a crystal vase and 15% gift card for FTD.com.

Retired 2001, Issue Price $27.50, '00
Set of 3

Purchased ________, Price $ ___________

☐ *It's A Banner Day, Congratulations,* 795259

$35.00
$32.50
$32.50
$32.50
$32.50
$32.50

Open, Issue Price $25.00, '01

Purchased ________, Price $ ___________

☐ *You Are The Wind Beneath My Wings,* 795267

$35.00 $32.50
$32.50 $32.50
$32.50 $32.50

Open, Issue Price $35.00, '01

Purchased___________,

Price $ ___________

☐ *You're As Sweet As Apple Pie,* 795275

$45.00
$43.00
$40.00
$35.00
$35.00

Suspended 2004, Issue Price $35.00, '01

Purchased ________, Price $ ___________

☐ *You're A Honey,* 795283

$40.00
$38.00
$35.00
$32.50
$32.50
$32.50

Open, Issue Price $35.00, '01

Purchased ________, Price $ ___________

☐ *O-Fish-Aly Friends For A Lifetime,* 795305

$60.00
$55.00
$50.00
$50.00
$50.00
$50.00

Open, Issue Price $50.00, '01

Purchased ________, Price $ ___________

☐ *Wishing You A Birthday Full Of Surprises,* 795313

$45.00
$40.00
$40.00
$40.00
$40.00
$40.00

Suspended 2005, Issue Price $40.00, '01

Purchased ________, Price $ ___________

☐ *No Bones About It — You're Grrreat,* 795321

$45.00
$40.00
$40.00
$40.00
$40.00

Open, Issue Price $40.00, '01
Series: *Special Wishes*

Purchased ________, Price $ ___________

☐ *Blessed With A Loving Godmother,* 795348

$45.00
$40.00
$40.00
$40.00
$40.00
$40.00

Open, Issue Price $40.00, '01

Purchased ________, Price $ ___________

☐ *Life Would Be The Pits Without Friends,* 795356

$50.00
$45.00
$40.00
$40.00
$40.00

Retired 2004, Issue Price $40.00, '01
Series: *Country Lane Collection*

Purchased ________, Price $ ___________

☐ *Bride (African-American),* 795364

$35.00
$30.00
$30.00
$30.00
$30.00
$30.00

Open, Issue Price $30.00, '01

Purchased ________, Price $ ___________

☐ *Groom (African-American),* 795372

$35.00 $30.00
$30.00 $30.00
$30.00 $30.00

Open, Issue Price $30.00, '01

Purchased____________,

Price $ ____________

☐ *Bride (Hispanic), 795380*

○	$35.00
✂	$30.00
♡	$30.00
♔	$30.00
✿	$30.00
☐	$30.00

Open, Issue Price $30.00, '01

Purchased ________, Price $ __________

☐ *Groom (Asian), 795410*

○	$35.00
✂	$30.00
♡	$30.00
♔	$30.00
✿	$30.00
☐	$30.00

Open, Issue Price $30.00, '01

Purchased ________, Price $ __________

☐ *Groom (Hispanic), 795399*

○	$35.00
✂	$30.00
♡	$30.00
♔	$30.00
✿	$30.00
☐	$30.00

Open, Issue Price $30.00, '01

Purchased ________, Price $ __________

☐ *Friendship Grows From The Heart, 795496*

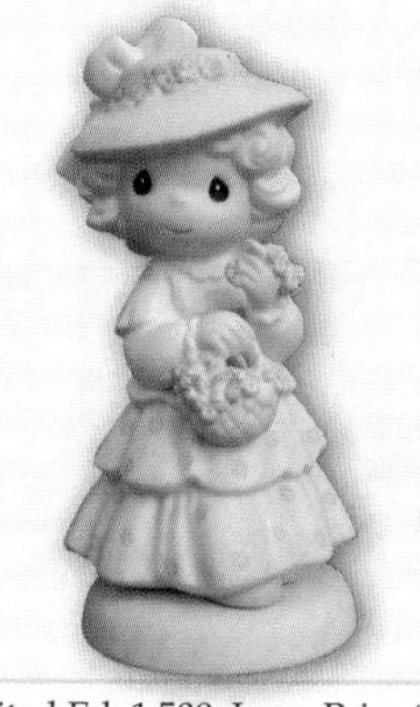

UM $60.00

Limited Ed. 1,500, Issue Price $35.00, '01
2001 Licensee Event Exclusive

Purchased ________, Price $ __________

☐ *Bride (Asian), 795402*

○	$35.00
✂	$30.00
♡	$30.00
♔	$30.00
✿	$30.00
☐	$30.00

Open, Issue Price $30.00, '01

Purchased ________,

Price $ __________

☐ *On Our Way To The Chapel, 795518*

UM	$40.00
✂	$35.00
♡	$32.50
♔	$32.50
✿	$32.50
☐	$32.50

Open, Issue Price $32.50, '00
Chapel Exclusive

Purchased __________,

Price $ __________

You Tug On My Heart Strings, 795526

$65.00
$60.00
$60.00
$60.00
$60.00
$60.00

Annual 2001, Issue Price $60.00, '01
Boys & Girls Club of America Exclusive
Purchased ________, Price $ __________

Your Love Keeps Me Toasty Warm, 795577 (Ornament)

$35.00

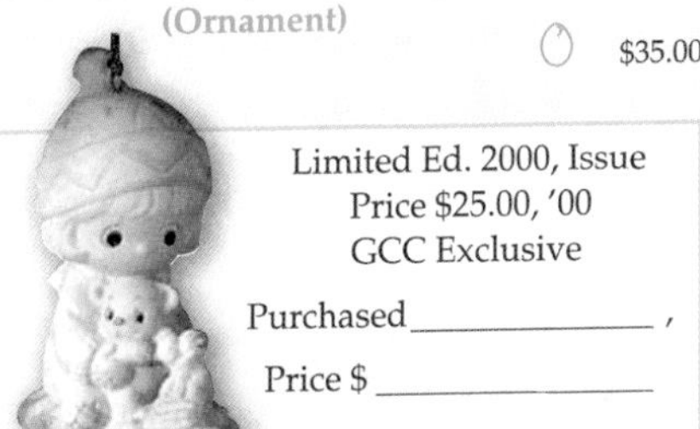

Limited Ed. 2000, Issue Price $25.00, '00
GCC Exclusive
Purchased ____________,
Price $ ____________

Konnichiwa Friends, 796581

$85.00

Open, Issue Price $35.00, '02
2001 Regional Event Exclusive
Purchased ____________,
Price $ ____________

You're Just Too Thweet, 797693 (Box)

$25.00
$22.50
$22.50
$22.50

Open, Issue Price $22.50, '02
Purchased ________, Price $ __________

Grandma, I'll Never Outgrow You! 798223

$35.00
$33.00
$30.00
$28.00

Limited Ed., Issue Price $25.00, '00
Purchased ________, Price $ __________

Grandma, I'll Never Outgrow You! 798231

$35.00
$33.00
$30.00
$28.00

Limited Ed., Issue Price $25.00, '00
Purchased ________, Price $ __________

Your Love Keeps Me Toasty Warm, 800813 (Ornament)

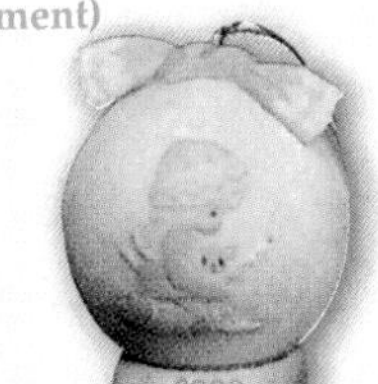

$35.00

Annual 2000, Issue Price $25.00, '00
Set of 2
Purchased ________, Price $ __________

☐ *I Give You My Heart,* 801313

Also issued in 2000 as a limited edition Carlton Cards Early Release (801313C); Egg mark, $45.00, Sandal mark, $40.00.

$40.00

Limited Ed., Issue Price $30.00, '01
CCR Exclusive
Purchased ________, Price $ __________

☐ *Sweetheart Safari,* 802484 (Medallion)

$85.00

Limited Ed. 1,200, Issue Price $20.00, '00
2000 Licensee Event
Purchased ________, Price $ __________

☐ *Let's Keep Our Eyes On The Goal,* 802557 (Ornament)

$28.00
$25.00

Limited Ed., Issue Price $20.00, '01
Canadian Exclusive
Purchased ________, Price $ __________

☐ *Ready In The "Nick" Of Time,* 804088

$90.00

Limited Ed. 1,500, Issue Price $45.00, '00
2000 Christmas Event
Purchased ________, Price $ __________

☐ *A Godchild Close To My Heart,* 804096

$30.00
$25.00
$25.00
$25.00
$25.00

Open, Issue Price $25.00, '01
Purchased ________, Price $ __________

☐ *Happy Anniversary,* 804444

$35.00
$35.00

Open, Issue Price $35.00, '03
DSR & CCR Exclusive
One day only, June 21, 2003
Purchased ________, Price $ __________

A Godchild Close To My Heart (Girl), 811807

$35.00
$35.00
$35.00
$35.00
$35.00

Open, Issue Price $35.00, '01

Purchased ________, Price $ ____________

A Godchild Close To My Heart (Boy), 811815

$35.00
$35.00
$35.00
$35.00
$35.00

Open, Issue Price $35.00, '01

Purchased ________, Price $ ____________

A Winning Spirit Comes From Within, 813044

$45.00
$43.00
$40.00
$38.00
$35.00
$35.00

Retired 2005, Issue Price $35.00, '01
Special Olympics Exclusive

Purchased ________, Price $ ____________

I Will Make My Country Proud, 820423

$50.00
$48.00
$40.00
$35.00
$35.00
$35.00

Open, Issue Price $37.50, '00
Canadian Exclusive

Purchased ________, Price $ ____________

Hisssterrically Sweet, 821969

$16.00
$16.00
$16.00
$16.00
$16.00

Open, Issue Price $15.00, '01
Japanese Exclusive

Purchased ________, Price $ ____________

Love One Another, 822426

$500.00
$450.00

Limited Ed. 1,500, Issue Price $500.00, '01
Easter Seals Commemorative

Purchased ________, Price $ ____________

A Beary Loving Collector, 823953C

★ $15.00

Limited Ed., Issue Price $15.00, '99
1999 Convention Exclusive
Purchased ________, Price $ __________

Our Love Will Never Be Endangered, 824119

Egg $55.00

Also issued in 2001 as a Reef Hallmark Fortieth Anniversary Limited Edition (824119S); Egg mark, $75.00.

Limited Ed., Issue Price $50.00, '01
CCR Exclusive
Purchased ________, Price $ __________

Mom (Blonde), 848735

UM $20.00

Open, Issue Price $20.00, '01
Series: *Build A Family — Little Moments*
Purchased ________, Price $ __________

Dad (Blond), 848743

UM $20.00

Open, Issue Price $20.00, '01
Series: *Build A Family — Little Moments*
Purchased ________, Price $ __________

Teenage Daughter (Blonde), 848751

UM $20.00

Open, Issue Price $17.50, '01
Series: *Build A Family — Little Moments*
Purchased ________, Price $ __________

Teenage Son (Blond), 848778

UM $17.50

Open, Issue Price $17.50, '01
Series: *Build A Family — Little Moments*
Purchased ________, Price $ __________

Toddler Daughter (Blonde), 848786

UM $17.50

Open, Issue Price $15.00, '01
Series: *Build A Family — Little Moments*
Purchased ________, Price $ ___________

Toddler Son (Blond), 848794

UM $15.00

Open, Issue Price $15.00, '01
Series: *Build A Family — Little Moments*
Purchased ________, Price $ ___________

Infant Daughter (Blonde), 848808

UM $12.50

Open, Issue Price $12.50, '01
Series: *Build A Family — Little Moments*
Purchased ________, Price $ ___________

Infant Son (Blond), 848816

UM $12.50

Open, Issue Price $12.50, '01
Series: *Build A Family — Little Moments*
Purchased ________, Price $ ___________

Dog, 848824

UM $10.00

Open, Issue Price $10.00, '01
Series: *Build A Family — Little Moments*
Purchased ________, Price $ ___________

Cat, 848832

UM $10.00

Open, Issue Price $10.00, '01
Series: *Build A Family — Little Moments*
Purchased ________, Price $ ___________

Bride And Groom, 848840 (Picture Frame)

$35.00 $35.00 $35.00
$35.00 $35.00

Open, Issue Price $35.00, '01
Purchased ________, Price $ ___________

☐ *Victorious In Jesus,* 850950

Also issued as a Chapel Exclusive Limited Edition of 2,400 in 2000 (850942) with an issue price of $85.00; Unmarked, $100.00.

UM $50.00
$50.00
$50.00

Open, Issue Price $50.00, '01
Chapel Exclusive
Purchased ________, Price $ __________

☐ *Mary Had A Little Lamb,* 850969

UM $40.00
$35.00
$35.00
$35.00
$35.00
$35.00

Open, Issue Price $35.00, '00
Chapel Exclusive
Purchased ________, Price $ __________

☐ *Bride (Brunette),* 874485

$35.00
$30.00
$30.00
$30.00
$30.00
$30.00

Open, Issue Price $30.00, '01
Series: *The Lord Bless You And Keep You*
Purchased ________, Price $ __________

☐ *Groom (Brunette),* 874493

$35.00
$30.00
$30.00
$30.00
$30.00
$30.00

Open, Issue Price $30.00, '01
Series: *The Lord Bless You And Keep You*
Purchased ________, Price $ __________

☐ *I Give You My Love Forever True,* 876143 (Musical)

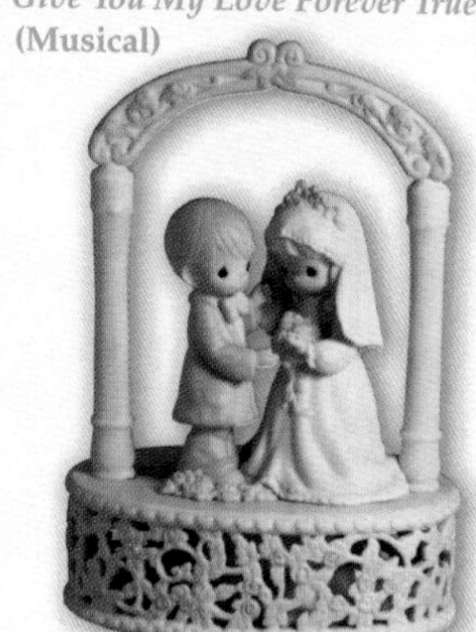

$135.00
$125.00
$125.00
$125.00
$125.00

Open, Issue Price $125.00, '01
Tune: "Pachelbel's Canon in D"
Purchased ________, Price $ __________

☐ *Bridal Arch,* 876151 (Musical)

$55.00
$50.00
$50.00
$50.00
$50.00
$50.00

Open, Issue Price $50.00, '01
Tune: "Pachelbel's Canon in D"
Purchased ________, Price $ __________

The Lord Is The Hope Of Our Future, 877123

$45.00
$40.00
$40.00
$40.00
$40.00
$40.00

Open, Issue Price $40.00, '01

Purchased ________, Price $ __________

The Lord Is The Hope Of Our Future, 877131

$45.00
$40.00
$40.00
$40.00
$40.00
$40.00

Open, Issue Price $40.00, '01

Purchased ________, Price $ __________

May Your Christmas Begin With A Bang! 877433

$35.00

Annual 2001, Issue Price $30.00, '01

Purchased ________, Price $ __________

May Your Christmas Begin With A Bang! 877441 (Ornament)

$25.00

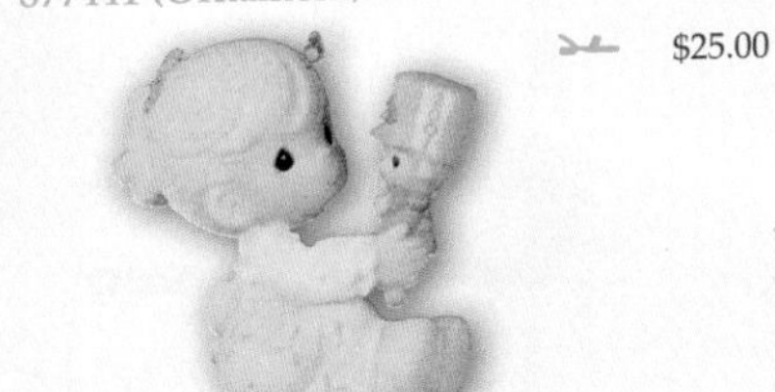

Annual 2001, Issue Price $19.00, '01

Purchased ________, Price $ __________

Baby's First Christmas, 877506 (Ornament)

$25.00

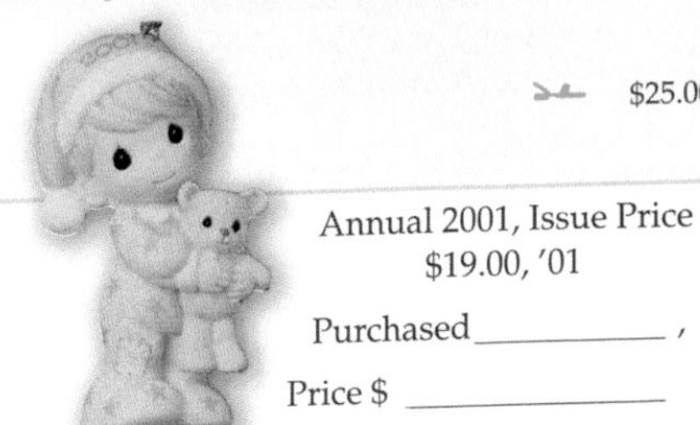

Annual 2001, Issue Price $19.00, '01

Purchased __________,

Price $ __________

Baby's First Christmas, 877514 (Ornament)

$25.00

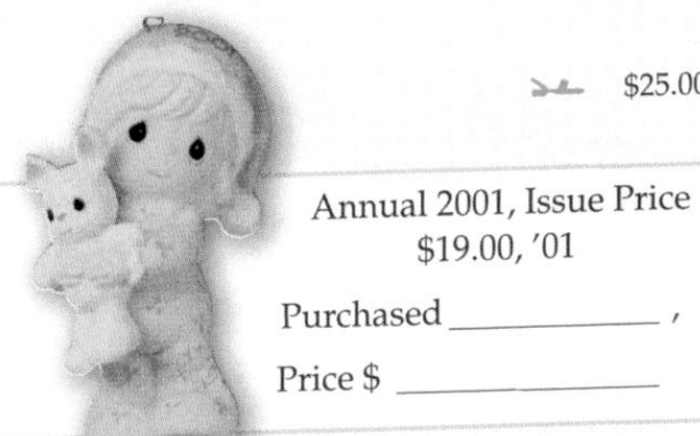

Annual 2001, Issue Price $19.00, '01

Purchased __________,

Price $ __________

Our First Christmas Together, 878855 (Ornament)

$30.00

Annual 2001, Issue Price $25.00, '01

Purchased ________, Price $ __________

May Your Days Be Merry And Bright, 878901

Bow & Arrow	$50.00
Heart & Cross	$45.00
Crown	$45.00
Clover	$45.00
Box	$45.00

Open, Issue Price $45.00, '01
Series: *Christmas Remembered*
Purchased ________, Price $ ________

The Royal Budge Is Good For The Soul, 878987

Bow & Arrow	$50.00
Heart & Cross	$45.00
Crown	$45.00
Clover	$45.00
Box	$45.00

Open, Issue Price $45.00, '01
Nativity Addition
Purchased ________, Price $ ________

On A Scale From 1 To 10 You Are The Deerest, 878944

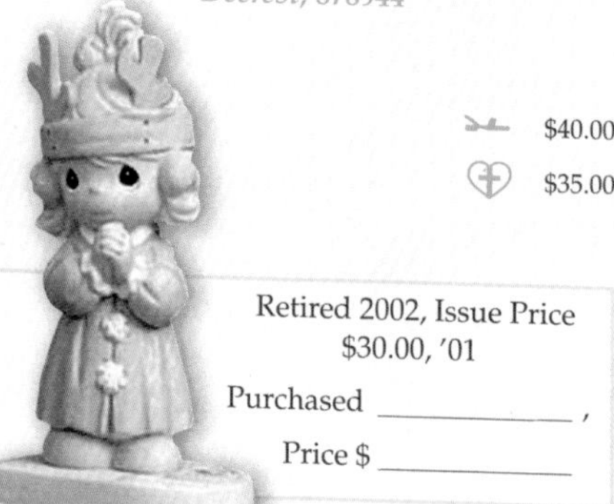

Bow & Arrow	$40.00
Heart & Cross	$35.00

Retired 2002, Issue Price $30.00, '01
Purchased ________,
Price $ ________

Life Is So Uplifting, 878995

Bow & Arrow	$40.00
Heart & Cross	$35.00
Crown	$35.00
Clover	$35.00
Box	$35.00

Open, Issue Price $35.00, '01
Purchased ________, Price $ ________

Celebrating His Arrival, 878952

Bow & Arrow	$45.00
Heart & Cross	$40.00
Crown	$40.00
Clover	$40.00
Box	$40.00

Open, Issue Price $40.00, '01
Purchased ________, Price $ ________

Roll Away, Roll Away, Roll Away, 879002

Bow & Arrow	$40.00
Heart & Cross	$35.00
Crown	$35.00
Clover	$35.00
Box	$35.00

Open, Issue Price $35.00, '01
Purchased ________, Price $ ________

☐ *Building Special Friendships, 879029*

$85.00
$80.00
$80.00
$80.00
$80.00

Annual 2001, Issue Price $80.00, '01
Boys And Girls Club Of America Commemorative

Purchased ________, Price $ ____________

☐ *Oh, What A Wonder-Fall Day, 879096*

$45.00
$40.00
$40.00

Open, Issue Price $40.00, '01
Series: *Country Lane Collection*

Purchased ________, Price $ ____________

☐ *Lord Let Our Friendship Bloom, 879126*

$50.00
$48.00
$45.00

Suspended 2003, Issue Price $40.00

Purchased ________, Price $ ____________

☐ *Our Friendship Was Made To Order, 879134*

$40.00
$35.00
$35.00
$35.00
$35.00

Open, Issue Price $35.00, '01

Purchased ________, Price $ ____________

☐ *Up To Our Ears In A White Christmas, 879185*

$70.00

Limited Ed., Issue Price $55.00, '01

Purchased ________, Price $ ____________

☐ *Count Your Many Blessings, 879274*

$55.00

Limited Ed., Issue Price $50.00, '01

Purchased ________, Price $ ____________

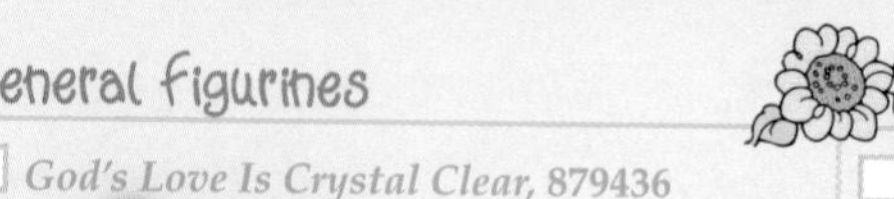

God's Love Is Crystal Clear, 879436

$50.00

Limited Ed., Issue Price $45.00, '01
CCR Event Exclusive

Purchased ________ ,
Price $ ____________

God's Love Is Crystal Clear, 879487 (Ornament)

$30.00

Annual 2001, Issue Price $25.00, '01
CCR Event Exclusive

Purchased ________, Price $ ____________

O Holy Night, 879428 (Nativity Scene)

$400.00

Limited Ed. 3,000, Issue Price $375.00, '01
GoCollect.com and CCR Exclusives
Worldwide, Hand Numbered

Purchased ________, Price $ ____________

Star Smith Vignette, 879568

$125.00
$100.00
$90.00

Retired 2003, Issue Price $85.00, '01
Series: *The Heavenly Daze* — First Issue
Set of 3

Purchased ________, Price $ ____________

Halo Maker, 879576

$125.00
$100.00
$90.00

Retired 2003, Issue Price $85.00, '01
Series: *The Heavenly Daze* —
Second Issue, Set of 3

Purchased ________, Price $ ____________

The Golden Gown Seamstress, 879606

$100.00

$90.00

Retired 2003, Issue Price $85.00, '02
Series: *The Heavenly Daze* — Third Issue
Set of 3

Purchased ____________,

Price $________________

House Of Bells Vignette, 879614

$100.00

$90.00

Retired 2003, Issue Price $85.00, '02
Series: *The Heavenly Daze* — Fourth Issue
Set of 3

Purchased ________, Price $ ___________

The Good Book Library, 879622

$100.00 $90.00

Retired 2003, Issue Price $85.00, '02
Series: *The Heavenly Daze* — Fifth Issue
Set of 3

Purchased ________, Price $ ___________

Dream Makers, 879630

$90.00

Retired 2003, Issue Price $85.00, '03
Series: *The Heavenly Daze* — Sixth Issue
Set of 3

Purchased ________, Price $ ___________

We Would See Jesus, 879681

UM $300.00

Limited Ed. 1,500, Issue Price $300.00, '01
Chapel Exclusive
Purchased ________, Price $ __________

He Is The Rose Of Sharon, 879703

UM $35.00 | (crown) $30.00
(heart) $30.00 | (trefoil) $30.00
(box) $30.00

Open, Issue Price $30.00, '01
Chapel Exclusive
Purchased __________,
Price $ __________

The Most Precious Place On Earth, 879711

(bow) $45.00
(heart) $40.00
(crown) $40.00
(trefoil) $40.00
(box) $40.00

Open, Issue Price $40.00, '01
Chapel Exclusive
Purchased ________, Price $ __________

The Lord Is Our Chief Inspiration, 879738 (Ornament)

(bow) $25.00 | (crown) $20.00
(heart) $23.00 | (trefoil) $20.00
(box) $20.00

Open, Issue Price
$20.00, '01
Chapel Exclusive
Purchased __________,
Price $ __________

Sleep In Heavenly Peace, 879746 (Ornament)

UM $30.00
(heart) $25.00
(crown) $25.00
(trefoil) $25.00
(box) $25.00

Open, Issue Price $25.00, '01
Chapel Exclusive
Purchased ________, Price $ __________

Sleep In Heavenly Peace, 879754

(bow) $40.00
(heart) $35.00
(crown) $35.00
(trefoil) $35.00
(box) $35.00

Open, Issue Price $35.00, '01
Chapel Exclusive
Purchased ________, Price $ __________

Mom (Brunette), 880833

UM $20.00

Open, Issue Price $20.00, '01
Series: *Build A Family — Little Moments*
Purchased __________,
Price $ __________

Dad (Brunette), 880841

UM $20.00

Open, Issue Price $20.00, '01
Series: *Build A Family — Little Moments*

Purchased ______________ ,

Price $__________________

Teenage Daughter (Brunette), 880868

UM $17.50

Open, Issue Price $17.50, '01
Series: *Build A Family — Little Moments*

Purchased ______________ ,

Price $ __________________

Teenage Son (Brunette), 880876

UM $17.50

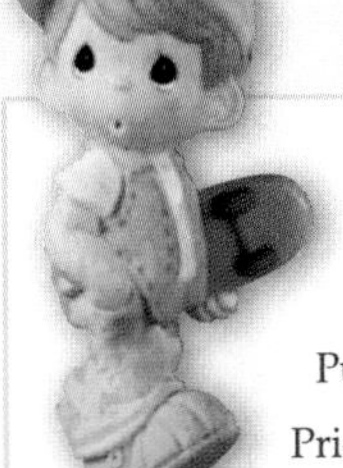

Open, Issue Price $17.50, '01
Series: *Build A Family — Little Moments*

Purchased ______________ ,

Price $__________________

Toddler Daughter (Brunette), 880884

UM $15.00

Open, Issue Price $15.00, '01
Series: *Build A Family — Little Moments*

Purchased ______________ ,

Price $ __________________

Toddler Son (Brunette), 880892

UM $15.00

Open, Issue Price $15.00, '01
Series: *Build A Family — Little Moments*

Purchased __________, Price $ ______________

Infant Daughter (Brunette), 880906

UM $15.00

Open, Issue Price $15.00, '01
Series: *Build A Family — Little Moments*

Purchased __________, Price $ ______________

Infant Son (Brunette), 880914

UM $15.00

Open, Issue Price $15.00, '01
Series: *Build A Family — Little Moments*

Purchased __________, Price $ ______________

You Decorate My Life, 881139

$40.00

Limited Ed., Issue Price $35.00, '01
2001 Fall Catalog Exclusive
Purchased ________, Price $ ___________

You Decorate My Life, 881147 (Ornament)

$25.00

Limited Ed., Issue Price $20.00, '01
2001 Fall Catalog Exclusive
Purchased ________, Price $ ___________

You Decorate My Life, 881163 (Ornament)

$33.00

Dated 2001, Issue Price $30.00, '01
Purchased ________, Price $ ___________

Grandma's Little Angel (Blonde), 887900

$25.00
$25.00
$25.00
$25.00
$25.00

Open, Issue Price $25.00, '01
Purchased ________, Price $ ___________

Grandma's Little Angel (Brunette), 887927

$25.00
$25.00
$25.00
$25.00
$25.00

Open, Issue Price $25.00, '02
Purchased ________, Price $ ___________

Daddy's Little Angel (Brunette), 887935

$25.00
$25.00
$25.00
$25.00
$25.00

Open, Issue Price $25.00, '02
Purchased ________, Price $ ___________

☐ *Daddy's Little Angel (Blonde)*, 887951

$25.00
$25.00
$25.00
$25.00
$25.00

Open, Issue Price $25.00, '02

Purchased ________, Price $ ____________

☐ *Grandma's Little Angel (Blond)*, 887978

$25.00
$25.00
$25.00
$25.00
$25.00

Open, Issue Price $25.00, '02

Purchased ________, Price $ ____________

☐ *Grandma's Little Angel (Brunette)*, 887986

$25.00
$25.00
$25.00
$25.00
$25.00

Open, Issue Price $25.00, '02

Purchased ________, Price $ ____________

☐ *Mommy's Little Angel (Brunette)*, 887994

$25.00
$25.00
$25.00
$25.00
$25.00

Open, Issue Price $25.00, '02

Purchased ________, Price $ ____________

☐ *Mommy's Little Angel (Blond)*, 888001

$25.00
$25.00
$25.00
$25.00
$25.00

Open, Issue Price $25.00, '02

Purchased ________, Price $ ____________

☐ *The Lord Is The Hope Of Our Future (Hispanic)*, 889563

$45.00
$40.00
$40.00
$40.00
$40.00

Open, Issue Price $40.00, '02

Purchased ________, Price $ ____________

Let's Have A Ball Together, 889849

$40.00

Annual 2001, Issue Price $35.00, '01
Boys and Girls Club of America Commemorative

Purchased ________, Price $ ____________

Let Love Reign, 890596

$70.00
$65.00

Limited Ed., Issue Price $60.00, '02

Purchased ______ ,

Price $ ________

You Have A Heart Of Gold, 890626

$30.00
$25.00
$25.00
$25.00
$25.00

Open, Issue Price $25.00, '02

Purchased ___________ ,

Price $____________

Nearer To The Heart Of God, 890731

$55.00
$50.00

Retired 2002, Issue Price $40.00, '02

Purchased_________ ,

Price $ ___________

God's Love Has No Measure, 890871

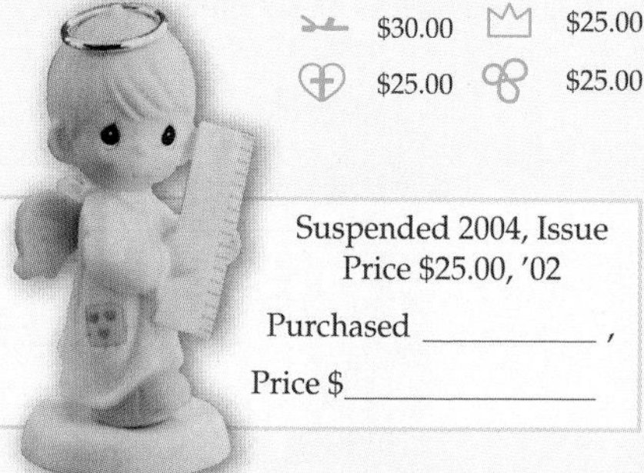

$30.00
$25.00
$25.00
$25.00

Suspended 2004, Issue Price $25.00, '02

Purchased ___________ ,

Price $_______________

You Are The Cat's Meow, 890952

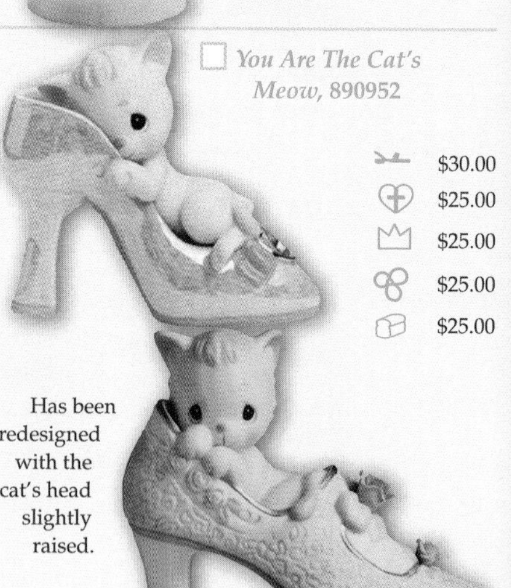

$30.00
$25.00
$25.00
$25.00
$25.00

Has been redesigned with the cat's head slightly raised.

Open, Issue Price $25.00, '02
Series: *Special Wishes*

Purchased ________, Price $ ___________

Just A Happy Note, 890960

$30.00
$25.00
$25.00
$25.00
$25.00

Open, Issue Price $25.00, '02
Series: *Special Wishes*

Purchased ________, Price $ ___________

Best Friends Share The Same Heart, 890987

$55.00
$50.00
$50.00
$50.00
$50.00

Open, Issue Price $50.00, '02
Set of 2

Purchased ________, Price $ ___________

Daddy's Little Girl, 891045

$45.00
$40.00
$40.00
$40.00
$40.00

Open, Issue Price $40.00, '02
Series: *Family*

Purchased ________, Price $ ___________

You Are My Gift From Above, 891738

$55.00
$50.00
$50.00
$50.00
$50.00

Open, Issue Price $50.00, '02
Series: *Family*

Purchased ________, Price $ ___________

Healing Begins With Forgiveness, 892157

$55.00
$53.00
$50.00

Suspended 2003, Issue Price $45.00, '02
Series: *Family*

Purchased ________, Price $ ___________

Ewe Are So Precious To Me, 892726

$50.00
$45.00
$45.00
$45.00
$45.00

Open, Issue Price $45.00, '02

Purchased ________, Price $ ___________

☐ *Overalls, I Think You're Special, 898147*

$53.00
$50.00
$48.00
$45.00
$45.00

Retired 2005, Issue Price $45.00, '02
Series: *Country Lane Collection*
Purchased ________, Price $ ____________

☐ *How Can I Says Thanks, 898309*

UM $35.00
$35.00

Open, Issue Price $35.00, '02
Chapel Exclusive
Purchased ________, Price $ ____________

☐ *How Can I Says Thanks, 898317 (Ornament)*

UM $20.00
$20.00

Open, Issue Price $20.00, '02
Chapel Exclusive
Purchased ________, Price $ ____________

☐ *Scent From Above To Share His Love, 898325*

$30.00

Open, Issue Price $30.00, '05
Chapel Exclusive
Purchased ________, Price $ ____________

☐ *Loving, Caring And Shearing, 898414*

$70.00

Limited Ed. 10,000, Issue Price $60.00, '01
Purchased ________, Price $ ____________

☐ *You Are My Favorite Dish, 898457*

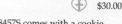

$35.00
$30.00

898457S comes with a cookie cutter, has Cross in Heart mark, and is valued at $25.00.

Retired 2002, Issue Price $25.00, '02
Purchased ____________,
Price $ ____________

☐ *Jesus Loves Me (Latino), 899526*

$25.00
$23.00
$20.00
$20.00
$20.00

Open, Issue Price $20.00, '01
Purchased ________, Price $ ___________

☐ *Jesus Loves Me (African-American), 899879*

$25.00
$23.00
$20.00
$20.00
$20.00

Open, Issue Price $20.00, '01
Purchased ________, Price $ ___________

☐ *Jesus Loves Me (Latino), 899542*

$25.00
$23.00
$20.00
$20.00
$20.00

Open, Issue Price $20.00, '01
Purchased ________, Price $ ___________

☐ *Jesus Loves Me (Asian), 900575*

$25.00
$23.00
$20.00
$20.00
$20.00

Open, Issue Price $20.00, '01
Purchased ________, Price $ ___________

☐ *Jesus Loves Me (African-American), 899771*

$25.00
$23.00
$20.00
$20.00
$20.00

Open, Issue Price $20.00, '01
Purchased ________, Price $ ___________

☐ *Jesus Loves Me (Asian), 901555*

$25.00
$23.00
$20.00
$20.00
$20.00

Open, Issue Price $20.00, '01
Purchased ________, Price $ ___________

☐ *Best Man (Hispanic), 901563*

$30.00
$28.00
$25.00
$25.00
$25.00

Open, Issue Price $25.00, '02
Purchased ________, Price $ __________

☐ *Maid Of Honor (African-American), 902039*

$30.00
$28.00
$25.00
$25.00
$25.00

Open, Issue Price $25.00, '02
Purchased ________, Price $ __________

☐ *Maid Of Honor (Hispanic), 901571*

$30.00
$28.00
$25.00
$25.00
$25.00

Open, Issue Price $25.00, '02
Purchased ________, Price $ __________

☐ *Best Man (Asian), 902047*

$30.00
$28.00
$25.00
$25.00
$25.00

Open, Issue Price $25.00, '02
Purchased ________, Price $ __________

☐ *Best Man (African-American), 902020*

$30.00
$28.00
$25.00
$25.00
$25.00

Open, Issue Price $25.00, '02
Purchased ________, Price $ __________

☐ *Maid Of Honor (Asian), 902055*

$30.00
$28.00
$25.00
$25.00
$25.00

Open, Issue Price $25.00, '02
Purchased ________, Price $ __________

Un Dia Muy Especial (A Very Special Day), 902098

$35.00
$30.00
$30.00
$30.00
$30.00

Open, Issue Price $30.00, '01
Purchased ________, Price $ ___________

Preparado Con Amor (Prepared With Love), 928445

$40.00
$35.00
$35.00
$35.00
$35.00

Open, Issue Price $35.00, '01
Purchased ________, Price $ ___________

Una Madres Es El Corazon De La Familia (A Mother Is The Heart Of The Family), 902101

$35.00
$30.00
$30.00
$30.00
$30.00

Open, Issue Price $30.00, '01
Purchased ________, Price $ ___________

Seguro In Los Brazos De Padrinos (Safe In The Arms Of Godparents), 928453

$55.00
$50.00
$50.00
$50.00
$50.00

Open, Issue Price $50.00, '01
Purchased ________, Price $ ___________

God's Precious Pearl Of The Ozarks, 927899

UM $38.00
$35.00
$33.00
$30.00
$30.00

Open, Issue Price $30.00, '01
Chapel Exclusive
Purchased ________, Price $ ___________

Mi Pequeno Amor (My Little Sweetheart), 928461

$35.00
$30.00
$30.00
$30.00
$30.00

Open, Issue Price $40.00, '01
Purchased ________, Price $ ___________

☐ *Una Bendesion Del Cielo (A Blessing From Heaven), 928488*

$45.00
$40.00
$40.00
$40.00
$40.00

Open, Issue Price $40.00, '01
Purchased ________, Price $ ___________

☐ *I Am A Bee-liever, 928534*

$35.00
$30.00
$30.00
$30.00

Open, Issue Price $30.00, '02
Series: *Trusting Is Bee-lieving*
Purchased ________, Price $ ___________

☐ *Precious Friends, 928542*

$45.00
$40.00
$40.00
$40.00
$40.00

Open, Issue Price $40.00, '02
Purchased ________, Price $ ___________

☐ *The Lord Is Always Bee-side Us, 928550*

$37.50
$37.50
$37.50
$37.50

Open, Issue Price $37.50, '02
Purchased ________, Price $ ___________

☐ *Worthy Is The Lamb, 928569*

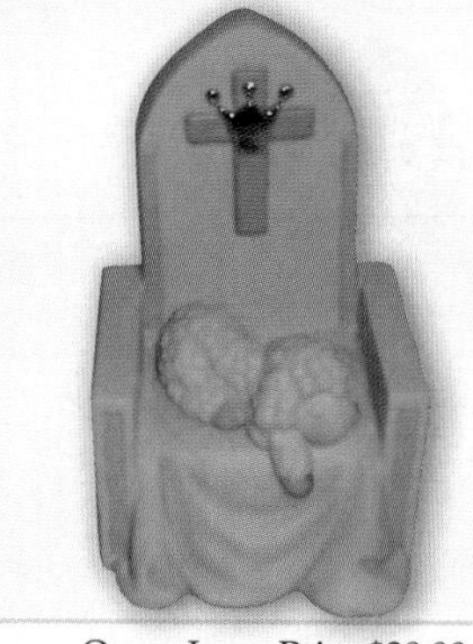

UM $35.00
$30.00
$30.00
$30.00

Open, Issue Price $30.00, '02
Chapel Exclusive
Purchased ________, Price $ ___________

☐ *Worthy Is The Lamb, 928577 (Ornament)*

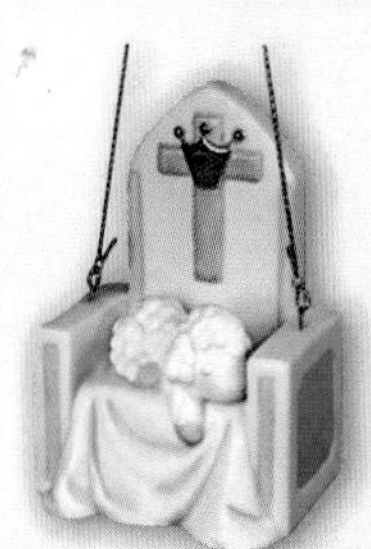

UM $20.00
$18.50
$18.50
$18.50

Open, Issue Price $18.50, '02
Chapel Exclusive
Purchased ________, Price $ ___________

It Came Upon A Midnight Clear, 928585 (Tree Topper)

UM $125.00

Limited Ed. 2,500, Issue Price $125.00, '02
Chapel Exclusive

Purchased ________, Price $ ___________

My Teacher, My Friend, 928607

UM $75.00
$73.00
$70.00
$70.00

Open, Issue Price $70.00, '02
Chapel Exclusive

Purchased ________, Price $ ___________

Ice See In You A Champion, 934852 (Ornament)

$25.00

Limited Ed., Issue Price $25.00, '02
Canadian Exclusive

Purchased ________, Price $ ___________

We've Got The Right Plan, 937282

$90.00
$85.00
$83.00
$80.00

Suspended 2004, Issue Price $80.00, '02

Purchased ________, Price $ ___________

Our Heroes In The Sky, 958832

$40.00
$35.00
$35.00
$35.00

Open, Issue Price $35.00, '02

Purchased ________, Price $ ___________

Our Heroes In The Sky, 958840

$40.00
$35.00
$35.00
$35.00

Open, Issue Price $35.00, '02

Purchased ________, Price $ ___________

☐ *Galloping Towards Tomorrow, 958859*

$25.00
$23.00

Retired 2003, Issue Price $17.50, '02
Japan Early Release
Purchased ________, Price $ ___________

☐ *I See Bright Hope In Your Future, 973912*

$60.00

Limited Ed., Issue Price $50.00, '02
2002 Show Exclusive
Purchased ________, Price $ ___________

☐ *Faith Is Heaven's Sweet Song, 975893*

$130.00
$125.00
$125.00
$125.00

Open, Issue Price $125.00, '02
Easter Seals Exclusive
Series: *Heaven's Grace* – 1st Edition
Purchased ______,
Price $ ___________

☐ *We're Behind You All The Way, 994863*

$25.00
$20.00
$20.00
$20.00

Open, Issue Price $20.00, '02
Series: *Animal Affections*
Purchased ________, Price $ ___________

☐ *Miracles Can Happen, 994871*

$25.00
$20.00
$20.00
$20.00

Open, Issue Price $20.00, '02
Series: *Animal Affections*
Purchased ________, Price $ ___________

☐ *Holy Mackerel It's Your Birthday! 994898*

$25.00
$20.00
$20.00
$20.00

Open, Issue Price $20.00, '02
Series: *Animal Affections*
Purchased ________, Price $ ___________

For His Precious Love, 0000364

$30.00

$30.00

Open, Issue Price $30.00, '04

Purchased ________, Price $ ___________

For His Precious Love, 0000365

$30.00

$30.00

Open, Issue Price $30.00, '04

Purchased __________,

Price $ ___________

A Family Of Love, 0000366

$45.00

$45.00

Open, Issue Price $45.00, '04

Purchased ________, Price $ ___________

You're Purr-fect, Pumpkin, 0000367

$37.50

$37.50

Open, Issue Price $37.50, '04

Purchased ________, Price $ ___________

Give With A Grateful Heart, 0000382

$30.00

$30.00

Open, Issue Price $30.00, '04

Purchased ________, Price $ ___________

Arose On Her Toes, 0000383

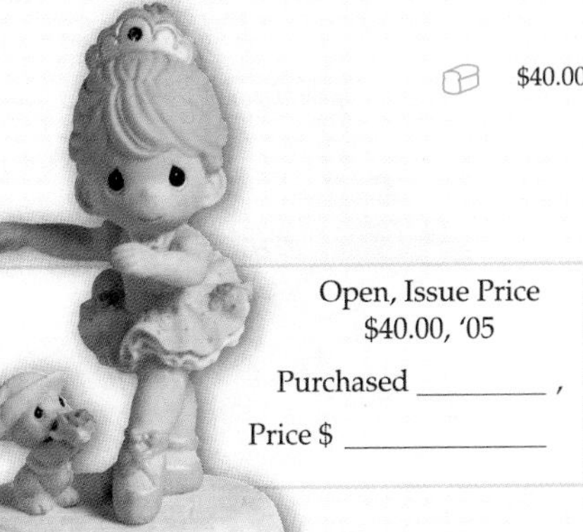

$40.00

Open, Issue Price $40.00, '05

Purchased ________,

Price $ ___________

Twinkle, Twinkle, You're A Star, 0000384

$37.50

$37.50

Limited Ed. 10,000, Issue Price $37.50, '04
Series: *Pretty As A Princess*

Purchased_____ ,
Price $ ________

Too Dog-Gone Sweet, 0000387

$37.50

$37.50

Limited Ed. 10,000, Issue Price $37.50, '04
Series: *Pretty As A Princess*

Purchased_______ ,
Price $ __________

Love Is Reflected In You, 0000385

$37.50

$37.50

Limited Ed. 10,000, Issue Price $37.50, '04
Series: *Pretty As A Princess*

Purchased _________, Price $ ____________

You Color My World, 0000615

$50.00

$50.00

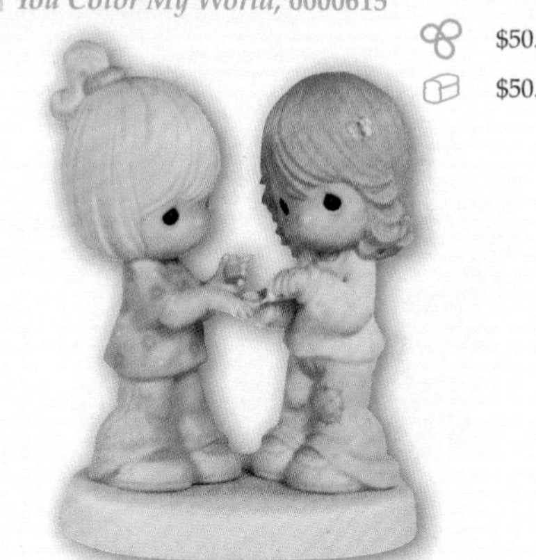

Limited Ed., Issue Price $50.00, '04
Carlton Cards/American Greetings Early Release

Purchased _________, Price $ ___________

Sunshine Brings A Purr-fect Friend, 0000386

$37.50

$37.50

Limited Ed. 10,000, Issue Price $37.50, '04
Series: *Pretty As A Princess*

Purchased _________, Price $ _________

I Give You My Heart, 0000974

$40.00

Open, Issue Price $40.00, '05

Purchased__________ ,
Price $___________

☐ *Calling All My Party Girls, 4001029*

$45.00

Open, Issue Price $45.00, '05

Purchased ________, Price $ __________

☐ *Some Bunny Loves You, 4001247*

$50.00

$50.00

Open, Issue Price $50.00, '04

Purchased________,

Price $ __________

☐ *Blooming In God's Love, 4001245*

$50.00 $50.00

Open, Issue Price $50.00, '04

Purchased __________,

Price $_________

☐ *Actions Speak Louder Than Words, 4001570*

"Actions Speak Louder Than Words"

$100.00

Limited Ed. 3,000, Issue Price $100.00, '05
Precious Moments Premier Collection
Charter Figurine

Purchased ________, Price $ __________

☐ *Love Will Carry You Through, 4001246*

$50.00 $50.00

Open, Issue Price $50.00, '04

Purchased _________,

Price $___________

☐ *Make Everything A Masterpiece, 4001571*

$135.00

"Make Everything A Masterpiece"

Limited Ed. 3,000, Issue Price $135.00, '05
Precious Moments Premier Collection
Charter Figurine

Purchased ________, Price $ __________

☐ *Praise Him With Resounding Cymbals,* 4001572

$115.00

Limited Ed. 3,000, Issue Price $115.00, '05
Precious Moments Premier Collection
Charter Figurine
Purchased ________, Price $ ___________

☐ *An Angel In Disguise,* 4001573

$115.00

Limited Ed. 3,000, Issue Price $115.00, '05
Precious Moments Premier Collection
Charter Figurine
Purchased ________, Price $ ___________

☐ *We Fix Souls,* 4001574

$135.00

Limited Ed. 3,000, Issue Price $135.00, '05
Precious Moments Premier Collection
Charter Figurine
Purchased ________, Price $ ___________

☐ *Always Close To My Heart,* 4001645

$35.00

Open, Issue Price $35.00, '05
Purchased ________, Price $ ___________

☐ *Count Your Blessings,* 4001646

$50.00

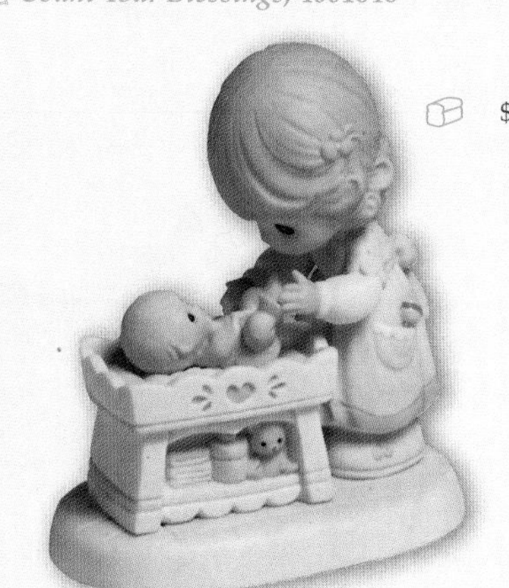

Open, Issue Price $50.00, '05
Purchased ________, Price $ ___________

S'More Time Spent With You, 4001647

$55.00

Open, Issue Price $55.00, '05

Purchased ________, Price $ ___________

Can I Have This Dance For The Rest Of My Life, 4001655

$50.00

Open, Issue Price $50.00, '05

Purchased ________, Price $ ___________

A Mother's Love Is A Warm Glow, 4001650

$45.00

Comes with a tulip candle.

Suspended 2005, Issue Price $45.00, '05

Purchased ________, Price $ ___________

You Are A Precious Gift, 4001656

$25.00

Open, Issue Price $25.00, '05

Purchased______________,

Price $ _______________

I'm Always Bee-Side You, 4001661

$45.00

$45.00

Open, Issue Price $45.00, '04 Easter Seals Exclusive

Purchased _______ ,

Price $ __________

'Til The End Of Time, 4001653

$60.00

Open, Issue Price $60.00, '05

Purchased ________, Price $ ___________

☐ *It's Time To Blow Your Own Horn*, 4001664

$50.00

Open, Issue Price $50.00, '05
Purchased ________, Price $ ____________

☐ *Tuning In To Happy Times*, 4001669

$50.00

Limited Ed. 7,500, Issue Price $50.00, '05
Series: *Through The Years*
Purchased ________, Price $ ____________

☐ *Cent With Love*, 4001667

$25.00

Open, Issue Price $25.00, '05
Purchased ________,
Price $____________

☐ *Hopping For The Best*, 4001670

$50.00

Limited Ed. 7,500, Issue Price $50.00, '05
Series: *Through The Years*
Purchased ________, Price $ ____________

☐ *I Love You This Much*, 4001668

$30.00

Open, Issue Price $30.00, '05
Purchased _______,
Price $__________

☐ *From Small Beginnings Come Great Things*, 4001671

$50.00

Limited Ed. 7,500, Issue Price $50.00, '05
Series: *Through The Years*
Purchased__________,
Price $ ___________

I Love You This Much, 4001673

$30.00

Open, Issue Price $30.00, '05

Purchased ________ ,

Price $ __________

By Your Side Forever And Always, 4001778

$90.00

Limited Ed. 1,500, Issue Price $90.00, '05
Chapel Exclusive

Purchased ________, Price $ ___________

I'm Yours Heart And Soul, 4001779

$100.00

Open, Issue Price $100.00, '05
Chapel Exclusive

Purchased ________, Price $ ___________

You Take The Cake, 4001780

$50.00

Open, Issue Price $50.00, '05
Chapel Exclusive

Purchased ________, Price $ ___________

Renew Faith, Restore Hope, Replenish Love, 4001784

$75.00

Limited Ed. 2,000, Issue Price $75.00, '05
Precious Moments Premier Collection
CCR Exclusive
Series: *Four Seasons Carousel Horse*

Purchased ________, Price $ ___________

Allow Sunshine And Laughter To Fill Your Days, 4001785

$75.00

Limited Ed. 2,000, Issue Price $75.00, '05
Precious Moments Premier Collection
CCR Exclusive
Series: *Four Seasons Carousel Horse*

Purchased ________, Price $ ___________

A Winter Wonderland Awaits, 4001787

$75.00

Limited Ed. 2,000, Issue Price $75.00, '05
Precious Moments Premier Collection
CCR Exclusive
Series: *Four Seasons Carousel Horse*

Purchased ________, Price $ ___________

Reflect And Give Thanks For All Of Life's Bounty, 4001786

$75.00

Limited Ed. 2,000, Issue Price $75.00, '05
Precious Moments Premier Collection
CCR Exclusive
Series: *Four Seasons Carousel Horse*

Purchased ________, Price $ ___________

I Picked You To Love, 4001810

$30.00

Open, Issue Price $30.00, '05

Purchased ________, Price $ ___________

☐ *I Picked You To Love, 4001811*

$30.00

Open, Issue Price
$30.00, '05

Purchased ________ ,

Price $____________

☐ *The Tassel Was No Hassle, 4001812*

$40.00

Open, Issue Price $40.00, '05

Purchased _________ , Price $ ____________

☐ *A Bead-azzling Friendship, 4001947*

$40.00

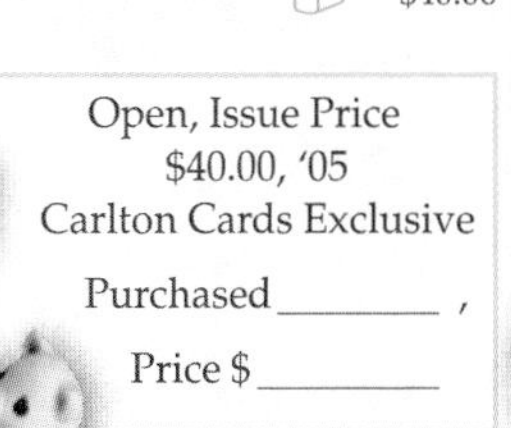

Open, Issue Price
$40.00, '05
Carlton Cards Exclusive

Purchased________ ,

Price $__________

☐ *May Your Holidays Be So-Sew Special, 4003161 (Ornament)*

$20.00

Open, Issue Price
$20.00, '05

Purchased ________ ,

Price $_____________

☐ *May Your Holidays Be So-Sew Special, 4003162 (Ornament)*

$30.00

Open, Issue Price $30.00, '05

Purchased _________ , Price $ ____________

☐ *Our First Christmas Together, 4003163 (Ornament)*

$20.00

Open, Issue Price
$20.00, '05

Purchased_____________ ,

Price $_______________

☐ *True Friends Have One Heart, 4003164*

$60.00

Open, Issue Price $60.00, '05

Purchased _________ , Price $ ____________

☐ *You Light Up My Holly-Days,* 4003165

$45.00

Open, Issue Price $45.00, '05

Purchased ________, Price $ ___________

☐ *Thankful For My Family,* 4003166

$70.00

Open, Issue Price $70.00, '05

Purchased ________, Price $ ___________

☐ *Merry Christmas To Ewe,* 4003168

$35.00

Open, Issue Price $35.00, '05

Purchased ________, Price $ ___________

☐ *Star Of Wonder,* 4003169

$45.00

Limited Ed., Issue Price $45.00, '05

Purchased ________, Price $ ___________

☐ *There's No Place Like Home For Christmas,* 4003172

$35.00

Comes with photo frame stocking ornament.

Open, Issue Price $35.00, '05

Purchased ________, Price $ ___________

☐ *Rejoicing In God's Gift Of You*, 4003174

$35.00

Open, Issue Price $35.00, '05

Purchased ________, Price $ ___________

☐ *Together Is The Nicest Place To Be*, 4003175

$75.00

Open, Issue Price $75.00, '05

Purchased ________, Price $ ___________

☐ *Sing Songs Of Praise To Him*, 4003176 (Musical)

$145.00

Limited Ed. 5,000, Issue Price $145.00, '05
Tune: "Silent Night"

Purchased ________, Price $ ___________

☐ *You're The Cymbal Of Perfection*, 4003177

$35.00

Open, Issue Price $35.00, '05
Nativity Addition

Purchased ________, Price $ ___________

☐ *His Truth Is Marching On*, 4003178

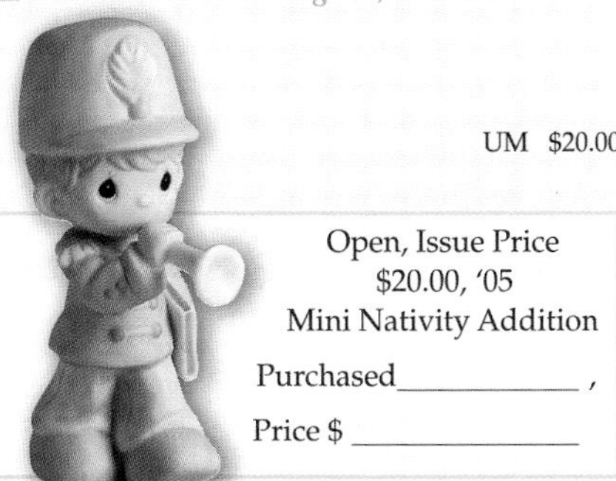

UM $20.00

Open, Issue Price
$20.00, '05
Mini Nativity Addition

Purchased___________ ,

Price $ ____________

☐ *Angels Keep While Shepherds Sleep*, 4003179

$65.00

Open, Issue Price $65.00, '05

Purchased ________, Price $ ___________

Sprinkled In Sweetness, 4003182

$60.00

Open, Issue Price $60.00, '05

Purchased ________, Price $ ___________

Until We Meet Again, 4003183

$40.00

Open, Issue Price $40.00, '05
Chapel Exclusive

Purchased ________, Price $ ___________

"A Hui Hou," Til We Meet Again, 4003245

$35.00

Limited Ed., Gift, '05
2005 Hawaii Event Exclusive

Purchased________,

Price $___________

"Pi'I Mai Ka Nalu," Surf's Up! 4003247

$35.00

Limited Ed., Gift, '05
2005 Hawaii Event Exclusive

Purchased ________,

Price $___________

"Mahlo Hawi'I," Thank You Hawaii, 4003248

$35.00

Limited Ed., Gift, '05
2005 Hawaii Event Exclusive

Purchased ________, Price $ ___________

"Aloha Kakou A Pau," Aloha Everyone, 4003249

$40.00

Limited Ed., Gift, '05
2005 Hawaii Event Exclusive

Purchased ________, Price $ ___________

"Aloha Aina" Love Of The Land, 4003250

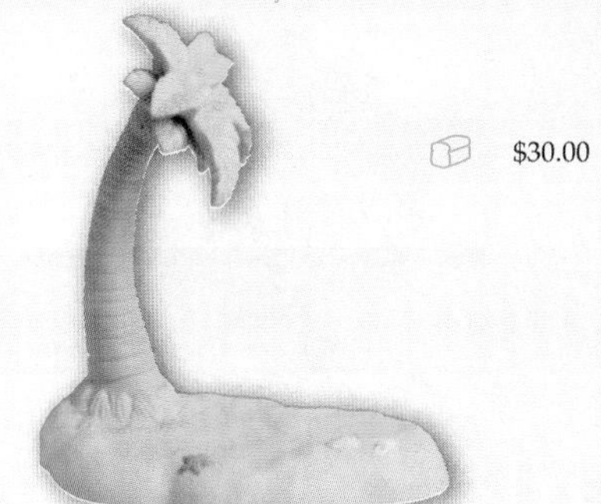

$30.00

Limited Ed., Gift, '05
2005 Hawaii Event Exclusive

Purchased ________, Price $ ___________

"Wiki Wiki Transit" Quick Transportation, 4003251

$45.00

Limited Ed., Gift, '05
2005 Hawaii Event Exclusive

Purchased ________, Price $ ___________

Snowman in Top Hat — Streetlight, 4003322

$15.00

Open, Issue Price $15.00, '05

Purchased ________, Price $ ___________

Snowman Christmas Tree, 4003323

$20.00

Open, Issue Price $20.00, '05

Purchased ________, Price $ ___________

Snowman Holding Lantern, 4003324

$15.00

Open, Issue Price $15.00, '05

Purchased ________, Price $ ___________

Snowman Holding Wreath, 4003325

$15.00

Open, Issue Price $15.00, '05

Purchased________,

Price $ ___________

Boy Placing Star On Tree, 4003327 (Nightlight)

$40.00

Open, Issue Price $40.00, '05

Purchased ________, Price $ ____________

Nativity, 4003328

$20.00

Open, Issue Price $20.00, '05

Purchased ________, Price $ ____________

Special Times With Mom Create Special Memories, 4003585

$50.00

Open, Issue Price $50.00, '05

Purchased ________, Price $ ____________

Happiness Is Best Shared Together, 4004156

$75.00

Open, Issue Price $75.00, '05
Disney Theme Park Exclusive

Purchased ________, Price $ ____________

Who Says A Mouse Can't Be Cute? 4004157

$35.00

Open, Issue Price $75.00, '05

Purchased ________, Price $ ____________

Everything's Better With A Friend, 4004158

$60.00

Open, Issue Price $60.00, '05

Purchased ________, Price $ ____________

Make Every Day Magical, 4004159

$45.00

Open, Issue Price $45.00, '05

Purchased ________, Price $ ___________

This Bears My Love For You (Girl), 4004371

$35.00

Open, Issue Price $35.00, '05

Purchased ________, Price $ ___________

I M The One You Love, 4004372

$25.00

Open, Issue Price $25.00, '05

Purchased ________, Price $ ___________

The Same Today, Yesterday And Forever, 4004373

$35.00

Open, Issue Price $35.00, '05

Purchased ________, Price $ ___________

Heaven Sent, 4004374

$37.50

Open, Issue Price $37.50, '05

Purchased ________, Price $ ___________

You Were Made For Me, 4004375

$35.00

Available at Distinguished Service Retailers during a special one-day event on November 19, 2005.

Event Piece, Issue Price $35.00, '05

Purchased ________, Price $ ___________

You Were Made For Me, 4004376 (Ornament)

$12.00

Available at Distinguished Service Retailers during a special one-day event on November 19, 2005.

Event Piece, Issue Price $12.00, '05

Purchased ______________ ,

Price $ ______________

Light Of Hope, 4004378

$40.00

Open, Issue Price $40.00, '05

Chapel Exclusive

Purchased ___________ ,

Price $ ___________

Light Of Hope, 4004379 (Ornament)

$25.00

Open, Issue Price $25.00, '05

Chapel Exclusive

Purchased ___________ ,

Price $ ___________

I'm So Glad I Picked You, 4004380

$35.00

Open, Issue Price $35.00, '05

Purchased ____________ ,

Price $ ____________

Baby's First Christmas, 4024080 (Ornament)

$20.00

Open, Issue Price $20.00, '05

Purchased ____________ ,

Price $ ____________

Baby's First Christmas, 4024081 (Ornament)

$20.00

Open, Issue Price $20.00, '05

Purchased ____________ ,

Price $ ____________

The Purr-fect Gift, 4024082 (Ornament)

$20.00

Open, Issue Price $20.00, '05

Purchased ___________ ,

Price $ ___________

This Bears My Love For You (Boy), 4024083

$35.00

Open, Issue Price $35.00, '05

Purchased _________ , Price $ _________

☐ *Love Is A Warm Heart On A Cold Day,* 4024084

$30.00

Open, Issue Price $30.00, '05

Purchased ________ ,

Price $ ____________

☐ *His Hope Lights My Way,* 4024085

$50.00

Open, Issue Price $50.00, '05

Purchased _________, Price $ ____________

☐ *Faithful Follower,* 4024086

$40.00

Open, Issue Price $40.00, '05

Purchased _________, Price $ ____________

☐ *Scatter Joy,* 4024087

$50.00

Open, Issue Price $50.00, '05

Purchased _________, Price $ ____________

☐ *May Your Holidays Be So-Sew Special,* 4024088

$35.00

Open, Issue Price $35.00, '05

Purchased _________, Price $ ____________

☐ *No Rest For The Weary,* 4024100 (Ornament)

$20.00

Open, Issue Price $20.00, '05

Purchased ___________ ,

Price $ ____________

☐ *Grandma, I'll Never Outgrow You!* 4024101 (Ornament)

$20.00

Open, Issue Price $20.00, '05

Purchased ____________ ,

Price $ ____________

☐ *Sister, You Have A Heart Of Gold*, 4024102 (Ornament)

$20.00

Open, Issue Price $20.00, '05

Purchased ____________ ,

Price $ ____________

☐ *Daughter, You'll Always Be My Princess*, 4024103 (Ornament)

$20.00

Open, Issue Price $20.00, '05

Purchased ____________ ,

Price $ ____________

☐ *Blessed With A Loving Godmother*, 4024104 (Ornament)

$20.00

Open, Issue Price $20.00, '05

Purchased ____________ ,

Price $ ____________

☐ *Grandma's Little Angel*, 4024105 (Ornament)

$20.00

Open, Issue Price $20.00, '05

Purchased ____________ ,

Price $ ____________

☐ *I Can't Give You Anything But Love*, 4024106 (Ornament)

$20.00

Open, Issue Price $20.00, '05

Purchased ____________ ,

Price $ ____________

☐ *You're A Gem Of A Friend*, 4024107 (Ornament)

$20.00

Open, Issue Price $20.00, '05

Purchased ____________ ,

Price $ ____________

☐ *A Nurse's Care Is The Best Medicine*, 4024108 (Ornament)

$20.00

Open, Issue Price $20.00, '05

Purchased ____________ ,

Price $ ____________

☐ *Teacher, You're A Precious Work Of Art,* **4024109 (Ornament)**

$20.00

Open, Issue
Price $20.00, '05

Purchased ______________ ,

Price $ ______________

☐ *You'll Always Be A Winner To Me,* **4024111 (Ornament)**

$20.00

Open, Issue
Price $20.00, '05

Purchased ______________ ,

Price $ ______________

☐ *Serving Up Fun,* **4024110 (Ornament)**

$20.00

Open, Issue
Price $20.00, '05

Purchased ______________ ,

Price $ ______________

☐ *Your Spirit Is An Inspiration,* **4024112 (Ornament)**

$20.00

Open, Issue
Price $20.00, '05

Purchased ______________ ,

Price $ ______________

Collector's Club

☐ *I Will Make You Fishers Of Men* (Lithograph)

UM $30.00

Club members entitled to this exclusive lithograph free with purchase of $25.00 on January 25, 2002.

Members Only, Gift, '02

Purchased ________, Price $ ___________

☐ *Bubble Your Troubles Away,* 101730

$45.00

$40.00

Members Only, Issue Price $45.00, '02

Purchased ________, Price $ ___________

☐ *God Bless Our Years Together,* 12440

There have been reports of this piece being completely unpainted.

$300.00

Members Only,
Issue Price $175.00, '85
Fifth Anniversary Club
Commemorative

Purchased ________, Price $ ___________

☐ *A Portrait Of Loving, Caring And Sharing,* 108543

Available for preorder from January 25 through February 19, 2003.

$400.00

$375.00

Members Only,
Issue Price $375.00, '03
Limited Ed.

Purchased ________, Price $ ___________

☐ *The Sweetest Treat Is Friendship, 110855*

$55.00

Members Only, Issue Price $55.00, '03

Purchased ________, Price $ __________

☐ *Teach Us To Love One Another, 211672*

$25.00

Members Only, Issue Price $7.00, '96

Purchased ________, Price $ __________

☐ *You Make My Heart Soar, 118316*

$35.00

$35.00

Open, Issue Price $35.00, '05

Purchased ________, Price $ __________

☐ *Celebrating A Decade Of Loving, Caring And Sharing, 227986 (Ornament)*

UM $15.00

Members Only, Issue Price $7.00, '89

Purchased ________,

Price $ __________

☐ *Our Club Is Soda-licious, 266841 (Ornament)*

$350.00

Members Only, Gift, '96 Convention Ornament

Purchased ________,

Price $ __________

☐ *A Perfect Display Of 15 Happy Years, 127817*

Club's fifteenth anniversary commemorative figurine.

$140.00

Members Only, Issue Price $100.00, '95

Purchased ________, Price $ __________

☐ *Rejoice In The Victory, 283541*

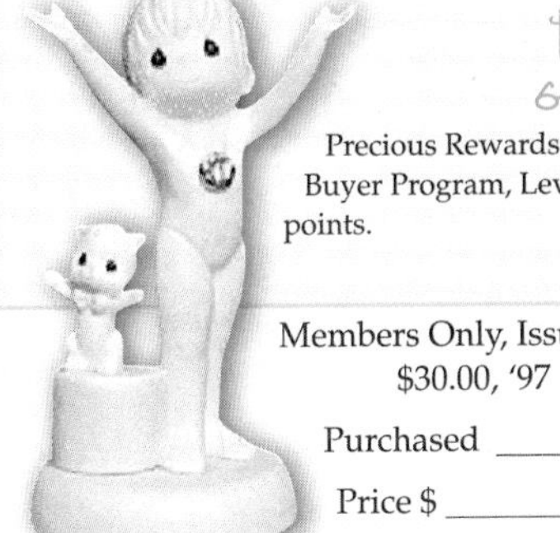

$60.00

$55.00

Precious Rewards Frequent Buyer Program, Level 1: 300 points.

Members Only, Issue Price $30.00, '97

Purchased ________,

Price $ __________

☐ *God Bless You With Bouquets Of Victory, 283584*

$75.00

$70.00

Precious Rewards Frequent Buyer Program, Level 2: 500 points.

Members Only, Issue Price $50.00, '97

Purchased ________, Price $ __________

☐ *Faith Is The Victory, 283592*

$135.00

$125.00

Precious Rewards Frequent Buyer Program, Level 3: 1,000 points.

Members Only, Issue Price $75.00, '97

Purchased ________, Price $ __________

☐ *Put On A Happy Face, 440906 (Mask)*

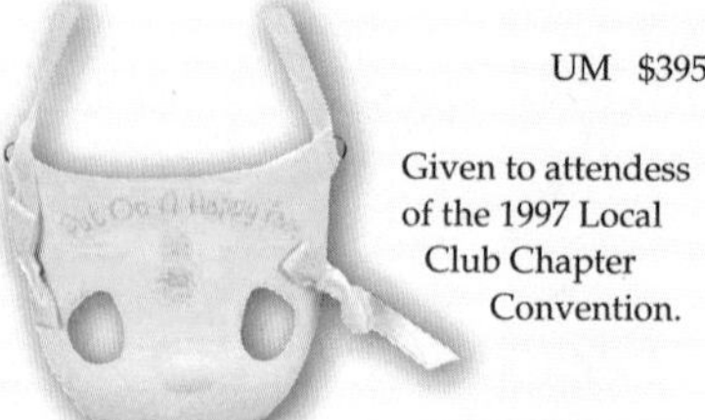

UM $395.00

Given to attendess of the 1997 Local Club Chapter Convention.

Convention Gift, '97

Purchased ________, Price $ __________

☐ *Delivering Good News To You, 488135*

$55.00

$50.00

Gift to club members who purchased $35.00 or more during June 21, 2003 event.

Members Only, Gift, '03 DSR & CCR Event

Purchased ________, Price $ __________

☐ *God Loveth A Cheerful Giver, 495891 (Box)*

UM $35.00

Gift to club members joining by June 30, 1998.

Members Only, Gift, '98

Purchased ________,

Price $ __________

☐ *A Growing Love, 520349 (Ornament)*

$80.00

Members Only, Issue Price $15.00, '88

Purchased ________,

Price $ __________

☐ *Always Room For One More, 522961 (Ornament)*

$85.00

Members Only, Issue Price $15.00, '89

Purchased ________,

Price $__________

This Land Is Our Land, 527386

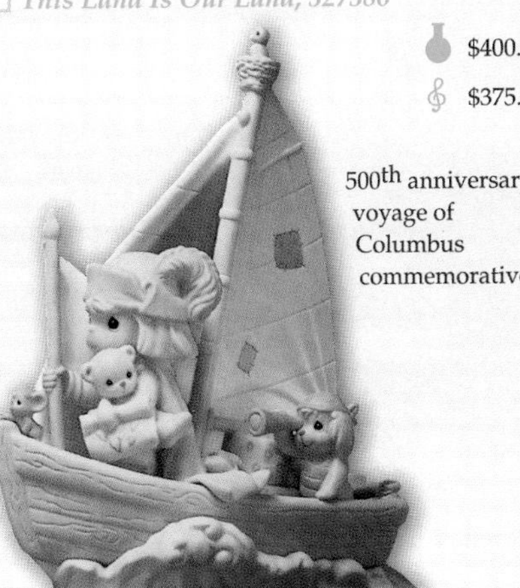

$400.00
$375.00

500th anniversary voyage of Columbus commemorative.

Members Only, Issue Price $350.00, '92

Purchased ________, Price $ ___________

You Fill The Pages Of My Life, 530980

$70.00

Came with collector's edition of the book, *Precious Moments Last Forever.*

Members Only, Issue Price $32.50, '94

Purchased ________, Price $ ___________

A Salute To Our Stars, 549614 (Medallion)

$350.00

Convention Gift, '98

Purchased ________, Price $ ___________

Thank You For Your Membership, 635243

$95.00
$85.00
$80.00
$75.00
$70.00

Five-year membership piece.

Members Only, Issue Price $30.00, '99

Purchased ________, Price $ ___________

A Club Where Friendships Are Made, 635251

$105.00
$100.00
$90.00
$80.00
$75.00

Ten-year membership piece.

Members Only, Issue Price $40.00, '99

Purchased ________, Price $ ___________

A Club Where Fellowship Reigns, 635278

$120.00
$110.00
$95.00
$90.00
$85.00

Fifteen-year membership piece.

Members Only, Issue Price $50.00, '99

Purchased ________, Price $ ___________

☐ *Companionship Happens In Our Club,* 635286

$130.00

$120.00

$105.00

$100.00

$95.00

Twenty-year membership piece.

Members Only, Issue Price $60.00, '99

Purchased ________, Price $ ____________

☐ *You Are The Heart Of Precious Moments,* 681016 (Medallion)

UM $450.00

1999 local club chapter convention.

Limited Ed. 600, Members Only, '99

Purchased ________, Price $ ____________

☐ *A Beary Loving Collector,* 823953

$45.00

$40.00

Members Only, Issue Price $15.00, '01
Club Exclusive

Purchased ________, Price $ ____________

☐ *Always Room For One More,* C-0009

$45.00 $38.00

Members Only pieces through C-0025 were also issued as Charter Members Only pieces, adding 100 to the item number (i.e., C-0009 was also issued as C-0109).

Members Only, Issue Price $19.50, '89

Purchased ________, Price $ ____________

☐ *My Happiness,* C-0010

$42.00

$40.00

Members Only, Issue Price $21.00, '90

Purchased ________, Price $ ____________

☐ *Sharing The Good News Together,* C-0011

$45.00

$43.00

Members Only, Issue Price $22.50, '91

Purchased ________, Price $ ____________

The Club That's Out Of This World, C-0012

$48.00

$45.00

Members Only, Issue Price $25.00, '92

Purchased _________, Price $ ___________

You're The Sweetest Cookie In The Batch, C-0015

$45.00

$43.00

Members Only, Issue Price $27.00, '95

Purchased _________, Price $ ___________

Loving, Caring And Sharing Along The Way, C-0013

$40.00

$35.00

Members Only, Issue Price $25.00, '93

Purchased _________, Price $ ___________

You're As Pretty As A Picture, C-0016

$33.00

$30.00

Members Only, Issue Price $25.00, '96

Purchased _________, Price $ ___________

You Are The End Of My Rainbow, C-0014

$35.00

$30.00

Members Only, Issue Price $26.00, '94

Purchased _________, Price $ ___________

A Special Toast To Precious Moments, C-0017

$40.00

$35.00

Members Only, Issue Price $25.00, '97

Purchased _________, Price $ ___________

☐ *Focusing In On Those Precious Moments, C-0018*

$35.00

$28.00

Members Only, Issue Price $28.00, '98

Purchased ________, Price $ __________

☐ *Wishing You A World Of Peace, C-0019*

$45.00

$43.00

Members Only, Issue Price $25.00, '99

Purchased ________, Price $ __________

☐ *Thanks A Bunch, C-0020*

$33.00

$30.00

Members Only, Issue Price $28.50, '00

Purchased ________, Price $ __________

☐ *Friends Write From The Start, C-0021*

$35.00

$33.00

Members Only, Issue Price $28.50, '01

Purchased ________, Price $ __________

☐ *It's Time To Bless Your Own Day, C-0022*

$35.00

$32.00

Members Only, Issue Price $25.00, '02

Purchased ________, Price $ __________

☐ *There's Always A Place In My Heart For You, C-0023*

$35.00

$33.00

Members Only, Issue Price $25.00, '03

Purchased ________, Price $ __________

☐ *The Road To A Friend Is Never Long,* C-0024

$35.00

$35.00

Members Only, Gift, '04

Purchased ________, Price $ ____________

☐ *Map A Route Toward Loving, Caring And Sharing,* C-0025

$40.00

$40.00

Members Only, Gift, '04

Purchased ________, Price $ ____________

☐ *But Love Goes On Forever,* E-0001

UM $200.00

$175.00

$165.00

Charter Members Only, Issue Price $15.00, '81

Purchased ____ ,

Price $ _______

☐ *Seek And Ye Shall Find,* E-0005

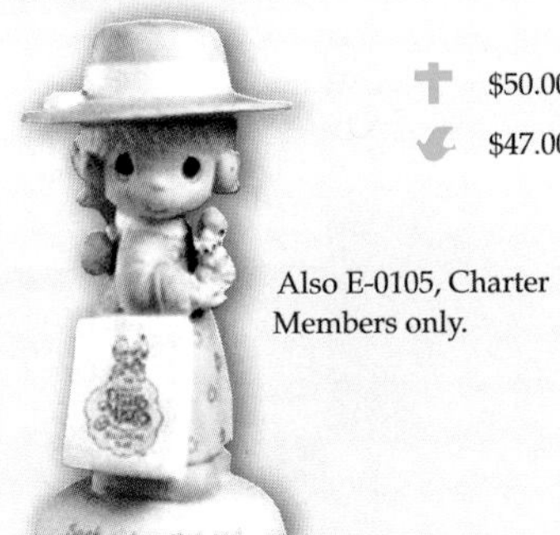

$50.00

$47.00

Also E-0105, Charter Members only.

Members Only, Issue Price $17.50, '85

Purchased ________, Price $ ____________

☐ *Birds Of A Feather Collect Together,* E-0006

$45.00

$42.00

Also E-0106, Charter Members only.

Members Only, Issue Price $17.50, '86

Purchased ________, Price $ ____________

☐ *Sharing Is Universal,* E-0007

$45.00

$40.00

Also E-0107, Charter Members only.

Members Only, Issue Price $17.50, '87

Purchased ________, Price $ ____________

☐ *A Growing Love*, E-0008

Tree $40.00

Anchor $38.00

Also E-0108, Charter Members only.

Members Only, Issue Price $18.50, '88

Purchased ______ ,

Price $__________

☐ *But Love Goes On Forever*, E-0102 (Plaque)

UM $150.00

Triangle $90.00

Hourglass $80.00

Also E-0202, Members only. *Precious Moments Last Forever* inscription on front confused many because the title of this piece is *But Love Goes On Forever.* Termed the "Canadian Plaque Error," approximately 750 pieces of this 1982 symbol of membership were produced in 1985 and shipped to Canada. These pieces are stamped TAIWAN and have a Dove annual production symbol. Value for the "Canadian Plaque Error" is $125.00.

Charter Members Only, Issue Price $15.00, '82

Purchased ________, Price $ ___________

☐ *Let Us Call The Club To Order*, E-0103

Hourglass $65.00

Fish $60.00

Also E-0303, Members only.

Charter Members Only, Issue Price $15.00 '83

Purchased _________ ,

Price $___________

☐ *Join In On The Blessings*, E-0104

Hourglass $100.00

Fish $65.00

Cross $60.00

Also E-0404, Members only.

Charter Members Only, Issue Price $17.50, '84

Purchased ________, Price $ ___________

☐ *Loving, Caring And Sharing*, PCC-112 (Medallions)

UM $30.00

Members Only, Issue Price $22.50, '93
Set of 3, with case

Purchased ________, Price $ ___________

☐ *Lord It's Hard To Be Humble*, PCC-489 (Lithograph)

UM $65.00

Signed lithograph, Precious Rewards Frequent Buyer Program, Level 4.

Members Only, Gift, '98

Purchased ________, Price $ ___________

☐ *My Collection, PM-001*

★ $35.00

◯ $30.00

Members Only, Issue Price $20.00, '00

Purchased ________, Price $ __________

☐ *Collecting Friends Along The Way, PM-002*

★ $120.00

◯ $110.00

Club's twentieth anniversary commemorative figurine.

Members Only, Issue Price $100.00, '00

Purchased ________, Price $ __________

☐ *Calling To Say You're Special, PM-0011*

◯ $55.00

$53.00

Members Only, Issue Price $50.00, '01

Purchased ________, Price $ __________

☐ *You're A Computie Cutie, PM-0012*

◯ $40.00

$35.00

Members Only, Issue Price $35.00, '01

Purchased ________, Price $ __________

☐ *You Are My In-Spa-ration, PM-0021*

$50.00

$47.00

Members Only, Issue Price $45.00, '02

Purchased ________, Price $ __________

☐ *You Are My Favorite Pastime, PM-0022*

$45.00

$40.00

Members Only, Issue Price $40.00, '02

Purchased ________, Price $ __________

☐ *Blessed With Small Miracles*, PM-0031

$45.00
$40.00

Members Only, Issue Price $40.00, '03
Purchased ________, Price $ __________

☐ *Safe In The Hands Of Love*, PM-0032

$60.00
$55.00

Members Only, Issue Price $55.00, '03
Purchased ________, Price $ __________

☐ *Others Pail In Comparison To You*, PM-0041

$30.00
$30.00

Members Only, Issue Price $30.00, '04
Purchased ________, Price $ __________

☐ *Friendship Is Waiting To Be Discovered*, PM-0042

$40.00
$40.00

Members Only, Issue Price $40.00, '04
Purchased ________, Price $ __________

☐ *Friends Help Us Keep Moving Up*, PM-0051

$50.00
$50.00

Members Only, Issue Price $50.00, '05
Purchased ________, Price $ __________

☐ *Getting There Is Half The Fun*, PM-0052

$65.00
$65.00

MembersOnly, Issue Price $65.00, '05
Purchased ________, Price $ __________

☐ *Mug, PM-032* UM $7.00

Members Only, Issue Price $7.00, '90

Purchased ________ ,

Price $ __________

☐ *Desk Flag, PM-034* UM $5.00

Members Only, Issue Price $4.00, '90

Purchased __________ ,

Price $__________

☐ *Sharing The Good News Together, PM-037 (Ornament)* $75.00

Members Only, Issue Price $17.50, '91

Purchased _________ ,

Price $ __________

☐ *The Club That's Out Of This World, PM-038 (Ornament)* $75.00

Members Only, Issue Price $17.50, '92

Purchased_________ ,

Price $ __________

☐ *Loving, Caring And Sharing, PM-040 (Ornament)* $35.00

Members Only, Issue Price $15.00, '93

Purchased_________ ,

Price $ _________

☐ *You Are The End Of My Rainbow, PM-041 (Ornament)* $35.00

Members Only, Issue Price $15.00, '94

Purchased ____________ ,

Price $ ____________

☐ *Blessed Are The Poor In Spirit, For Theirs Is The Kingdom Of Heaven, PM-190 (Ornament)* UM $25.00

Members Only, Issue Price $15.00, '90

Purchased ___________ ,

Price $____________

☐ *Blessed Are They That Mourn, For They Shall Be Comforted, PM-290 (Ornament)* UM $25.00

Members Only, Issue Price $15.00, '90

Purchased __________ ,

Price $____________

☐ *Blessed Are The Meek, For They Shall Inherit The Earth, PM-390 (Ornament)* UM $25.00

Members Only, Issue Price $15.00, '90

Purchased ___________ ,

Price $____________

Blessed Are They That Hunger And Thirst After Righteousness, For They Shall Be Filled, PM-490 (Ornament)

UM $25.00

Members Only, Issue Price $15.00, '90

Purchased ____________,

Price $____________

Blessed Are The Merciful, For They Shall Obtain Mercy, PM-590 (Ornament)

UM $25.00

Members Only, Issue Price $15.00, '90

Purchased ____________,

Price $____________

Blessed Are The Pure In Heart, For They Shall See God, PM-690 (Ornament)

UM $25.00

Members Only, Issue Price $15.00, '90

Purchased ____________,

Price $____________

Blessed Are The Peacemakers, For They Shall Be Called Sons Of God, PM-790 (Ornament)

UM $25.00

Members Only, Issue Price $15.00, '90

Purchased ____________,

Price $____________

Hello Lord, It's Me Again, PM-811

▲ $425.00

⧗ $400.00

Members Only, Issue Price $25.00, '81

Purchased ________, Price $ ________

Smile, God Loves You, PM-821

⧗ $200.00

Fish $190.00

Members Only, Issue Price $25.00, '82

Purchased ________, Price $ ________

Put On A Happy Face, PM-822

⧗ $225.00

Fish $205.00

✝ $195.00

Members Only, Issue Price $25.00, '83

Purchased ________, Price $ ________

Dawn's Early Light, PM-831

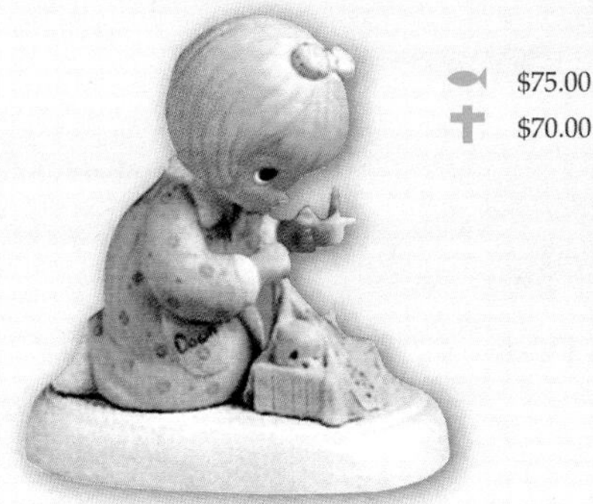

$75.00
$70.00

Members Only, Issue Price $25.00, '83
Purchased ________, Price $ ___________

Trust In The Lord To The Finish, PM-843 (Crossstitch)

UM $20.00

Members Only, Issue Price $11.00, '84
Purchased ________, Price $ ___________

God's Ray Of Mercy, PM-841

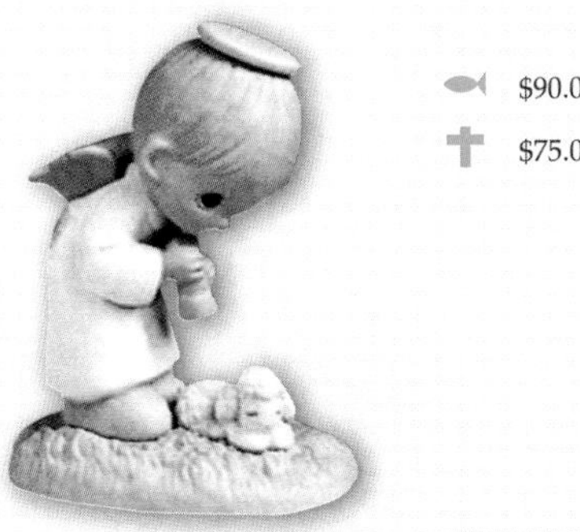

$90.00
$75.00

Members Only, Issue Price $25.00, '84
Purchased ________, Price $ ___________

The Lord Is My Shepherd, PM-851

$85.00
$80.00

Members Only, Issue Price $25.00, '85
Purchased ________, Price $ ___________

Trust In The Lord To The Finish, PM-842

$72.00
$65.00

Members Only, Issue Price $25.00, '84
Purchased ________, Price $ ___________

I Love To Tell The Story, PM-852

$70.00
$65.00

Members Only, Issue Price $27.50, '85
Purchased ________, Price $ ___________

☐ *The Lord Is My Shepherd,* PM-853 (Crossstitch)

UM $20.00

Members Only, Issue Price $13.00, '85

Purchased ________, Price $ ___________

☐ *Grandma's Prayer,* PM-861

$95.00

$85.00

Members Only, Issue Price $25.00, '86

Purchased ________, Price $ ___________

☐ *I'm Following Jesus,* PM-862

$75.00

$65.00

Members Only, Issue Price $25.00, '86

Purchased ________, Price $ ___________

Members Only, Issue Price $25.00, '87

Purchased ________, Price $ ___________

☐ *I'm Following Jesus,* PM-863 (Mugs)

UM $22.00

Members Only, Issue Price $17.50, '86 Set of 2

Purchased ________, Price $ ___________

☐ *Birds Of A Feather Collect Together,* PM-864 (Ornament)

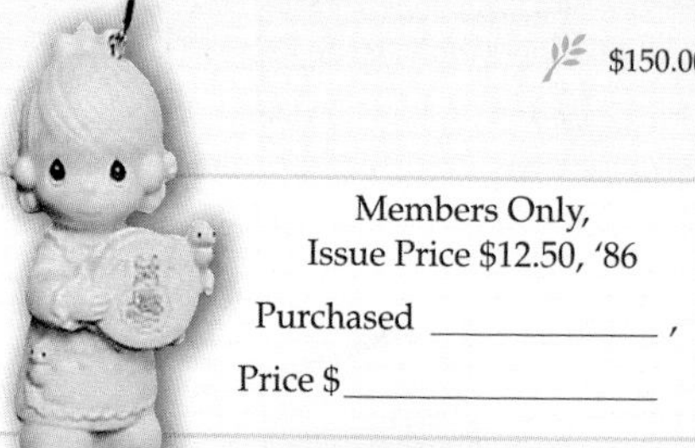

$150.00

Members Only, Issue Price $12.50, '86

Purchased ___________, Price $___________

☐ *Feed My Sheep,* PM-871

$90.00

$80.00

Members Only, Issue Price $25.00, '87

Purchased ________, Price $ ___________

☐ *In His Time,* PM-872

$65.00

$60.00

☐ *Loving You Dear Valentine (Boy)*, PM-873

$45.00

$40.00

Members Only, Issue Price $25.00, '87

Purchased ________, Price $ ___________

☐ *Loving You Dear Valentine (Girl)*, PM-874

$55.00

$50.00

Members Only, Issue Price $25.00, '87

Purchased ________, Price $ ___________

☐ *God Bless You For Touching My Life*, PM-881

$70.00

$65.00

Members Only, Issue Price $27.50, '88

Purchased ________, Price $ ___________

☐ *You Just Cannot Chuck A Good Friendship*, PM-882

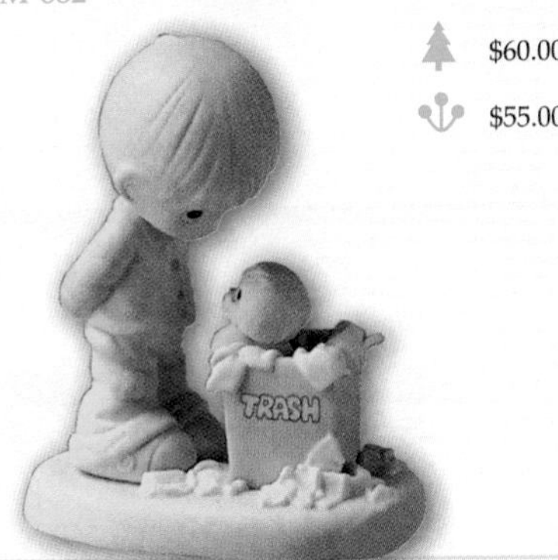

$60.00

$55.00

Members Only, Issue Price $27.50, '88

Purchased ________, Price $ ___________

☐ *Beatitudes Ornament Series*, PM-890 (Ornaments)

UM $145.00

Members Only, Issue Price $105.00, '90
Set of 7, Individually Numbered PM-190 through PM-790

Purchased ________, Price $ ___________

☐ *You Will Always Be My Choice*, PM-891

$50.00

$45.00

Members Only, Issue Price $27.50, '89

Purchased ________, Price $ ___________

☐ *Mow Power To Ya, PM-892*

$65.00

$60.00

Members Only, Issue Price $27.50, '89

Purchased ________, Price $ ___________

☐ *Ten Years And Still Going Strong, PM-901*

$55.00

$50.00

Members Only, Issue Price $30.00, '90

Purchased ________, Price $ ___________

☐ *You Are A Blessing To Me, PM-902*

$65.00

$60.00

Members Only, Issue Price $27.50, '90

Purchased ______,

Price $ __________

☐ *You Are A Blessing To Me, PM-903 (Needlepoint Pillow)*

UM $10.00

Members Only, Issue Price $7.00, '90

Purchased ________,

Price $ ___________

☐ *My Happiness, PM-904 (Ornament)*

$80.00

Members Only, Issue Price $15.00, '90

Purchased __________,

Price $ ___________

☐ *One Step At A Time, PM-911*

$55.00

$50.00

Members Only, Issue Price $33.00, '91

Purchased ________, Price $ ___________

☐ *Lord, Keep Me In Teepee Top Shape, PM-912*

$65.00

$60.00

Members Only, Issue Price $27.50, '91

Purchased ________,

Price $ ___________

Only Love Can Make A Home, PM-921

$70.00

$65.00

Members Only, Issue Price $30.00, '92

Purchased ________, Price $ __________

Sowing The Seeds Of Love, PM-922

$45.00

$40.00

Members Only, Issue Price $30.00, '92

Purchased ________,

Price $ __________

His Little Treasure, PM-931

$50.00

$45.00

Members Only, Issue Price $30.00, '93

Purchased ______________,

Price $______________

Loving, PM-932

$75.00

$70.00

Members Only, Issue Price $30.00, '93

Purchased ______________,

Price $ ______________

Caring, PM-941

$60.00

$55.00

Members Only, Issue Price $35.00, '94

Purchased ________, Price $ __________

Sharing, PM-942

$65.00

$60.00

Members Only, Issue Price $35.00, '94

Purchased ________, Price $ __________

You're One In A Million To Me, PM-951

$50.00

$45.00

Members Only, Issue Price $35.00, '95

Purchased ______________,

Price $______________

☐ *Always Take Time To Pray,* PM-952

$55.00
$50.00

Members Only, Issue Price $35.00, '95
Purchased ________, Price $ __________

☐ *Teach Us To Love One Another,* PM-961

$60.00
$55.00

Sam Butcher honors Aunt Cleo.

Members Only, Issue Price $40.00, '96
Purchased ________, Price $ __________

☐ *Our Club Is Soda-licious,* PM-962

$60.00
$55.00

Members Only, Issue Price $35.00, '96
Purchased________ ,
Price $ __________

☐ *You Will Always Be A Treasure To Me,* PM-971

$60.00
$55.00

Members Only, Issue Price $50.00, '97
Purchased ________, Price $ __________

☐ *Blessed Are The Merciful,* PM-972

$50.00
$45.00

Members Only, Issue Price $40.00, '97
Purchased ________, Price $ __________

☐ *Happy Trails,* PM-981

$55.00
$50.00

Members Only, Issue Price $50.00, '98
Purchased ________, Price $ __________

Lord Please Don't Put Me On Hold, PM-982

$50.00
$45.00

Members Only, Issue Price $40.00, '98
Purchased ________, Price $ ___________

How Can Two Work Together Except They Agree, PM-983

$135.00
$130.00

Members Only, Issue Price $125.00, '98
Purchased ________, Price $ ___________

Jumping For Joy, PM-991

$38.00
$35.00

Members Only, Issue Price $30.00, '99
Purchased _________ ,
Price $ ____________

Members Only, "Gift To Go" Program, Limited Ed., Issue Price $25.00, '01
Purchased ________, Price $ ________

God's Speed, PM-992

$45.00
$40.00

Members Only, Issue Price $30.00, '99
Purchased ____________ ,
Price $ ____________

He Watches Over Us All, PM-993

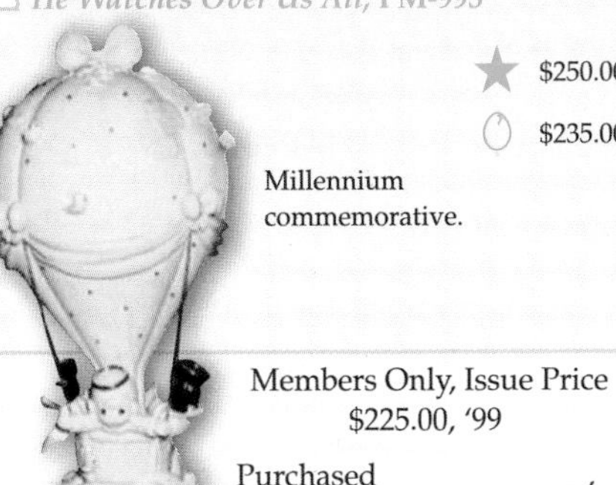

$250.00
$235.00

Millennium commemorative.

Members Only, Issue Price $225.00, '99
Purchased ____________,
Price $ _______________

You Fill The Pages Of My Life, PMB-034 (Book & Figurine)

$85.00
$80.00

Members Only, Issue Price $67.50, '94
Special Edition
Purchased ________, Price $ ___________

Home For The Holidays, PMB-225 (Ornament)

UM $25.00

Comes with Christmas collection CD.

Cecilia, 100018

UM $12.00

Members Only, Gift, '02
Tender Tails, Club Exclusive
Purchased ________, Price $ ___________

I'm So Glad You Sled Into My Life, 101731

$20.00

Members Only, Issue Price $20.00, '02
Purchased ________, Price $ ___________

Friendship Begins With Caring, 110858

$50.00
$48.00
$45.00
$40.00

Members Only, Issue Price $35.00, '02
Purchased ________, Price $ ___________

Boots, 546593

UM $15.00

Can be personalized using attached pen.

Members Only, Gift, '99
Tender Tails, Club Exclusive
Purchased ________, Price $ ___________

Gorilla, 602361

UM $10.00

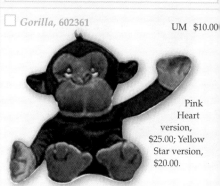

Pink Heart version, $25.00; Yellow Star version, $20.00.

Members Only, Gift, '99
Tender Tails
Purchased ________, Price $ ___________

Twinkle The Star, 646237

UM $20.00

Members Only, Gift, '99
Tender Tails
Purchased ________, Price $ ___________

Iris The Caterpillar, 720976 (Attachable)

UM $20.00

Members Only, Gift, '00
Tender Tails, Club Exclusive

Purchased ________, Price $ ___________

Iris The Caterpillar, 721050

UM $18.00

Add wings to make her a butterfly.

Members Only, Gift, '00
Tender Tails, Club Exclusive

Purchased ________, Price $ ___________

Zelda The Zebra, 819417

UM $15.00

Members Only, Gift, '01
Tender Tails, Club Exclusive

Purchased ________, Price $ ___________

Zelda The Zebra, 826758 (Attachable)

UM $12.00

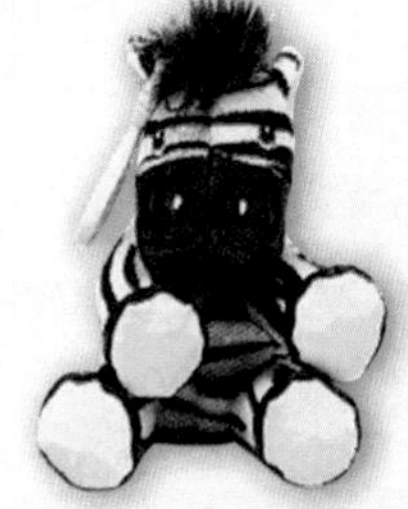

Members Only, Gift, '01
Tender Tails, Club Exclusive

Purchased ________, Price $ ___________

Our Club Can't Be Beat, B-0001

(dove) $85.00
(olive branch) $80.00

Members Only, Issue Price $10.00, '86

Purchased ________, Price $ ___________

A Smile's The Cymbal Of Joy, B-0002

(olive branch) $85.00
(tree) $80.00

Also issued as B-0102 for Charter Members only.

Members Only, Issue Price $10.00, '87

Purchased ________, Price $ ___________

The Sweetest Club Around, B-0003

$50.00

$45.00

Also issued as B-0103 for Charter Members only.

Members Only, Issue Price $11.00, '88

Purchased ________, Price $ ___________

Have A Beary Special Birthday, B-0004

$45.00

$40.00

Also issued as B-0104 for Charter Members Only.

Members Only, Issue Price $11.50, '89

Purchased ________, Price $ ___________

Our Club Is A Tough Act To Follow, B-0005

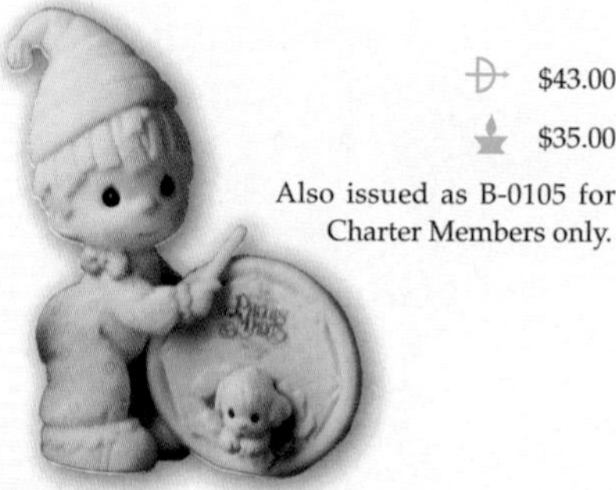

$43.00

$35.00

Also issued as B-0105 for Charter Members only.

Members Only, Issue Price $13.50, '90

Purchased ________, Price $ ___________

Jest To Let You Know You're Tops, B-0006

$40.00

$35.00

Also issued as B-0106 for Charter Members only.

Members Only, Issue Price $15.00, '91

Purchased ________, Price $ ___________

All Aboard For Birthday Club Fun, B-0007

$38.00

$33.00

Also issued as B-0107 for Charter Members only.

Members Only, Issue Price $16.00, '92

Purchased ________, Price $ ___________

Happiness Is Belonging, B-0008

$35.00

$30.00

Also issued as B-0108 for Charter Members only.

Members Only, Issue Price $17.50, '93

Purchased ________, Price $ ___________

Can't Get Enough Of Our Club, B-0009

$35.00

$30.00

Also issued as B-0109 for Charter Members only.

Members Only, Issue Price $17.50, '94

Purchased ________, Price $ ___________

The Fun Starts Here, B-0012

$30.00

$27.00

Also issued as B-0112 for Charter Members only.

Members Only, Issue Price $22.50, '97

Purchased ________, Price $ ___________

Hoppy Birthday, B-0010

$35.00

$30.00

Also issued as B-0110 for Charter Members only.

Members Only, Issue Price $20.00, '95

Purchased ________, Price $ ___________

Scootin' By Just To Say Hi! B-0011

$35.00

$30.00

Also issued as B-0111 for Charter Members only.

Members Only, Issue Price $21.00, '96

Purchased ________, Price $ ___________

You Are My Mane Inspiration, B-0014

$50.00

$48.00

Also issued as B-0114 for Charter Members only.

Members Only, Gift, '97

Purchased ________, Price $ ___________

Fishing For Friends, BC-861

$130.00

$120.00

Members Only, Issue Price $10.00, '86

Purchased ________, Price $ ___________

☐ *Hi Sugar, BC-871*

$110.00
$100.00

Members Only, Issue Price $11.00, '87
Purchased ________, Price $ __________

☐ *Somebunny Cares, BC-881*

$60.00
$55.00

Members Only, Issue Price $13.50, '88
Purchased ________, Price $ __________

☐ *Can't Bee Hive Myself Without You, BC-891*

$60.00
$55.00

Members Only, Issue Price $13.50, '89
Purchased ________, Price $ __________

☐ *Collecting Makes Good Scents, BC-901*

$50.00
$45.00

Members Only, Issue Price $15.00, '90
Purchased ________, Price $ __________

☐ *I'm Nuts Over My Collection, BC-902*

$45.00
$40.00

Members Only, Issue Price $15.00, '90
Purchased ________, Price $ __________

☐ *Love Pacifies, BC-911*

$45.00
$40.00

Members Only, Issue Price $16.00, '91
Purchased ________, Price $ __________

☐ *True Blue Friends, BC-912*

$45.00

$40.00

Members Only, Issue Price $15.00, '91

Purchased ________, Price $ ____________

☐ *Put A Little Punch In Your Birthday, BC-931*

$40.00

$35.00

Members Only, Issue Price $15.00, '93

Purchased ________, Price $ ____________

☐ *Every Man's House Is His Castle, BC-921*

$40.00

$35.00

Members Only, Issue Price $16.50, '92

Purchased ________, Price $ ____________

☐ *Owl Always Be Your Friend, BC-932*

$38.00

$32.00

Members Only, Issue Price $16.00, '93

Purchased ________, Price $ ____________

☐ *I Got You Under My Skin, BC-922*

$40.00

$35.00

Members Only, Issue Price $16.00, '92

Purchased ________, Price $ ____________

☐ *God Bless Our Home, BC-941*

$42.00

$38.00

Members Only, Issue Price $16.00, '94

Purchased ________, Price $ ____________

☐ *Yer A Pel-I-Can Count On, BC-942*

$35.00

$33.00

Members Only, Issue Price $16.00, '94

Purchased ________, Price $ ___________

☐ *Making A Point To Say You're Special, BC-951*

$35.00

$30.00

Members Only, Issue Price $15.00, '95

Purchased ________, Price $ ___________

☐ *10 Wonderful Years Of Wishes, BC-952*

$75.00

$70.00

Members Only, Issue Price $50.00, '95

Purchased ________, Price $ ___________

☐ *There's A Spot In My Heart For You, BC-961*

$35.00

$30.00

Members Only, Issue Price $15.00, '96

Purchased ________, Price $ ___________

☐ *You're First In My Heart, BC-962*

$35.00

$30.00

Members Only, Issue Price $15.00, '96

Purchased ________, Price $ ___________

☐ *Hare's To The Birthday Club, BC-971*

$30.00

$25.00

Members Only, Issue Price $16.00, '97

Purchased ________, Price $ ___________

Holy Tweet, BC-972

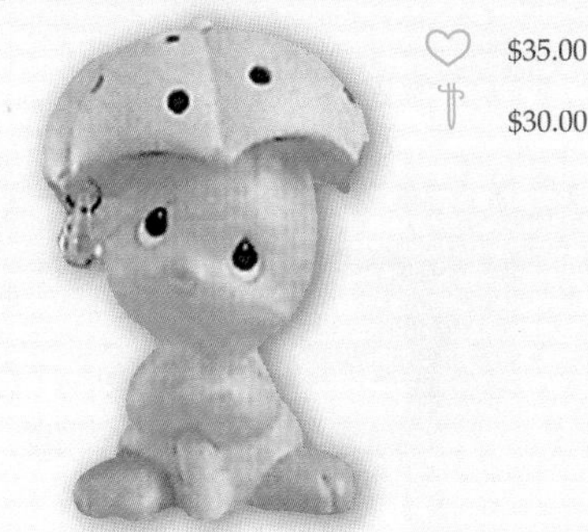

$35.00

$30.00

Members Only, Issue Price $18.50, '97

Purchased ________, Price $ ___________

Slide Into The Celebration, BC-981

$28.00

$25.00

Commemorates the twentieth anniversary of Precious Moments.

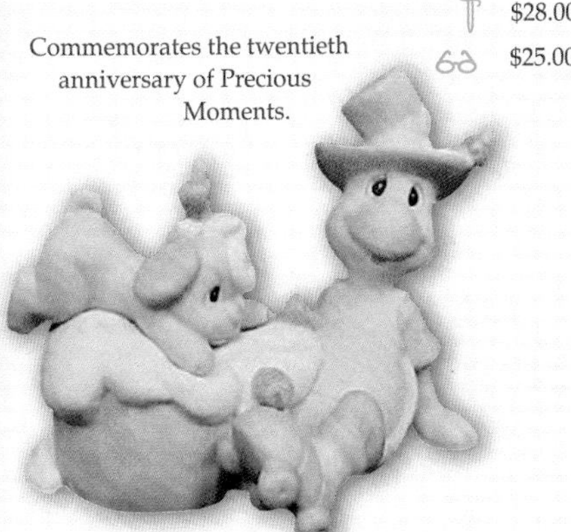

Members Only, Issue Price $15.00, '98

Purchased ________, Price $ ___________

Ewe Are So Special To Me, BC-991

$35.00

$30.00

Members Only, Issue Price $25.00, '99

Purchased ________, Price $ ___________

Chester, BC-992

UM $8.00

Members Only, Issue Price $7.00, '99
Tender Tails

Purchased ________, Price $ ___________

Chippie, BC-993

UM $7.00

Members Only, Issue Price $10.50, '99
Tender Tails

Purchased ________, Price $ ___________

Don't Fret, We'll Get There Yet! F-0002

$30.00

$25.00

Also issued as F-0102 for Charter Members only.

Members Only, Gift, '00

Purchased ________, Price $ ___________

True Friendship Is A Precious Treasure, F-0003

$32.00

$28.00

Also issued as F-0103 for Charter Members only.

Charter Members only, Issue Price $30.00, '01
Purchased ________, Price $ ___________

Seal-ed With A Kiss, F-0004

$30.00

$28.00

Also issued as F-0104 for Charter Members only.

Members Only, Gift, '02
Purchased ________, Price $ ___________

I'm All Ears For You, F-0005

$30.00

$25.00

Also issued as F-0105 for Charter Members only.

Members Only, Gift, '03
Purchased ________, Price $ ___________

Be You And The Rest Is Cool, F-0006

$25.00

$25.00

Also issued as F-0106 for Charter Members only.

Members Only, Gift, '04
Purchased ________,
Price $ ___________

When You Play With Heart, Music Is Art, F-0007

$25.00

$25.00

Also issued as F-0107 for Charter Members only.

Members Only, Issue Price $25.00, '04
Purchased ________,
Price $ ___________

Daring To Have True Fun, F-0008

$50.00

$50.00

Also issued as F-0108 for Charter Members only.

Members Only, Gift, '05
Purchased ________, Price $ ___________

☐ *Reed The Centipede*, FC-001

UM $12.00

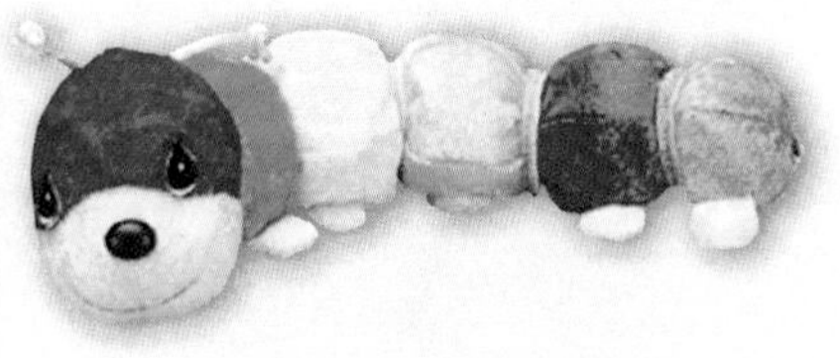

Members Only, Issue Price $6.99, '00
Tender Tails
Purchased ________, Price $ ___________

☐ *Ronnie The Rhino Beetle*, FC-002

UM $12.00

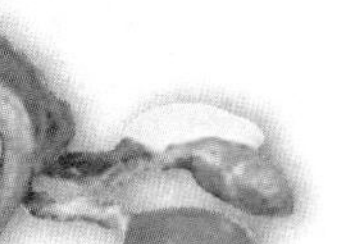

Members Only, Issue Price $6.99, '00
Tender Tails
Purchased ________, Price $ ___________

☐ *Hold On To The Moment*, FC-003

★ $32.00
◯ $28.00

Members Only, Issue Price $25.00, '00
Purchased ________, Price $ ___________

☐ *I'm Always Happy When You're A-long*, FC-011

◯ $25.00
$22.00

Members Only, Issue Price $18.50, '01
Purchased ________, Price $ ___________

☐ *Chris The Crocodile*, FC-012

UM $12.00

Members Only, Issue Price $6.99, '01
Tender Tails
Purchased ________, Price $ ___________

☐ *Monty The Mandrill*, FC-013

UM $12.00

Members Only, Issue Price $6.99, '01
Tender Tails
Purchased ________, Price $ ___________

☐ *Wade The Water Buffalo,* FC-014

UM $12.00

Members Only, Gift, '01
Tender Tails, Club Exclusive
Purchased ________, Price $ __________

☐ *You Are The Coolest Friend,* FC-021

$45.00
$40.00

Members Only, Issue Price $35.00, '02
Purchased ________, Price $ __________

☐ *Gwen The Penguin,* FC-022

UM $12.00

Members Only, Issue Price $9.99, '02
Tender Tails
Purchased ________, Price $ __________

☐ *You're So Bear-y Cool,* FC-023

$25.00
$23.00

Members Only, Issue Price $20.00, '02
Purchased ________, Price $ __________

☐ *So Happy To Be Together,* FC-031

$24.00
$22.00

Members Only, Issue Price $20.00, '03
Purchased ________, Price $ __________

☐ *Lost Without You,* FC-032

$43.00
$40.00

Members Only, Issue Price $40.00, '03
Purchased ________, Price $ __________

☐ *Sam*, FC-033

UM $12.00

Members Only, Issue Price $9.99, '03
Tender Tails

Purchased ________, Price $ ___________

☐ *Shelly The Turtle*, FC-034

UM $12.00

Shell opens. Comes with frog figurine.

Members Only, Issue Price $9.99, '03
Tender Tails

Purchased ________, Price $ ___________

☐ *Brought Together Through The Beat*, FC-041

$35.00

$35.00

Members Only, Issue Price $35.00, '04

Purchased ________, Price $ ___________

☐ *Never Too Young For Sleepover Fun*, FC-051

$35.00

$35.00

Members Only, Issue Price $35.00, '05

Purchased ________, Price $ ___________

☐ *The Best Is Yet To Comb*, FC-052

$45.00

$45.00

Members Only, Issue Price $45.00, '05

Purchased ________, Price $ ___________

Websites

Precious Moments Chapel And Store	www.preciousmoments.com
Precious Moments Community	www.preciousmomentscommunity.com
Enesco Corporation	www.enesco.com
Gocollect Collector's site	www.gocollect.com
Precious Moments Company Dolls	www.pmcdolls.com
Limited Of Michigan	www.limitedweb.com/index.vml
eBay online auction site	www.ebay.com
Precious Memory	www.preciousmemory.com
Collector Books	www.collectorbooks.com

Glossary

Annual (Non-Dated): Pieces sold once a year or introduced only once a year.

Care-A-Van Exclusive: Piece that is only sold when the Precious Moments Van travels to different cities.

Carlton Cards Exclusive: Special pieces made just for the Carlton Cards Company.

CCR: Century Circle Retailer.

Chapel Exclusive: Special pieces made just for the Precious Moments Chapel in Carthage, Missouri.

Dated Annual: A piece with a date on that bottom that was released for only one year.

Discontinued: Pieces not being made presently.

DSR: Distinguished Service Retailer, a recognition given by Enesco for a retailer's high level of goods and services.

Easter Seals Commemorative: Limited edition pieces made to benefit the National Easter Seals Society.

GCC: Gift Creation Concept; retailer receives special Limited Edition pieces made exclusively for their stores.

Limited Ed.: Pieces of which only certain amounts were produced.

Limited To One Day Only: A collector is given a specific date to order a piece. Only that one-day order is manufactured.

Open: A piece that is still in production that can be purchased on the open market.

Original "21": The first 21 figurines manufactured in 1979.

Regional Event: Special pieces made just for events held in certain parts of the country.

Re-Introduced: A Suspended piece that has been changed and brought back to the open market. These pieces can vary from a color change to a sculptor change.

Retired: A mold of a bisque piece that has been destroyed and permanently removed from production.

Suspended: Removed from production for an undetermined period of time.

Unmarked: Having no Annual Production mark on the bottom of the base.

Variation: Certain pieces that have different coloring or were fired differently. Variations can be caused by human error or be deliberate production changes made by the company.

Numerical Index

General Index